CRITICAL SURVEY
OF
DRAMA

CRITICAL SURVEY
OF
DRAMA

Supplement

Edited by
FRANK N. MAGILL

SALEM PRESS

Pasadena, California   Englewood Cliffs, New Jersey

Library of Congress Cataloging-in-Publication Data
Critical survey of drama. Supplement.
    Bibliography: p.
    Includes index.
    Summary: Critical essays examine representa-
tive plays and identify themes and characteristics
employed by fifty dramatists not covered in the
original series. Also updates the original series
with more recent information on prizes, achievements, and awards of the literary form.
    1. Drama—History and criticism—Dictionaries.
2. Drama—Bio-bibliography. [1. Drama—History
and criticism—Dictionaries. 2. Drama—Bio-bib-
liography] I. Magill, Frank Norhen, 1907-   .
PN1625.C74   1986   Suppl.   809.2'003   87-15810
ISBN 0-89356-389-7

PUBLISHER'S NOTE

The present volume is a supplement to the *Critical Survey of Drama*, English Language Series (1985) and Foreign Language Series (1986). It is being published in conjunction with comparable supplements to the other sets in Magill's Salem Press genre series, which together constitute a forty-five-volume, worldwide study of the major figures in the fields of short fiction, poetry, long fiction, and drama.

The primary purpose of this supplement is to extend coverage to significant dramatists who were not included in the earlier volumes—particularly contemporary playwrights, who could be covered only very selectively in the original survey. Thus, of the forty-nine dramatists included in the supplement (ten of whom are women), all but three are from the twentieth century; most of them are still active. Slightly more than a third of the dramatists included are from the United States; in all, nineteen countries are represented on the list, which includes dramatists from England and Ireland, Canada and Australia, Eastern and Western Europe, Africa and the West Indies, and Latin America.

Some of the most vital work in contemporary theater emphasizes dance, music, and other elements of spectacle rather than the traditional resources of the stage play; this trend is reflected in the supplement by the inclusion of figures such as JoAnne Akalaitis, Martha Clarke, and Robert Wilson. Also included is the Polish director and playwright Tadeusz Kantor, whose innovative productions blur the distinction between adaptation and original creation.

The format of the individual articles in this volume is consistent with that of the earlier volumes. Pertinent top matter is followed by a listing of the dramatist's plays, with dates of first production and publication, a brief survey of work in literary forms other than drama, a summary of the subject's professional achievements, a biographical sketch, and a critical analysis of the subject's canon, which is the body of the article. Following these critical overviews is a list of major publications other than plays and a bibliography of significant criticism.

In addition, the supplement updates information provided in the *Critical Survey of Drama*. For dramatists who were living when those earlier volumes were published, the supplement provides a record of subsequent publications and awards received and, when applicable, a death date. These listings appear in a separate section following the articles on individual dramatists.

A comprehensive Index to the volume supplements the original *Critical Survey of Drama* index, listing all major playwrights, titles, and terms discussed. Entries for playwrights who appear in the volume are in boldface type, followed by an alphabetical listing of those of their works which are analyzed in the text.

CONTRIBUTORS

Ehrhard Bahr

Rebecca Bell-Metereau

Timothy Brennan

J. R. Broadus

Lorne M. Buchman

C. L. Chua

Ada Coe

Sandra Messinger Cypess

Jill Dolan

Ayne C. Durham

Gerald A. Fetz

Edward Fiorelli

Robert J. Forman

Christopher Griffin

Steven Hart

Albert E. Kalson

Anne Mills King

Frank S. Lambasa

Michael Loudon

Jonathan Marks

Joseph Marohl

Anne Laura Mattrella

Barbara Mujica

Helen H. Naugle

Gregory Nehler

Kirsten F. Nigro

Peter Petro

John Povey

Diane Quinn

Michael Quinn

James R. Reece

Joseph Rosenblum

Robert Ross

Victor Anthony Rudowski

Richard J. Sherry

P. Jane Splawn

Thomas J. Taylor

Ian C. Todd

Mara R. Wade

James M. Welsh

LIST OF AUTHORS

CRITICAL SURVEY
OF
DRAMA

JOANNE AKALAITIS

Born: Chicago, Illinois; June 29, 1937

Principal drama
Dressed Like an Egg, pr. 1977, pb. 1984; *Southern Exposure*, pr. 1979; *Dead End Kids*, pr. 1980, pb. 1982; *Green Card*, pr. 1986.

Other literary forms
JoAnne Akalaitis is known primarily as a playwright, director, and actress.

Achievements
Akalaitis and Mabou Mines, the theater company which she helped form in 1969, are best known for their contributions to multimedia, collaborative work. Akalaitis has received support from the National Endowment for the Arts, as well as from the New York State Creative Artists Public Service Program. Mabou Mines did not originally consider itself to be performance theater; its conceptual collaborations, such as *Red Horse Animation* (1970) and *The Saint and the Football Player* (1976), evolved slowly, taking place first as visual performance pieces in New York's Solomon R. Guggenheim Museum, the Museum of Modern Art, and the Berkeley and Pasadena art museums. Other multimedia events by Akalaitis include performances with the 1976 American Dance Festival. Composer Philip Glass, who was once married to Akalaitis, provided music for Mabou Mines in such productions as *Dressed Like an Egg* and *Dead End Kids*, which was the only New York avant-garde play included in the Toronto Theatre Festival in 1980.

Biography
The influence of JoAnne Akalaitis' background appears in various forms in her work. Born in Chicago, Illinois, in 1937, she was reared in a predominantly Lithuanian Catholic neighborhood. She studied philosophy at the University of Chicago and Stanford University, training that emerges in her constant fascination with the nature of being. She worked at the Actor's Workshop in San Francisco in 1962, where she first met Lee Breuer and Ruth Maleczech, with whom she formed the theater collective Mabou Mines in 1969. Her acting teachers included Herbert Berghof, Bill Hickey, and later Spalding Gray and Joyce Aaron of Open Theatre.

Analysis
JoAnne Akalaitis' place in the history of theater is, according to her own assessment, not connected with the American theater tradition of such artists as Tennessee Williams, Arthur Miller, and Edward Albee, who, despite their apparent differences, all have family and relationships at the core of their

work. Solidly nested in avant-garde theater, Akalaitis' work with Mabou Mines is more international and multimedia in flavor. Surrealist and expressionist elements appear in nontraditional use of objects and lighting. Like Bertolt Brecht, Mabou Mines creates a reflexive world in which the actors call attention to the existence of the stage and their own acting, through nonconcealment of set changes, onstage narration, shifting of character portrayal among various actors, and partial set designs that reveal the bare bones of the stage.

At once grounded in history and deliberately detached from context, Akalaitis' work is highly conceptual, tempting the audience to decipher or create the play's patterns while deconstructing these patterns, even as they grow. Her views on acting include a firm determination not to manipulate actors or audiences but rather to allow whatever works for the moment to happen. The methods of Akalaitis and Mabou Mines stem from their notions of group consciousness, and they aim to create theater from the dialectic between past and present, traditional theater and nontheatrical media, and group and individual.

Her first widely successful production, *Dressed Like an Egg*, first presented by the New York Shakespeare Festival in May of 1977, is a collage piece with ten segments: "Prologue," "The Dance," "The Cage," "The Bath," "The Seaside," "The Cage (Part II)," "The Pantomime," "Opium," "The Novel," and "Age." Based on the writings of Colette, each of the segments deals in some manner with the issue of gender. The prologue begins with a brief recitation on carrying a child high in the womb. The play moves quickly to "The Dance," which explores relationships between men and women, juxtaposing such romantic elements as a Chopin polonaise to the obvious movements of a stagehand who offhandedly whistles the tune as he works. Flowers and lines about the ecstasy of love are delivered by males and females wearing turn-of-the-century undergarments and gazing into hand mirrors as they speak, thus undercutting the emotion and sentimentality of their words. "The Cage," and "The Bath" feature trapeze work and a bathing scene, followed by "The Seaside," in which a man claims that he writes out titles the library should have, a service he claims preserves the honor of the Catalogue. These comic scenes focus audience attention on the concept of the ideal in sexuality, romance, and intellect.

The structure of the play is not at first apparent, but on closer inspection, the second half seems more serious, less playful, despite occasional absurdities which may draw audience laughter. "The Cage (Part II)" deals with the ending of romance, and the last line, "I'm cold," hints at death, a line reiterated as the last phrase of the final scene. In absurd recapitulation of the theme of physical passion, a stagehand commands a woman to "let loose a breast!" in "The Pantomime." "Opium" and "The Novel" quote extensively from Colette on the topics of opium dens and the power play of romantic involvements. These two segments both depict decadent phases of development, one within an individual or culture and one within a relationship. The historical connections and recurrence of themes achieve full circle in "Age," which combines images of American planes and the cycle of Venus, a planet that grows into its period of greatest brilliance every eight years. The section on Venus indirectly comments on the waxing and waning of romantic impulses, at both an individual and a cultural level.

As in most of Akalaitis' works, visual and aural richness play an integral role in the production. *Dressed Like an Egg* contrasts the soft romantic elements of seashell footlights, pastel pinks, blues, and grays, with the crudity of modern fabrics, silver lamé, a Celastic dress, a mylar rug, and the startling image of hairy male arms and hands dancing in women's shoes. Stereotypically feminine symbols, such as carnations and irises, act as counterpoint to a woman snoring loudly. *Dressed Like an Egg* explores sexual ambiguity in other visually shocking scenes: for example, when a woman dressed as a mummy passionately kisses another woman who is dressed as a man, an allusion to Colette's intimate friendships with other women.

Akalaitis works well with historical information, weaving facts into the fabric of a purely modern vision, including abstract philosophy and absurdist elements of theater performance. *Southern Exposure*, performed at The New Theatre Festival, Baltimore, in 1979, is an exploration of exterior and interior poles. The play offers tribute to early explorers of the Antarctic, at the same time that it explores interior or mental uncharted territory, areas of the mind untouched by civilization, perhaps seeking the blank spot of pure being, nonbeing, or Nirvana. As in *Dressed Like an Egg*, past and present commingle in delightful ways, with the idea of blankness as the element which draws people to superimpose definitions and "culture" on empty space. In the prologue, a woman dressed in Edwardian style builds a penguin nest as she explains the penguin family system, in which the father warms the eggs. Blackout follows this touching scene, after which a film of a modern couple visiting aquarium penguins appears, accompanied by a female voice-over describing the timeless penguin burial ground, where dead penguins float, layer upon layer, preserved in the ice of Antarctica.

In the "Shackleton Story," a scene in *Southern Exposure*, a couple in bed recount the disastrous mission of Ernest Shackleton's Trans-Antarctic Expedition from 1914 to 1917. The melancholy quality of this historical document diminishes as the woman drops black cubes into the man's lap. In "Mirage," a man draws the word "horizon" on a blank paper, then rips and crinkles it, underscoring the failure of art to capture the immediate quality of the environment, just as the explorer fails to encompass the vastness of physical space. "Bed" and "Food" bring the play to a humorous, mundane level, with the account of the Shackleton party's obsession with fantasies of huge repasts. The next segment, "Quilt," takes the audience to the domestic scene of a man and a woman sewing a pattern on the quilt as they discuss the failure of Robert Falcon Scott and Roald Amundsen, as slides are projected onto the background. The quilt and the final reading from the explorer's journal point to humanity's drive to trace the pattern of life, even if this attempt is utterly futile.

The stark set serves as an additional character in the piece. Whites predominate, with only the gray stones of a penguin nest, a book, a grayish chair, and the gray shadow of a canted bed offering contrast to the stark simplicity of the set. The set, costumes, slides, film, and props all call attention to the connections between art and life, between the exploration of geographical domains and the intellectual and spiritual realms of art. Human beings' attempts to impose a design on this blank space are portrayed simultaneously as the origin of nobility and the destruction of the very openness necessary to creativity.

Dead End Kids, one of the group's most widely publicized works and clearly their most didactic, is worthy of detailed analysis. The play's opening at The Public Theatre in November of 1980 exemplifies the group's attempt to break down boundaries between audience and performers, between theater and life, with the performance beginning even before the audience enters the theater. In the lobby, patrons view a 1950's-style science fair, whose theme is "Atoms for Peace." As people enter the theater, they hear the droning voice of a girl describing effective construction and use of home bomb shelters, a haunting recapitulation of many of the defense department films of the 1950's. The girl's speech ends with an admonition to be prepared and to remember President Franklin D. Roosevelt's famous line, "There is nothing to fear but fear itself," a statement whose irony becomes more apparent as the play continues.

The appearance of such characters as alchemists, Madame Marie Curie, Albert Einstein, a lecturer, a magician, a young female doctoral student, and an announcer, underscore humanity's communal responsibility for the development of nuclear energy and weapons. When Mephistopheles and Faust appear, reciting in German as Madame Curie conducts a simultaneous commentary, the link between nuclear power and the desire for metaphysical power becomes apparent. In the next scene, army generals and a sexy stenographer join with Mephistopheles, sitting around a conference table, smoking and guffawing at double entendres laced through descriptions of the first nuclear explosion. This scene portrays military knowledge as a means to establish virility and provide male bonding.

After this relatively comic interlude, the intermission actually returns the audience to more sober aspects of the play's nuclear theme, with the fallout shelter tape continuing throughout. Upon return to their seats, audiences witness a film compilation of 1950's government propaganda films for nuclear power and arms. A man and woman recite back and forth all that they have seen in the universe, and they are then joined by a series of characters, including a boy nerd, a Cub Scout, an older woman, and a teenager, all of whom begin dancing the Jerk, until the music ceases and they end frozen in grotesque, strained poses, as a voice recites statistics about the risk of lung cancer caused by plutonium particles. The lecturer continues with graphic information about the effects of radiation sickness, as various listeners display a disturbing lack of emotion. The play closes much as it began, with voices of two girls reciting definitions of nuclear terms; as the audience exits, the fallout shelter tape resumes. The play accomplishes its purpose quite effectively, showing at once the absurdity and logic behind the development of nuclear power, as a natural outgrowth of human intellectual curiosity and the self-destructive impulse toward ultimate domination over life itself.

In keeping with Akalaitis' interest in social responsibility for individual suffering, *Green Card* addresses the issue of United States immigration policies. Through what Akalaitis calls a "collage" of characters, the play presents information about the lives and viewpoints of aliens, from a Salvadoran refugee to a Jewish immigrant of the late 1900's. As with *Dead End Kids*, the opening occurs as the audience enters, with loudspeaker voices delivering lines relevant to the play's theme. A woman's recitation of Emma Lazarus' poem, "Send these, the homeless, tempest-tost to me," fades under a booming male voice reeling off racial slurs and epithets. A spotlight shines on a master of ceremonies who cheerfully calls out insulting terms for different ethnic and racial groups. As if in answer, the light on him fades and another appears, highlighting a collection of men and women grouped together. To the sound of blasting rock music, they break into dance, and then, just as suddenly, stop, paralyzed and frightened-looking, as before.

Green Card opened in Los Angeles' Mark Taper Forum in 1986, a location appropriate to the play's immediate concern. At one point the Salvadoran refugee comments that El Centro, near Los Angeles, is "really a jail," thus bringing the play's suffering into the backyard of the audience. Personal histories of individual men and women interweave with ethnic tidbits in this sometimes humorous, always biting, commentary on the new "melting pot" on the West Coast. The play repeatedly suggests the United States' complicity in the bloody wars and political repression that has driven people from their homelands in Central America and elsewhere in the world. The issue of citizen and government responsibility is not resolved, nor is the fate of the aliens whose lives have been briefly displayed. *Green Card* closes with a line of men and women waiting at a bus stop, all gazing hopefully down the line into a less than rosy future. Some viewers find the play painful to watch, oppressive in its grim depiction of apparently futile struggles. Others see more optimism and a call for action, but regardless of one's interpretation, Akalaitis' work demands that its audience grapple with disturbing political realities.

If Akalaitis creates a stir by her selection of controversial subject matter, she creates an even greater controversy in her treatment of other playwrights' work in her role as director. The most outstanding case is the much-disputed American Repertory Theater production of Samuel Beckett's 1957 *Endgame*, performed in Cambridge, Massachusetts, in 1984. Beckett's stage directions call for an empty room with two small windows, but director Akalaitis placed the work in a subway station with a derailed train in the background. Beckett threatened to halt production but finally agreed to allow the performance to take place with his disclaimer attached to the playbill. Such conflicts between playwrights and performers appear frequently in theater of the 1980's, particularly in the protests of minorities seeking more casting of nontraditional actors in traditional roles.

The whole issue of the nature of performance, the extent to which directors and actors may tamper with original casting, set design, and text, is central to the fate of directors and groups such as Akalaitis and Mabou Mines. As is the case with many artists, within the strengths of works by Akalaitis reside her limitations and perhaps her downfall. Dedication to timely topics and a collaborative theater style make her work vibrant and electric, but these virtues may condemn her to the same kind of relative obscurity endured by such innovative and polemical artists as Clifford Odets and Elmer Rice. Indeed, Akalaitis and Mabou Mines hope that *Dead End Kids* will become dated, that the dangerous use of nuclear power which inspired their work may someday be eliminated, erasing any need for protest. At the same time, all of their works deal with concepts and human concerns that are timeless. The survival of their plays, however, may not be assured without a change in the very nature of the theater canon. As long as it is a body of literature created by individuals and preserved through conventional publishing methods, dynamic groups such as Mabou Mines and truly collaborative artists such as Akalaitis will remain in the realm of theater ephemera—which may be exactly where they wish to reside.

Bibliography
Cohen, Debra. "The Mabou Mines' *The Lost Ones*," in *The Drama Review*. XX (June, 1976), pp. 83-87.
Fox, Terry Curtis. "The Quiet Explosions of JoAnne Akalaitis," in *The Village Voice*. May 23, 1977, p. 77.
Kalb, Jonathan. "JoAnne Akalaitis," in *Theater*. XV (May, 1984), pp. 6-13.
Lacayo, Richard. "Directors Fiddle, Authors Burn," in *Time*. CXXV (January, 1985), p. 74.
Marranca, Bonnie, ed. *The Theatre of Images*, 1977.
Mehta, Xerxes. "Notes from the Avant-Garde," in *Theatre Journal*. XXXI (March, 1979), pp. 20-24.
_____. "Some Versions of Performance Art," in *Theatre Journal*.

XXXVI (May, 1984), pp. 164-191.
Sommer, Sally R. "JoAnne Akalaitis of Mabou Mines," in *The Drama Review*. XX (September, 1976), pp. 3-16.

Rebecca Bell-Metereau

PETER BARNES

Born: London, England; January 10, 1931

Principal drama

The Man with a Feather in His Hat, pr. 1960 (teleplay); *Sclerosis*, 1965; *The Ruling Class: A Baroque Comedy*, pr. 1968, pb. 1969; *Leonardo's Last Supper*, pr. 1969, pb. 1970; *Noonday Demons*, pr. 1969, pb. 1970; *Lulu*, pr. 1970, pb. 1971 (conflation of Frank Wedekind's *Der Erdgeist* and *Die Büchse der Pandora*); *The Bewitched*, pr., pb. 1974; *The Frontiers of Farce*, pr. 1976, pb. 1977 (adaptations of Georges Feydeau's *On purge Bébé!* and Wedekind's *Der Kammersänger*); *Antonio*, pr. as radio play 1977, staged 1979 (adaptation of John Marston's plays *Antonio and Mellida* and *Antonio's Revenge*); *Laughter!*, pr., pb. 1978; *Barnes' People I: Seven Monologues*, pr., pb. 1981 (radio play); *Barnes' People No. 2: Seven Dialogues*, pr., pb. 1984 (radio play); *Red Noses*, pr., pb. 1985; *The Real Long John Silver and Other Plays: Barnes' People III*, pr., pb. 1986 (radio play).

Other literary forms

Peter Barnes is known primarily for a wide range of theater-related activities. He is an editor, adapter, and director of stage and radio plays and cabaret. He has also written many screenplays as well as working as a story editor for Warwick Films. Barnes draws an important distinction between his filmwork, in which he is simply practicing a craft, and his stage plays, which are the product of an inner compulsion.

Achievements

Barnes is a controversial English playwright with an international reputation. His plays are all complex, seriocomic or satirical studies in opposites and extremes. For the most part, he writes highly theatrical, nonrealistic, antiestablishment plays, which employ elements of farce; alienation or dislocation effects such as the rapid succession of short, contrasting scenes or the unexpected introduction of songs and dance; and surrealistic devices. His work contains echoes of English Renaissance dramas, English music hall, American vaudeville, musical comedy, and motion pictures. His theatrical language is richly textured, full of neologisms, literary, biblical, and historical allusions, and British and American slang. In his historical plays, he creates special, eccentric languages with their own period flavor. Most of his own radio plays are more realistic, but his characters and situations are always extraordinary or disturbing. Barnes constantly attacks the corruption of the powerful, the greedy, and the obsessed, and defends the victims of society: the lonely, the old, the dispossessed, the disadvantaged.

Although Barnes' view of the world is pessimistic, there is, particularly in the plays after 1978, a glimmer of hope that the world can be improved. Laughter can be used by the powerful to divert attention from their oppression of the less fortunate, but it can also be a major source of good, and Barnes' plays reverberate with irreverent laughter at social or religious pretensions and an absurd universe. Barnes' work is distinguished by its disturbing subject matter, its rough, often vulgar energy, and its spectacular stage effects. His universe is in turmoil, with no clear direction or purpose. Barnes mirrors ontological anxiety by playing on the paradoxes and ambiguities of life and by juxtaposing contrasting moods, which ultimately prevent any true comic or tragic resolution.

Barnes has also made considerable contributions to the theater and to radio drama as reviver, editor, adapter, and director of plays, both English and European, hitherto neglected in England. His own collections of radio plays for the British Broadcasting Corporation (BBC) earned for him the Giles Cooper Award for Radio Drama in 1981 and 1984. For his stage plays he won the John Whiting Award in 1968 and the *Evening Standard* Award in 1969 for *The Ruling Class*, and the Olivier Award for Best Play of the Year, 1985, for *Red Noses*.

Biography

Peter Barnes was born in the East End of London on January 10, 1931. His parents, assimilated Jews, later moved the family to the holiday resort of Clacton-on-Sea, Essex, where they ran an amusement arcade on the pier. He has one younger sister. During World War II, Barnes was evacuated to the county of Gloucestershire. After the war, he returned to Clacton and completed his formal education at a local grammar school, followed by a year's compulsory military service. He continued his education at night school in London while working as a civil servant for the Greater London Council and as a free-lance film critic. In 1954 he was film critic for *Films and Filming*, and the following year he became a story editor for Warwick Films. From about 1958 to 1967, he worked free-lance on a number of screenplays, including *Violent Moment* (1958), *The Professionals* (1960), *Off Beat* (1961), and *Ring of Spies* (1964). In 1961, he married Charlotte Beck, a secretary at the British Film Institute.

His own first play, *The Man with a Feather in His Hat*, was produced for television in 1960. His first stage play, *The Time of the Barracudas*, was produced in San Francisco and Los Angeles in 1963, but it failed, and Barnes refused permission for any subsequent productions. In 1965, his one-act play *Sclerosis* was produced at the Edinburgh Festival and later at the Aldwych Theatre, London, directed by Charles Marowitz. In 1968, Barnes achieved considerable public success with his award-winning play, *The Ruling Class*, at the Nottingham Playhouse, later performed at the Piccadilly Theatre, London, directed by Stuart Burge. This play, more than any other of Barnes' works, has been staged all over the world, and a film version, starring Peter O'Toole, with screenplay by Barnes, released in 1972, established his international reputation.

Also in 1969, Barnes' two one-act plays *Leonardo's Last Supper* and *Noonday Demons* were played at the Open Space Theatre, London, directed by Charles Marowitz. His next full-length play, *The Bewitched*, was produced in 1974 by the Royal Shakespeare Company at the Aldwych, directed by Terry Hands, and received mixed reviews. *Laughter!* was produced by the Royal Court Theatre in 1978, directed by Charles Marowitz, Barnes having correctly anticipated that this work would displease most critics. That same year he completed *Red Noses, Black Death*, which, thanks at least in part to the unfavorable reception of *Laughter!*, was not to be seen until 1985 in a production by the Royal Shakespeare Company at the Barbican, London, directed by Terry Hands, the title shortened to *Red Noses*.

Barnes occupied himself between stage productions by editing, conflating, or adapting, and occasionally directing, plays by Ben Jonson: *The Alchemist* (1610) and *The Devil Is an Ass* (1616) at the Nottingham Playhouse, co-directed by Stuart Burge; *Bartholomew Fair* (1614) at the Roundhouse, London, under his own direction; and also plays by Thomas Middleton, George Chapman, Thomas Otway, Georges Feydeau, and Frank Wedekind, both for the stage and for radio. One notes particularly the success of *Lulu*, produced in Nottingham and London in 1970; *Antonio*, an adaptation/conflation of John Marston's *Antonio and Mellida* (1599) and *Antonio's Revenge* (1599), first heard on BBC radio in 1977 and later staged at the Nottingham Playhouse in 1979; and *The Frontiers of Farce*, produced at the Old Vic in 1976.

In a conscious effort to refine his skills and experiment with plays employing smaller casts, Barnes worked on three sets of short radio dramas—monologues, duologues, and three-character plays—produced by the BBC in 1981, 1984, and 1986 respectively, under the headings of *Barnes' People I*, *Barnes' People No. 2*, and *Barnes' People III*. These plays, acted by such great performers as Sir John Gielgud, Dame Edith Evans, Paul Scofield, Alec McCowen, Peter Ustinov, and Ian McKellen, were very well received in Great Britain and won two drama awards.

Analysis

Peter Barnes' plays are a heady mixture of many theatrical forms in which the visual elements are important; the written text falls far short of offering the true effect of a good production. Barnes claims that "the aim is to create, by means of soliloquy, rhetoric, formalized ritual, slapstick, songs and dances, a comic theatre of contrasting moods and opposites, where everything is simultaneously tragic and ridiculous." Most reviewers and critics agree about the theatrical brilliance and ingenuity of his plays, but opinion is divided about the significance or depth of his views of the human condition. Barnes is concerned with the pressures of society (authority) which suppress openness of feeling and deny happiness (freedom). His plays attack class, privilege, and whatever prevents the realization of individual or group fulfillment; revolution, even anarchy, may be better than meek submission. Above all, Barnes reveals the fierce tenacity with which groups or individuals hold on to or grasp at power and make society less human. Even devotion to God often conceals selfishness, encourages persecution, or is a form of madness or obsession. Barnes is constantly preoccupied with man's inhumanity to man and with God's seeming indifference to human suffering. While most of his plays suggest that the world is beyond redemption, there are small but significant gleams of hope in the darkness, especially in the plays after 1978, and the comic vitality in all of his works mitigates Barnes' anger and pessimism.

Barnes' first published play, *The Ruling Class*, ridicules the English upper classes, the House of Lords, the Anglican Church, public schools (expensive private upper-class institutions), the police, English xenophobia, psychiatrists, snobbery, and complacency. The play begins with the death of the thirteenth Earl of Gurney. Dressed in a tutu and military dress hat and jacket, and brandishing a sword, the Earl indulges in a recreational mock-hanging in order to induce intoxicating visions; he accidentally kills himself. His son, Jack, the fourteenth Earl, becomes the focus of the family's efforts to marry him off to Grace Shelley, have him produce an heir, and then certify him insane. He is a threat because of his egalitarian views; he believes himself to be the God of Love reincarnated.

The loving Earl is a paranoid schizophrenic with enormous energy and an eccentric verbal exuberance, but his delusions make him an easy victim. When asked why he thinks he is God, he replies, "Simple. When I pray to Him I find I'm talking to myself." His uncle, Sir Charles, persuades Grace, his mistress, a former actress and stripper, to impersonate Marguerite Gautier, the Lady of the Camelias, to whom the Earl thinks he is already married. She arrives at a crucial moment dressed as the heroine of Giuseppe Verdi's *La Traviata* (1853), complete with wax camelias, singing the famous "Godiam" aria. In this splendid theatrical scene, the Earl sings and dances with her.

The main focus of the play is on Jack as the New Testament God of Love and what he becomes after Dr. Herder's "cure": the Old Testament God of Wrath and Justice, and Jack the Ripper. No longer open, spontaneous, and joyful, Jack becomes repressed, Victorian, and as such acceptable to the ruling class. The pivotal scene is the confrontation arranged by Dr. Herder between the madman McKyle, the High-Voltage Messiah, and Jack, the God of Love. This scene presents the symbolic death of Jack as Jesus, and his rebirth, coinciding with the birth of Jack's son and heir, as God the Father.

Jack's "change" is demonstrated by his being attacked by a surreal, apelike monster dressed in Victorian garb, a Victorian Beast which possesses him, although it is unseen by the others onstage, and Jack's pummeling seems to be an epileptic seizure. Act 2 shows Jack's successful efforts to establish his normality, dominate his family, and become a bulwark of respectability, while as Jack the Ripper he carries on a private war against sexuality by murdering his amorous Aunt Claire and, ultimately, his wife. His maiden speech in the House of Lords on the need of the strong to crush the weak receives rapturous applause: He is one of them at last.

Noonday Demons also deals with religion, this time the folly of the "saintly" anchorite's wish to purge himself of the sins of the flesh. Saint Eusebius is shown in his cave in the Theban desert, ragged and in chains, attempting to rid himself of "old style man": "In destroying my body I destroyed Space and Time," he claims. He can see into the future, and communes with angelic voices. Challenged and tempted by an inner demon, he successfully resists wealth, lust, and power. When another anchorite, Saint Pior, arrives and lays claim to Saint Eusebius' cave, conflict between the two holy men quickly develops, each saint being convinced that he alone interprets God's will and that the other must be a demon. Saint Eusebius kills Saint Pior, and he is again able to commune with the angels, but the play's ending undercuts his triumph as, transported to the present, he can see how the theater audience watching *Noonday Demons* regards his life as meaningless and bizarre.

Leonardo's Last Supper, set in the grisly Ambois charnel house to which Leonardo da Vinci's corpse has been taken, introduces the audience to the squabbling Lasca family, forerunners of modern morticians, fallen on hard times. They toast their good luck in having been sent a "golden carcass" which will restore their wealth and reputation. Yet Leonardo is not dead, although when he awakes in such a place he finds it hard to believe that he is alive. The Lascas are not interested in the gratitude of future generations for preserving "the universal man." They are the new men: "Men o' trade, o' money, we'll build a new heaven and a new earth by helping ourselves." To them, Leonardo is a luxury, as are the things he represents: beauty, truth, knowledge, humanity. Seeing their trade being taken away from them, they seize, kill, and prepare Leonardo for burial, a family happily reunited in their business pursuits.

The Bewitched is long and complex, but one can recognize in it many of the themes explored in Barnes' earlier plays, with a heightened savagery and ironic intensity to them: cruelty and violence performed in the name of a God of Love; demoniac possession and angry confrontations between "holy" men; the professional pride and dedication of destroyers of men, from doctors and astrologers to torturers for the Inquisition; the absurd tenacity with which the Spanish grandees cling to their often ludicrous privileges; and the unscrupulous ways in which men behave when driven to pettiness, greed, folly, jealousy, murder. *The Bewitched* is a concentrated attack on the madness of man's blind respect for hierarchical order.

The play deals in particular with the reign of Carlos II, the last of the Spanish Habsburgs. The end product of prolonged inbreeding, Carlos is sickly, impotent, epileptic, and the pawn of unscrupulous politicians, leaders of church and court. The play records some of the intrigues and incredible devices used to keep Carlos alive and to induce him to produce an heir to the Spanish throne and thus preserve the privileged caste. Carlos dies childless, his throne passes to the Bourbons, and the terrible War of the Spanish Succession follows: "One million dead. Two million wounded. Western Europe is in ruins." The reign of Carlos is "a glorious monument to futility." In one of his few lucid moments in the play, Carlos presents Barnes' most open attack on the system when he says,

> Now I see Authority's a poor provider.
> No blessings come from 't
> No man born shouldst ha' t', wield 't . . .
> 'Twill make a desert o' this world
> Whilst there's still one man left t' gi' commands
> And another who'll obey 'em.

Laughter! is the most extreme and most controversial of Barnes' plays. Its thesis is voiced by the character of the Author, who introduces the play: "Comedy is the enemy," the ally of tyrants. "It softens our hatred. An excuse to change nothing, for nothing needs changing when it's all a joke." He asks the audience to root out laughter, "strangle mirth, let the heart pump sulphuric acid, not blood." This plea is accompanied by some diverting, zany stage business, including a whirling bow tie and trousers falling to reveal spangled underpants.

Part 1 deals with the reign of Ivan the Terrible; part 2 with Auschwitz. Ivan is reluctant either to wield power or to surrender it; nevertheless, in the name of authority he slaughters thousands and kills his own son to protect him from the pain of exercising power. Finally, an Angel of Death, dressed like a seedy office clerk, confronts Ivan. After wrestling with this relentless antagonist, Ivan is petrified into a statue, befouled by bird droppings.

In part 2, the setting is Berlin, where petty bureaucrats Else Jost, Victor Cranach, and Heinz Stroop live out their working lives. It is Christmas Eve, 1942. They are visited by the snooping, fanatical Nazi, Gottleb. In spite of wartime shortages and constant fear of the authorities should they deviate from the expected norm, they manage a kind of drunken festivity, and induce an ambiguous vision of the truth behind their façade of loyalty. They rail against their superiors and intellectuals, and finally fire off a round of subversive anti-Hitler jokes. Gottleb then summons a vision of what their paperwork is really masking: the production of flues for the crematoriums at Auschwitz. Onstage, a graphic, horrible representation of the death agonies of those gassed by hydro-cyanide is shown with dummies in place of human beings. Horrified, the bureaucrats cannot translate coded office numbers into the brutal facts. They throw out Gottleb and find solace in being "ordinary people, people who like people, people like them, you, me, us." The epilogue introduces the farewell Christmas concert appearance of the Boffo Boys of Birkenau, Abe Bimko and Hymie Bieberstein, whose awful dance and patter routine comes to an end as the gas does its work.

Red Noses, a most complex play, elaborates many of the themes found in *The Bewitched*, and modifies some of the ideas expounded in *Laughter!* Faced with the horror of the Black Death, which has removed more than a third of the population of Europe, what can a small, bizarre group of entertainers do to improve the world? Given the facts that the Church, prayers, medicine, and wealth are helpless against the plague, Father Flote and his group of "Christ's Clowns," wearing red noses, can at least give the dying some consolation. They are sanctioned by Pope Clement VI and become agents of Church power, a distraction from the real world.

Yet Barnes also suggests that laughter can be associated with revolution and redemption. Opposed to the Floties are the Black Ravens, who see the plague as a chance to create an egalitarian society. Another opposing group, the Flagellants, seek no social change but defy the Church establishment and wish to atone for sin by self-inflicted punishment and direct appeal to God. Inevitably the Church cannot tolerate such deviations and eventually destroys both the Black Ravens and the Flagellants. The Church tolerates the Floties, however, even after the end of the plague, until Father Flote, realizing that there are valuable qualities in the beliefs of the two outlawed groups—that laughter is in fact revolutionary as well as a corrective to sin—defies papal authority and advocates SLOP, "Slow, Lawful, Orthodox Progress." Laughter will no longer be only for losers but can be a force for social and personal improvement. The Church regards Father Flote's defiance as a threat, and the Red Noses are executed. The importance of the individual, the need for social reform, and the positive power of "the laughter of compassion and joy" are at last united in a new and more positive way in a play that is highly complex and richly textured.

The three collections of radio plays, too numerous to discuss here, are particularly interesting as illustrations of the transition Barnes makes from deep pessimism to a more positive view of the world. The outstanding play in *Barnes' People I* is "Rosa," about an aging, disillusioned, but still dedicated social worker. She has a brief, devastating vision of an army of geriatrics on the rampage, raging against the waste of their lives; her vision ends, however, and she knows that she must go on, working with the system, however imperfect it may be: "Slow, Lawful, Orthodox Progress." "The Three Visions," the last play of *Barnes' People III*, is a discussion between Barnes at ages thirty-one, Barnes at age fifty-five, and Barnes at age seventy-four. It is clear that however little he believes he has contributed to his profession, he goes on with the struggle, and never compromises.

Bibliography

Dukore, Bernard F. "Peter Barnes," in *Contemporary British Drama*, 1981.
_____. *The Theatre of Peter Barnes*, 1981.
Elsom, John. *Post-War British Theatre*, 1976.
Esslin, Martin. "The Bewitched," in *Plays and Players*. XXI (June, 1974), pp. 36-37.
_____. "The Ruling Class," in *Plays and Players*. January, 1969, p. 55.
Shafer, Yvonne. "Peter Barnes and the Theatre of Disturbance," in *Theatre News*. December, 1982, pp. 7-9.
Taylor, John Russell. *The Second Wave: British Drama for the Seventies*, 1971.
Worth, Katherine J. *Revolutions in Modern English Drama*, 1972.

Ian C. Todd

VOLKER BRAUN

Born: Dresden, Germany; May 7, 1939

Principal drama

Die Kipper, wr. 1962-1965, pr., pb. 1972; *Freunde*, wr. 1965, pb. 1971; *Mink*, wr. 1965, pr. 1972; *Hinze und Kunze*, pr. 1968 as *Hans Faust*, revised pb. 1973; *Schmitten*, wr. 1969-1978, pr. 1982, pb. 1981; "Lenins Tod," wr. 1970; *Tinka*, pb. 1975, pr. 1976; *Guevara: Oder, Der Sonnenstaat*, pr., pb. 1977; *Grosser Frieden*, pb. 1978, pr. 1979 (*The Great Peace*, c. 1980); *Simplex Deutsch*, pr., pb. 1980; *Dmitri*, pb. 1983; *Siegfried Frauenprotokolle Deutscher Furor*, pr. 1986.

Other literary forms

Volker Braun is as well-known for his work as a lyric poet as he is as a playwright. He made his literary debut in 1965 with the collection of poetry titled *Provokation für mich* (1965; provocation for me), and, in spite of his steady involvement in the theater, he has kept active as a poet throughout his career, publishing his work at regular intervals in both East and West Germany. Among the best-known volumes of his poetry are the collections *Wir und nicht sie* (1970; we and not they), *Gegen die symmetrische Welt* (1974; against the symmetrical world), and *Training des aufrechten Gangs* (1978; training of the upright posture). Numerous poems by Braun have appeared in English translation in major anthologies devoted to contemporary German poetry.

While his literary reputation is in large part based on his work as a poet and dramatist, Braun has published important prose fiction as well. The three "reports" in *Das ungezwungene Leben Kasts* (1972, 1979; the unconstrained life of Kast) are based on his experiences respectively as a construction worker, a student, and a beginning playwright. A fourth story, focusing on the leadership role of the writer-intellectual in Socialist society and corresponding to Braun's own increased prominence in the East German literary establishment, was included in an expanded version of the book that appeared in 1979. Braun's novella *Unvollendete Geschichten* (1975; *Unfinished Story*, 1979), which offers a frank portrayal of an East German state overly prone to distrust its young people, was the center of a minor literary storm when it was withdrawn from circulation shortly after its publication. In addition, Braun has published two prose works that draw and expand upon the relationship he first explored in the play *Hinze und Kunze*. *Geschichten von Hinze und Kunze* (1982; stories of Hinze and Kunze) is a collection of seventy anecdotes centering on the relationship between the worker Hinze and the party secretary Kunze. Written in conscious imitation of Bertolt Brecht's Keuner stories (*Geschichten vom Herrn Keuner*, 1930, 1958), each anecdote reveals some aspect of the complex relationship between the party leadership and working people in contemporary Socialist society. The Hinze-Kunze relationship is developed in depth in Braun's *Hinze-Kunze-Roman* (1985; Hinze-Kunze-novel), in which the two representative figures assume more specific fictional identities as a high-ranking party official and his chauffeur.

Finally, Braun has published one collection of essays and assorted "notes" under the title *Es genügt nicht die einfache Wahrheit* (1975; the simple truth is not enough). Several of the essays included there, especially "Die Schaubühne nicht als moralische Anstalt betrachtet" (1968; the theater not regarded as a moral institution) and "Über die Bauweise neuer Stücke" (1973; about the making of new plays), are important expressions of Braun's views on the function and practice of theater after Brecht.

Achievements

When Braun's first plays were finally published and performed in the early 1970's, he was hailed in both the East and the West as the most promising young talent among the dramatists of his generation. While his career as a dramatist has had its ups and downs, he has emerged as one of East Germany's leading dramatists and as a principal heir to and adapter of the Brechtian theatrical tradition in East Germany. One indication of Braun's stature as a playwright is the positive reception given his work in West Germany, where seven of his plays have been published and three have appeared in the repertory of major stages. Among East German dramatists, only Braun and his colleagues Peter Hacks and Heiner Müller have managed in the long term to find an audience for their work in both German states—an accomplishment made the more remarkable when one considers the political-ideological context in which inter-German cultural exchange takes place. Since the early 1970's, Braun's international reputation as both a poet and a dramatist has grown steadily and has led to a following for his work outside German-speaking Europe, most notably in France, Italy, England, and the United States.

Although Braun had no direct contact with Brecht or with his historic productions at the Berliner Ensemble in the 1950's, Braun's plays clearly show the influence of Brecht and the theatrical tradition that he began. More than the work of any of his East German contemporaries, Braun's drama represents a continuation of Brecht's tradition, which he adapts to and for the situation of the Socialist state in the 1960's and 1970's. While Brecht's drama focused on the dialectic of the class struggle, Braun's theater moves to new conflicts that are to be found within Socialist society itself. The dialectic tension inherent in these "non-antagonistic" conflicts—by which Braun means conflicts within one social system rather than between competing social systems—is essential to the evolution of socialism and is the focal point of Braun's dramatic method.

Braun's refusal to provide solutions to the problems he presents in his drama (that is, to suggest positive models of behavior) has been one reason for the uneven reception given his plays in his native East Germany. Especially during the early stages of his career in the 1960's, a time during which East German cultural policy encouraged affirmative theater celebrating the accomplishments of the new Socialist German state, Braun's insistence on focusing on unresolved problems and unpleasant realities clearly worked against the publication and performance of his work. It would be misleading, however, to overemphasize Braun's difficulties with cultural authorities in his country. He, like many critical writers in East Germany, views himself as a committed Socialist, who, in posing difficult and even unanswerable questions, seeks to encourage change in the direction of a better society. His stance as a writer is one of "critical solidarity" with the cause of socialism. Thus, in spite of the mixed performance history of his plays, Braun remains an influential force in the East German theater, a fact evidenced by his nearly continuous involvement throughout his career as a dramaturge and artistic consultant for several major East German stages.

Braun's work has been recognized with three major East German literary awards: the Erich Weinert Medal for young writers, presented in 1964, and since then the important Heinrich Heine and Heinrich Mann prizes for literature, awarded in 1971 and 1980 respectively.

Biography

Volker Braun was born on the eve of World War II, on May 7, 1939, in Dresden, Germany. His father was killed in the last weeks of the war, leaving his mother to rear him and four brothers alone. In 1948, the nine-year-old Braun spent a brief period of time in the care of the International Red Cross in Switzerland, where he was treated for acute malnutrition; he soon returned to his family in the Soviet Occupation Zone, which officially became the German Democratic Republic in October of 1949. In spite of the traumatic conditions under which he grew up, Braun does not generally deal with the war and its immediate aftermath in his writing. In contrast to his older colleagues, who experienced the war as adolescents or adults and whose work often returns to this experience, Braun's work, like that of many writers of his generation, has tended to focus on the postwar efforts to build a new Socialist state in the void left by the defeat of Fascism.

Braun finished his basic schooling in 1957 with the successful completion of the university qualifying exam, the *Abitur*; he was initially unsuccessful, however, in gaining admission to the university. Over the next four years, he worked variously as a printer in his native Dresden, then as a mine construction worker at the coal and steel cooperative Schwarze Pumpe, and finally, after completing a technical apprenticeship, as a machine mechanic at the open-pit coal mine Burghammer. His work experiences during these four years were to leave a profound mark on his early writing and are especially apparent in the subject matter and the setting of his first several plays.

It was during this period that Braun wrote his first poetry, and in 1959 he completed the first of the four prose reports that would together make up *Das ungezwungene Leben Kasts*. More directly than in any of his other writing, the Kast stories illustrate Braun's strong personal identification with the young Socialist state. The autobiographically inspired accounts reflect in the figure Kast important stages in both Braun's personal development and the parallel development of his country.

In 1960, Braun was admitted to the University of Leipzig, where he studied philosophy until 1964. Upon completion of his studies, he traveled for a time in the Soviet Union (in Siberia) before accepting an invitation from Brecht's widow, Helene Weigel, to work as a dramaturge and assistant director at the Berliner Ensemble in East Berlin. He held this position for one year before leaving to devote himself full-time to his writing.

These first years in Berlin were an especially productive period for Braun's writing. In addition to his poetry and the work on the first Kast stories, the period between 1964 and 1971 saw him work on no fewer than six plays, all but one of which (*Hans Faust*) were to remain unpublished and unperformed until after a general liberalization of cultural policy in 1971. The more liberal cultural policies announced that year by new party chief Erich Honecker coincided with Braun's return to a direct involvement in theater work when he accepted a one-year position as consultant and playwright-in-residence with the civic theaters of the city of Leipzig. In Leipzig and over the next few years, Braun was able to play a part in the first successful productions of his early plays. Braun has been involved with the theater continuously since 1971, working from 1972 to 1977 with the Deutsches Theater in East Berlin, and thereafter with the Berliner Ensemble. These two theaters have become the principal proponents and producers of his work in East Germany.

In 1973, Braun was elected to the executive council of the East German Writers' Union, a post that reflects both his strong Socialist convictions and the prominence and respect that he enjoys among his colleagues. He resides and works in East Berlin.

Analysis

Volker Braun's plays are concrete expressions of his dissatisfaction with the present, his unwillingness to accept the current state of things in his own society and in the world. His plays focus, therefore, on the unresolved problems and troubling contradictions of a Socialist state, not so much as a criticism of its failings—although this criticism is clearly important—but as a challenge to his audience to join in the enormous task of building a new society. Braun's dramatic method is, as the critic Katherine Vanovitch has observed, to present his audience with the challenge that a Socialist society in its imperfection offers, and "to excite them, as individuals, to share in the poetry by grasping their opportunity to mould their own environment and, in the process, themselves."

One basic question is at the heart of all Braun's drama. It concerns the dialectical relationship between the various contradictory forces that reside within all revolutions. Braun's plays portray in manifold variation the continual struggle between utopian vision and reactionary impulse. They examine in the lives and fates of his individual protagonists the conflicts between the desire for progress and the conservative tendency to preserve what currently exists, and between the subjective desires of the individual and the objective limitations inherent in real-life situations. In Braun's view, these conflicts are most apparent in the contradictory relationship between the political leaders of the society "who consciously orchestrate the transformation of the society or who consciously or unconsciously impede it," and those who are led and "who consciously or unconsciously put the plans into action or who criticize and resist them." Accordingly, the relationship between the political leadership and individual citizens is an important focus in his plays.

A second, related question posed in Braun's drama concerns the costs, in particular the human costs, associated with the building of the new society. Thus, Braun's plays often examine the effect that larger political and economic issues have upon the lives of individuals—that is, upon the people who either willingly or under duress have taken on the task of moving the society forward.

In terms of both the choice of subject matter and their dramatic approach, Braun's plays fall into two fairly distinct periods. The first extends from the early 1960's and his first work on the play *Die Kipper* (the dumpers) through the mid-1970's and the completion of the dramas *Schmitten* and *Tinka*. During this roughly fifteen-year period, Braun's plays focused almost exclusively on the problems connected with the development of socialism in East Germany. With the lone exception of the unpublished play "Lenins Tod" (Lenin's death), which deals with the still-taboo subject of the transition of power in the Soviet Union in the 1920's, all the major plays of this period are set in the German Democratic Republic of the 1950's and early 1960's, in the so-called *Aufbau*, or "building," period, in which the fledgling East German state struggled to build a new industrial economy.

In his first play, *Die Kipper*, Braun focuses on the continuing existence of demeaning and dehumanizing work in the context of socialism. The case in point is the physically and spiritually ruinous work of the dumpers, who spend their entire shift dumping trainloads of sand and dirt. While it is technologically possible to automate the dumping process, the country's fragile economy in the 1950's does not make automation feasible, and workers remain bound to the methods of production borrowed from the old system. The play begins with a prologue in which one of the actors presents a short synopsis of the play's essential content, a synopsis that should focus the audience's attention on the play's central concerns. The play will recount one year in the life of the unskilled worker Paul Bauch, who discovers one day that "in addition to the arm that he needs for his work, he has yet another arm, and what's more two legs and even a head." Braun's point is clear: The new society does not make use of the entire person. The individual worker now, as before, is reduced to the one procedure he or she performs, and the traditional division between headwork and handwork, between the "bosses" who lead and the workers who follow, is kept intact.

In the figure Paul Bauch, Braun embodies the energy and legitimate aspirations of the individual worker, who demands that work be meaningful and that he be involved in it completely, head and hand. Like the figures Hinze and Tinka in later plays, Bauch demands an immediate and complete change in the methods of production. He demands an ideal socialism while disregarding the very real factors that still hamper its realization. When, through an unlikely series of events, he is made *Brigadier*, the foreman of his work brigade, he throws himself into his work, driving himself and the brigade on to meet ever higher production goals. By making the tedious labor of the dump into a kind of sport, he is able to help each of his coworkers to realize the importance of the individual's contribution to the success of the whole. His innovative measures are at first successful in increasing both the level of production and the involvement of the individual brigade members in their work; they ultimately collapse, however, as Bauch's subjective demands surpass the objective reality of the young country's ability to support them. Bauch's methods culminate in an accident that destroys some of the brigade's antiquated equipment and seriously injures one of the workers. Bauch, who is held responsible, is relieved of his post and sent to prison.

On the one hand, by not being content to accept that which is "objectively possible" under existing conditions, Bauch is able to accomplish something previously considered impossible. On the other hand, his individual efforts frustrate the ultimate goal of true collective work, for the brigade members have become mere extensions of his energy. They have become his "arm," relying on his head rather than using their own. Somewhat ironically, Bauch's revolutionary energy, while contributing somewhat to the society's progress, serves to frustrate the ultimate goal of the Socialist revolution. In like manner, the outdated and inadequate machinery that the dumpers must use suggests the limits within which the revolution must proceed. The young Socialist state does not yet possess the objective basis for true and complete socialism, a fact that dictates the country's continuing reliance on remnants of the old social order.

While Paul Bauch fails, the play nevertheless ends optimistically. Bauch's "unreasonable" demands have awakened a new consciousness among his co-workers, who will now proceed on their own in the direction that Bauch has pushed them—if now at a more measured and moderate pace. As foretold somewhat enigmatically in the prologue, in the end, Paul Bauch "loses a brigade, but the brigade wins." Braun's protagonists are not exemplary figures; they are not the positive heroes and heroines called for in the literary program of Socialist Realism. This fact is suggested in the title of the final 1972 version of the play, which places the dumpers as a group in the forefront, while two earlier versions of the play, entitled first "Der totale Mensch" (the total person) and then "Kipper Paul Bauch" (dumper Paul Bauch), emphasized the individual's central importance.

In his second major drama, *Hinze und Kunze*, Braun returns to some of the same issues he examined in *Die Kipper*. Like his first play, *Hinze und Kunze* went through a number of revisions and rewritings before it appeared in its final form in 1973. (An early version of the play with the title *Hans Faust* had premiered in Leipzig in 1968 but was withdrawn from production shortly after its premiere.) One significant result of the long revision process is reflected in the changing of the play's title, which in the 1973 version gives equal billing to the play's two central figures. The play follows the career and development of the construction worker Hinze, the Hans Faust of the earlier version. A figure in many ways similar to Paul Bauch, he is impatient and discouraged by the slow progress of socialism. Although he no longer goes by the name Faust, Hinze's impatient dissatisfaction with the status quo clearly links him to Johann Wolfgang von Goethe's hero, and the text is full of allusions to Goethe's masterpiece. The most obvious point of connection to the Faust theme is made in the pact between Hinze and the local party secretary Kunze. Like Mephistopheles in Goethe's play, Kunze will urge Hinze on to new experience; rather than diverting him in the manner of his predecessor, however, his Kunze will ultimately keep Hinze on track. Here, each partner is dependent on the other if their common cause is to succeed. Thus, they agree to remain together as long as either is dissatisfied.

In the relationship between Faust and Mephistopheles, Braun has discovered a useful model with which to explore what he has termed "the most disturbing contradiction" in the Socialist revolution: the contradiction between the society's leaders and those whom they seek to lead, or, stated somewhat differently, the continuing division between the subjective needs of the individual and the collective interest of the society as represented by the Party. Here, as throughout his work, Braun calls attention to the disparity that exists between the goals and accomplishments so effortlessly announced in his country's newspapers and by its leaders, and the actual costs that the realization of these goals exacts in the lives of individuals. Kunze must use his best persuasive skills to win the disillusioned and skeptical Hinze for the cause; once having won him, he must push and cajole Hinze to a full commitment of himself in the slow and costly process of building the new society. As the result of their pact, Hinze develops gradually from a worker who must be manipulated by Kunze's clever arguments into carrying out the work of the new society, into one who is capable and willing to change, that is, who is capable of assuming an equal role in shaping the future of his country.

Hinze's acceptance of Kunze's challenge is not, however, without problems for his personal life. In order to pursue the work at hand and later to qualify himself through additional schooling for a leadership position, he must leave his wife, Marlies. Rather than passively accepting her abandonment, however, Marlies heeds Kunze's advice to go to work. By accepting Kunze's challenge, she, like Hinze, can make a greater contribution at the industrial plant where they later both work. To Hinze, who barely recognizes her when they meet again, she is a changed person. She is, as Kunze comments ironically, "her own man"; that is, she is no longer dependent on her husband. While Hinze has acquired the needed education for the leadership role he now assumes at the plant, he remains the individualistic self-helper he has always been, a fact that will lead to his eventual failure as a leader. Now reunited with Hinze, Marlies provides a striking and important contrast to her husband. When Hinze's visionary plans for the future of the factory are frustrated by a decision of the Party's central planners, he rebels and forsakes his agreement with Kunze. Marlies is torn between the two men who have thus far been her life, between Hinze, whose child she now carries and who wants her to leave with him, and Kunze, who urges her to stay and continue the important work she has just begun.

Marlies remains to complete the work originally undertaken with Hinze. She succeeds without him and in spite of his desertion; as Kunze later comments, however, she has progressed so far (in her Socialist awareness) that she goes too far. Faced with the choice between her unborn child and following through with the work that her efforts have made possible, she chooses the latter and aborts the fetus. Through no fault of her own, she loses both husband and child because she wished to complete the tasks for which she is so desperately needed. In the broken relationship between Hinze and Marlies and in the loss of their unborn child, Braun is able to suggest the considerable human costs associated with the building of the new society. Beyond their personal tragedy, the fact that Marlies believes that she must make such a choice at all is itself a comment on the transitional and imperfect nature of the society in which such choices are in any sense necessary. Still, the play ends with a measure of hope. Shaken by the events that have taken place in his absence, Hinze is drawn back to the factory and to the cause it represents. As the play ends, he enters anew into his pact with Kunze and resolves to start again from the beginning.

In the plays *Tinka* and *Schmitten*, Braun continues to examine issues related to women and to their role in the building of socialism. In the two title figures, Braun dramatizes opposite responses of women to the challenges that the new society presents. In *Schmitten*, he constructs his drama around the difficulties of workers who under all previous social systems have been the "dumb ones," those workers who have traditionally had no say in the work that they perform. Jutta Schmitten, a model worker whose example has always served to encourage others, is asked by the Party to seek a higher level of qualification and responsibility by returning to school. After persuading others to do so, she refuses herself for the simple reason that she lacks confidence in her ability to learn something new. While her coworkers attempt to shame her into compliance, the factory's chief engineer, Kolb, who is also her lover, is in the position to "spare" her. His attempt to treat her humanely, to spare her possible future embarrassment, is, however, a throwback to the thinking of the old, pre-Socialist society, in which such gestures based on gender were often also a form of and an excuse for the subjugation of women. Her lover's patronizing treatment of her evokes a violent response in Schmitten and her female coworkers, who, in a mad outbreak, castrate the hapless Kolb. Ironically, it is through this act of madness that Schmitten is able to break out of the restrictive role that has limited her development.

In *Tinka*, Braun presents the opposite case, the worker who has accepted the challenge to further her training. Tinka has just returned from three years of technical studies when the factory is informed that the planned automation for which she was trained will not take place. Tinka protests and is bitter over the passivity of her coworkers, who seem content to accept whatever decisions are handed down from above. She is especially bitter over the apparent lack of resistance by her fiancé, Brenner, who is the plant's technical director. Brenner and the local Party secretary Ludwig have, in fact, begun working behind the scenes in the belief that a cautious, tactical approach will eventually restore some portion of the original automation plans. In the manner of her predecessors Paul Bauch and Hinze, Tinka is unwilling to accept less than was originally promised, and her insistent protests lead finally to her dismissal from the factory. She refuses to give in, however, and relentlessly pursues Brenner, from whom she demands complete honesty, something which his tactical maneuverings prevent him from giving. In the play's climactic final scene, the drunken Brenner kills Tinka, who has become for him a constant reminder of his own dishonesty and inadequacy.

Tinka is in part written against tactics of the kind that Brenner and Ludwig employ. Brenner's tactical maneuvering, while well-intentioned, is, in its indirectness and conciliatory avoidance of conflict, dishonest. It alienates Brenner from himself (his true beliefs) and from those around him, and it ultimately leads to violence and tragedy.

In the mid-1970's, Braun's drama entered a new, somewhat more philosophical stage. While the issues that concern him remained in this second period essentially the same as they were in his early work, the plays written after 1975 were no longer so narrowly focused on the specific situation and problems of East Germany. Instead, Braun turned increasingly to history and to literary sources for the material for his plays.

Revolution remains Braun's central theme in the plays of this second period, a fact that is immediately clear in his choice of material. Three of the plays, *Guevara: Oder, Der Sonnenstaat* (Guevara: or, the sun state), *The Great Peace*, and *Dmitri*, have as their central focus revolutions that fail. In spite of the fact that all three plays are based on historical events, Braun does not intend them merely to be interesting case studies. Rather, they are parables in the Brechtian sense, which are meant to create a dialectical tension between the past and the present such that the events in the past provoke a response in the present. Each revolution portrayed is relevant to the modern audience to the extent that the past example can suggest what remains to be done. In *Guevara*, for example, Braun exposes the naïve revolutionary romanticism of the title figure, who fails to recognize the real situation of the peasants whom the revolution seeks to liberate. Without their involvement, there can be no revolution, only the replacement of one set of rulers by another. Braun's reversal of the normal chronological sequence of events allows for an especially effective analysis of Guevara's failure. The play begins with Guevara's death and leads the audience back, step-by-step, to the optimistic beginnings of the ill-fated guerrilla campaign, a technique which encourages an analytical examination of the play's action.

Of the plays written after 1975, *The Great Peace* stands apart as Braun's most fully realized dramatic parable. Set in ancient China, the play dramatizes the course of a "successful" peasant uprising. Having disposed of the aristocracy that tyrannized them, the peasants proclaim the "Great Peace," which, according to ancient texts, is to be more than the mere absence of war; it is a state of total equality in which there are no class differences and therefore no need for either violence or rules. The land descends quickly into chaos, however, as the absence of rules and leaders brings the normal functioning of society to an abrupt halt. At this point, the clever poet Tschu Jün takes the lead. He persuades the peasant Gau Dsu to become Emperor and then proceeds to reestablish many of the rules and distinctions that previously existed. In effect, he "saves" the revolution by subverting it. While the new reign of Gau Dsu may initially represent an improvement over that of his predecessor, the advances of the revolution remain modest. Only at the end of the play, when his reign is beset by new enemies, one of whom is the very peasant class from which he rose, does Gau Dsu realize that his rule has in fact reestablished the structures of oppression that his revolution sought to overthrow.

In the end, it is the poet-philosopher Wang who provides the key to understanding Braun's parable. Wang is Braun's spokesman for the utopian ideals of the revolution and is, accordingly, persecuted by both regimes in the play.

His experience leads him to conclude that a revolution can preserve its ideals only if it is successful in truly changing society "from the ground up." In Braun's view, the "ground" that forms the basis for the society and its successful functioning is work; it is here, in the nature of work, that Braun sees the reason that change is so difficult to achieve. As long as there remains a distinction between headwork and handwork, between those who plan and organize the work with their heads and those who carry out the work with their hands, the structures of class oppression will continue to exist.

While recognizing the revolution's failure, it is not Braun's intention here or in his other plays to recant his utopian view of the future. If the peasants' uprising in China failed, it was not because of the actions or omissions of Gau Dsu; it was rather because the society was not at a point in its development that would support so drastic a change "from the ground up." Similarly, in plays such as *Simplex Deutsch* (simplex German), Braun suggests that a process of human development and change must accompany any external transformation of society. The ten outwardly unrelated scenes in this play portray examples of human immaturity that continue to frustrate the process of becoming a full and autonomous human being.

Braun does not provide ready solutions to the contradictions he perceives in society. Rather, he attempts only to show his audience how both objective and subjective resistance to the achievement of revolutionary goals continues to hinder true progress toward a better society. As was the case in early dramas that examined the problems and failures of socialism in his own country, the later plays, for all their apparent pessimism, seem to suggest that what was not possible at an earlier stage in human and social development may indeed be possible in the future. As Braun notes in one of his theater essays, it is not the theater's role in his time to offer solutions to society's problems, but rather to show that solutions to its problems are possible. In the true Brechtian tradition, it is left to the audience to act upon what it has witnessed on the stage and to choose for itself an alternative that will avoid the failures of the past.

Other major works

NOVELS: *Das ungezwungene Leben Kasts*, 1972, 1979; *Unvollendete Geschichte*, 1975 (*Unfinished Story*, 1979); *Geschichten von Hinze und Kunze*, 1982; *Hinze-Kunze-Roman*, 1985.

POETRY: *Provokation für mich*, 1965; *Vorläufiges*, 1966; *Wir und nicht sie*, 1970; *Gegen die symmetrische Welt*, 1974; *Poesiealbum 115*, 1977; *Der Stoff zum Leben*, 1977; *Training des aufrechten Gangs*, 1978; *Archaische Landschaft mit Losungen*, 1983.

NONFICTION: *Es genügt nicht die einfache Wahrheit*, 1975.

Bibliography

Huettich, H. G. "Theater in the Planned Society," in *Contemporary Drama in the German Democratic Republic in Its Historical, Political, and Cultural Context*, 1978.

Profitlich, Ulrich. "Das Drama der DDR in den siebziger Jahren," in *Literatur der DDR in den siebziger Jahren*, 1983. Edited by P. U. Hohendahl and P. Herminghouse.

Rosellini, Jay. *Volker Braun*, 1983.

Vanovitch, Katherine. "Volker Braun," in *Female Roles in East German Drama, 1949-1977: A Selective History of Drama in the G.D.R.*, 1982.

James R. Reece

HOWARD BRENTON

Born: Portsmouth, England; December 13, 1942

Principal drama

Ladder of Fools, pr. 1967; *Gargantua*, pr. 1969 (adaptation of François Rabelais' novel); *Gum and Goo*, pr. 1969, pb. 1972; *Revenge*, pr. 1969, pb. 1970; *Heads*, pr. 1969, pb. 1970; *The Education of Skinny Spew*, pr. 1969, pb. 1970; *Christie in Love*, pr. 1969, pb. 1970; *Wesley*, pr. 1970, pb. 1972; *Cheek*, pr. 1970; *Fruit*, pr. 1970; *Scott of the Antarctic: What God Didn't See*, pr. 1971, pb. 1972; *Lay By*, pr. 1971, pb. 1972 (with Brian Clark, Trevor Griffiths, David Hare, Steven Poliakoff, Hugh Stoddart, and Snoo Wilson); *Hitler Dances*, pr. 1972; *How Beautiful with Badges*, pr. 1972; *Measure for Measure*, pr. 1972 (adaptation of William Shakespeare's play); *England's Ireland*, pr. 1972 (with David Elgar, Tony Bicât, Brian Clark, Francis Fuchs, Hare, and Wilson); *A Fart for Europe*, pr. 1973 (with Elgar); *Mug*, pr. 1973; *Magnificence*, pr., pb. 1973; *Brassneck*, pr. 1973, pb. 1974 (with Hare); *The Churchill Play: As It Will Be Performed in the Winter of 1984 by the Internees of Churchill Camp Somewhere in England*, pr., pb. 1974; *The Saliva Milkshake*, pr. 1975, pb. 1977 (adaptation of Joseph Conrad's novel *Under Western Eyes*); *Weapons of Happiness*, pr., pb. 1976; *Government Property*, pr. 1976; *Epsom Downs*, pr., pb. 1977; *Deeds*, pr. 1978 (with Griffiths, Ken Campbell, and Hare); *Sore Throats*, pr., pb. 1979; *A Short Sharp Shock!*, pr. 1980, pb. 1981 (with Tony Howard); *The Romans in Britain*, pr. 1980, pb. 1981; *Thirteenth Night*, pr., pb. 1981 (based on Shakespeare's play *Macbeth*); *The Genius*, pr., pb. 1983; *Sleeping Policemen*, pr. 1983, pb. 1984 (with Tunde Ikoli); *Bloody Poetry*, pr. 1984, pb. 1985; *Pravda: A Fleet Street Comedy*, pr., pb. 1985 (with Hare).

Other literary forms

Although known primarily as a playwright, Howard Brenton has published two collections of poetry: *Notes from a Psychotic Journal and Other Poems* (1969) and *Sore Throats and Sonnets of Love and Opposition* (1979).

Achievements

Brenton belongs to a small group of radical English playwrights known as the "wild bunch," which includes Snoo Wilson, Howard Barker, and David Hare. Brenton's achievements in drama have been principally in openly agitprop theater in the interest of revolutionary socialism. His plays depict matters of current public interest in Great Britain, though frequently he sets the drama in a specific, noncontemporary historical period, such as Roman Britain or nineteenth century Italy. Despite the directness of their Marxist propaganda, the plays hold their own in terms of dramatic plot and characterization. Like Edward Bond, Brenton employs graphic violence and pornographic images to convey his outrage against the social complacency he detects in his country. The plot forms resemble Samuel Beckett's Theater of the Absurd and Bertolt Brecht's epic drama, but Brenton dissociates himself from both playwrights: Beckett he has criticized for being a philosophical pessimist, Brecht for lacking awareness of the theater event. Brenton's play *Weapons of Happiness* won the *Evening Standard* Drama Award for Best Play of 1976, and he received commissions to write plays for the Royal Shakespeare Company and the National Theatre. Frequently, his plays are collaborations with other writers, notably his friend David Hare.

Biography

Howard Brenton was born in Portsmouth, England, on December 13, 1942, during the German blitzes of World War II. His parents were Donald Henry and Rose Lilian (née Lewis) Brenton. Donald Brenton retired in the early 1960's after twenty-five years as a law-enforcement officer and joined the Methodist Church, eventually becoming an ordained minister in that denomination. His avocations included the theater, in which he participated frequently as an amateur stage actor and director. Howard Brenton's interest in writing and the theater began quite early in life in imitation of his father. Traveling all over England and Wales with his family, Brenton was glum and rebellious even as a child, enjoying the nonauthoritarian environment of the stage and the privacy of writing. At age nine, he adapted a comic strip into a short play. The youthful Brenton also wrote poems and three novels, in addition to completing a biography of Adolf Hitler at age seventeen. Brenton attended grammar school and was graduated from Chichester High School in West Sussex. He initially wanted to be a visual artist specializing in abstract paintings, and with that end in mind, he enrolled at Corsham Court, an art college in Bath. Changing his mind at the last minute, he dropped art school and made plans to attend St. Catherine's College, Cambridge, to study writing. In later years, Brenton said that he hated his Cambridge years despite the fact that he was a promising student there. Majoring in English, he took courses with George Steiner, the distinguished literary critic; Brenton greatly admired Steiner for his social views and for his teaching. In 1965, Brenton saw the first production of one of his plays, *Ladder of Fools*, at Cambridge and received a B.A. degree with honors.

Upon leaving Cambridge, Brenton worked odd jobs, stage-managed, and acted part-time while continuing to write plays. In 1969, he performed as an actor with the Brighton Combination, for whom he also wrote the short experimental plays *Gargantua* and *Gum and Goo*. Later the same year, he worked with Chris Parr's theater group at Bradford University, which produced *Gum and Goo*, *Heads*, and *The Education of Skinny Spew* in conjunction with rock concerts given at the university. During this time, Brenton submitted a play script to the Royal Court Theatre and was invited for an interview. *Revenge*, his first full-length play, was produced at the Royal Court Theatre Upstairs, London, in September, 1969. During the production of *Revenge*, Brenton met and befriended David Hare, a fellow playwright and director. Hare's company, the Portable Theatre, commissioned Brenton to write *Christie in Love*, which Hare directed in November, 1969, and for which Snoo Wilson (who, like Hare, was later to be professionally associated with Brenton) built the set and stage-managed. The play moved to the Royal Court Theatre Upstairs early the following year and received favorable reviews. As a result of *Christie in Love*, Brenton won the Arts Council's John Whiting Award in 1970 and received an Arts Council Drama Bursary for the next season. The play was the beginning of a long and prodigious professional relationship between Brenton and Hare. On January 31, 1970, between productions of *Christie in Love*, Brenton married Jane Margaret Fry.

As a playwright on the "Fringe" in the early 1970's, Brenton wrote a number of plays to be produced in unusual spaces. His play *Wesley* was performed at the Eastbrook Hall Methodist Church in Bradford, and *Scott of the Antarctic: What God Didn't See* was produced in an ice-skating rink. These works appeared as part of the Bradford Festival in 1970 and 1971. The playwright was also involved in several collaborative efforts during this time, notably *Lay By* and *England's Ireland*. In 1972, Brenton became a resident playwright at the Royal Court Theatre. It was at the Royal Court that Brenton began a succession of "anti-Brechtian" epic plays, which cemented his reputation: *Magnificence*, *Brassneck*, *The Churchill Play*, *Weapons of Happiness*, and *Epsom Downs*. *Weapons of Happiness*, which took its title from a phrase spray-painted on the set of *Magnificence*, was the first play to debut at the National Theatre's new Lyttelton Theatre. Brenton wrote *Epsom Downs* in 1977 for the Joint Stock Theatre Group. During the same period of time, Brenton wrote three plays for television: *Lushly* (1971), *The Saliva Milkshake*, and *The Paradise Run* (1976). *The Saliva Milkshake* was later adapted for the stage and eventually was performed in New York, marking Brenton's debut in the United States. In 1973, Brenton wrote a short screenplay for the British Film Institute, *Skin Flicker*, based on a novel by Tony Bicât, who worked with him at the Portable Theatre (founded by Bicât and Hare).

In its 1978-1979 season, the Royal Shakespeare Company staged a successful revival of *The Churchill Play* at the Warehouse Theatre in London. The next year, *Sore Throats*, also performed by the Royal Shakespeare Company at the Warehouse, departed from the theatrical epics which established Brenton as an important playwright in the 1970's. The play, which the writer calls "an intimate play in two acts," occurs in a Pinteresque *mise en scène* (an empty South London flat), with only three characters: two women and a man. Brenton followed *Sore Throats* with *A Short Sharp Shock!* in 1980, a collaboration with Tony Howard. The year 1980 was to become a landmark year for Brenton with the National Theatre production of *The Romans in Britain* at the new Olivier Theatre. The play, his second for the National Theatre, provoked a strong critical reaction that did not abate during its entire run. Indeed, not since Edward Bond depicted the brutal stoning of an infant in a perambulator in his 1965 play *Saved* had London theater critics raised such an outcry against a play and a playwright. Most of the outrage was directed at the production's liberal use of male nudity and the graphic representation onstage of a Roman soldier's attempted rape of a young Celtic priest. The director Michael Bogdanov was charged with obscene behavior under the Sexual Offenses Act of 1967, and there was an effort to stop the play and withdraw the Greater London Council's subsidy to the National Theatre. Despite, or perhaps because of, all the puritan indignation over the play's visual content, *The Romans in Britain* played to full houses during its six-month run in London. Also in 1980, the National Theatre presented Brenton's *The Life of Galileo* (1980; adaptation of Bertolt Brecht's play *Leben des Galilei*) which ran for more than a year.

The Royal Shakespeare Company's performance of *Thirteenth Night* in 1981 was a little less controversial than *The Romans in Britain*. The play, a political satire loosely adapted from William Shakespeare's tragedy *Macbeth*, drew criticism for its pointed, allegedly libelous references by name to prominent living British conservatives. A number of the play's offensive lines were subsequently deleted from performances. Brenton criticized academia and technology in *The Genius*, which the Royal Court Theatre produced in 1983. In the same year, the Foco Novo Theatre Company commissioned Brenton and Tunde Ikoli to write separate plays involving three black characters and three white characters. The two plays were then synthesized by the director Roland Rees into a single play, *Sleeping Policemen*. The next year, the same theater company commissioned Brenton to write *Bloody Poetry*, a play about Percy Bysshe Shelley, which the company produced at the Haymarket Theatre at Leicester. *Bloody Poetry* was subsequently moved to the Hampstead Theatre in London. In 1985, Howard Brenton and David Hare collaborated on a comedy called *Pravda*, a satire on the more commercial and sensationalistic aspects of English newspaper journalism. Presented under Hare's direction at the National Theatre, the play was both a popular and a critical success, with Anthony Hopkins' performance in the leading role being singled out for special praise.

Analysis

Howard Brenton's plays aggressively and unapologetically exploit contemporary public issues to promote revolutionary socialism and antiestablishment social causes. Whether the dramatic setting is historical (*The Romans in Britain, Bloody Poetry*) or contemporary (*Magnificence, Sore Throats*) or futuristic (*The Churchill Play, The Genius*), the plays depict class struggle and the necessity of nonviolent change on a universal scale. Brenton's drama is, nevertheless, remarkably evenhanded in its treatment of the characters, sometimes critical of the radicals for their fuzzy thinking about politics and sometimes sympathetic toward the human foibles of the rich and powerful. It portrays even political conservatives, usually the villains of Brenton's stage conflicts, in the best possible light, notably in the touching dialogue between Alice and Babs in scene 4 of *Magnificence*, and in the sympathetic characterization of Captain Thompson, the physician at the English concentration camp in *The Churchill Play*. Brenton's plays frequently make the point that self-interest and misspent passion occur on all sides of a political issue, thus contributing to the general malaise in society. It is a point scored expertly in the 1969 play *Revenge*, in which opposing sides of the law are represented by a single actor.

Brenton's early one-act play, *Christie in Love*, demonstrates the writer's interest in the criminal mind and the banality of evil. Based on the case of the 1950's mass murderer John Reginald Halliday Christie, the play combines elements of psychological naturalism and self-conscious structuralist theater. The Constable and the Inspector, the only actors in the drama besides Christie, are intentionally flat characters, offsetting Christie himself, who is (after his initial entrance) dramatically believable and psychologically complex. In the first two scenes, the two law-enforcement officers exchange inane comments about their activity and sexist jokes which are painfully ill-timed and unfunny. When Christie appears, in scene 3, he arises slowly out of a grave of newspapers in the manner of a Count Dracula, wearing a large, disfiguring fright mask. In all the subsequent scenes, Christie is maskless, revealing a quite ordinary looking and surprisingly defenseless man. The contrasting imagery suggests that the concocted tabloid image of Christie (or, for that matter, any "villain") as a monster is a false one, and that the real person who was Christie performed his heinous crimes out of love, peculiarly defined and experienced by the individual. Moreover, in the context of the play, Christie is far more genuine in his passions than his interrogators, who delude themselves with ideas of normality and morality which they enforce through violence, willful ignorance, and deprecation of sex and love.

Certain elements of the play have appeared again in Brenton's later work. Christie's theatrical resurrection from the dead is very similar to Winston Churchill's escape from the catafalque in the play-within-a-play at the beginning of *The Churchill Play*. The startling synthesis of exclamations of true love and images of brutality appears again in *Sore Throats*, in which sudden dramatic reversals and extremely contradictory actions muddle the real nature of the characters' emotions. The bleak, Cold War background and the surrealistic middle-class setting of the play recur in numerous other Brenton works, including *The Churchill Play* and *The Genius*. At the same time, *Christie in Love* is unique among Brenton's plays in the comparative subtlety of its politics and theatrical violence. In the plays most characteristic of the playwright, revolutionary socialism is openly espoused, and terrorism and violence are gruesomely reified on the stage.

Critics and reviewers frequently complain that Brenton's theater is too violent, that it is in reality only sensationalistic. A certain amount of the outcry against his play *The Romans in Britain* was directed against its graphic portrayal of torture and murder, as well as its profuse male nudity. Brenton deliberately uses shock techniques, violence, profanity, nudity, and scatology to provoke his audiences. There is a prophetic intensity about his writing, particularly in the plays of the middle 1970's and early 1980's, which are public spectacles condemning oppression and collaboration with oppression through passivity. Brenton calls this element in drama "aggro," a British slang term which suggests a mix of aggression and aggravation. Its purpose is to draw the audience together into the play's (and playwright's) outrage. Brenton has commented that his agitprop theater frequently succeeds better at agitation than at propaganda, and the usual critical and public response to his plays seems to bear him out on this point.

Another aspect of Brenton's writing that draws criticism on occasion is the unevenness of his dramatic style. Scenes that are dark with pessimism and brooding alternate with slapstick comedy, and sensitive character drama intermixes with pornographic and Grand Guignol stage effects. For example, the ironically titled revenge play *Magnificence* begins with five young radicals occupying an abandoned flat in protest against the landowner's legal oppression of the poor tenants. The opening scenes center mainly on the two female members of the group: Mary, who is pregnant and whose approach to revolution is largely aesthetic, and Veronica, who formerly worked for the British Broadcasting Corporation (BBC) and who is the most intellectual (and moderate) member of the group. A sort of climax is reached in the play at the end of scene 3, when Mr. Slaughter, the landlord, in the company of a constable, breaks into the room and bodily attacks the occupants. In the process, he kicks Mary in the stomach, accidentally causing a miscarriage. The setting of the play then changes to Cambridge College and two new characters are introduced: two men who are friends, Tory bureaucrats in government and academia, who go by the nicknames Alice and Babs. The scene, which is the center of the play, is peaceful, full of reminiscences and flirtations between the two old friends as they punt a flat-bottomed boat across the stage. In the course of the scene, Babs reveals to his friend that he is about to die, and at the scene's end, he expires quietly in Alice's arms. The final third of the play centers on Jed, a minor and mostly silent character in the opening scenes, who now seeks revenge for the death of Mary's child. The other members of the radical group have chosen a less active public course; in Jed's opinion, they have debased the principles for which they stood at the beginning. The play concludes with a riveting horror scene in which Jed attacks Alice and forces him to wear a bomb in the form of a mask upon his head. When, after agonizing dramatic suspense, the explosive fails to detonate, Jed and Alice attempt to strike some sort of bargain, and then unexpectedly the bomb explodes, killing them both.

In the end, *Magnificence* leaves the audience with a sense of having watched three individual plots, each with its own impetus and tone, and—except for the obvious continuation of characters from scene to scene—little coherence is evident between the three principal parts. Brenton treats each scene on its own terms without imposing unity of action. In respect to this professedly unconscious stylistic element, Brenton categorizes himself, along with Snoo Wilson and David Hare, as a "maximalist" playwright, in contrast to the dramatic minimalism of Samuel Beckett and Harold Pinter. Brenton's goal is to depict a situation realistically by incorporating into the play as many facets or aspects of the situation as possible. The result is a deliberate hodgepodge of styles, characters, and events.

Perhaps the quintessential Brenton protagonist is Josef Frank in *Weapons of Happiness*. Like Christie and Churchill, Frank is an actual historical figure whom Brenton "resurrects" in order to make a point about political activism. The real Josef Frank was one of the twelve prominent members of the Czechoslovakian Communist Party hanged by the Stalinists in Prague in 1952. Brenton's Frank survives to 1976 by emigrating to England, where he inadvertently becomes involved in a workers' strike at a potato chip factory. Frank, a sullen and silent old man plagued with painful memories of his interrogation in the 1950's and nightmare fantasies about Stalin, is alienated not only from the factory owner and managers but also from the youthful rebels who attempt a minor coup by taking over the factory. Unable to side with the capitalists and reactionary police who want him to betray the young radicals and also unable to side with the Communists for whom violent force and half-digested Marxist ideology are legitimate tools of revolution, Frank is forced once again into a solitary position. In the end, he is able to confide in Janice, one of the young English Communists, and warns her against the utopian and terrorist tendencies which have become a part of the radical movement. He dies alone in a drain leading out of the factory. The final scene shows Janice and her comrades establishing a Socialist commune in Wales, hopefully modeled on Frank's Trotskyism.

Aspects of Josef Frank's character are typical of Brenton's antiheroes—lapsed idealists who fall, at least temporarily, into inactivity because of disillusionment and embitterment about the status quo and the state of the revolution. In *The Genius*, the American physicist Leo Lehrer, perhaps modeled on Brecht's Galileo, invents a weapon capable of destroying the whole world at once. Distressed that the American military establishment has perverted his mathematical genius in the interest of power and oppression, he flees the United States for a small university in England, full of self-loathing and paranoid fears. There he meets Gilly Brown, another mathematical genius, who has accidentally completed the formula for the weapon also. In the closing scene, Gilly and Leo have left the university to camp outside the wire fences surrounding a military installation, which they, along with another student and the university bursar's wife, periodically invade in order to publicize the vulnerability of lethal military weapons to outside attack.

Another disillusioned radical is Percy Bysshe Shelley in *Bloody Poetry*. Like Frank and Lehrer, Shelley is a refugee. He has fled from England, where his female entourage (Mary Shelley and Claire Clairemont) and he are viewed with suspicion and moral repugnance, and sets up residence in Switzerland and Italy with George Gordon, Lord Byron, a fellow radical and anarchist whose moral dissipation is portrayed in his continual drunkenness and unawareness of the consequences of his sexual liaisons. Like Frank, Shelley is haunted by the ghosts of his past life, in this case the ghost of Harriet Westbrook, Shelley's first wife, who was unable to live the life of a revolutionary (or a revolutionary's wife) and so was abandoned, eventually to go mad and kill herself. Shelley's dilemma in the play is that his wild libertarian ideology contradicts his social conscience. The puritan indignation of his countrymen and the irresponsible self-destruction of Byron do not represent his own conscience and his own concept of personal liberty, which, moreover, he cannot quite reconcile within himself. The play concludes with Shelley jubilant and adrift at sea shortly before his death. He sings about the utopian future when the men of England will rid themselves of tyrants and become free. After a blackout, Byron is seen on stage with the sail-draped corpse of Shelley and the silent, brooding ghost of Harriet. Dismayed at the unexpected death of his friend, Byron shouts, "Burn him! Burn him! Burn him! Burn us all!" thus crying down the old order in a renewed spirit of social revolution.

The Genius and *Bloody Poetry* also present examples of another class of Brenton character: the sideline observer who lacks the courage or will to act on his convictions. In *The Genius*, the university bursar, Graham Hay, is a liberal humanist who is initially sympathetic to Lehrer, even after, midway through act 1, Lehrer cuckolds the old man. Hay is a gentle man with somewhat rarefied academic tastes, but he is the lackey of the university vice-chancellor. In the end, Hay is interrogated by the English secret police and betrays Lehrer. Despite his right-thinking liberal humanist philosophy, Hay fails in the end for lack of moral passion. In *Bloody Poetry*, the sideline figure is Dr. William Polidori, whom Byron's publisher has sent to spy upon the circle of radical friends in Italy. Polidori lacks the involvement in the dramatic action which would make him a sympathetic character; his moralizing commentary on Shelley's and Byron's actions is invalidated by his own lack of commitment. In his final appearance, Polidori circulates solo in the theater with a glass of wine in one hand, lying to his listeners about his close ties with the Shelley circle and supplying grisly details about Shelley's "suicide."

Both Polidori and Hay are part of the "vast conspiracy of obedience" Morn describes in the last act of *The Churchill Play*. It is a bureaucratic conspiracy for which everyone is and is not responsible—one which leads ultimately, so Morn thinks, to military dictatorship. The most seductive aspect of the conspiracy is its anonymity. No one needs to feel individually accountable for the atrocities which one's government (or one's private organization) perpetrates. The conspiracy of obedience absolves the individual participant from personal guilt. Polidori accepts this absolution as a matter of fact. Hay, on the other hand, has to be "taught" through intimidation not to feel responsible. The character of Captain Thompson, the concentration camp physician in *The Churchill Play*, is perhaps the best developed of Brenton's sideline observers, and the play delineates a certain progress in the ethical development of Thompson.

Thompson is the chief supporter of the seditious entertainment the prisoners of the Churchill Camp are preparing for the visiting Members of Parliament. When first seen, Thompson is defending the play to Colonel Ball, the commanding officer of the prison. Shortly thereafter, Sergeant Baxter attempts to intimidate Thompson into withdrawing his support for the play. Thompson is so shaken by the threat that he becomes deaf to the story that the new prisoner Reese tries to tell him and walks officiously away. In act 3, Thompson takes an evening walk with his wife Caroline. Their conversation reveals that their position at the camp is repulsive to their liberal humanist ideals, but at the same time, Thompson feels powerless to take a stand. He is shocked at the unjust, murderous treatment of the prisoners, but since the injustice is apparently no one person's responsibility, he does not know where he can turn for justice. Thompson and Caroline's ideology, represented by their wish for seclusion and a quiet home, tends to be obscurantist; they are unable to face the harsh reality of the camp, much less to fight against it. At the end, Thompson offers to accompany the prisoners as they attempt to escape from the camp. To the prisoners, however, Thompson is a collaborator, and despite his professed goodwill toward them, he is not one of them. They turn from him in disgust, leaving him in the company of the right-wing Members of Parliament and the camp guards.

Howard Brenton's plays represent an important contribution to radical and poststructuralist English drama. He belongs to the second wave of modernist English theater, the generation after Arnold Wesker, John Osborne, and Harold Pinter. Though sometimes attacked for the political content of the writing, Brenton's theater is vivid and powerful propaganda. As a playwright, he has never failed to excite critical and public comment and to stir controversy.

Other major works

SCREENPLAY: *Skin Flicker*, 1973.
TELEPLAYS: *Lushly*, 1971; *The Saliva Milkshake*, 1975; *The Paradise Run*, 1976.
POETRY: *Notes from a Psychotic Journal and Other Poems*, 1969; *Sore Throats and Sonnets of Love and Opposition*, 1979.

Bibliography

Beacham, Richard. "Brenton Invades Britain: The *Romans in Britain* Controversy," in *Theatre*. XII (Spring, 1981), pp. 34-37.

Cameron, Ben. "Howard Brenton: The Privilege of Revolt," in *Theatre*. XII (Spring, 1981), pp. 28-33.

Dunn, Tony. "Pravda o Pravde (Truth About the Truth)," in *Plays and Players*. CCCLXXXI (June, 1985), pp. 18-20.

Itzin, Catherine, and Simon Trussler. "Petrol Bombs Through the Proscenium Arch," in *Theatre Quarterly*. XVII (March, 1975), pp. 4-20.

Merchant, Paul. "The Theatre Poems of Bertolt Brecht, Edward Bond, and Howard Brenton," in *Theatre Quarterly*. IX (Summer, 1979), pp. 49-51.

Roberts, Philip. "Howard Brenton's Romans," in *Critical Quarterly*. XXIII (Autumn, 1981), pp. 5-23.

Soto-Morettini, Donna. "Disrupting the Spectacle: Brenton's *Magnificence*," *Theatre Journal*. XXXVIII (March, 1986), pp. 82-95.

Taylor, John Russell. "In and Out of Court," *Plays and Players*. CCCXL (January, 1982), pp. 12-14.

Weiner, Bernard. "The *Romans in Britain* Controversy," in *TDR: The Drama Review*. XXV (Spring, 1981), pp. 57-68.

Joseph Marohl

AIMÉ CÉSAIRE

Born: Basse-Pointe, Martinique; June 25, 1913

Principal drama
Et les chiens se taisaient, pb. 1956, pr. 1960; *La Tragédie du Roi Christophe*, pb. 1963, pr. 1964 (*The Tragedy of King Christophe*, 1964); *Une Saison au Congo*, pb. 1966, pr. 1967 (*A Season in the Congo*, 1968); *Une Tempête, d'après "La Tempête" de Shakespeare: Adaptation pour un théâtre nègre*, pr., pb. 1969 (*The Tempest*, 1974).

Other literary forms
Aimé Césaire has produced major works in a wide range of literary forms, including poetry (*Cahier d'un retour au pays natal*, 1939, 1947, 1956; *Memorandum on My Martinique*, 1947; also as *Return to My Native Land*, 1968), history (*Toussaint Louverture: La Révolution française et le problème coloniale*, 1960), treatises (*Discours sur le colonialisme*, 1950; *Discourse on Colonialism*, 1972), speeches (*Commemoration du centenaire de l'abolition de l'esclavage: Discours prononces à la Sorbonne le 27 avril 1948*, 1948), and numerous essays on poetry, politics, and culture in a wide variety of French, West Indian, and African publications. Césaire has delivered a large number of his speeches before the French National Assembly in his capacity as deputy of the Department of Martinique. As a consequence, much of his occasional work (telegrams, letters, interviews) has historical interest in its own right.

Achievements
As poet, dramatist, politician, historian, and essayist, Césaire helped transform the French colonial world over a period of more than six decades. His reputation depends chiefly on his lengthy autobiographical poem *Return to My Native Land*, a passionate indictment of colonialism that the French poet and novelist André Breton hailed as "nothing less than the greatest lyrical monument of our time."

As a virtuoso performance and as a portrayal of the pain and anguish of Martinique's dispossessed, the poem burst upon the literary scene, challenging the image of the French Antilles as the "happy isles" filled with inferior beings and unable to produce writers equal to those of Europe. Representing the culmination of almost a decade of intellectual dialogue among Africans and West Indians within the Parisian student community of the 1930's, the poem poignantly rejected assimilation for blacks, denounced the domination of the Western powers, and exalted the contributions of the black race. This sense of a unique black consciousness and common heritage—what Césaire himself described as "the awareness of being black . . . a taking charge of one's destiny as a black man, of one's history and culture"—was expressed in the term "*négritude*," first coined in the poem itself and later used to describe the movement led by Césaire, the French Guianan poet Léon Damas, and the Senegalese poet and statesman Léopold Senghor.

Césaire was instrumental in bringing African, Caribbean, and Afro-American artists together in a common cultural front, whose various literary expressions in the 1920's and 1930's included the magazines with which he was directly involved—*L'Étudiant noir*, *Tropiques*, and *Présence africaine*. *Négritude* in this sense found evidence of black vitality and originality equally in the civilizations of ancient Africa and in the already distinctive cultural achievements of Afro-American jazz, blues, dance, and the literature of the Harlem Renaissance.

The most renowned French-speaking poet of the Caribbean, Césaire is at the same time an accomplished dramatist. Turning to theater in the 1960's in an effort to reach audiences that either could not read or could not understand his difficult poetry, Césaire composed three plays with conventional formats and easily discernible political themes. In *The Tragedy of King Christophe*, he treated the rise and fall of an early nineteenth century Haitian revolutionary. Moving from the Caribbean to Africa in *A Season in the Congo*, he considered the downfall of Congolese leader Patrice Lumumba. Finally, in 1969, using William Shakespeare's *The Tempest* (1611) as a source, he wrote an allegory of colonial conflict, *The Tempest*, which may have been modeled on the debates in the American black power movement between Malcolm X and Martin Luther King. As a statesman, Césaire has been central in promoting the policies of autonomy in Martinique and has written extensively on governmental affairs.

Biography

Aimé Césaire was born on June 25, 1913, in Basse-Pointe, Martinique, in the French West Indies. Part of a large family, Césaire attended the Lycée Victor Schoelcher in Fort-de-France in 1924 and received a scholarship to study in France in 1931. In the years that immediately followed in Paris, Césaire met many of his major intellectual collaborators, including the future president of Senegal, Senghor; the French Guianan poet, Damas; and others.

In an environment marked by the popularity of the French Communist Party and the surrealism of André Breton, Césaire, Senghor, and Damas founded the journal *L'Étudiant noir* in 1934, calling for a "cultural revolution" and declaring themselves against the chains of logic and the "bourgeois ego." Following his admission to the prestigious École Normale Supérieure in 1935, Césaire began an intense period of poetic activity.

A few months after the publication of *Return to My Native Land* in August

of 1939, Césaire returned to Martinique to teach at the Lycée Victor Schoelcher, where one of his students was the future psychologist and theorist of
decolonization, Frantz Fanon. Despite restrictions imposed by the Vichy regime during the war years, Césaire founded the journal *Tropiques* with his
wife, Suzanne Roussy, and others. Deeply impressed by the journal's honesty
and verve, Breton (who arrived in Martinique in 1941) wrote a preface to the
1944 edition of *Return to My Native Land* which contributed to Césaire's
international reputation. Partly as an outcome of the invigorating effects of
this meeting, Césaire published his next volume of poetry, declaring his
embrace of the "miraculous weapons" of surrealist poetic style, *Les Armes
miraculeuses* (1946; *Miraculous Weapons*, 1983).

Inspired by a six-month tour of Haiti in 1944, Césaire came to pay homage
to this site of the first successful slave rebellion in the early nineteenth century. Haiti's legacy plays an important role in his later work—particularly his
drama *The Tragedy of King Christophe* and his history of the Haitian revolution, *Toussaint Louverture*.

In 1945, Césaire was elected mayor of Fort-de-France and deputy to the
French Assembly, positions to which he has been repeatedly reelected. In
1946, he voted for, and played a key role in promoting, controversial legisla-
tion demanding the assimilation of Guadeloupe and Martinique as depart-
ments of France. Still active in cultural affairs, in 1947 he helped create, with
Alioune Diop, Paul Niger, and others, the influential journal *Présence
africaine*, with the patronage of such French intellectuals as André Gide,
Jean-Paul Sartre, and Albert Camus. Despite his other activities, he published another volume of poetry, *Soleil cou coupé* (1948; *Beheaded Sun*,
1983).

Outraged by the massacres of the *Malgaches*, the peoples of Madagascar,
in 1947, he delivered a scathing attack on the "civilizing" mission of colonialism at the 1948 World Congress of Intellectuals for Peace in Poland, which
would later be published as his *Discourse on Colonialism*, in the same year as
his fourth volume of poetry, *Corps perdu* (1950; *Disembodied*, 1983). In
1956, as a result of the Soviet occupation of Hungary, Césaire officially resigned from the Communist Party in a public letter to the Party's general secretary, *Lettre à Maurice Thorez* (1956). As a result of leaving, he launched
the Parti Progressiste Martiniquais.

Turning increasingly to the writing of drama in the 1960's, Césaire participated in the Festival of Black Arts in Dakar in 1966, where he presented his
play *A Season in the Congo*. In 1972, he founded an annual Martinican cultural festival dedicated to the expression of West Indian culture.

Analysis

Aimé Césaire's drama marks a conscious departure in style and artistic attitude from the main body of his poetry. With the exception of *Et les chiens*

se taisaient (and the dogs grew silent), which was first included as a dramatic poem in *Miraculous Weapons* and only later revised in a special "theatrical arrangement" in 1956, all of Césaire's plays were composed and performed in the 1960's. In these years, the opportunities for decolonization had apparently increased abruptly. Several African states were for the first time winning their independence, and in the United States, the Civil Rights movement was at its height. As a longtime spokesman for *négritude*, Césaire apparently wanted to reach audiences put off by the dense imagery of his surrealist poetry—especially audiences from the largely illiterate countries in which decolonization was occurring. In the speeches of his characters, Césaire debates the entirely new set of problems created by independence: the problems of rebels in power, of former slaves who enslave others, and of anticolonialists who fight one another instead of the enemy.

As a group, Césaire's four plays can be said to touch on the principal concerns of his life's work. If *Et les chiens se taisaient* belongs to the world of *Return to My Native Land*, with its exotic invocations of revolt in a general or a metaphysical sense, the next three plays situate themselves in the history of the black movement: *The Tragedy of King Christophe* in the Caribbean of postindependence Haiti of the early nineteenth century, *A Season in the Congo* in the Congo of contemporary Africa, and *The Tempest* in the spiritual landscape of Afro-American politics.

Et les chiens se taisaient describes Césaire's journey from poetry to theater, and the play has been staged only in German translation. The play's hero, referred to simply as "the Rebel," carries on the obsessive interest in *négritude* from *Return to My Native Land*—at once enchained and wildly free, eloquent and mute, a descendent of slavery and of royalty. While the play opens to a more-or-less conventional prison setting, where the Rebel has been condemned to death for killing his "master," the apparent order rapidly disintegrates into a series of hallucinatory tableaux representing various stages of colonization from Columbus to the present. Here, one finds sudden changes of scenery and quick jumps in time and place. The entire tapestry of characters and events therefore is located, fantastically, within what the play calls "a vast collective prison, peopled by black candidates for madness and death."

The play is a phantasmagoric record of rebellion and subjugation in their pure states, in which characters with emblematic titles such as "The Administrator" and "The Great Promoter" march before the reader hypocritically lamenting the "burden of civilization," while a Chorus representing the West Indian people admires the Rebel's example from a distance, without being able to follow it. "Bishops" and "High Commissioners" confront "Lovers"; statistics confront poetry. The play nevertheless establishes motifs that recur in Césaire's later dramatic work—particularly the image of the leader who contains perfectly within him the conscience of his race, who retains the memory of both the African royal splendor and its bondage, who employs beautifully the power of the word, but who (in spite of these things) remains isolated from a people who cannot attain his heights.

Césaire's next two plays, although emotionally and thematically linked to *Et les chiens se taisaient*, employ a very different theatrical strategy. Both *The Tragedy of King Christophe* and *A Season in the Congo*—the best-known and most widely performed of his plays and among the few translated into English—are frankly historical and rooted in specific social situations. All three of his remaining plays, in fact, were deeply influenced by Jean-Marie Serreau, a follower of the German playwright Bertolt Brecht's "epic" school of theater which sought to dramatize historical conflicts in such a way that the audience might participate in solving them. Serreau produced all three of these plays and commissioned *The Tempest*.

The Tragedy of King Christophe is a tragedy of revolutionary decline. Based on an actual historical personage—one of the generals of Toussaint Louverture who became ruler of Haiti in the early 1800's—the problem of power after independence is plainly meant to apply to the Third World leaders of the early 1960's: for example, Ben Bella of Algeria, Fidel Castro of Cuba, and Senghor of Senegal. The play's action revolves around the irony that Christophe, in order to outmaneuver his French colonial enemies, abolishes the republic and establishes himself as king. The question thus becomes: Can one defeat one's opponent by becoming like him? As portrayed in the play, the monarchy is a disturbing sight: Christophe conscripts workers to build a royal Citadel on the model of the pyramids, rants about there being "no freedom without labor," executes his own bishops and emissaries, and calls his people "niggers." The dramatic tension, however, is in no way one-sided. One is constantly reminded of Christophe's heroic defiance of the colonizer, his admirable ability to rely on "the will and the grace of [his] two fists."

The play is strikingly popular in its formal appeals. In an early monologue, for example, the Commentator explains the historical background needed to understand the action. Songs in dialect everywhere punctuate the longer speeches, a court jester entertains and instructs with his lyrical jabs and satirical jokes, and the number of crowd scenes underlines the communal (and not merely personal) significance of the tragic events.

A Season in the Congo is basically a repetition of *The Tragedy of King Christophe*, which is merely transplanted to the soil of the modern Congo. Here, the black revolutionary Patrice Lumumba is examined. The play has not generally been received as well as *The Tragedy of King Christophe*. It is packed with long monologues that are really declarations of positions and little more. Character itself becomes synonymous with a social position and is expressed typically in names such as "First Banker," "Second Banker," or "First Belgian Policeman" and "Second Belgian Policeman," and so on. The broad social nature of the drama is reflected also in the many fleeting glimpses of mass movements, demonstrations, strikes, appeals, and backroom negotiations, all of them contributing to a kind of pastiche of exemplary moments in the history of the Congo (modern Zaire).

The Tempest, as indicated by its French title, calls attention to the unique concerns of "black theater" and seeks to illustrate them all the more clearly by adapting (and intentionally distorting) a well-known Shakespearean play. Prospero is the original colonial intruder, subjugating the black slave Caliban, in his own tropical home, while Ariel, a mulatto slave, makes his own deals with the master, often at Caliban's expense. As suggested here, the setting is neither the transhistorical mental realm of *Et les chiens se taisaient* nor the fixed locales of the historical plays, but a symbolic model of Caribbean society as a whole, ruled by the dialectic of master and slave and complicated by the unequal status of the subjects themselves: a relationship already seen clearly in Basilio, Lumumba, and Kala Lubu of *A Season in the Congo*.

According to comments by Césaire, the play was intended to address problems within the black power movement of the United States; if it did, however, it did so indirectly. Given Césaire's intention, many have seen Martin Luther King in Césaire's Ariel and Malcolm X in his Caliban; evidence for this reading can be found in black power slogans such as "Freedom now," which appear in English in the original text.

In some respects, the play returns to Césaire's earlier lyricism. Described in Césaire's stage directions as having the "atmosphere of a psychodrama," the work plays up this unreality in at least two ways: by using anachronisms, usually with a satirical twist, as when the crew of the sinking ship in the first scene sings "Nearer My God to Thee"; and the stipulation in the stage notes that actors entering the stage may choose a mask at their discretion. Nevertheless, the specific Caribbean and North American motifs and the implicit challenge to Shakespeare's own imaginative vision make the play clearly political satire.

The plays of Césaire are essential to a full understanding of his career— the career not only of a poet and historian but of a politician as well. Forming a coherent body of work, written almost a decade after he first assumed his post as deputy to the French Assembly, and in the very midst of the African revolution he had long predicted and hoped for, the plays bring together in new combinations the ecstatic poetry, polemical speech, and acute awareness of colonial injustice of Césaire's work generally.

Other major works

POETRY: *Cahier d'un retour au pays natal*, 1939, 1947, 1956 (*Memorandum on My Martinique*, 1947; also as *Return to My Native Land*, 1968); *Les Armes miraculeuses*, 1946 (*Miraculous Weapons*, 1983); *Soleil cou coupé*, 1948 (*Beheaded Sun*, 1983); *Corps perdu*, 1950 (*Disembodied*, 1983);

Ferrements, 1960 (*Shackles*, 1983); *Cadastre*, 1961 (revised editions of *Beheaded Sun* and *Disembodied*; *Cadastre: Poems*, 1973); *State of the Union*, 1966 (includes abridged translations of *Miraculous Weapons* and *Shackles*); *Aimé Césaire: The Collected Poetry*, 1983.

NONFICTION: *Commemoration du centenaire de l'abolition de l'esclavage: Discours prononces à la Sorbonne le 27 avril 1948*, 1948; *Discours sur le colonialisme*, 1950 (*Discourse on Colonialism*, 1972); *Lettre à Maurice Thorez*, 1956; *Toussaint Louverture: La Révolution française et le problème colonial*, 1960.

MISCELLANEOUS: *Œuvres complètes*, 1976.

Bibliography

Arnold, A. James. "Césaire and Shakespeare: Two Tempests," in *Comparative Literature Studies*. XXX, no. 3 (1978), pp. 236-248.

Benamou, Michel. "Demiurgic Imagery in Césaire's Theatre," in *Présence africaine*. No. 93 (1975), pp. 165-177.

Cohen, Henry. "The Petrified Builder: Césaire's Roi Christophe," in *Studies in Black Literature*. V, no. 3 (1974), pp. 21-24.

Cohn, Ruby. "Black Power on Stage: *Emperor Jones* and *King Christophe*," in *Yale French Studies*. No. 46 (1971), pp. 41-47.

Frutkin, Susan. *Aimé Césaire, Black Between Worlds*, 1973.

Irele, Abiola. "Post-colonial Negritude: The Political Plays of Aimé Césaire," in *West Africa*. No. 27 (1968), pp. 100-101.

Kesteloot, Lilyan. *Black Writers in French: A Literary History of Negritude*, 1974. Translated by Ellen Conroy Kennedy.

Songolo, Aliko. "Surrealism and Black Literatures in French," in *The French Review*. LV, no. 6 (1982), pp. 724-732.

Timothy Brennan

FRANK CHIN

Born: Berkeley, California; February 25, 1940

Principal drama

The Chickencoop Chinaman, pr. 1972, pb. 1981; *The Year of the Dragon*, pr. 1974, pb. 1981.

Other literary forms

In addition to his plays, Frank Chin has published a collection of short stories, as well as numerous essays and articles on Chinese American literature and culture.

Achievements

Chin is the first Chinese American playwright to have had serious drama produced on the New York stage (at the American Place Theater) and on national television (by the Public Broadcasting Service). Having come into prominence in the 1960's and 1970's, he represents the consciousness of Americans of Chinese descent—those born and reared in the United States, who thus have only tenuous ties to the language and culture of China. Chin has sometimes been considered the John Osborne, the angry young man, of his generation of Chinese Americans. His plays turn on themes of identity—anguished and indignant probings into ethnic identity, gender identity, and self-identity. In them, Chin mirrors the issues and realities of Chinese American life and history as lived in Chinatown ghettos; they seek to expose and explode generally held stereotypes of Chinese Americans as an emasculated model minority with a quaintly exotic culture. Painful truths told with exuberant verbal pyrotechnics are trademarks of Chin's theater, and the characteristic gamut of his language ranges from black ghetto dialect to hipster talk to authentic Chinatown Cantonese (not Hollywood's "Charlie Chan–ese").

In addition to his achievement as a playwright, Chin is important as an editor of Asian American literature, a short-story writer, and an essayist. Chin's work has been recognized by many awards, among them prizes and grants from the Rockefeller Foundation, the American Place Theater (New York), and the National Endowment for the Arts.

Biography

Frank Chew Chin, Jr., was born on February 25, 1940, in Berkeley, California, some distance from Oakland, where his parents lived and worked. He grew up in the Chinatowns of Oakland and San Francisco and was graduated from the University of California at Berkeley, where he won several prizes for fiction writing. In 1961, he was awarded a fellowship at the Writers' Workshop at the University of Iowa.

After Iowa, Chin spent some time with the Southern Pacific Railroad, becoming the first Chinese American to work as a brakeman on the rails laid by his forefathers. Chin eventually left the railroad company to become a writer-producer for KING-TV in Seattle, and several of his shows were aired by the Public Broadcasting Service (PBS) and on *Sesame Street.*

Chin left Seattle to teach Asian American studies at San Francisco State University and the University of California, Davis. With a group of scholars, he organized the Combined Asian American Resources Project (CARP), which collected materials now housed in the Bancroft Library of the University of California, Berkeley. CARP has since been responsible for the publication of key Asian American texts by the University of Washington Press. In 1972, Chin founded the Asian American Theater Workshop in San Francisco with the support of the American Conservatory Theater (where he has been a writer-in-residence).

Analysis

Both of Frank Chin's published plays center on a protagonist's confrontation with the problematics of identity. *The Chickencoop Chinaman* is the more experimental in technique, with an almost cinematic use of montage, flashbacks, symbolic stage sets, and surrealistic, dreamlike sequences. *The Year of the Dragon* is more conventional, a drama of family and psychological conflict set in a San Francisco Chinatown apartment.

The Chickencoop Chinaman is a play that treats the theme of identity through dispelling stereotypes and myths. The play is divided into two acts. Each act has a scene in Limbo (a surreal transitional time-space located between realistic time-spaces), a sequence recollecting a past obsession with a mythic figure (for example, the miracle-working Helen Keller in act 1, the popular-culture hero the Lone Ranger in act 2), and scenes set in the realistic location of 1960's Pittsburgh, where the problem of the protagonist's identity is worked out.

The play's action centers on Tam Lum, a Chinese American filmmaker who is making a documentary about a black boxing champion named Ovaltine Jack Dancer, a boyhood idol with whom he once shared a moment of mystic brotherhood urinating in unison in a roadside bush. Tam comes to Pittsburgh from San Francisco in search of Dancer's father, Charley Popcorn, who was a quintessential formative figure for Dancer and who now runs a Pittsburgh theater. Allegorically, Tam's making a film about Dancer is an effort to express an identity for himself, and his search for Charley is his search for a father figure.

Before arriving in Pittsburgh, Tam is introduced in a Limbo scene on his airliner from San Francisco. The air hostess is transformed into a Hong Kong Dream Girl clad in a drill team uniform and twirling a baton (hence an American dream girl, too). Indeed, the woman represents the American stereotype of Asian women—attractive, compliant, trained to give pleasure. Although Tam scoffs at the Hong Kong Dream Girl's stereotypical identity, it becomes apparent that his own identity is problematic. For example, when asked what his mother tongue is, Tam can speak no Chinese, but instead begins speaking in tongues, using a startling array of American dialects. Tam also points out that Chinese American identity is not one ordained by nature; Chinese Americans are not born to an identity but must synthesize one out of the diverse experiences of living in crowded Chinatown tenements, metaphorical chickencoops. This opening sequence, then, poses the play's central theme: the problem of stereotyping and identity.

In Pittsburgh, Tam stays with a boyhood friend, a Japanese American dentist named "Blackjap" Kenji. Kenji's apartment in Pittsburgh's black ghetto, Oakland, ironically underlines the circularity of Tam's search (since San Francisco has its Oakland too), and its location within earshot of a railroad yard is a symbolic reminder of the Chinese American contribution to American history. Tam and Kenji, who grew up in the black ghetto of Oakland, California, talk in exuberant black dialect and express themselves by slapping skin; they have, to a great degree, adopted the style and expressiveness of a black identity.

Kenji's ménage includes Lee, a part-Chinese woman who is passing for white. She has a young son, Robbie, by a previous liaison or marriage. Lee has a love-hate relationship with men of color, men whom she collects and then uses her whiteness and sexuality to dominate and intimidate. Thus, Lee lives platonically and parasitically with Kenji, in fact reducing him to a sexless host.

During their reunion scene in act 1, Tam and Kenji reenact a past obsession that they had with the figure of Helen Keller, imitating and parodying her. This may seem pointlessly cruel until one realizes that, in Chin's play, Keller symbolizes the myth of the disadvantaged person who overcomes all handicaps and pulls herself up by her own bootstraps. In other words, she epitomizes what American society fondly thinks that every disadvantaged minority group can do for itself. When Tam and Kenji mock and demythologize the figure of Helen Keller, they are, in particular, rejecting the popular American myth that Asian Americans are a model minority capable of miracles of self-help.

Act 2 opens with another scene in which Tam and Kenji again recollect a mythic figure, this time the Lone Ranger. As a boy, Tam had fantasized that, behind his mask, the Lone Ranger was a Chinese, and Tam had therefore identified with him as a heroic role model who represented the possibility that a Chinese American could become an idol of the American public. As Tam reenacts his past fantasy in his adulthood, however, he realizes that the Lone Ranger is a racist, as is clear in his treatment of Tonto, and that he is not by any means a Chinese. In fact, the Lone Ranger is an obese white man who sadistically shoots Tam in the hand (symbolically handicapping him physically), then lays on him the curse of being an honorary white (handicapping him psychologically with this false identity). This episode, then, demythologizes the private fantasies of any Chinese American who might believe that he can easily achieve heroic status in the American imagination; it also shows the wounding consequences of the Chinese American fantasy that they can be accepted as honorary whites.

Tam and Kenji then track down Charley Popcorn. They are crushed, however, when Charley reveals that he is not, in fact, Dancer's father—that Dancer had constructed a myth around his memories of their association. Thus Tam's search for a surrogate and idolized father figure in a black man ends in disillusionment.

Returning to the apartment, Tam and Kenji undergo another identity crisis, this time precipitated by Lee's former husband, Tom. His name suggests the stereotype of the subservient minority, "Uncle Tom," and he is the very model of the minority that has attained middle-class success. Tom has heard of Kenji's decent but sexless relationship with Lee and wants to take Lee and Robbie back. Yet now Kenji authoritatively stands his ground, sends Robbie to bed, and asserts that he wants Lee to stay and that he will father children with her.

Tam, too, appears to recover from his shattering disillusionment with Charley. In the surrealistic penultimate scene, he is shown being borne to Kenji's apartment on Charley's back, and in this position, Tam recalls the unmanning events when his wife left him on his birthday. In the play's last scene, however, Tam makes a great effort and stumbles into Kenji's apartment carrying Charley on his back. This reversal of position symbolically denotes Tam's freedom from his past reliance on an identity borrowed from the blacks and a new determination to find the wherewithal for a future identity from sources within himself. He is thus able to keep his integrity despite the needling of Lee and the blandishments of Tom's imitation whiteness. Just as Kenji and Lee are united in a new relationship, so Tam is shown coming to terms with an identity grounded on his own ethnicity. Before the curtain falls, Tam is shown in the kitchen unashamedly practicing the craft of his ethnic group *par excellence*. As he prepares the food, he reminisces about the Chinese American legend of the Iron Moonhunter, a mythic train which the Chinese railroaders supposedly created out of parts stolen from the railroad companies, and which wanders the West searching out the souls of dead Chinese to bear them home to their families. Chin seems to understand that people need myths, and in the end, his protagonist, disillusioned with the black myth that is unavailable to him and rejecting a white myth that he finds contemptible, shapes his own myth of identity in the heroism and craft of Chinese America.

Chin's second play, *The Year of the Dragon*, is more conventionally structured than its predecessor and was accorded a national audience in a television production on "PBS Theatre in America" in 1975. This play also treats the theme of identity, but it focuses more sharply and poignantly upon the question of self-worth: the worth of an individual self to loved ones (family) and the worth of a minority ethnic group to the majority society (white-dominated America). Again, stereotypes form the chief factor that obscures individual worth and identity—stereotypes about family relationships, stereotypes about ethnicity. These thematic strands are worked out in the exposition of the many psychological conflicts and confrontations in the well-established Eng family of San Francisco's Chinatown.

The exposition, and exposé, of ethnic stereotypes is presented chiefly through two elements of the play: the family business of providing tours of Chinatown and the new Anglo son-in-law whom their daughter has brought from Boston. The family owns Eng's Chinatown Tour and Travel agency, and the eldest son, forty-year-old Fred, conducts tours of San Francisco's Chinatown. For the sake of business, however, Fred cannot show Chinatown as it really is; rather, he must pander to the stereotypes of Chinatown held by the American public—that it is an exotic place of delicious foods, mysterious (but safe) goings on, and incomprehensible (but happy) inhabitants composed of attractively available women, complaisant men, and harmonious families with above-average children. Fred knows that he is being false to himself and his people when he gives his happy tour-guide's spiel, and he mutters curses at his customers under his breath beneath his patter. In reality, Fred would like to tell the truths of Chinatown, which he sets down in short stories, but no one will publish his work. Through Fred's situation, then, Chin portrays the stifling effects of ethnic stereotypes.

The other element in the play that deals with ethnic stereotypes is presented through the character Ross, the Eng family's Boston-bred son-in-law on a honeymoon visit from the East. He is portrayed as a well-meaning but oafish Sinophile who has studied Chinese (albeit in a dialect different from the Eng family's), admires Chinese culture and customs, and thinks of Chinese Americans as the only minority group that does not dislike white dominance. Such stereotypes prevent him from seeing the Chinese American realities which trip him up constantly. His type of cultural voyeurism is subtly captured in the play's final scene, in which he is appointed photographer to take posed pictures of the Eng family. In this technically effective scene, Chin uses spatial form as adroitly as did Gustave Flaubert in the "agricultural fair" scene of *Madame Bovary* (1857). Through a kind of auditory montage, Chin creates an ironic counterpoint commenting on Ross's photography by interspersing the scene with the sounds and spiel of a tour guide describing a Chinese New Year's parade offstage. Just as the tourists are gawking at the Chinatown parade, so is Ross ogling his new Chinese American family.

In probing the stereotypes of familial relationships, Chin makes a painful but necessary criticism of stereotypes held by his own ethnic group. He also dispels the Charlie Chan–esque stereotype held by many Americans, that Chinese families are uniformly harmonious and hierarchical.

Much of the conflict in the family swirls around its patriarch, Pa Eng, who came to the United States in 1935 accompanied only by his infant son Fred, for he was forced to leave his wife in China because United States immigration laws excluded Chinese women from entering America. Pa Eng soon married a fifteen-year-old American-born Chinese girl (Ma Eng), who risked losing her American citizenship by marrying the man she loved (her citizenship was at risk not because she married a bigamist but because another American anti-Chinese law forbade American-born women to marry Chinese men on pain of forfeiting their citizenship). Ma Eng bore and reared two children, meanwhile pampering Pa Eng in his stereotypical Chinese view of the patriarch as a kind of semidivinity.

When the play opens, Pa Eng has prospered, to the point that he has been elected mayor of Chinatown. Yet he is now old and ill, and he believes that his days are numbered. He wants to die in the bosom of his family, so he has sent for his first wife (China Mama). This he has done without communicating his intent to his family. (In fact, throughout the play, the family members can hardly be said to communicate; they never bother to listen to what others have to say.) China Mama's arrival, as can be expected, precipitates several crises during which Pa Eng appears an inconsiderate, uncomprehending, ego-bound patriarch. For example, he commands Ma Eng, who is unnerved by this presence in her household, either to relinquish her home or to be subservient to China Mama and begin teaching her English. It is in his relationship with Fred, however, that Pa Eng's authoritarian role becomes most apparent.

Pa Eng's patriarchal dominance and his Chinese values have acted as long-standing denials of Fred's identity and self-worth. Fred had aspired to be a writer, but his father scoffed at this: According to stereotypes he holds, if one is not a doctor or a lawyer, one is nothing at all. Pa Eng gives his mayoral speech to Ross to edit, not to Fred, who majored in English. Nevertheless, Fred is a dutiful son, nursing his father when he spits blood and even going through a daily ritual of accompanying him to the toilet and wiping him after a defecation, a viscerally affecting scene to stage. Fred has also sacrificed his own college career to work and provide for his sister's college expenses, but his father does not appreciate that, probably because his stereotypical values do not accord much importance to daughters. Fred also is aware that his younger brother, Johnny, is deteriorating into a gun-wielding Chinatown mobster and wants him to leave his environment and go to college in the East. This Johnny resists. Fred knows that Johnny will comply if Pa Eng orders him to go, but Pa Eng refuses. Instead, Pa Eng wants Fred to accompany him as he delivers his mayoral speech. In this speech, he plans to acknowledge Fred as his heir, but he will do it in such a way that Fred will always be fitted with the stereotypical identity of a Number One Son, a person who has no self-worth beyond that which derives from his father. This is unacceptable to Fred, who refuses to go with his father as long as he refuses to order Johnny to leave Chinatown. In attempting to impose his will on his son, Pa Eng resorts to violence and slaps him repeatedly. Yet the physical exertion is too much for the sick old man, and he dies in this pitiable moment of futile tyranny. Tragically, Pa Eng's death does not free Fred. The closing tableau of the play shows Fred being submerged by his milieu as he slips into the spiel of the Chinatown tour guide, and as the spotlight singles him out, Fred is shown dressed glaringly in white, the Chinese symbol of death.

In sum, it may be said that Frank Chin has pioneered in the field of Asian American literature. His daring and verbally exuberant theater has asserted the presence of the richly unique and deeply human complexities of Chinese American life, and his work has brought this presence to the attention of the American public. He has criticized the false myths and the deadening stereotypes of self and ethnicity held by Asians and whites alike. At a time when it was ripe and necessary to do so, Chin proclaimed and proved that there is such an entity as Asian American literature. American literary history must henceforth reckon with that claim if it is to be true to itself.

Other major works
SHORT FICTION: *The Chinaman Pacific and Frisco R.R. Co.*, 1987.
TELEPLAYS: *S.R.T., Act Two*, 1966; *The Bel Canto Carols*, 1966; *A Man and His Music*, 1967; *Ed Sierer's New Zealand*, 1967; *Searfair Preview*, 1967; *The Year of the Ram*, 1967; *And Still Champion...*, 1967; *The Report*, 1967; *Mary*, 1969; *Rainlight Rainvision*, 1969; *Chinaman's Chance*, 1971.

Bibliography
Kim, Elaine H. *Asian American Literature: An Introduction to the Writings and Their Social Context*, 1982.
_____. "Frank Chin: The Chinatown Cowboy and his Backtalk," in *Midwest Quarterly*. XX (Autumn, 1978), pp. 78-91.
Kroll, Jack. "Primary Color," in *Newsweek*. LXXIX (June 19, 1972), p. 55.
McDonald, Dorothy Ritsuko. Introduction to *The Chickencoop Chinaman and The Year of the Dragon: Two Plays by Frank Chin*, 1981.
Oliver, Edith. "Off Broadway," in *The New Yorker*. XLVIII (June 24, 1972), p. 46.

C. L. Chua

JOHN PEPPER CLARK

Born: Kiagbodo, Nigeria; April 6, 1935

Principal drama

Song of a Goat, pr., pb. 1961; *The Masquerade*, pb. 1964, pr. 1965; *The Raft*, pb. 1964, pr. as radio play 1966, revised pr. 1978; *Three Plays*, pb. 1964; *Ozidi*, pb. 1966; *The Boat*, pr. 1981.

Other literary forms

John Pepper Clark is recognized as a major poet for his collections *Poems* (1962), *A Reed in the Tide: A Selection of Poems* (1965), *Casualties: Poems, 1966-68* (1970), and *A Decade of Tongues* (1981). He has also published literary criticism with *The Example of Shakespeare: Critical Essays on African Literature* (1970) and a travel diary, *America, Their America* (1964).

Achievements

Clark was a member of an extraordinary group of creative young Nigerian writers and artists who began their careers in the early 1960's with publication in the legendary magazine *Black Orpheus*. Contributors besides Clark included Chinua Achebe, the Nobel Prize winner Wole Soyinka, and Christopher Okigbo. The nature of this publication defined Clark's subsequent work. He wished to establish and confirm the importance and dignity of his Ijaw inheritance in the river delta of Nigeria and yet communicate these roots through publication in English. Both in his poetry and in his drama, Clark presented with affectionate sensibility his ancestry. Yet because he had become an academic within the formal university system which the British had exported to West Africa, he was committed to linking this antecedence with the wider concept of international, universal human issues. His major works draw from the specific environment of his birth. He uses English to make profound statements about the conditions of humanity in the contemporary world, but an English skillfully adapted to express its African context.

Biography

John Pepper Clark was born in the Western Rivers area of Nigeria in Kiagbodo, Warri Province, on April 6, 1935. His father, Clark Fuludu Bekederemo, was a chief. He attended several local schools, the most important being Government College in Ughelli. In 1954, he spent a year as a clerk in a government office before earning entrance to a college in Ibadan which would subsequently become the distinguished University of Ibadan. At the university he rapidly entered the literary milieu and became editor first of *Beacon* and later of *Horn*, student magazines that offered early opportunities for publication to several writers who would become the first generation of

Nigerian authors. In 1960, he was graduated with a B.A. in English, worked briefly as Information Officer with the Ministry of Information at Ibadan, and then was appointed an editorial writer for the *Express*, a Lagos newspaper. It was this position that permitted his appointment as Parvin Fellow at Princeton during the 1962-1963 academic year. For various reasons, this opportunity occasioned mutual dissatisfaction. For Clark, it provided the basis for a rather bad-tempered diary of that year, *America, Their America*. On his return to Nigeria, he spent a year as Research Fellow at Ibadan and began the field research that produced the *Ozidi* saga. In 1964, he married a Yoruba woman, Ebun Odutola, a talented actress. They had three children: two daughters, Ebiere and Imoyadue, and a son, Ambakederemo. That same year, he joined the faculty of the University of Lagos and in 1972 was appointed professor of English. The years 1975 and 1976 saw him as Distinguished Fellow at Wesleyan University in Connecticut. In 1979, however, he chose to give up an academic career in order to concentrate on writing. Indicatively, he returned to his birthplace at Kiagbodo. He became influential in Nigerian theater, and in 1982 he formed the PEC Repertory in Lagos.

Analysis

John Pepper Clark's first play was *Song of a Goat*. Its title indicates the multiple cultural elements he integrates into his drama. There is obvious reference to classic Greek in that the very term "tragedy" translates as "goat song" (*tragos* meaning "goat," and *oide* meaning "song"). There is also a parallel tradition from Africa. By Ijaw custom, a goat is the appropriate sacrifice—in the manner of the Hebraic concept of scapegoat. Similarities with the Irish playwright John Millington Synge are also apparent. Clark accepts Synge's view of the tragic dignity of humble people.

The plot of *Song of a Goat* presents a conflict between traditional and modern beliefs, though this does not seem to be the central element. The tragedy itself derives from urgent human responses. Zifa's wife, Ebiere, consults a "masseur," who is both doctor and priest, concerning her infertility. From her diffident explanations it becomes clear that the husband has become impotent: "I keep my house/ Open by night and day/ But my lord will not come in." The doctor argues that "some one has to go in, or they will take rust." He advises the tribal custom that someone within the family, such as Tonye, his younger brother, substitute for the husband. "That'll be a retying of knots" and there will be continuity of issue. Clark presents a curious psychological ambivalence in response to this advice. Even though presumably the practice is legalized by long-term custom ("What I suggested our fathers did not forbid"), Ebiere is as horrified as any Western wife would be. "I'll not stay here longer to hear this kind of talk," she says. With ominous perception, she answers, "That will be an act of death." Her husband Zifa is also violently shocked by the suggestion. He prefers to wait: "The thing may come back any day." He is shamed that he will receive public scorn for his impotence. "Everybody will be saying, there/ Goes the cock. . . ." There are continuing hints that his problem is imposed by the gods as punishment for some very vaguely defined and unpurged offense committed by his father.

After some months of barrenness, Ebiere, bitter against her husband and lusting with thwarted passion, teases Tonye into seducing her. He resists at first, for the deed is wicked, but he embraces her with such ardor that there is no possible pretense that he is simply obeying the decrees of custom. This is naked adultery passionately performed. Zifa finds his incestuous brother in his bed and berates him: "I can't believe it. . . . My own brother who I have looked after." Zifa decides that he will kill the adulterer, but before he can do this, in shame Tonye goes and hangs himself. It seems there is nobility in this decision, for he takes upon himself the crime of suicide and frees Zifa from the penalty for committing the most heinous crime conceivable in Ijaw life: a deed that offends the gods. Zifa recognizes this sacrifice. "I thought to kill/ You but in that office you have again performed my part." Only now does his guilty self-condemnation confirm the possible justice of the act. "He went to my wife. . . . Was that not a brotherly act?" Ebiere is said to have miscarried in giving birth to his brother's son. Despairing at the disaster his own anguish and jealousy have wrought, Zifa commits suicide by drowning himself in the sea, yielding to the power of the gods whom in his life he has opposed. The masseur concludes by attempting words of comfort and reconciliation, rather than blame, in the face of tragedy that reduces men to misery and defeat. "It is enough/ You know now that each day we live/ Hints at why we cried at birth." Here is the moral essence of the tragic condition. The urgency in this play does not rest with the external cultural conflict, though this is often mentioned. The conflict between human passion and moral duty provides the trigger for the inescapable disaster constantly prophesied by an old woman who leads the neighbors in the role of Chorus. Cassandra-like, she issues warnings that are perceived but not heeded. This makes for absorbing drama in the classic tradition.

The richness of the language more than sustains the tension of the events. Clark enjoys the long, extended poetic metaphor. Ebiere's unpregnant womb is compared to a "piece of fertile land—run fallow with elephant grass," an analogy he carries through to extreme development. This technique connects with the Ijaw preference for the riddle when matters are too intimate to be spoken of directly. There is the almost Shakespearean invective: "You lame thing, you crawling piece/ Of withered flesh." Clark also employs the profoundest declamatory poetry. "You may well cry. But this is nothing/ To beat your breast. It was how/ We all began and will end." Here is something rare on the contemporary stage—a modern tragedy, a form that Western playwrights have only rarely achieved in this century.

The Masquerade closely links with the earlier play. It is essentially similar in mood and structure. One of the chief characters derives from *Song of a Goat*. It is now determined that Ebiere died giving birth to Tonye's son, Tufa. The earlier play spoke of her surviving a miscarriage. That minor point indicates that the two plays were not conceived originally as part of a single cycle. Tufa grows up and travels from his home, hoping like Oedipus to escape from the curse of his illegitimate origin. The play begins with a sense of foreboding. Without knowing the reason ("as far as I know no feasts have been left out," says one), the villagers see ominous signs: "The tilt [of the moon] is prominent,/ It is never so but there is disaster."

Into this situation comes Tufa. Titi is the local belle. A neighbor's description of her almost parodies the famous report of Cleopatra by Enobarbus: "Her head high in that silver tiara so/ Brilliant it was blindness trying to tell/ Its characters." Tufa immediately falls for her, and at first the affair seems blessed. The couple make love in lyric poetry: "Your flesh under flush/ Of cam flashes many times lovelier than gold/ Or pearls." Soon, however, gossip informs of the tragic but polluting events of Tufa's past: "His father/ Usurped the bed of his elder brother, yes,/ Brazenly in his lifetime, and for shame/ Of it hanged himself." Titi's father, Diribi, immediately condemns Tufa and forbids the marriage: "Consider the taint." He fears that the curse Tufa bears will spread among the entire family. If they associate with him, the gods will threaten them, too. The mother is equally dismissive, saying, "the man is no more your husband now happily/ His past and back are in full view." Tufa is told "leave my daughter alone, . . . and go your curse-laden way." To her father's horror, Titi defies him and argues that she will marry Tufa in spite of "this prospect of pollution." Her father curses Titi, calling her "this witch and bitch/ Who has quite infected her breed." Tufa, however, is touched by the generosity of her love and recognizes her devotion. Titi "called herself my wife, my bride ready to go with me/ In spite of my shame." Her father, in spite of his great affection, is more concerned with his consequent family shame and determines to kill her. Though "she tried tears, tried prayers," he shoots her with the very gun Tufa had given him as a present. He turns the gun upon Tufa and wounds him mortally. Tufa staggers out to join Titi, after confessing, "I am that unmentionable beast/ Born of woman to brother." Borrowing from Greek, Clark has the priests observe, "Who/ The gods love they visit with calamity." No action need be taken against the father. In this situation, no human punishment can add to the misfortune imposed. He has destroyed himself. He "who was so tall and strong/ Before. . . . Now at one stroke/ See him splintered to the ground." The tragedy that began with *Song of a Goat* has now worked itself out, purging the crime from which it originated in the manner of the great Greek tragedies.

Again, one should observe the controlled poetry which Clark employs. Like that of Shakespeare, it can range without any apparent contradiction

between colloquial conversation and great poetic feeling. Beautiful are the
lines: "It is the time/ Of night. There is a catch in the air/ Will not hold. Not
a rustle of leaves,/ Not a cry of a bird, nor the sudden charge/ Of sheep or
goats. . . ."

The Raft explores a new topic, a circumstance reminiscent of Stephen
Crane's famous short story "The Open Boat." It describes four workers:
Olotu, the educated townsman; Kengide, the cynic; Ogro, the traditionalist,
and Ibobo, the priest figure. They are camping on a huge raft of hard wood
logs, sailing it downriver to the port. Owing to mischance or carelessness, the
ropes tying it during the night come away and they drift helplessly down the
river, unable to control direction or, since a heavy fog comes down, to determine where they are. This danger frightens them, and one by one these men
are brought to the breaking point and die. The raft itself would seem to be a
general symbol of man's inability to be master of his environment, indicating
his weakness when pitted against the superior power of circumstance. Some
critics have argued that, since this was written when Nigerian political events
seemed to be equally drifting before the resolution of an army coup, direct
reference must be intended. The times may conceivably have been in Clark's
mind when he invented this plot, but the play is certainly far more universal
in its concept than any political tract would be. The characters in the play do
not represent public persons, even obliquely, nor are they conceived as representing generalized attitudes of the time. They are individuals battling fierce
problems in a highly realistic setting. The play succeeds on the stage because
the potential allegory is never allowed to intrude into the actual events.

The raft begins to drift when by some inexplicable means its mooring ropes
break. "What I can't understand is how all/ The seven gave way. . . . Some
madman/ Came aboard and cut us loose?/ Some ghost or evil god." The
speculations indicate the cosmic nature of their plight. They find that they
are being carried out to sea on the ebb tide. Desperately they apply all of
their skill. As they contemplate the prospect of death, they agonize and discuss their chances, reminisce about their pasts, their families, their jobs,
their hopes. Yet disaster cannot be avoided. First, Olotu is taken away when
a part of the raft breaks off and he is unable to swim back. "He's adrift and
lost!" is the cry. The greater truth comes in the responsive observation, "We
are all adrift and lost!" Then they hear a ship coming. Ogro decides his best
chance is to swim to it and be hauled aboard. The sailors see him and beat
him away until he becomes entwined in the stern wheel and is killed. None
will assist in escape. Now only Ibobo and Kengide remain. Ibobo thinks that
he recognizes a small town they are passing and decides to jump overboard.
Kengide holds him back, warning him of sharks, but Ibobo asks, "are/ You
afraid to be alone?" With a more generalized recognition that typically links
actual event to universality, Kengide says, "Aren't you afraid to be left alone/
In this world, aren't you?" They decide to shout in the hope of attracting

attention. The last lines of the play are their forlorn and feeble voices crying "Ee-ee-eee!" which, in a stage direction, Clark reminds his readers is "the long squeal as used when women go wood-gathering and by nightfall have still not found their way home." In a sense, the tragedy here is less personal, more cosmic. The suffering is not imposed upon the characters because there is some taint in their past, some evil to be assuaged. Here is the more pessimistic conclusion that all men are doomed to suffer in a universe which is implacably indifferent to their fate. This view does not allow the note of hope that occurs in the final resolution of many tragedies when even death can be seen as a kind of liberation from the pains of enduring the arrows of life. Here, death is an end without purpose and without meaning imposed by powers beyond man's control and indifferent to his fate.

Ozidi brings a major change in the direction of Clark's work. The original *Ozidi* is a traditional poetic saga of the Ijaw people. Clark affirms its epic status, calling it "an old story, truly heroic in proportion, arising out of a people's sense of their past." In its original form, its performance lasts seven days and is embellished with dance, music, ritual masks, and costumes. In drawing upon the historical event, Clark has departed from the universalist ideas of his earlier plays and immersed himself deeply in his African inheritance. This involvement makes it difficult for him to extract a sequence of action that will be appropriate for a formal theatrical presentation, inevitably restricted both in time span and area.

Clark's concern for *Ozidi* has an extended history. He first heard the tale when Afoluwa of Ofonibenga recited it to an eager school audience. It had such an impact that he worked for ten years as a researcher to record permanently this oral, public event. The results were a film, a record of the music, and, in 1977, an Ijaw/English side-by-side transcription of nearly four hundred pages. While continuing this long-term study, in 1966 he attempted to distill the extensive epic into an English-language dramatized version. The result presents barriers to the non-African reader. The fullest comprehension may seem to require anthropological knowledge. Nevertheless, the play has moments of dramatic intensity and the basic plot is clear enough, even though compression requires external explication.

The story spans two generations. A new king must be selected, this time from the house of Ozidi. He refuses the honor and is amazed when his younger brother, Temugedege, a discreditable and feeble figure "dribbling with drink," demands his rights to the throne. He greedily imagines his power, intending to become "terror of all our/ Territories." The populace consider his pretensions ridiculous. Ozidi agrees with their judgments but insists that, as his brother has been made king, all the normal honors are due him, including lavish gifts: "A god is/ A god once you make him so," he says. His subjects have no intention of gratifying so feeble a monarch, for "nobody is going to serve Temugedege; he is an idiot." When Ozidi insists that the traditional generosities are required no matter how inadequate the recipient, there are murmurs of revolt. Rather than tax themselves for safety from the ruthless Ozidi, they prefer to plan his death. Since one of the expectations of a new king is a symbolic skull, they attack Ozidi, cunningly destroy his magic security, and send his head to his brother. "There is our tribute to you, King." He is too weak to do other than flee. Ozidi's grandmother Oreame escapes with his pregnant wife Orea, who delivers a child also called Ozidi.

The second section deals with young Ozidi's upbringing largely at the hands of his grandmother, who uses her skills in magic to develop his courage so that he will be the means of revenge for his father's murder. She intends that he "must go forth and scatter death among/ His father's enemies." He returns to his father's home and reinstates himself: "Let's raise again the compound of my fathers." Urged by his grandmother and protected by her magic, he seeks out his enemies and throws down a challenge by shamefully and publicly stripping their wives. He singles out his opponents and fights them one by one. Though they confront him boldly, "Ozidi, I am going to eat you up today," he is always victorious. Others seeking to avenge their friends are equally eliminated, their magic brought to nothing against Oreame's spells. The sequence of deaths affects Ozidi, until a woman can ask, "is there nothing else you can do except kill?" Finally blinded by herbs, he kills both enemy and grandmother, for she has not thought to protect herself from her own grandson. He is attacked by fever and nursed by his mother. He wins that bodily battle and thus defeats King Smallpox, the ultimate enemy of the people, who will not "set foot again on this shore." The end is somewhat surprising, but it is clear that some general victory other than satisfied revenge is required to achieve Ozidi's full heroic status.

The events in this play are repetitive and sometimes confusing. The language, seeming sometimes close to Ijaw, makes for difficult interpretation. At other times, it has the familiar Clark lyrical conviction. "What need have/ We to stand up when silk cotton trees lie prostrate/ We are reeds only, mere reeds in the storm, and must/ Stretch our broken backs on the ground." *Ozidi* is less immediately accessible to a non-Nigerian reader, but it has the same tragic power and evocative language found in the earlier plays and exhibits Clark's determination to draw ever more deeply from his African experience and culture.

For many years after his writing of *Ozidi*, Clark seems to have preferred to concentrate on poetry, and perhaps his reputation in this genre is higher than his reputation as a dramatist; yet in the 1980's, his contribution to the theater continued with production of *The Boat*. Clark would not separate poetry from drama, and his ability to bring poetry and an African context and sensibility to the modern stage establishes his importance in contemporary world literature.

Other major works

POETRY: *Poems*, 1962; *A Reed in the Tide: A Selection of Poems*, 1965; *Casualties: Poems, 1966-68*, 1970; *A Decade of Tongues*, 1981.

NONFICTION: *America, Their America*, 1964; *The Example of Shakespeare: Critical Essays on African Literature*, 1970.

Bibliography

Cartey, Wilfred. *Whispers from a Continent*, 1969.

Connor, William. "Diribi's Incest," in *World Literatures Written in English*. XVIII, no. 2 (1979), pp. 278-286.

Egudu, R. N. "The Poetry and Drama of J. P. Clark," in *Introduction to Nigerian Literature*, 1971. Edited by B. King.

Ferguson, John. "Nigerian Drama in English," in *Modern Drama*. XI (May, 1968), pp. 10-26.

Obeakaran, Paul. "John Pepper Clark and Stephen Crane," in *Research in African Literatures*. XIII (Spring, 1982), pp. 53-59.

Okpewho, Isidore. *The Epic in Africa*, 1979.

Povey, John. "Two Hands a Man Has," in *African Literature Today*. I (1968), pp. 36-47.

Wren, Robert. *J. P. Clark*, 1984.

John Povey

MARTHA CLARKE

Born: Baltimore, Maryland; June 3, 1944

Principal drama

A Metamorphosis in Miniature, pr. 1982; *The Garden of Earthly Delights*, pr. 1984 (music by Richard Peaslee); *Vienna: Lusthaus*, pr. 1986 (text by Charles Mee, Jr., music by Peaslee); *The Hunger Artist*, pr. 1987 (text by Richard Greenberg, music by Peaslee, set by Robert Israel; adaptation of Franz Kafka's story and diaries).

Other literary forms

Martha Clarke is known for her extensive work as a choreographer and performer for the dance companies of Pilobolus and Crowsnest. Her dramatic works do not fall easily into any one genre: They incorporate elements of dance, music, and visual arts, as well as use of text, and involve collaborations with other artists.

Achievements

Clarke was already a highly acclaimed dramatic modern dancer performing in a world-renowned dance company Pilobolus Dance Theater when she crossed over into creating theatrical works. Her contributions as a choreographer include, with Pilobolus, *Ciona*, *Monkshood's Farewell*, and *Untitled*. These dances remain in the repertory of Pilobolus and are also presented by other major dance companies. Clarke has been compared to other experimental theater directors such as Robert Wilson, Ping Chong, and Meredith Monk for her ability to create multimedia theater pieces. Clarke's are noted for their visual beauty and a characteristic use of movement and timing. Clarke's innovative approach to her work encourages dancers, actors, designers, composers, and writers to work in a highly collaborative way toward a complex and richly textured performance-art object. Her first major theatrical production, *The Garden of Earthly Delights*, won a Village Voice Obie Award for Richard Peaslee's lush musical score. With the popular and critical success of this work and the later *Vienna: Lusthaus* and *The Hunger Artist*, Clarke has proved to be a successful synthesizer of dance and theater.

Biography

Martha Clarke was born in Baltimore, Maryland, on June 3, 1944. As the second child and only daughter in a financially secure and artistically inclined family, she was encouraged to pursue her creative interests at an early age. Her father was a lawyer who had been a jazz musician and songwriter. Her mother played the piano, and her mother's father, a businessman, presented string quartets at his home on Tuesday nights and collected antique musical instruments. Shirley Clarke, the avant-garde filmmaker, was Martha's aunt, on whose suggestion her niece was named after dancer/choreographer Martha Graham.

Clarke's childhood was spent in Pikesville, Maryland. She attended a small private school in Baltimore, at which her father was on the board of trustees. At age six, she began studying dance at the Peabody Conservatory of Music and taking drawing lessons on Tuesday afternoons at the Baltimore Museum. Horseback riding was another favorite activity and one she pursued in the summers at the Perry-Mansfield Camp in Colorado. There, in 1957, she met Helen Tamiris, who cast her, at age thirteen, as a child in *Ode to Walt Whitman*. Clarke says that she was hooked on dancing from the first time she worked with Tamiris.

When Clarke was fifteen, Tamiris and Daniel Nagrin asked her to attend their first summer workshop in Maine Nagrin hoped to make Clarke an apprentice in the new company they were forming. Instead, Clarke chose to attend the American Dance Festival in Connecticut, where she first met Louis Horst, Merce Cunningham, Martha Graham, José Limón, Charles Weidman, and Alvin Ailey, and where she first saw the work of Anna Sokolow, whose dramatic dances greatly impressed her.

The next year, when she applied to the Juilliard School, Horst was on her jury, and he encouraged her to begin classes immediately and skip her senior year in high school. At Juilliard, she studied dance composition with Horst, who inspired and intimidated her. Horst's class in modern forms, in which dance studies are composed based on medieval and primitive art and Impressionist painting, was instrumental in developing her theatrical style.

Although Clarke was a Graham major and Horst was Graham's associate, it was the work of Sokolow and Anthony Tudor to which the young student was attracted. For two years, she studied with Tudor and as a sophomore danced a large part in a small ballet which he choreographed. She admired Tudor's work and its musicality. Also at Juilliard, she danced in the companies of Ethel Winter and Lucas Hoving, performing *Suite for a Summer Day* by the latter in 1962. She was in the first Dance Theater Workshop production with Jeff Duncan, after which she joined Sokolow's company. During her three years with the company she appeared in *Session for Six*, (at Juilliard), *Lyric Suite, Time + 7*, and *Dreams*. Clarke left the company because she found the work bleak and believed that she was becoming artistically limited.

Shortly after she was graduated from Juilliard, she married sculptor Philip Grausman, a Prix de Rome winner. For the first five years of their fifteen-year marriage (they were divorced in 1980), Clarke stopped dancing. The couple lived in Italy for part of this time, immersing themselves in the art world. Shortly after their return to the United States, their son David was born. Grausman was named artist-in-residence at Dartmouth College, but Clarke saw herself as a twenty-seven-year-old mother and retired Anna Sokolow dancer. She and her husband moved into a large farmhouse, which resembled her childhood home, and built a dance studio for Clarke.

By this time, the four men who started Pilobolus were already touring. Clarke met Alison Chase, the Pilobolus men's dance teacher at Dartmouth, and the two became close friends. One of the members of Pilobolus, Robert Morgan Barnett, was an art major at Dartmouth and an assistant to Grausman. Barnett and Clarke began improvising dances in her studio after Barnett was forced to return early from a tour because of an injury. Clarke and Chase soon joined the previously all-male company. What drew her to Pilobolus was the company's irreverence and its rediscovery of the body. She believed that the inclusion of women in the company would allow the possibility of romance, gentleness, and delicacy to the male-oriented humor and gymnastics which were the company's trademarks. As a member of Pilobolus, she developed and performed *Ciona, Monkshood's Farewell*, and *Untitled*. In the seven years she was with Pilobolus, from 1972 through 1979, she created six solos, *Pagliaccio, Fallen Angel, Vagabond, Grey Room, Nocturne*, and *Wakefield*.

Her years with Pilobolus identified her as a clown and as a serious dramatic performer, but she wearied of the company's hectic touring schedule. Encouraged by Charles Reinhart, director of the American Dance Festival, and Lyn Austin, producer/director of the Music/Theater Group, Clarke left Pilobolus to start her own company, Crowsnest. Clarke joined with Felix Blaska, the French dancer and choreographer, whom she had met in Paris during her touring years with Pilobolus, and Pilobolus dancer Barnett. The trio worked collaboratively, and their work was described as a form of imagist movement-art when they first appeared at the American Dance Festival. Clarke and Blaska created *La Marquese de Solana*, and, with Barnett, *Haiku, The Garden of Villandry*, and *Fromage Dangeureux*.

Clarke's first step into theater from dance was as choreographer for the Long Wharf Theater's production of Igor Stravinsky's *L'Histoire du Soldat* in New Haven. For Lyn Austin, who first suggested that she direct, Martha Clarke and Linda Hunt created a two-woman dance-drama collage for the company's season in Stockbridge, Massachusetts. This work was followed by a production of *Elizabeth Dead*, a play by the humorist for *The New Yorker* George W. S. Trow. Clarke's debut as a New York theater director came with *A Metamorphosis in Miniature*. The late David Rounds and Linda Hunt performed Clarke's dramatization of the Kafka story with a ten-page script and much physicalization.

In 1984, under the auspices of Music-Theater Group/Lenox Arts Center, Clarke created *The Garden of Earthly Delights*. The hour-long work, based on the painting of Hieronymus Bosch, was a collaboration with Crowsnest and other dancers, with composer Richard Peaslee and musicians, and with lighting designer Paul Gallo. After a successful engagement at St. Clement's in New York, *The Garden of Earthly Delights* toured the United States and Europe.

By this time, Clarke was working on *Vienna: Lusthaus*. Like the Bosch piece, *Vienna: Lusthaus* began with visual images, initially inspired by an exhibition about *fin de siècle* Vienna which Clarke had seen in Venice. Once again, the project was a collaboration with dancers, musicians, composer Peaslee, set and costume designer Robert Israel, lighting designer Gallo, and with a text written by historian and playwright Charles Mee, Jr. Music-Theater Group/Lenox Arts Center again produced the work, which opened at St. Clement's for a two-week run before moving to The Public Theater on June 4, 1986.

Like the works before it, Clarke's next project was a collaborative creation. Clarke returned to the literary inspiration of Franz Kafka's writings to begin *The Hunger Artist*. This time, she used not only the story, "A Hunger Artist," but also the writer's own life in letters and diaries for inspiration. The company of dancers, actors, and musicians, along with Clarke, designer Israel, composer Peaslee, and playwright Richard Greenberg, focused on the themes of starvation and death, physical, emotional, and artistic. *The Hunger Artist* was also produced by the Music-Theater Group and opened at St. Clement's Theater on February 26, 1987. Clarke has successfully crossed the threshold from dancer/choreographer to theatrical director and has consistently applied the best of both disciplines to her individual artistic vision.

Analysis

Martha Clarke's works are in a performance genre which, as yet, has no name. It is a blending and fusion of dance, drama, music, gesture, light, scenic design, and text into performance pieces which mirror her unique artistic vision. Clarke is in a group of experimental performance artists as various as Robert Wilson, Ping Chong, Meredith Monk, and Peter Brook. Clarke's work as a conceptual director is distinguished from that of her peers by its painstaking use of movement and its density in a typically brief (usually one-hour) performance. Clarke achieves this synthesis of mediums by a collaborative, collagelike approach to composition.

Collaboration begins when rehearsals begin. Each performer, musician, composer, or designer is free to offer suggestions for the assemblage of fragments which will grow into a finished object of art. A long trial-and-error period ensues, during which the director develops movement phrases out of gestures and begins to keep a notebook of the ideas that work in rehearsal. She begins to distill the images and to dovetail the events while she looks for the contradictory images which will give the work texture and solidity. Clarke looks for a through-line that will unify her ideas, and she arranges and rearranges the scenes until they are compressed into their final form. She searches in works of art and writings for ideas that can be interpolated into the work. The final product is the result of the creativity of many people, but Clarke is responsible for the ultimate examination, selection, adaptation, and direction of all the elements.

Traces of Clarke's earlier work with Pilobolus Dance Theater can be seen in her theatrical direction and in her use of movement within the new works. In one of Pilobolus' best-known dances, *Monkshood's Farewell*, the members of the company, for the first time, began to organize the material with a dramatic logic instead of simply from an abstract point of view. The piece is reportedly based on the work of James Thurber, Hieronymus Bosch (for whose painting Clarke's work is named) Breughel the Elder, Geoffrey Chaucer's *The Canterbury Tales* (1387-1400), Sir Thomas Malory's *Le Morte d'Arthur* (1485), and a Craig Claiborne soup recipe, among other things. The four male members of the company joust, using the women as lancers, but later all six appear as the cretinous characters from the Bosch and Breughel paintings.

In *The Garden of Earthly Delights*, Clarke uses the Bosch painting as a point of departure for her own exploration and animation of the depicted world. She was attracted to the extremes of human emotion and behavior evident in the painting. The work is conceived as a left-to-right reading of the triptych, beginning in the Garden of Eden. The Garden of Earthly Delights and Hell are interrupted by an interpolation of the Seven Deadly Sins, the subject of another Bosch painting.

The director attempts to extract the qualities of the painting and condense its crowded, bustling panorama by giving Bosch's figures kinetic life. Though Clarke consulted science-fiction writer Peter Beagle, who wrote a book on the painting in 1982, for an interpretation of the qualities in the painting, her approach to the creation of *The Garden of Earthly Delights* is primarily choreographic. Each vignette in the work has some characteristic movement idea repeated rhythmically until it dissolves to make way for the next image.

In Clarke's hour-long enactment, seven dancers and three musicians are incorporated into a series of *tableaux vivants*. The vignettes include scenes of Eve wrapping her long hair around Adam, a serpent who produces the apple from between her thighs, performers who appear as musical instruments and trees, bawdy peasants, putti flying overhead, and angels falling through the heavens, transformed into demons, crashing in midair, and plummeting into Hell. Clarke summons the entire Bosch landscape, from the dreamlike Garden of Eden to medieval poverty to a nightmarish eternity.

The grotesque, acrobatic, and allegorical use of the human body always interested Clarke and the other members of Pilobolus. Clarke's exploration of metaphorical dance imagery developed differently, however, in the solo works she choreographed for Pilobolus and Crowsnest. Her work is characterized by its use of movement repetition, its languid, deliberate pacing, and the eroticism of the movement images. She believes that the slow pace allows the audience members time to respond to the complete scope of visual and textual associations with their own, more personal set of references.

The pleasure-garden idea returns in Clarke's *Vienna: Lusthaus*, but this time the director has chosen an entire city and culture, turn-of-the-century Vienna, as her point of departure. Clarke had worked at least twice before on a similar theme. One of the first dances by Alison Chase and Clarke, *Cameo*, was a study of the relationship between two Victorian women. In Pilobolus' *Untitled*, two nine-foot women dance about the stage in flowing Victorian dresses until two nude men appear from beneath their skirts. *Vienna: Lusthaus* conjures an entire world, a dreamlike world of images that gradually shifts from a sensuous dream to an intensely disturbing nightmare, similar to the progression in *The Garden of Earthly Delights*.

Clarke's *Vienna: Lusthaus* was inspired by the art of the period, particularly that of Gustav Klimt and Egon Schiele, and by the political and social atmosphere at the traumatic beginning of the twentieth century in Vienna. The suicide of Prince Rudolf at Mayerling and the assassination of Archduke Ferdinand in 1914 provide the margins between which Clarke's surrealistic series of vignettes is set. Clarke was interested in a closer study of the veneer of graciousness, civility, and manners in Vienna that concealed the dark beginnings of twentieth century pyschosis and warfare.

On this work, Clarke enlisted a playwright, Charles Mee, Jr., to help develop a performance text. Mee used material from Sigmund Freud's *The Interpretation of Dreams* (1900), historical sources, and his own dreams to produce a text consisting of reminiscences spoken as monologue. These spoken memories, whose themes are primarily love and death, have an unashamed directness that makes them sound like dreams. Clarke and the performers worked to distill the text into vignettes, which are connected thematically rather than dramatically. Clarke thinks of this as an instinctual process rather than an intellectual one, and one that evokes the internal world of actors and audience.

The walls of the set are slanted, and a scrim is placed between the stage and the audience to distort the view. While some of the images are quite beautiful, others are ominous. A young couple caress and embrace each other on the floor in an erotic scene until the young woman is replaced by an old woman, whom the young man continues to kiss. Most of the men are dressed as soldiers, and the women are dressed in Victorian petticoats and long slips. Beautiful nudes pose as artists' models. Actors read fragments of Freud's letters. Skaters in plumed hats and waltzing soldiers and girls glide through the moonlight to fragments of the music of Richard Strauss. A booted man with a riding crop flicks it menacingly across a girl's face and then over her body.

A woman recalls her mother carrying an armful of flowers through the house on a summer day but then says that when her mother's mind began to wander, she walked through an open window and fell to her death. A half-dressed soldier appears with a girl in a petticoat, who sits in his lap and acts like a puppet. A clarinetist and accordion player begin tuneless renditions of carnival music. The waltzing young soldiers begin marching to a resounding martial drumbeat. At the end, snow begins to fall. A woman embraces the body of a dying soldier. She raises his dead body and bangs it against the floor. Eventually, she stops. The snow keeps falling as the dead man speaks. He asks, "What colors does the body pass through in death?" Another man answers dispassionately, "First pink, then red, light blue, dark blue, and finally purple-red." Until this ending, these images are not presented linearly, but with amplifications, double meanings, contradictions, and a definite dramatic progression from the frivolous to the sinister.

Throughout, there is a sensuality and a surreal lack of logic. More than half the scenes are wordless but incorporate movements based on the same themes as those in the text. Clarke, once again, uses her characteristic technique of condensing, slowing down, and sharp-focusing the movement. Clarke finds that in working with actors and texts there is a natural sense of timing that corresponds to music. The speed and variation of certain phrases has a musical sense. She is interested in the slow development of a scene onstage which can mesmerize and stimulate the viewer's imagination. One of the actors turns into a horse, demonstrating the movements of the horse's arched legs and completing the transformation in one gesture. His foot becomes a hoof, and the man becomes an animal. Throughout *Vienna: Lusthaus*, the performers conjure scenes of the elegance and the decadence of this city of contradictions.

Following this work, Clarke began the process of researching, discussing, probing, and distilling new material once again. *The Hunger Artist* is not a revival of her earlier *A Metamorphosis in Miniature*, but a complete reworking of the Kafka material. Letters and diaries, as well as Kafka's body of fictional work, were consulted. Playwright Richard Greenberg worked with the actors to bring the letters to life. Scenic designer Robert Israel created a set which outlines a triangular house with striped walls, and placed a large box filled with earth onstage. Bentwood chairs are planted in the earth bed along with Dresden china and silverware, a nineteenth century rocking horse and cabbages. Peaslee's musical score contains phrases of Czech folk songs.

Clarke found a through-line in the theme of starvation and dying. In Kafka's famous story "A Hunger Artist," the main character earns his living by fasting and eventually starves himself to death. In Kafka's personal life, Clarke found evidence of emotional starvation in his relationships with his father and his fiancée Felice, and in his hunger for a normal life. One performer in *The Hunger Artist* resembles a Kafka insect when seen behind a

World War II gas mask. Another performer poses in a small doorway, holding a hatchet, while one of the women performs a lyrical dance movement with a cabbage on her head.

In their final forms, Clarke's works seamlessly blend theater and dance. The entire theater becomes the canvas for Clarke's moving images. Clarke's innovative approach to synthesizing these media gives her work its unique identity.

Bibliography

Acocella, Joan Ross. "Body and Soul: A Review of Martha Clarke's *Vienna: Lusthaus*," in *Dance Magazine*. August, 1986, pp. 40-45.

Blake, Betty, and Joan Marlowe, editors. *New York Theater Critics Reviews*, 1986.

Croce, Arlene. "Grand pas Petipa," in *Going to the Dance*, 1982.

Fanger, Iris M. "Pilobolus," in *Dance Magazine*. July, 1974, pp. 38-42.

Feingold, Michael. Review of *The Hunger Artist* in *Village Voice*. XXXII (March 17, 1987), p. 89.

Greskovic, Robert. Review of Crowsnest in *Ballet News*. III (September, 1981), p. 39.

Gruen, John. "Dancevision," in *Dance Magazine*. June, 1981, p. 110.

Gussow, Mel. "Clarke Work," in *The New York Times Magazine*. January 18, 1987, pp. 30-34.

Horn, Laurie. Review of Crowsnest in *Ballet News*. II (July, 1980), pp. 37-38.

Jowitt, Deborah. Review of *The Hunger Artist* in *Village Voice*. XXXII (March 17, 1987), p. 81.

Kendall, Elizabeth, and Don Daniels. "A Conversation with Martha Clarke," in *Ballet Review*. XII (Winter, 1985), pp. 15-25.

Lewis, Julinda. Review of *Fallen Angel* and *Haiku* in *Dance Magazine*. December, 1981, pp. 36-42.

Martin, Carol. Review of *Vienna: Lusthaus* in *Performing Arts Journal*. X, pp. 88-90.

Smith, Amanda. "Inside the Fellini-Esque World of Martha Clarke," in *Dance Magazine*. April, 1986, pp. 70-74.

Zimmer, Elizabeth. Review of *The Garden of Earthly Delights* in *Dance Magazine*. September, 1984, pp. 85-88.

Diane Quinn

MART CROWLEY

Born: Vicksburg, Mississippi; August 21, 1935

Principal drama

The Boys in the Band, pr., pb. 1968; *Remote Asylum*, pr. 1970; *A Breeze from the Gulf*, pr. 1973, pb. 1974.

Other literary forms

Mart Crowley is known primarily for his plays. He wrote the screenplay for a 1970 film adaptation of *The Boys in the Band*.

Achievements

Crowley brought the subject of male homosexuality into the open in the American theater with his 1968 comedy-drama *The Boys in the Band*. His plays are characterized by a clashing mix of personality types and a keen comic sense for one-liners. The significance of Crowley's work rests entirely on his first play and its introduction of a once-taboo subject. The play and the subsequent film adaptation of it are important milestones in the history of gay activism in the United States. Unlike Tennessee Williams, William Inge, and Edward Albee, who kept the topic of homosexual passions on the periphery of their work, Crowley made the initial leap which openly established gay drama and unapologetically linked his own life with his writing. The playwright's outrageously comical dialogue and his daring display of his own emotional failures are the most impressive and perhaps the most enduring of his contributions to the stage.

Biography

Martino Crowley was born in Vicksburg, Mississippi, on August 21, 1935. Crowley's parents were conservative and religious, and they scrupulously brought up Mart, their only child, in the teachings of the Roman Catholic Church, enrolling him in a parochial high school in Vicksburg. His father, an Irishman from the Midwest, owned a pool hall called Crowley's Smokehouse, which bore the motto "Where all good fellows meet." As a child, Crowley was asthmatic and sickly, a condition which changed, he claims, immediately after his departure from Vicksburg. An avid filmgoer and starstruck reader of Hollywood gossip magazines since early childhood, he left home in the early 1950's, moving to Los Angeles, where he took a number of low-paying jobs in order to be near the motion-picture studios. His father, who had cherished the hope that his only son should attend Notre Dame, finally compromised and convinced Mart to attend Catholic University of America in Washington, D.C. After two years there, Crowley, unhappy with the conservative social atmosphere in Washington, returned to Hollywood and began working on a degree in art at the University of California, Los Angeles, hoping to become a scenic designer in films. Crowley returned to Catholic University not long afterward and worked in the university theater. At one point, he collaborated with fellow collegian James Rado, later one of the writers of the rock musical *Hair* (which ran concurrently in New York with Crowley's hit *The Boys in the Band* in 1968), and the two of them produced a revue sketch. Crowley also worked in summer-stock theater in Vermont.

After his graduation from Catholic University in 1957, Crowley briefly considered joining the Foreign Service but moved back to Southern California instead, where he wrote a number of unproduced scripts for motion pictures and television. He took jobs with various film production companies, working on such films as *Butterfield 8* (1960) and *Splendor in the Grass* (1961). He also worked as a scriptwriter in the early 1960's for several television production companies. The popular film star Natalie Wood, whom Crowley met while both were working on *Splendor in the Grass*, hired him as a private secretary in 1964, a position he held until 1966. During this time, he wrote a screen adaptation of Dorothy Baker's novel *Cassandra at the Wedding* (1962) expressly for Wood and French director Serge Bourguignon. The film was never produced. Ridden with anxiety and depression, Crowley moved to Rome for a winter, staying with film star Robert Wagner and his wife, Marion.

In 1967, Paramount Studios completed a film from an original screenplay by Crowley entitled *Fade In*. The project was a hectic and disappointing experience for the young writer, and after all of his effort, the studio did not release the film. After six months of rest and psychoanalysis to cope with this ego-flattening experience, Crowley got the idea to write a play about homosexual friends at a birthday party. (His notes on the theme of homosexuality, including fragments of dialogue and character sketches, were begun as early as 1959.) Crowley finished the play, *The Boys in the Band*, in five weeks during the summer of 1967 while he was house-sitting in the Beverly Hills home of performer Diana Lynn. The agent he subsequently contacted about the script replied that although the play was very good, she did not believe the American stage was ready for a drama almost exclusively about homosexual men. She nevertheless sent a copy of the play to producer Richard Barr, who liked it and decided to produce it at his Playwrights Unit workshop. Robert Moore, an actor who had known Crowley at Catholic University and in summer stock, expressed interest in making his debut as a stage director with the play. More difficult, however, was the task of finding performers willing to be cast in the play. A number of actors read the play and liked it but refused to risk their professional images by performing homosexual characters onstage. The play was finally cast with an ensemble of largely unknown performers.

The Boys in the Band first appeared at the Vandam Theatre in January of

1968. Three months later, the play made its debut on the New York stage at Theatre Four. It was a success both at the box office and with most of the theater reviewers. Apart from viciously homophobic reviews from critics such as Martin Duberman and John Simon, the reviewers judged the play for its composition and production, rather than for its subject matter. Surprisingly, the play became controversial not so much in the heterosexual as in the homosexual community. The source of the contention may be inferred from the emphasis and wording of some of the favorable mainstream reviews, which commented on the play's portrayal of the "tragic" or even "freakish" aspects of the "homosexual life-style." Such generalizations were not, however, necessarily invited by the play. The production ran for more than one thousand performances in New York and was produced with great success in London, in regional theaters across the United States well into the 1970's, and as a 1970 film featuring the original Off-Broadway cast directed by William Friedkin. The play's director, Robert Moore, won a Drama Desk Award, and Cliff Gorman, who played the role of Emory, received an Obie Award (for performances in Off-Broadway theaters). The play was also included in several lists and anthologies of "best plays" of the 1960's. Many persons accounted for the play's success by observing that it offered the homosexual community a chance to see and hear itself represented onstage and the heterosexual community a chance to eavesdrop upon the former. By the time the play had been made into a motion picture, however, a considerable portion of the gay public objected to the play on the grounds that it made homosexuality seem like a form of neurosis characterized by religious guilt, loneliness, and self-loathing.

The year the film adaptation of *The Boys in the Band* was released, an earlier play by Crowley, *Remote Asylum*, was produced in California to universally unfavorable reviews. Opening at the end of 1970 at the Ahmanson Theatre in Los Angeles, *Remote Asylum* was not subsequently produced in New York. A third play, *A Breeze from the Gulf*, opened at the Eastside Playhouse in New York in October of 1973 to a somewhat better response. The writer's most intimate play, *A Breeze from the Gulf*, though praised for its competent writing and acting, lacked the audience appeal and the ability to stir up controversy which had made his first play a success. Its run was scarcely longer than *Remote Asylum*'s, but it took second place for a New York Drama Critics Circle Award. Crowley thereafter retired from playwriting and returned to television.

Analysis

Mart Crowley's plays are autobiographical to a large extent. Each contains a character named Michael, whom the audience is invited to let stand for the playwright himself. Crowley's persona is spared little in the psychological flayings which are characteristic of the writer's work. Contrary to what one might expect of an autobiographical protagonist, Michael/Mart does not embody positive, ideal, or necessarily healthy outlooks on life. In all of Crowley's plays, but especially in *The Boys in the Band*, Michael is characterized as self-pitying, debt-ridden, guilt-stricken, and vindictive; a failure as a friend, son, lover, and artist; a victim of excessive, intense self-scrutiny. The other characters stand in contrast to this negative image, or, to be more accurate perhaps, their personalities are in tension with his, caught in a web which alternately feeds and falls prey to Michael's repression, egotism, and anger.

Each play divulges a different part of the author's life, and consequently each play presents a separate but related galaxy of affection and social belonging. As they were produced, the plays run in reverse chronological order. *The Boys in the Band* presents a thirtyish Michael in the company of · his homosexual friends and former lovers in his rented lower-Manhattan apartment. The setting for *Remote Asylum* is a run-down mansion in Acapulco, and its *dramatis personae* include a bizarre assortment of misfits and outcasts surrounding an aging female film star. The characters abuse one another in a sort of shark frenzy of emotions, and the result is a more vicious, more bleak version of Lanford Wilson's multicharactered comedies, with Crowley's emphasis falling more definitely upon decadence. *A Breeze from the Gulf* presents Michael from age fifteen to age twenty-five. It is the most intimate of the three plays. Its only characters are Michael, his mother, Loraine, and his father, Teddy. Most of the dramatic action occurs in their family home in Mississippi, though the stage setting is only suggestive, avoiding naturalism or a sense of definite place. The play is not a simple exercise in nostalgia. The Connelly family is pathogenic; each of the three members is both victim and abuser of the other two. The play does not idealize bygone times. Its focus, which becomes gradually evident in the first act, is the painful psychological interdependency of son, father, and mother. The second act portrays a scene out of the playwright's life to which Crowley's previous two plays had only referred: the father's dying confession in the arms of his son on the floor of a hospital ward. The impact of this scene in the context of all the others is to assert that family relationships can be, and often are, morbidly corruptive to the individual human spirit.

Of the three plays Crowley produced within half a decade, only one, *The Boys in the Band*, earned a reputation for its writer. Twenty years after its New York opening, the play was still regarded as a landmark (historical, if not ideological) of gay drama. Its chronological proximity to the Stonewall Riots of June, 1969, lends added significance to its first production. Critic James W. Carlsen made the play the dividing point in the dramatic representation of gay men on the stage, his subtitles demarcating "Pre–*The Boys in the Band* perceptions" and "Post–*The Boys in the Band* Portraits." The changing attitudes toward homosexuality that the play helped to inspire turned eventually against the neurotic and self-demeaning "boys" in the drama. Without making an undue claim to "literary greatness" for the play, it is possible to defend it against its detractors, whose objections are primarily ideological, by asserting its social importance as a vehicle for making gay men more visible, and thus more vocal and politically viable, in American society. While the play does reinforce certain stereotypes of male homosexuality in the characters of Michael and Emory, *The Boys in the Band* also includes a number of other "types" which were hitherto unrepresented on the stage: The gay man as athletic, virile, capable of both fidelity and promiscuity, self-knowing, "ordinary," or "masculine" appeared in this play for the first time. The play also debunked a number of flattering truisms about homosexuals, such as that all gay men are more sensitive, tasteful, or witty than heterosexual men.

The focus of most of the criticism the play has received is its central character, Michael, who experiences more than his share of bitterness and self-loathing because of his homosexuality. As his friend Harold points out to him at the end of the play, Michael's problem is not his homosexual nature but his failure to accept himself as he is. Psychologists call this type of homosexuality "ego-dystonic," and the condition is considered a treatable psychological problem. It is thus possible to interpret Michael's personality as indicative of a real psychological disorder and not as symbolic of an inherent or typical maladjustment of the homosexual mind. That it is not the latter is evident in that other characters, such as Harold, Hank, and Larry, do not appear to suffer from the same self-hatred, and in that Michael's identity problem is explicitly compared to Bernard's, who struggles with feelings of inferiority because he is black. The charge that the play reinforces the prejudice that all gay men are really unhappy and that homosexual relationships are spurious is largely accurate, but it fails to take into account the tremendous step that was taken by the playwright in presenting even a somewhat compromising portrait of gay culture.

The Boys in the Band falls into a category of mid-twentieth century American drama sometimes labeled "comedy of exacerbation": An assortment of characters reveal themselves to themselves and to one another through some sort of excruciating ordeal, often, ironically, a party game. Whatever device is used, the veneer of each participant is stripped in order to bare the fact that the basis for much of his existence is rationalization, repression, or fantasy. The characters' relationships with one another flicker between love and loathing, and the repartee is savagely witty and unnervingly accurate. The epitome of this style of drama is Edward Albee's comedy-drama *Who's Afraid of Virginia Woolf?* (1962), to which *The Boys in the Band* is often compared. Albee's "Get-the-Guests" scene is structurally similar to Crowley's second act. In both, the device of a game is used in order to trick one of the participants into making a painful admission. Yet Michael's obsessive attempt to make his college friend Alan admit that he had a homosexual affair with a mutual friend fails and, like George and Martha's "game," backfires on him, revealing his own vulnerability and sadness.

The least that can be said for Crowley's contribution to the American theater is, sadly, also the most that can be said for it: His play *The Boys in the Band* opened up the subject of homosexuality to dramatic treatment. Though less positive than its successors, the play is no less forthright, and dramas such as Harvey Fierstein's *Torch Song Trilogy* (1978-1979) and Jane Chambers' *Last Summer at Bluefish Cove* (1982) would have perhaps never been were it not for Crowley's timely and trailblazing effort.

Other major work
SCREENPLAY: *The Boys in the Band*, 1970.

Bibliography
Carlsen, James W. "Images of the Gay Male in Contemporary Drama," in *Gayspeak: Gay Male and Lesbian Communication*, 1981. Edited by James W. Chesebro.

Duberman, Martin. Review of *The Boys in the Band* in *Partisan Review*. XXXV (Summer, 1968), p. 418.

Gussow, Mel. Review of *The Boys in the Band* in *Newsweek*. LXXI (May 20, 1968), p. 115.

Reed, Rex. "Mart Crowley," in *Conversations in the Raw*, 1969.

Simon, John. Review of *The Boys in the Band* in *Commonweal*. LXXXVIII (May 31, 1968), pp. 335-336.

West, Anthony. Review of *The Boys in the Band* in *Vogue*. August, 1968, p. 64.

Joseph Marohl

SHELAGH DELANEY

Born: Salford, England; November 25, 1939

Principal drama
A Taste of Honey, pr. 1958, pb. 1959; *The Lion in Love*, pr. 1960, pb. 1961; *The House That Jack Built*, televised and pb. 1977, revised for stage 1979.

Other literary forms
Three of Shelagh Delaney's screenplays have become successful films: *A Taste of Honey* (1961, with Tony Richardson), based on her stage play of the same title; *Charlie Bubbles*, (1968), based on one of her short stories; and *Dance with a Stranger* (1985), based on a celebrated murder case and trial in the mid-1950's. Three other screenplays were not as successful: *The White Bus* (1966), from a Delaney short story, filmed but never released; *Did Your Nanny Come from Bergen?* (1970); and *The Raging Moon* (1970). Delaney has done several teleplays, including *St. Martin's Summer* (1974) and *Find Me First* (1979). She has one television series to her credit, *The House That Jack Built* (1977), adapted for stage performance in New York in 1979. She has also written two radio plays, *So Does the Nightingale* (1980), and *Don't Worry About Matilda* (1983), which was very favorably reviewed. In 1963, a collection of semiautobiographical short stories appeared: *Sweetly Sings the Donkey*. A number of her essays appeared in the 1960's in *The New York Times Magazine* and *Cosmopolitan*.

Achievements
Delaney is highly regarded for her ability to create working-class characters and to express the difficulties of their lives in industrial northern England. She is a playwright of a particular region and social class. Both *A Taste of Honey* (which won the New York Drama Critics citation as best foreign play of 1961) and *The Lion in Love* employ such settings and characters. Her focus on the domestic tensions in the lives of working-class families is especially sympathetic to women, though never sentimental. Delaney's early work for the stage and her later television, film, and radio plays seem to revolve around the dreams and frustrations of women in contemporary society. While she was at first mistaken as an "Angry Young Woman," her focus has generally not been on large social issues but on individuals confronting their economic and social limitations and dealing with their illusions. *A Taste of Honey*, *The Lion in Love*, and several of her works in other media study characters who belong to families yet who are isolated even from those closest to them. That her characters face their difficulties with humor and wit sets her apart from many of her contemporaries, such as John Osborne.

Biography

Shelagh Delaney was born on November 25, 1939, in Salford, Lancashire, England. She remembers her father, Joseph, a bus inspector, as a great story-teller and reader. Delaney's education was erratic, marked by attendance at three primary schools and her failure of the eleven-plus qualifying examinations for grammar school. She was admitted to the Broughton Secondary School, and after a fair record of achievement, she was transferred to the more academic local grammar school. At fifteen, she took her General Certificate of Education, passing in five subjects, and at age seventeen she left school. She held a number of jobs in succession, as a shop assistant, as a milk depot clerk, as an usherette, and finally as an assistant researcher in the photography department of a large industrial firm.

The encouragement Delaney received at Broughton School led her to continue her writing later. She had already begun a novel when she saw a performance of Terence Rattigan's *Variation on a Theme* (1958), which she disliked and which she thought she could better. This experience served as a catalyst for reshaping her novel into the play which became *A Taste of Honey*. She sent the revision to Joan Littlewood, leader of a radical London group called Theatre Workshop, who began rehearsals immediately. Its initial run began May 27, 1958, at the Theatre Royal, Stratford East, and lasted a month. Restaged six months later at the Theatre Royal, it eventually opened in London, on February 10, 1959. When it opened in New York, in October, 1960, it was very well received, and ran for 391 performances.

Delaney's second play, *The Lion in Love*, was heavily criticized on its opening in Coventry in September, 1960. Attacked as verbose, without unity and focus, its London run was brief. After *The Lion in Love*, Delaney turned her efforts to television and film, and even some of this material has been adapted from her short stories. In 1961, she worked with director Tony Richardson to produce a successful film version of *A Taste of Honey*, one which differed markedly from the stage version in its realism. The production won for her a British Film Academy award. Her 1963 collection of short stories, *Sweetly Sings the Donkey*, also contains a version of "The White Bus," later filmed but never released. Her successful screenplay for *Charlie Bubbles*, reportedly based on a short story, won for her a Writers' Guild Award. Throughout the 1970's, most of her work was in television, including a series, *The House That Jack Built*, which she adapted for an Off-Off-Broadway production in 1979. Her 1985 screenplay *Dance with a Stranger* is her first work based on historical, rather than imagined, characters and situations. She has worked for a number of years as a director for Granada Television Network.

Analysis

Shelagh Delaney's stage plays *A Taste of Honey* and *The Lion in Love*, though very different in style, share several themes and emphases. Despite early critics' comments that the plays have "no ideas" and nearly no plot, both communicate effectively the loneliness of their working-class characters and their dreams and frustrations as they deal with the realities of love. In both plays, families are portrayed who, except by accident of birth and location, are strangers. Cut off from security and stability by education, social class, and economics, these characters are further isolated by a peculiar stubbornness and pride, in part a defense against the vulnerability love must bring.

A Taste of Honey is briefly told in two acts. As the play opens, Helen, a "semi-whore," and her sixteen-year-old daughter Josephine, or Jo, are moving into a desolate two-room flat in Manchester. Helen soon decides to marry Peter, a raffish one-eyed car salesman, and the two abandon Jo. Jo, too, has a love interest, in a black sailor, who proposes to her and consoles her as Helen and Peter leave. The second act, set six months later, introduces Geof, a homosexual art student, who moves in with Jo, now pregnant from her Christmas affair. He fixes up the apartment, attempts to help Jo accept the child, and eventually offers to marry her. In Jo's last month of pregnancy, Helen returns, her marriage having broken down. She bullies Geof into leaving and takes over as Jo goes into labor. When she discovers that the baby may be black, she leaves, ostensibly for a drink, promising to return. Jo's last lines are from a nursery rhyme of Geof's, holding out the promise of a benefactor who will care for her.

A Taste of Honey succeeded in part because of its daring plot, but primarily because of the strength of its characterizations, especially of Jo. Delaney's realistic dialogue creates a sense of authenticity of character which masks considerable implausibility. Particularly in the opening scenes with Helen and Jo, the rhythm of attack and defense, the revelation of past failures, the barely concealed insults, the self-deprecation, the sharpness and sustained talk tantalize the audience. Out of fragments of conversation, partial revelations, and even asides to the audience, Delaney creates individuals with deep and universal human needs. Out of this battle of words, partially revealing Jo's hope for love and her need for affirmation from her mother, come the forces which propel her into her love affair.

Delaney's male characters are significantly weaker than her women. Peter is more a caricature, some of his mannerisms suggesting a middle-class dropout now slumming with Helen. His villainy is stereotypical: Complete with eyepatch for a war wound, he carries a walletful of pictures of other girlfriends, though courting Helen. Geof is equally vague, in part because of his homosexuality. He is clearly the more sympathetic, in that he makes no demands on Jo, but is an easy and deferential target for Helen when she returns.

Although it may be said that little happens in the play, its physical and verbal compression makes the interaction of the characters overwhelming. Jo and Helen's two-room flat reflects a world lacking intellectual and physical privacy, in which the characters literally lack room to grow and develop. Similarly, the play's allusiveness contributes to a sense of the mythic nature of the action: References to other works of literature ranging from nursery rhymes to Sophocles' *Oedipus Tyrannus* (c. 429) are embedded in the dialogue. That they are suggested, rather than developed fully, may reflect Delaney's youthfulness.

The play's style, a result of the production techniques of the Theatre Workshop, makes it a mixture of gritty realism and dreams. Both the dialogue and the situation seem realistic: The language has the distinct flavor of a region and a class, and the characters' reactions to their situation seem authentic. Yet the text also seems stylized and Brechtian in its rapid pacing, asides in the third person to the audience, and a music-hall style of humor, including insults and songs. A small jazz band plays between scenes and provides music to which the characters enter and exit, many times dancing as they do. Significantly, the play never becomes abstract or allegorical, as do Bertolt Brecht's *Der kaukasische Kreidekreis* (1944-1945; *The Caucasian Chalk Circle*, 1948) and *Der gute Mensch von Sezuan* (1938-1940; *The Good Woman of Setzuan*, 1948), dealing with similar situations.

The collaboration of the Theatre Workshop is important, for *A Taste of Honey* was significantly reshaped from the original text. John Russell Taylor studied the original text of the play as it went to the Theatre Workshop and the final printed version. Aside from minor cutting to tighten dialogue, two major changes in the performance version are evident. First, the character of Peter is much weakened in performance, and he becomes a much more sinister figure. His marriage to Helen, successful in the original draft, now fails. The original draft employs his marriage to Helen as the basis for a more radical plot change from performance: He offers to take in both Jo and the baby. As the play ends, Jo seems destined to return to her mother. Geof is left onstage, holding the doll he had given Jo, all that he will have of the relationship. This seems to suggest much greater optimism in the original text than in performance and also a significant focus on and greater sympathy for Geof.

A Taste of Honey, by structure and characterization, indicates both the intense needs of its characters for love and affirmation and the likelihood of their failure to meet those needs. Most of the characters voice a longing for affection and love, but nearly all are defensive and uneasy in relationships with others. While Jo is the most fully realized character, Geof is, though shadowy, more sympathetic, for his willingness to become what Jo needs. Yet his love for her leads to his willingness to leave when Helen pushes him out. Despite Helen and Jo's reunion at the play's end, the inability of the characters to adapt their personal needs to those of others leaves only guarded optimism about the future.

The Lion in Love, a three-act play set in the,north of England, is both more compressed than *A Taste of Honey* and simultaneously more diverse. Delaney has extended her range of characters with an entire family, the Freskos: grandfather Jesse, his daughter Kit and her husband Frank, and their children, Banner and Peg. She further includes minor characters such as Nora, who is having an affair with Frank, Loll, Peg's boyfriend and fiancé, and Andy and Nell, the former an injured acrobat and pimp for the latter.

Instead of nine months' action, as in her previous play, Delaney dramatizes three days several weeks apart. Yet this does not tighten the structure of the play. Although characters confront opportunities for fulfillment, through hesitation or fear most of them lose their chance. The action consequently seems either directionless or circular, with little external change. Frank, who sells toys from a suitcase stand in the marketplace, spends most of his time with Kit arguing and being insulted. Either a permanent booth or Nora's offer to set up a shop with him would mean personal and economic security. In the end, Frank gains neither, and he remains trapped in his complex and antagonistic relationship with Kit. Peg and Loll, though able to see what has happened to the older generation, seem no wiser or better able to govern their emotions, and Peg apparently elopes with Loll. Only Banner, in his departure for Australia, is able to escape the limitations of marriage, but at the cost of abandoning his family and any support it may offer. Even Nell and Andy and their dreams of a new act for performance are blighted: He is not as good a dancer as she thought.

The title of the play is from an Aesopian fable in which a lion permits a forester to remove his claws and teeth as preconditions for marrying the forester's daughter. Once he submits, the forester kills him. The moral, "Nothing can be more fatal to peace than the ill-assorted marriages into which rash love may lead," applies to both the parents and children of the Fresko family. Both Kit and Frank seem to have lost by their marriage, and Loll and Peg may do the same. The banter of the partners back and forth, the attempt at friendship and intimacy, the defensiveness and caution are the same in both the younger and older lovers.

Once again, Delaney focuses more on the women of the play than the men. Although Kit does not enter immediately, she dominates the action and provides the center of interest. In a sense, the other members of her family exist only in their reaction to her. Her love of life and excitement, her determination not to behave as an adult and accept adult limitations, her chosen independence from children, husband, and father, make her a dynamic figure in an otherwise unchanging situation. She seems always to transcend the limitations of situation, class, and economic factors. Yet her "liveliness" is in fact destructive, provoking her husband's affairs and her daughter's disillusionment and eventual elopement. Although Peg is much less developed than Kit, her history will likely be the same. She has the wit, insight, and longings of her mother.

Delaney's men are, once again, shadowy or insufficient figures. While each has plans and dreams, none seems able to realize them or even develop commitment to them. They wander aimlessly, which may communicate a psychological truth but which confuses audiences. Jesse, the grandfather, the garrulous commentator on life, the link with the past, seems despite his history to have little to offer. Frank is much more fully realized, but his motives are still confused, and he is unable to confront his motives for returning to Kit. Banner and Loll are undeveloped, each with a dream which necessitates leaving and which has only vague longings to support it.

The Lion in Love has a quite different production style from that of *A Taste of Honey*. Gone are the Brechtian elements, the asides, the jazz band in the wings, the dancing entrances and exits. Although the stage directions indicate that the set is "suggested rather than real," with a backdrop which is "a fantastic panorama" of the city and "the local bombed-site" at the back, the play is much more conventionally realistic. While the stage action is at points quite lively, as at the opening of act 2, set on market day, the pacing throughout is measured. The biting humor of *A Taste of Honey* remains, but not the mixture of fantasy and reality.

Delaney has been applauded for her realism, especially in her language and her treatment of relationships. She deserves, however, equal praise for her creation of a mythic world, filled with powerful symbols of brokenness. When the plays appeared, critics recognized her regionalism, humor, and vivid women characters. Yet Delaney's early critics frequently assumed that the plays should be closed, climactic, showing issues resolved and measurable growth. Neither *The Lion in Love* nor *A Taste of Honey* fulfills such expectations. Instead, Delaney's world is one in which change is slight and in which circularity is common: Sons behave like fathers, and daughters follow their mothers. This world is, despite Delaney's humor, a difficult one. Her characters fear and hurt too much to become vulnerable, and they are ultimately detached from one another save for brief moments of consolation followed by antagonism.

Other major works
SHORT FICTION: *Sweetly Sings the Donkey*, 1963.
SCREENPLAYS: *A Taste of Honey*, 1961 (with Tony Richardson); *The White Bus*, 1966; *Charlie Bubbles*, 1968; *The Raging Moon*, 1970; *Dance with a Stranger*, 1985.
TELEPLAYS: *Did Your Nanny Come from Bergen?*, 1970; *St. Martin's Summer*, 1974; *The House That Jack Built*, 1977 (series); *Find Me First,*. 1979.
RADIO PLAYS: *So Does the Nightingale*, 1980; *Don't Worry About Matilda*, 1983.

Bibliography
Anderson, Lindsay. "A Taste of Honey," in *Encore*. V (July/August, 1958), pp. 42-43.
Armstrong, W. A., ed. *Experimental Drama*, 1963.
Delaney, Shelagh. "How Imagination Retraced a Murder," in *The New York Times*. CXXXIV (August 4, 1985), sec. 2, p. 15.
Kitchin, Laurence. *Mid-Century Drama*, 1960.
MacInnes, Colin. "A Taste of Reality," in *Encounter*. XII (April, 1959), pp. 70-71.
Oberg, Arthur K. "*A Taste of Honey* and the Popular Play," in *Wisconsin Studies in Contemporary Literature*. VII (Summer, 1966), pp. 160-167.
Taylor, John Russell. *Anger and After: A Guide to the New British Drama*, 1962.
Wellwarth, G. E. *The Theatre of Protest and Paradox*, 1965.

                                                         Richard J. Sherry

DENIS DIDEROT

Born: Langres, France; October 5, 1713
Died: Paris, France; July 30, 1784

Principal drama
Le Fils naturel: Ou, Les Épreuves de la vertu, pr., pb. 1757 (*Dorval: Or, The Test of Virtue*, 1767); *Le Père de famille*, pb. 1758, pr. 1761 (*The Father of the Family*, 1770); *Est-il bon? Est il méchant?*, pb. 1834, pr. 1913.

Other literary forms
In his own day, Denis Diderot was best known for his numerous unsigned contributions to the *Encyclopédie* (1751-1772), his reviews of the biennial art exhibitions in Paris (*Salons*, 1845, 1857), and his philosophical writings. Diderot also wrote extensively on the theater, and he produced a number of fictional works, beginning with the erotic *Les Bijoux indiscrets* (1748; *The Indiscreet Toys*, 1749). The best of his novels, however, appeared only posthumously: *La Religieuse* (1796; *The Nun*, 1797), *Jacques le fataliste et son maître* (1796; *Jacques the Fatalist and His Master*, 1797), and *Le Neveu de Rameau* (1821, 1891; *Rameau's Nephew*, 1897). His letters were edited by Georges Roth and Jean Varloot and have been published in sixteen volumes (*Correspondance*, 1955-1970).

Achievements
To his contemporaries, Diderot was known as "Monsieur le Philosophe." As coeditor and then sole editor of the *Encyclopédie*, he guided that masterpiece to its completion despite the desertion of collaborators and censorship by the government. This work, along with his philosophical writings, set forth the fundamental ideas of the French Enlightenment and challenged the old regime's politics and thoughts. Although the fiction that appeared in his own lifetime—*The Indiscreet Toys*, *Les Deux Amis de Bourbonne* (1773), *Entretien d'un père avec ses enfants: Ou, Le Danger de se mettre au-dessus des lois* (1773)—was not well received, his posthumously published works have established him as a leading prose writer of the eighteenth century, a worthy contemporary of Samuel Richardson and Laurence Sterne in England. Similarly, as a dramatist he was known in his own day as the author of two relatively unsuccessful plays. After two performances in 1757, *Dorval* did not appear onstage again for fourteen years. *The Father of the Family* fared better; the King of Naples requested it four nights in a row, and it was frequently revived throughout the eighteenth and early nineteenth centuries. Both were popular in book form, *Dorval* going through four editions in its first year and some twenty-five in France alone by 1800. *The Father of the Family* was even more successful: thirty-two editions in French before 1800 as

well as ten in German, three in English and Dutch, two in Russian, Danish, Polish, and Italian, and one in Spanish. As with his fiction, though, Diderot's most enduring work in this genre appeared posthumously. *Est-il bon? Est-il méchant?* has not been absent from the theater for long since the amateur theater Équipe began performing the piece in Paris in 1951. More significant for the eighteenth century stage were the essays that Diderot wrote about the theater, challenging the rule-bound attitudes of playwrights and actors and impelling the stage toward more natural presentations in both content and manner.

Biography

Denis Diderot was born in Langres, France, on October 5, 1713. His father, Didier Diderot, was a master cutler; his mother, Angélique Vigneron, was the daughter of a tanner. The family was thus decidedly bourgeois; while Diderot was to quarrel with his family's religious values, he remained true to his middle-class origins in the plays he wrote in the 1750's. Destined by his father for the priesthood, Diderot was enrolled in the local Jesuit college. In 1728, he went to Paris to continue his religious studies; four years later, he received a master of arts degree from the University of Paris. By then, he had lost all interest in a clerical career, so for two years he studied law under Clément de Ris. This occupation also failed to suit him, and for the next decade he earned a precarious living as tutor and hack writer.

Following his secret marriage in 1743 to Anne-Toinette Champion, the daughter of a lower-middle-class widow who owned a linen shop, Diderot sought a more stable income. Therefore, he began to translate into French a series of English works that would help shape his thinking and culminate in the monumental *Encyclopédie*. In 1745, he published *Principes de la philosophie morale: Ou, Essai de M.S*** sur le mérite et la vertu, avec réflexions*. The "M. S***" of the subtitle was Anthony Ashley Cooper, third Earl of Shaftesbury, whose *An Inquiry Concerning Virtue or Merit* (1699) formed the basis of this modified translation. The work introduced Diderot to the optimistic, natural morality of Shaftesbury, a view that would color Diderot's writings for the rest of his life. Further translations followed, making Diderot a logical choice to work on a French version of Ephraim Chambers' *Cyclopaedia: Or, Universal Dictionary of the Arts and Sciences* (1728).

Although Diderot was not initially named editor, he eventually assumed this post, first with Jean Le Rond d'Alembert and then, in 1758, by himself; in addition, he contributed many articles to this work. Though such responsibilities might have been sufficient to occupy his time, he wrote prolifically during these years, producing numerous philosophical essays, an erotic novel, and two plays.

His early writings led Diderot into conflict with the government. *Pensées philosophiques* (1746; *Philosophical Thoughts*, 1916) was condemned by the

Parlement of Paris in July, 1746, shortly after it was published. In 1747, the manuscript of *La Promenade du sceptique* (1830), an attack on Christianity, was seized before publication. For his speculations on the origins of the universe, he was imprisoned in the fortress of Vincennes outside Paris for three months in 1749. These experiences, coupled with the official suppression of the *Encyclopédie* a decade later, made Diderot cautious about exposing his manuscripts even to friends. Consequently, the works for which he is best known did not appear in his own lifetime, and his reputation in the eighteenth century did not rival that of contemporaries he has come to overshadow in the twentieth.

He did, however, have his admirers in his own time. Among them was Catherine the Great of Russia, who in 1765 engaged in a clever bit of patronage. She bought Diderot's library and made him curator for life, agreeing to take possession only after Diderot's death. This generosity guaranteed Diderot's financial security. To thank her, he traveled to Russia in 1773, where he frequently discussed political reforms with his patron. After returning to France in 1774, he continued to send advice to Catherine, who kept her fondness for Enlightenment ideas limited to the theoretical. Until his death on July 30, 1784, Diderot continued writing for posterity. His final treatise on moral philosophy, *Essai sur les règnes de Claude et de Néron* (1782), is a fitting capstone for his work, revealing his bitterness about the past but also his hopes for a future that he did so much to shape.

Analysis

Although Denis Diderot was in his mid-forties before he wrote his first play, his interest in drama was long-standing. Later in life, he commented that, "I myself, when I was young, hesitated between the Sorbonne and the Comédie. In winter, in the worst sort of weather, I used to recite roles from Molière and Corneille out loud in the solitary walks of the Luxembourg [Gardens]." In his *Lettre sur les sourds et muets* (1751; *Letter on the Deaf and Dumb*, 1916), he again recalled his early fondness for and knowledge of the drama: "Formerly I used to visit the theater very often, and I knew most of our good plays by heart." He would astonish those sitting around him by putting his fingers in his ears—a way of testing his memory—and surprise them even more by weeping at the tragic parts even though he apparently could not hear anything being said onstage.

This interest in the theater is also evident in his early writing. *The Indiscreet Toys* criticizes the artificiality of the theater. Diderot imagines someone being told that he is going to witness the intrigues and actions at court; instead, he is led to a spot overlooking a stage. According to Diderot, the spectator would not be fooled for an instant because contemporary stagecraft lacked realism. Another of Diderot's concerns emerges from a contribution of his to the third volume of the *Encyclopédie*. Under the heading "Comédiens," he defends actors by stressing their ability to incite in audiences a love of virtue and a dread of vice.

By the time he wrote *Dorval*, then, Diderot had acquainted himself with the great French theatrical tradition of the seventeenth century as well as contemporary drama, and he had spent at least a decade thinking about the kind of plays he thought most appropriate for the stage. *Dorval* was the first of his two attempts to create an example that would illustrate his precepts. Thus, the play rejects the rigid distinction between comedy and tragedy. The piece ends happily, with the appropriate people marrying each other and a supposedly lost fortune recovered; before this cheerful resolution, however, Dorval several times contemplates fleeing society and comes close to marrying his half sister, Rosalie. Also, Clairville narrowly escapes death in a duel and almost loses the woman he loves.

This serious treatment of middle-class characters was unconventional, though not unprecedented. It represented a new genre of serious comedy, which Diderot called *drame*, and it declared that the bourgeoisie was no longer to serve only as the butt of satire. Indeed, through Clairville Diderot praises the commercial class, observing, "Commerce is almost the only endeavor in which great fortunes are proportional to the effort, the industry, and the dangers that render them honest." Constance adds, "Our birth is given to us, but our virtues are truly ours," suggesting that the only distinctions worth making among people derive from their behavior, not their inherited rank in society. A century earlier, the very title of Molière's *Le Bourgeois Gentilhomme* (1670; *The Would-Be Gentleman*, 1675) would have made it clear to an audience that the play mocked middle-class pretensions. By the mid-eighteenth century, though, Diderot, the son of middle-class parents, portrays the middle class as dignified. Alexis de Tocqueville, in *De la démocratie en Amérique* (1835-1840; *Democracy in America*, 1835-1840), would observe that "the tastes and propensities natural to democratic nations, in respect to literature, will . . . first be discernible in the drama." Diderot's plays, along with those of his contemporaries, such as Pierre-Claude Nivelle de La Chaussée, Philippe Néricault Destouches, and Paul Landois, herald the ascendancy of the French middle class.

Dorval also puts into practice Diderot's belief in the power of the stage to reform society. Although Dorval observes that people speak of virtue too much, none of the characters, Dorval included, tires of moralizing. The piece's subtitle, "The Test of Virtue," indicates the play's moral theme, and Constance expresses Diderot's view on the potential of the theater as a moral agency when she tells Dorval, "The effect of virtue on our soul is no less necessary, no less powerful, than that of beauty on our senses. There is in the heart of man a yearning for order . . . which makes us sensible of shame. . . . Imitation is natural to us, and there is no example that compels us more forcefully than that of virtue."

This virtue that Diderot preaches in his play is less personal than social. Dorval is not condemned for being born out of wedlock, and the danger that Dorval escapes in renouncing Rosalie is less the union with his half sister than the betrayal of his best friend. Constance, his first love, persuades Dorval that personal inclinations must yield to duty, and Dorval agrees before he learns of his relationship to Rosalie. Constance repeats Diderot's views about man's social obligations when Dorval proposes to resolve his dilemma of loving both Constance and Rosalie by fleeing society completely. In a speech that ended a fifteen-year friendship between Diderot and the reclusive Jean-Jacques Rousseau, Constance tells Dorval, "You have received rare talents, and you must give an account of them to society. . . . I appeal to your heart. Ask it, and it will tell you that the good man belongs in society, and only the wicked person remains alone."

Dorval was intended to instruct not only Diderot's audiences but also the play's performers. According to a preface that Diderot included in the published version of the work, all the actors are supposedly the people they are representing, and they are reenacting events that actually befell them. Moreover, the production is intended only for themselves; they are performing in a salon without an audience. Dorval does allow Diderot to observe, but no one else knows he is present. This elaborate fictional frame emphasizes Diderot's belief that actors were paying too much attention to their audiences and so not behaving naturally. The result was a loss of realism, for the performers who were supposedly interacting with one another or meditating in private were always addressing the spectators. Hence, Diderot banished all asides from the play and included elaborate stage directions to encourage the players to behave as if the curtain had not risen. He wanted them to imagine an impenetrable barrier between themselves and the viewers, for Diderot believed that, paradoxically, only by ignoring the audience would an actor be able to please it.

A short time after its completion, the play was produced twice at Saint-Germaine-en-Laye, twelve miles west of Paris, where the action of the piece supposedly occurred. The first performance was well attended; on October 1, 1757, Alexandre Deleyre, a minor contributor to the *Encyclopédie*, wrote to Rousseau that he had been at "the first performance, where I wept copiously, although not intending to." According to Élie-Catherine Fréron, though, no one came to the second performance, and the Comédie-Française refused to produce the play until 1771.

Despite Diderot's disappointment over this poor reception, he quickly penned a second, similar work, *The Father of the Family*. Like *Dorval*, this play revolves around a dual courtship: Saint-Albin woos the poor Sophie while the poor Germeuil pursues Saint-Albin's sister, Cécile. Whereas in the first piece the only obstacle to the marriages is the characters' divided love— Dorval loves both Rosalie and Constance, and Rosalie loves both Clairville and Dorval—here, the Père de famille and his imperious brother, the Commander, object to the matches as unsuitable. Diderot draws on his own experiences for the plot, for his own father opposed his marriage to Anne-Toinette Champion precisely because she, like Sophie, was poor. Moreover, just as the Commander tries to use a *lettre de cachet* to separate the lovers by imprisoning Sophie, so Diderot was briefly locked in a monastery by his father.

Since Diderot portrays himself in Saint-Albin, one might expect that his sympathies would lie with the son rather than with the father. Instead, Diderot remains neutral, casting the play as a battle between parental prudence and youthful impetuosity. The Père is generous—he gives money to the poor and has willingly supported Germeuil; he is reasonable—he agrees to see Sophie before reaching any decision and then patiently explains his objections. He is also honest, dismissing a servant who lies to him. These good qualities become even more evident as Diderot contrasts the Père with his brother, who would achieve his ends by force rather than reason and who exhibits all the prejudices of the old regime. The Père opposes the marriage because of what he foresees as its negative social consequences, "the disorder of society, the confusion of blood and rank, the degradation of families." In other words, the Père upholds solid bourgeois values. Happily, Sophie proves to be sufficiently wellborn to deserve Saint-Albin; in fact, she is his first cousin.

Like Constance in *Dorval*, the Père has urged that personal considerations yield to social responsibility. When Cécile says that she wants to enter a convent, again he places society ahead of the individual, asking her, "Who will repopulate society with virtuous citizens, if the women the most worthy of being mothers of families refuse that role?"

Once more, Diderot used the theater as a vehicle for demonstrating his critical as well as his social theories. The middle-class characters are treated seriously, and the piece emphasizes their station in life rather than their peculiarities. Diderot had objected to the tradition, dating from Roman times, of portraying such types as the miser, the braggart soldier, or the wily servant. Instead, he urged that actors present the father, the lawyer, and the tradesman as they should ideally behave, thus heightening realism and morality in the play.

Another dramatic concern evident in this play is the tableau. Believing that the theater should present a series of "living pictures," Diderot provided numerous examples in this piece. His stage directions are so extensive as to remind the reader of George Bernard Shaw's lengthy instructions. Diderot thought that French actors were so concerned with speaking that they did not perform, so he tried to introduce elements of the pantomime to redress the imbalance.

Although more successful than its predecessor, *The Father of the Family* still did not meet as favorable a reception as Diderot had hoped; it was the last play Diderot offered his contemporaries. Nevertheless, his interest in the theater did not diminish. In 1760, he worked on translating Edward Moore's middleclass tragedy *The Gamester* (1753) and circulated the manuscript among his friends; the translation was finally published in 1819. He continued to write about the stage if not for it, and he utilized dramatic devices such as dialogue in his fiction. A number of these pieces have been successfully produced in this century: *The Nun* was made into a motion picture, and *Rameau's Nephew* was staged in Paris in 1963 to warm reviews.

The work that has won for Diderot the most respect as a dramatist, however, is *Est-il bon? Est-il méchant?*, which began in 1775 as *Plan d'un divertissement*, progressed to *La Pièce et le prologue* in 1777, and in 1781 emerged as a four-act play. Unknown in his own lifetime and rejected repeatedly by the Comédie-Française in the nineteenth century, it is the only one of Diderot's plays to be revived repeatedly in the twentieth. In this piece, Diderot made no attempt to instruct, no effort to implement his dramatic theories. Instead, he created a highly entertaining, fast-paced, witty comedy built around the crafty, semiautobiographical Hardouin.

Everyone asks favors of this person, and he obliges them, but in such a way as to raise the questions of the play's title. Madame Bertrand wants to be able to transfer her pension to her son and turns to Hardouin to use his influence on her behalf. He succeeds by persuading his friend Poultier that Madame Bertrand's son is also his (Hardouin's) own, thus making Madame Bertrand appear to be an adultress and her son a bastard. De Crancy wants to marry Mademoiselle de Vertillac, and when the girl's mother objects, he asks Hardouin to intercede. Hardouin does; he forges letters that convince the girl's mother that Mademoiselle is pregnant and so should marry even De Crancy to avoid disgrace. Hardouin is involved in so many plots, and deals with each so ingeniously, that the audience constantly marvels at his cleverness. At the same time, one wonders how long the charade can continue. Eventually, everyone learns of the humiliating ways in which Hardouin has secured for them what they wanted, but in the climactic trial scene (act 4, scene 4), he is pardoned without being totally exonerated. Hence, the play's title questions remain unanswered; each spectator must decide for himself whether Hardouin is good or wicked.

Absent from this play are the long, moralizing speeches and the tearful resolutions that mar Diderot's earlier pieces. He had at last discovered that the true end of the theater is to entertain and to ask questions, not to answer them. Not that his other works are unimportant in the history of French theater. In 1759, for example, the Comédie-Française banished audiences from the stage for precisely the reason Diderot had given for ending the practice: It detracted from the realism of the performance. The genre of serious comedy which he advocated enjoyed some decades of popularity both on the

Continent and in England, and his views on the didactic power of the stage remained influential well into the nineteenth century. One sees such ideas reflected even in the works of Henrik Ibsen and Shaw. Yet only when he abandoned theory in *Est-il bon? Est-il méchant?* could he himself create a work of sufficient stature to grant him his wish to be remembered as a first-rate dramatist.

Other major works

NOVELS: *Les Bijoux indiscrets*, 1748 (*The Indiscreet Toys*, 1749); *Jacques le fataliste et son maître*, wr. c. 1771, pb. 1796 (*Jacques the Fatalist and His Master*, 1797); *Les Deux Amis de Bourbonne*, 1773; *Entretien d'un père avec ses enfants: Ou, Le Danger de se mettre au-dessus des lois*, 1773; *La Religieuse*, 1796 (*The Nun*, 1797); *Le Neveu de Rameau*, 1821, 1891 (*Rameau's Nephew*, 1897). Although the official complete edition of Diderot's novels is found in the twenty-volume *Œuvres complètes* (1875-1877), edited by Jean Assézat and Maurice Tourneax, they are readily available in the Classiques Garnier, edited by Henri Bénac (1962). An updated edition of *Œuvres complètes* is in process under the editorship of Herbert Dieckmann, Jean Fabre, and Jacques Proust. All the novels are available in English in various popular editions.

SHORT FICTION: *Supplément au voyage de Bougainville*, 1796 (*Supplement to Bougainville's Voyage*, 1927); *Rameau's Nephew and Other Works*, 1964.

NONFICTION: *Pensées philosophiques*, 1746 (*Philosophical Thoughts*, 1916); *De la suffisance de la religion naturelle*, wr. 1747, pb. 1770; *La Promenade du sceptique*, wr. 1747, pb. 1830; *Lettre sur les aveugles*, 1749 (*An Essay on Blindness*, 1750; also as *Letter on the Blind*, 1916); *Notes et commentaires*, 1749; *Lettre sur les sourds et muets*, 1751 (*Letter on the Deaf and Dumb*, 1916); *Pensées sur l'interprétation de la nature*, 1754; *Entretiens sur "Le Fils naturel,"* 1757; *Concerning the Education of a Prince*, wr. 1758, pb. 1941; *Discours sur la poésie dramatique*, 1758 (English translation of chapters 1-5 in *Dramatic Essays of the Neo-Classical Age*, 1950); *Salons*, serialized 1759-1781, pb. 1845-1857; *Le Rêve de d'Alembert*, wr. 1769, pb. 1830 (*D'Alembert's Dream*, 1927); *Entretien d'un père avec ses enfants*, 1773 (*Conversation Between Father and Children*, 1964); *Paradoxe sur le comédien*, wr. 1773, pb. 1830 (*The Paradox of Acting*, 1883); *Essai sur Sénèque*, 1778 (revised and expanded as *Essai sur les règnes de Claude et de Néron*, 1782); *Diderot's Early Philosophical Works*, 1916 (includes *Letter on the Blind, Letter on the Deaf and Dumb, Philosophical Thoughts*); *Correspondance*, 1955-1970 (sixteen volumes); *Œuvres philosophiques*, 1956; *Œuvres esthétiques*, 1959; *Œuvres politiques*, 1962.

TRANSLATIONS: *L'Histoire de Grèce*, 1743 (of Temple Stanyan's *Grecian History*); *Principes de la philosophie morale: Ou, Essai de M. S*** sur le mérite et la vertu, avec réflexions*, 1745 (of the Earl of Shaftesbury's *An Inquiry*

Concerning Virtue or Merit); *Dictionnaire universel de médecine*, 1746-1748 (of Robert James's *A Medical Dictionary*).

MISCELLANEOUS: *Encyclopédie*, 1751-1772 (editor, seventeen volumes of text, eleven volumes of plates); *Œuvres*, 1798 (fifteen volumes); *Œuvres complètes*, 1875-1877 (twenty volumes); *Diderot, Interpreter of Nature: Selected Writings*, 1937 (includes short fiction); *Selected Writings*, 1966.

Bibliography
Fellows, Otis. *Diderot*, 1977.
France, Peter. *Diderot*, 1983.
Taylor, S. S. B., ed. *The Theatre of the French and German Enlightenment: Five Essays*, 1978.
Wilson, Arthur M. *Diderot: The Testing Years, 1713-1759*, 1957.

Joseph Rosenblum

90

TANKRED DORST

Born: Oberlind, Germany; December 19, 1925

Principal drama

Gesellschaft im Herbst, pr. 1960, pb. 1961; *Die Kurve*, pr. 1960, pb. 1962 (*The Curve*, 1963); *Freiheit für Clemens*, pr. 1960, pb. 1962 (*Freedom for Clemens*, 1967); *Grosse Schmährede an der Stadtmauer*, pr., pb. 1961 (*Great Tirade at the Town-Wall*, 1961); *Die Mohrin*, pr., pb. 1964; *Toller: Szenen aus einer deutschen Revolution*, pr., pb. 1968; *Eiszeit*, pr., pb. 1973; *Auf dem Chimborazo*, pb. 1974, pr. 1975; *Die Villa*, pr., pb. 1980; *Merlin: Oder, Das wüste Land*, pb. 1980, pr. 1981; *Der verbotene Garten*, pb. 1983, pr. 1984; *Heinrich: Oder, Die Schmerzen der Phantasie*, pb. 1984, pr. 1985.

Other literary forms

While Tankred Dorst is known primarily as a dramatist, he has written essays and other prose works which he often used as springboards for his plays. In addition to serious drama, he has extensively written and produced plays for children and fables for grown-ups, at times intended for and performed in puppet theaters. Dorst is also known for his radio plays and scripts for television, and in the 1970's and 1980's he distinguished himself in the German film industry by writing and directing motion pictures. In addition, Dorst has supplied libretti for several operas and ballets, and he translated several plays from the French and English. "Die Bühne ist der absolut Ort" (the stage is the unequivocal place), an article which he published in 1962, contain's Dorst's views of the theater, its role, its relationship to reality, and the theatrical devices he employs.

Achievements

At a time when only a handful of German dramatists were able to contribute anything original for the stage, Dorst—though inspired by already established German (Bertolt Brecht) as well as by some foreign, especially French, models (Jean Giraudoux, Jean Anouil, and Eugène Ionesco)— appeared in the German theater as a fresh and independent voice endowed with an innate sense of theater and stage technique. Unflinchingly, Dorst persevered in cultivating his vision, often in face of critical or political pressure to "take sides," especially in plays dealing with controversial figures or issues. That he was quite successful in his pursuit is demonstrated by prizes and awards received not only in Germany but also abroad. His theater debut, *Gesellschaft im Herbst* (autumn party), won for him the prize of the city of Mannheim (in 1959), which was followed by the Villa Massime stipend for a sojourn in Rome. Other awards came almost yearly: the Gerhart

Hauptmann Prize in 1964; the prize of the city of Munich in the same year and again in 1969; the prize of the city of Florence and the Theater Prize of Lisbon in 1970; the Bavarian Academy of Fine Arts Prize for Literature in 1983; and the Royal Film Institute of Belgium's L'Age d'Or award in 1984.

Biography

Tankred Dorst was born on December 19, 1925, in Oberlind near Sonneberg in Thuringia, an area which now constitutes the border between East and West Germany. His father was an engineer and manufacturer. As a teenager, Dorst became fascinated with the theater and dreamed of becoming a theater dramaturge. In 1942, as a seventeen-year-old high school student, he was drafted into the army. He was taken prisoner of war and placed in various English and American camps in Belgium, Great Britain, and the United States. Released in 1947, he first finished his interrupted high school studies (*Abitur*) in 1950, and then studied literature, art history, and drama at the Universities of Bamberg and Munich, without getting a degree. After 1952, he resided in Munich.

Dorst went through his theater apprenticeship while working with a students' puppet theater (*Das kleine Spiel*, the little play) in Schwabing, a bohemian section in Munich. He detailed his experiences there in a collection of essays, *Geheimnis der Marionette* (1957; the secret of the puppet) and in *Auf kleiner Bühne: Versuche mit Marionetten* (1959; on a small stage: experiments with puppets).

Soon, however, Dorst was acclaimed as a new talent in the German postwar theater, first gaining attention through a prize given by the city of Mannheim for his draft of *Gesellschaft im Herbst* and then by having the play produced almost simultaneously in several German theaters. Even more successful were his one-act plays: *Freiheit für Clemens* (freedom for Clemens), *The Curve*, and *Great Tirade at the Town-Wall*, all three performed in more than 150 theaters as well as translated into various languages. His new versions of some old plays (Ludwig Tieck's *Der gestiefelte Kater*, 1797; *Puss-in-Boots*, 1913-1914) and legends such as the old French love story of Aucassin and Nicolette (*Die Mohrin*) gave Dorst an opportunity to display his mastery of the stage by intermingling the most diverse theatrical techniques and devices, from play-within-a-play to masks and variety-show sketches and interludes. *Die Mohrin* (the Saracen girl) he also revised as a libretto for an opera.

In 1967, at the time of widespread student unrest in Germany and elsewhere, Dorst became a center of controversy with his new play, *Toller: Szenen aus einer deutschen Revolution* (Toller: scenes from a German revolution). Ernst Toller (1893-1939), a great German poet and dramatist of Expressionism, took part in a short-lived but violent revolution at the end of World War I and was elected president of the Bavarian Soviet Republic, which was soon suppressed by the right-wing militarists. Condemned to prison for a relatively short term (unlike other revolutionaries, who were summarily executed), Toller, after the rise of the Nazis, became a refugee in the United States, where he committed suicide in 1939. Based partly on Toller's autobiographical memoirs, Dorst portrays Toller as a sincere but muddle-headed idealist who plays a role of a revolutionary as if he were an actor on the stage; with such a leader the revolution was bound to fail. The widow of another prominent revolutionary presented in the play accused Dorst of having falsified the facts to suit his theatrical idea, while students and the leftist press claimed that he had exposed to ridicule the whole concept of revolution. In spite of, or because of, the controversy, the play was staged by numerous theaters in Germany and abroad, and a version of it ran on German television. That he was not afraid to create social and political debate, Dorst proved with other semidocumentary plays, among which *Eiszeit* (ice age) was just as contentious. It treats Knut Hamsun (1859-1952), Norwegian novelist and dramatist, the winner of the Nobel Prize for Literature (1920), who, when Germans occupied Norway during World War II, sided with the collaborationist government of Vidkun Quisling and after the war was locked in an old people's home.

In 1970, Dorst was invited to spend some time as a writer in residence at Oberlin College in Ohio, and in 1973 he lectured at universities in Australia and New Zealand. Starting in 1974, Dorst worked together with his life's companion, Ursula Ehler, on a long history of an upper-class German family which is in part rooted in the experiences of his own family. This family chronicle yielded several self-contained plays as well as prose works, television dramas, and films.

In the 1970's and 1980's, Dorst achieved a considerable success as a film director, his films gaining honors at various festivals. He has also been elected to a number of German academies, and he is a prominent member of the writers' association, PEN.

Analysis

Tankred Dorst's plays are distinguished above all by their craftsmanship and theatrical sensibility, which arise no doubt from Dorst's early preoccupation with puppet theater and his conviction that the stage is an instrument through which a dramatist can filter his creative ideas. With his first performed play, *Gesellschaft im Herbst*, Dorst exhibited his talent for presenting not only the characters of his play but also the setting and situations in which they find themselves as a theatrical artifice. Only rarely does he allow "the truth of life" or "the tragic sense of disillusionment" to be sensed from behind the scrim that he intentionally places between his play and the audience. While this first play may remind one of Jean Giraudoux's *La Folle de Chaillot* (1945; *The Madwoman of Chaillot*, 1947) in its effete, aristocratically seedy milieu as well as its burlesquing of the material greed of the aggressive commercial class, Dorst's play fundamentally differs from the older model. His play seems to be concerned less with the conflict between old values and twentieth century avariciousness and barbarism than it is with the prevalent human tendency to prefer illusion to reality, the ease with which people are ready to believe in the most preposterous suggestions—in this case, that an enormous treasure lies buried in the foundations of a castle. Thus, from the very beginning, Dorst was less interested in psychological realism than in playing out universal themes by way of theatrical magic.

Dorst's next performed dramas reiterate some of his basic ideas, which are expertly developed in three one-act plays which immediately followed. In *Freedom for Clemens*, he subtly manipulates the conceit that human beings can readily be convinced by others to accept the conditions of slavery as being those of freedom; in *The Curve*, the common assumption of social order and purpose in the world is quickly turned upside down, to reveal a vision of frightening absurdity; finally, in *Great Tirade at the Town-Wall*, the authorities toy with ordinary citizens until they are reduced to ranters lamenting their fate with no one to hear them.

Dorst's dramas, however, should not be reduced to a few overriding ideas, for this would deny his virtuosity, the skill with which he constructs his plays. The Countess de Villars-Brancas in *Gesellschaft im Herbst* appears at first to be easy prey for unscrupulous treasure diggers and other social vultures and hangers-on. Soon, however, she is revealed as a metaphor for an "autumn society" which has outlived its usefulness and is ready to decamp, but not before the rest of society's dregs and their frenzied "dance around the Golden Calf" are exposed. In *Freedom for Clemens*, Dorst underscores the Everyman features of Clemens, who is imprisoned for an undisclosed transgression, by giving him and other actors in the play puppetlike movements. They are supposed, however, to possess the agility of jugglers and acrobats.

While Dorst borrows from the French absurdist theater, the techniques employed in several of his plays hark back to the old Italian *commedia dell'arte* and beyond, including masks and plays-within-plays. The absence of seriousness on the surface of his plays is contradicted, however, by disturbing thoughts at their core. Thus in *Freedom for Clemens*, the question arises as to the meaning of freedom in general: If one is nestled comfortably in any one place, protected from viewing the outside world—like Clemens in his cell—and thus voluntarily relinquishing the freedom of often precarious commitment outside, preferring the safe containment within the four walls, is one then free or captive? Can one avoid seeing, by extension, parallel examples in the world at large? Is the word "freedom" merely a slogan to be placed on banners, a cliché without any deeper meaning?

The grotesque one-act play *The Curve* is similarly disturbing. It presents two symbiotic brothers (one works with his hands, the other with his head, like Gogo and Didi in Samuel Beckett's *Waiting for Godot* of 1952) who exist in an almost idyllic way at a dangerous bend in the road. They are creatures of ordinary, even cozy, domesticity who make their living from accidents that regularly happen at the curve. Their absurd profession—fashioning coffins for victims, burying them with proper ritual, repairing and then selling the victims' cars—parodies respectable and industrious ways of making a living. The latest victim, a highly placed government official who ignored the brothers' letters to him in reference to the dangerous curve, while appearing dead, suddenly recovers from the accident and pledges to remove the fatal hazard. At the prospect of losing their livelihood, the brothers murder the official and he is solemnly buried like the rest. The conditions whereby some people die and others benefit from their death are thus perpetuated. The farcical tone and the absurdity of the plot are underscored by the hypocritical rhetoric, the contrast between those who have "our best interests at heart," on one hand, and the gruesomeness of the underlying reality, on the other.

Great Tirade at the Town-Wall, which has as its source an ancient Chinese shadow play, immediately impresses the spectator with its simple but powerful setting, which recalls the Chinese costume plays by Bertolt Brecht. A fisher-woman beats against an enormous wall guarded by the imperial army, pleading that her soldier-husband be returned to her. Since he is dead, another soldier feigns to be her husband, and the imperial officers decide to have fun at the expense of the unfortunate woman. She is to prove that the man who claims to be the missing soldier is indeed her husband, for she is quite prepared—though knowing the truth—to take him as such. She fails, not because she cannot pretend, which she masterfully does, but because the passion with which she pursues her cause frightens the soldier away. Having lost, she laments her fate before the silent city wall.

While some critics have seen in the play the metaphor of an ever-present barrier dividing those in power, who toy with other people's lives, and the abject supplicants, who are always losers in their quest, other critics consider the central play-within-a-play representative of the perennial difficulty of establishing a mutual understanding between man and woman. The man flees from the all-embracing protectiveness of a strong, articulate woman to the more adventurous, albeit more dangerous, life of a soldier.

Dorst's semidocumentary plays, based on politically engaged historical figures, made him a celebrated if controversial dramatist. Toller, as noted above, appeared at a critical point in the political and social life of Germany. After more than two decades of apparently acquiescing to the idea of "not shaking the boat," accepting as normal the utter commercialization and even militarization of one Germany and the collectivization and Sovietization of the other, German young radicals clamored against all authority, proclaiming the necessity of wholesale social revolution. When Dorst branded Toller as a self-dramatizing idealist who plays roles from his own plays—notably *Masse-*

Mensch (1920; *Masses and Man*, 1924)—thus belying the bloody political as well as human reality of the revolution, that was more than the rebellious youth or liberal intellectual press could take. Students especially felt betrayed by a member of the intelligentsia from whom they would have expected support for their struggle for a more just society. When Dorst, in *Toller*, presented both sides of the uprising, showing the revolutionaries as well as the right-wing militarists to be contemptuous of human lives, the leftists charged that Dorst's play had distorted the truth, advocating the bourgeois view of revolution as an aberration of normal social behavior.

Aside from its questionable political import, *Toller* succeeds as an effective though disconcerting spectacle: Scenes of political caucusing are placed against scenes of private life; impassioned humanitarian appeals against macabre scenes of anti-Semitic students masked with clownishly exaggerated Jewish noses chanting and dancing; the servant girl's indifference to her student lover's attempt of raising her social conscience against executions and trials which in themselves mock justice and humanity. All these scenes, independently arranged in the Brechtian manner, dramatically reinforced with films, placards and oversized puppets, present a show of shattered dreams and painful nightmares.

Dorst's disdain for all preconceived political opinions and his disregard for the prevalent ideological pressure were made even more explicit in *Eiszeit*. The subject, a Quisling collaborator, was provocative, especially when the man in question is Knut Hamsun, an acknowledged giant of Norwegian and world literature. That there was no outright condemnation of the traitor was, to the majority, altogether appalling. Though Hamsun's arrogance and contempt for democracy, his shameless recalcitrance and political perversity were in no way concealed in the play, there was at least a tinge of admiration for his "being true to himself," for not yielding to this or that suggestion of what he should do or think. Dorst is interested in questions of morality, human decency, and integrity, but he loads the questions when he posits them in such a way that they appear somewhat blunted: Why, he asks, should a writer have deeper political insights than other citizens? Does literary fame have anything to do with a writer's political and moral integrity? *Eiszeit*, however, is not as effective theater as *Toller* is. The young partisan who mopes, full of hatred for the old writer, around the old people's home where Hamsun is kept under investigation is supposed to be Hamsun's antagonist and counterweight in the scale of social values and political morality. His enmity, however, is inadequately articulated, and his challenges in no way balance out the old man's arguments; moreover, his suicide—an admission of defeat in the face of Hamsun's fascinating impenetrability—is dramatically unconvincing. Ultimately, Dorst's portrayal of Hamsun does not add much to the audience's understanding of a man whose only regret is that he is now old and helpless, frozen in his "ice age."

Another play which centers on a famous writer—one who, like Hamsun, evoked as much denunciation and ridicule, as he did admiration—is *Der verbotene Garten* (the forbidden garden), which was first produced as a radio play and then, in 1984, as a stage drama. The work revolves around Gabriele D'Annunzio, the Italian poet, novelist, dramatist, and aviator. Physically unprepossessing, he cleverly cultivated his image as a great lover (his liaison with the famous actress Eleonora Duse was well publicized in his novel *Il fuoco* (1900; *The Flame of Life*, 1900), and a great national hero (based on his Fiume expedition in 1919). D'Annunzio's "patriotic" exploits and his intimate friendship with Benito Mussolini contributed to the general rise of chauvinistic and Fascistic sentiments in Italy after World War I.

In the late 1970's, Dorst, in cooperation with Ursula Ehler, wrote a number of plays dealing with a German family which were in part based on autobiographical details. The comedy *Auf dem Chimborazo* (on the Chimborazo) and his subsequent plays *Die Villa* (the villa) and *Heinrich: Oder, Die Schmerzen der Phantasie* (Henry: or, the pain of fantasy), in addition to his prose and television works, represent various stages in a long family chronicle, which depicts a well-to-do German family caught in the historical upheaval and catastrophic events of the crucial years between the 1920's and the 1950's. The destiny of Germany is juxtaposed to the fortunes of the family members, each with different political as well as social loyalties, biases, hopes, and preconceptions. While Dorst continued to avoid making any judgments, political or otherwise, the underlying tone of these plays is darker, and a sense of pessimistic disillusionment has crept in. The characters in the family chronicle cannot learn from their painful experience and continue clinging to their self-deluding images until they perish, which seemingly they must. The chance to begin anew, either on a personal or a national level, has been frittered away, often through stubborn foolishness and a false sense of pride. What remains is an individual as well as a national wasteland, as Dorst makes clear in the subtitle to his monumental Arthurian spectacle, *Merlin*. *Merlin* is the story of our own world: the bankruptcy of all utopian ideals. Consisting of ninety-seven scenes covering 375 pages, *Merlin* is a kaleidoscope composed with most diverse elements: fairy tales and comic-strip-like scenes, myth and farce, bits of dialogue and colorful but loose episodes, history and legend. Merlin, the Celtic magician, is the central character and at the same time the master of ceremonies who puts into motion this spectacular vision. To give the play its proper cosmic significance, Dorst introjects a Faustian bet which concerns nothing less than the destiny of mankind. The outcome is never in doubt, as the subtitle indicates. The human beings will senselessly destroy themselves in a chimerical ideological battle and leave this earth a wasteland.

That Dorst would gravitate toward television and cinema seemed natural. His dramatic flair, his large theatrical visions, are perhaps constrained by the physical confines of the stage. In whatever medium Dorst chooses to create, however, he will continue to astound his audiences with his inventiveness and theatrical mastery.

Other major works

NONFICTION: *Geheimnis der Marionette*, 1957; *Auf kleiner Bühne: Versuche mit Marionetten*, 1959; "Die Bühne ist der absolut Ort," 1962.

Bibliography

Hayman, Ronald, ed. *The German Theater: A Symposium*, 1975.
Innes, Christopher. *Modern German Drama: A Study in Form*, 1979.

Frank S. Lambasa

CHRISTOPHER DURANG

Born: Montclair, New Jersey; January 2, 1949

Principal drama

The Greatest Musical Ever Sung, pr. 1971; *The Nature and Purpose of the Universe*, wr. 1971, pr. as radio play 1975, staged 1979, pb. 1979; *Better Dead than Sorry*, pr. 1972 (libretto, music by Jack Feldman); *I Don't Generally Like Poetry but Have You Read "Trees"?*, pr. 1972 (with Albert Innaurato); *The Life Story of Mitzi Gaynor: Or, Gyp*, pr. 1973 (with Innaurato); *The Marriage of Bette and Boo*, pr. 1973, pb. 1976, rev. pr. 1979, pb. 1985; *The Idiots Karamazov*, pr. 1974, pb. 1976 (with Innaurato, music by Feldman); *Titanic*, pr. 1974, pb. 1983; *Death Comes to Us All, Mary Agnes*, pr. 1975, pb. 1979; *When Dinah Shore Ruled the Earth*, pr. 1975 (with Wendy Wasserstein); *'dentity Crisis*, pr. 1975, pb. 1979; *Das Lusitania Songspiel*, pr. 1976 (with Sigourney Weaver, music by Mel Marvin and Jack Gaughan); *A History of the American Film*, pr. 1976, pb. 1978; *The Vietnamization of New Jersey (A American Tragedy)*, pr. 1976, pb. 1978; *Sister Mary Ignatius Explains It All for You*, pr. 1979, pb. 1980; *The Actor's Nightmare*, pr., pb. 1981; *Beyond Therapy*, pr. 1981, pb. 1983; *Christopher Durang Explains It All for You*, pb. 1983; *Baby with the Bathwater*, pr., pb. 1983.

Other literary forms

Christopher Durang is known primarily for his plays. He has written a screenplay of *Beyond Therapy* (1987).

Achievements

Durang belongs to a tradition of black humorists and fabulists who first emerged in the 1950's with the novelists Joseph Heller, Kurt Vonnegut, Jr., and Thomas Berger. His plays are ridiculous comedies which agitate the audience without propagating a particular political viewpoint, attacking every "Great Idea" of Western literature and philosophy merely because it is assailable. His writing centers on the enduring questions of human suffering and authority. His most popular play, *Sister Mary Ignatius Explains It All for You*, was hotly debated by theologians and theater critics alike and won an Obie Award as the best new Off-Broadway play of 1980. His other honors include grants from the Rockefeller Foundation and the Lecomte du Nuoy Foundation, fellowships with Guggenheim and the Columbia Broadcasting System, and a Tony nomination for his musical *A History of the American Film*. His work is characterized by energy and a sense of the ridiculous in life and art, sustained by anger and despair. The targets of his abusive wit are the sacred cows of contemporary American society: religion, family life, hero-worship, law and order, and success.

Biography

Christopher Durang was born in Montclair, New Jersey, on January 2, 1949. A very humorous autobiographical sketch is given in the introduction to his plays in *Christopher Durang Explains It All for You*, beginning with his conception and ending with the reviews of *Beyond Therapy*. His parents, Francis Ferdinand and Patricia Elizabeth Durang, were devout Catholics who fought constantly until they were divorced, when Durang was still in grade school. Durang's interest in theater and playwriting became evident early in life. He wrote his first play while in the second grade in a Catholic elementary school. He subsequently attended a Catholic preparatory high school run by Benedictine priests. He continued to write plays, and though a fairly conservative and conventional student, he often inserted hints of sex for their shock effect. In high school, Durang was overcome with religious zeal and the desire to enter a monastery upon graduation, but soon afterward he lost his faith and his interest in the Roman Catholic religion.

He attended Harvard University with the hope and expectation of discovering a more intellectual and less conservative dimension of Catholicism but was disappointed. In his second year at Harvard, he entered psychoanalysis with a priest. He became obsessed with motion pictures and neglected his academic studies. Although he had been a prodigious writer in high school, he wrote almost nothing in college until his senior year, when he wrote (as a form of therapy for his feeling of religious guilt) a musical-comedy version of the life of Christ called *The Greatest Musical Ever Sung*, which included such irreverent show-tune lampoons as "The Dove That Done Me Wrong" and "Everything's Coming up Moses." The play stirred up a local religious controversy but was well received by audiences, encouraging the young playwright to write more. His next effort, the ambitiously titled *The Nature and Purpose of the Universe*, was eventually produced in New York and, following Durang's graduation from Harvard in 1971, was submitted as part of his application to the Yale School of Drama.

At Yale, Durang met and worked with a number of actors and playwrights who were, along with him, to make their marks in the American theater. Among his classmates were Albert Innaurato (with whom Durang collaborated on several plays), Meryl Streep (who appeared in a Durang play in college), Wendy Wasserstein (with whom Durang wrote *When Dinah Shore Ruled the Earth*), and Sigourney Weaver (who appeared in several Durang plays in New York and with whom he wrote *Das Lusitania Songspiel*). His chief supporter at Yale and later in New York was Robert Brustein, who was dean of the drama school while Durang was enrolled there and artistic director of the Yale Repertory Theater. Durang received his M.F.A. in 1974 but remained in New Haven for an extra year, performing and writing at Yale, teaching drama at the Southern Connecticut College in New Haven, and working as a typist at the medical school.

Durang moved to New York in 1975. *Titanic*, which he wrote for a class at Yale, and *The Nature and Purpose of the Universe* were produced in Off-Broadway theaters. In 1976, his musical play *A History of the American Film* was produced in Waterford, Connecticut, as part of the Eugene O'Neill Playwrights Conference, and in 1977 it was produced simultaneously on both coasts at the Hartford Stage Company in Connecticut, the Mark Taper Forum in Los Angeles, California, and the Arena Stage in Washington, D.C. In 1978, the play opened on Broadway at the American National Theatre. The play's subsequent failure on Broadway precipitated a period of depression which climaxed with the death of Durang's mother in March of 1979. Watching his mother die of incurable bone cancer and reassessing his Catholic upbringing, Durang started writing the play upon which his reputation as a playwright would be secured, *Sister Mary Ignatius Explains It All for You*. The play was first produced in December of 1979 by Curt Dempster's Ensemble Studio Theatre in New York, along with other one-act plays by David Mamet, Marsha Norman, and Tennessee Williams. Two years later, Andre Bishop's Playwrights Horizons produced the play Off-Broadway with two members of the original cast of six, along with Durang's *The Actor's Nightmare*, which he wrote as a curtain raiser.

Sister Mary Ignatius Explains It All for You brought Durang to the public's attention, not only through the show's popularity but also through several battles against censorship when various Catholic organizations attempted to close down the play. The Phoenix Theatre commissioned Durang to write *Beyond Therapy*, which opened in 1981 and then, almost a year and a half later, was rewritten and produced on Broadway at the Brooks Atkinson Theater. Later, Durang revised and expanded two plays he originally wrote at Yale, *Baby with the Bathwater* and *The Marriage of Bette and Boo*, which also were produced in New York. In 1987, Robert Altman released an unsuccessful film adaptation of *Beyond Therapy*, starring Glenda Jackson.

Analysis

The plays of Christopher Durang are remarkable for their absurdist approach to the important questions of modern philosophy, for their hilarious disregard for social conventions and traditional sexual roles, and for their uncompromisingly bleak assessment of human politics and society. As early as the satirical travesties he produced in college, Durang's abiding themes have been suffering and paternalism. The cutting edge of his humor is his insistence on the commonplaceness of suffering in the world. His plays are populated by archetypal sadists and victims, and the comedy is usually cruel (as the audience is made to laugh at the exaggerated and grotesque misery of the characters) and nearly always violent; death, suicide, disaster, and murder are never too far away in typical Durang slapstick. In a note accompanying the publication of *The Nature and Purpose of the Universe*, the writer explains that the violence of the play must appear simultaneously vicious and funny, demanding that performers make the audience sympathize with the victim and yet feel sufficiently "alienated" (in the sense of Bertolt Brecht's "alienation-effect") from the theatrical action to be able to laugh at it. Presiding over the sufferers is a figure of authority, always coldly detached and frequently insane, who "explains" the suffering with banal truisms taken from philosophy, religion, and pop psychology, while in fact he or she acts as the instrument of the oppression and mindless malice.

Fear and insecurity are the principal components of Durang's comedy of paranoia. While his plays are repeatedly criticized for not being positive and for not suggesting any remedy to the problem of human evil, they are in fact relentlessly moral, fueled by a profound sense of outrage at the crimes against human dignity. Like Eugène Ionesco, Joe Orton, and Lenny Bruce, Durang attempts to shock the audience out of its complacency through the use of vulgarity, blasphemy, violence, and other forms of extremism. If his endings seem less than perfectly conclusive, and if his characters seem to be no more than cartoons, still, underneath all the madcap and sophomoric nonsense is a serious and humane plea for tolerance, diversity, and individual liberty. The object of the writer's most satirical attacks is the incompetent guardian, a sometimes well-intentioned but always destructive figure of patriarchal authority who appears in many different guises: parent, husband, teacher, analyst, hero, nanny, doctor, author, and even deity. This figure embodies for Durang all the evil elements of human nature and social hierarchy.

Durang's drama of the mid-1970's, the plays which grew out of his college exercises at Yale, is chiefly parodic and yet contains kernels of the preoccupation with suffering characteristic of his later works. *The Idiots Karamazov*, which he wrote with Innaurato, is a musical-comedy travesty of the great Russian novelists of suffering, Fyodor Dostoevski and Leo Tolstoy. The principal character, Constance Garnett, is the translator, an older woman confined to a wheelchair and attended by a suicidal manservant, Ernest. In Durang and Innaurato's version of Dostoevski's *The Brothers Karamazov*, the holy innocent and idiot savant Alyosha becomes a pop music star, and the "Great Books," along with other academic pretensions to cultural importance, are thus trivialized as commodities in a money-and-glitter-oriented enterprise. Durang ridiculed Hollywood and the motion pictures in *A History of the American Film*, a 1976 musical which opened on Broadway in 1978. The five principal characters are caricatures based on familiar Hollywood types. Loretta (as in Loretta Young) is the long-suffering and lovingly innocent heroine. Jimmy (as in James Cagney) is the tough guy, part hoodlum and part romantic hero. Bette (as in Bette Davis) is the vamp, a vindictive but seductive figure who enjoys nothing more than making Loretta suffer. Hank (as in Henry Fonda) is the strong and silent all-American good guy, who eventually turns psychotic. Eve (as in Eve Arden) is the ever-present true friend, who covers up her own sexual frustration with dry witticisms and hard-boiled mottoes. True to its title, the play satirizes the gamut of Hollywood kitsch, including jabs at *Birth of a Nation* (1915), *The Grapes of Wrath* (1940), *The Best Years of Our Lives* (1946), *Psycho* (1960), *Who's Afraid of Virginia Woolf?* (1966), and *Earthquake* (1974). On a deeper level, the play exposes the American motion-picture industry as a manufacturer of glamorous façades for real-life misery and fear. In *The Vietnamization of New Jersey*, Durang takes on the legitimate theater itself. Using David Rabe's controversial Vietnam-era satire *Sticks and Bones* (1969) as a starting place, Durang makes the social and political pretensions of "serious theater" seem silly, while castigating the various "isms" of contemporary culture: liberalism, consumerism, racism, militarism, and sexism. The play treats the horrors of war, mental illness, inflation, unemployment, and suicide with chilling comedy.

In the late 1970's, when Durang wrote *'dentity Crisis*, *The Nature and Purpose of the Universe*, and the phenomenally successful *Sister Mary Ignatius Explains It All for You*, the playwright challenged the idea of authority or expertise itself. Inspired by R. D. Laing's controversial theories about schizophrenia, *'dentity Crisis* is an oddly moving comedy in one act and two scenes. The action centers on a young, depressed woman named Jane and her mother, Edith. The play opens as Edith returns from the dry cleaner with Jane's bloodstained dress, which has been ruined after an unsuccessful suicide attempt. Despite the initial impression, it soon appears that Jane is the only character in the play who is "sane." Edith manufactures and discards versions of reality with breathless speed, and Robert, the other occupant of the house, manifests four distinct personalities, alternately Jane's brother, father, and grandfather, as well as the Count de Rochelay, a foreign suitor of the perversely promiscuous Edith. Even Jane's psychoanalyst, Mrs. Summers, is bizarrely inconsistent. In scene 1, the role is played by a man, and in scene 2, after a sex-change operation, by a woman (the actor who plays Mr. Summers in the first scene plays his wife in the second). Jane reveals the motive behind her suicide attempt in a poignant and surrealistic monologue concerning a production of *Peter Pan* she had seen as a girl. Life is not worth continuing, she says, if it only leads to death in the end. The play ends with the daughter's loss of her identity, but the audience's sympathy remains with her because it has entered her version of reality and regards the others as mad.

The authoritative Mr. and Mrs. Summers in *'dentity Crisis* are remarkably similar to Ronald and Elaine May Alcott, the two "agents of God" who borrow various guises in *The Nature and Purpose of the Universe*. Like its glib title, the play pokes fun at those who would offer easy explanations of the mysteries of existence and evil. It is a play in thirteen "chapters," each chronicling a different aspect of the tragicomic downfall of the hapless Eleanor Mann. Presiding over the events of the drama are Ronald and Elaine, who pretend to render meaningful the random catastrophes which they inflict upon the Job-like Eleanor. Every now and then they enter the action of the play, purportedly to offer heavenly guidance and solace but actually to intensify the poor woman's suffering. Durang's comedy springs from the characters' absurdly cool responses to horror. When Eleanor is knocked to the kitchen floor and kicked by her drug-peddling son, her husband chides the boy, saying, "Donald, have a little patience with your mother." The play ends as, in a parody of Old Testament piety, Ronald and Elaine bind and gag Eleanor and sacrifice her to a distant and passively vicious God.

Sister Mary Ignatius, teacher at Our Lady of Perpetual Sorrow and the menacingly maternal protagonist of *Sister Mary Ignatius Explains It All for You*, is the writer's classic realization of the banality and willful ignorance of human evil. The play falls into three sections. In the first, Sister Mary catechizes the audience on basic doctrines and practices of the Roman Catholic Church. As Durang noted in several interviews, the humor of this section stems from the unexaggerated reportage of the irrational but devoutly held beliefs of certain Christians: the existence of Heaven, Hell, and Purgatory within the physical universe; the supernatural births of Jesus Christ and Mary; the efficacy of Christ's suffering and death on a cross; the exclusively procreative function of sex; and God's everlasting vengeance against wrongdoers such as Zsa Zsa Gabor, Brooke Shields, and David Bowie. Repeatedly, however, Sister Mary dodges the more interesting issue of God's responsibility for the existence of evil and suffering in the world. The second section presents a Nativity play performed by four of Sister Mary's former students. More than anything else, the play demonstrates the triumph of dogma over narrative in traditional Christianity and portrays an absurdly abbreviated life of Christ. With only three characters, Mary, Joseph, and Misty the camel (two actors impersonate separate humps), and a doll as the infant Jesus, the play spans the time from the Immaculate Conception (of Mary) to the Ascension (of Jesus, Mary, Joseph, and Misty). The third section of the play involves the Nativity-scene actors' disclosure to Sister Mary of the courses their lives have taken after leaving Our Lady of Perpetual Sorrow. Philomena (Misty's front end) has borne a daughter out of wedlock. Aloysius (Misty's back end) has become a suicidal alcoholic who regularly beats his wife. Gary (Joseph) has had homosexual relationships. Diane (Mary), whom Sister Mary especially detests, has had two abortions. Diane engineers the climactic confrontation in order to embarrass Sister Mary and then reveals her intention to kill her, much to the surprise of her three cohorts. Victorious in the end, Sister Mary whips out a gun and kills Diane; then, after assuring herself that he has made a recent confession of his sexual sins, she kills Gary as well. The play ends with a recitation of the catechism by Thomas, a boy currently enrolled in the parochial school.

In the 1980's, Durang turned his attention to other kinds of oppression in society, specifically the normalization of sexuality and family relationships. In *Beyond Therapy*, he again attacks psychoanalysis from a Laingian perspective, portraying the analysts in the play as more bizarre versions of Mr. Summers and his wife in *'dentity Crisis*. Their clients are a heterosexual woman and a bisexual man who meet through an advertisement in the personals column of a newspaper. The complex relationship they form is played mainly for laughs, but the butt of most of the jokes is pop psychology, as well as the notion of anyone's being an expert about how other people ought to live their lives.

Both *Baby with the Bathwater* and *The Marriage of Bette and Boo* have their origins in plays Durang wrote while in college and pertain to American family life. *Baby with the Bathwater* is a grim but humorous indictment of the science of child-rearing. Born as a boy but reared as a girl, Daisy, the baby of the title, is the victim of two inept parents and a manipulative nanny; in the last act he appears in his analyst's office wearing a dress, clearly suffering from a sexual identity crisis. *The Marriage of Bette and Boo* takes the form of a college student's memories of his parents, both of whom are emotionally unbalanced and (for their son Matt, the narrator) unbalancing. The play is a parody of the family dramas of American dramatists Thornton Wilder and Eugene O'Neill. The mother, Bette, idolizes babies but is able to produce only one living descendant because her blood type is incompatible with her husband's. The several stillborn infants she produces she names after animal characters in Winnie the Pooh storybooks. The father, Boo, is an alcoholic whose life is a cycle of a reformation and backsliding. Though a comedy, the play touches on serious philosophical questions concerning God, suffering, death, the absurdity of life, and the meaning of love. It is also the most autobiographical of Durang's plays.

Christopher Durang belongs to the postmodernist wave of American playwrights who emerged during the 1970's, including A. R. Gurney, Tina Howe, and Sam Shepard. These writers fused the experimental techniques of the structuralist theater experiments of the 1960's with the "traditional" domestic drama of the early twentieth century American realists, creating a new form of theater that is simultaneously naturalistic and self-consciously theatrical. Evolving as it did from collegiate travesties and comedy sketches, Durang's drama violates many of the established principles of the well-made play. However sloppily constructed and politically unsophisticated his plays may be, Durang's genius is to create comedies out of existential anger and to infuse them with energy, thought, and an unbounded sense of liberty.

Other major work
SCREENPLAY: *Beyond Therapy*, 1987.

Bibliography

Brustein, Robert. "The Crack in the Chimney: Reflections on Contemporary American Playwriting," in *Theater*. IX (Spring, 1978), pp. 21-29.

Denby, David. "Chris Durang—Funny Baby," in *Vogue*. CLXXIV (February, 1984), pp. 358-359.

Durang, Christopher. Introduction to *Christopher Durang Explains It All for You*, 1983.

Flippo, Chet. "Is Broadway Ready for Christopher Durang?" in *New York*. XV (March 15, 1982), pp. 40-43.

Simon, John. Review of *Baby with the Bathwater* in *New York*. XVI (November 21, 1983), pp. 67-68.

Weales, Gerald. Review of *Sister Mary Ignatius Explains It All for You* in *Georgia Review*. XXXVI (Fall, 1982), pp. 523-525.

Joseph Marohl

DARIO FO

Born: San Giano, Italy; March 24, 1926

Principal drama

Poer Nano, pr. as radio play 1951, staged 1952; *Il dito nell' occhio*, pr. 1953 (with Franco Parenti and Giustino Durano); *I sani da legare*, pr. 1954 (with Parenti and Durano); *Ladri, manichini e donne nude*, pr. 1958; *I cadaveri si spediscono, le donne si spogliano*, pr., pb. 1958; *Comica finale*, pr. 1959 (includes *Quando sarai povero sarai re*, *La Marcolfa*, *Un morto da vendere*, and *I tre bravi*); *Gli arcangeli non giocano a flipper*, pr. 1959, pb. 1966; *Aveva due pistole con gli occhi bianchi è neri*, pr., pb. 1960; *Chi ruba un piede è fortunato in amore*, pr., pb. 1961; *Gli imbianchini non hanno ricordi*, pb. 1962; *Non tutti i ladri vengono per nuocere*, pb. 1962; *Isabella, tre caravelle è un cacciaballe*, pr., pb. 1963; *Settimo: Ruba un po meno*, pr., pb. 1964; *La colpa è sempre del diavolo*, pr., pb. 1965; *La signora è da buttare*, pr., pb. 1967; *Grande pantomima con bandiere e pupazzi piccoli e medi*, pr. 1968, pb. 1975; *La fine del mondo*, pr. 1969; *Mistero buffo*, pr. 1969, pb. 1970; *Legami pure che tanto spacco tutto lo stesso*, pr. 1969, pb. 1975 (includes *Il telaio* and *Il funerale del padrone*); *L'operaio conosce trecento parole, il padrone mille: Per questo lui è il padrone*, pr. 1969, pb. 1970 (*The Worker Knows Three Hundred Words, the Boss Knows a Thousand: That's Why He's the Boss*, 1983); *Vorrei morire anche stasera se dovessi pensare che non è servito a niente*, pr., pb. 1970; *Morte accidentale d'un anarchico*, pr. 1970, pb. 1972 (*Accidental Death of an Anarchist*, 1979); *Tutti uniti! Tutti insieme! Ma scusa, quello non è il padrone?*, pr., pb. 1971; *Fedayn*, pr., pb. 1972; *Ordine per DIO.000.000!*, pr., pb. 1972; *Pum, pum! Chi è? La Polizia!*, pb. 1972, pr. 1973; *Guerra di popolo in Cile*, pr., pb. 1973; *Non si paga! Non si paga!*, pr., pb. 1974 (*We Can't Pay! We Won't Pay!*, 1978); *Il Fanfani rapito*, pr., pb. 1975; *La giullarata*, pb. 1975, pr. 1976; *La marijuana della mama è la più bella*, pr., pb. 1976; *Le commedie di Dario Fo*, pb. 1977 (five volumes); *Parliamo di donne*, televised 1977 (with Franca Rame); *Ulrike Meinhof*, pr. 1978 (English translation, 1980); *Tutta casa, letto è chiesa*, pr., pb. 1978 (with Rame; adapted as *Female Parts*, 1981; also known as *One Woman Plays*); *La storia della tigre*, pr. 1978, pb. 1980; *La storia di un soldato*, (libretto by C. F. Ramuz; adaptation of Igor Stravinsky's opera *The Soldier's Tale*); *La tragedia di Aldo Moro*, pr. 1979; *Clacson, trombette è pernacchi*, pr. 1981 (*About Face*, 1983); *L'opera dello sghignazzo*, pr. 1981 (music by Kurt Weill; adaptation of Bertolt Brecht's play *The Threepenny Opera* and John Gay's play *The Beggar's Opera*); *Il fabulazzo osceno*, pr. 1982; *Pata pumfete*, pr. 1983; *Coppia aperta, quasi spalancata*, pr. 1983 (with Rame; *An Open Couple— Very Open*, 1985); *Elisabetta: Quasi per caso una donna*, pr. 1984; *Hellequin, Arlekin, Arlecchino*, pr. 1986; *Dio li fa e poi li accoppa*, pb. 1986.

Other literary forms

Dario Fo's songs and poems are collected in *Ballate è canzoni* (1974; ballads and songs). He has also designed sets and written scripts for several films, including Carlo Lizzani's *Lo Svitato* (1956). *Ci ragiono è canto* (1966), *Ci ragiono è canto No. 2* (1969), and *Ci ragiono è canto No. 3* (1973)—which can be translated as "I think things out and sing about them," numbers one, two, and three—are spectacles based on Italian folk and traditional songs.

Achievements

Fo is concerned above all with reviving a tradition of "popular" theater, presenting a satirical critique of modern society, especially of authority and the powers that be, and highlighting corruption and injustice. He is deeply involved in contemporary issues, and his texts remain flexible so as to reflect current changes (some plays—for example, *Accidental Death of an Anarchist*—present the critic with at least three, sometimes more, versions, differing slightly from one another, as the situation which engendered them changed and developed). Fo himself traces his inspiration back to the Medieval *giullare*, the joker, who performed at fairs and in marketplaces, entertaining the people, expressing their complaints and grievances in a popular form of political satire (for which he was not infrequently persecuted or even executed by the authorities). In spite of the political content of his plays, however, Fo stresses the fact that he does not belong to the Communist or to any Marxist Party, because bureaucracy, in whatever guise, is "destructive." As a modern-day *giullare*, beyond political commentary and satire, Fo aims at all times at entertaining his audience, at making people laugh, "because laughter activates intelligence." The label most often applied to Fo is that of "clown": not so much a circus clown, although clownish antics often form part of his act, but a farcical Chaplinesque clown, with a sharp bite behind the laughter. Fo is a virtuoso performer of immense skill and dynamism, described as a superstar by enthusiastic reviewers. With the serious popular tradition of the *giullare*, he has combined the stage antics and tricks of the *commedia dell'arte*, along with its tradition of improvisation.

In what is a close working partnership with his wife, Franca Rame, he takes his theater to the working class, performing in labor halls, workers' cooperatives, factories, and market squares. With his wife and members of his company, he has traveled widely abroad, arousing both enthusiasm and polemic. In 1977, he was nominated for the Nobel Prize; in 1981, he was awarded the Danish "Sonnig" Prize.

Biography

Dario Fo was born in 1926, in San Giano, Italy, a small town in Lombardy on the shores of Lake Maggiore, near the Swiss border. His father was a railway worker who enjoyed acting in an amateur theater company, and his mother came from a peasant family. As a boy, Dario was very much influenced by the *fabulatori* and *cantastorie*, traveling storytellers and ballad singers who wandered around the shores of the lake entertaining the local fishermen. As a youth, he went to Milan, where he studied painting at the Brera Academy and architecture at the Polytechnic Institute, abandoning his studies when he was close to obtaining his degree. When he suffered a nervous breakdown in the late 1940's, he was advised to pursue what he found most enjoyable, and he thereafter turned more and more to theater. During the 1950's, Fo tried his hand at radio, revues, and films. During the period between 1958 and 1959, he wrote, produced, directed, and performed in one-act farces and short comic pieces, inspired by theatrical traditions ranging from the *commedia dell'arte* to the "French Farce" of Ernest Feydeau. "These farces were a very important exercise for me in understanding how to write a theatrical text. I learned how to dismantle and re-assemble the mechanisms of comedy," Fo has said. "I also realized how many antiquated, useless things there were in many plays which belong to the theatre of words."

In 1954, Fo married actress Franca Rame, a member of a popular touring theater family. (Their son, Jacopo, in 1977 provided the illustrations for two scenarios from *Poer Nano*, which were published in cartoon form.) In 1959, the Fos formed their own company, La Compagnia Dario Fo–Franca Rame, in Milan.

The years 1959 to 1968 are usually described as Fo's "bourgeois period," because the company performed mainly before middle-class audiences, working in traditional boulevard or Broadway-type commercial theaters. The plays had consistent plot lines and character development, but they all satirized and criticized the government and existing political and social conditions in Italy. "Having accepted this circuit and these audiences," Fo recalls, "we had to put across political and social truths under the guise of satiric licence."

In 1959, Fo and Rame were invited to present some of their farces on the government-controlled national television, RAI-TV. In 1962, they worked in a popular Italian television series, *Canzonissima*. Fo's sketches, highly satirical and explicitly political, were censored, causing Fo and Rame to resign in protest. The Fos were then sued by RAI and effectively excluded from Italian television for some fourteen years. *Ci ragiono è canto* was an uneasy collaboration with a musical group interested in reviving peasant and working-class songs. Fo directed the show, and rewrote some of the songs.

The Paris revolts in May, 1968, the protests against the Vietnam War, the cultural revolution in China, and revolts in Latin America and Africa all helped to influence Fo's decision to break away from establishment, mainstream, bourgeois theater and lend his voice to the class struggle and to political revolt. He declared that he no longer wanted to be "the court jester of the bourgeoisie," preferring instead to serve as the "the jester of the proletariat."

The year 1968 also witnessed the dissolution of La Compagnia Dario Fo–Franca Rame to be replaced by the Associazione Nuova Scena, a cooperative theater company, organized under the auspices of Associazione Ricreativa Culturale Italiana (ARCI), the cultural and recreational organization of the Italian Communist Party (PCI). Yet Fo's refusal to toe any party line and his indiscriminate satirical attacks on bureaucracy soon brought him into conflict with the PCI, leading to their boycott of the group's performances.

In 1970, after internal debates and conflicts, Fo and Rame withdrew from Nuova Scena and founded Il Collettivo Teatrale "La Comune," an independent, self-supporting political theater group allied to organizations of the extraparliamentary Left.

Rame was abducted and tortured by a Fascist group in 1973. In a separate incident later that year, Fo was arrested and briefly imprisoned in Sassari (Sardinia) but was released after his company organized a demonstration outside the police station.

After a highly successful tour of *Mistero buffo* (comic mystery-play) in France, in 1974, the reorganized Il Collettivo Teatrale "La Comune" set about finding itself a permanent location. The group finally occupied an abandoned building, the Palazzina Liberty, close to the center of Milan. This led to a struggle with the authorities, which developed into a major national issue, but eventually the group was given temporary permission to remain. The painter Matta was closely involved and painted murals in the Palazzina.

The decade of the 1970's saw the beginning of Fo's and Rame's extensive trips and performances abroad, although the United States denied them visas in 1980 and again in 1984, a denial based on the "ideological exclusionary clauses" of the McCarthy-era immigration law. Not until 1985 were Fo and Rame allowed to enter the United States, and then for less than a week, to attend final rehearsals and previews of a Broadway production of *Accidental Death of an Anarchist*. In 1986, however, they were allowed to visit the United States for a six-week performance tour; they returned again in 1987.

In 1977, Fo performed *Mistero buffo* on Italian television, arousing bitter protests from Church and government. In the same year, collaborating for the first time with Rame, he wrote *Female Parts*, a series of monologues dealing with the condition of women, which she subsequently performed. Other monologues followed, dealing with the frustration of women at their role of second-class citizens, or "sub-proletariat."

Mistero buffo was presented at the Berlin International Festival in 1978. There was something of a return to the bourgeois theater in that year, with the touring of *La storia della tigre* around Italy. For the 1978-1979 season at the world-famous La Scala opera theater, Fo directed a politically oriented adaptation of Igor Stravinsky's *The Soldier's Tale* (1918), to the disgust of opera connoisseurs. Fo's collaboration with La Scala was short-lived. Eviction from the Palazzina Liberty was followed by further tours abroad for Fo and Rame, who were ever more in demand. Since the loss of the Palazzina Liberty, Fo and Rame have had no permanent base in Italy, although from time to time they have made a provisional home in the Teatro Cristallo in Milan a former music hall. Abroad, however, theater locations have never been a problem. Fo's plays have been produced in so many countries and translated into so many languages that he has been described as the most widely performed living Italian dramatist.

Analysis

One of the problems which faces agitprop theater is that of combining a militant political message with a powerful dramatic and artistic effect, since each may tend to weaken the other. Dario Fo's theater successfully maintains a balance between the two. While the intensity and actuality of the political message, being too close to the bone, have created problems for the Fos in their own country, the effectiveness of their theater has contributed much to their popularity abroad, where the political implications are less specific. Fo's theater is not nihilistic: It aims at making people think, and it does this chiefly through laughter because, as Rame says, when one laughs, one's mind is suddenly opened to be pierced by the nails of reason." Fo's laughter is the uneasy one which goes naturally "with a degree of cynicism" that satire induces, or "a kind of *grand guignol* scream," resulting from those "nails of reason" piercing one's head.

After various one-act farces and playlets, *Gli arcangeli non giocano a flipper* (archangels don't play pinball machines), a three-act play with music and a traditional structure which approximates that of the well-made play, introduced Fo's bourgeois period. As its title page notes, one of the main incidents is inspired by a short story by Augusto Frassineti, but the treatment is Fo's own. Through a complex plot of farcical twists and reversals, surrealistic dream sequences, and stylized, balletlike stage business, Fo attacks the stupidity and narrow-mindedness of Italian bureaucratic red tape and the inefficiency and corruption of government ministers. The starting point of the play is a group of petty criminals, "good-natured, sulphuric louts, a kind of proletariat of the outer suburbs who survive on expedients." They are responsible for introducing the main character, Lanky, to the girl of his dreams, the Blonde, through the elaborate theatrical practical joke they construct. Theater within theater, and a fusion to the point of confusion of theatricality and reality, are elements that would continue to run through Fo's plays. Interesting also is the mention, for the first time in a Fo drama of the *giullare* tradition, which would play such a dominant role in the development of his theater.

The underworld returned, but with gangsters, in Fo's next play, *Aveva due pistole con gli occhi bianchi è neri* (he had two pistols with white and black eyes). The plot remains farcical, based upon a "double" and a series of mistaken identities, and the play is again interspersed with musical numbers. The political satire is predominant, however, and in an interview Fo described the company's difficulties with censorship (not for the last time in Fo's career). Problems of madness and psychiatry, themes which recur in Fo's theater, here make a brief appearance, as the main character struggles with amnesia and with the difficulty of establishing his identity in a psychiatric hospital. The influence of Bertolt Brecht can be clearly sensed in this play—an influence which causes Fo to refer to certain aspects of his drama as "epic."

This influence can be found, too, in *Isabella, tre caravelle è un cacciaballe* (Isabella, three sailing ships and a con man), a play in two acts and an interlude, which has certain similarities to Brecht's *Leben des Galileo* (1943, revised 1955-1956; *Life of Galileo*, 1947), which had enjoyed a memorable production in Milan in the same season; although the way Fo's Columbus comes into conflict with the established political powers differs from that of Brecht's hero. *Isabella, tre caravelle è un cacciaballe* is a historical play which relies on detachment and distancing of the audience. Fo's aim was to "dismantle a character who had been embalmed as a hero in school history books"; the critique of a Columbus, who is at once an intellectual and a political opportunist, a "sailor" and an "adventurer," is developed in a highly satirical vein through a play-within-the-play. A recurring figure throughout Fo's theater, that of the madman, or simple fool, is embodied in this play in Isabella's daughter, Giovanna la Pazza (Joanna the Mad). Fo's use of songs differs from Brecht's, inasmuch as they are more strongly a means of political or social comment rather than part of the action.

Mistero buffo is among the best-known and most popular of Fo's works outside Italy. It has been described as the culmination of Fo's research into popular culture. It consists of a series of texts developed over several years and divided into two sections. To the first part belong sketches such as "Bonifacio VIII," a merciless satire of Pope Boniface VIII, attacked by Dante in the *Inferno*, but Fo also alludes to Pope John Paul II. "La resurrezione di Lazzaro" is presented from the point of view of the crowd as a once-in-a-lifetime spectacle not to be missed; "La nascita del giullare" describes how a victimized, downtrodden peasant, about to hang himself, is stopped by Christ, who praises him for resisting the tyranny of the authorities and gives him the gift of telling stories so that he may share his experiences with others and encourage them also to resistance and revolt.

The second part comprises sketches such as "Maria viene a conoscere della condanna imposta al figlio," in which the Virgin Mary learns that the joyful crowds which she thought might be going to a wedding are in fact going to her son's crucifixion; "Gioco del matto sotto la croce" is a gruesomely comic sketch dealing with the difficulties of driving in the nails at the Crucifixion, and an aborted attempt by the madman to rescue Jesus from the Cross. The historical aspect of these *giullarate* is emphasized by Fo's introductions, complete with reproductions of ancient manuscripts or paintings; the contemporary message, on the other hand, is stressed by topical allusions which may change, if not always from one night to the next, at least over a period of weeks or months. The text is never definitive; it remains fluid. Fo is always responsive and flexible to dynamic interaction and intimate rapport with his audience.

Most of the texts are in a language which Fo describes as "fifteenth century Padano," an amalgam of various Northern Italian dialects. Fo adapts these dialects, sometimes modernizes them, and invents words, so that the language functions as a codified system of sounds. Furthermore, it was in *Mistero buffo*, in some of the sketches, that Fo introduced what he calls "grammelot," a mainly invented language which uses some real or recognizable words. Thus, he has developed a French grammelot, an American grammelot, and so on. Although some of the grammelot sketches, such as "Il sogno dello Zanni" ("Johnny's dream," but also "the Zanni's dream," the Italian title meaning either or both), are among Fo's most famous performance pieces, they have been found to defy transcription or publication, as opposed to those sketches in dialect, which are published side by side with a translation into modern Italian. Fo ascribes the use of an amalgam of dialects, or of grammelot, as deriving from the itinerant nature of the *giullare*, who had to be understood by all the people wherever he went and who could not learn an unlimited number of dialects. Yet grammelot has the advantage of providing legal protection, inasmuch as it is, strictly speaking, a nonlanguage. In all of his plays, Fo makes use of nonverbal noises: In *Mistero buffo*, belches, farts, and other uncouth sounds become an integral part of the text. The Chinese-inspired *Storia della tigre, La giullarata* (which includes an essay concerning the origin of the *giullare*), and *Il fabulazzo osceno*, which is based on fabliaux, continue along the lines of *Mistero buffo*.

Almost equally well-known and popular in the English-speaking world is *Accidental Death of an Anarchist*, directly inspired by a headline event: the death, accidental or otherwise, of the anarchist Giuseppe Pinelli, supposedly responsible for the bombing of a bank in Milan in 1969 in which sixteen people were killed and some one hundred injured. Ostensibly, the play treats of the death, in 1921, of the anarchist, Salsedo, who "fell" out of a window while being interrogated by the police in New York, although characters within the play refer on more than one occasion to the "transposition": A character will confuse Milan and New York, Rome and Washington, then correct himself, excusing himself for having forgotten that the story has been "transposed." The central character is a madman (somewhat inaccurately translated into English as "maniac"), a favorite figure with Fo, since a madman, or simpleton, or fool, can speak unpalatable truths with impunity. Having been arrested for impersonation and taking money under false pretenses, the Madman proceeds to impersonate various figures of high authority, not only turning the police station topsy-turvy in the best farcical tradition but also bringing to light the corruption and the dishonesty of the authorities. This play, along with *Mistero buffo*, is one of the best examples of Fo's flexible, living text, since the play developed and changed to keep up with the investigation into Pinelli's death. The various published versions of the play (three in Italian and two in English) reveal differences, some more significant than others. Although strongly political, the play is also highly farcical. Fo explains this in a postword to the 1974 Italian publication: "So painfully grotesque" did he and his company find the actions of the authorities, from the documents of the inquiry they were allowed to see. On the other hand, Fo has also criticized English-speaking productions for being so slapstick that the political element was lost in the madcap farce. The exact, careful balance of the two opposing elements of farce and political criticism lies at the heart of Fo's genius and artistic achievement.

Some of the themes of *Mistero buffo*, such as hunger, poverty, and oppression, return in an updated setting in *We Can't Pay! We Won't Pay!*. The play is based on happenings in Italy in 1974, when in various cities working people refused to pay rising prices in supermarkets, public transport, utility bills, and so on, limiting themselves to paying only what they considered a fair price. The structure is farcical, based on plot complications and reversals of situation. It has been described as Fo's "first feminine comedy" for the prominence it gives to the two women characters and the sympathetic treatment of the problems working women face while trying to run a household successfully and smoothly in the face of low wages and rising prices. Stolen goods hidden under the women's skirts or inside a coffin, an unconscious constable stashed into a closet together with stolen loot, are among the farcical elements which provide the laughter in the play.

Collaboration between Fo and Rame produced various monologues which she performed, collected under the title *Parliamo di donne*, produced for television in 1977, and *Female Parts* the following year. To some extent, these might be described as feminine *giullarate*, paralleling Fo's monologues. The Fos have also collaborated on a one-act play *An Open Couple—Very Open*, somewhat reminiscent of Edward Albee's *Who's Afraid of Virginia Woolf?* (1962) in the tensions and conflicts which separate and draw together a husband and wife, although the problems involved are quite different. The two quarrel, insult each other, attack each other verbally and physically, and relapse into tenderness. Unlike Albee's play, however, that of Fo and Rame is basically a farce, although once again Fo has expressed dissatisfaction with foreign productions which stress the comedy element to the detriment of the tragedy, upsetting his own carefully contrived balance.

About Face is based on the farcical device of mistaken identity. In dealing with the issues of terrorism and its possible connections with high finance and the Italian government, this play, more than others, shows a tendency to lengthy speeches and lectures. In spite of this weakness, as forceful political theater the play drew large audiences in Milan, and has attracted a certain amount of attention abroad (in "adaptations," which have usually made a number of cuts).

In 1981, Fo was invited by the Berliner Ensemble to adapt Brecht's *The Threepenny Opera* (1928) for a modern public. His version, however, proved to be too original and was rejected by those who had commissioned it. Fo himself claimed that he was following Brecht in spirit by showing disrespect for a "classic." At another time, he explained that Brecht utilized cabaret-theater because it was linked to the German popular tradition, stressing that any "epic" theater bases itself on its own popular tradition. As for what has become *L'opera dello sghignazzo*, Fo admitted that his play owes more to the original *The Beggar's Opera* (1728) by John Gay than to Brecht's adaptation of it. Fo introduced many of his own concerns and preoccupations into the work. Peachum, for example, deals with visas for people from Africa and Asia and specializes in sickness benefits for false cripples and false drug addicts, while Mackie is an Italian Mafia-style gangster. Fo also introduces some of his own songs.

Terrorism, allied to corruption in high places, reappears in *Dio li fa e poi li accoppa* (God makes them and then kills them), in which an eminent surgeon, Professor Bernari, a drug addict and appropriator of government grants, and leader of one clique or band, has organized the terrorist-style assassination of another eminent doctor, a neurologist, leader of a rival organization, not knowing that there is a third rival organization trying to get him. Echoes of *An Open Couple—Very Open* return as the Professor's wife, rebelling against his jealousy, tries to affirm that what is sauce for the goose is sauce for the gander. The farce in this play derives from a slapstick operation onstage, as the Professor tries to deal with one of the hired killers who has been shot in the stomach; from a series of impersonations; and from a wild exchange of roles and personages. The political criticism is filtered through the farcical situation but is emphasized at the end, when most of the characters are about to murder one another, as the characters step briefly outside their roles to discuss what was or was not in the script, and which of them are worth saving.

It is sometimes asked whether, and to what extent, a statement which is so closely rooted in contemporary events can be expected to retain its interest. Many years, or even decades, already separate certain of Fo's plays from their inspiration, and some of the plays do seem to have somewhat fallen from favor, but since this has happened often in the case of plays which were never published, it is difficult to judge for oneself the possible reasons for the public's loss of interest. Much of Fo's theater continues to play to an ever-growing following. The recurring themes in his work, his protest against injustice and oppression, are at once contemporary expressions and universal concerns, much as the grammelot is both a nonlanguage and a language accessible to all. Built on a series of contradictions, drawing together and carefully balancing disparate elements such as comedy and tragedy, farce and political back-benching, Dario Fo's forcefully committed theater also emerges at all times as highly successful entertainment.

Other major works
SCREENPLAY: *Lo Svitato*, 1956.
POETRY: *Ballate è canzoni*, 1974.

Bibliography
Artese, Erminia. *Dario Fo parla di Dario Fo*, 1977.
Binni, Lanfranco. *Attento te . . . ! Il teatro politico di Dario Fo*, 1975.
Cowan, Suzanne. "Dario Fo: Bibliography, Biography, Playography," in *Theatre Quarterly*. No. 17, 1978.
"Dario Fo Explains," in *The Drama Review*. XX, no. 1 (1978), pp. 33-48.
Fo, Dario. "Popular Culture," in *Theater*. XIV, no. 3 (1983), pp. 50-54.
Fo, Dario, and Franca, Rame, et al. *Dario Fo and Franca Rame: Theatre Workshops at Riverside Studios, London*, 1983.
Jenkins, Ron. "Clowns, Politics, and Miracles: The Epic Satire of Dario Fo," in *American Theatre*. June, 1986, pp. 10-16.
Mitchell, Tony. *Dario Fo: People's Court Jester*, 1984.
_____. "Dario Fo's *Mistero buffo*: Popular Theatre, the Giullari, and the Grotesque," in *Theatre Quarterly*. IX, no. 35 (1979), pp. 3-16.
Valentini, Chiara. *La storia di Fo*, 1977.

Ada Coe

RICHARD FOREMAN

Born: New York, New York; June 10, 1937

Principal drama

Angelface, pr. 1968, pb. 1976; *Elephant-Steps*, pr. 1968 (music by Stanley Silverman); *Ida-Eyed*, pr. 1969; *Real Magic in New York*, pr. 1970; *Total Recall: Or, Sophia = (Wisdom) Part II*, pr. 1970, pb. 1976; *Dream Tantras for Western Massachusetts*, pr. 1971 (music by Silverman); *HCohtienla: Or, Hotel China: Parts I and II*, pr., pb. 1972; *Dr. Selavy's Magic Theatre*, pr. 1972 (music by Silverman, lyrics by Thomas Hendry); *Evidence*, pr. 1972; *Sophia = (Wisdom) Part III*, pr. 1972, pb. 1973; *The Cliffs*, pr., pb. 1973; *Honor*, pr. 1973; *Particle Theory*, pr. 1973; *Une Semaine sous l'Influence de . . .*, pr. 1973, pb. 1976; *Vertical Mobility*, pb. 1974; *Pain(t), and Vertical Mobility: Sophia = (Wisdom) Part IV*, pr. 1974, pb. 1976; *Pandering to the Masses: A Misrepresentation*, pr. 1975, pb. 1977; *Hotel for Criminals*, pr. 1975 (music by Silverman); *Rhoda in Potatoland (Her Fall-starts)*, pr. 1975, pb. 1976; *Livre de Splendeurs (Part I)*, pr., pb. 1976; *Book of Splendors (Part II): Book of Levers: Action at a Distance*, pr. 1977, pb. 1986; *Boulevard de Paris (I've Got the Shakes)*, pr. 1977, pb. 1986; *Madness and Tranquility (My Head Was a Sledgehammer)*, pr. 1979; *Luogo + Bersaglio*, pr. 1979, pb. as *Place + Target*, 1986; *Penguin Touquet*, pr. 1980, pb. 1986; *Madame Adare*, pr. 1980 (music by Silverman); *Cafe Amerique*, pr. 1981, pb. 1986; *Egyptology (My Head Was a Sledgehammer)*, pr. 1983, pb. 1986; *La Robe de Chambre de Georges Bataille*, pr. 1983; *The Golem*, pr. 1984; *Miss Universal Happiness*, pr. 1985; *Birth of the Poet*, pr. 1985 (with Kathy Acker); *The Cure*, pr. 1986; *Largo Desolato*, pr. 1986.

Other literary forms

Richard Foreman has been involved in all aspects of theater. In addition to his plays, he has written several manifestos that explain the genesis of his theater work from a philosophical point of view, and he has also directed several plays and produced numerous videos.

Achievements

Foreman is one of the founders of the contemporary American theatrical avant-garde. His Ontological-Hysteric Theatre—for which Foreman is the sole playwright, director, and designer—is influenced by the theories of Bertolt Brecht and Gertrude Stein. Foreman's intent is to distance the audience from their normal expectations of a pleasurable theater experience and to make spectators aware of the process of perception. To force this awareness, he often obscures the stage picture with bright lights, leaves his scripts meaningless, non-narrative, and nonlinear, and uses loud sounds to unsettle the spectator from passive complacency. Foreman has also applied his avant-garde aesthetic to texts by other writers, and even as a director, his signature remains unmistakable. Foreman's style was the harbinger of the postmodern theater work of artists such as the Wooster Group and John Jesurun. Foreman has received three *Village Voice* Obie Awards, two New York State Creative Artists Public Service Awards, a Rockefeller Foundation Playwrights Grant, a Guggenheim Playwriting Fellowship, and a Ford Foundation Playwrights Grant.

Biography

Richard Foreman was born in New York City on June 10, 1937, and was reared in Scarsdale, an affluent New York suburb in Westchester County. He became interested in theater as an adolescent, encouraged by an indulgent high school teacher who allowed him to express his already iconoclastic vision in inappropriately surreal set designs for school plays. During this time, Foreman studied the writings of Brecht, whose theories permeated Foreman's thought and would later profoundly influence his theater work. At Brown University, from which he was graduated magna cum laude in 1959, Foreman became interested first in film and then in playwriting, and was introduced to the writings of José Ortega y Gasset, which also influenced his later, rigorous style. Foreman studied with John Gassner at Yale University, from which he received his M.F.A. in 1962.

Foreman married his high school friend Amy Taubin in 1962. They moved to New York City, where Taubin pursued an acting career and Foreman wrote conventionally plotted plays. From 1962 to 1967, Foreman and Taubin immersed themselves in the New American Cinema movement evolving in Lower Manhattan, and became captivated by the avant-garde work of filmmakers Ken Jacobs, Michael Snow, and Jack Smith. Foreman gradually began applying the avant-garde film aesthetic to his own playwriting, leaving gaps and rough spots where he had once sought closure and polish. He presented *Angelface*, his first Ontological-Hysteric Theatre production, in 1968, at the Cinematheque on Wooster Street in Manhattan's Soho district, and began collaborating with musician Stanley Silverman on experimental musical productions for the Music Theatre Group/Lenox Art Center.

Foreman dislodged his productions from his Wooster Street loft in 1976 and began working occasionally in Europe through the early 1980's. He spent most of this period either in Paris or touring to different performance spaces in Europe, such as Teatro Nuovo in Turin, Italy, and the Mickery Theatre in Amsterdam, Holland. Some of Foreman's later works were first performed in Europe: *Livre de Splendeurs* was first shown in Paris, and *Luogo* + *Bersaglio* was first performed, in Italian, in Rome.

In 1982, Foreman began directing occasional productions for Joseph

Papp's New York Shakespeare Festival, where he mounted Botho Strauss's *Trilogie des Wiedersehens* (1976; *Three Acts of Recognition*, 1982) and Molière's *Don Juan: Ou, Le Festin de Pierre* (1655; *Don Juan*, 1755) in 1982, H. Leivick's *Der Golem* (1921; *The Golem*, 1966) in 1984, and Vaclav Havel's *Largo Desolato* (1985; English translation, 1985) in 1986. He has also directed productions of *Don Juan* for the Guthrie Theatre in Minneapolis, Minnesota (1981), and Arthur Kopit's *End of the World with Symposium to Follow* (1984) for the American Repertory Theatre (1987) in Cambridge, Massachusetts. Although his Ontological-Hysteric Theatre no longer has a home base, Foreman still writes, designs, and directs his own productions, often using space borrowed from other avant-garde performance artists, such as the Wooster Group.

Analysis

Richard Foreman began his theater career as a playwright and progressed toward international recognition as one of the most influential auteurs of the contemporary American avant-garde. Foreman's writing style helped to establish what has come to be called the postmodern aesthetic, in which character no longer exists as a theatrical element, and the "theater of images," in which aural and visual elements of a production become more important than the literary. His scripts for the Ontological-Hysteric Theatre represent only the workings of his mind while he writes them.

As a designer, Foreman constructs a playing space jumbled with objects and sensory input, which he then obscures from the spectator by shining blinding white lights into their eyes. Although he still presents Ontological-Hysteric Theatre productions, over which he maintains absolute control, Foreman has begun to direct other classic and contemporary plays, yet his unique directorial style is always apparent in his work.

Foreman established his Ontological-Hysteric Theatre in 1968, in a long, narrow loft that he converted into a performance space in the Soho neighborhood of Manhattan. The name Ontological-Hysteric, although chosen rather capriciously, has come to symbolize many of Foreman's preoccupations. In both his playwriting and his subsequent staging of his own texts and those of other playwrights, Foreman's goal is to materialize the workings of consciousness and to make spectators aware of how they perceive their world.

Foreman sees consciousness as a perceptual mechanism that filters the world through the senses, and he believes that habit has taught people to limit their sensory input. To free them to explore their perceptual potential, Foreman constructs a rigorous attack on habitual ways of seeing the world and seeing art. Foreman's early Ontological-Hysteric Theatre works, such as *Sophia = (Wisdom) Part III, Pain(t), and Vertical Mobility, Pandering to the Masses*, and *Rhoda in Potatoland (Her Fall-starts)*, insistently aimed to reshape spectators' perceptions by focusing on form and structure. He created a perceptually challenging environment that forced the audience to participate actively in constructing the theater experience.

In contrast to realistic theater (which strives to provide catharsis and to resolve its ambiguities and questions in a happy conclusion), Foreman's art avoids moral issues and the linear development of traditional plots. He forces spectators to expend their energies on "blasting" themselves into productions in which the entire framework of traditional theater—plot, characterization, and settings—has been discarded. The required perceptual work replaces the usual theater experience, in which the audience passively awaits catharsis through identification with a hero.

Foreman was considerably influenced by the theories of Brecht, whose alienation effect forced spectators into critical contemplation of the actions presented in his epic dramas. Brecht discouraged the identification processes of more realistic theater, which he believed rendered spectators passive and unable to move toward political change. Brecht's stagings were presentational. He used placards to announce his drama's episodes, intentionally interrupting the seductive narrative flow. His performers were taught to present quoted characterizations that maintained the separation between actor and character and gave the spectators room to contemplate the play's meanings.

Where Brecht encouraged critical distance in order to allow political self-determination, however, Foreman is emphatically apolitical: He wants his spectators to contemplate purely perceptual concerns. His work, however, departs from traditionally Brechtian techniques. Particularly in his early Ontological-Hysteric Theatre pieces, he discouraged his performers from acting as anyone other than themselves, and he directed them to deliver their lines in a flat monotone. Sometimes, performers' dialogue was recorded on tape and played back during performance, dissociating them from their voices. The performers moved through a series of complex, carefully choreographed movements and tasks. Actors in Foreman's early productions were merely demonstrators for his perceptual experiments.

Foreman established his unique style while other artists were also disrupting the conventions of traditional theater. In the late 1960's and early 1970's, the Performance Group, the Living Theatre, and the Open Theatre staged their productions environmentally, using the whole theater instead of only the stage behind the proscenium. All three encouraged their performers to interact physically with the audience and created texts that were often didactic, reflecting the radical political sentiment of the era.

Foreman, a staunch formalist, was at that time diametrically opposed to what he called such "expressionistic" theater. He maintained the proscenium/spectator arrangement, carefully orchestrating his stage pictures in static or slow-moving tableaux behind the proscenium frame; he prohibited his actors from interacting with spectators and maintained the "fourth wall" convention, in which spectators expect to feel as though they are looking into a world from which they cannot be seen; and he offered no didactic meanings for his spectators to consider from a political perspective. Within these conventional outlines, however, Foreman's theater was revolutionary in other ways.

Along with Robert Wilson and Lee Breuer, Foreman's work helped coin the term "theater of images." Despite his theoretical concern with language, Foreman's theater is distinctly nonliterary. The theater of images increases the value of its visual and aural elements, displacing the text's primacy as the motivating principle. As a result, plot and character lose their places as the predominant bearers of meaning. Since the theater of images is dominated by sights and sounds that occur in space and time, within the immediate theater experience, sense impressions and the present-tense manipulation of perception become primary.

It is impossible to understand the full impact of a Foreman play by reading it on a page, because the experience of time and space is so important to his work. The atomization of movement and motion allows spectators' minds to roam freely, considering each part of the stage picture. The carefully constructed tableaux allow theatrical time to pause or even slow to a standstill, so that the spectator can choose which elements of the complex picture to relish visually and which objects to connect with others placed around the space.

Foreman takes a phenomenological approach to the stage space and his props. His aesthetic is similar to Gertrude Stein's, whose "present moment" landscape plays also stripped things to their essences. Wrenched out of context, objects become things without associations that impose meaning. To this end, Foreman constructs his scenography to render the ordinary extraordinary. Potatoes in *Rhoda in Potatoland (Her Fall-starts)* become larger-than-life. Clocks, such as the grandfather clock in *Sophia = (Wisdom) Part III*, become animate objects that enter the playing space. People become objects related to other objects. The potatoes that come crashing through windows in *Rhoda in Potatoland (Her Fall-starts)* are as much performers as the human beings inhabiting Foreman's cerebral landscape.

Spectators are also kept from finding meaning in Foreman's plays by the intentionally disorienting, uncomfortable process of perceiving the work. Lights shine directly in the spectators' eyes, making it difficult to see the stage. Loud noises startle the spectators out of passive contemplation, jolting them back into full awareness. The texts constantly comment on Foreman's process of creating them, calling attention to the arbitrary nature of words themselves. Snatches of familiar music are used to seduce the spectator into a feeling of ease, then are abruptly curtailed.

Foreman's scripts are plotless, self-reflective meditations on the act of writing. Although nothing ever happens in the conventional sense of action and linear narrative in a Foreman play, his scripts are often humorous and ironic, and they invite spectators to share in their witty investigations of how meaning is being created or withheld in the present theatrical moment. Where Brecht's writing was episodic, Foreman's is atomic, a succession of brief, discrete moments intended to replicate the workings of his mind in the process of writing his plays.

Although there are no carefully crafted, fictional characters in Foreman's work, each person onstage represents a part of Foreman's consciousness. In his early work, a group of characters reappeared in different productions over several years. His works from this early period resembled something of a soap opera, in that the plotless productions never gave spectators the pleasure of a satisfactory ending. The character Max, whom some critics saw as Foreman's fictional counterpart, was a kind of artist figure constantly defining himself intellectually in relation to Rhoda. Rhoda, who was always played by Foreman's lover, Kate Mannheim, represented women. She symbolized the dark continent of sexuality and repressed psychology that could not be explained by rational male intellect. These strict gender dichotomies, which some feminist critics find misogynous, are very apparent in Foreman's early work and, despite minor alterations, operate throughout his oeuvre.

While Foreman's theater is clearly ontological because of its obsession with questions of consciousness and being, his theater is aptly named "hysteric" in that it also deals with a more surrealist world of dreams, sexual desire, and anxieties. Foreman uses the ubiquitous Max and Rhoda to represent his consciousness and fears. Rhoda, in particular, represents Foreman grappling with the nature of sexuality and a more irrational world not easily explained by his otherwise rampant intellect.

Foreman's scenography further illustrates his theoretical and philosophical preoccupations. Foreman's sets are distinguished by their jumble of outsized objects, the strings stretched in a maze across the performance space that carves it into geometric patterns, the words or phrases of language decorating the space as though they, too, were objects, and the brightly colored streamers and other fanciful or bizarre props and materials that make for something of a carnivalesque atmosphere. Foreman's scenography is intended to force the eye to scan the stage picture. No one object or person is more important than another, and the taut strings are used to move the eye around the playing space. Miscellaneous words often dangle from the strings in Foreman's design, inviting the spectators to read the stage in a careful, perceptive way.

Foreman is preoccupied with the mechanisms of perception, which his scenography continually challenges. The hallmark of Foreman's productions are the bright white lights turned to shine in spectators' eyes, obscuring often tantalizing images within the stage picture; loud, irritating buzzers that interrupt the dialogue; bells that determine the beginning and the end of bits of action; and taped voices that dissociate the performers from their bodies or order them around. During productions at his Wooster Street loft, Foreman would sit at a table directly in front of the playing space, controlling the lights and the sound. Because many of the performers' cues were on an audiotape, he could change a performance's pace by adjusting the speed of the tape.

After spending a period from the late 1970's to the early 1980's in Europe, where his Ontological-Hysteric Theatre preoccupations were translated into French and toured avant-garde performance spaces, Foreman returned to the United States and began to focus on directing. Since he brings his own unique aesthetic to any play he undertakes, Foreman is often accused of "trashing" classical texts. His unusual scenography and presentational directing style might indeed seem out of place in plays such as Vaclav Havel's *Largo Desolato*, which has its own internal meanings that some critics believed were obscured by Foreman's external devices. His treatments of Molière's *Don Juan* and the classic folktale *The Golem*, however, were applauded for rejuvenating these texts from a new, contemporary perspective.

Still, Foreman's most exciting directorial work seems to be accomplished on the fringes of established theater, in conjunction with avant-garde performance groups. Foreman's *Miss Universal Happiness*, for example, was a collaboration with the Wooster Group at the Performing Garage in Soho. The Wooster Group's performances for this piece were physical and presentational, in the post-Brechtian style that is the Group's hallmark.

Miss Universal Happiness was purportedly a political piece, although Foreman is avowedly apolitical. The *mise en scène* had revolutionary overtones: The men wore combat clothes, the women dressed in rags and ripped stockings, and all the performers wore sombreros, vaguely referring to Third World revolutions and political strife. Yet more than revolutionary struggle, the performance was a self-reflexive commentary on how meaning is produced in theater. A teenage boy, the youngest member of the Wooster Group, began the piece by displaying his "lead lined" raincoat, which "protects you from ambiguities and obscurities" in the script. The remark was a wry warning to spectators that they should not try hard to look for meaning.

In the mid-1980's, Foreman departed from the slow, static tableaux that had once characterized his style. The stage images in *Miss Universal Happiness*, for example, were created by manic direction. The performers played musical chairs, but every time the music stopped, there was one chair too many, and another player was added to, instead of subtracted from, the game. Miss Universal Happiness, a parody of the Statue of Liberty, ran about the space dressed in black, wearing a black crown, and holding a tennis racket instead of a flame. Foreman did, however, maintain the artifice of his trademark scenography. A man in a rabbit suit appeared with two oversize oblong objects that could have been either missiles or cold capsules. Two big painted eyes were set up on easels in the back of the space, to watch *Miss Universal Happiness* progress.

Foreman's piece *Birth of the Poet*, with a script by Kathy Acker, was presented in Rotterdam, Holland, and then at the Brooklyn Academy of Music's Next Wave Festival in 1985. Acker's text was as disjunctive and fragmented as Foreman's. There were no characters in *Birth of the Poet*, which consisted of many long, rambling speeches about workers, productivity, and nuclear energy, delivered along with aggressively pornographic imagery and language. To emphasize the technological theme, the performers maneuvered golf carts around the space and moved manically among huge set pieces by sculptor David Salle.

Each of the three production elements—script, set, and music by Peter Gordon—were conceived individually, then brought together by Foreman's direction, a method that echoed the chance performances of Composer John Cage. Foreman's signature devices were missing from this production. There were no strings pulled taut across the stage, and Foreman's usually witty, ironic text was replaced by Acker's pornographic script, which the performers shouted through microphones worn like headsets. Yet Foreman's concerns were still in evidence. Part of Foreman's theatrical project is to expose the process of creating performance. In *Birth of the Poet*, the battery packs that feed the microphones the performers wore were visibly strapped to their waists, and the dissociation of their voices from their source through amplification was intentional.

Foreman's concern with language was still clear in *Birth of the Poet*. A tubular steel structure hung from the flies with colorful cloth banners stretched from end to end. For the first hour or so of performance, one word—"talent"—and fragments of other words were on view. These fragments were meaningless until later in the performance. When the structure was moved offstage—by stagehands whose presence also emphasized the process of creating performance normally hidden from the audience's view—complementary word fragments at other angles formed complete words.

Foreman's trademark bright lights were present, but obscuring the spectators' view was meaningless in *Birth of the Poet*, since little happened onstage. The space looked empty and disinterested, despite designer David Salle's unusual images: gigantic, two-dimensional ears of corn, a full-stage human body made of steel tubing and purple cloth, a giant steel hand that becomes a cage, a giant steel vagina, and expressionistic painted backdrops of a man's head, a dog's head, and a woman bent over at the waist peering through her legs at the audience.

As a director, Foreman's style is to bring his own aesthetic theory to bear on any text. Instead of evoking images through simple description or suggestion, Foreman's *mise en scène* intentionally creates obstacles to the spectator's search for meaning in the production. He interrupts the textual flow with loud noises and creates a performance space so packed with images and information that it thwarts spectators' expectations of managing, consuming, or knowing the space. Through his long career, Foreman's preoccupations have remained the same, even as his role continually shifts among those of playwright, designer, and director.

Other major works

FILM/VIDEO PRODUCTIONS: *Out of the Body Travel*, 1975 (video); *City Archives*, 1977 (video); *Strong Medicine*, 1978 (16mm film).

Bibliography

Davy, Kate. *Richard Foreman and the Ontological-Hysteric Theatre*, 1981.
Foreman, Richard. *Plays and Manifestos of Richard Foreman*, 1976. Edited by Kate Davy.
_____. *Reverberation Machines: The Later Plays and Essays*, 1985.
Kirby, Michael. "Richard Foreman's Ontological-Hysteric Theatre," in *The Drama Review*. XVII (June, 1973), pp. 5-32.
Marranca, Bonnie. "The Ontological-Hysteric Theatre of Richard Foreman," in *The Theatre of Images*, 1977.
Scarpetta, Guy, and Jill Dolan. "Richard Foreman's Scenography: Examples from his Work in France," in *The Drama Review*. XXVIII (Summer, 1984), pp. 23-31.

Jill Dolan

MICHAEL FRAYN

Born: London, England; September 8, 1933

Principal drama

The Two of Us, pr., pb. 1970; *The Sandboy*, pr. 1971; *Alphabetical Order*, pr. 1975, pb. 1977; *Donkeys' Years*, pr. 1976, pb. 1977; *Clouds*, pr. 1976, pb. 1977; *Liberty Hall*, pr. 1980; *Make and Break*, pr., pb. 1980; *Noises Off*, pr., pb. 1982; *Benefactors*, pr., pb. 1984; *Plays: One*, pb. 1985.

Other literary forms

Michael Frayn began his career as a journalist, contributing reviews, then satirical essays, and later personal observations about his travels to *The Guardian* and *The Observer*. Much of his journalistic writing has been republished in collections of his work. Frayn turned to the novel while still writing for newspapers, eventually abandoning journalism. Frayn has written five novels, most of them published before he moved on to the theater, where he has enjoyed his greatest success. In addition to his original drama, he has translated and adapted plays by Anton Chekhov (of which Frayn's adaptation of *Three Sisters* in 1985 has received especially favorable notice), Leo Tolstoy, and Jean Anouilh and has written documentaries as well as original scripts for television; with *Clockwise* in 1986, he became a screenwriter. Interested in moral sciences since his Cambridge University days, when he was especially influenced by the work of philosopher Ludwig Wittgenstein, he has also written a nonfiction work, *Constructions* (1974), which is best described as a philosophical treatise on perception, language, and time.

Achievements

Already established as a respected journalist and novelist, in middle age Frayn won even greater acclaim as a playwright. His first plays, amusing and well-crafted comedies, suggested that yet another clever farceur, someone akin to the early Alan Ayckbourn, had arrived on the scene. More discerning viewers, however, began to note that beyond the laughter, Frayn was a serious writer employing comedy to explore philosophical themes—the relationship of language and perception, of order and misrule, of man's illusory control of self and environment. Soon after arriving on the theatrical scene, Frayn was winning awards as author of the best comedy of the year (for *Alphabetical Order*, *Donkeys' Years*, and *Noises Off*). In 1980, *Make and Break*, more reflective than his previous plays, won awards as both the year's best comedy and the year's best play. In 1984, *Benefactors*, his darkest comedy, not only won awards as the year's best play but also established Frayn as a writer of the first rank, to be considered alongside such contemporary British dramatists as Harold Pinter, Tom Stoppard, and Edward Bond. After *Benefactors*, critics as well as theatergoers eagerly awaited new work by Michael Frayn.

Biography

Michael Frayn's family lived in Mill Hill in northwest London but moved to Holloway soon after his birth and then to Ewell, a southwest suburb, where he was reared. His father was an asbestos salesman who occasionally took Michael and his sister to the nearby Kingston Empire, a music hall, as a special treat. Frayn remembers borrowing some music-hall routines for the home entertainments—puppet shows and conjuring acts—that he devised for an audience of three—father, mother, and sister. At Christmastime, the elder Frayn became the star performer in the comic sketches that he himself wrote. Michael and his sister were relegated to supporting roles, and Mrs. Frayn comprised an audience of one. Michael Frayn's mother, who had earlier worked as a shop assistant and occasional model in Harrods, London's grandest department store, died when he was twelve, a disorienting experience for the boy. At that time, his father removed him from the private day school, which the boy hated, and enrolled him in the good state-run Kingston Grammar School, where he was far more comfortable.

Frayn got along with his chums by playing the fool and by cleverly mimicking his teachers while doing a minimum of schoolwork. That changed when an English master, aware of the boy's incipient talent for writing, challenged him to produce even better work. These were the years in which Frayn discovered poetry, music, religion, and politics. He and his friends declared themselves atheists and formed a model communist cell in the school. Although his interest in Communism soon waned, it led him to study the Russian language. He has since traveled in the Soviet Union, employing it as the setting of his *The Russian Interpreter* (1966), a spy novel. In addition, he has become Great Britain's foremost translator of Russian drama, specifically the plays of Chekhov, which are peopled with characters as bewildered, as troubled, and as comic as Frayn's own.

Frayn actually perfected his Russian when he was drafted into the army in 1952 and sent to language school at Cambridge University. He returned to Cambridge as an undergraduate after completing his national service in 1954. In addition to studying philosophy, he dabbled in university theatricals, collaborating on a musical revue and playing a servant in a production of Nikolai Gogol's *Revizor* (1836; *The Inspector General*, 1890). Trapped onstage in Gogol's play for what seemed an eternity when a door refused to open and the audience started a slow handclap, he vowed never again to tread the boards, an experience that may have provided an inspiration for *Noises Off*, a play about theatrical mishaps.

After being graduated from Cambridge in 1957, Frayn worked for *The*

Guardian (Manchester) and two years later began a satirical humor column, which he has himself likened to the work of American columnists Russell Baker and Art Buchwald. Like Joseph Addison and Richard Steele in *The Spectator* (1711-1712), Frayn invented a cast of characters, among them two couples reappearing with great frequency: Christopher and Lavinia Crumble, who knew everything, and Horace and Doris Morris, who knew nothing at all. The relationship of contrasting couples, the fortunate Kitzingers and the unfortunate Molyneuxs, would become the basis of his most acclaimed work, *Benefactors*.

After further newspaper work on *The Observer*, Frayn decided that the novel would allow him greater latitude for the exploration of character and ideas. Between 1965 and 1973, he published five novels to generally favorable reviews, the most effective among them *Towards the End of the Morning* (1967; U.S. edition, *Against Entropy*, 1967), a comic exploration of Frayn's familiar newspaper world. A television script brought him to the attention of theatrical producer Michael Codron, who urged him to write a play. Frayn's first attempt was *The Two of Us*, a collection of four one-acts, with all the characters played by two actors and ending in a farcical disaster of a dinner party. Although it entertained audiences for half a year, the play did not amuse the critics. Intrigued, nevertheless, by the possibilities of dramatic presentation, Frayn believed that he could do better. The eight plays he produced in the ensuing fifteen years have proved him right.

Frayn married Gillian Palmer in 1969 and has three daughters with whom he enjoys a close relationship, but he and his wife separated in 1981. He lives in London with Claire Tomalin, literary editor of the London *Sunday Times*.

Analysis

Like Chekhov, his inspirational mentor, Michael Frayn is at his best when he allows his audience an intimate glimpse of characters attempting to make order out of the routine chaos of their mundane existence. There are no grand confrontations, no melodramatic plot twists, merely bursts of wasted energy frequently followed by a deepening frustration as his characters— reporters, salesmen, actors, and architects—perceive a world that ought to be changed, but their ineffectual efforts and plans make no impression upon it. Only the characters change, surrendering to the inevitable, as, comically, a disordered world continues its mad spin, signifying nothing.

Frayn's third play and first critical success, *Alphabetical Order*, locates what would become his abiding concerns. In the library of a provincial newspaper office, several middle-aged reporters, who resemble little boys lost, take refuge amid the office debris. Their daily routine dictates that they enlighten the surrounding world, yet they would rather run and hide from the world, mothered by the head librarian, Lucy, who indulges their whims just as she allows a haphazard filing system to take care of itself. Their personal lives are in as much disarray as the room itself, cluttered with baskets and boxes of news items, even a broken chair. Lucy lives with John, is interested in Wally, and offers sympathy to Arnold, whose unloved wife, Megan, is in the hospital.

When Lucy hires a young woman, Leslie, as her assistant, the newcomer immediately takes control. When a reporter cuts his hand and Lucy cannot find the key to the first-aid kit, Leslie's first act is to break open the kit with a smartly delivered blow with a leg from the broken chair. Not only does Leslie rearrange the furniture, but also all the clutter is soon neatly filed away. More significant, Leslie imposes order on chaos by rearranging relationships as well. She enters into an affair with John, freeing Lucy for Wally; Lucy resists the neat arrangement, however, and takes Arnold into her home instead, thus dashing the hopes of Nora, the features editor.

The newly imposed order is short-lived. A seemingly more efficient library has no effect on a newspaper that is failing. When the paper's closing is announced, the library's habitués, with Leslie out of the room, revolt. Throwing caution to the winds, grown men reduced to little boys convert folders and clippings into missiles to pelt one another. Chaos has dictated order, which in turn has dictated chaos. When Leslie, the youngest and most recent employee, enters to announce that she is in the vanguard of those who will take over the paper to run it themselves, she reasserts the notion that order will rule once more, but to what purpose? Her fellow employees' lives are as messy as ever, and Leslie's failing relationship with John further suggests that her compulsion for efficiency does not extend to that area of her life that really matters.

Critics have viewed Leslie as the villain of the piece, seeing her as the symbol of arid organization in confrontation with the confused humanity of Lucy, the heroine. Frayn himself takes a different view. Perhaps, he suggests, *Alphabetical Order* demonstrates that order and disorder are interdependent, that any extreme provokes its opposite. Lucy's inefficiency is only a perception; her library functions. Leslie's order, too, is only a perception. She is hardly responsible for the paper's failure, but as she rules her roost, the paper grinds to a halt. A semblance of change occurs, but the essential remains the same.

In an essay entitled "Business Worries," originally written for *The Observer* and collected in *At Bay in Gear Street* (1967), Frayn offers a reason for not going to the theater: An audience sits in fear—a fear of something going wrong onstage. A carefully rehearsed play represents an ordered world that should comfort an audience that lives in an uncertain world in flux. Actors, however, can trip and fall, cigarette lighters can fail to light, cues can be missed. In *Noises Off*, Frayn takes theatrical accidents to their extreme, but an audience can view it all happily, knowing that the disorder onstage is, in fact, the order of art. Frayn's award-winning farce presents a predetermined world in which accidents are programmed to occur. First produced in 1982, *Noises Off*, a play in which an actual unforeseen mishap occurring to an actor is accepted by the viewer as yet one more comic disaster planned by the author, so delighted audiences that it achieved a four-and-a-half-year run, breaking all records at London's Savoy Theatre, and has afforded Frayn financial independence. In addition to its nearly two-year Broadway run, *Noises Off* has been translated into thirty-six languages including Russian, the language that Frayn has so frequently translated into English. *Noises Off* is easily the most successful farce of the last quarter-century. What has, however, surprised its author is that the laughter has obscured for most audiences, who may consider it mindless entertainment, that the play has a general application even for them. It is about, Frayn insists, what everyone does in his life—keeping a performance going.

Noises Off, whose title derives from a British stage term for offstage sound effects, parodies the innocuous sex farces, such as Anthony Marriott and Alistair Foot's *No Sex Please, We're British* (1973), which have become a staple of London's commercial theater. In act 1, the audience witnesses the combination technical dress rehearsal of the first act of a farce called "Nothing On," performed by third-rate actors whose careers have been limited to barely professional companies that play middle-class seaside resorts such as Weston-Super-Mare. Whatever can possibly go wrong does, but only mildly in act 1. In act 2, Frayn changes the perspective. The audience witnesses the performance of "Nothing On" again, but this time from a backstage view. The actors are seen directly behind their set preparing to make their entrances. In act 1, an inept company at least attempted to work together to put on a play. Four weeks later, the inevitably developing professional jealousies and personal entanglements have turned the backstage area into a battlefield. As a result, "Nothing On" is falling apart. In act 3, the perspective is reversed again. Four more weeks have gone by, and the audience witnesses that first act yet again from an audience's usual point of view. By then, however, "Nothing On," the play-within-the-play, has totally collapsed as *Noises Off*'s actual audience, perceiving the changes brought to the performance by the realities of human involvements, collapses from laughter.

Perhaps in repeating the first act of "Nothing On" three times with variations within the framework of *Noises Off*, Frayn had in mind the repetition of the two acts of Samuel Beckett's *En attendant Godot* (1952; *Waiting for Godot*, 1954), another play about actors of sorts keeping a performance going. In *Waiting for Godot*, too, the essential does not change, but the characters' despair—and the audience's—deepens. What keeps the audience happy at *Noises Off* is that, as the characters fail to find solace in the rehearsed world of performance, the audience knows that for once everything has gone right. Here, chaos represents order.

Frayn's view of *Noises Off* being about the necessity of keeping life going provides a key to his darkest comedy, *Benefactors*, whose subtleties took playgoers by surprise following, as it did, a knockabout farce. For the author, it is the petty jealousies and pique, the link to *Noises Off*, that is at the root of what he considers to be, within the context of a thought-provoking domestic comedy, society's "progressive collapse." The bleakest aspect of *Benefactors* is that, in wrecking their own lives, the two couples who constitute its cast—friends who are white, middle-class, reasonably comfortable, basically good, and committed to helping others—unwittingly destroy the hopes of a better, more comfortable life for a class of people further down the social and economic scale, the residents, some white, more of them black, of a public housing enclave in southeast London. The real victims, who never come onstage in the play, are the inhabitants of a slum area, euphemistically referred to by the local housing authority as a "twilight area," who pay for the casual bickering and increasingly strained relationships between the two couples in the foreground of the play and provide *Benefactors* with its too-easily ignored "noises off."

Like the self-deluded architect-protagonist of Frayn's failed second play, *The Sandboy*, liberal-minded David Kitzinger believes he is helping others by designing high-rise local housing. When his wife, Jane, brings their hapless neighbor Sheila into their home as general factotum, Sheila's husband, Colin, an unemployed journalist, is upset by the growing relationship between Sheila and David, supposedly his best friend. He takes action by turning public sentiment against David's housing scheme. The relationships among the four persons who had thought of themselves as two friendly couples undergo obvious and subtle shifts that end with the collapse of one marriage and a total change in dependency in the other. No one by the end, as the four characters relate their own perceptions of what took place some years earlier, is quite sure just what did happen, but people, David finally understands, have a way of wrecking any possibility of meaningful change. The Kitzingers had played at being benefactors for the Molyneuxs, but if Sheila's marriage is destroyed, she has at least achieved a measure of independence she had never known before. Colin, too, is a benefactor. Whatever his motive for opposing David's plan, he has, he convinces himself, actually saved the inhabitants of the area undergoing redevelopment from the dehumanizing conditions that David's efficient scheme would impose upon them. Colin even provides Jane a new career working for another housing trust that plans to rehabilitate rather than rebuild.

What adds impact to the play is Frayn's choice of names for the streets bounding the area for which David has been designing the new housing— "Basuto Road, Bechuana Road, Matebele Road, Mashona Road, and Barotse Road." "Basuto Road" becomes an evermore despairing refrain as the architect's plans undergo extensive modifications until they are at last rejected. By evoking, through the dispossessed people of the Basuto Road enclave, an echo of Basutoland, once an outpost of the British Empire, now the independent enclave of Lesotho surrounded by a hostile South Africa, Frayn suggests that Great Britain's privileged class has not only failed itself but also, ultimately, betrayed its responsibilities to those who had come there from the far reaches of the empire in search of a better life. In like manner, South Africa has exploited the Basutos, who must leave their infertile land to search for a livelihood among a people who oppress them. In *Benefactors*, chaos breeds chaos, and the need for order is implied by the discipline of the dramatist's art. Basuto Road, for Frayn, becomes a ruined Eden. Lured by false hopes, desperately in need of help, the dispossessed are betrayed even by their so-called benefactors, who are too involved in their own petty concerns to comprehend the damage that their intentioned good works can do.

Benefactors concludes ambiguously with the audience only certain that David, Jane, Colin, and Sheila—each one pitted against the others in a quest for self-fulfillment—have been involved in "progressive collapse." By the end of the play, the phrase has become not merely an architectural term but a dramatist's diagnosis of an unhealthy society's desperate need for change while it perpetuates, in a frantic flurry of compromise and accommodation, the desperation of stasis. Possessing wider implications than any of his other plays, *Benefactors*, still within a comic framework, reinforces Frayn's pessimistic view of man's search for order, sanity, and humanity in the twentieth century.

Other major works

NOVELS: *The Tin Men*, 1965; *The Russian Interpreter*, 1966; *Towards the End of the Morning*, 1967 (U.S. edition, *Against Entropy*, 1967); *A Very Private Life*, 1968; *Sweet Dreams*, 1973.

SCREENPLAY: *Clockwise*, 1986.

NONFICTION: *The Day of the Dog*, 1962; *The Book of Fub*, 1963 (U.S. edition, *Never Put Off to Gomorrah*, 1964); *On the Outskirts*, 1964; *At Bay in Gear Street*, 1967; *Constructions*, 1974; *The Original Michael Frayn: Columns from the "Guardian" and "Observer,"* 1983.

TRANSLATIONS: *The Cherry Orchard*, 1978 (of Anton Chekhov's play *Vishnyovy sad*); *The Fruits of Enlightenment*, 1979 (of Leo Tolstoy's play *Plody prosveshcheniya*); *Number One*, 1984 (of Jean Anouilh's play *Le Nombril*); *Wild Honey*, 1984 (of an untitled play by Chekhov); *Three Sisters*, 1985 (of Chekhov's play *Tri sestry*).

Bibliography

Gross, Miriam. "A Playwright of Many Parts," in *The Sunday Telegraph*. November 30, 1986, p. 17.

Jack, Ian. "Frayn, Philosopher of the Suburbs," in *Sunday Times*. April 13, 1975, p. 43.

Kaufman, David. "The Frayn Refrain," in *Horizon*. XXIX (January/February, 1986), pp. 33-36.

Albert E. Kalson

ALEKSANDER FREDRO

Born: Surochów, Poland; June 20, 1793
Died: Lwów, Poland; July 15, 1876

Principal drama

Intryga na prędce, pr. 1817; *Pan Geldhab,* pr. 1821, pb. 1826; *Mąż i żona,* pr. 1822, pb. 1826 (*Husband and Wife,* 1969); *Damy i huzary,* pr. 1825, pb. 1826 (*Ladies and Hussars,* 1925, 1969); *Śluby panieńskie, czyli Magnetyszm serca,* wr. 1827, revised pr. 1833, pb. 1834 (*Maidens' Vows: Or, The Magnetism of the Heart,* 1940, 1969); *Pan Jowialski,* pr. 1832, pb. 1838; *Zemsta,* pr. 1834, pb. 1838 (*The Vengeance,* 1957, 1969); *Dożywocie,* pr. 1835, pb. 1838 (*The Life Annuity,* 1969); *Wielki człowiek do małych interesów,* wr. 1852 or 1854, pr., pb. 1877; *Wychowanka,* wr. 1855 or 1856, pr., pb. 1877; *Ożenić się nie mogę,* wr. 1859, pr., pb. 1877; *Rewolwer,* wr. 1861, pr., pb. 1877; *Godzien litości,* wr. 1862, pr., pb. 1877; *The Major Comedies of Alexander Fredro,* pb. 1969.

Other literary forms

Aleksander Fredro wrote autobiographical and patriotic poetry intermittently throughout his adult life. These poems, however, are not of major importance. Also of modest literary merit is Fredro's only novel, *Nieszczęścia najszczęśliwego męża* (1841; the misfortunes of the happiest husband). On the other hand, his posthumously published book of reminiscences, *Trzy po trzy* (1880; topsy-turvy talk), has been acclaimed as one of the masterworks of Polish prose. This work, apparently written in the late 1840's, is composed in a style similar to the one employed in Lawrence Sterne's *A Sentimental Journey Through France and Italy* (1768). Fredro's *Trzy po trzy,* moreover, is highly esteemed by Polish historians as a firsthand account of their nation's military participation in the Napoleonic Wars. Another noteworthy work of nonfiction is the collection of sardonic aphorisms posthumously printed under the title *Zapiski starucha* (1880; notes of an old man).

Achievements

The most productive phase in Fredro's literary career as a writer of comedy coincided with the Romantic epoch in Polish literature. Yet Fredro was relatively unaffected by its literary tenets. In the period following the suppression of the November Insurrection of 1831, moreover, the most prominent Polish writers—men such as Adam Mickiewicz, Juliusz Słowacki, and Zygmunt Krasiński—believed that those who engage in literary activity are morally obliged to act as adjuncts to the cause of national restoration. Owing to the lack of any overt political content in his comedies, Fredro's achievements in this genre tended to be underrated by a literary establishment that had been seduced by the siren song of Romanticism. It was not until after the debacle of the January Insurrection of 1863 that the Polish intelligentsia appeared to wash its collective hands of the doctrines of Romanticism and abandoned the quixotic quest for national independence by means of political conspiracy and armed rebellion. This change in the climate of opinion permitted an objective reappraisal of Fredro's merits as a playwright, and he was henceforth duly recognized as the foremost writer of comedy in the annals of Polish theatrical history.

Biography

The entire territory that comprised the Polish Commonwealth was divided up by its neighbors in a series of partitions that occurred in 1772, 1793, and 1795. As a result of the first partition, the southern area of Poland that is commonly designated as Galicia came under Austrian rule, and it was in the eastern part of this region that Aleksander Fredro was born on June 20, 1793. His birth took place in a manor house of a country estate belonging to his family that was located at Surochów near Jarosław. His parents, Jacek and Maria Fredro, had a total of nine offspring, six of whom were males. Among these were two older brothers, Maksymilian and Seweryn, who were to exert a strong influence on their younger sibling. Aleksander's father, for his part, was a prosperous member of the landowning gentry, who managed to obtain the hereditary title of count from the Austrian regime, chiefly by virtue of a talent for business that enabled him to accumulate a vast personal fortune through the purchase of other estates. Aleksander received the conventional education befitting the son of a country squire on the family estate of Beńkowa Wisznia near Lwów, a city of forty thousand inhabitants that served as the capital of Galicia. Upon the death of his mother in 1806, Aleksander's family took up residence in Lwów proper. The fourteen-year-old boy was also concurrently deprived of the company of both older brothers, for it was decided to enhance their education by having them serve at the court of a powerful Galician magnate named Adam Czartoryski.

At the time when Fredro was coming of age, the greater part of the Polish gentry came to believe that the person of Napoleon Bonaparte represented the best hope for the restoration of Poland's independence. All three occupying powers—Russia, Prussia, and Austria—were united in a continental coalition whose aim it was to thwart the political ambitions of the French emperor. In order to exploit Polish money and manpower on behalf of his military ventures, Napoleon held out the prospect of national restoration as a reward for services rendered to his cause. Shortly after inflicting a crushing defeat on the Prussians at Jena in 1806, Napoleon set up a modest political entity known as the Duchy of Warsaw, comprising those areas that Prussia had annexed during the partitions of 1793 and 1795. The Polish army itself was then reconstituted under the command of Prince Józef Poniatowski, a nephew of the last king of Poland. Owing to another overwhelming French victory over Austrian forces at Wagram in 1809, the territory of the Duchy was subsequently expanded to include the area that was occupied by Austria in 1795. As soon as Poniatowski's men marched into Galicia in support of the French, both Maksymilian and Seweryn decided to enlist. Fredro, though only a teenager, was quick to follow the example set by his older brothers and he, too, became a member of Poniatowski's army. Within a few months, Fredro was promoted to the rank of lieutenant in an elite cavalry unit. After two further years of service, moreover, he rose to the rank of captain. During this same period, he also led an active social life and cut a gallant figure in many a fashionable salon in the district of Lublin where he was stationed.

The course of Fredro's life altered abruptly when, in the spring of 1812, Napoleon launched a grandiose military operation against Russia for the purpose of coercing Czar Alexander to join a continental alliance in opposition to England. The move to attack the czar met with enthusiastic approbation from a majority of the Polish gentry, for they envisioned the recovery of the Russian-occupied eastern provinces in the aftermath of a French victory. Poland's contribution to the multinational army of a half-million men that crossed the Russian frontier numbered one hundred thousand, all but twenty thousand of whom were destined to perish during the ill-fated campaign against the forces of the czar. While most Polish soldiers were assigned to multinational units of the invasion force, Prince Poniatowski was given command of an exclusively national contingent of thirty-five thousand men that was designated as the Fifth Army Corps. Fredro and his older brothers served in this Polish Corps, and it thus fell to their lot to be in the vanguard of the initial attack and in the rearguard of the subsequent retreat. Despite such hazards, each of the three brothers came through the campaign without permanent injury. Owing to a case of typhus, which he contracted during the retreat, however, Fredro was captured by the Russians and imprisoned in a military hospital located near Wilno. Shortly after recovering, he managed to escape and eventually rejoined Poniatowski's forces in time to participate in the last desperate battles that the Grande Armée fought against a reactivated anti-French coalition consisting of Russia, Prussia, and Austria. Poniatowski, notwithstanding several offers of amnesty on the part of the czar, proved steadfast in his commitment to Napoleon and died heroically in the savage three-day struggle known as the Battle of Nations, which was fought near Leipzig during the autumn of 1813. Further defeats of his forces on French soil led to the emperor's abdication at Fontainebleau on April 6, 1814.

The remnant of the Polish Corps—then under the command of General Wincenty Krasiński—was subsequently repatriated to its homeland, where it was to form the nucleus of the armed forces of the czarist protectorate that was established by the Congress of Vienna in 1815 and officially designated as the Kingdom of Poland. With respect to Fredro and his brothers, he and Seweryn chose to be discharged in June, 1814, so as to assist their father in the management of his properties while Maksymilian decided to remain in military service. In addition to receiving high honors from France in recognition of his valorous service in the emperor's cause, Fredro was also awarded his own country's highest military decoration, the Order of the Virtuti Militari.

After his discharge from the army, Fredro returned to Austrian-occupied Galicia by way of Vienna. There he made the acquaintance of Countess Zofia Skarbek (née Jabłonowska), a young woman trapped in an unhappy marriage to a powerful magnate. The attraction that he felt for Zofia proved to be mutual, and they maintained contact with each other once back in Galicia. Fredro took up residence in a village near the estate of Beńkowa Wisznia, whose management had been entrusted to his brother Seweryn. More than a decade later, Fredro moved into Beńkowa Wisznia when his father's health deteriorated abruptly, and he continued to reside there from that time onward. His father died in 1828, and in the same year Fredro was finally able to wed Zofia. They had formed a permanent relationship in 1819, but their wedding had to be deferred until her marriage to Count Skarbek was formally annulled. His wife subsequently bore him a son, Jan Aleksander, in 1829, and a daughter, Zofia, in 1837.

Fredro, while still a member of the Polish Corps in France, took the opportunity to attend the theaters in Paris and thereby familiarized himself with the plays of Molière as well as those of more recent French writers of comedy. His own literary career began in earnest a few years after his discharge from military service. He achieved a modest success with a comedy in one act entitled *Intryga na prędce* (intrigue in a hurry) when it was staged in Lwów in March of 1817. This work was soon followed by a number of full-length plays, as well as an occasional one-acter, which met with increasing approbation on the part of the public. These literary activities were temporarily interrupted by the terminal illness of his father and later by the outbreak of the November Insurrection in 1830. Even though this uprising was confined to the Russian-occupied region of Poland, Fredro feared that it might spread to Galicia. For safety's sake, he thought it best to move to Vienna along with his wife and infant son until the cessation of hostilities. Soon after the capitulation of Warsaw on September 8, 1831, Fredro and his family returned to Galicia, and he once again resumed the career of dramatist with great zeal. In 1835, however, the Romantic poet Seweryn Goszczyński published an article in which he dismissed Fredro's plays as second-rate imitations of foreign models whose content did nothing to foster the cause of Polish independence. Emotionally devastated by these charges, as well as by other critics' attacks against him, Fredro did not find the courage to write another play until the early 1850's. He did, however, continue to work intermittently on other literary projects, including the preparation of a new and expanded edition of his collected writings.

Throughout this period, Fredro also managed to play an active role in the political life of Galicia. His efforts to promote sorely needed social and political reforms in his native province were, however, seriously compromised by his son's decision to join the Polish legions, under the command of General Józef Bem, which had gone to the aid of the Hungarian insurgents engaged in a struggle against the forces of the Hapsburg emperor during the Revolution of 1848. After the Hungarian revolt was crushed, Fredro's son found himself banished from all territory under the control of Austria, and he eventually took up residence in Paris. In subsequent years, his parents spent more time in the French capital than they did in Galicia. On one of his visits to his homeland, Fredro compounded his political difficulties by delivering a seditious speech to the members of a Polish patriotic organization and was subjected to a lengthy legal inquiry that ended with his formal acquittal on March 8, 1854. Three years later, his son was also politically rehabilitated and permitted to return home. In the 1850's, Fredro resumed writing plays; none of these late works, however, was produced or published during his lifetime. With his family in attendance, Fredro died on July 15, 1876, in Lwów, the city where the majority of his earlier plays had received their premiere performances. Lwów today is called L'vov and is located within the Soviet Ukraine as the result of territorial changes that occurred in the course of World War II.

Analysis

Prior to 1835, the year when he was unjustly vilified in Goszczyński's article "Nowa epoka poezji polskiej" (the new epoch of Polish poetry), Aleksander Fredro had already written some twenty plays for the theater. His first full-length play was called *Pan Geldhab* (a title that may be literally rendered as "Mister Has Money" or more colloquially as "Mister Moneybags"). The theme of this three-act comedy in verse manifests a strong affinity with Moliére's *Le Bourgeois Gentilhomme* (1670; *The Would-Be Gentleman*, 1675). Pan Geldhab is a rich merchant who seeks to enhance his own social status by marrying his daughter to a titled aristocrat who is desperately in need of money. Even though the daughter is already engaged to an impoverished member of the gentry who genuinely loves her, she readily acquiesces to her father's plans. To forestall this scheme from being implemented, her fiancé challenges the aristocrat to a duel. The aristocrat, who has in the meantime come into a sizable inheritance from his late aunt, has no desire to risk his life over a woman whom he does not really love and promptly withdraws his offer of marriage. In the light of these events, the merchant is now willing to allow his daughter to marry her fiancé. The young man is, however, thoroughly disgusted with the antics of both father and daughter and therefore decides to have nothing further to do with either of them. While the play is not overtly didactic, it fully reflects Molière's dictum that "the purpose of comedy is to correct men by entertaining them."

Plots involving marital infidelity have been used with great frequency by writers of comedy throughout the ages, and it may seem that there is little room for novelty in works of this type. Fredro, however, takes a strikingly new approach to this theme in the play entitled *Husband and Wife*. Here, four persons who are both young and attractive engage in multiple breaches of trust. The scene is set in the town residence of Count Wacław, the husband of a woman named Elwira. Finding his marital relationship with Elwira to be routine and unexciting, he attempts to find amorous titillation by engaging in a romantic dalliance with his wife's servant, Justysia. His closest personal friend, Alfred, decides to take advantage of the disarray that prevails within the Count's household and proceeds to seduce Elwira. Before long, however, Alfred himself comes to find his relationship with Elwira somewhat tiresome and therefore enters into an amatory liaison with Justysia as well. This soubrette manages deftly to balance the needs of her two lovers, but her duplicity is finally uncovered and she is forced to enter a convent against her will. Count Wacław proves to be far more charitable toward Elwira and Alfred, however, and readily forgives both of them in view of their apparent repentance. The play ends with the Count, Elwira, and Alfred pledging to observe mutual fidelity in their future relations. In addition to the novelty of the plot, *Husband and Wife* is noteworthy for its metrical virtuosity. Whereas convention dictated the use of a thirteen-syllable line with a caesura after the seventh syllable for all lines of dialogue, Fredro composed lines of varying length so as to achieve greater expressiveness by having the number of syllables in a line match the mood of the speaker.

As a lighthearted comedy, *Ladies and Hussars* is generally considered to be at least equal, if not superior, to *Husband and Wife*. *Ladies and Hussars* is also noteworthy for being one of the few plays that Fredro composed in prose prior to 1835, when the first phase of his career as a writer of comedy came to an abrupt end. Being in prose, the dialogue in *Ladies and Hussars* presents few obstacles to the process of translation and suffers very little when recast into another tongue. The play takes place during the period when the army of Prince Józef Poniatowski seized the province of Galicia in 1809 and is set on a country estate belonging to a character designated as the Major. While on official leave, the Major plays host to a captain and a lieutenant from his own regiment, as well as to a pair of older hussars. Suddenly, this exclusively masculine domain is invaded by the Major's three sisters. Of these sisters, two are married and the third is a spinster. Also members of the party are three vivacious maids in their employ and a pretty young woman named Zofia, who is the Major's niece. The sole purpose of the sisters' visit is to persuade their old bachelor brother to marry his niece. Before long, the Major accedes to their wishes and agrees to marry Zofia. Things get a bit out of hand, however, when his spinster sister gets herself engaged to the captain and one of the maids becomes betrothed to one of the old hussars. The Major is the first to recognize the folly of the situation and cancels his nuptial plans. The other males are quick to follow suit. Once all of these mismatches have been eliminated, the way is clear for a marital union between a true pair of lovers: Zofia and the young lieutenant. Although lacking in seriousness of purpose, *Ladies and Hussars* has proved itself to be a favorite among Polish theatergoers.

Maidens' Vows is, on one level, a comedy which aims at contravening the tragic view of love that pervades the writings of the Romanticists. The dramatic embodiment of Fredro's anti-Romantic sentiments is the central figure of Gustaw, whose attitude toward life in general is a combination of both realism and optimism. With intentional irony, Fredro selected the name of Gustaw, because it had previously been used by Adam Mickiewicz to designate the arch-Romantic protagonist in part 3 of his projected dramatic tetralogy titled *Dziady* (1823, 1832; *Forefathers' Eve*, 1925, 1944-1946). By calling attention to the disparity between their respective heroes in this odd way, Fredro hoped to underscore the anti-Romantic aspect of *Maidens' Vows*. As the play opens, Gustaw's uncle, Radost, is attempting to promote a marriage between his nephew and a young lady named Aniela. Her mother also favors the match, but Aniela's cousin, Klara, has talked her into making a vow that neither of them is ever to marry. Accordingly, Aniela refuses Gustaw's offer and Klara rejects her own suitor, Albin. Gustaw, however, is determined to get Aniela to break her vow and devises a clever stratagem to activate the magnetism of the heart. He makes Aniela into his confidante and pretends to be in love with another woman who bears the same name as she does. She soon finds her resolve to remain immune to the passions of the heart weakening when Gustaw, feigning an injury to his hand, dictates a letter to her that is addressed to the imaginary Aniela. Shortly thereafter, Gustaw reveals the true state of affairs to Aniela, and she is quick to accept his offer of marriage. Gustaw also takes revenge on Klara by tricking her into believing that her father will disinherit her if she does not marry Radost. To circumvent this eventuality, Klara decides to enter into marriage with Albin as the lesser of two evils. Except for *The Vengeance*, no other play of Fredro's ranks as high as *Maidens' Vows* in terms of both critical and popular esteem.

There can be little doubt that *The Vengeance* represents the high point of Fredro's career as a writer of comedy. Many critics also consider it to be the finest of all Polish comedies irrespective of period. The plot of the play is extremely complex and revolves around a quarrel between two neighbors over the boundaries dividing their estates. One of them is an elderly nobleman who bears the archaic hereditary title of "royal cupbearer" (*czesnik*) and the other is a petty lawyer who is proud to hold the rank of "notary" (*rejent*).

When the lawyer takes it upon himself to hire masons to erect a wall that will separate the two properties, the nobleman instructs his own servants to drive away the masons. To even the score, the lawyer pressures his son, Wacław, into making a marriage proposal to a rich widow who is the object of the nobleman's affections. Wacław finds the prospect of marrying the widow most distasteful, for he is secretly in love with the nobleman's niece, Klara. Furious at the impending marriage between Wacław and the widow, the nobleman has the young man seized and brought to his home. There he forces Wacław to wed Klara. Both the bride and the groom are delighted by this turn of events. The nobleman and the lawyer, for their part, promptly resolve their dispute in the light of the new relationship that now exists between them. Much of the humor in this play stems from the grandiloquent speech of a soldier-braggart named Papkin. While not directly involved in the main events of the play, this impoverished hanger-on is always on hand to add a touch of drollery to the happenings. The other major characters are depicted more realistically, and the play as a whole presents a vivid tableau of the traditional Polish manners and customs that prevailed among the gentry with whom Fredro spent his entire life.

Two other plays written prior to 1835 are worthy of mention: *Pan Jowialski* and *The Life Annuity*. The former, a work written in prose, may be weak from a dramatic point of view, but it contains innumerable jokes, proverbs, and versified fables that are related by the eponymous hero of the play, whose name is best translated as Mister Joviality. The latter was the last play of Fredro to be produced or published during his own lifetime. In this work, a young rake sells his life annuity to a usurer. Since the annuity will lose its value once its official beneficiary dies, the usurer attempts to coerce the young rake into altering his dissolute life-style. While this premise is highly amusing, Fredro chooses to focus most of the action on the competition between the young rake and the usurer to win the hand of the same woman.

Fredro resumed writing plays in the 1850's and eventually added another sixteen comedies to his dramatic oeuvre. (Most of these works, it should be noted, were written in prose.) Despite a few successful contemporary revivals, none of these late plays has become a permanent part of the classical repertory of the Polish theater. Fredro's reputation as Poland's greatest writer of comedy still rests on those works that were written and produced prior to 1835.

Other major works

NOVEL: *Nieszczęścia najszczęśliwego męża*, 1841.
NONFICTION: *Trzy po trzy*, 1880; *Zapiski starucha*, 1880.
MISCELLANEOUS: *Pisma wszystkie*, 1955-1968 (thirteen volumes).

Bibliography
Kridl, Manfred. *A Survey of Polish Literature and Culture*, 1956.
Krzyżanowski, Julian. *A History of Polish Literature*, 1972.
——————. *Polish Romantic Literature*, 1931, 1968.
Miłosz, Czesław. *The History of Polish Literature*, 1969, 1983.
Segel, Harold B., ed. *The Major Comedies of Alexander Fredro*, 1969.

Victor Anthony Rudowski

GRISELDA GAMBARO

Born: Buenos Aires, Argentina; July 28, 1928

Principal drama

Las paredes, pr. 1964, pb. 1979; *El desatino*, pr., pb. 1965; *Matrimonio*, pr. 1965; *Los siameses*, pr., pb. 1967 (*The Siamese Twins*, 1967); *El campo*, pb. 1967, pr. 1968 (*The Camp*, 1970); "Información para extranjeros," wr. 1971; *Nada que ver*, pr. 1972, pb. 1983; *Solo un aspecto*, pb. 1973, pr. 1974; *Sucede lo que pasa*, pr. 1976, pb. 1983; *Decir sí*, pb. 1978, pr. 1981; *El despojamiento*, pr., pb. 1981; *La malasangre*, pr. 1982, pb. 1984; *Real envido*, pr. 1983, pb. 1984; *Del sol naciente*, pr., pb. 1984.

Other literary forms

Although Griselda Gambaro is known primarily for her plays, she has also written short stories and novels which have received literary prizes. A number of her most successful plays have been derived from prose pieces, including *Las paredes* (the walls), *El desatino* (the blunder), and *The Camp*, which were first short stories, while *Nada que ver* (out of it), is related to the novel *Nada que ver con otra historia* (1972; nothing to do with another story).

Achievements

Of the many successful Argentine dramatists, Gambaro is consistently named among the top playwrights of her country and of Latin America in general. Despite working within a confined sociopolitical context, she has been successful in creating a theatrical experience that relates to the particular problems of her country yet is couched in a universal theatrical idiom. For critics and spectators beyond Argentina, her plays offer formal and structural affinities with the Theater of the Absurd and the Theater of Cruelty, while within Argentina, the roots of her theater are considered to be bound up with the native Argentine expression of the *grotesco-criollo* originated by Francisco Defilippis Novoa and Armando Discepolo. Gambaro, however, does not tend to situate her dramatic world in any specific time or geographic location. All of her plays focus on the recurring themes of power relations in society and the abuses of authority, and are characterized by attention to the whole theatrical experience: dialogue as well as other sounds, gestures, movements, dress, lighting, use of stage space, and so on.

Few images from the Latin American stage have survived with such vitality as those created by Gambaro: the slowly encroaching walls of the Youth's room in *Las paredes*; the entrapped Alfonso of *El desatino*, helpless because of the iron object attached to his foot; the macabre parody of Siamese attachment in *The Siamese Twins*, in which Lorenzo and Ignacio crisscross the stage in a pantomime of two persons joined at the hip; Lorenzo, alone on an empty stage, in a fetal position paralleling that of his dead brother, Ignacio; Emma of *The Camp* grandly gesturing as if playing the piano in a macabre, silent concert; the barber of *Decir sí* (say yes) using his knife to cut off the head of his client instead of shaving him; the sad striptease of the aging actress in *El despojamiento* (the divestore).

Because her view of the human condition transcends national boundaries and her plays are richly textured in terms of theme and technique, Gambaro's work has been the focus of an increasing number of articles and dissertations in the United States, Canada, and Europe. In general, her work may be characterized as having a contemporary sociopolitical message which is conveyed with intense visual images of compelling dramatic interest that work well onstage.

Biography

Griselda Gambaro was born in Buenos Aires, Argentina, and has spent her life there, aside from a year in Rome in 1970 and almost three years in Barcelona (1977-1980). She is the daughter of a postal worker, and because she came from a family with limited economic means, after she finished high school in 1943 she went to work in the business office of a publishing company. Through her writing and its successes, including such awards as a Guggenheim Fellowship in 1982, she has enjoyed greater financial security. She is married to the sculptor Juan Carlos Distefano and is the mother of two children, Andrea, born in 1961, and Lucas, born in 1965. Many of the critics who meet Gambaro in Argentina or during one of her trips abroad are struck by her gentle manner and gracious demeanor, which belie the brutality, vigor, and cruelty expressed in her texts. Although she once called herself "a cowardly person," any reader or spectator of her work soon realizes that the texts also disprove this evaluation, for the writer of these plays must be brave indeed to face the types of bleak and cruel situations that are portrayed. The expectation is implied, however, that the works will bring forth the kind of participation needed to correct the real problems of today's sociopolitical environment.

According to her recollections, she was always writing; that is, from the moment she learned to read she also began to write. She threw away many pieces of work until she was sufficiently satisfied to offer as her first effort worthy of publishing *Madrigal en ciudad* (1963; madrigal in the city), a collection of three short novellas which won the Prize of the Argentine Fondo Nacional de las Artes for narrative in 1963. Soon after, she received the Premio Emece in 1965 for the collection *El desatino* (1965), also containing novellas and short stories. At the same time, two plays emerged from the prose pieces, *Las paredes* and *El desatino*, each winning theatrical prizes: for *Las paredes*, the Premio de la Asociacion de Teatros and the Fondo Nacional de las Artes in 1964, and for *El desatino*, the Prize of the Revista Teatro XX in 1965. One of the characteristics of her writing production which emerged from the beginning was her development of some of the prose pieces as dramatic works almost at the same time that she was writing the prose pieces. She continued this practice until 1972, the year in which she completed work on the novel *Nada que ver con otra historia* and the play *Nada que ver*. She no longer works in that almost parallel fashion in the two genres, finding that she now writes either a play or a piece of fiction independent of one or the other; the plays, however, have become more famous than her fiction and have been translated into several languages and staged around the world. In Argentina, she was closely associated with the experimental art group located at the Centro de Experimentacion audiovisual del Instituto Torcuato Di Tella, a foundation formed in 1958 to patronize the fine arts and foster sociological investigations. The Institute, which unfortunately closed in 1971, worked in part as a theatrical laboratory for young writers who were able to experiment with techniques and representation by adapting audiovisual phenomena to the stage. As part of its promotion of vanguardist and creative talents, the Institute published as well as produced a number of her plays. Jorge Petraglia, a noted Argentine director and actor, has also been associated with Gambaro's work in both of his talented capacities.

As a woman who writes in Latin America, Gambaro is often asked about her role as a woman writer, with questions ranging from the problematics of a feminine discourse to extraliterary problems concerning whether she has faced discrimination in her career because of gender. Her response is usually to present her own specific experiences rather than offer observations applicable to women in Latin America. Argentina, for example, has a long tradition of women writers, and there are many well-established women in literary circles. She sees any difficulties she may have in promoting her as related more to social class than to gender; all the successful women in Argentina have been from the upper class and appear to act with an inborn sense of security absent in a person from the lower classes. In regard to feminine discourse, she was asked to present a paper on the question, "¿Es posible y deseable una dramaturgia especificamente femenina?" (1980; is it possible or desirable to have a specifically feminine dramaturgy?), and her answer is that one writes naturally, without thinking of gender, and the result is the particular view of the writer, showing his or her particular characteristics. The women characters in her own work fit no particular pattern and seem to reflect the greater division Gambaro has perceived in human behavior: Some people are victims of the oppressive acts of others, but at any one moment, anyone can become a victim.

Gambaro has been invited to many international theater conferences. Her first visit to the United States in 1968 was as the guest of the International Exchange Program; she has returned to the United States frequently as an invited speaker at various conferences and university programs, such as the

First International Drama Festival in San Francisco in 1972 and the symposium on Latin American theater at Florida International University in 1979. She has also made frequent trips to France, Italy, and Spain, countries in which her work is well-known and well received critically.

Analysis

Griselda Gambaro is one of the Argentine dramatists who has maintained steady theatrical activity since 1964, when her first produced play, *Las paredes*, also won theatrical prizes. Since then, her productions have consistently been well received in national and international theatrical circles. Critics often compare her plays with European currents, especially the Theater of the Absurd and the Theater of Cruelty, because of the obvious similarities in tone, techniques, and themes. In particular, it is possible to see the relationship between Antonin Artaud's theories for a Theater of Cruelty and Gambaro's skillful use of nonrhetorical language integrated with gestures and movements and her manipulation of the space of the stage to create a physical environment which first moves deeply the emotions of the audience before its intellect is engaged. In the manner Artaud envisioned for his theater, she makes good use of violent physical images as a potent means to express her own vision of the cruelty of existence.

In response to comments associating her work with international movements, Gambaro generally stresses the importance of the Argentine context in the formation of her dramatic vocabulary. While the four plays of the 1960's, which formed the basis of her dramatic reputation, utilize a general Spanish-language expression, her later plays, from the 1970's onward, are written with the more specific Argentine language form of the *voseo* (the use of the familiar singular form of *vos* instead of the more generalized *tu* form), openly marking the language of the plays with a particularly national flavor. She prefers to see the effect of the Argentine dramatic tradition called the *grotesco-criollo*, as well as the real absurdities of the Argentine political situation, as the true inspiration for her tone of black humor and her treatment of man's inhumanity to man, of that paradox in human nature—the capacity of ordinary human beings to participate in atrocities. Although she may deal with real facts and situations in the real world, all of Gambaro's plays may be considered tragicomedies based on variations of the grotesque rather than on realistic conventions.

In form, Gambaro's plays are generally structured with two parallel acts or one act with many fast-moving scenes. Despite anecdotal differences, a recurring pattern of action is found in most of the plays: An average person finds himself in a not unusual setting which soon becomes transformed into a threatening environment because of the inexplicable, menacing actions of adversaries who are often from his intimate circle of family and friends. The relationships among the characters are generally that of oppressor to oppressed; the authority figure may be an unsuspected type, as the mother of *El desatino*, who belies her traditional role as a positive nurturing figure, or an obvious dictatorial character, such as Franco in *The Camp*, or the neighborhood barber, as in *Decir sí*. The victim is generally an unassuming individual who does not rise to the challenge of the situation with heroism, but sinks into an abyss of passive cowardice.

It also should be noted that in Gambaro's plays dialogue functions differently from both the traditional presentation and the innovations of the Theater of the Absurd. Traditionally, dramatic action progressed by means of the dialogic exchanges, a rational sequencing which the absurdists parodied when their characters would speak alternatively without communicating an intellectually viable argument, as in Eugène Ionesco's *La Cantatrice chauve* (1950; *The Bald Soprano*, 1956). In Gambaro's plays, on the other hand, there is an attempt by the victim to communicate, but he is generally deliberately deceived by his tormentors. When the Youth of *Las paredes* remarks that the walls of his room seem to be growing smaller or that he hears pitiful screams from his invisible neighbors, these real observations are noticed, too, by the spectators; the Custodian ignores or denigrates the observations with the effect that the Youth soon distrusts his own senses and resignedly accedes to whatever the Custodian claims, no matter how "absurd," or out of harmony with the real world. This pattern is found in most of Gambaro's plays written in the 1960's and 1970's: The victim's observations are verified by the spectators, but the oppressor figures purposely question and discredit the veracity of the real observations in an attempt to undermine the individual's sense of integrity and well-being. The individual is gradually deprived of his ability to discern for himself between real events and the deceptive interpretations offered by the authorities. His attempts to communicate and to make sense of his universe are overwhelmed, and he is rendered passive, a victim prepared to accept whatever the authorities decide or demand. Gambaro presents this extreme picture of victimization in order to shock her spectators out of their own passivity.

In *El desatino*, the contrast between dialogue and actions is especially menacing because the unidentified youth and the tormentors of *Las paredes* are replaced by a circle of family and friends. When Alfonso attempts to extricate himself from the iron object attached to his foot, his mother, Doña Viola, is too preoccupied with her own needs to pay attention to the problems of her son. She gives all of her attention to Luís, Alfonso's best friend, although Luís acts the opposite of the caring companion. Luís verbalizes the typical solicitations of a friend, but by his actions he actively threatens Alfonso with physical injury. "I'll warm you, I'll protect you," says Luís as he ties a scarf around Alfonso's neck, and in the process nearly strangles him. None of Alfonso's closest companions tries to help him, and only one character in the play appears to take his problem seriously. El muchacho (the boy), identified only as a road-construction worker, offers to do whatever possible to help Alfonso, but his aid is rejected because of his social class. His goodness and concern for others are contrasted with the selfishness of Alfonso's group and Alfonso's own cowardice. The play has been read as an allegory of the problems of the middle class in contemporary Argentina and Latin America, Alfonso representing the middle class, which is dominated by tradition and arrogantly scornful of the efforts of the well-meaning working class.

The contrast between words and actions typical of Gambaro's dramatic images is graphically demonstrated in *The Siamese Twins*. The play develops as a series of encounters in which Lorenzo, the dominant member of the pair alluded to in the title, is driven by envy to cause the destruction of Ignacio. This relationship re-creates the Cain and Abel motif, yet the play never makes explicit that the two are blood brothers; their fraternal relationship seems to be a myth exploited by Lorenzo or, if true, a fact not willingly accepted by Ignacio. Lorenzo's attempt at domination is dramatically expressed in the scene in which he forces Ignacio to walk with him as if the two were real Siamese twins, attached physically. This theatrical gesture contradicts the verbal messages which indicate that the two are physically separate and psychologically different as well. Lorenzo is cunning, envious, and treacherous while Ignacio is ingenuous, compassionate, and good-natured. The docile character Ignacio is the victim of Lorenzo's various dirty tricks and destructive behavior. His need to rid himself of Ignacio is predicated on the erroneous belief that without Ignacio he will somehow be more whole, more independent. By the end of the play, Lorenzo has finally succeeded in implicating Ignacio in some deed for which the police torture and kill him. In the final scene, Lorenzo realizes too late that his destruction of Ignacio has not left him whole but deficient, and has caused his own victimization.

The impact of the final scene is strengthened by its power to recall the final moments of Samuel Beckett's *En attendant Godot* (1952; *Waiting for Godot*, 1954). Lorenzo is alone on an empty stage, ironically assuming the identity of Ignacio by re-creating the latter's fetal position as a dead man. Like Estragon's famous *allons*, which brings no action, Lorenzo, too, announces his imminent departure but goes nowhere. His inability to act contradicts his words and his very existence; the completion of his goal has brought his own destruction.

While Gambaro's use of visual images and stage space is not to be underestimated, neither should the importance of her explorations of language be ignored. Gambaro's choice of words is meant to point out the multiplicity of meanings inherent in any sign. Her titles are an obvious indication of this play with language, with *The Camp* offering a particularly rich demonstration of her technique. In Spanish, *el campo* refers to the countryside and carries connotations of peace and tranquillity, fresh air, open skies, and physical freedom from constraints. In the play with that title, Martin comes to the *campo* to work, yet the place soon becomes transformed from its traditional reference to assume the particular twentieth century meaning of a *campo de concentración*, a concentration camp. The central character, Martin, freely enters the camp on assignment as a bookkeeper. He is directed in his duties by Franco, who is dressed in a Gestapo uniform and armed with a whip. Franco's outfit, the prison garb of the character Emma, and the presence of guards and inmates all suggest that the camp is a prison. Yet Franco claims to see and hear children and farmers singing at work to support the illusion of the first, more harmless, meaning of camp. Franco treats Emma as a great lady and a renowned pianist despite her obvious prison attire. His true relationship to Emma is dramatized when he repeatedly strikes the ground with his whip and Emma gestures in agony as if she has been physically hit.

Martin never finds peace or freedom at the camp; the menacing treatment of the armed guards, the smell of charred flesh and screams of torture, and his own victimization become the reality of his environment. Like Emma, whose wounds and prison markings aroused his sympathy and stimulated him to become involved in her predicament, Martin ends up as another victim in the camp. The trajectory of his experiences, from innocent worker to prisoner, from positive to negative, was first suggested by the ambiguous meaning of the play's title.

Nada que ver is another equivocal title which anticipates a play based on actions of irony and counterpoint. Literally it means "nothing to see," an irony in a play which is a spectacle meant to be seen. In addition, the phrase is part of a Spanish idiom which conveys the idea that something has nothing to do with another thing, as in "esto no tiene nada que ver con eso" (this has nothing to do with that). The title implies that the play has nothing to do with anything else, yet this implication is seen to be patently false once the action begins. Unlike the brief allusion to *Waiting for Godot* at the end of *The Siamese Twins*, *Nada que ver* clearly wishes to elaborate on its relationship with another well-known text, Mary Wollstonecraft Shelley's *Frankenstein* (1818). The two-act play offers some interesting new aspects not only to Shelley's story but also to the basic patterns of Gambaro's dramaturgy. Gambaro offers a parody of the earlier work in order to comment on sociopolitical events relevant to her own time. With ironic humor, in contrast to the serious tone and anguished characters of Shelley's work, Gambaro relates the story of Manolo, an Argentine version of Shelley's scientist-inventor Frankenstein, who speaks with the typical Argentine *voseo* and mannerisms. Manolo is a poor veterinary student who works within a cockroach-infested room that serves as home and laboratory. From whatever castoffs he could find, he creates his own monster, Toni, a Boris Karloff spin-off in appearance only. Toni never acts like the cruel and threatening creature on which he is based; as he gains in experiences and interacts with human beings, he slowly becomes more human in appearance and behavior. Whereas Shelley's monster kills Dr. Frankenstein's betrothed, Toni falls in love with Brigita María, Manolo's girlfriend. She overcomes her initial repugnance to his appearance and reciprocates his amorous feelings.

Although Toni learns to respect and cherish other human beings, he lives in a society which acts in a monstrous way, that is, indiscriminately attacking people and causing senseless deaths. Brigita María becomes the victim of one of these gratuitous acts, and her violent death is deeply mourned by both Manolo and Toni; creator and creature become equal through their shared grief. As a birthday present for Toni, Manolo fabricates another monster in the image of Brigita María, a tasteless simulacrum of the dead woman. Toni and Manolo both learn, however, that human beings are not easily replaceable, and the injustices are not easily corrected. Although Toni has witnessed actions that can be classified only as monstrous, the progression of his own behavior has proceeded from monsterdom to humanity; to carry the analogy to its logical conclusion, one sees by means of the play's actions that the true monsters are not made but are defined by their actions. In a subtle manner, the typical Argentine linguistic expressions employed in the play and the references to political acts of violence recall Argentine political history of the 1970's, during which time a military junta ruled the country almost as a monster gone wild, creating many victims by its inhumane treatment of dissenters. *Nada que ver* purposely offers no clear reference, however, to any specific political system; as the title indicates, it has nothing to do with specifics. In a typical ironic movement which has been a constant of her technique, Gambaro recalls Shelley's text in order to reinterpret the general nature of monsterdom in terms of twentieth century events. Her farces *Real envido* (royal bidding) and *Del sol naciente* (from the rising sun) can also be read as political allegories which offer critiques of totalitarian regimes.

Gambaro's "Información para extranjeros" (information for aliens), subtitled "Cronica en ventiún escenas" (chronicle in twenty-one scenes), is another political allegory that was written in the early 1970's but not published then because of its obvious political content. Unconventional in its dramatic structure, it is a multi-focused work composed of a collage of vignettes, episodes, and spectacles. The physical structuring of the stage space is also unconventional as it is envisioned by the stage directions: either a house of empty rooms with stairs and corridors or a theater where the seats have been removed and replaced by numerous enclosed spaces and narrow hallways. The spectators are expected to move about the alternately darkened and illuminated spaces, interspersed with actors, a situation which creates a dynamic space that corresponds to the dynamic events surrounding the spectators. No story is developed, and the sequence of events is variable; only the last scene takes place at a specified point in the performance, when both spectators and actors are brought together. A guide leads the audience through a series of violent spectacles characterized by black humor, abusive and vulgar language, nudity, and incongruous childish games. Some scenes portray kidnappings, murders, bombings, and the trials of political activists.

Because the spectators are positioned in the midst of the events enacted, they are forced to be more than passive witnesses to the scenes. The boundary between stage and life becomes blurred as the guides ask the spectators to comment on the acting they have just seen as well as on the reality of the events enacted. To the spectators, the guide does not seem to be an actor, but rather the link between the actors and the spectators; the guide functions as an authoritarian figure in his relationship to both actors and audience, telling them what to do, where to go, how to behave. The political implications of the content become evident, then, for the spectators cannot act on their own and their well-being is threatened since they cannot escape their proximity to people who are being tortured and persecuted. "Información para extranjeros" becomes more than an interesting theatrical experiment, as it forces the spectators to recognize their general passivity and requires them to question and respond more fully to the nature of events in their environment. In the earlier plays, only the actors were involved with trying to determine the nature of the reality presented to them by the authority figures, but in "Información para extranjeros" the spectator is made a part of the process as well. Because of its dramatic self-consciousness, the work can be seen as a metaplay, transforming the world into a stage, the stage into the world.

The spatial and formal innovations of "Información para extranjeros" were not developed further in Gambaro's later plays. The play which has been her most successful and has caused the greatest impact on the Argentine public is *La malasangre* (bitter blood). It is set in the 1840's, during the time of the dictator Juan Manuel de Rosas, whose cruelty and barbarous excesses were being repeated by the military dictatorship under which Gambaro presented the play. As is common in her dramatic technique, Gambaro creates a provocative visual text that relates to the Argentine present and to universal issues dealing with power and the abuses of authority.

For the first time she creates a historical drama that develops a naturalistic plot which is a love story. All the action takes place in one room of a castle ruled by a father who acts the stereotype of the patriarch—a domineering, cruel, and insensitive figure. The room is covered with deep, blood-red tapestries, and all the clothes worn by the characters are in shades of red, echoing the allusion to blood in the title and foreshadowing the bloody acts to follow. The father, never given a proper name, acts brutally toward his wife and daughter and brooks no opposing will to his own. He has apparently killed the daughter Dolores' last tutor because of supposed moral improprieties between the two, and he is about to hire a new tutor, Rafael, who is a hunchback. The father believes that Rafael's deformity will be an obstacle to any sexual contact between his daughter and the tutor. While the characters interact onstage, the noise of a wagon is heard outside; from the comments made, it becomes clear that the wagoneer is not selling melons, as is first suggested, but rather is transporting the severed heads of the father's victims. At the outset, Dolores appears insensitive to her father's cruelty, but through her experiences with Rafael, she is taught not only to treat others with respect but also to rebel against the authority of her evil father.

Rafael represents a new character in Gambaro's dramatic world, for he is not a passive person and he recognizes the dangers of the system in which authority is not challenged. That he becomes another of the victims of the father's wrath does not obviate the success he has in converting the daughter of the dictator to a new state of consciousness. After the death of Rafael, Dolores continues his challenge to authority by rebelling against her father. Just as Rafael, as one individual, was unable to overwhelm the power of the dictator, Dolores, too, is unable to topple him. Yet the dictator is shown to be powerless to destroy the courage and dignity of those individuals who are willing to stand up and cry out. The repression of the individual voices will not go on forever, suggests Gambaro, as more people speak up. Gambaro's characters have come a long way from the automaton-like figure of the Youth of *Las paredes*, who lost his dignity and power to act by his cowardly compliance with the authorities.

In the same way that Rafael stands out for his willingness to challenge the system, Dolores is a new type of character for Gambaro, appearing as a decisive and assertive rebel. Previously, Gambaro developed relatively few women on her stage, and those who appeared seemed to fit well the stereotypes of the patriarchal woman. Doña Viola of *El desatino*, for example, is typical of the domineering woman corrupted by the patriarchal society of Latin America, while Lily, Alfonso's wife, is merely a figment of his imagination and another stereotype of the sexy female. Emma of *The Camp* is also a victim of patriarchy. The woman monologuist of *El despojamiento* is the most pathetic female figure of Gambaro's theater, for in her outpouring of words she reveals that she has been physically abused and psychologically dominated by family, friends, and strangers, to the point that she readily submits to subjugation at the slightest provocation. She has no reserves of strength or dignity left, and by her own actions she divests herself of her clothes and her emotional protective covering. Brigita María of *Nada que ver*, in contrast, is active and politically engaged, but she, too, ends up a victim of a senseless society. Dolores is never passive and leaves the stage fighting and shouting her defiance to authority. Perhaps the image of Dolores is a fitting image of Gambaro's entire production, for she has also challenged the imposition of silence of a dictatorial system and succeeded in creating lasting images of intense dramatic power.

Critical Survey of Drama

Other major works

NOVELS: *Una felicidad con menos pena*, 1967; *Nada que ver con otra historia*, 1972; *Ganarse la muerte*, 1976; *Dios no nos quiere contentos*, 1979; *Lo impenetrable*, 1984.

SHORT FICTION: *Madrigal en ciudad*, 1963; *El desatino*, 1965.

MISCELLANEOUS: *Conversaciónes con chicos*, 1966.

Bibliography

Cypress, Sandra Messinger. "Physical Imagery in the Plays of Griselda Gambaro," in *Modern Drama*. XVIII, no. 4 (1975), pp. 357-364.

_____. "The Plays of Griselda Gambaro," in *Dramatists in Revolt: The New Latin American Theatre*, 1976. Edited by George W. Woodyard and Leon F. Lyday.

Foster, David William. "The Texture of Dramatic Action in the Plays of Griselda Gambaro," in *Hispanic Journal*. I, no. 2 (1979), pp. 57-66.

Holzapfel, Tamara. "Griselda Gambaro's Theatre of the Absurd," in *Latin American Theatre Review*. IV, no. 1 (1970), pp. 5-12.

Mendez-Faith, Teresa. "Sobre el uso y abuso de poder en la producción dramatica de Griselda Gambaro," in *Revista Iberoamericana*. LI (1985), pp. 831-841.

Sandra Messinger Cypress

GÜNTER GRASS

Born: Danzig, Germany; October 16, 1927

Principal drama

Noch zehn Minuten bis Buffalo, pr. 1954, pb. 1958 (*Only Ten Minutes to Buffalo*, 1967); *Hochwasser*, pr. 1957, pb. 1960, revised pb. 1963 (*Flood*, 1967); *Onkel, Onkel*, pr. 1958, revised pb. 1965 (*Mister, Mister*, 1967); *Beritten hin und zurück*, pb. 1958, pr. 1959 (*Rocking Back and Forth*, 1967); *Zweiunddreissig Zähne*, pr. 1959; *Die bösen Köche*, pr., pb. 1961 (*The Wicked Cooks*, 1964); *Poum: Oder, Die Vergangenheit fliegt mit*, pb. 1965; *Die Plebejer proben den Aufstand*, pr., pb. 1966 (*The Plebeians Rehearse the Uprising*, 1966); *Four Plays*, 1967; *Davor*, pr., pb. 1969 (partial translation as *Uptight*, 1970; complete translation as *Max: A Play by Günter Grass*, 1972); *Theaterspiele*, 1970.

Other literary forms

In addition to drama, Günter Grass is known for his novels, shorter fiction, poetry, political essays and speeches (indeed, he is an active Socialist), and ballet libretti. His first novel, *Die Blechtrommel* (1959; *The Tin Drum*, 1961), reflects its author's concern with the rehabilitation of man in postwar Nazi Germany in particular and in a nearly absurd postwar society in general. Grass is also an artist, having published prints and sketches, some in conjunction with his literary works.

Achievements

Called by *Newsweek* the author who "put postwar German literature back on the market," Grass has enjoyed the critical acclaim of his peers as well. John Irving called *The Tin Drum* "the greatest novel by a living author" as late as 1982, and Grass himself "the most versatile and original writer alive."

Grass's involvement in and dedication to Social Democratic politics and the peace movement no doubt has much to do with the vitality and social preoccupations of his writing. His works not only record the personal and societal struggles of postwar, post-Nazi Germany but also grapple—at times comically and even grotesquely—with the orientation of the individual in such an absurd world. In turn, his writings (especially *The Tin Drum*), which have enjoyed international distribution, have provided their author with an international forum for his beliefs on a wide range of issues—political, environmental, nuclear, and more.

Grass is the recipient of numerous literary awards, among them the prestigious Gruppe 47 award in 1958, the Georg Büchner Prize in 1965, the Fontane Prize in 1968, and the Premio Internationale Mondello in 1977. He himself established the Alfred Döblin Prize in 1978.

Biography

Günter Grass was born in Danzig (now Gdańsk, Poland) on October 16, 1927. His parents owned a grocery store in the suburb Langfuhr. His father's family included workers and carpenters; his mother's family was Kaschubian. Biographical elements from his working-class youth appear throughout his literary works, especially in the *Danziger Trilogie* (1980). Grass attended the Conradinum *gymnasium* in Danzig. As a teenager, he served in an antiaircraft battery during World War II, was wounded, and became an American captive. Subsequently, he worked his way from Bavaria to Düsseldorf, where he became an apprentice stonecutter (1946-1947) in order to earn money for art school. He studied both graphic design and sculpture in Düsseldorf (1948-1952) and sculpture in Berlin under Karl Hartung (1953-1956).

During these years, Grass also began to write; his initial efforts were in the area of lyric poetry. In 1954, he married Anna Schwarz, a Swiss ballerina. He resided in Paris from 1956 to 1959. He first read before the literary group Gruppe 47 in 1955, winning the group's prize in 1958 for excerpts from his novel *The Tin Drum*, which catapulted him to fame after its publication in 1959. Grass participated in Gruppe 47 until its last meeting in 1967.

In the elections of 1961, Grass actively took up the cause of the Social Democrats and campaigned intensively for Willy Brandt, former mayor of West Berlin and chancellor of the Federal Republic of Germany. Grass has drawn frequent criticism from both the extreme Left and Right political groups. He openly criticized the East German government at the East Berlin Writers' Congress and wrote an open letter to the East German writer Anna Seghers after the construction of the Berlin Wall on August 13, 1961.

The early phase of Grass's literary career, during the mid-1950's, includes poetry, shorter prose fiction, and absurdist dramas, although it was also during these early years that he wrote *The Tin Drum*. His first collection of poetry, *Die Vorzüge der Windhühner*, appeared in 1956. He also won third prize in a poetry contest sponsored by the South German Radio in 1954. In 1956 he first exhibited his drawings in Stuttgart; in 1957 his sculpture and drawings were exhibited in Berlin. In 1957 *Flood* had its premiere in Frankfurt, and a ballet, *Stoffreste*, also enjoyed its first performance, in Essen. Further absurdist dramatic works appeared in rapid succession: *Mister, Mister* in 1958 in Cologne, and in 1959 a ballet (*Fünf Köche*, in Aix-les-Bains) and a farce, (*Rocking Back and Forth*, in Frankfurt and Hamburg). A poetry collection, *Gliesdreieck*, with illustrations by the author, appeared in 1960. With the publication in 1961 of *Katz und Maus* (*Cat and Mouse*, 1963) and in 1963 of *Hundejahre* (*Dog Years*, 1965)—which together with *The Tin Drum* constitute the *Danziger Trilogie*—Grass firmly established himself as the leading German novelist since World War II. In 1961 the drama *The Wicked Cooks* premiered, and in 1964 another ballet, *Goldmäulchen* in Munich. Grass also revised *Mister, Mister* at this time.

Grass's career in the 1960's was characterized by increased political activity, reflected in such works as *The Plebeians Rehearse the Uprising*, the novel *Örtlich betäubt* (1969; *Local Anaesthetic*, 1969), and poems from his collection *Ausgefragt* (1967; *New Poems*, 1968). The tale *Aus dem Tagebuch einer Schnecke* (1972; *From the Diary of a Snail*, 1973) is a transitional work in that the author employs a relatively new narrative technique—one which anticipates subsequent works—while simultaneously drawing on themes from earlier novels. Grass discusses here the elections of 1969 which led to Willy Brandt's victory as well as the treatment of Jews during World War II and the Third Reich, both in relation to the postwar Federal Republic of Germany. After the publication of this work, and until the appearance of his next long novel, *Der Butt* (1977; *The Flounder*, 1978), Grass withdrew from the public eye and concentrated on lyric poetry and graphic art. In 1978, Grass was divorced, and in 1979 he married Ute Grunert, a musician. This period in the mid-1970's might be compared to the similar one during the mid-1950's before the publication of *The Tin Drum*.

The publication of *The Flounder* in 1977 reaffirmed Grass's position as the leading contemporary German novelist. In the earlier *Danziger Trilogie*, Grass used several narrators to relate different perspectives of German-speaking lands under Nazi domination. In these works the narrator looks back from the 1950's and early 1960's to the time just before, during, and after World War II. In *The Flounder*, Grass employs a radically new narrative technique: He has a single first-person narrator tell his story from the Stone Age until the 1970's. In rapid succession appeared *Das Treffen in Telgte* (1979; *The Meeting at Telgte*, 1981) and *Kopfgeburten: Oder, Die Deutschen sterben aus* (1980; *Headbirths: Or, The Germans Are Dying Out*, 1982). *The Meeting at Telgte* is the expansion from *The Flounder* of a chapter which occurs during the Thirty Years' War. The fanciful meeting of baroque poets in 1647 at Telgte is an imaginative analogue to the initial meeting of twentieth century poets in 1947 as the Gruppe 47. *Headbirths* discusses other, more contemporary political issues raised in *The Flounder*. Since *The Flounder* is formally divided into nine months from the conception of a child in October, 1973, until its birth in the summer of 1974, this birth is a physical parallel to the subsequent intellectual, or "head," birth. Grass illustrated a volume of poems, *Ach Butt, dein Märchen geht böse aus* (1983), a lyric and artistic treatment of themes from *The Flounder*. Grass's novel *Die Rättin* (1986; *The Rat*, 1987) continues and elaborates on narrative techniques and themes begun in *The Flounder*.

Analysis

Günter Grass's dramatic works are generally divided into two categories. The earlier group, which includes *Flood*, *Mister, Mister*, *Only Ten Minutes to Buffalo*, and *The Wicked Cooks*, features the absurd or grotesque, while *The*

Plebeians Rehearse the Uprising and *Max* represent the new dramaturgical impetus of dialectical theater in the Brechtian sense. The two groups are distinct in the treatment of thematic material as well as in dramatic elements and structures. In all the plays, however, there is a marked tendency to avoid dramatic situations and the resolution of the plot in a traditional manner. The author refuses to provide any answers to the many provocative questions posed in his dramatic works.

Grass himself relegated the early plays to the category of "poetic" theater, a designation which reflects the integral relationship of his early lyrics and plays. Poems which bear the same name and/or which treat themes similar to those of the corresponding drama exist in many instances. Grass explains his procedure in this way:

> And so the transition from poetry to drama happened like this: poems were written in dialogue form, and were then extended. That was shortly after the war. Then slowly, gradually, stage directions were added, and so, parallel with my main occupation at that time, sculpture, I evolved my first play. That is why in a relatively short time, between 1954 and 1957, I wrote four full-length and two one-act plays, which, just like my poems and my prose, contain fantastic and realistic elements; these fantastic and realistic elements rub against each other and keep each other in check.

The two-act play *Flood* depicts humankind's uncanny ability to deal nonchalantly with periodic catastrophe and the inability to learn anything at all from this experience. Noah, together with his sister-in-law Betty, moves his cherished collection of antique inkwells to a higher story; she, in turn, is worried about her photo collection. Noah's daughter, Jutta, and her fiancé, Henn, are listless youths, too bored to help or even to make love. The arrival of the aggressive duo, Leo (Noah's son) and Kongo (Leo's friend and an erstwhile boxer), from out of a packing crate catalyzes the situation. Leo and Kongo force Henn out on the roof, where a pair of wise rats, Strich and Perle (their names allude to rain), observe and comment on history and human behavior. Henn is not at all perturbed by Jutta's liaison with Kongo; everyone is aware that their attraction for each other will last only as long as the flood.

Meanwhile, Noah naps and Betty sews parasols for the sunny weather ahead. What strikes the audience is that no one is worried about the rain and the rising water, no one considers the imminent peril; all are content to wait until their previous life-styles can be resumed. The notion of rats abandoning a sinking ship receives an ironic twist: Here the wise rats, who suspect a return to normality and therefore to rattraps, embark for Hamelin as soon as the water recedes. Henn returns to Jutta, Noah sees to his inkwells, and Leo and Kongo depart for Liverpool (or maybe the North Pole), taking along Noah's grandfather clock, from which emerges an official insurance inspector, who is anxious to assess the damages incurred during the flood.

Biblical elements and their parodies abound: Noah, the dove with some "weeds" in its beak, the dove on the armband of the insurance assessor, the cyclical rain and high waters versus the biblical Flood, and the moldy rainbow which whets the rats' appetite. The unusual juxtaposition of persons, objects, and animals, typical of Grass's early works, returns to "normal" after the flood. The play points to the absurdity of human behavior in the face of disaster—with a minimum amount of action. As in *Rocking Back and Forth*, there is emphasis on motion leading nowhere—back and forth, up and down the stairs to avoid the rising water.

In the one-act *Only Ten Minutes to Buffalo*, Grass similarly flouts the tradition of forward-moving motion of the plot and action. The countdown to only ten minutes to Buffalo contrasts starkly to the immobility of the rusty locomotive in an alpine meadow. The marine terminology used by Krudewil and Pempelfort in their train, which is presumed to be speeding toward Buffalo, is further underscored by the painter Kotschenreuter's nautical scene as well as his conversation with the cowherd, Axel, in which he maintains that language is arbitrary and distinctions between "cow, ship, professor, and buttercup" must be seen as mere conventions. The nautical tone is appropriate to the title of the play, a literary spoof on Theodor Fontane's ballad *John Maynard* about a Lake Erie boat captain who, at the cost of his own life, saves his passengers. As it happens, the two men on the locomotive encounter Fregate, their former captain, a tough female smoking three cigars, and together they row across the meadow. Axel, however, realizes the true artistic potential of the scene and climbs into the locomotive, which promptly chugs away.

Mister, Mister reflects Grass's return to a more strictly composed drama, although the theme is nevertheless absurd and grotesque. Each of the four acts is preceded by a prologue. Two tough inner-city kids, Sprotte and Jannemann, also serve to structure the work, which concerns a serial murderer, Bollin, whom none of his intended victims takes seriously. In the first prologue, Sprotte and Jannemann accost Bollin as he sits on a park bench. Their singsong encounter with him anticipates several macabre aspects of the play. They do not accept candy from him, not because he is a stranger, but because they want something else. Their mindless aggression is reminiscent of the corrupt and violent duo Leo and Kongo from *Flood*. The pair taunt Bollin: "Mister, mister, aintcha got a thing, aintcha got a thing . . . maybe in your pocket."

The play proper consists of Bollin's encounter with prospective victims. None of them is in the least perturbed by his appearance. In fact, the adults seem even flattered to be chosen by this notorious killer. In the last act, Bollin appears much older, more decrepit, and somewhat lame. Usually a loner, he has agreed to meet an accomplice to stake out a potential victim. While he lurks outside waiting for his rendezvous, Sprotte and Jannemann persuade Bollin to give them first his pen, then his watch, and finally his revolver. Jannemann inadvertently fires the gun and kills Bollin. Further associations of sex and violence become manifest, as Sprotte and Jannemann run off to have sex. Based on their sexual misinformation, it seems that they have little sexual experience.

The four prologues perform an expository function, as structural elements incorporating the Sprotte-Jannemann plot and revealing the blacker and more abstract elements of the protagonist's nature. For example, in the second prologue, Bollin twice stabs and repairs the doll Pinkie, stolen from a sick girl, one of the intended victims who unwittingly thwarted the planned molestation and murder. He then hangs the doll on a hook and shoots it. Bollin's grotesque methodology and penchant for systematic detail echo Nazi tactics. As a serial murderer, he has enjoyed numerous past successes, yet all current attempts fail. He himself is carelessly killed by two children who rely on no system. His methodological ideology dies with him.

In *The Wicked Cooks*, Grass's characteristic gastronomical motifs are applied to the nature of the artist. Themes related to food and cooking occur throughout his fiction and poetry. The art of cooking is transformed into a metaphor for art itself, and the cook becomes identical with the artist. In the play, Herbert Schymanski, the Count, has learned to cook a certain gray soup. The wicked cooks—Petri, Vasco, Grün, Stach, and Benny—try to force the Count to give them the recipe. A competing band of cooks, led by one Kletterer, attempts to get the recipe first and disrupt a party which Vasco's fiancée, Martha, is forced to attend. The cooks suggest an exchange: love for the recipe. Martha goes with the Count, and he promises to give them the recipe at a later date. The situation becomes problematic when the Count's sexual encounter causes him to forget the recipe. The cooks threaten the pair; the Count and Martha commit suicide.

The recipe can be interpreted as a symbolic formula for artistic creativity which simply cannot be transferred. The Count's behavior can also be seen as active resistance to the unscrupulous methods of the cooks. At the first performance of the play, the actor portraying the Count wore a mask in the likeness of Günter Grass, a theatrical interpretation which supports the contention that the play represents the artistic dilemma of an author.

The Plebeians Rehearse the Uprising relates fictive events around a historical occasion, a revolt on June 17, 1953, in the Soviet sector of Berlin (now East Berlin). Grass takes up the theme of the politically engaged artist as the focus of this four-act drama. Many characteristics of the theater director "Boss" allude to Bertolt Brecht, who was director of the Theater am Schiffbauerdamm. As the fictitious theater ensemble rehearses the Boss's adaptation of William Shakespeare's *Coriolanus*, the plebeians, who have the function of messengers, enter the theater from the outside and report various stages of the revolt. There is little physical action in the play; the verbal arguments for and against the rebellion provide the focus of the drama, which bears the subtitle "A German Tragedy."

Early reception of the play, the only one of Grass's dramas to enjoy a Berlin premiere, reflected only moderate success. Many critics saw it merely as an anti-Brecht play or a documentary drama. Although Grass does attempt to assimilate the Brechtian legacy here, the Boss represents not only Brecht but also the position of many Marxist intellectuals. The fact that most of the *dramatis personae* do not have personal names but are known by their functions (Boss, Bricklayer) or by their roles in the Shakespeare play (Volumnia, Flavis) is an indication that the play-within-the-play is meant to serve as a model. The realities of the revolt and the play, of Berlin and Rome, overlap. Only as the Shakespeare production progresses does it occur to the Boss that the actual, unrehearsed uprising, which he gives little chance for success, poses grave questions for his theater and his rehearsed revolt. With the noble intentions of a liberal intellectual, the Boss had wanted to enlighten the workers through theater, to show them how to make a revolution. As the drama closes, the Boss admits that Shakespeare cannot be adapted or changed unless people themselves change. The Boss fails, not because he does not provide the workers with a manifesto, but because he cannot give them his theoretical knowledge of revolution. The Boss, the only character who is correct in his estimation of the uprising, is morally wrong. He has failed all those who have pinned their hopes on him in the expectation that a single renowned public figure might change the historical process. The Boss abandons his production and goes to the country to write poetry. In Shakespeare's *Coriolanus*, the protagonist is not a plebeian but a friend of the patricians. Brecht's adaptation idealizes the plebeians, who triumph. In view of Grass's own literary production and growing political involvement at the time, the play emerges as a statement about the dilemma of the politically involved artist.

Max, a play in thirteen scenes, derives from Grass's novel *Local Anaesthetic*, but it takes the perspective of the dentist and Eberhard Starusch, Philp (Flip) Scherbaum's teacher. The dramatic core of the play is not action itself but discourse about an action. Should Flip protest the use of napalm in Vietnam by burning his dog Max in front of the café at the Hotel Kempinski and disgust the well-heeled, overweight Berlin women, known for their love of canines and cake? Flip's Maoist girlfriend, Vero, encourages him to act. The dentist and another teacher, Fräulein Seifert, also support his decision to burn the dog, not because they approve of or believe in his own protest but because they want him to act vicariously on their behalf. The various scenes of the drama represent Starusch's attempt to dissuade his student. In the end Flip does not burn the dog and he assumes the editorship of the school paper. Vero, who boycotts the first editorial meeting, vows to go to the Hotel Kempinski and eat cake in her own protest.

Grass's polyhistorical interests permeate all aspects of his artistic production, both graphic and literary. The dramas demonstrate the author's command of form as expressed in the idiom of the theater and, by comparison to his other works, the control and manipulation of content. All of his plays experiment with traditional dramatic elements, themes, and structures. Grass's plays have met with only limited success, a fact which might be attributed to the topical nature of the plays, to the dearth of any real action and the focus on verbal argument, and to their inherent tendency to be nondramatic. For example, temporal as well as geographic proximity of themes in *The Plebeians Rehearse the Uprising* and *Max*—Brecht, the revolt of 1953, the Berlin Wall, student rebellions—may have prompted the initially mixed reception of these works.

Nevertheless, few modern writers exhibit a scope, diversity, and depth of artistic production comparable to that of Günter Grass. As a playwright he provides witty dialogues and clever situations as well as black humor; his use of theatrical techniques is adept. Together with his novels, poetry, and graphics, Grass's plays constitute an oeuvre which is unsurpassed in postwar German literature.

Other major works

NOVELS: *Die Blechtrommel,* 1959 (*The Tin Drum,* 1961); *Katz und Maus,* 1961 (*Cat and Mouse,* 1963); *Hundejahre,* 1963 (*Dog Years,* 1965); *Örtlich betäubt,* 1969 (*Local Anaesthetic,* 1969); *Aus dem Tagebuch einer Schnecke,* 1972 (*From the Diary of a Snail,* 1973); *Der Butt,* 1977 (*The Flounder,* 1978); *Das Treffen in Telgte,* 1979 (*The Meeting at Telgte,* 1981); *Danziger Trilogie,* 1980 (includes *Die Blechtrommel; Katz und Maus; Hundejahre*); *Kopfgeburten: Oder, Die Deutschen sterben aus,* 1980 (*Headbirths: Or, The Germans Are Dying Out,* 1982); *Die Rättin,* 1986 (*The Rat,* 1987).

POETRY: *Die Vorzüge der Windhühner,* 1956; *Gleisdreieck,* 1960; *Selected Poems,* 1966; *Ausgefragt,* 1967 (*New Poems,* 1968); *Poems of Günter Grass,* 1969 (includes *Selected Poems* and *New Poems*; also in a bilingual edition as *In the Egg and Other Poems,* 1977); *Gesammelte Gedichte,* 1971; *Mariazuehren, Hommageàmarie, Inmarypraise,* 1973 (trilingual edition); *Liebe geprüft,* 1974; *Love Tested,* 1975; *Ach Butt, dein Märchen geht böse aus,* 1983 (with illustrations).

NONFICTION: *Über das Selbstverständliche,* 1968 (partial translation as *Speak Out!,* 1969); *Über meinen Lehrer Döblin und andere Vorträge,* 1968; *Der Bürger und seine Stimme,* 1974; *Denkzettel,* 1978; *Aufsätze zur Literatur,* 1980; *Widerstand lernen: Politische Gegenreden 1980-1983,* 1984; *On Writing and Politics, 1967-1983,* 1985.

BALLET SCENARIOS: *Fünf Köche,* 1959; *Stoffreste,* 1959; *Goldmäulchen,* 1964.

Bibliography

Cunliffe, W. Gordon. *Günter Grass*, 1969.
Durzak, Manfred. "Günter Grass," in *West German Poets on Society and Politics*, 1979. Edited by Karl H. Van D'Elden.
Hollington, Michael. *Günter Grass: The Writer in a Pluralist Society*, 1980.
Lawson, Richard H. *Günter Grass*, 1985.
White, Ray Lewis. *Günter Grass in America: The Early Years*, 1981.
Willson, A. Leslie, ed. *A Günter Grass Symposium*, 1971.

Mara R. Wade

ALBERT GURNEY

Born: Buffalo, New York; November 1, 1930

Principal drama

Three People, pb. 1956; *Turn of the Century*, pb. 1958; *Love in Buffalo*, pr. 1958; *The Bridal Dinner*, pb. 1961, pr. 1962; *The Comeback*, pr. 1964, pb. 1966; *The Open Meeting*, pr. 1965, pb. 1968; *The Rape of Bunny Stuntz*, pr. 1966, pb. 1976; *The David Show*, pr. 1966, pb. 1968; *The Golden Fleece*, pb. 1967, pr. 1968; *The Problem*, pb. 1968, pr. 1969; *The Love Course*, pb. 1969, pr. 1970; *Scenes from American Life*, pr., pb. 1970; *The Old One-Two*, pb. 1971, pr. 1973; *Children*, pr., pb. 1974 (based on John Cheever's short story "Goodbye, My Brother"); *Who Killed Richard Cory?*, pr., pb. 1976; *The Middle Ages*, pr. 1977, pb. 1978; *The Wayside Motor Inn*, pr. 1977, pb. 1978; *The Golden Age*, pr. 1981; *The Dining Room*, pr., pb. 1982; *What I Did Last Summer*, pr. 1982; *The Perfect Party*, pr. 1985; *Another Antigone*, pr. 1986; *Sweet Sue*, pr. 1986.

Other literary forms

Albert Gurney has written for television and film as well as for the stage; in addition, he has published the novels *The Gospel According to Joe* (1974), *Entertaining Strangers* (1977), and *The Snow Ball* (1984).

Achievements

Gurney is often labeled the dramatist of the WASP (white Anglo Saxon Protestant) enclave. He laughs at, ridicules, even satirizes WASPs but at the same time understands them and in some ways sympathizes with them. Being born and reared a WASP, he knows his material. His characters live and breathe. They vividly represent a passing culture. Their motivations are clearly depicted, along with their frustrations and emotional tensions. Never really damnable, they are bored, fenced in, stifled. They crave freedom and self-realization. Gurney's mastery of concise form reflects his classical bent. His plays are brief and to the point. They exemplify glories of artistic structure similar to those of the sonnet or sonata form. No excesses mar their impact. They abound with thrilling resonance of offstage events.

Gurney is in like manner a master of dramatic dialogue. The clichés and literary reflections of his characters are consonant with their status and emotions. Like Henrik Ibsen's plays, Gurney's are well wrought. Stage settings, props, and costumes are carefully detailed. Following in the tradition of such American innovators of drama as Eugene O'Neill, Arthur Miller, Tennessee Williams, and Edward Albee, Gurney loosens space, opening up the stage. Hamlet-like, his characters address the audience, who at times even become participants in the play. The rueful humor of Gurney's highly polished, smoothly crafted plays makes for entertaining theater, despite the underlying pessimism of his work.

Biography

Albert Ramsdell Gurney, Jr., was born in Buffalo, New York, on November 1, 1930, the son of Albert Ramsdell Gurney, Sr., a dealer in real estate and insurance, and Marion Spaulding Gurney. The young Gurney grew up in the exclusive suburbia he depicts in his plays. From St. Paul's school he went to Williams College, where he was graduated in 1952 with a B.A. degree in English literature. After graduation, he served three years (1952-1955) in the navy as an officer and then attended the Yale School of Drama, where he earned the M.F.A. degree in 1958. In 1984, he was awarded an honorary D.D.L. degree. In 1960, he began a long, distinguished career as teacher of literature and humanities at Massachusetts Institute of Technology.

In June, 1957, Gurney married Mary Forman Goodyear, who bore him four children: George, Amy, Evelyn, and Benjamin. They lived in Boston until 1983, when Gurney moved his family to New York to be near the theater, television, and publishers while he was on sabbatical from M.I.T. All this time he was concerned with the contrast between the values instilled in him as a youth and those of the world he was experiencing.

From early childhood, he had a passion for drama. He wrote his first play in kindergarten. His passion was fostered by his aunt, who liked to attend matinees but could find no one to go with her. It fell Gurney's lot to go, and he enjoyed every minute of the saturation. He also liked to listen to dramas on the radio and through them learned the importance of sound to drama, especially the spoken word. He developed an accurate ear for the kinds of things certain kinds of people say. While at Williams College, it might be said he began his writing career by creating college revues. In the Navy, as special services officer, he wrote and produced revues on a grander scale. Finally, in drama school at Yale, his playwriting career began in earnest, and he published his first drama, the one-act play *Three People*, in 1956.

While teaching he had little time to write, but he always had writing on his mind. As he lectured and read, ideas for drama would come to him; during summer vacations, he would write. Following this routine, he managed to publish more than fifteen plays between the late 1960's and the early 1980's.

Gurney has received many notable awards. In 1971, he was the recipient of the New York Drama Desk Award, and in 1977, the Rockefeller Playwright Award.

The National Endowment for the Arts bestowed on him the Playwriting award for 1981-1982. He is a member of the Dramatists Guild (council) and the Writers Guild. His *Three People* was included in the *The Best Short Plays of 1955-56*; *Turn of the Century* appeared in *The Best Short Plays of 1957-58*;

and *The Love Course* was selected for *The Best Short Plays of 1970*. His plays have won acclaim in London as well as in the United States.

Analysis

Albert Gurney crafts his plays about the people he knows—WASPs. The setting of most of his plays is New England suburbia. The stage is never crowded with actors or furniture; rather, Gurney's sets suggest moods and situations. Often the audience become participants, and offstage actions, sounds, and characters are central to the play. Though writing with classical constraint, he is innovative in staging. In several plays, multiple scenes go on simultaneously. Music is also an integral part of many of his plays; Gurney deftly employs songs for atmosphere and tone. His plays are notable for their structure and polish; not a word is wasted.

Gurney's first published play, *Three People*, written while he was in the Yale School of Drama, deals with his major theme: freedom. Two of the three characters—a university professor and his wife—are sympathetically presented in their struggle to accept the fact that their child is mentally deficient. They struggle magnificently with their broken dreams. The tragedy of this tightly knit one-act, one-scene play is that the third character, the baby, gets very little consideration as a person. Gurney manages the pathos of the situation without being morbid or sentimental. The baby is never onstage. He is talked about and tended to, but he is never seen. Much dialogue is exchanged from the offstage nursery as the wife talks to her husband from the nursery. The characters are honestly and sympathetically drawn, each encased in a tragic plight from which there is no release.

Gurney's first three-act play, *The Bridal Dinner*, is typical of his classical restraint of setting and time. All action takes place in one room where a bridal dinner is held during an evening and a morning in June. The characters are also typical of Gurney: high livers in high society, concerned with money and status, acting out their lives of boredom. Gurney masterfully presents a play-within-a-play wherein the bride and groom look into themselves and their future. WASPish standards are humorously, satirically, and delightfully paraded before the bridal party and the audience. The play is full of telling vignettes and repartee as the young couple feel alone, isolated, apart—all the links broken. They recognize the empty ritual of the bridal dinner for what it is and discard symbolic relics of the past. The problem, ever-present in Gurney plays, is what to do next. Are they strong enough to cast off the old armor and face up to a new and challenging future? Where can they go from here? They feel wobbly, so they decide to dance. This parody of marriage in a "rotten world" has enough reality to make the caricature believable. As the characters themselves admit, it smacks of Thornton Wilder, Luigi Pirandello, and "the worst from Broadway"; still, it is delightful and thought-provoking. As in most of Gurney's plays, literary references abound, and clichés and old saws are subversively employed. Finally, reflecting Gurney's patriotic theme in the 1960's, the marriage assumes global scope with a vision of world peace through the marriage of nations in love. Gurney's wit saves the play from melodrama by posing the question, "But can she cook?"

Gurney continued in this seriocomic vein in *The David Show*, where he sets the biblical story of the coronation of King David in a modern television studio. This one-set, one-scene, five-character parody is good fantasy. The characters are catchy, if a bit overdrawn. David is portrayed as a Madison Avenue type who uses people for his benefit; Bathsheba, with her cliché-studded dialogue, is a combination of charm and clowning. She comes across as a true philistine, while Jonathan is a playboy seeking only "the good life." Gurney's characterization is vivid and entertaining, and the dialogue sparkles. Clichés are cleverly sprinkled throughout; there is much witty wordplay. Undergirding the spoof is Gurney's usual seriousness. Problems of war, the good life, moral fiber, and ethnic groups are aired until in contrast with the surface hilarity, David is forced to face up to the reality that Goliath is David himself: his own rotten soul looming larger than life. Though not always successful onstage, this satire laced with wit and underlying seriousness is good reading.

Scenes from American Life, as the title indicates, is a montage depicting the upper-middle-class society that Gurney knows so well. Like most of his plays, this one lends itself to easy production. The set is attractive, simple, and functional, with the action flowing around a burnished baby-grand piano. To achieve this feeling of flow, no curtain is used and few blackouts; one scene blends naturally into the next, with the actors setting up the stage and carrying on and off their props and costumes. Music plays an integral part in this drama, establishing the time and tone of each scene. Props, accessories, and costumes also help anchor the date of a particular scene.

The play is set in Buffalo; the time fluctuates from the early 1930's of the opening scene to the mid-1980's. One character, Snoozer, serves to unify the diverse vignettes. From the opening scene of his christening to the final scene, when inebriated, he participates in the burning of a canoe, the play depicts the passing of an old order of Americanism. Four male actors and four female actors are all that are required for producing these vignettes. These eight characters may act various roles in the various scenes, with the stipulation that the same actor and actress play the father and mother in the first and last scenes. In the intermittent scenes, sons play fathers and mothers daughters so as to keep the play from appearing to be about only one or two families. A sense of virtuosity prevails. Here is a kaleidoscope of scenes from America.

Here again, Gurney satirizes upper-middle-class society. The characters are self-centered, modish, pampered, misguided, opinionated, and bored.

They speak in clichés and find their world disappearing. Like an unmoored boat, they float along. At times the satire is more biting than in Gurney's earlier plays, but the message is clear and the entertainment delightful. The language, typical of these characters, helps reveal their plight. A toast to the Father, the Son, and the best gin ever smuggled across Niagara River is followed by chatter about a pusher and manners at meals. The characters' names underscore the satire. Snoozer earns his name by sleeping through everything; Grace, Snoozer's godmother, to the tune of "The Star Spangled Banner" boozily proposes a one-word toast to Snoozer, "responsibility." From the Depression days of Franklin D. Roosevelt to an apocalyptic vision of a Fascist America in the 1980's (a decade in the future when the play was produced), Gurney depicts a vapid society that lacks any moral foundation.

In one of the drama's strongest scenes, a father takes his son, who is in trouble for draft evasion, out for a day's sailing. Quoting his own code of honor, which is anachronistic to the boy, the father tries to persuade his son to stand trial and go to prison. His son tells him off with one epithet. In another scene typical of Gurney's dramas, a Yale graduate dictates a letter to a classmate declaring that he will not contribute to the alumni animal fund; midway into the letter, however, he resorts to the usual clichés, sending his wife's regards and an enclosed check. Gurney's recurring theme of freedom and coercion is evident in a luncheon scene with a mother and daughter. The mother says that the daughter may do as she pleases, choosing between a coming-out party and a college education, yet in spite of the daughter's protests in favor of an education, the mother ultimately decides on the party.

Not surprisingly, Gurney has often been compared to novelist and short-story writer John Cheever, the rueful chronicler of suburbia. Gurney's play *Children*, based on Cheever's story "Goodbye, My Brother," is another satire on the old gentry as they conduct themselves when they come face-to-face with the upheavals of the present. *Children* provides actors with a number of splendid roles, but, as in several other Gurney plays, the characters who motivate much of the action are never seen onstage. These include Pokey, scion of the genteel family at the center of the action, who stands ominously in the shadows offstage; his braless Jewish wife, who holds a doctoral degree; and their uninhibited child. Also unseen but significant to the action is the rich local builder, who once worked as a yard boy for the WASP family.

Set in a summer house on an island off the Northeast coast during a Fourth of July weekend in 1970, *Children* includes four characters who appear onstage: an affluent, attractive mother; her daughter, Barbara, a divorceé; her son, Randy; and his wife, Jane. Though a slight disruption threatens and slight violence erupts, the play ends in unrelieved, unenlightened stasis. The characters prefer withdrawing into their status quo, staying put, deeply embedded in the customary ground of their past. Here, as in *Scenes from American Life*, Gurney presents intelligent entertainment for a wide audience, offering an ironic portrait of a classic WASP family that is losing its identity in a changing America. Subversive forces are undermining what is eventually revealed as the hypocrisy of an entire way of life.

The Wayside Motor Inn, like *Scenes from American Life*, is composed of scenes that flow into each other. Five separate subplots take place simultaneously in one room of a suburban motor lodge outside Boston during the late afternoon and early evening of a spring day in the late 1970's. Like other Gurney plays, *The Wayside Motor Inn* deals with decadent Americans. Each of the five plots dramatizes the plight of WASP society, underscoring the characters' inability to escape to freedom. Such key words as "door," "escape," and "choose" hint at a choice, but the characters cannot bestir themselves to act decisively. They are not so much enthralled as self-entrapped. They and their language ring true to themselves and to life. They mirror, enlighten, and entertain.

A Willy Loman–type father confronts his Biff-like son to no avail, while a couple pondering divorce look out from the balcony at the world, then come back inside for a drink. A traveling salesman bitterly chafes under the domination of the computerized world, while a young college couple can make love only when hyped up by dope and a hot tub. Another couple snap at each other between fits of sympathy, contempt, and boredom. The television in the background amplifies and extends the drama of ordinary life. These ten ordinary people find themselves at the wayside of their lives, wondering which turn to take. Their difficulties and conflicts are commonplace, but Gurney succeeds in giving them resonance by presenting them side by side, simultaneously, onstage, thereby making the ordinary seem somehow extraordinary. The diverse scenes flow into an organic whole, commenting on the dark undercurrents of modern life.

Gurney scored his greatest hit with *The Dining Room*. In this play, the dining room becomes a metaphor for the continuity of bourgeois values, challenged by the younger generation in the latter part of the twentieth century. The space of the dining room itself—and the changing use of the space as scenes from different time periods are going on simultaneously—dramatizes the ways in which these values have been distorted. Through a humorously poignant series of vignettes, Gurney dramatizes the changing role of the classical, formal dining room through the course of three generations of WASPs. The changes are bittersweet—in some ways inevitable, but lamentable—a combination of continuity and change. Like Gurney, the little boy in the play views his great aunt's Waterford crystal finger bowls with fascination, seeing in them the habits of a vanishing culture, a neurotic obsession with cleanliness associated with the guilt of the last stages of capitalism. In its combination of moral critique, satiric wit, and humane sympathy, *The Dining Room* epitomizes Gurney's contribution to contemporary American drama.

Other major works

NOVELS: *The Gospel According to Joe*, 1974; *Entertaining Strangers*, 1977; *The Snow Ball*, 1984.

SCREENPLAY: *The House of Mirth*, 1972.

TELEPLAY: *O Youth and Beauty*, 1980 (based on a short story by John Cheever).

Bibliography

Curtis, Charlotte. "The Fadeout of a Culture," in *The New York Times*. April 5, 1983, p. C9.

Gurney, A. R., Jr. "Pushing the Walls of Dramatic Form," in *The New York Times*. CXXXI (July 27, 1982), sec. II, p. 1.

Levett. "A. R. Gurney Writing About the World He Knows," in *Dramatists*. LVI (October, 1984), p. 5.

Oliver, Edith. "The Theatre," in *The New Yorker*. XLIV (November 9, 1968), pp. 115-116.

_____. "The Theatre," in *The New Yorker*. XLVII (April 3, 1971), pp. 95-97.

Helen H. Naugle

TAWFIQ AL-HAKIM

Born: October 9, 1898; Alexandria, Egypt

Principal drama

Khatim Sulayman, pr. 1924; *al-Mar'ah al-jadidah*, pr. 1926, pb. 1952; *Ahl al-kahf*, pb. 1933, pr. 1935 (partial translation, *The People of the Cave*, 1955-1957); *Shahrazad*, pb. 1934, pr. 1966 (English translation, 1955); *Muhammad*, pb. 1936 (partial English translation, 1955); *Nahr al-junun*, pb. 1937 (*The River of Madness*, 1963); *Piraksa: Aw, Mushkilat al-hukm*, part 1 pb. 1939, part 2 pb. 1960; *Salah al-mala 'ikah*, pb. 1941 (*Angels' Prayer*, 1981); *Pijmalyun*, pb. 1942, pr. 1953 (*Pygmalion*, 1961); *Sulayman al-hakim*, pb. 1943 (*The Wisdom of Solomon*, 1981); *Himari qala li*, pb. 1945 (short plays, one translated as *The Donkey Market*, 1981); *al-Malik Udib*, pb. 1949 (*King Oedipus*, 1981); *Ughniyah al-mawt*, pb. 1950, pr. 1956 (*The Song of Death*, 1973); *al-Aydi al-na'imah*, pb. 1954, pr. 1957 (*Tender Hands*, 1984); *Bayna al-harb wa-al-salam*, pb. 1956 (*Between War and Peace*, 1984); *Rihlah ila al-ghad*, pb. 1957 (*Voyage to Tomorrow*, 1984); *al-Sultan al-ha'ir*, pb. 1960, pr. 1961 (*The Sultan's Dilemma*, 1973); *Ya tali' al-shajarah*, pb. 1962 (*The Tree Climber*, 1966); *al-Ta'am li-kull fam*, pb. 1963, pr. 1964 (*Food for the Millions*, 1984); *Shams al-Nahar*, pr. 1964, pb. 1965 (*Princess Sunshine*, 1981); *Masir Sursar*, pb. 1966, pr. 1969 (*Fate of a Cockroach*, 1973); *Kullu shay' fi mahallihi*, pb. 1966 (*Not a Thing Out of Place*, 1973); *al-Wartah*, pb. 1966 (*Incrimination*, 1984); *Ahl al-qamar*, pb. 1969 (*Poet on the Moon*, 1984); *al-Dunya riwayah hazaliyah*, pb. 1971, pr. 1972. Many of al-Hakim's dramatic works may be found in collections such as *Masrahiyat* (1937, two volumes), *Masrah al-mujtama'* (1950), and *al-Masrah al-munawwa'* (1956). The most important collections of plays in English translation are *Fate of a Cockroach: Four Plays of Freedom* (1973) and *Plays, Prefaces, and Postscripts of Tawfiq al-Hakim* (1981, 1984, two volumes).

Other literary forms

In addition to the drama, Tawfiq al-Hakim has been active in a number of genres. Among his novels, written rather early in his career, *al-Qasr al-mashur* (1936; the enchanted palace) is notable as a collaborative effort composed with the distinguished man of letters Taha Husayn. His most celebrated work of long fiction, *Yawmiyat na'ib fi al-aryaf* (1937; *Maze of Justice*, 1947), draws upon al-Hakim's experience as a legal functionary and deftly combines social commentary with satire. Other novels are significant as indications of al-Hakim's propensity to experiment with this form of fiction. At intervals during his career, al-Hakim wrote short stories, which are most readily accessible through the two-volume collection *Qisas*, published in

1949. He has also published a number of essentially autobiographical works, of which *Sijn al-'umr* (1964; the prison of life) deserves particular mention; *Zahrat al-'umr* (1943; life in flower) is a compilation of letters, translated from the French, from al-Hakim's correspondence with those he met during his student days in Paris. Reflections on drama, art, and life are presented in works of literary criticism such as *Min al-burj al-'aji* (1941; from the ivory tower) and *Fann al-adab* (1952; the art of literature), as well as other studies. For a number of years, beginning in 1943, al-Hakim has written columns for the influential newspapers *Akhbar al-yawm* (news of the day) and *al-Ahram* (the pyramids) of Cairo. His collection of political essays, *'Awdat al-wa'y* (1974; *The Return of Consciousness*, 1985), and a companion volume of documents published the next year, aroused criticism in some circles and wonderment in others, for their unfavorable commentary on the government of Egypt under President Gamal Abdel Nasser.

Achievements

At the beginning of the twentieth century, drama in Egypt and the Arab world remained a derivative and largely secondary form of creative expression; puppet and shadow plays were produced alongside adaptations drawn for the most part from French and Italian playwrights. Some innovations were introduced on the Egyptian stage with the production of works by Salim Khalil al-Naqqash, Ya'qub Sannu' (James Sanua), and Ahmad Shawqi. After World War I, important new plays were written by Mahmud Taymur; Najib al-Rihani's performances in comic roles also aroused interest in the theater. Nevertheless, with only an exiguous native tradition, Tawfiq al-Hakim came to the forefront of modern Egyptian dramatists with strikingly original depictions of time-honored Middle Eastern themes. His earlier work, particularly that beginning with *Ahl al-kahf*, achieved the fusion of regional themes with European techniques. More than that, al-Hakim's work came to be classed as pioneering on at least three other fronts as well. He has brought to the Egyptian and Arab stage unique and distinctive interpretations of Western works, notably versions of classical Greek drama. Many of his works have a surrealistic bent, suggesting analogies, which he has encouraged, with the Western Theater of the Absurd. He has also been among the first Arab dramatists to write dialogue in colloquial language; purists, who insisted upon the use of classical Arabic, were outraged, but others have conceded that the effects may have heightened the contrasts between the timeless and the mundane that are integral concerns of al-Hakim's productions. His efforts to introduce idiomatic usage into the language of the stage have been followed by those of other notable playwrights; this trend in itself marks the extent to which, largely as a result of al-Hakim's influence, drama has developed from the stylized, ritualistic forms that characterized the early Arab theater.

Notwithstanding the decidedly mixed reception accorded his works during the early phases of his career, Tawfiq al-Hakim has received a number of awards and honors in his native country. In 1951 he was made director general of the Egyptian National Library, and three years later he became a member of the Academy of the Arabic Language in Cairo. He was awarded the cordon of the republic in 1958, and he served as Egypt's representative to UNESCO, in Paris, during the following two years. He received the State Literature Prize in 1961, and in 1963 a theater in Cairo was formally named for him. His position as the preeminent modern dramatist in the Arab world was underscored when a Tawfiq al-Hakim Festival was held at the University of Cairo in 1969; at that time he also presided over a Congress of Arab Dramatists that was held in the Egyptian capital. In 1974, he became president of his country's Story Writers' Club. Although personally at times he may have been inclined to overstate his own importance—during the early 1960's he announced his candidacy for the Nobel Prize for Literature— Tawfiq al-Hakim's stature has been imposing among Middle Eastern playwrights, and on the international level his works are almost certainly the most widely recognized of any Arab dramatic productions.

Biography

For some time, the date of Tawfiq al-Hakim's birth was in doubt—in places the year 1902 was cited, but later October 9, 1898, was accepted as proved. It is certain that he was born in Alexandria, Egypt, of an Arab doctor and a mother who was descended from a family of Ottoman officials and army officers. Although his education moved forward slowly during his early years, al-Hakim evinced an early interest in dramatic storytelling. In 1915, he entered the Muhammad Ali Secondary School in Cairo, and he received the baccalaureate in 1921. His youth evidently was marred somewhat by difficult relations with his mother, and a brief, unrequited love affair did nothing to improve his attitude toward women. During the short-lived revolution of 1919, which was provoked by the exile of Sa'd Zaghlul, a prominent national leader, to Malta, al-Hakim was imprisoned for composing patriotic songs. His incarceration was brief and hardly unpleasant; at about that time he wrote his first play, a work that Cairo producers would not stage because of its defiantly anti-British standpoint.

For four years, until 1925, al-Hakim studied law at the state university in Cairo; increasingly it became evident that his proclivities, and his real calling, lay elsewhere. His further efforts at the writing of drama brought forth *al-Mar'ah al-jadidah* (modern woman), which was composed in 1923 and produced on the stage three years later. Three other short plays, including *Khatim Sulayman* (the ring of Solomon), were produced in 1924, shortly after he had committed them to paper. In spite of an undistinguished academic record—he graduated third from last among those who were promoted in his class—he entered the Collège des Lois at the Sorbonne in Paris. At that time he was still guided in part by his father's wish that he should become a lawyer, and evidently he was otherwise undecided about which direction his career should take. During his student years in France— between 1925 and 1928—he spent much of his time reading, sightseeing, and absorbing as much European culture as possible. In addition to philosophy and narrative fiction, he delved at length into published drama and attended performances of major plays. It would seem that he was particularly fascinated by the works of Henrik Ibsen, George Bernard Shaw, and Luigi Pirandello; classical Greek theater also left a lasting impression on him. The lack of an Arab dramatic tradition, which had troubled him during his first efforts in Egypt, was brought home to him more definitely; along the way, two love affairs, which turned out badly, added further poignancy to his outlook. In 1928, having passed all but one of his examinations, he returned to Egypt, ostensibly to commence work within the legal profession, but with his creative aspirations probably now foremost in his mind.

After an apprenticeship of one year in Alexandria, al-Hakim served as a public prosecutor in various rural communities between 1929 and 1934; he then became director of the investigation bureau of the Ministry of Education, and in 1939 he was appointed to a position in the Ministry of Social Affairs. In 1943 he left public service to devote himself entirely to writing; it may readily be inferred from his fictional and autobiographical works that he regarded government positions as sinecures, an attitude he also detected in those around him. The decisive event of his career as a playwright was the publication in 1933 of his *Ahl al-kahf*; al-Hakim's transfer from legal to bureaucratic responsibilities may have been a result of the uproar that greeted this work. Although Taha Husayn, a leading critic, and other men of letters praised its bold, unconventional approach, others castigated it for its use of informal, even ungrammatical, language. *Shahrazad* had already been published (in 1934) when an outcry broke out over the staged version of *Ahl al-kahf*; audiences rejected it as far too long and too far removed from the formal routines that they had come to expect from the theater. Typical of other dramatic works from this period are *Muhammad*, a lengthy treatment of episodes from the life of the Prophet, and other works set in classical times. In 1936, al-Hakim, on a visit to Europe, attended the Salzburg Theater Festival, and in 1938 he vacationed in the Alps, in an effort again to maintain cultural contacts abroad.

The next period of al-Hakim's creative life is sometimes associated with the title of his book *Min al-burj al-'aji*, which refers to the literary life as being led in an "ivory tower." To be sure, some of his writings expressed concern about Nazi ambitions during World War II; in a more general light, he also wrote about his fears for world peace during an age dominated by brute militarism and technology. Other works explored classical Greek themes or considered episodes from the Old Testament that are also part of Islamic lore. In 1946 he was married, and thereafter fathered a son and three daughters; critics later have tried to determine the effect his family life has had upon the obvious though sometimes playful misogyny of his literary efforts.

His reputation as a playwright detached from ideological concerns was reinforced during the period surrounding the Egyptian revolution of 1952 and the ultimate withdrawal of British forces from that country in 1956. In 1953, al-Hakim's version of Shaw's *Pygmalion* was staged at the Salzburg Theater Festival; in 1960, *The Sultan's Dilemma* was published simultaneously in Cairo and, in a French translation, in Paris. He was honored by President Gamal Abdel Nasser, who secured official awards for him and attended the production premiere of *Tender Hands* in 1957. The author thus had reason to believe that his renown and acceptance of his works were on the rise. His works were also produced in other Arab countries; some of them were successfully adapted for the cinema. Quite apart from experiments with language, he turned increasingly to futuristic, global concerns or to the bemused contemplation of the absurdities in everyday life. Students of the theater struggled to find political allusions in al-Hakim's later plays; some of them were set in remote historical periods and others took place in future ages.

In January, 1973, the dramatist became directly embroiled in public concerns; he presented President Anwar el-Sadat with a letter on behalf of forty-six writers, protesting the nation's indecisive stance against Israel. Although for a brief period publication and production of al-Hakim's work were suspended, in October of that year war broke out, and the aging author vociferously supported Egypt's military efforts. By 1974 a short treatise that al-Hakim had written which criticized the excesses and extravagances of the Nasser years was cleared for publication, in keeping with Sadat's efforts to chart a political course of his own. Although this work, *The Return of Consciousness*, was denounced by Nasser's remaining supporters (who, among other questions, asked why al-Hakim had remained silent until four years after their leader's death), it became a best-seller for some time; in 1975, it was reported that a companion volume, which presented documents from the author's work, in its turn had become the most popular book in Egypt. Although he has not gone further in his professed intention to open the political files from his country's recent past, al-Hakim has remained an important and widely cited newspaper columnist. In line with the nation's foreign policy, at times he has suggested that Egypt and Israel may serve as islands of security in the Middle East. He has also edited and supervised the collection of the numerous dramatic writings and other works that he has composed over the years. Moreover, as the senior representative of an important modern tradition in Arabic and Egyptian literature, his works have been reprinted and have been made available in many parts of the world. Translations of al-Hakim's writings exist in French, Spanish, Italian, German, Hebrew, Russian, and Japanese, as well as other Middle Eastern languages; English language compilations of his major plays have also done much to increase his following.

Analysis

The drama of Tawfiq al-Hakim displays a remarkable diversity of outlook, and his breadth of vision inspires respect mingled slightly with awe. His cosmopolitan standpoint, coupled with his relentless quest for the new and untried, is in evidence across the span of his career. He has been extraordinarily prolific; one recent count yielded eighty-four titles of dramatic works that he has composed, quite apart from his writings in other genres. His plays have been set in historical periods from the times of King Solomon of the Old Testament, through the age of classical Greek drama, across early and medieval periods of Islamic history, on to modern times in Egypt, and beyond, into the space age. He has depicted the rustic peasant landscapes of his native country, the courts of great monarchs from the past, and the cosmic scenery of new worlds to come. It may well be argued that his work is uneven, both in its technical execution and where depth of characterization is involved. It would seem that his penchant for the unexpected and the unusual at times may have affected the direction of his dramatic efforts; any facile attempt to devise categories for his works is doomed to frustration. Nevertheless, although even a chronological approach would be subject to anomalies and overlapping impulses may be observed in many areas, there are some broad elements of thematic continuity that may be discerned in the development of al-Hakim's repertory.

The historical contexts for major early works were derived from Islamic religious and literary traditions. *Ahl al-kahf*, the work which in 1933 was hailed as heralding the onset of a new era in Arab drama and which elicited stormy protests on the part of subsequent audiences, deals with the Christian legend of the Seven Sleepers of Ephesus, which is also cited in the Koran. In this play, visions of the miraculous, hope, and despair are presented in a light that is broadly consonant with the convictions of Muslim believers, but without prejudice to the Christian values that are also affirmed by Islam. *Shahrazad* is al-Hakim's effort to supply a continuation of the *The Arabian Nights' Entertainments*; when the fabled storyteller survives and marries the monarch from the tale, some poignant and revealing reflections on nature, beauty, and mortality are recorded. *Muhammad*, which serves as a sort of Muslim Passion play, is a sweeping pageant that was meant to demonstrate al-Hakim's belief that suitable dramatic forms could be found to evoke themes from the life of the Prophet. This play may also point to the author's contention that the drama is meant to be read as much as it is meant to be viewed: in one edition there are a prologue, three acts, and an epilogue, comprising, in all, ninety-five scenes.

Absolute power and helplessness are treated in plays taken from past epochs of Oriental despotism. In *The River of Madness*, a one-act production, a monarch's subjects drink mystical waters which render them impervious to his commands; at the end, the unnamed ruler also seeks wisdom in this form of supposed madness. It is not clear who is sane and who is not, or from whence real authority springs. For all of his powers, the biblical King Solomon is unable to win the favor of a beautiful woman, in one of al-Hakim's longer works, *The Wisdom of Solomon*. This effort, which draws upon characters depicted in one of the author's earliest plays, *Khatim Sulayman*, opens when a jinni appears to a humble fisherman and informs him of his quarrel with the king. He hopes for reinstatement into Solomon's good graces. When the Queen of Sheba, the most beautiful of all women, is brought before the mighty monarch, Solomon in all his glory is unable to win her favor. He is tempted to enlist the spirit, but is reluctant to summon unearthly powers. The queen remains demure as ever, and for all his countless treasures and innumerable wives, the great ruler falls prey to the frailties of the flesh; he becomes old and dies. At the end, the jinni warns that love and power will provoke struggle on this earth for centuries and ages to come.

Themes of punishment and justice converge with concerns about past politics in some of the author's later plays. In *The Sultan's Dilemma*, which is set in late medieval Egypt, a man is sentenced to death for maintaining that the sultan is a slave; a lady intervenes on his behalf, demonstrates that the condemned man is indeed correct, and in the end the ruler's place before the people must be redeemed by a complicated process of manumission. By emphasizing the absurdities of a bygone political system (where in fact under the Mamluk Dynasty the loftiest as well as the lowliest positions were occupied by those who in a technical legal sense were held in bonded servitude), al-Hakim implies that authority and official dignity are transitory attributes that are real only to the extent that society accepts them. *Princess Sunshine* has an unspecified medieval setting, during the reign of a certain Sultan Nu'man. He rules over an odd kingdom: Princes from all around are flogged to deter them from courting the princess; executions must be halted because the gallows rope has been stolen. Harmony is achieved, however, when the princess agrees to marry one of her suitors, even after she learns that he is actually a commoner and his real name is the unprepossessing Dindan.

Works that are borrowed from Western traditions exhibit another facet of al-Hakim's conception of the drama. Aristophanes was the original source for *Piraksa: Aw, Mushkilat al-hukm* (Praxagora: or, the difficulties of government). The Egyptian playwright's version turns out to be an exercise in political discourse; some ludicrous problems arise when the protagonist of the title subjects ancient Athens to a form of feminist communism. *Pygmalion*, though suggested by George Bernard Shaw's work, also takes up classical concerns. A Cypriot Greek artist calls upon the goddess Venus to endow one of his statues with life; when he falls in love with his creation, Pygmalion, the title character, fears that he will have to abandon sculpture. This work, published in 1942, highlights the conflicting demands of life, love, and art in a felicitous union of several disparate approaches to the drama. A major work in al-Hakim's canon is *King Oedipus*, which is an adaptation of Sophocles' *Oedipus Tyrannus* (c. 429 B.C.); in this version, the tragic denouement takes place when the monarch learns that he is not of royal birth. He is driven by a zealous pursuit of the truth even beyond the doors that should not be opened. Curiosity is Oedipus' tragic flaw; when he learns that he was adopted, he is blinded. It is noteworthy here that, without introducing overt references to Islam, the pantheon of Greek gods from the original tragedy is replaced with suggestions of a monotheistic purpose. Countervailing concerns with predestination and free will arise when al-Hakim points to problems of divine intentions in this world.

Contemporary social issues figure in many of al-Hakim's plays, sometimes in a bizarre, mocking sense; but a more straightforward presentation of these themes may be found in *Tender Hands*, which concerns the place in society of university graduates who have more formal learning than practical training. Whether grammatical usage has any relevance to the management of an oil company is a problem that is no more readily resolved than the just division of household tasks for a prospective couple. Nevertheless, all ends happily when a marriage uniting two leading characters is secured.

Whimsical and broadly comic themes have been pursued in several of al-Hakim's works; this is the case with *Himari qala li* (my donkey said to me). In this group of dramatic sketches, the author's donkey asks him questions about life's predicaments; in some sequences the roles of human and animal almost seem to be reversed, as ordinary logic appears inadequate to explain the anomalies of man's condition. In some of his works, al-Hakim has acknowledged the examples of European playwrights such as Bertolt Brecht, Samuel Beckett, and Eugène Ionesco; in 1962 he announced that his most recent play had an irrationalist inspiration, and some affinities with the Theater of the Absurd, in the introduction to one of his best-known works. *The Tree Climber* opens as a retired railway inspector is perplexed by the simultaneous disappearance of his wife and a female lizard that had lived under their orange tree. After police interrogation, and with the testimony of a bizarre dervish who appears at the train station, the old railwayman confesses to murder and claims that by burying his wife's body under the tree he had hoped to increase its yield of fruit. The lawmen begin digging, but they uncover nothing; the wife reappears later, and, when her husband questions her about her absence, he becomes enraged by her evasive answers. He strangles her, puts the body in the hole the police have left under the tree, and then is distracted by the mysterious dervish. During their conversation, the wife's body vanishes; in its place they find the body of the lizard, the man's talisman of good fortune.

Another notable effort in the same vein is *Fate of a Cockroach*, which commences with a satirical view of order and legitimacy in the insect world. The cockroach king takes precedence over the queen because his whiskers are longer, but the female talks of mobilizing her sex for a war against predatory ants; the two seem to agree, however, that their species is the most advanced on the planet. Unknown to them, a married couple is arguing about the equitable disbursement of household funds. The wife asks the husband to kill a cockroach in their bathtub; when first the man and then the woman begin instead to contemplate the insect in admiration, a doctor is called in. He cannot understand either one of them because he has never been married. For a certain time, the husband and the wife quarrel about rank and obedience in a way that recalls the argument between the cockroach king and queen; relations seem more strained than ever after the maid, in the course of her cleaning routine, drowns the insect without a second thought. *Not a Thing Out of Place* is a brisk one-act piece which has villagers talking of melons that resemble human heads and a philosophically inclined donkey when they go off to join a local dance.

Themes of violence and guilt—notably those that elude any judicial resolution—are taken up in certain works. The one-act play *The Song of Death* deals with a blood vendetta between peasant families in Upper Egypt; a young university graduate is unable to persuade them that they would be better concerned with technological means to improve their living standards. While power, punishment, and the political order have been considered in plays set in earlier periods, an absurdist treatment of crime during modern times is presented in *Incrimination*. Here a law professor who has written learned treatises on criminal psychology, but has never met any lawbreakers, is introduced to some local gang members. When a policeman is shot to death during a jewel theft, the scholar agrees to defend his acquaintance from the underworld in court; by a strange transposition of the clues, however, the evidence in the end points to the professor. It would seem, then, that in the author's view guilt and innocence have no more fixed constancy than visual illusions. *Voyage to Tomorrow* begins with a crime story and ends with some of the ironic, futuristic twists that are notable in al-Hakim's later drama. A man who perpetrated murder while in the throes of romantic infatuation is allowed to participate in an experimental, and extremely hazardous, space flight; his companion is a fellow convict who had committed four murders for personal gain. Against all the odds they survive and return to earth during a future age when all material wants are provided for and people routinely live several hundred years; this state, however, is actually a despotism wherein love and romance are regarded as unwanted, somehow subversive relics of the past. The first convict, after a brief flirtation with a sympathetic brunette, threatens to kill a security guard who tries to separate them; he comes close to committing murder again for the sake of a woman. Here the great themes of conscience and emotional commitment are interwoven with the author's visionary and speculative concerns.

A final grouping of al-Hakim's works might include those that deal with global issues. Here a question that is frequently posed is whether science will benefit humanity or assist in its mass destruction; this issue has been taken up at intervals across much of al-Hakim's career. In his attitude toward World War II, and in his considerations on the advent of nuclear weapons and rivalries in space exploration, al-Hakim has dealt with important developments in advance of many other Arab authors. The short play *Angels' Prayer* depicts an angel who comes to earth; he finds a monk and a scientist quarreling over responsibility for the wayward path of the human race. The angel is later captured, tried, and executed at the behest of two tyrants who resemble Adolf Hitler and Benito Mussolini. When he returns to Heaven, still holding his apple of peace which the dictators have vainly tried to take from him, he urges the other angels to pray for the inhabitants of the earth. The one-act play *Between War and Peace* has an odd bit of personification: characters named War and Peace meet in the boudoir of a lady named Diplomacy, where their deliberations resemble the intrigues of a lovers' triangle. Human issues in the nuclear age are examined in *Food for the Millions*. A scientific prodigy claims to have made a discovery more important than the atom bomb: Food can be produced at an infinitesimal fraction of its original cost, and families everywhere will be able to have it in abundance. Others compare this project to the fond dreams of science fiction, and it falls by the wayside when the youth and other family members learn that their mother, before remarrying, may have acted to hasten the death of their seriously ill father. Toward the end of the drama there are some homely but portentous musings on water stains that repeatedly appear on their apartment walls; these may be symbolic of guilt in the household that has not yet been expunged. In one of his last plays, *Poet on the Moon*, al-Hakim describes a flight to the moon on which, in spite of some misgivings from the authorities, a poet is allowed to accompany two astronauts. When they arrive, the poet is the only one who can hear the voices of moon creatures, who warn against any attempt to remove precious or hitherto unknown minerals from their domain. Upon the return of the spacecraft to earth, the creatures effect the mysterious transmutation of moon rocks into ordinary vitreous earth, thus averting any premature or unprincipled exploitation of outer space.

Although al-Hakim's dramatic imagination has ranged across at least three millennia of human experience, touching down at particularly evocative points along the way, some generalizations may be made about common features in much of his work. Characterization has been important, but something less than a vital issue in his efforts; for that matter some leading personages have been typecast as abstract categories, such as war and peace, while others have been significant not for their intrinsic qualities but as participants in seemingly irrational situations. Characters in the plays based on medieval themes might possibly be interchanged with others from similar works. The domestic dramas also feature some stock types who seem to appear under various names in works of this kind. The author never claimed to have developed a florid, polished style—indeed, he purposely avoided such tendencies—and his dialogue has a crisp, staccato ring that often serves to heighten dramatic tension. There are, in many of his works, series of exclamations and interjections that, particularly in the absurdist dramas, merge with scenes taken up mainly with the exchange of questions. Even the most carefully constructed plays have been meant as much for the reader as for the theater audience. While some works have enjoyed considerably more success on the stage than others, the structure of al-Hakim's major dramatic efforts has been determined more by his thematic concerns than by the requirements of actual production. Many plays have long sequences of brief scenes, or sometimes present lengthy acts alternating with short, abrupt transitional passages. On another level, regardless of whether, during his classical or his absurdist phases, al-Hakim has resolved the perennial questions of love, art, guilt, and social division, his works have posed these issues in unusual and distinctively original variations. Although at times he has complained that during thirty years he attempted to accomplish for the Arab theater what it had taken Western civilization two thousand years to achieve, the freshness of his works, and the extent to which he has realized the conjunction of diverse aesthetic and moral concerns, should signify the magnitude of Tawfiq al-Hakim's efforts within and indeed beyond the limits of the drama as he had found them.

Other major works

NOVELS: *'Awdat al-ruh*, 1933; *al-Qasr al-mashur*, 1936 (with Taha Husayn); *Yawmiyat na'ib fi al-aryaf*, 1937 (*Maze of Justice*, 1947); *'Usfur min al-Sharq*, 1938 (*Bird of the East*, 1966); *Raqisat al-ma'bad*, 1939; *al-Ribat al-muqaddas*, 1944.

SHORT FICTION: *Qisas*, 1949 (two volumes); *Arini Allah*, 1953.

NONFICTION: *Tahta shams al-fikr*, 1938; *Tahta al-misbah al-akhdar*, 1941; *Min al-burj al-'aji*, 1941; *Zahrat al-'umr*, 1943; *Fann al-adab*, 1952; *Sijn al-'umr*, 1964; *Qalabuna al-masrahi*, 1967; *'Awdat al-wa'y*, 1974 (*The Return of Consciousness*, 1985); *Watha'iq fi tariq 'Awdat al-wa'y*, 1975; *Nazarat fi al-din, al-thaqafah, al-mujtama'*, 1979; *Mamalih dakhiliyah*, 1982.

Bibliography
Audebert, C. F. "Al-Hakim's *Ya Tali' al-Shajara* and Folk Art," in *Journal of Arabic Literature*. IX (1978), pp. 138-149.

Awad, Louis. "Problems of the Egyptian Theatre," in *Studies in Modern Arabic Literature*, 1975. Edited by R. C. Ostle.

Cachia, Pierre. "Idealism and Ideology: The Case of Tawfiq al-Hakim," in *Journal of the American Oriental Society*. C, no. 3 (1980), pp. 225-235.

Landau, Jacob M. *Studies in the Arab Theatre and Cinema*, 1958.

Long, Richard. *Tawfiq al Hakim: Playwright of Egypt*, 1979.

Somekh, Sasson. "The Diglottic Dilemma in the Drama of Tawfiq al-Hakim," in *Israel Oriental Studies*. IX (1979), pp. 392-403.

Starkey, Paul. "Philosophical Themes in Tawfiq al-Hakim's Drama," in *Journal of Arabic Literature*. VIII (1977), pp. 136-152.

J. R. Broadus

DAVID HARE

Born: Bexhill, England; June 5, 1947

Principal drama

Inside Out, pr. 1968 (with Tony Bicat; adaptation of Franz Kafka's diaries); *How Brophy Made Good*, pr. 1969, pb. 1971; *What Happened to Blake?*, pr. 1970; *Slag*, pr. 1970, pb. 1971; *The Rules of the Game*, pr. 1971 (adaptation of Luigi Pirandello's play); *Lay By*, pr. 1971, pb. 1972 (with Howard Brenton, Brian Clark, Trevor Griffiths, Stephen Poliakoff, Hugh Stoddart, and Snoo Wilson); *Deathsheads*, pr. 1971; *England's Ireland*, pr. 1972 (with others); *The Great Exhibition*, pr., pb. 1972; *Brassneck*, pr. 1973, pb. 1974 (with Brenton); *Knuckle*, pr., pb. 1974; *Fanshen*, pr. 1975, pb. 1976 (adaptation of William Hinton's book *Fanshen: A Documentary of Revolution in a Chinese Village*); *Teeth 'n' Smiles*, pr. 1975, pb. 1976 (music by Nick Bicat, lyrics by Tony Bicat); *Plenty*, pr., pb. 1978; *A Map of the World*, pr., pb. 1983; *Pravda: A Fleet Street Comedy*, pr., pb. 1985 (with Brenton); *The Bay at Nice*, pr. 1986; *Wrecked Eggs*, pr. 1986.

Other literary forms

While continuing to work in the theater, David Hare turned to television in 1973 to write and produce *Man Above Men* for the British Broadcasting Corporation (BBC), followed by *Licking Hitler*, which Hare authored and directed for the BBC in 1978, *Dreams of Leaving* (1980), and *Saigon: Year of the Cat* (1983). In 1985, Hare adapted his play *Plenty* for the motion-picture screen and also wrote and directed *Wetherby*, which some critics regarded as a better film than *Plenty*. *Wetherby* demonstrated that Hare could work effectively in the medium of film as a total artist.

Achievements

Hare has been identified as a Socialist playwright, a committed artist whose concerns are predominantly moral and often satiric. His work reflects the stance of the "angry" writers of the 1950's carried forward into a second generation of "furious" playwrights, as Jack Kroll has aptly described them. Hare's English characters are shaped by the postwar realities of British life; some of them (such as Susan, the central character of *Plenty*) have not properly adjusted to a changing world, while others (such as Curly, the central character of *Knuckle*) have adjusted at the expense of becoming hardened and cynical or morally complacent. Hare has a genius for drawing strong, distinctive characters who often behave outrageously. Although many of the plays are set in his native England, his concerns are global, as reflected by increasingly international and exotic settings for the later plays: New York,

Leningrad, Saigon, India, and the People's Republic of China, for example. He has also extended his work from the stage to film and television. Hare has a unique talent for dramatizing people under pressure and confronted with crises—social, commercial, moral, revolutionary, and political. His scope is impressively broad, and his concerns in general involve issues of truth, honesty, and integrity. Indeed, the title of one of his most successful plays of the 1980's, *Pravda*, means "truth." Hare has been favorably compared with Bertolt Brecht (for *Fanshen*, his documentary play about the Chinese Revolution, "the nearest any English contemporary writer has come to emulating Brecht," in the estimation of Michael Coveney) and Harold Pinter, perhaps the most gifted playwright of the previous generation. Among younger talents, the volume and quality of his work may perhaps be matched by Tom Stoppard, but few others. After the success of *Slag* in 1970, Hare won the *Evening Standard* Award for Most Promising Playwright. In 1974, *Knuckle* won for him the John Llewellyn Rhys Award. In 1979, the British Academy of Film and Television Arts voted *Licking Hitler* the Best Television Play of the Year. In 1985, the film *Wetherby*, which Hare both wrote and directed, won the Berlin Film Festival's Golden Bear Award.

Biography

David Hare was born in Bexhill, England, on June 5, 1947, the son of Clifford Theodore Rippon and the former Agnes Gillmour, his wife. Hare was first educated at Lancing College before going on to Jesus College, Cambridge, where he earned a master's degree, with honors, in 1968. Hare began writing plays at the age of twenty-two. In 1970, his first full-length play, *Slag*, about three women teachers locked into a power struggle over a failing English boarding school, won for him the Most Promising Playwright Award granted by the *Evening Standard*, even though the play was not favorably received by some feminists, who considered the playwright to be sexist; others went so far as to call him a misogynist. *The New York Times* drama critic Clive Barnes described *Slag* as a metaphor for the decline of English society, following Hare's suggestion that the play was not so much about women as institutions. Also in 1970, Hare married Margaret Matheson, a marriage that produced three children before ending in divorce in 1980.

From the beginning of his theatrical career in 1968 when he cofounded the Portable Theatre Company (with Howard Brenton and Snoo Wilson), an experimental troupe that toured Great Britain, Hare demonstrated an interest in creative dramatic collaboration and in theatrical direction, as well as in writing plays. In 1969, Hare became literary manager of the Royal Court Theatre, and in 1970 he was appointed resident dramatist. (*Slag* was first produced at the Hampstead Theatre Club before being moved to the Royal Court.) After working at the Royal Court, Hare served as resident playwright at the Nottingham Playhouse, where his play *Brassneck* (written in collaboration with Howard Brenton), which traced corruption through three generations of a Midlands family, premiered in 1973. In 1974, Hare cofounded Joint Stock, another fringe company; *Fanshen* was done as a Joint Stock production in the city of Sheffield.

As a young man, Hare once worked for Pathé Pictorial and went on to write for television productions after having established himself as a successful playwright. *Saigon: Year of the Cat* was directed by Stephen Frears for Thames Television in 1983, for example, but his earlier award-winning teleplay, *Licking Hitler*, Hare wrote and directed himself for the BBC in 1978. In 1985, his film *Wetherby*, which Hare also wrote and directed, earned the Golden Bear Award at the Berlin Film Festival and received a large measure of critical acclaim internationally. Hare wrote the screenplay adaptation of *Plenty*, his most successful play to date, for a major motion picture that starred Meryl Streep, Charles Dance, and Sir John Gielgud and was directed by Fred Schepisi and released by Twentieth Century-Fox. Having earned a reputation as a sometimes controversial national playwright during the 1970's, Hare had established himself by the mid-1980's as a multifaceted writer and director of international scope and importance.

Analysis

David Hare's creative work can be sorted into three categories: plays he wrote and directed himself, scripts written for film and television productions, and plays written in collaboration with Howard Brenton and others. In discussing Hare for the journal *Modern Drama*, C. W. E. Bigsby described the playwright as having been shaped by his times, the political turmoil and social upheaval of the student rebellions of 1968 and the growing dissent over Western policy in Southeast Asia. Bigsby also noted that 1968 was the year that "marked the beginnings of the theatrical fringe in London." Active in fringe theater from the beginning of his dramatic career, Hare became one of the architects of the fringe movement.

Early in his career, for example, Hare became interested in dramatic collaboration, which later led to successful partnerships with Howard Brenton—*Brassneck* in 1973 and *Pravda* in 1985. At the Royal Court Theatre in 1971, Hare instigated an experiment in group collaboration that resulted in the play *Lay By*, a group effort of seven writers (Trevor Griffiths, Brian Clark, Stephen Poliakoff, Hugh Stoddard, and Snoo Wilson, along with Brenton and Hare), stimulated by a *Sunday Times* feature by Ludovic Kennedy, concerning an ambiguous rape case that might have resulted in an erroneous conviction. The Royal Court rejected the play, but Hare's colleagues in the Portable Theatre Company mounted a production directed by Snoo Wilson in conjunction with the Traverse Theatre at the Edinburgh Festival Fringe. The Portable Theatre also produced another collective effort in which Hare was involved as a writer, *England's Ireland*, in 1972.

The rationale for the Portable Theatre was political. The idea was to have a touring company that would address working-class audiences, an "antagonistic theatre," as Brenton described it, designed for "people who have never seen the theatre before." The plays produced were intended to be controversial in nature (*Lay By* was an exercise in sexual politics, for example, reconstructing a rape and interspersing the reconstruction with a pornographic photo session) and to challenge conventional assumptions and the traditional forms and methods of the established theater.

In this context, Hare may be regarded as a social critic functioning as a practicing dramatist with a flair for satire. His play *The Great Exhibition* is a political satire treating a Labour M.P., Charles Hammett, swept into office during the great Labour victory of 1965 and swept out of office when the Conservative Party returned to power in 1970. Peter Ansorge has called the play a parody of "middle-class playwrights who have turned to working-class communities both for inspiration and as an escape from the more subtle dilemmas of their own environment and class."

Hare's interest in politics is also obvious in *Fanshen*, a play based on a book by William Hinton, an American who went to China "as a tractor technician," as Hare has described him, "both to observe and help the great land reform programmes of the late 1940's." Hare felt "an obligation to portray Chinese peasants" of the village of Log Bow "in a way which was adequate to their suffering," but was "not interested in portraying the scenes of violence and brutality which marked the landlords' regime and its overthrow." After seeing the play, Hinton objected to Hare's "liberal slant" and urged the playwright to revise the play so as to provide a clear Marxist emphasis, but Hare incorporated only a few of Hinton's list of 110 suggested emendations. *Fanshen* (the title is translated as "to turn the body," or, alternatively, "to turn over") was written for the Joint Stock Company in 1974 and opened in Sheffield before moving on to the ICA Terrace Theatre in London in April of 1975.

As has been noted, Hare's artistic sensibilities were no doubt influenced by the events of 1968, and his early work suggests a theater of political commitment and protest, carried into the 1970's. His play *Teeth 'n' Smiles*, produced in 1975 at the Royal Court Theatre, has been called "a metaphor for British society," and in the way it treats rock music and popular culture, "an elegy for the vanished visions of the late Sixties."

The action is set at Cambridge on June 9, 1969, and centers on a performance of a rock band for the May Ball of Jesus College. This concert proves to be a disaster when Maggie, the lead singer of the group, gets drunk, insults the audience, and is finally sent to prison on a drug charge. The musicians regard their privileged audience with contempt: "Rich complacent self-loving self-regarding self-righteous phoney half-baked politically immature evil-minded little shits." Interviewed about the play by *Theatre Quar-*

terly, Hare claimed it was intended to question "whether we have any chance of changing ourselves."

In his survey *British Theatre Since 1955: A Reassessment* (1979), Ronald Hayman criticizes the play for setting up Cambridge as symbolizing a repressive capitalist system, concluding that "this kind of play bases its appeal on giving the audience a chance to believe that there is a common enemy which can be fought." Hare's targets in this play are self-delusion, class guilt, and class war, but the play mainly attacks the upscale educational establishment, represented by Cambridge (which Hare knew at firsthand), and has been regarded as an indictment of the detached university intellectuals.

The protagonist of *Knuckle*, which opened at London's Comedy Theatre in March of 1974, is far removed from the privileged setting of Cambridge. He is a tough-minded vulgarian who is pragmatic and cynical about the hypocrisy of his world and his own family. Curly Delafield has returned to his home in Guildford seeking information about the disappearance of his sister Sarah, who had worked as a nurse in a psychiatric hospital. Curly is a blunt and brutal man. He had not seen his sister in twelve years, but he is determined to discover what has happened to her.

Sarah's overcoat was found on the beach at Eastbourne, famous for a ghastly murder that was committed there in the spring of 1924. Apparently Sarah either committed suicide or was murdered. The play therefore involves a process of detection, as those close to Sarah, a journalist named Max, her friend Jenny, and her father, are subjected to Curly's relentless interrogation. The mystery of her disappearance is solved at the end, after a sordid story of scandal and blackmail has been brought to light.

Curly is extremely cynical, a man who has been involved in selling arms, and in this regard he resembles in his amoral outlook the character of Andrew Undershaft in George Bernard Shaw's play *Major Barbara* (1905). Curly is habitually skeptical of men and their motives, including his own father. His view of the world is revealed by his motto: "Every man has his own gun. That's not a metaphor. That's a fact." In a mean world, Curly does not "pick fights" but merely provides weapons: "They're going to kill each other with or without my help," he claims. London is viewed as the corrupt center of a corrupt and fallen world, and the corruption has spread to Guildford. As Curly remarks at the end of the play, "In the mean square mile of the City of London they were making money. Back to my guns." Nearly everyone in this play is contaminated by money.

Knuckle is experimental in the way it mixes genres. The play develops as an apparent murder mystery, a whodunit that leaves open the possibility of suicide but turns out to be merely a parody of a conventional thriller. The sleuth Curly is like a stripped-down, plain-spoken Andrew Undershaft wearing a Mike Hammer mask, a very private eye. In fact, however, the play is an allegory of family betrayal, capitalist greed, and corruption. Hare's declared intention in writing it was "to subvert the form of the thriller to a serious end."

Curly is not a likable character because he is so cynical and so crude, but his character, shaped by the world that has molded it, is at least redeemed by his brutal honesty. He is not self-deluded, as so many of Hare's characters seem to be. One of Hare's most ambitious plays that attempts to take on human delusion on a global scale is *A Map of the World*, first performed at London's Lyttleton Theatre in January of 1983. The title comes from Oscar Wilde: "A map of the world that does not include Utopia is not worth even glancing at. . . ," and the central conflict is a philosophical argument between a Marxist idealist, Stephen Andrews, and a conservative "realist," an expatriate celebrity Indian writer named Victor Mehta; the two have been invited to address a UNESCO conference on world poverty in Bombay.

The play is complicated by the way it is framed, with the action shifting from the original confrontation to a filmed reconstruction being shot in London, as the audience realizes when scene 1 gives way to scene 2. This polemical play has been criticized for being too experimental in its framework and conception and too ambitious in scope, taking on issues of artistic freedom, world poverty, Third World nationalism, political compromise, and the decline of Western civilization, in the midst of a rhetorical contest partly based on sexual jealousy. "Unarguably," Hare has confessed, "I was trying to do too many things at once, and although I have now directed three productions of the play, I cannot ever quite achieve the right balance between the different strands."

Hare describes *A Map of the World* as a "disputatious play" that intended "to sharpen up people's minds, to ask them to remember why they believe what they do." Perhaps this goal was better achieved in the earlier play, *Plenty*, despite the puzzlement over motivation evident in the reviews of the later film version. *Plenty* was one of Hare's most successful plays but also one of his most ambiguous. It was first performed at London's Lyttleton Theatre in 1978, starring Kate Nelligan as Susan Traherne, the protagonist, before going on to Broadway. In 1985, Hare reshaped the script for the motion picture adaptation. The film version rearranged the opening, starting the action at St. Benoît, France, in November of 1943, rather than in the Knightsbridge area of London in 1962, presumably to establish Susan's character from the start as a young Englishwoman serving the French Resistance behind enemy lines during World War II.

Thereafter, in general, the film follows the chronology of the play, which mainly concerns Susan's difficulty in adjusting to civilian and domestic life in England after the war in the time of "plenty" that was to follow. The play seems to document a movement from innocence to insanity, as Susan restlessly moves from one job to another and from one relationship to another, presumably trying to recapture the excitement she knew with her wartime lover, a British agent in France known only by his codename, Lazar. After a brief flirtation with a working-class lover named Mick, whom she had selected to father a child in a liaison that only proved frustrating to both of them, she agrees to marry a career diplomat, Raymond Brock, whose career she later destroys for no clearly explained reason.

With regard to Susan, Hare has written that he was struck by a statistic "that seventy-five percent of the women flown behind the lines for the Special Operations Executive were subsequently divorced after the war." The play, which dramatizes Susan's restlessness in this context, has been criticized for its failure to explain her motives. After all, Raymond Brock seems to be a decent character who sincerely cares for his disturbed wife. Hare describes him as a young man of "delightful ingenuousness," and has noted that it would be a mistake to play him as a fool. His character is blemished, however, by the corrupt institution he serves, the Foreign Office. In a less obvious way than Andrew May in *Pravda*, Brock is ruined by his professionalism and his dedication to an unworthy career.

On the surface, Susan may appear to be maladjusted and irrational. She expresses the need to "move on" several times during the course of the play, but at first glance it seems that she is only able to "move on" from one job to another or from one relationship to another. Psychologically, she does not seem to be able to "move on" from the excitement of love and life behind enemy lines during the war. When she is much later reunited with Lazar in England, she discovers that he has "moved on" to shabby domesticity and a life without joy or enthusiasm. The danger of "moving on" in the sense of adjusting to a changing commonplace world is that this could mean nothing more than accepting banal conformity.

Susan's character is vibrant because she resists that kind of commonplace adjustment. Hare has written that men "are predisposed to find Susan Traherne unsympathetic." The commonplace judgment likely to be made about Susan is that she is emotionally unstable, if not completely deranged. "It's a common criticism of my work," Hare notes in his postscript to the play, "that I write about women whom I find admirable, but whom the audience dislikes."

The case against Susan "makes itself, or is made by the other characters," Hare adds, but the character is remarkable in her fierce independence and quite extraordinary in her behavior, which Hare believes should create "a balance of sympathy" throughout the play. Hare has written that he intended to show through Susan "the struggle of a heroine against a deceitful and emotionally stultified class." Her motives are submerged and complex, no doubt, but if that is a criticism of the character, it is one that could also be leveled at Hamlet. The mystery of motivation is not necessarily a flaw in a complex and enduring drama.

Hare's most critically acclaimed play after *Plenty* was *Pravda*, a biting satire of farcical dimensions on the newspaper industry in Great Britain and the dangers of collusion between Whitehall and Fleet Street, between government and the press. *Pravda* was written with Hare's earlier collaborator Brenton and appears to be a not-so-thinly-veiled attack upon the brand of journalism represented by the Australian press tycoon Rupert Murdoch, who took over *The Times* of London, just as *Pravda*'s central character, Lambert Le Roux (from South Africa rather than Australia) takes over the most influential establishment in Brenton and Hare's fictional London, *The Victory*.

Pravda premiered at the National Theatre in 1985, with Anthony Hopkins gaining rave notices for his caricature of Le Roux. Murdoch was reportedly angered by the play. Trevor Nunn, enjoying the limelight of *Les Misérables* (1985), which he directed and adapted as a musical from Victor Hugo's novel, told *Newsweek* that Murdoch "was extremely incensed and sent out the word to get the National and the RSC [Royal Shakespeare Company, whose London home is the Barbican Arts Centre], the two subsidized theatres" in Great Britain. Nunn and Peter Hall, who was instrumental in creating the three-auditorium National Theatre complex on London's South Bank, were both disappointed that the government of Margaret Thatcher did not support the integrity of the National Theatre in the "totally corrupt campaign" (as Hall described it) that followed. When government subsidies to the arts were cut (threatening to close down the National's smallest experimental auditorium in the complex), the director of the National must have sensed political pressure nearly as bizarre and dangerous as what is imagined in the Brenton and Hare play. ·

Pravda shows Hare's skill as a gadfly, questioning not only journalistic ethics but the larger issue of truth in journalism as well. This "comedy of excess" (as Hare described it) concerns the monopolizing of newspapers in England by the ruthless Lambert Le Roux. The action opens with Le Roux's takeover of a provincial paper, the *Leicester Bystander*, hardly a paradigm for journalistic ethics even before Le Roux's bid. Moira Patterson, a local shop-owner maligned by the newspaper by mistake, goes to the editorial offices to demand a retraction. The cynical editor, Harry Morrison, and his subordinate, Andrew May (soon to become the new editor-in-chief) tell her "we . . . don't publish corrections," because "what is printed must be true," and so "to print corrections is a kind of betrayal" of the public trust. May considers this perverse logic a matter of journalistic ethics.

This satiric introduction to an already corrupt world of journalism hardly inspires confidence in the *Leicester Bystander* and what it represents. The corruption of this provincial paper, however, pales in comparison to Andrew's later experiences as editor of *The Victory*, a national paper, a "paper for England."

Although billed as a comedy and often howlingly funny, *Pravda* is an extremely bitter satire that manages to strike out at corruption in high places and to spoof newspapers at all levels and television journalism as well. Besides *The Victory*, Le Roux owns a gutter tabloid (famous for its nudes) called *The Tide* and also attempts to take over a Left Wing paper called *The Usurper* (shades of *The Guardian?*). Once in power, Le Roux fires underlings with the gleeful abandon of the Queen of Hearts in Lewis Carroll's *Alice's Adventures in Wonderland* (1865). A fired journalist from *The Victory* regrets most that he will never again appear on a television talk show called *Speak or Shut Up*. Now, he will have to "sit at home shouting at the television like ordinary people."

In his bluntness, Le Roux resembles the unsentimental Curly of *Knuckle*, blown up to monstrous proportions, a vindictive Citizen Kane running amok. There is no clever Hamlet to counter the villainy of this Claudius, as Hare's satire seems to be moving in the direction of tragedy. The tragic vision depends on a sense of justice, however, and finally all that appears in Hare's bitter satiric world is a sense of the absurd so total that railing against it is clearly pointless.

Andrew's wife, Rebecca, gives him a "leaked" document that indicates a breach of public trust by the Minister of Defence concerning the transport of plutonium in flasks that are demonstrably unsafe. When Andrew decides to print the story in *The Victory*, Le Roux fires him. When Andrew and other fired *Victory* journalists take over *The Usurper*, Le Roux and his subordinate trick them into running libelous stories about their former employer, then threaten Andrew with litigation and bankruptcy.

At the end, Andrew is humiliated into begging Le Roux's forgiveness and editing *The Tide* as a means of penance. Practicing journalism is more important to him, finally, than ethics, integrity, truth, or love. A muddled idealist not fully understanding his presumed convictions, Andrew deserves to become a lacky to the demonic Le Roux, devoting his skill to purveying falsehood and smut, the foreman of what Le Roux calls his "foundry of lies."

Rebecca, who loves Andrew, is forced to abandon him after he succumbs to his bloodlust for revenge against Le Roux (his tragic flaw, if this play could be a tragedy) and after he finally sells his soul to the demon magnate who believes "No one tells the truth. Why single out newspapers?" Rebecca is the only character clever enough to see through Le Roux's deviousness, but she is powerless to take action against him. Otherwise, this bitter, satiric world is populated by mean-spirited, unscrupulous, dishonest people.

Hare has a particular genius for designing ingeniously constructed, unpredictable plots and strong, ambiguous characters that defy immediate classification and interpretation. The male characters tend to be flawed, either because they are infirm of purpose and self-deceived, or because they are all too purposeful and self-assured, in some instances even brutal. In Hare's male characters, civilized behavior and even signals of basic decency can be signs of weakness. Andrew May's apparently "good" qualities (bourgeois ambition, a dedication to the work ethic, a capacity for moral outrage) are in fact merely the product of an unthinking liberal idealism, which easily gives way to his monstrous hatred for Le Roux and his absolute thirst for vengeance. Brock, the diplomat in *Plenty*, is also misled by his emotions.

"Decent" people are not survivors in the kind of world Hare imagines, a world that requires intellectual toughness for survival. The idealist, like the sympathetic Darwin of *Plenty*, cannot stand a chance when countered by the unfeeling pragmatists who operate the machinery of State. Hare's men, often dominated by career ambitions, gradually lose their integrity while serving the corrupt and corrupting Establishment of government and big business. They give themselves to these enterprises and are transformed into cogs in the machinery of State, disposable and interchangeable parts. The career diplomat Darwin of *Plenty*, for example, has given a lifetime of loyal service to the Foreign Office but is betrayed by his superiors during the Suez Crisis. Determined to speak his mind and tell the truth, an honorable course of action, he is crushed and his career ruined. This is the sort of career from which Susan extricates her husband, but Brock, lacking her perspective, can only regret the career loss and resent Susan's interference.

The male characters, then, are driven by ambition and the lure of professional success; their vision will be clouded and their integrity compromised. Brock is not a fool, but he will not conclude, as Susan apparently does, that a state bureau that will betray a career loyalist such as Darwin and make a scapegoat of him is not worthy of one's service. In *Pravda*, with its broad, satiric distortions, Andrew can be seen as a fool because his self-betrayal is expanded to farcical proportions. In a more restrained context, Andrew might be seen as a parallel figure to Brock. In the end, Andrew's integrity is compromised when he goes back to Le Roux to edit the sleaziest tabloid in England, but the man is so stupidly devoted to his profession that he hardly seems to care that he has lost his integrity and self-respect. Rebecca has attempted to clarify his decision and to explain the consequences, but to no avail. In a more subtle way, Susan performs a similar function for Brock in *Plenty*, but Brock is so ordinary, so average, and so typical in his ambition that audiences may miss the point.

Plenty may be mistaken for domestic melodrama (even though Susan is hardly a typical melodramatic heroine), but the movement is toward pathos and tragedy in the way men allow themselves to be transformed and corrupted into banality. The meaning of *Pravda* is the more easily recognized by its satiric approach and farcical distortions. Even so, Gavin Millar, in *Sight and Sound*, praised *Plenty* as "one of the few recent texts, in theatre or cinema, that undertakes an unpretentious but serious review of postwar Britain's decline."

Other major works

SCREENPLAYS: *Plenty*, 1985 (adaptation of his stage play); *Wetherby*, 1985.
TELEPLAYS: *Man Above Men*, 1973; *Licking Hitler*, 1978; *Dreams of Leaving*, 1980; *Saigon: Year of the Cat*, 1983.

Bibliography

Ansorge, Peter. "Running Wild," in *Disrupting the Spectacle: Five Years of Experimental and Fringe Theatre in Britain*, 1975.

Bigsby, C. W. E. "The Politics of Anxiety: Contemporary Socialist Theatre in England," in *Modern Drama*. XXIV (December, 1981), pp. 393-403.

Brown, John Russell. *A Short Guide to Modern British Drama*, 1982.

Grant, Steve. "Voicing the Protest: The New Writers," in *Dreams and Deconstructions: Alternative Theatre in Britain*, 1980.

Gussow, Mel. "David Hare: Playwright as Provocateur," in *The New York Times Magazine*. CXXXV (September 29, 1985), pp. 42-47, 75-76.

Hayman, Ronald. *British Theatre Since 1955: A Reassessment*, 1979.

Lawson, Steve. "Hare Apparent," interview in *Film Comment*. XXI (September/October, 1985), pp. 18-22.

Millar, Gavin. "The Habit of Lying," in *Sight and Sound*. LIV (Autumn, 1985), pp. 299-300.

Myerson, Jonathan. "David Hare: Fringe Graduate," in *Drama*. No. 149 (Autumn, 1983), pp. 26-28.

Poole, Mike, and John Wyver. *Powerplays: Trevor Griffiths in Television*, 1984.

James M. Welsh

BETH HENLEY

Born: Jackson, Mississippi; May 8, 1952

Principal drama

Am I Blue, pr. 1973, pb. 1982; *Crimes of the Heart*, pr. 1979, pb. 1981; *The Miss Firecracker Contest*, pr. 1980, pb. 1982; *The Wake of Jamey Foster*, pr., pb. 1982; *The Debutante Ball*, pr. 1985; *The Lucky Spot*, pr. 1986.

Other literary forms

In addition to her works for the stage, Beth Henley has written screenplays, including *The Moon Watcher* (1983), *Nobody's Fool* (1986), and the film version of her play *Crimes of the Heart* (1986).

Achievements

Henley is often compared to fiction writers Eudora Welty and Flannery O'Connor for her sympathetic portrayals of eccentric characters who lead deceptively simple lives in small Southern communities. Her work has also been identified with the literary traditions of the grotesque and the absurd. Henley's unique achievement, however, is the intermingling of absurdism and realism. Her plays realistically capture the Southern vernacular and take place in authentic Southern settings, yet they also exaggerate the recognizable and push the bizarre to extremes to reveal the underlying absurdity of the human condition. Whereas Henley's characters are rooted in her Southern heritage, the meaning of their experiences is not limited to time and place. Loss and renewal, the vulnerability of loving, and the frail but indomitable human spirit are among her recurring themes; Henley delivers these serious concerns, however, through unpredictable characters, outrageously witty dialogue, and offbeat humor. It is her insistence on the value of laughter in the face of adversity that places her within the tragicomic tradition of modern dramatic literature. Another of Henley's strengths is that she approaches her craft with a keen insight into what is stageworthy. This awareness, no doubt, is one of the reasons that her first full-length play, *Crimes of the Heart*, won the Pulitzer Prize for Drama in 1981 with the distinction of being the first play to win the coveted award before appearing on Broadway. *Crimes of the Heart* also received the New York Drama Critics' Circle Award in 1981, and, in the same year, Henley captured the prestigious George Oppenheimer/*Newsday* Playwriting Award.

Biography

The second of four daughters, Elizabeth Becker Henley was born May 8, 1952, in Jackson, Mississippi. Her parents, Charles Boyce and Elizabeth Josephine Becker, were reared in the neighboring communities of Hazelhurst and Brookhaven, locales that Henley adopts for two of her plays. Henley's father, an attorney, served in both houses of the Mississippi legislature. A shy child plagued with chronic attacks of asthma, Henley, often bedridden, entertained herself by reading play scripts that were in production at the New Stage Theatre in Jackson, where her mother, an amateur actress, regularly performed.

Henley attended high school in Jackson. During her senior year, she took part in an acting workshop at the New Stage Theatre, an experience that influenced her decision to become an actress. Selecting drama as her major, Henley enrolled at Southern Methodist University in Dallas, Texas, in 1970. While a sophomore, she wrote her first play as an assignment for a playwriting class. The play, a one-act comedy titled *Am I Blue*, was produced at the university under a pseudonym in her senior year. After graduation from Southern Methodist University in 1974 with a bachelor of fine arts degree, Henley taught creative dramatics and acted for the Dallas Minority Repertory Theatre. She earned a livelihood at odd jobs as a waitress, file clerk, and photographer of children at a department store. In 1975, she received a teaching scholarship from the University of Illinois, where she taught acting classes while pursuing graduate studies in drama. In the summer of 1976, she acted in the *Great American People Show*, a historical pageant presented at the New Salem State Park.

Hoping to break into films as an actress, Henley moved to Los Angeles in the fall of 1976. Failing to get auditions for parts, Henley turned to writing screenplays as a creative outlet, but without an agent to represent her, the studios would not read her scripts. Thinking that stage plays would have a better chance of getting performed, especially in small theaters, Henley began working on a comedy (set in Hazelhurst, Mississippi) about a crisis in the lives of three sisters. With production costs in mind, she deliberately limited the play to six characters and one indoor set. She finished *Crimes of the Heart* in 1978 and submitted it to several regional theaters without success, but Henley's friend and fellow playwright Frederick Bailey had faith in the play. Without Henley's knowledge, he entered *Crimes of the Heart* in the annual drama competition of the Actors Theatre of Louisville, Kentucky, where it was selected as a cowinner for 1977-1978. In February, 1979, the Actors Theatre produced the play as part of the company's annual Festival of New American Plays. The play was an immediate success. After productions in Maryland, Missouri, and California, *Crimes of the Heart* opened to full houses on off-Broadway on December 21, 1980. The public's high regard for the play was matched by critical acclaim. In April, 1981, at the age of twenty-nine, Henley was awarded the Pulitzer Prize for drama for *Crimes of the Heart*, the first woman so honored in twenty-three years. In the fall of 1981, after having been recognized by the New York Drama Critics' Circle as the best American play of the season, *Crimes of the Heart* premiered on Broadway; it ran for 535 performances. Subsequent productions were staged in England, France, Israel, and Australia.

Meanwhile, Henley was writing a television pilot entitled "Morgan's Daughters" for Paramount Pictures and a screenplay called *The Moon Watcher* about a historical pageant set in Petersburg, Illinois. She also took a small role as a bag lady in Frederick Bailey's *No Scratch*, produced in Los Angeles in the summer of 1981. In January, 1982, the New York Repertory Company staged Henley's *Am I Blue* with two other one-acts under the collective title *Confluence*. Theater critics found weaknesses in the playwright's student effort but also acknowledged that the comedy showed the promise of her later work.

Within the next three years, two other comedies written before Henley won the Pulitzer Prize were produced in New York City. *The Wake of Jamey Foster* opened on Broadway on October 14, 1982, but closed after only twelve nights. Critics found the play, which was also set in Mississippi, too repetitious of *Crimes of the Heart*. Written before *The Wake of Jamey Foster*, *The Miss Firecracker Contest* was staged in the spring of 1984. Again critics faulted the play for its similarity to her earlier works. Undaunted by these box-office failures, Henley kept writing for the stage. In the spring of 1985, the South Coast Repertory Theatre in Costa Mesa, California, produced her next play *The Debutante Ball*. In the following year, Henley's *The Lucky Spot* was staged as part of the Williamson Theatre Festival and scheduled for a New York premiere in the spring of 1987. As a Pulitzer Prize winner, the young playwright/actress also found herself in demand as a screenwriter. While continuing to write stage plays, Henley wrote the screenplay for the acclaimed film version of *Crimes of the Heart*, released in late 1986; the script for another film, *Nobody's Fool*; and a teleplay for the Public Broadcasting Service titled *Survival Guides* (1986).

Henley's plays have reached audiences far beyond the regional theaters for which she first wrote, making her a significant contributor to American dramatic literature. Although the plays written after *Crimes of the Heart* have failed to bring her the critical praise she earned with that first full-length comedy, her dramatic output as a whole reveals a consistency in tone and theme unsurpassed by her American contemporaries.

Analysis

While the plays of Beth Henley are well constructed and provide ample conflict and suspense, the playwright's keen sense of place and character and her humorous yet compassionate view of the human predicament most typify her work. Her plays are set most often in her home state of Mississippi, where the innocent façade of friendly small-town life belies the horror and lunacy within. The dark side of humanity—the unpredictable, the irrational, the abnormal—attracts Henley, and her plays abound with stories of sickness, disease, and perversions. Ironically, however, Henley creates comedy out of the grotesque and shapes endearing characters out of eccentricity.

Usually, Henley's plays depict the family in crisis joined by a close circle of friends and neighbors. From this basic situation, Henley makes her case for emotional survival. Guilt, despair, and loneliness are typical experiences of Henley's failed heroines, but each continues to search for some measure of happiness and often finds it, if only momentarily, in the community of others. Whereas Henley doggedly exposes human frailties, in the final analysis her view is a charitable one and her plays are optimistic, despite the fact that they offer no lasting resolutions to her characters' problems. The key to understanding Henley's optimism lies in the laughter that her plays evoke; laughter functions to undercut that which is horrifying in life—to render it less horrifying.

Henley's reputation as a major American playwright was established with three full-length plays, *Crimes of the Heart*, *The Miss Firecracker Contest*, and *The Wake of Jamey Foster*. These plays also best illustrate the qualities that shape her unusual talent: a uniquely comic but sad voice, a distinguishing preoccupation with the bizarre, and a gift for working out variations on the themes of loneliness, guilt, loss, and renewal. Set in Hazelhurst, Mississippi, five years after hurricane Camille, *Crimes of the Heart* is about three sisters—Lenny, Meg, and Babe McGrath. The immediate crisis is that the youngest sister, Babe, has shot her husband, Zackery Botrelle, who is the richest and most powerful man in the community. The plot is fairly easily resolved when Zackery recovers and his threat to confine Babe in a mental institution is thwarted. This, however, hardly accounts for the sisters' bizarre tale, which Henley unravels through exposition that is brilliantly interspersed with the main action. Babe's trouble is only one more disaster among many that the McGrath women have experienced, beginning with their father's desertion and their mother's suicide (she hanged herself and the family's cat). The mother's death left the sisters under the supervision of their grandfather, and now the care of the sick old man has fallen to Lenny, the oldest sister, because Babe married young and Meg escaped to California to pursue a singing career. Growing up in the shadow of their mother's inexplicable suicide and the notoriety it brought, each of the sisters suffers silently and alone. Meg was especially affected. Fearing to show pity as a sign of weakness, she tested herself as a youngster by staring at a book full of pictures of people with horrible skin diseases. Remarkably, Henley wrings laughter out of the McGraths' misfortunes: The sisters suspect that Mama McGrath killed herself because she was having a bad day; Lenny's prospects for marriage are bleak because she has a deformed ovary; and Babe shoots Zackery because she does not like his looks. To Henley's credit, the laughter is never at the expense of her characters, and there is a kind of bizarre logic to their eccentric behavior that makes the incredible credible. After Babe attempts suicide twice (because she, too, is having a bad day), she learns why her mother hanged the cat: She was afraid to die alone.

Of the same eccentric mold as the McGrath women, twenty-four-year-old Carnelle Scott, the central character of *The Miss Firecracker Contest*, seeks to overcome her well-earned reputation as the town trollop by becoming Miss Firecracker at the annual Fourth of July celebration in her hometown of Brookhaven, Mississippi. Since Carnelle's determination to succeed is exceeded only by her lack of talent, the outcome is predictable. Carnelle loses (she comes in fifth in a field of five), but she manages to overcome her despondency over the loss and joins her friends to watch the fireworks display at the close of the play. Henley enlivens the simple plot with a number of very odd characters, all of whom, like Carnelle, seek redemption from their unhappy pasts. Delmount Williams, Carnelle's cousin, is a former mental patient who wants to be a philosopher; his sister Elain finds it easier to desert her husband and sons than to abandon her clock collection; and Carnelle's seamstress, Popeye Jackson, who learned her trade by making dresses for frogs, hears voices through her eyes. Henley's propensity for the grotesque is even more marked in *The Miss Firecracker Contest* than in *Crimes of the Heart*. Carnelle recalls a childhood bout with ringworm, the treatment for which was to shave her head and cover it with a disgusting ointment; Delmount's last job was scraping up dead dogs from county roads; and all fondly remember Ronelle Williams, Delmount and Elain's mother, who died looking like a hairy ape after having her cancerous pituitary gland replaced by one from a monkey. Although in *The Miss Firecracker Contest* Henley tries too hard to be amusing at times, her characters are distinctly drawn and believable despite their whimsicality.

Henley pushes the morbid to extremes in *The Wake of Jamey Foster*, which is set at Easter time in Canton, Mississippi. The inevitability of death, an underlying theme in Henley's earlier work, is the central focus of this very black comedy in which Marshael Foster, the thirty-three-year-old widow of Jamey Foster, endures the embarrassment of holding the wake of her estranged husband in her home. Marshael faces the ordeal with anger and remorse; she has only recently filed for divorce because her alcoholic husband left her for another woman. The widow finds little comfort from the strange group of friends and relatives who gather to pay their last respects to Jamey, who is laid out in the cheapest pine box available and dressed in a bright yellow sports coat. Among the mourners are Marshael's brother, Leon Darnell, a turkey jerker in a chicken factory; the orphan Pixrose Wilson, Leon's betrothed, who is planning a career washing dogs; Collard Darnell, Marshael's promiscuous sister, whose whole life has been marred by a low score on an IQ test that she took when she was twelve years old; Jamey's brother, Wayne Foster, a successful banker, and his wife, Katie, who turn up their noses at the other guests; and Brocker Slade, a pig farmer who is in love with Marshael. Very little that is significant happens in the play. As the group waits for morning and Jamey's funeral, they eat, drink, play cards, and take pictures of the corpse, but mostly they talk about gruesome things that have happened to them or others they know: arson, brain damage, miscarriages, automobile accidents, the cow that kicked Jamey in the head and killed him, and exploding pigs. Although plot is subsumed by character and character borders on caricature, *The Wake of Jamey Foster* is both entertaining and convincingly human, especially in the solace the characters find in the calamities of others.

Beth Henley's rise to prominence in the American theater is remarkable considering the regionalism that characterizes her work. The weaknesses of her plays, a penchant for telling tall tales that stretch credulity and a tendency to write gags that force laughter, are overcome by her gift for creating memorable characters. Whereas Henley's dramatic material is confined to small Southern towns and the misfits who inhabit them, her humorous but sympathetic treatment of human foibles has a universality and originality that make her one of the most imaginative dramatists writing for the American theater.

Other major works

SCREENPLAYS: *The Moon Watcher*, 1983; *Nobody's Fool*, 1986; *Crimes of the Heart*, 1986 (adaptation of her play).

TELEPLAY: *Survival Guides*, 1986.

Bibliography

Berkvist, Robert. "Act I: The Pulitzer, Act II: Broadway," in *The New York Times*. CCXXXI (October 25, 1981), pp. 4, 22.

Brustein, Robert. "Broadway Inches Forward," in *The New Republic*. CLXXXV (December 23, 1981), pp. 25-27.

Haller, Scot. "Her First Play, Her First Pulitzer Prize," in *Saturday Review*. VIII (November, 1981), pp. 40-44.

Simon, John. "Living Beings, Cardboard Symbols," in *New York*. XIV (November 16, 1981), pp. 125-126.

_____. "Sisterhood Is Beautiful," in *New York*. XIV (January 12, 1981), pp. 42-43.

Ayne C. Durham

ALBERT INNAURATO

Born: Philadelphia, Pennsylvania; June 2, 1948

Principal drama

Urlicht, pr. 1971, pb. 1980; *I Don't Generally Like Poetry but Have You Read "Trees"?*, pr. 1972 (with Christopher Durang); *The Life Story of Mitzi Gaynor: Or, Gyp*, pr. 1973 (with Durang); *Wisdom Amok*, pr. 1973?, pb. 1980; *The Transfiguration of Benno Blimpie*, pr. 1973, pb. 1976; *The Idiots Karamazov*, pr., pb. 1974, augmented pb. 1981 (with Durang, music by Jack Feldman, lyrics by Durang); *Earth Worms*, pr. 1974, pb. 1980; *Gemini*, pr. 1976, pb. 1977; *Ulysses in Traction*, pr. 1977, pb. 1978; *Passione*, pr. 1980; *Bizarre Behavior: Six Plays*, pb. 1980; *Coming of Age in Soho*, pr. 1985.

Other literary forms

Albert Innaurato is known only for his dramatic works.

Achievements

Innaurato enjoyed enormous popularity with the simultaneous success of *Gemini* and *The Transfiguration of Benno Blimpie* in 1977: Both plays received Obie Awards. Since that time, Innaurato has struggled to fulfill the high expectations of his audience, and none of his subsequent efforts has met the high level of critical acclaim that the earlier plays enjoyed. Innaurato has received Rockefeller and Guggenheim grants and has served as resident playwright at the Circle Repertory Company and The Public Theater. *Coming of Age in Soho* underwent a widely publicized revision during the course of its Public Theater production and received a measure of praise. Nevertheless, Innaurato continues to be remembered for his first two New York productions, which established his place as a major contemporary dramatist.

Biography

Albert Innaurato was born and reared in Philadelphia, the son of Italian immigrants. The ethnic world of south Philadelphia provides the background for his most successful plays; though precise autobiographical parallels have not been revealed by Innaurato, the events and characters in the plays are transformations of his own experiences and acquaintances. His portrayals of Italian-American life are sufficiently realistic that Innaurato's opinions about ethnic identity have been sought out by reporters.

Many of Innaurato's plays were begun when he was quite young; a version of *Urlicht*, for example, dates from his late teens. He continued to write prolifically during his undergraduate years at Temple University, where he received his B.A. Many of these early works were lost or destroyed, though some of the titles are known. Innaurato develops scripts rather slowly, so some of the material may eventually surface again in new plays.

Perhaps the most persistent early influence on Innaurato was his taste for opera. He taught himself to play the piano and made some early experiments in operatic composition, but its influence lingers mostly through frequent allusions to opera in plays such as *Gemini* and in the leitmotif structure of the plays, which also feature set speeches designed as arias. Innaurato collects opera recordings and has written about his fascination with the form for *The New York Times*.

After attending Temple University, the young writer spent a year at the California Institute of the Arts. His experience there was unsettling, causing him to question his assumptions about art, politics, and society, and he left the school to return to the East Coast.

During the early 1970's, Innaurato studied playwriting at Yale University under Howard Stein and Jules Feiffer. The discipline of regular writing and constructive feedback seems to have provided an unusually productive routine for Innaurato, who developed his serious dramatic talents in plays such as *Earth Worms*. Feiffer's influence seems important to Innaurato's development as a satirist, too—his concern for grotesque, seriocomic characters who exist beyond social conventions.

Equally important to Innaurato's development at Yale was his association with Christopher Durang. The two young writers shared a virulent anti-Catholicism, most concisely demonstrated in the famous monologue by the title character of Durang's play *Sister Mary Ignatius Explains It All for You* (1979). Durang is more important to Innaurato for having collaborated with him on a number of madcap comic satires. The ridiculous mayhem of *Gemini* does not seem eccentric in Innaurato's oeuvre when considered in relation to plays such as *The Idiots Karamazov*, *I Don't Generally Like Poetry but Have You Read "Trees"?*, and *The Life Story of Mitzi Gaynor: Or, Gyp*, all written during the Yale years with Durang. These works also provided the experience with allusion and the manipulation of theatrical conventions that Innaurato used later in *Ulysses in Traction*.

In 1974, Innaurato was graduated from Yale with a master of fine arts degree in playwriting. He had also directed and acted in some of the plays, which even in their student productions featured talented, capable casts. His work was published in Yale's *Theater* magazine and was produced by the Yale Repertory Theatre. Some of his plays also received readings and critical feedback at the Yale summer session, the O'Neill Theater Center's National Playwrights' Conference.

In 1975, Innaurato received a Guggenheim Fellowship and began his career as a full-time playwright. The first production of *Gemini*, at the PAF playhouse in Huntington, Long Island, was so successful that a subsequent production was arranged at the Circle Rep. When this Off-Broadway staging was acclaimed by critics, the play was moved downtown to a small Broadway house where it ran for more than a thousand performances. This bona fide hit, following close upon the heels of a heralded performance by James Coco as Benno Blimpie, made Innaurato the most talked-about young playwright of the season. His work received especially close scrutiny from the gay press, where Innaurato's theme of sexual confusion was furiously debated.

Since the mid-1970's, Innaurato's progress has been uneven as he has tried to support his playwriting activity through a series of odd jobs. *Ulysses in Traction* was very coolly received, as were productions of some of the early plays. Innaurato directed the Playwrights' Horizons production of *Passione* in 1980, which was then transferred to Broadway with Frank Langella supervising the performance. The personal financial and health problems that have slowed Innaurato's production were eventually made public in 1985, during his work with Joseph Papp on the production of *Coming of Age in Soho*. Still, Innaurato's commitment to dramatic writing seems strong, and he is likely to continue to produce new material if circumstances allow him to do so.

Analysis

Albert Innaurato's plays alternate in their effect from farcical comedy to unrelenting pathos. The consistent aspect of his work is not a matter of genre or formula, but one of theatrical style. Innaurato populates his plays with grotesque misfits, vivid personalities that depart from traditional theatrical types. The settings are drawn from contemporary lower-class dwellings and ground the desires of his sympathetic characters in a run-down atmosphere that predicts their eventual defeat. Actions, too, are frequently grotesque, particularly when the plays' themes combine death, eating, and debased sexuality. Innaurato's vision disturbs and fascinates audiences because he has created new voices for the expression of obsessive concerns, new ways to dramatize important themes through characterization. Innaurato's work is uneven, however, almost equally divided between adeptly constructed scripts that shift cleanly from one scene to the next and plays that diffuse his obsessions into shrill, unfocused energy. If any single work can be said to predict the themes and style of Innaurato's work, it is John Guare's *The House of Blue Leaves* (1971).

The Innaurato hero is usually unhappy, from a depressed family, sexually confused, but in love with beauty. The most concise expression of this character's unhappiness comes in Innaurato's *The Transfiguration of Benno Blimpie*, perhaps his best work. Benno, "an enormously fat young man," narrates his story while seated on a stool apart from the main acting area. Benno's desire for love and beauty, expressed by his passion for great paintings, is contradicted by everything around him. His combative Italian parents ignore and abuse him, his grandfather carries out a sordid affair with a foul young Irish girl, while Benno, eventually raped by a gang of schoolboys, takes solace in eating.

The performance begins with Benno's announcement that he plans to eat himself to death. The plot then proceeds through a series of flashbacks, which establish in turn the cruelty of his parents, the depravity of his grandfather's sexual activity, and the incongruity of his passion for art. Much of the story is narrated by Benno, who remains stationary and participates in the flashback action only vocally, altering his voice to indicate youth while the other actors behave as if a Benno figure were present in the scene. This choice to disrupt the conventional structure of the acting event causes the behavior of the other characters toward the phantom Benno to be more noticeable than usual. When they ignore his needs and requests, or send him away, the audience is conscious of the theatrical parallel that objectifies his rejection. Once Benno's story is complete, Innaurato repeats the first scene; this time, however, Benno adds a gesture with a cleaver, showing that he will literally eat himself—consume his own body until he dies.

The economy of construction and unrelenting plot progression in *The Transfiguration of Benno Blimpie* are especially impressive when compared to Innaurato's other early works, such as *Wisdom Amok*, *Urlicht*, and *Earth Worms*. In the first two of these plays, Innaurato's anti-Catholic feelings are so virulent that the plays surrender any pretension of credible mimesis to a free-associative, vengeful attack on the Church. Nothing like reality, the plays also fail to achieve any internal, formal coherence, dissolving instead into a disintegrated barrage of images. In *Wisdom Amok*, there are no sympathetic characters; the action begins with grotesquely disrupted public events, then immerses itself in a sacrilegious madhouse. The power and fascination of charismatic madness were important themes in other plays popular at the time of *Wisdom Amok*'s composition, such as Peter Weiss's *Marat/Sade* (1964), but Innaurato's attempt to explore the plunge of a cleric into insanity and murder sheds no new light on the repressive qualities of religion, nor is his character sufficiently interesting to maintain sympathetic attention. *Urlicht* is slightly more compact, substituting the extravagance of opera for the decadence of the Church but still surpassing credibility with its grotesque extremes of imagery and action.

In *Earth Worms*, Innaurato's work remains diffuse, but the characters evolve along with the dramatic events to create a number of unique, fascinating personalities. The most flamboyant of these characters is Bernard, an aged transvestite and retired English professor who takes the dominant role in the action, performing a Pygmalion-like transformation on the central female. This character, Mary, who reappears in *Passione* as Aggy, is an uneducated young Appalachian woman who becomes mature enough eventually to push the other crippled characters away. Innaurato's trademark of sexual confusion is stamped not only on the professor but also on Arnold,

Mary's serviceman husband. He brings her back to his childhood home, now grown filthy and decayed, then abandons her when his guilt over the death of their child overcomes him. These roles and a few others make *Earth Worms* a fascinating play for actors, though as of the mid-1980's its challenges had been met in only one professional production (by Robert Goldsby at the Berkeley Stage Company).

The anti-Catholic theme is communicated in a different, symbolic mode in *Earth Worms*. Nuns who resemble Furies or the witches from *Macbeth* terrorize the husband and perform actions that reflect back upon the play's dramatic events. The most terrifying of these is the surreal dance they perform with the dead infant impaled on a cross. Innaurato's alternation of these horrible symbolic gestures with squalid realistic scenes provides a loose form that supplies striking effects almost at random.

In *Gemini*, Innaurato deals with a similar group of people but shows them at an earlier age, when their environment is less decayed, their dreams still intact. This shift, accompanied by the change into a quick, complex, but more conventionally comic dialogue structure, transforms the same themes and grotesque character images into the material of farce. The audience, no longer directly addressed by a Benno figure, gains some perspective on the action; this distance from the bizarre world of Italian south Philadelphia is at least partially supplied by the introduction of two visitors from Harvard. The consternation of these attractive outsiders at the rude characters and strange twists of action guides the audience's response. In addition, Innaurato finally omits his obsessive, distracting attack on Catholicism, allowing full attention to be focused on the construction of the play itself.

The title character of the play, Francis Geminiani, is probably the most autobiographical hero in the playwright's first group of plays. A young Harvard (not Yale) student whose name symbolizes his split sexual inclinations, Francis acts out his sexual indecision in the playwright's old neighborhood. The hero also loves opera, using the music to express his moods and provide inspiration for important decisions. While Francis, like the playwright, thinks that he is pudgy, the genuinely grotesque traits of Benno Blimpie have been foisted off onto Herschel, a young next-door neighbor who is still childish enough that he arouses more laughter than pathos. In the serious plays, all kinds of sexuality seem disgusting, but in *Gemini* Innaurato introduces Bunny, a robust, tolerant neighbor who finds such humor and pleasure in her sex life that when Francis finally leaves home to work out his sexual preference, either choice on his part would seem to offer a healthy, comfortable conclusion. In *Gemini*, the parents are benevolent and encouraging, if embarrassingly provincial; they want to help Francis answer his questions about social and sexual values. Innaurato reduces his own didactic impulses to the level of a gentle, implied satire, and so raises issues without seeming maudlin or pathetic.

One of Innaurato's most striking intellectual skills is his facility for comic allusion. He uses this talent sparingly in most cases, as a way to develop character voices. He has also, however, written whole plays based on allusion. The most successful of these plays is *The Idiots Karamazov*, a lampoon of nineteenth century Russian literature that was written with Christopher Durang at Yale. Apart from Fyodor Dostoevski, the play includes numerous references to Anton Chekhov; perhaps the most amusing moments are those when the two sources are combined, as when the Karamazov brothers enact portions of *Three Sisters*. The rapid-fire flow of allusive material includes many such incongruous turns, as well as several bizarre song-and-dance numbers that help to pace the laughter while providing a measure of relief from the intellectual demands of the dialogue scenes. Apart from the Russian sources, major roles are given to Constance Garnett, the aged "translatrix" whose wandering mind presides over the play, and feminist writers Anaïs Nin and Djuna Barnes. These last two characters begin to control the action in act 2, when Innaurato's obsessions with death and decay emerge to dominate the play. Unfortunately, the comic effects subside proportionately in this second half of the text, giving way to a kind of enervated morbidity as the corpses pile up. Though it loses some steam at the end, the fantastic complexity and inspired satire of the first act is probably impossible to sustain for two hours; even a master allusionist such as Tom Stoppard takes time out for weighty issues in the second act of *Travesties*. It is, however, a shame that the serious parts of *The Idiots Karamazov* cannot sustain the attention that the first half attracts.

Ulysses in Traction suffers from much the same gradual loss of energy. The first act manages to entertain through a number of devices: a satire of the David Rabe–style Vietnam drama, the gossipy sexual intrigue between cast members, and a world-as-drama-department twist on the *theatre mundi* theme. So long as the clever devices keep coming, the play retains an engaging novelty. In the second act, however, when a race riot outside the theater confines the actors, an introspective group analysis session begins that fails to reveal anything unusual or particularly moving about the selfish characters. Certain biographical parallels are obvious: Chapel University for Temple; Detroit for Philadelphia; a sexually disturbed M.F.A. playwright from Yale. Yet Innaurato seems to push away the personal aspect of the material, instead embracing sentimental abstractions to conclude the action and reconcile the characters. Innaurato's inability to pull political themes into the play, to develop a range of characters sympathetically, or to sustain his formal innovations reveals many of his limitations as a playwright. *Ulysses in Traction* begins with a pretentious premise, adopts a self-righteous tone, and then does not deliver; it has been the least successful of Innaurato's plays in professional production.

In *Passione*, Innaurato retreats considerably from the challenges of *Ulysses in Traction*, and in doing so constructs one of his most appealing plays. Using familiar elements such as the south Philadelphia setting, Italian song, and vivid, obese characters, Innaurato composes an entertaining domestic play about giving relationships a second chance. This limited theme carries the play because it applies to a number of the characters. Aggy, a self-possessed woman who abandoned her family a decade ago, has returned to her husband's apartment to claim her belongings. Though she brings with her a hard-nosed sister named Sarah and expects no complications, the patient appeals of Berto, her former husband, finally convince her to remain. She also comes to accept her son, who had disappointed her by forsaking professional ambition for the love of a fat girl. Meanwhile, Sarah, strong and hostile, develops feelings for Renzo, a willful friend of Berto. The serious moments are interrupted throughout by the comic antics of Berto's senile father and Francine, a magnetic, robust beauty who works as the fat lady in a children's circus. There is little in the way of intrigue or character development, apart from Aggy's change of heart, and some of the rough-and-tumble action spins out of control, but *Passione*'s modest, conventional goals are well realized. The grotesque has become something cozy and commercial in *Passione*, a fact that perhaps says more about the changing taste of American theater audiences than it does about Innaurato's artistic development. The play is unmistakably Innaurato's, but it is also solidly second-rate.

After *Passione*'s lukewarm reception, Innaurato suffered a serious difficulty coming up with new material. He finally emerged from his dry spell with *Coming of Age in Soho*, a play that marks an important shift in several aspects of his work. Rather than Philadelphia, the setting is Soho, where the play's hero, having abandoned a comfortable but sexless marriage to declare his homosexuality, is now coincidentally trying to get over a case of writer's block. Unlike some of the earlier characters, such as Benno, this man, named Beatrice, is openly autobiographical, even if the precise circumstances of the play are fictitious. Innaurato seems to do his best work when he believes that it is both honest and witty, and with Beatrice he invented a strong vehicle for expression.

The play underwent an unusually extreme revision after its first tryouts. The script began with a female composer named Gioconda at its center; she was confronted by an unacknowledged son and his companion, a boy with whom she fell in love. Bartholomew Dante, or Beatrice, was merely the downstairs neighbor who harbored the rejected son. In the revised version, Gioconda was eliminated, the son was attributed to Beatrice, and the other boy's attraction was made homosexual. Many of the lines remained unchanged, and the author/director resumed production with a new confidence in the play.

Some of *Coming of Age in Soho* remains far-fetched, such as the Mafia connections of the former wife, yet the play generates a confident charm without resorting to grotesque images for its effects. The most successful aspect of the play is the character of the son, a German computer whiz whose frank appraisals of foreign situations lend a precocious, fresh tone to the whole work, much like that supplied by the two visitors in *Gemini*. The supporting characters tend to be young and tolerant, rather than old and decayed, so that Beatrice is able to indulge in his introspection in an encouraging atmosphere that is simple rather than barren. Once again, as with *Passione*, the themes are scarcely world-shaking—frequent references to the "health crisis" do not amount to confronting the impact of AIDS—yet the story is engaging and the dialogue articulate.

Innaurato's early acclaim caused the critical expectations about his subsequent work to be very high. Unlike many young playwrights, Innaurato was given little time to develop; instead his work was consistently condemned as disappointing. Tangential debate over his portrayals of homosexual characters only tended to fuel the critical fire. Yet in retrospect Innaurato's achievements are great for such a young writer. Like Tennessee Williams, he developed a personal, slightly grotesque seriocomic style that was rooted in a particular environment. Within this paradigm he has created a number of good plays, and two outstanding ones: *The Transfiguration of Benno Blimpie* is a kind of miracle of ugliness, and *Gemini* is the sort of popular comedy that also has the power to change public perceptions. If Innaurato has settled into a pattern with the last two plays, it is as a writer of competently constructed domestic comedies with unusual characters. This role may be a disappointment to some critics, but with the state of commercial theater in contemporary America, Innaurato is a writer for whom the public can be grateful—one who should be encouraged to continue.

Bibliography

DiGaetani, John. "An Interview with Albert Innaurato," in *Studies in American Drama, 1945-Present.* II (1987).

Freedman, Samuel G. "Reshaping a Play to Reveal Its True Nature," in *The New York Times.* February 24, 1985, sec. II, p. 1.

Innaurato, Albert. Introduction to *Bizarre Behavior*, 1980.

Katz, Mark. "Albert Innaurato: An Interview," in *New York Arts Journal.* No. 10 (July/August, 1978), pp. 7-9.

Lester, Elenore. "Innaurato: His Passion for Outcasts Is Finding a Place on Stage," in *The New York Times.* May 29, 1977, sec. II, p. 4.

Ventimiglia, Peter James. "Recent Trends in American Drama: Michael Christopher, David Mamet, and Albert Innaurato," in *Journal of American Culture.* I (Spring, 1978), pp. 195-204.

Wetzsteon, Ross. "Gay Theatre After Camp: From Ridicule to Revenge," in *The Village Voice.* XXII (April 18, 1977), p. 87.

Michael Quinn

TADEUSZ KANTOR

Born: Wielopole, Poland; 1915

Principal drama

Directed: Juliusz Słowacki's *Balladyna* (1834), pr. 1943; Stanisław Wyspiański's *Powrót Odysa* (1907), pr. 1944; Pierre Corneille's *Le Cid* (1637), pr. 1946; Pedro Calderón de la Barca's *El alcalde de Zalamea* (1643), pr. 1951; George Bernard Shaw's *Saint Joan* (1923), pr. 1956; Stanisław Ignacy Witkiewicz's *Mątwa: Czyli Hyrkaniczny światopogląd* (1923; *The Cuttlefish*, 1970), pr. 1956; Kazimierz Mikulski's *Circus* (c. 1957), pr. 1957; Witkiewicz's *W małym dworku* (1923), pr. 1961; Witkiewicz's *Wariat i zakonnica: Czyli, Nie ma złego, co by na jeszcze gorsze nie wyszło* (1923; *The Madman and the Nun: Or, There Is Nothing Bad Which Could Not Turn into Something Worse*, 1966), pr. 1963; Witkiewicz's *Kurka wodna* (1922; *The Water Hen*, 1969), pr. 1968; Witkiewicz's *Szewcy* (wr. 1934, pb. 1948; *The Shoemakers*, 1968), pr. 1972; Witkiewicz's *Nadobnisie i koczkodany: Czyli, Zielon pigułka* (wr. 1922, pb. 1948; *Dainty Shapes and Hairy Apes: Or, The Green Pill*, 1980), pr. 1973.

Wrote and directed: *Umarła Klasa*, pr. 1975 (based partly on Witkiewicz's *Tumor Mózgowicz*, Witold Gombrowicz's *Ferdyduke*, and Bruno Schulz's "The Pensioner"; *The Dead Class*, 1979); *Wielopole, Wielopole*, pr. 1980 (English translation, 1982); *Niech Sczena Artysci*, pr. 1985 (*Let the Artists Die*, 1985).

Other literary forms

Tadeusz Kantor is best known in the West as a theater director because of his avant-garde, highly unusual and individualized productions. His career has, however, touched on many other aspects of the arts. He originally studied painting and achieved a reputation as a painter; he then gained extensive recognition as a creator/director of "happenings" in the 1960's and 1970's and has written several free-verse tracts or "manifestos" on his theories of the theater. In addition to the areas of expertise already listed, Kantor's work is internationally recognized in graphics, stage design, and costume design.

Achievements

Throughout his long career, Kantor has remained an uncompromised force in the postwar avant-garde in the theater and in other creative fields, such as painting. As a disciple of the ideas of Gordon Craig, he has achieved an extraordinary integration of all the different art forms that compose the theater's *mise en scène*, from innovative notions of acting and the treatment of dramatic literature to the imaginative redefinition and selective reduction of the theater's auditory and visual elements.

Kantor was twice appointed to the faculty of the Academy of Fine Arts in Cracow, in 1948 and in 1968. On both occasions, the professorship was revoked within one year because of his courageous unwillingness to follow government orthodoxy concerning the arts. He was, however, awarded a Polish State Prize for his work in 1962.

Significantly, Kantor's theater company, Cricot 2, has never received support from the Polish government, despite its enormous international success. That success is a mark of the high regard in which Kantor's work is held among theater artists and the theatergoing public in Poland and elsewhere. Perhaps the most remarkable achievement of his theatrical career is the visceral and intellectual impact of his later, intensely personal productions, such as *Wielopole, Wielopole.* The play deals with Kantor's memories of his early life between the wars, and despite the fact that it is performed in Polish, it has become a landmark of the modern theater even for international audiences that know nothing of Polish language, history, and culture.

Biography

Tadeusz Kantor was born in 1915 in Wielopole, a small town not far from the southern city of Cracow, in Poland. His father, a teacher, was killed in World War I, and thus Kantor grew up in the house of his grandmother's brother, a priest. He took an early interest in the theater but decided instead to become a painter, learning drawing and painting under the influence of the Polish Symbolists: Stanisław Wyspiański, Witold Wojtkiewicz, and Jacek Malczewski. From 1934 to 1939, he attended the Academy of Fine Arts in Cracow, where he studied scene design with Karol Frycz, who was himself a highly innovative stage designer as well as a painter, theatrical director, theater manager, and follower of the ideas of Gordon Craig and Wyspiański. Frycz's and Kantor's careers are in keeping with the twentieth century traditions of Cracow, a Polish center for both stage design and for the avant-garde in the visual arts where visual artists often become theater directors and managers.

In 1942, Kantor and a group of young painters formed the underground, experimental Independent Theatre during the German occupation. In 1946, Kantor began his career as a scene designer, creating sets and costumes for theaters throughout Poland until he went to study in France in 1947. He returned in 1948 to organize the first postwar exhibition of modern Polish art in Cracow and was appointed to the faculty of the Cracow Academy of Fine Arts.

The Stalinist period began in Poland in 1949, marked in the arts by the official imposition of Socialist Realism. Kantor's professorship was revoked, and he began to collaborate with Maria Jarema, a widely recognized painter and sculptor who had done scene design for Cricot 1, an important Cracow avant-garde theater between the world wars. Kantor continued designing in this manner until the collapse of Stalinism under Khrushchev in 1956. With the increased independence of Poland, at least in areas of culture, Polish theater began to flourish. During this time, Kantor's style began to intensify and vary. It was also in 1956 that Kantor opened Cricot 2, which would eventually be housed in the basement of the Gallery Krysztofory in the old city of Cracow. Cricot 2 became Kantor's base of operations and a homing point for actors, painters, and poets who sought to explore new dimensions in the arts.

During the late 1950's, Kantor mounted productions at Cricot 2 while traveling and exhibiting his painting in various parts of Western Europe. In 1961, he published the first of his theoretical works on theater, *Teatr Informel* (1961; *The Manifesto of the Informel Theatre*, 1982), which dealt with the concept of a fluid theater composed of "shapeless matter" in which the substance of the performance lay in the artist's struggle with the material, not in the aggregate result of the performance. Kantor was, in the early 1960's, a professor at the Akademie Kunste in Hamburg, where in 1961 he published "Ob die Ruckkehr von Orpheus moglich ist?" (is Orpheus' comeback possible?)

In 1962, Kantor wrote his *Emballage Manifesto*, which propounded the creation of art objects from the lowliest of wrappings, such as discarded sacks, bags, and envelopes, which, from their despised position as disposable receptacles, acquired an autonomous but utterly empty existence. The *Teatr Zerowy* (1963; *Theatre Zero Manifesto*, 1982) followed, and it argued that a play ought not to be enacted but commented on by the performers, its text is to be destroyed and replaced by a theatrical universe of humdrum, discarded objects that are transformed in performance and interact with the actors in a struggle with them for presence on the stage.

From this point on, Kantor continued to create productions in which the text—in many cases the plays of Stanisław Ignacy Witkiewicz ("Witkacy")—had been radically altered. He also continued to mount happenings, to paint, to design, and to write. By the mid-1970's, Kantor was working away from the texts of others by combining parts of other works and adapting them to his special theatrical form as in the case of *The Dead Class*, until he began on his two major autobiographical pieces, *Wielopole, Wielopole* and *Let the Artists Die*. Also during this time, he published his *The Theatre of Death Manifesto* (1975) in which he argues that life can only be expressed in the theater through reference to death.

Throughout his career, Kantor traveled extensively to the major international theater festivals with his productions. Long recognized in Eastern and Western Europe, he first gained attention in North America when he presented *The Dead Class* in Mexico and in the United States at La Mama in 1979. His subsequent tours of *Wielopole, Wielopole* and *Let the Artists Die* have secured Kantor's position as a world-class director and one of the creative forces in the twentieth century avant-garde theater.

Analysis

Tadeusz Kantor's theater can be characterized to a large extent as a theater of objects, a description that applies to both his actors and himself. In his later productions, Kantor has been the subject of his own work, and he appears onstage as a visual element of his own productions—giving directions to the actors and technicians, musing over the action, and playing the role of Tadeusz Kantor in his black jacket and trousers and tieless, plain white shirt. His stage presence is greatly enhanced by his long, gaunt face, which he sets in a mask of haunted contemplation briefly interrupted with small bursts of irritation or humor.

That Kantor's work reflects such an imaginative and insightful ability to transform objects and people into complex, unique performances is in large part because of his background in the visual arts. He clearly subscribes to Craig's notion of the total theater artist and, as such, personally designs and shapes every aspect of his productions. His dramatic works employ virtually none of the conventions of traditional theatrical staging, and his scenography is completely composed of discarded, worn-looking objects and clothing, which he alters to bring them into his special theatrical universe and puts to ingenious, surprising use. The colors in his productions are predominantly flat, pale grays, bone, and black, with accents of purple and red.

The other cause of his theatrical inventiveness has been necessity. His early productions with the Independent Theatre had to be staged in secret because artistic activity of any sort was prohibited by the Germans under penalty of death. In the case of Wyspiański's *Powrot Odysa* (the return of Odysseus), Kantor staged this brooding and sinister play as a modern story of a soldier returning home from the front. Performed in a room of an apartment which had been partially destroyed by the war, without benefit of a stage or set, Kantor transformed the space through the use of objects into the metaphoric waiting room of a train station. Odysseus returns to find his homeland under Nazi domination. Partly as a reaction against the then fashionable school of constructivism, Kantor employed objects such as a decayed wooden board, a muddy broken cartwheel, a mastlike object, an object that looked like the barrel of an old rifle, large, anonymous parcels covered with dust, and a soldier's uniform to create a total environment. In this way, he meant to overwhelm the text with the historical circumstances and the style of performance into which it had been thrust.

After the war, Kantor went to Paris, where he became familiar with Surrealism and abstract expressionism, both hitherto unknown in Poland. He was appointed to the faculty of the Cracow Academy of Fine Arts but subsequently lost his professorship after he refused to participate in official cultural life after the imposition of Socialist Realism. His paintings continued to be exhibited underground, and he made his living as a scene designer. With the collapse of Socialist Realism and the onset of the "thaw" in government cultural repression in the late 1950's, Kantor tried again to insinuate his theatrical aesthetic into the official theaters.

When this proved impossible, he limited his work to the Cricot 2 Theatre, which had been in the planning stages for several years. In 1960, Kantor staged the first postwar performance of Stanisław Witkiewicz's *The Cuttlefish*, which had previously been banned. This production, which was staged as a happening, illustrated Kantor's concept as described in *Teatr autonomiczny* (1963; *The Autonomous Theatre*, 1986) in the following manner: "The theatre which I call **autonomous**/ is the theatre which is not/ a reproductive mechanism,/ i.e., a mechanism whose aim is to/ present an interpretation of a piece of literature/ on stage,/ but a mechanism which/ has its own **independent**/ **existence**."

Kantor's ideas have continued to evolve throughout his complex career. While these shifts often run parallel to current trends in the arts, Kantor is not a follower of movements. For example, when he visited the United States in 1965, he met people who also made happenings. He would later remark that he had been staging happenings since the end of World War II, lacking only the popular name given these events. He would eventually reject happenings because of their necessary physicality, preferring an increasingly reduced theater of essential images. His production of Witkiewicz's *Dainty Shapes and Hairy Apes* in 1973 paralleled his new theory espoused in *Le Théâtre impossible* (1972; *The Impossible Theatre*, 1973). Audience participation, used in the happenings, was abandoned, and the actors performed the play in a cloakroom where, bereft of their humanity, they hung like lifeless objects. Through these methods, Kantor hoped to work beyond the borders of art into an aesthetic space so rarefied and charged with an extraordinary theatrical reality that art would be impossible.

Kantor's work as a director has also been a struggle against illusion in the theater in the service of reality. Thus, for example, he often uses dummies in his productions, as in *The Dead Class*. The principal character, an old man, has decided to return to school at the end of his life. He carries a wax dummy that mirrors his appearance but in a cheap, debased form, a problem that Kantor finds with all imitation in the arts.

His autobiographical works—*Wielopole, Wielopole* and *Let the Artists Die*—are representative of the essence of Kantor's theatrical structure. It has been said of his work that it is as much musical as it is theatrical. Images and themes are presented not through narrative chains of causation, as in most conventional drama, but rather through varied repetitions and recapitulations. In *Let the Artists Die*, the cast appeared again and again repeating a pattern of movement or series of actions that had already been performed with minor variations. These become reexplorations of these themes and images for the audience and for Kantor, who both watches and participates in the production. The effect is not so much one of the musicality of harmonics as one of juxtaposition through contrasts. For example, several times in the production a general, reminiscent of Józef Piłsudski, is wheeled onstage riding a comic-grotesque skeleton of a horse. With each turn, depending on the actions surrounding each circuit, the feeling the general evokes is enriched and slightly transformed.

Kantor's work does not draw conclusions for the spectator. Like his own theoretical evolution and artistic development, it invites the audience to experience the process of his work in performance rather than carry away homiletic messages.

Other major works

NONFICTION: *Teatr Informel,* 1961 (*The Manifesto of the Informel Theatre,* 1982); *Emballage Manifesto,* 1962; *Teatr Zerowy,* 1963 (*Theatre Zero Manifesto,* 1982); *Teatr autonomiczny,* 1963 (*The Autonomous Theatre,* 1986); *Le Théâtre impossible,* 1972 (*The Impossible Theatre,* 1973); *The Theatre of Death Manifesto,* 1975.

Bibliography

Gerould, Daniel."Tadeusz Kantor (1915-   ): A Visual Artist Works Magic on the Polish Stage," in *Performing Arts Journal.* IV, no. 3 (1979), pp. 28-38.

Jenkins, R. "Ring Master in a Circus of Dreams," in *American Theatre.* II (March, 1986), pp. 4-11.

Kłossowicz, Jon."Tadeusz Kantor's Journey," in *The Drama Review.* XXX (Fall, 1986), pp. 98-114.

Kobiałka, Michał. "Kantor—Candor: An Interview with Tadeusz Kantor," in *Stages.* VI, pp. 6-37.

_____. *The Theatre of Essence,* 1984.

Kott, Jon. "The Theatre of Essence: Kantor and Brook," in *Theatre.* III, pp. 55-58.

Steven Hart

ADRIENNE KENNEDY

Born: Pittsburgh, Pennsylvania; September 13, 1931

Principal drama

Funnyhouse of a Negro, pr. 1962, pb. 1969; *The Owl Answers*, pr. 1963, pb. 1969; *A Rat's Mass*, pr. 1966, pb. 1968; *The Lennon Play: In His Own Write*, pr. 1967, pb. 1969 (with John Lennon and Victor Spinetti); *A Lesson in Dead Language*, pr., pb. 1968; *Sun: A Poem for Malcolm X Inspired by His Murder*, pr. 1968, pb. 1971; *A Beast's Story*, pr., pb. 1969; *Boats*, pr. 1969; *Cities of Bezique: Two One Act Plays*, pb. 1969; *An Evening with Dead Essex*, pr. 1973; *A Movie Star Has to Star in Black and White*, pr. 1976, pb. 1984; *A Lancashire Lad*, pr. 1980; *Orestes and Electra*, pr. 1980; *Black Children's Day*, pr. 1980.

Other literary forms

In addition to her plays, Adrienne Kennedy has published a wide-ranging memoir, *People Who Led to My Plays* (1987).

Achievements

Kennedy departs from the theatrical naturalism used by other black American playwrights in favor of a surrealistic and expressionistic form. Her plays capture the irrational quality of dreams while offering insight into the nature of the self and being. Most of her works are complex character studies in which a given figure may have several selves or roles. In this multidimensional presentation lies Kennedy's forte—the unraveling of the individual consciousness.

The playwright received an Obie Award in 1964 for *Funnyhouse of a Negro*, her best-known play; held a Guggenheim Fellowship in 1967; and has received grants from the Rockefeller Foundation, the New England Theatre Conference, the National Endowment for the Arts, and the Creative Artists Public Service. She was a lecturer at Yale University from 1972 to 1974 and a Yale Fellow from 1974 to 1975. In addition to lecturing at Yale, Kennedy has also taught playwriting at Princeton and Brown universities.

Biography

Adrienne Kennedy was born on September 13, 1931, in Pittsburgh, Pennsylvania, the daughter of Cornell Wallace Hawkins, a social worker, and the former Etta Haugabook, a teacher. She grew up in Cleveland, Ohio, and attended Ohio State University, where she received a bachelor's degree in education in 1953. A few years later, she moved to New York and enrolled in creative writing classes at Columbia University and the New School for Social

Research. In 1962, she joined Edward Albee's Playwrights' Workshop in New York City's Circle in the Square. She wrote *Funnyhouse of a Negro* for Albee's workshop. A decade later she became a founder of the Women's Theater Council. In 1953, the playwright married Joseph C. Kennedy, whom she divorced in 1966. She has two sons.

Analysis

Adrienne Kennedy's plays are consistent in their exploration of the double consciousness of Afro-Americans who are themselves inheritors of both African and European American culture and tradition. Symbolically represented by the split in the head of Patrice Lumumba, one of the selves in *Funnyhouse of a Negro*, this double identity frequently results in a schizophrenic division in which a character's selves or roles are at odds with one another. Typically it is the African identity with which the protagonist—who is often a sensitive, well-read young woman—is unable to come to grips. By using a surrealistic form to treat such a complex subject, Kennedy is able to suggest that truth can be arrived at only through the unraveling of distortion. Indeed, what Kennedy's protagonist knows of Africa and of blacks has come to her filtered through the consciousness of others who are eager to label Africans and their descendants "bestial" or "deranged." This seems to be what theater critic Clive Barnes means when he says that Kennedy "thinks black, but she remembers white." For this reason, animal imagery, as well as black and white color contrasts, dominates Kennedy's plays.

Kennedy's concerns with isolationism, identity conflict, and consciousness are presented primarily through character. She has called her plays "states of mind," in which she attempts to bring the subconscious to the level of consciousness. She achieves this essentially by decoding her dreams. Indeed, many of the plays were actually dreams that she later translated into theatrical form. This surrealistic or dreamlike quality of her work has been compared to August Strindberg's dream plays, in that both dramatists render reality through the presentation of distortion. Extracting what is real from what is a distortion as one would with a dream is the puzzle Kennedy establishes for her characters, as well as for her audience, to unravel in each of her major plays: *Funnyhouse of a Negro*, *The Owl Answers*, *A Rat's Mass*, and *A Movie Star Has to Star in Black and White*.

As in life, truth in Kennedy's plays is frequently a matter of subjectivity, and one character's version of it is often brought into question by another's. This is the case in *Funnyhouse of a Negro*, Kennedy's most critically acclaimed play. From the moment a somnambulist woman walks across the stage "as if in a dream" at the beginning of the play, the audience is aware that it is not viewing a realistic performance. Such figures onstage as the woman sleepwalker, women with "wild, straight black hair," a "hunchbacked yellow-skinned dwarf," and objects such as the monumental ebony bed, which resembles a tomb, suggest a nightmarish setting. The action of the play takes place in four settings: Queen Victoria's chamber, the Duchess of Hapsburg's chamber, a Harlem hotel room, and the jungle. Nevertheless, it is not implausible to suggest that the real setting of *Funnyhouse of a Negro* takes place inside the head of Sarah, Kennedy's protagonist. As Sarah tells the theater audience in her opening speech, the four rooms onstage are "[her] rooms."

As with the four sets that are really one room, Sarah has four "selves" who help to reveal the complexity of her character. At first, Sarah appears to be a version of the kindhearted prostitute, or perhaps a reverse Electra who hates rather than loves her father. Kennedy builds upon these types to show Sarah's preoccupation with imagination and dreams, as well as her divided consciousness as a partaker of two cultures. Queen Victoria and the Duchess of Hapsburg are identified with Sarah's mother, or with her white European identity. The other two personalities, Jesus and Patrice Lumumba, the Congolese leader and martyr, on the other hand, are identified with Sarah's father, or with her black African heritage. Significantly, Sarah's four personalities tell the story of the parents' marriage and subsequent trip to Africa and the rape of the mother, which results in the conception of Sarah, each of which events can be called into question by the dreamlike atmosphere of the play and by the mother's insanity. One by one, the four alter egos add details to the story which allow the picture of Sarah's family to build through accretion. Even so, this story is undermined by the final conversation between the landlady and Sarah's boyfriend, Raymond. Doubling as "the Funnyman" to the landlady's "Funnylady," Raymond comes onstage after Sarah's suicide to tell the audience the truth about Sarah's father in the epilogue to the play. Although Sarah claimed to have killed her father, Raymond tells the audience that the father is not dead but rather "liv[ing] in the city in a room with European antiques, photographs of Roman ruins, walls of books and oriental carpets."

The same eschewal of linear progression in *Funnyhouse of a Negro* occurs in *The Owl Answers*, the first of two one-act plays appearing with *A Beast's Story* in the collection titled *Cities of Bezique*. Clara Passmore, the protagonist in *The Owl Answers*, like Sarah in *Funnyhouse of a Negro*, is a sensitive, educated young woman torn between the two cultures of which she is a part. Riveted by her fascination for a culture which seems to want no part of her, Clara, a mulatto English teacher from Savannah, Georgia, learns from her mother that her father, "the richest white man in town," is of English ancestry. She comes to London to give him a fitting burial at Saint Paul's Cathedral, among the "lovely English." Once there, she has a breakdown and is imprisoned in the Tower of London by William Shakespeare, Geoffrey Chaucer, and William the Conquerer, who taunt her by denying her English heritage. Clara, who is both the daughter of the deceased William Mattheson and the Reverend Mr. Passmore (who, with his wife, adopted Clara when she was a child), is as firm in her claim to English ancestry as she is in her plans to bury her father in London. Like Sarah in *Funnyhouse of a Negro*, Clara's true prison exists in her mind. Ironically, Clara Passmore, whose name suggests racial passing, passes only from human into animal form. In a final, violent scene in which the third movement of Haydn's Concerto for Horn in D accentuates the mental anguish of Clara and her mother, Clara's mother stabs herself on an altar of owl feathers. Clara, in the meantime, fends off an attack from a man whom she calls "God," who has assumed that the love she seeks from him is merely sexual. Sarah, who has grown increasingly more owl-like as the play has progressed, utters a final "Ow... oww." In this play, as in *Funnyhouse of a Negro*, Kennedy leaves the audience with questions about the nature of spiritual faith in a world in which one calls upon God, yet in which the only answer heard comes from the owl.

Similar preoccupations with the clash of African and European culture in *Funnyhouse of a Negro* and *The Owl Answers* can be seen in *A Rat's Mass*, a one-act play set in the time of the marching of the Nazi armies. Brother and Sister Rat, who have a rat's head and a rat's belly, respectively, are both in love with Rosemary, a descendant of "the Pope, Julius Caesar, and the Virgin Mary." The two rat siblings struggle to atone for the dark, secret sin they committed when they "went on the slide together," which has forced them into hiding in the attic of their home. Alone together in their misery, Kay and Blake, the sister and brother, remember a time when they "lived in a Holy Chapel with parents and Jesus, Joseph, and Mary, our wise men and our shepherd." Now they can only hear the gnawing of rats in the attic. In desperation, they turn to Rosemary to help them atone for their sins. Rosemary refuses, stating that only through their deaths will there be a way of atonement. The way comes when Jesus, Joseph, Mary, two wise men, and the shepherd return as the Nazi army to open fire on the rats, leaving only Rosemary, like the evergreen shrub for which she is named, to remain standing.

The animal motif employed in *The Owl Answers* and *A Rat's Mass* is less apparent in *A Movie Star Has to Star in Black and White*. Clara Passmore of *The Owl Answers* returns for a "bit role" in which she reads from several of Kennedy's plays. The English literary tradition highly esteemed by the protagonist in *Funnyhouse of a Negro* and *The Owl Answers* is replaced by the American film tradition. Reinforcing the theme of illusion versus reality begun in *Funnyhouse of a Negro*, *A Movie Star Has to Star in Black and White* is actually a series of plays-within-a-play in which scenes from the films *Now, Voyager*, *Viva Zapata*, and *A Place in the Sun* take place in a hospital lobby, Clara's brother's room, and in Clara's old room, respectively. As the title of the play indicates—as well as a stage note directing that all the colors be shades of black and white—Kennedy continues her experimentation with black and white color contrasts onstage. As in other plays by Kennedy, linear progression is eschewed and the illusion of cinema merges with the reality of the life of Clara, a writer and daughter to the Mother and Father, the wife of Eddie, the mother of Eddie Jr., and the alter ego to the film actresses.

Through lines spoken in the first scene by Bette Davis to Paul Henreid, the audience learns of Clara's parents' dream of success in the North, which ends in disappointment when they learn that racial oppression is not confined to the South. The scene takes place simultaneously in an ocean liner from *Now, Voyager* and a hospital lobby where Clara and her mother have come to ascertain the condition of Wally, Clara's brother, who lies in a coma.

Scene 2 moves to Wally's room, while Jean Peters and Marlon Brando enact lines from *Viva Zapata*. History repeats itself when it is revealed that Clara, like her mother before her, is having marital problems with her husband, Eddie. In the meantime, Marlon Brando's character changes the bed sheets onto which Jean Peters' character has bled, reminding the audience of Clara's miscarriage while Eddie was away in the armed services.

In the following scene, Shelley Winters and Montgomery Clift appear onstage in a small rowboat from the film *A Place in the Sun*. In this scene, Clara reveals her frustration as a writer who is black and a woman. She says that her husband thinks that her life is "one of my black and white movies that I love so . . . with me playing a bit part." The play ends with the news that Wally will live, but with brain damage. In the interim, Shelley Winters' character drowns as Montgomery Clift's character looks on, suggesting a connection between Clara's fantasy life in motion pictures and the real world, from which she struggles to escape.

Kennedy's other plays deal with themes similar to those in the works discussed. The animal motif, coupled with the theme of sexuality, is continued in *A Beast's Story* and *A Lesson in Dead Language*. In *A Beast's Story*, Beast Girl kills her child with quinine and whiskey and then kills her husband with an ax after he attempts to make love to her. Her parents, Beast Man and Beast Woman, preside over the dark course of events as shamans anxious for their daughter to rid the household of the "intruder" whose presence has caused a black sun to hover above them. Animal imagery is paired with the rite-of-passage motif in *A Lesson in Dead Language*. In this play, a schoolteacher who is a white dog "from the waist up" instructs seven young girls about menstruation. Similarly, the dreamlike quality of earlier plays continues in *Sun*, a play-poem written about the death of Malcolm X, and in *An Evening with Dead Essex*, based on the assassination of black sniper Mark James Essex.

With the 1980's, Kennedy branched out into the writing of children's plays on commission. Among these plays are *A Lancashire Lad*, *Orestes and Electra*, and *Black Children's Day*.

Adrienne Kennedy dares to be innovative both in her subject matter and in theatrical form. She writes difficult plays that raise questions rather than provide answers. From *Funnyhouse of a Negro* onward, Kennedy chose a subjective form that she has retained throughout her literary career. Her plays grow out of her own experiences as a sensitive and gifted black American who grew up in the American Midwest. There may be little plot in Kennedy's plays, but there is, to be sure, a wealth of symbolism concerning the inherent tensions of Afro-American experience.

Other major work

NONFICTION: *People Who Led to My Plays*, 1987.

Bibliography

Benston, Kimberly W. "*Cities in Bezique*: Adrienne Kennedy's Expressionist Vision," in *CLA Journal*. XX (1976), pp. 235-244.

Brown, Lorraine A. " 'For the Characters Are Myself': Adrienne Kennedy's *Funnyhouse of a Negro*," in *Negro American Literature Forum*. IX (Fall, 1975), pp. 86-88.

Cohn, Ruby. "Black on Black: Baraka, Bullins, Kennedy," in *New American Dramatists, 1960-1980*, 1982.

Curb, Rosemary. "Fragmented Selves in Adrienne Kennedy's *Funnyhouse of a Negro* and *The Owl Answers*," in *Theatre Journal*. XXXII (1980), pp. 180-195.

Tener, Robert L. "Theatre of Identity: Adrienne Kennedy's Portrait of the Black Woman," in *Studies in Black Literature*. VI (1975), pp. 1-5.

P. Jane Splawn

PAVEL KOHOUT

Born: Prague, Czechoslovakia; July 20, 1928

Principal drama

Dobrá píseň, pr., pb. 1952; *Zářijové noci*, pr. 1955, pb. 1956; *Sbohem smutku!*, pr. 1957, pb. 1958; *Taková láska*, pr. 1957, pb. 1958; *Třetí sestra*, pr., pb. 1960; *Říkali mi soudruhu*, pr. 1961; *Cesta kolem světa za 80 dní*, pr., pb. 1962 (adaptation of Jules Verne's novel *Le Tour du monde en quatre-vingts jours*); *Válka s mloky*, pr., pb. 1963 (adaptation of Karel Čapek's novel); *Dvanáct*, pr., pb. 1963; *Josef Švejk*, pr. 1963, pb. 1966 (adaptation of Jaroslav Hašek's novel *Osudy dobrého vojáka Švejka ve světove války*); *August, August, august*, pr. 1967, pb. 1968; *Aksál*, pb. in German as *Evol*, 1969, pr. 1970?; *Válka ve třetím poschodé*, pr., pb. in German as *Krieg im dritten Stock*, 1971; *Ubohý vrah*, pb. in German as *Armer Mörder*, 1972, pr. 1974 (*Poor Murderer*, 1977); *Život v tichém domě*, pr. 1974; *Pech pod střechou*, pr., pb. in German as *Pech unterm den Dach*, 1974; *Požár v suterénu*, pr., pb. in German as *Brand im Souterrain*, 1974 (*Fire in the Basement*, 198?); *Ruleta*, pr., pb. in German as *Roullette*, 1975; *Atest*, pr. in German as *Attest*, 1979 (*Permit*, 198?).

Other literary forms

Apart from his dramatic works, Pavel Kohout has written several success-ful novels: *Bílá kniha* (first published in German, as *Weissbuch*, in 1970; *White Book*, 1977), *Katyně* (1978; *The Hangwoman*, 1981), and *Nápady svaté Kláry* (1982; the ideas of Saint Claire). He has also written poetry, literature for children, screenplays, essays, translations, and lyrics.

Achievements

Kohout belongs to the group of outstanding Czech authors that includes Milan Kundera, Josef Škvorecky, and Václav Havel, who—with the exception of Havel—following a brilliant career in Czechoslovakia left their home-land some time after the Soviet occupation in 1968. At its most essential, Kohout's dramas, as well as his novels, have a common theme: disillusion-ment with the product of modern rationalism and with rationalism itself. His work challenges official explanations of reality, whether of political, philo-sophical, or even scientific origin. Kohout achieves this in a number of ways: by recasting, through creative adaptation, an established literary or dramatic work; through his original dramatic works; and finally, by joining other play-wrights in a cooperative venture that documents the evils of his age and then exorcises them through comedy. His plays have enjoyed tremendous success not only in Czechoslovakia but also in the Soviet Union, Western Europe, and even the United States and Canada. In 1978, he was awarded the Austrian State Prize for his work.

Biography

Pavel Kohout was born in Prague, Czechoslovakia, in 1928, ten years after the creation of the Czechoslovak Republic, and ten years before it was handed over to Adolf Hitler to appease him, in 1938. Again, ten years after this tragic date, in 1948, Czechoslovakia was taken over by the Communists. When the Communist regime tried to liberalize the country from within, the Soviet Union invaded and occupied Czechoslovakia, in 1968. These dates, all of them important historical milestones, define the moving and tragic history of that Central European country and have politicized writers of Kohout's generation.

Born into a middle-class family, Kohout was graduated from high school in 1947 and then studied arts at the Charles University in Prague, from which he was graduated in 1952. He simultaneously embarked on his literary career by publishing, in 1945, his first verses. Between 1947 and 1949, Kohout worked for the Czechoslovak Radio and, after the Communist coup in 1948, experienced a meteoric rise in his career as he became cultural attaché in Moscow (1949-1950), the editor in chief of the satiric weekly *Dikobraz* (*Porcupine*, 1950-1952), and then the editor of the *Czechoslovak Soldier* (1953-1955). Finally, after the inauguration of television broadcasting, he worked as an editor for Czechoslovak Television (1955-1957). This unusually successful decade in Kohout's life, after which he worked as a professional writer, without need of any other employment, is a testimonial to his enthusiastic endorsement of and active participation in the establishment of the Communist system. Even the Czech literary sphere, in which Kohout was most involved, was by no means free from totalitarian horror and outright terror: Poets were hanged and thousands were locked up in labor camps mining uranium or coal. Kohout could not have been unaware of all this.

Following the call for de-Stalinization in 1956, however, Kohout was among the first to subject his beliefs and his work to a critical analysis, and he emerged from this examination of his conscience—personal and literary—a better writer. This fundamental change was not merely a matter of practical expediency. On the contrary, the political situation in Czechoslovakia was such that only after 1962 did a gradual and wildly fluctuating process of liberalization set in. To join the process of liberalization actively still entailed tremendous risks—and few potential rewards—for the courageous, liberal writers. It is entirely to Kohout's credit that he took the risks so early and at a time when Stalinists were so firmly in control.

Kohout's first stage triumph was his play *Taková láska* (such a love), which became the most performed play in Czechoslovakia, with 770 performances within four years of its appearance. It ran for more than five hundred performances in neighboring East Germany and was performed abroad—in the Soviet Union, Israel, South America, and South Africa. Kohout's surprising success has to be considered in the light of the stilted, sterile dramatic productions of dogmatic Socialist Realism, which inhibited not only theater but also all the arts in the countries that subscribed to it. In *Taková láska* Kohout rejected Socialist Realism in a play which, although by no means revolutionary or highly original by today's standards, was nevertheless a courageous application of techniques that had been pioneered by such playwrights as Luigi Pirandello and Bertolt Brecht. This was enough to win for him the fame that he continues to enjoy.

Kohout engaged in a dialogue with Günter Grass in 1967, during the highly politically charged atmosphere on the eve of the heady experience that resulted in the Prague Spring, the short-lived period known as "socialism with a human face." The dialogue was ostensibly an attempt to establish communication between two writers separated not so much by personal inability to communicate as by the fact that the authors belonged to inimical worlds. The side effect of this association was that it elevated Kohout, previously unknown internationally, to a level of European celebrity. Since Kohout had already enjoyed some professional success in the German-speaking world, the publication, in 1968, of his letters to Grass only cemented the image of someone who is on the same level as Grass, an impression fortified by a remarkable degree of agreement between the two.

In 1967 and 1968, Kohout was among the most politically active writers during the remarkable congress of the Czechoslovak Writers' Union (1967) and during the process of liberal reforms (1968). He stood in the forefront of those who pressured the Communist government to undertake such reforms as would turn the country away from the inhumanity inherent in the Communist system and make it respectful of the democratic and humanistic values befitting a central European country with a Christian heritage and a pluralistic cultural tradition. For this activity, he was later, following the Soviet military invasion of Czechoslovakia in 1968, branded a "counterrevolutionary." Kohout's characteristic and courageous reply to the regime which successfully managed to turn the clock back was to accept the challenge expressed in the label "counterrevolutionary" and to publish abroad his *Aus dem Tagebuch eines Konterrevolutionaers* (1969; *From the Diary of a Counterrevolutionary*, 1972). Indeed many of Kohout's works written in the late 1960's and throughout the 1970's were first published in German, although written in Czech.

In 1977, the opposition to the regime's attempt to terrorize the population took the form of a manifesto called Charta 77. This document attempted to hold the government to its previous agreements, such as its signing of the Helsinki Accord, which committed Czechoslovakia to a far-reaching acceptance of international norms of behavior that respected human rights. Kohout was among the signatories of Charta 77, together with his fellow playwright and friend Václav Havel. The authorities tried to make life more difficult for him, although, unlike Havel, he was not sent to prison. On the contrary, he was allowed, in 1978, to go to Vienna, Austria, to direct Nikolai Gogol's *Revizor* (1836; *The Inspector General*, 1890) in Vienna's Burgtheater. Mercifully, Kohout was happy to find in Austria many loyal supporters among the theatergoers as well as among the influential personalities, a fact reflected in his winning the prestigious Austrian State Prize.

Being realistic about the true motivation behind the Czechoslovak authorities' permission that allowed him to stay in Austria, Kohout brought along an Austrian television crew as he returned to the border crossing, sensing that he might not be allowed back. He was right, and this incident at the border, where he not only was prevented from returning to his homeland but also learned that he was stripped of his Czechoslovak citizenship, made an interesting television program, illustrating better than anything the true attitude of his government to the Helsinki Accord. Kohout then decided to make his home in Vienna.

Analysis

If an entity called "Central European literature" truly exists, as some believe (and their most persuasive spokesman is Milan Kundera, a novelist, playwright, and Kohout's countryman), then it would exhibit features that could define the work of Pavel Kohout as well. It would be literature (and drama) concerned with the nature of reality. It would have an obsessive urge to unmask, to demythologize, to tear off the disguises. It would try to approach the truth mindful of the fact that the ultimate truth remains hidden.

Rationalism, the belief underpinning the modern doctrine of progress, is itself challenged when the results of the application of the most progressive thought are as disappointing as the Central European experience suggests. Furthermore, there are areas in human life which resist cool, rational analysis, where the inquisitor is helpless. Kohout dramatizes this belief in his triumphantly successful early play *Taková láska* through the ostensibly trivial but eternal love triangle, in which A loves B, but B loves C (who is unfortunately already married). The twist is that the love of two men and one woman leads to a tragedy, the suicide of the woman, Lida, and that this suicide is treated as a social case, like a murder, for which a judge—in the play identified only as "The Man in a Legal Robe"—attempts to find a cause, that is, a guilty party.

Formally, the interesting premise of the play is fortified by a judicious use of elements borrowed from avant-garde dramatists such as Pirandello and Brecht. Although the play has about it an air of absurdity, in the light of far more absurd stage trials (in which obviously innocent victims perished) such an air of absurdity paradoxically brings to the stage a semblance of normality rather than contrived absurdity. Compared to the lifeless propaganda plays of Socialist Realism, the viewers in Czechoslovakia and elsewhere in the Eastern Bloc viewed the play as refreshingly authentic: It dealt with human problems that are impervious to neat solutions and that are offered wholesale in a world in which ideology attempts to eliminate uncertainty and present the world as monochromatic. The very fact that the play's topic has absolutely nothing to do with politics or ideology of any kind (since the tragedy is derived from the timeless theme of love) itself makes the play political: It proves there are limits to politics, as well as to reason.

In a Brechtian move, the audience is asked to make its own judgment, to become the judges establishing the guilt of those responsible for the death of Lida. It turns out that it is impossible to make a clear-cut judgment, that life is too complex even in the case about which one knows the details. There is a Pirandello-like minimalism about the staging that underlines the philosophical implications of the play. A courtroom set is transformed into a variety of locations, without elaborate stage sets, by the use of light. The play progresses through carefully administered doses of "illuminations," gradually stripping the certainty from the heretofore rather predictable plot. While the series of flashbacks does illuminate the past, it also paradoxically relativizes it: The audience moves closer to the truth, only to see it (the truth) become more elusive.

After this success, Kohout embarked on a series of dramatic adaptations of novels and short stories from a variety of sources. Not all of them merit much critical interest, but some are definitely masterpieces. Perhaps it is unfortunate that the modern age puts such a stress on originality. Kohout would have found a more sympathetic audience in a Shakespearean age. It is refreshing, however, that Kohout himself lacks any embarrassment on this score, regarding his dramatic adaptations as a challenge, whether he is adapting Jules Verne's *Le Tour du monde en quatre-vingts jours* (1873; *Around the World in Eighty Days*, 1873), Karel Čapek's *Válka s mloky* (1936; *War with the Newts*, 1939), or Jaroslav Hašek's *Osudy dobrého vojáka Švejka ve světove války* (1921-1923; *The Good Soldier Schweik*, 1930). Each of these projects posed a truly formidable challenge, and in each case, Kohout surmounted the difficulties imaginatively. Verne's novel, with its huge cast of characters and locations, is staged with half a dozen characters playing ten roles each, with a twentieth century commentator/*raisonneur* supplying an additional dimension as well as a bridging device. *Válka s mloky* was staged as a television broadcast featuring the apocalyptic destruction of the world. Yet it was Hašek's *The Good Soldier Schweik* that presented Kohout with the biggest challenge. No fewer than thirty dramatists had tried to stage the novel, from Erwin Piscator to Bertolt Brecht. Brecht's adaptation was particularly unsuccessful, but it taught Kohout a lesson. Where Brecht put Švejk in a German uniform sending him to fight in World War II, Kohout decided to let Švejk be Švejk. He did it by concentrating on the first of four books of the novel and on a single theme: little Josef Švejk against the entire Austro-Hungarian Empire. Kohout further preserved the original flavor of Hašek's work by incorporating quotations with minimal changes and transforming the play into a multimedia extravaganza with the use of music and projection techniques.

Each of the three plays is much more than an adaptation of an entertaining novel with comical and satirical possibilities. *Cesta kolem světa za 80 dni* contrasts the travel and technology of the nineteenth century with the technology of the twentieth century, with its space travel. Yet the audience in Prague could not even travel to Vienna, because it was "in the West," though only in the political sense (geographically, Vienna is east of Prague). The freedom to move freely where one wants was among the most desired in the liberal 1960's and remains the dream of intellectuals and ordinary people alike. Technological advances did nothing to enable one to travel to neighboring Vienna, hence the disappointment. Furthermore, the rational application of technology, which harnessed the labor of the newts, results in an apocalyptic war instead of a millennium. Švejk is an example of a man who turns the very thought of rational organization of society (best exemplified in the military) into a joke.

Švejk is a clown who knows that he is clowning in order to survive. His wits are all that keep him from ending up as common cannon fodder, as did his comrades. What makes him special is his analysis of reality and his strategy to deal with it, both of which escape a common soldier. Švejk is not only amusing but also cynical and cruel. He is the opposite of the dreamer. In fact, he is the bane of all dreamers, as becomes abundantly clear in Švejk's clashes with many-hued dreamers in Hašek's novel. It is perhaps because of Kohout's deep involvement with the character of Švejk that he turned, in his next play, to an original creation of an anti-Švejk: the clown-dreamer hero of his *August, August, august* (August, August, the clown).

August is a clown-dreamer, as opposed to the clown-cynic of the Švejk type. Instead of cynicism, one finds lyricism; instead of the war, there is circus; instead of the Austro-Hungarian monarchy, a circus manager. The play deals very artfully with the timeless problems through allegories which are purposefully transparent but nevertheless effective. It was also the last major play which Kohout saw staged in his own country.

Three one-act plays—*Pech pod střechou* (bad luck under the roof), *Fire in the Basement*, and *Válka ve třetím poschodí* (war on the third floor)—were staged in Ingolstadt, Bavaria, in 1974 as a trilogy under the common title *Život v tichém domě* (life in a quiet house). These are plays that could not be shown in Czechoslovakia and that one could define as dissident plays, if only because their common theme is the powerlessness of ordinary people confronting an all-pervasive totalitarian machinery that invades the "quiet" private space of an individual like a Kafkaesque nightmare.

Without any doubt, the most powerful of Kohout's plays is his creative adaptation of a short story by Leonid Andreyev, "Mysl'" ("Thought"), entitled *Poor Murderer*. It is an example which, better than other Kohout adaptations, provides an ample justification for adaptations in general. It is also a borderline case in the sense that Kohout has taken liberties with the story, making some important changes that invest the original with possibilities that it did not have as a short story. In the original story, a physician, Kerzhentsev, is interrogated by a board of psychiatrists in order to determine whether he is sane, since he is to be tried for murder. As Kerzhentsev reconstructs the murder, it becomes clear that some time before he attempted the murder, he had decided to pretend to be insane in order to evade legal responsibility for the crime. Kerzhentsev's tragedy follows his realization that his pretense was so thorough that even he no longer knows for sure whether he is normal.

In Kohout's play, Kerzhentsev is turned into an actor and allowed to reenact his crime with the help of his fellow inmates in a mental hospital, under the watchful eye of the chief psychiatrist, who attempts to understand Kerzhentsev's problem through the reenactment of a "play" written by Kerzhentsev. The wealth of meanings and different levels of interpretation enter through the device of the play-within-a-play. Kerzhentsev was in love with a woman (who did not reciprocate his love) married to an unworthy has-been of an actor, a philanderer, a drinker, and a man of very little talent. Kerzhentsev believed that he was a much better man and feigned madness in order to kill his actor/rival. When he reenacts the murder in the play-within-a-play, he is stopped, and it is revealed to him that he never murdered his rival. Crushed, Kerzhentsev is seen smiling dementedly as his beloved actress finally realizes the depth of Kerzhentsev's passion and, blaming herself for his insanity, decides to dedicate her life to nursing Kerzhentsev. At this point, the rival admits defeat and congratulates Kerzhentsev for his successful "killing." The ambiguity inherent in this ending is not resolved. It is impossible to know what Kerzhentsev is truly thinking, whether he is in fact insane. One thing is clear: Kerzhentsev planned to get rid of his rival and planned a revenge and a "killing." Although not a drop of blood was spilled, Kerzhentsev carried out his threat of revenge and even succeeded in getting the attention of his beloved.

The play is a masterpiece of tense, concentrated, highly choreographed dance macabre, in which meaning suddenly shifts and the focus moves among several levels of reality. One message is relentlessly driven home: Rationality has its limits. If Kerzhentsev's plan truly did work, did it not work perhaps too well? There are serious doubts about Kerzhentsev's sanity no matter what the outcome. Perhaps even more relevant, bearing in mind the general direction of Kohout's long-standing preoccupation with rationalism, the play provides yet another example of rationality in the service of evil. As an outstanding example of Kohout's disillusionment with rationalism, the play has no rivals in his dramatic repertoire. The theme has ample support, however, in Kohout's novels. In *White Book*, a high school teacher challenges the traditional understanding of physics symbolized by the law of gravity when he levitates at will (to the distress of the local scientific and political authorities). In *The Hangwoman*, modern education produces an executrix versed in the art of execution and torture after being systematically trained by several knowledgeable, even scholarly, executioners. In *Nápady svaté Kláry*, a high school girl causes consternation by her accurate fortune-telling.

The irrationality of the three novels clashes with an only apparent rationality of the authorities, be they political or scientific. The outcome of such clashes is the underlying doubt about the rationality of a wide variety of beliefs. In this, Kohout joins the chorus of other Eastern European dramatists and novelists, whose experience motivates them to regard the nature of belief in all of its guises with suspicion. It is a suspicion well-founded, as Kohout convincingly demonstrated in his first truly internationally successful play, *Taková láska*. It was perhaps his desire to convey this conclusion clearly that motivated him to turn to adaptations and rely on transparent allegories. The effect of such cautionary tales as he provides in his plays and novels is often liberating. Far from encouraging a pessimism, disdain, or contempt, they promote understanding, sympathy, and compassion, even toward those authorities who so richly deserve his censure.

Other major works

NOVELS: *Bílá kniha*, 1970 (in German as *Weissbuch*; *White Book*, 1977); *Katyně*, 1978 (*The Hangwoman*, 1981); *Nápady svaté Kláry*, 1982.

NONFICTION: *Briefe über die Grenze: Versuch eines Ost-West-Dialogs*, 1968 (with Günter Grass); *Aus dem Tagebuch eines Konterrevolutionaers*, 1969 (*From the Diary of a Counterrevolutionary*, 1972).

CHILDREN'S LITERATURE: *Jolana a Kouselnik*, 1980 (in German as *Jolana und der Zauberer*).

MISCELLANEOUS: *Verse a pisne z let 1945-1952*, 1952.

Bibliography
Goetz-Stankiewicz, Marketa. *The Silenced Theatre: Czech Playwrights Without a Stage*, 1979.
Trensky, Paul I. *Czech Drama Since World War II*, 1978.

Peter Petro

HUGH LEONARD
John Keyes Byrne

Born: Dublin, Ireland; November 9, 1926

Principal drama

The Italian Road, pr. 1954; *The Big Birthday,* pr. 1956; *A Leap in the Dark,* pr. 1957; *Madigan's Lock,* pr. 1958, pb. 1987; *A Walk on the Water,* pr. 1960; *The Passion of Peter McGinty,* pr. 1961; *Stephen D,* pr., pb. 1962 (adaptation of James Joyce's novels *A Portrait of the Artist as a Young Man* and *Stephen Hero*); *The Poker Session,* pr., pb. 1963; *Dublin One,* pr. 1963 (adaptation of Joyce's short-story collection *Dubliners*); *The Saints Go Cycling In,* pr. 1965 (adaptation of Flann O'Brien's novel *The Dalkey Archives*); *Mick and Mick,* pr. 1966, pb. as *All the Nice People,* 1966; *The Au Pair Man,* pr., pb. 1968; *The Patrick Pearse Motel,* pr., pb. 1971; *Da,* pr., pb. 1973; *Summer,* pr. 1974, pb. 1979; *Irishmen: A Suburb of Babylon,* pr. 1975, pb. 1983 (includes *Irishmen, Nothing Personal,* and *The Last of the Mohicans*); *Liam Liar,* pr. 1976 (adaptation of Keith Waterhouse and Willis Hall's play *Billy Liar*); *Time Was,* pr. 1976, pb. 1980; *A Life,* pr. 1979, pb. 1981; *Kill,* pr. 1982; *Scorpions,* pr. 1983; *Pizzazz,* pr. 1984, pb. 1987; *The Mask of Moriarty,* pr. 1985, pb. 1987.

Other literary forms

Home Before Night: Memoirs of an Irish Time and Place by the Author of "Da" (1979) is a charming, humorous memoir, which includes many of the characters, incidents, conversations, and witticisms in *Da*. "Out After Dark" is a forthcoming sequel to his autobiography. Hugh Leonard has been a regular contributor of amusing topical commentaries in such Irish newspapers as *Hibernia,* the *Sunday Independent,* and the *Sunday Tribune.* He has also reviewed theater for *Plays and Players.*

Achievements

Among contemporary Irish playwrights, Leonard is the most widely produced. His plays have achieved commercial success in Ireland, Great Britain, and the United States. Exceptionally prolific and yet polished, Leonard has been a good journeyman author in various media. Leonard honed his dramatic skills by writing extensively not only for the stage but also for radio, television, film, and newspapers, always with entertainment as a prime consideration. (His television play *Silent Song,* 1966, received the Italia Award.)

Leonard's reputation as an Irish Neil Simon suggests the aspects for which he has been both admired and criticized. His greatest asset as a playwright is essential to any commercially successful dramatist: He knows how to keep an audience entertained with humorous dialogue and situations. Conversely, his detractors have usually complained that his main weakness is a facile, glib superficiality. His best plays combine a theatrical flair for clever language and situation comedy with thoughtful depth of human understanding.

For example, his greatest achievement on the stage has been *Da*, which in 1978 won the Tony Award, New York Drama Critics' Circle Award, Outer Critics' Circle Award, and Drama Desk Award for Best Play. Mel Gussow of *The New York Times* claimed that *Da* is "in a class with the best of O'Casey." Even the fastidious John Simon of *New York* magazine found it "complex and graceful" and "entertaining, endearing and gently moving."

A new play by Leonard has often been a highlight of the Dublin Theatre Festival. At the same time, the theatrical facility and universal accessibility of his plays allow them to be transplanted with ease from Dublin's Abbey or Olympia theaters to London's West End and America's Broadway or regional companies.

Biography

Hugh Leonard is the pen name of John Keyes Byrne, who was born on November 9, 1926, in Dublin, Ireland. Leonard was adopted and reared by a couple in Dalkey, in south County Dublin, who were the prototypes for the foster parents in *Da*.

In 1945, at age eighteen, Leonard started work in the Land Commission for five pounds per week. He was always expecting to leave soon but remained for fourteen years, by which time his salary was ten pounds, eight shillings. In 1955, he married Paule Jacquet, a Belgian who lived in Moscow and Los Angeles during World War II. They had a daughter, Danielle.

To escape from the drudgery of his civil service job, Leonard joined a dramatic society. Amateur theater has been the seedbed for some of Ireland's best playwrights, and this was true for Leonard as well. *The Italian Road* was given an amateur production but was turned down by the Abbey Theatre. Then Leonard submitted *The Big Birthday* (which had an amateur production as *Nightingale in the Branches* in 1954), taking his pseudonym from the psychopath Hughie Leonard in the rejected play. *The Big Birthday* was produced in 1956 by the Abbey. He also wrote serial radio dramas, including the daily *The Kennedys of Castleross*, which was the main dramatic experience for the non-theatergoing, pretelevision majority in Ireland. He resigned from the Land Commission in 1959 to become a full-time professional writer.

Leonard wrote for Granada television in Manchester, England, and then moved there, and he later lived in London from 1963 until 1970, writing adaptations and original scripts for television. His numerous adaptations for television have included *The Hound of the Baskervilles* (1968), *Dombey and Son* (1969), *Great Expectations* (1967), *The Moonstone* (1972), *Nicholas Nickleby* (1968), *The Possessed* (1969), *A Sentimental Education* (1970), and

Wuthering Heights (1967). He claimed that he could write an original television play in six to eight weeks or an episode of adaptation in two days. Leonard wrote the script for a major Irish television production in 1966, *Insurrection*, for the commemorations of the 1916 Easter Rising. He also wrote for film, including *Great Catherine* (starring and coproduced by Peter O'Toole) and *Interlude* (both 1968). Leonard's first play to open in London's West End was *Stephen D*, his adaptation of fellow Dubliner James Joyce's *Portrait of the Artist as a Young Man* (1916) and *Stephen Hero* (1944). Before *Stephen D* was produced in New York in 1967, it had its American premiere at the Olney Theater, near Washington, D.C., which has often introduced Leonard plays to the United States, with James Waring as the director, working closely with the playwright.

In 1970, Leonard returned with his family to Dalkey in south Dublin. Productions of *The Patrick Pearse Motel*, *Da*, *Summer*, *Irishmen*, *Time Was*, *A Life*, *Kill*, *Scorpions*, and *The Mask of Moriarty* attracted large audiences and generally favorable reviews. He continued to write for television, including the adaptation of *Strumpet City* (1981) for Radio Telefis Eireann with Peter O'Toole and Peter Ustinov featured in a major Irish production.

Leonard has been quite successful financially, and he especially benefited from a 1970's Irish tax law regarding artistic income as nontaxable. A segment of the television program *Sixty Minutes*, focusing on the Irish tax law, revealed that Leonard's large royalties from *Da* were not taxable whereas actors in Irish productions of Leonard's plays were taxed as usual. An article in the *Sunday Independent* entitled "Leonard's 'Da' Gives Him £4,000 a Week!" quoted Leonard as saying that the Broadway production of *Da* was grossing eighty thousand dollars a week, of which he got ten percent, amounting to £200,000 a year tax-free. He expected another two thousand pounds per week from United States touring productions. Moreover, he claimed to have sold the film rights for $150,000 with an extra $100,000 for writing the screenplay.

Some of his compatriots may have seen the prolific writer as a prodigal son, returned yet rich and unrepentant. Leonard has lived out much of his life in the public eye, particularly in the Irish newspapers. Whereas his new plays often appeared annually, his essays often appeared weekly, covering similar material in a different genre but containing what could be scenarios, scenes, themes, or quips from plays-in-progress. Leonard's humorous columns in Irish periodicals, such as *Hibernia*, the *Sunday Independent*, and the *Sunday Tribune*, have given his opinions high visibility, even notoriety. In his articles, private reminiscences have mingled with public declarations, winning him praise and blame as a wise man and a foolish egotist. He has used such extratheatrical forums to sound off wittily and sometimes bitterly on diverse subjects, including Irish provinciality or modishness, contraception, narrow nationalism, prudery or vulgarity, Abbey Theatre policy, inefficient services, political shibboleths, demagoguery and skulduggery, and the violence of the Irish Republican Army, a daring target for ridicule. Indeed, few issues in Irish public life have gone unnoticed in Leonard's satirical essays. Allusions to "my present wife" in a country without divorce teased those who might regard this cosmopolitan author as a jet-set Don Juan contaminated by alien life-styles and ideas. He has been among the celebrities that some Irish love to hate. While some would praise him as a brave clear voice with sharp barbs against deserving enemies, others would blame him for cheap, cynical, glib wisecracks. For example, his review of events in the year 1986 in the *Sunday Independent* (January 4, 1987) included sardonic put-downs of both God and an Irish prime minister in the same paragraph: "The Gobshite of the Year Award goes to God, for having His chance and missing it." Such comments, direct from the author rather than filtered through a mouthpiece in a play, add to Leonard's vivid public persona in Holy Ireland.

Analysis

As a playwright, Hugh Leonard is a dependable professional. He may not be of the first rank (few are), but unlike many a would-be dramatist, he can hold an audience. His plays are usually of some interest if not always of great depth. In short, his plays show great talent but no genius, which is perhaps all an audience requires for the price of admission. In adapting Joyce's novels for the stage as *Stephen D*, Leonard showed a command over the special demands of theater as a genre. His play *The Poker Session* used a little humor, a staple of much of his work, but held the audience's attention with a Pinteresque menace, as a patient from a mental asylum takes revenge on his family with both method and madness. *The Au Pair Man* was an interesting allegory about the relationship between a dying British Empire and an emerging Ireland. *Summer* and *Irishmen* showed both Leonard's compassion for, and critique of, his compatriots. *Time Was* stretched Leonard's theatrical powers but did not really amount to a satisfying work. *The Mask of Moriarty* was a clever and original Sherlock Holmes story but did nothing more than tell a detective yarn with slick theatrical aplomb. Three plays that stand out among Leonard's large oeuvre and that will be examined in this analysis are *The Patrick Pearse Motel*, *Da*, and *A Life*.

The Patrick Pearse Motel is a hilarious two-act farce meticulously constructed and cleverly written. This bedroom farce is in the style of a Georges Feydeau, Eugène Labiche, or Alan Ayckbourn, with the unusual distinction that it is set in Ireland. It is not only an amusing sex romp but also an outrageous satire ridiculing the Dublin nouveau riche anxious to get more money and to forget their humble pasts. Set after the 1966 commemorations of the 1916 Easter Rising, the play portrays a new Ireland with a confused identity, invoking the pieties of nationalistic heroism while scrambling to assimilate with the worst of Anglo-American culture. The very title of *The Patrick*

Pearse Motel suggests the contradictions of the new Ireland willing to peddle its devalued cultural icons as it enters the Common Market of international mediocrity and homogeneity.

Such a theme may seem rather heavy for a farce, but Leonard handles all aspects of his play with a light, sure touch. The setting is the upscale suburb of Foxrock in Dublin's "vodka-and-bitter-lemon belt," but the names of the characters are from Irish myths. There are three couples: Dermod and Grainne, Fintan and Niamh, and James Usheen and Venetia Manning. Usheen is obsessed with the English Miss Manning but is too full of self-love to share himself with any one woman. A talk-show host on British television, he is an outrageous parody of the modern celebrity whose character is profoundly shallow.

Dermod is a get-rich-quick businessman and social climber who, with Fintan, is opening the Patrick Pearse Motel in the Dublin mountains and the Michael Collins Motel in Cork. He and his beautiful wife, Grainne, have risen from a working-class housing estate to a Foxrock home with all the material goods that a *parvenu* couple could want. There is still something more, however, that Grainne desires: one "night of harmless innocent adultery." The man she is luring is Usheen, and the site for the consummation is to be the Patrick Pearse Motel, the setting for act 2.

The set for the motel is two bedrooms, which are mirror images of each other, with a corridor between. Nearly all the eighty-four rooms in the motel are identical (the Manchester Martyrs' room has three single beds), and all are named after the pantheon of Irish patriots, including Brian Boru, Thomas Davis, Michael Davitt, O'Donovan Rossa, and Bernadette Devlin. The action takes place in the Charles Stewart Parnell room (appropriate for adultery), where Grainne intends to have Usheen, and the Robert Emmet room, where her husband is being seduced by Venetia Manning.

Moreover, Fintan, who madly desires only his plain wife Niamh and wrongly suspects her of adultery, is trying to kill her as she hides in a wardrobe. The characters are not aware of the proximity of the other characters, because as one enters a space, another exits with split-second timing. A letter, wet trousers, a negligee, a fur coat, a shillelagh, and brandy, as well as husbands and wives, go astray and lead to all kinds of comic confusion. Despite the complications, the dramatist, like a master puppeteer, never loses control of the characters or the action, and as a social satirist, never loses sight of the thrust of the comedy to ridicule and correct human folly.

Da is Leonard's most successful play both commercially and artistically. As much as in any other Leonard play, entertaining humorous dialogue and situations are mingled with a depth of compassion. In this autobiographical memory play, the humor is mirthful without malice and moves toward forgiveness. *Da* was conceived and premiered at the Olney Theater near Washington, D.C. Leonard's program notes for the 1973 world premiere at

Olney said that during rehearsals for *The Patrick Pearse Motel* at Olney in 1972, someone (perhaps James Waring, the longtime American director of Leonard's plays) suggested that Leonard's stories about his father could be the basis for an amusing play. Within a year, Leonard had turned the suggestion into perhaps his best play. The original production, with John McGiver in the title role, was a success at Olney, in Chicago, and at the 1973 Dublin Theatre Festival. In 1978, *Da* featured Barnard Hughes in the successful Broadway production at the Morosco Theater and won many awards, including a Tony for best play.

"Da, in my part of the world, means father," writes Samuel Beckett in *Molloy* (1951; English translation, 1955). Leonard is also from Beckett's part of the world, south Dublin, but his treatment of his da is quite different from Beckett's stark, mordant style. Leonard's coming to terms with his dead father is bathed in a nostalgic, almost sentimental, glow. The tone of Charlie, the narrator, may indeed be resentful throughout the drama, but the overall tone of the play is light, generous, and forgiving. John Keyes Byrne the man may indeed have drawn on bittersweet personal experiences for this memory play, but Hugh Leonard the entertainer refined and altered that autobiographical material for the sake of a good yarn.

Charlie is a playwright in his early forties who has returned from London to Dalkey for his father's funeral in present time May, 1968. In the play as well as in Leonard's life, his "Da" and "Ma" were not his real parents but a couple who adopted him as a baby. As he is straightening up in the house in which he was reared, he has flashbacks to his childhood and is haunted by the memories of his (foster) parents and by his own younger selves (played by a second actor). Unlike Thornton Wilder's *Our Town* (1938), in which the dead observe the living and cannot communicate with them, Charlie observes those now dead and even argues with them. He quarrels even with his younger self. The theatrical device of Charlie Now and Charlie Then, played by two actors, two decades apart but in lively debate, is more than a gimmick and is very effective for both humor and insight. It is interesting to note that Irish playwrights Brian Friel and Thomas Murphy have used similar antinaturalistic techniques in plays dealing with similar subjects. In *Philadelphia, Here I Come!* (1964), Friel split his main character into public and private selves played by two actors. In *A Crucial Week in the Life of a Grocer's Assistant* (1967), Murphy's protagonist slips from present time into fantasies of what might be. Such antinaturalistic techniques can use entertaining devices to reveal insight into interior life.

Another theatrical dimension that gives the play fluidity to move in time and place is the set. The main playing area in *Da* is the kitchen ("the womb of the play"), but this play is not the mere "kitchen-sink" realism of the stereotypical early Abbey drama, as there are several playing spaces. Moreover, as most of the characters now supposedly exist in the haunted mind of

Charlie, they break the conventions of literal realism by walking through walls and crossing boundaries of playing areas, as well as moving forward and backward in their ages. The areas include a seafront and a hilltop. "On the other side of the stage is a neutral area, defined by lighting," to signify various locales.

In the opening scene, as Charlie Now meets his old friend Oliver (who can be played by the same actor who will play Oliver at a younger age), a remark about the dead father is the cue for Da to pass through the kitchen and contradict the remark. When Charlie is again alone, Da nonchalantly returns to comment on his own funeral. He disregards his son's order to "Piss off." About one of his catch phrases, "Yis, the angels'll be having a pee," Da says, "You ought to put that down in one of your plays." The protagonist playwright replies, "I'll die first." This irony is typical of how this reflexive play makes the playwright figure a target of humor, whereas Da, the "ignorant man," "lop-sided liar," "an old thick, a zombie, a mastodon," "a sheep," is the life of the drama. Charlie is learning that "love turned upside down is love for all that."

The dramatic conflict is not only between father and son but also within the son himself. In the fine scene that opens act 2, Charlie is berated by his younger self for not properly taking care of Da: "All the dirty bits over with when you got here." In fact, young Charlie finds the man he is to become "jizzless" and "a bit of a disappointment." In return, Charlie finds his younger self naïve and self-righteous.

An important theme in *Da* as in other Leonard plays is class differences. Having worked as a gardener for the upper-class Prynne family for fifty-four years, Da received a mere twenty-five pounds as severance pay. Charlie castigates Da for being so obsequious in accepting the mean, condescending patronage of the rich. In order to help his son, Da works for another four years for "Catholics with money, letting on they're the Quality." Charlie's debt to Da goes beyond the grave: The allowance that Charlie had been sending Da was saved as an inheritance. Da proclaims, "I didn't die with the arse out of me trousers like the rest of them—I left money!" The curtain falls as Da's ghost follows Charlie back to England.

Da's 1978 American success was followed by a 1979 sequel, *A Life*, premiered at the Abbey for the Dublin Theatre Festival and featuring Cyril Cusack. From *Da*, Leonard takes the thin, acerbic Mr. Drumm, the man who gets Charlie into the Irish civil service, the foil to Da, and makes him the central character of *A Life*. In the bittersweet *Da*, the sweetness of the title character gave the play its warm, even sentimental quality, triumphing over the bitter aspects of Charlie and Mr. Drumm. So it was a daring move to make the testy Drumm the chief protagonist of a sequel and yet retain the audience's interest in and sympathy for him. Mr. Drumm's attempts at humor are his cold caustic quips against his wife and few friends, and yet the play engages an audience's compassion for the dying central character despite his life of nastiness. Desmond Drumm is described at various ages as "prickly," "a dry stick," "a nun," "a bitter old pill," with "a face on you like a plateful of mortal sins" (an Irishism also used by James Joyce and Brendan Behan). Foils to Mr. Drumm are his dotty wife, Dolly; exuberant, teasing Mary ("Mims"), whom Des loves when young but with whom he seems to be incompatible because she had "a mind like a mayfly"; and the man whom Mary marries instead, "feckless, good-humored" Lar Kearns. All four characters (Mr. Drumm, Dolly, Mary, and Kearns) are about sixty and have corresponding selves about forty years younger (Desmond, Dorothy, Mibs, and Lar) played by four other actors.

Like *Da*, *A Life* is set in May, but the mood is more autumnal and melancholy. Instead of looking forward to a well-earned retirement, Mr. Drumm is facing death and looking back on his life, with a sad realization of what was and what might have been. He visits Mary and Lar Kearns in order to redeem the time, perhaps not only the previous six years of silence but also a lifetime of opportunities for love wasted by selfish righteousness. As in *Da*, the set is inventively designed and lighted with various spaces to accommodate flashbacks to youth. As two older characters cross from a parlor into a kitchen, the scene jumps back forty years to their younger selves.

There are beautiful symmetries of comparison and contrast among the characters, the time periods, the stage areas, and various other mirror images. Such techniques are not only clever in themselves, but also, by distilling time and space, they reveal to the audience the importance of using well a life's short precious time. Drumm has such an epiphany in the play's last minutes: "Three hundred days a year for forty years . . . I've spent twelve thousand days doing work I despise. Instead of friends, I've had standards . . . Well, *I* failed."

Other major works

SCREENPLAYS: *Great Catherine*, 1968; *Interlude*, 1968.

TELEPLAYS: *Silent Song*, 1966; *Great Expectations*, 1967 (based on Charles Dickens' novel); *Wuthering Heights*, 1967 (based on Emily Brontë's novel); *Nicholas Nickleby*, 1968 (based on Dickens' novel); *The Hound of the Baskervilles*, 1968 (based on Arthur Conan Doyle's story); *The Possessed*, 1969 (based on Fyodor Dostoevski's novel); *Dombey and Son*, 1969 (based on Dickens' novel); *A Sentimental Education*, 1970 (based on Gustave Flaubert's novel); *The Moonstone*, 1972 (based on Wilkie Collins' novel); *Strumpet City*, 1981 (based on James Plunkett's novel).

NONFICTION: *Home Before Night: Memoirs of an Irish Time and Place by the Author of "Da,"* 1979; *Leonard's Year*, 1987.

Bibliography
Hickey, Des, and Gus Smith. *A Paler Shade of Green*, 1972.
Hogan, Robert. *After the Irish Renaissance: A Critical History of the Irish Drama Since The Plough and the Stars*, 1967.
Kakutani, Michiko. "Today's Irish Dramatists—and the Literary Ghosts That Haunt Their Imagination," in *The New York Times*. November 2, 1980, sec. D, p. 1.
King, Kimball. *Ten Modern Irish Playwrights: A Comprehensive Annotated Bibliography*, 1979.
Rosenfeld, Megan. "'A Life' in the Theater: Olney's Support System (Hugh Leonard Writes, and James Waring Puts It on Stage)," in *The Washington Post*. August 9, 1981, sec. D, p. 1.

Christopher Griffin

ROMULUS LINNEY

Born: Philadelphia, Pennsylvania; September 21, 1930

Principal drama

The Sorrows of Frederick, pb. 1966, pr. 1967; *Goodbye Howard*, pr. 1970; *The Love Suicide at Schofield Barracks*, pr. 1972, pb. 1973; *Democracy and Esther*, pb. 1973 (adaptation of Henry Adams' novels *Democracy* and *Esther*; revised as *Democracy*, pr. 1974, pb. 1975); *Holy Ghosts*, pr. 1974, pb. 1977; *The Seasons, Man's Estate*, pr. 1974; *Appalachia Sounding*, pr. 1975; *Old Man Joseph and His Family: A Play in Two Acts*, pr. 1977, pb. 1978; *Childe Byron*, pr. 1977, pb. 1981; *Just Folks*, pr. 1978; *The Death of King Philip*, pr. 1979; *Tennessee*, pr. 1979, pb. 1980; *The Captivity of Pixie Shedman*, pb. 1980, pr. 1981; *El Hermano*, pr., pb. 1981; *Laughing Stock*, pr., pb. 1984 (includes *Tennessee, Goodbye Howard*, and *F.M.*); *Why the Lord Come to Sand Mountain*, pr., pb. 1984; *The Soul of a Tree*, pr. 1984; *Sand Mountain*, pr., pb. 1985 (includes *Why the Lord Come to Sand Mountain* and *Sand Mountain Matchmaking*); *A Woman Without a Name*, pr. 1985, pb. 1986; *Pops*, pr. 1986, pb. 1987 (six short plays).

Other literary forms

Romulus Linney is the author of three novels—*Heathen Valley* (1962), *Slowly, by Thy Hand Unfurled* (1965), and *Jesus Tales* (1980)—as well as innumerable articles, reviews, poems, and short fiction, published in *The New York Times Sunday Book Review*, *New York Quarterly*, and elsewhere.

Achievements

Linney's dramatic achievements are in two areas: historical biography and Appalachian mountain tales. He is ranked high among the few American playwrights writing historical drama for the contemporary theater. Without sacrificing theatricality, Linney brings to the stage the soaring language and large ideas that have been attributed to other great dramatic eras. In addition, through his folk plays dealing with Appalachian areas, he has become a voice for the rural life-styles in danger of extinction in America. Like John Millington Synge in Ireland and Federico García Lorca in Spain, Linney captures the unique features of the speech of the rural areas of the Carolinas, Virginias, and Tennessee.

The much-produced Linney has been the recipient of virtually every major playwriting award and fellowship in the United States, including those of the National Endowment for the Arts (1974), the Guggenheim Foundation (1980), and an Obie Award (1980). In 1984, he was honored with an Award in Literature from the American Academy and Institute of Arts and Letters.

While his plays have been performed all over the United States and Europe, he has a special relationship with the Whole Theatre in New Jersey and the Philadelphia Festival Theatre.

Biography

Romulus Linney was born in Philadelphia and reared in Madison, Tennessee. His father, a doctor and an avid outdoorsman, greatly influenced Linney's life but died when Linney was thirteen. He and his mother moved to Washington, where she taught public speaking. After he was graduated from Oberlin College in 1953, Linney attended Yale School of Drama, where he received an M.F.A. degree in directing in 1958. He began his writing career as a novelist, writing *Heathen Valley* in 1962 and *Slowly, by Thy Hand Unfurled* in 1965. After some struggling, he wrote his first play, *The Sorrows of Frederick*, and found his true voice. Since that time, Linney has written many plays. He was a member of New Dramatists for seven years, and he writes, lectures, and conducts workshops at several colleges in the New York area, where he also makes his home.

Analysis

Despite his rural childhood, Romulus Linney is a sophisticated and very well-read author, drawing on his education and scholarly research as much as on his personal experiences to bring a surprisingly simple but authentic worldview to his work. Fascinated by the storytelling traditions of Appalachia, Linney finds a gold mine of material in the folktales of that region. Yet what separates his work from the anthropologist's is his ability to exploit the inherent dramatic qualities of the storytellers themselves. In Linney's mountain plays, he makes use of the natural storytelling power of the stage to spin fascinating yarns about simple folk whose intuitive understanding of human relationships is expressed in superstitious old wives' tales. The action is often the dramatization of a story to witnesses—a play-within-a-play device that works well because the characters are natural storytellers. Linney's own storytelling powers are enhanced by this format, because the characters, by their attitudes toward the value of tall tales, reinforce for the audience the magical qualities of theatrical reenactment. Yet Linney's work never descends to simple recitation; the personality of the storyteller, the reactions of the character-listener, and the presence of "something at stake" for both always keep the dramatic tension intact.

The best illustration of the texture of Linney's mountain plays is the one-act play *Why the Lord Come to Sand Mountain*, which, together with *Sand Mountain Matchmaking*, constitutes the evening of drama *Sand Mountain*. An old mountain woman named Sang Picker (she gathers ginseng root for a living) asks the audience if they know any good "Smoky Mountain head benders," and proceeds to tell one of her own, a story which comes alive before her as the Lord and Peter enter, looking for Sand Mountain. When they find Jack, Jean, and Fourteen Children (played by one actor), the Lord and Peter are treated to another story: a reenactment of the conception, birth, and childhood of Jesus, reared by Joseph (acted by Jack) and Mary (acted by Jean), embellished with apocryphal details. "He'd come to Sand Mountain," Sang Picker tells the audience, "to hear tell about his Daddy, and Mary and hisself as a child, and he had." Jean supplies the moral (a favorite of Linney): "Hit ain't the ending whut's important. Hit's the beginning."

One early success, which has been re-created in many regional theaters, is *Holy Ghosts*, about a primitive Fundamentalist sect that uses snakes in its worship services. A convert to this religion, Nancy Shedman, leaves her husband, Colman, to marry the old father of the religion, Obediah Buckhorn; Colman follows her to the church and debunks her quasi-religious conversion. At the play's climax, however, Nancy chooses neither her husband nor her "savior"; she exercises a newfound independence from both and leaves for business school. Thematically, Linney deals with the shortcomings of unquestioning obedience (implied in Obediah's name), but Nancy's decision is a typical Linney signature: women turning their backs on men, the weaker sex. *Sand Mountain Matchmaking* pursues the dramatic potential of the courtship ritual. The widow Rebecca listens patiently to three suitors (in the traditional folktale format), then follows the bizarre but effective advice ("Cure a cold sore—kiss a dog") of an old mountain woman. The final match is an equal partnership based on mutual honesty. In *A Woman Without a Name* (based on Linney's novel *Slowly, by Thy Hand Unfurled*), serious in theme and tone, the nameless central figure keeps a journal, clumsily at first, but more and more articulately as the years pass. In the journal, she collects her feelings about the loss of her children one by one, the guilt she feels because she believes that she has somehow caused their deaths, and the indifference of the men in her life to her longing to express herself and to live a full life. The outcome of the play, partially drawing on historical fact, finds her the leader of a temperance society: "Anneal, Journal, Standard Dictionary: to put to the fire, then to freezing cold. To temper. To toughen. To make enduring. That is the word I understand now." The play bears a resemblance to *The Captivity of Pixie Shedman*, in which a young man reads the diary of his grandmother and learns of her exploitation by the men in her life, who treated her like property.

Linney's erudition and penchant for scholarly research are most clearly seen in his historical dramas, which in his hands become dramatic expressions of the chasm between the conceived ideal and the practical application of that ideal in an imperfect world. Frederick II, in *The Sorrows of Frederick*, abandons an important battle to attend the funeral of his dog; his greatest military triumphs are always marred by a personal loss. In Linney's portrait, Frederick is forceful, clearheaded, and single-minded in public af-

fairs but almost pathetically inept in dealing with his personal life. His friendship with Voltaire, his unconsummated marriage to Elizabeth Christine, and
especially his love for Fredersdorf, a childhood comrade, are all clumsily
handled, while his military victories often come fortuitously, without effort.
Linney dramatizes the complex career of Frederick through a series of time
changes, moving backward and forward from pivotal public events to the
significant personal events that exacerbate or ameliorate them.

Democracy and Esther, later titled simply *Democracy*, is a dramatic combination of two Henry Adams novels. As in *Holy Ghosts*, the women in the
play prove to be the strongest characters, declining offers of marriage from
seemingly eligible men whose strength of character does not fulfill the wom-
en's expectations. Another historical drama, *Childe Byron*, deals with an
imaginary meeting of Lord Byron and his estranged daughter, Ada, who
challenges her father to justify his wretched life, in a mock trial at the moment of her death. One of the most complex storytelling devices Linney has
ever employed is used in the essentially antiwar play *The Love Suicide at
Schofield Barracks*. Here, by the specific instructions of the General of
Schofield Barracks, his own public suicide, along with his wife's, is reenacted
by the officers and witnesses to the tragedy on the morning after the deaths.
By means of disparate testimonies, which give a multiple perspective of the
General's personality, the complex motives of his act are examined.

Linney is perhaps most comfortable in the short-play format, where his
storytelling abilities transform human relationships into entertaining yarns
with warm-hearted morals. *Laughing Stock* consists of three fairly short
pieces, at the same time comic and touching. *Tennessee* tells the story of a
woman whose husband promised to take her to Tennessee, only to drive in
circles until she was only seven miles from her childhood home. *Goodbye,
Howard*, despite its hospital setting, is a comedy in which three elderly sisters prematurely announce the death of their brother, only to discover that
they have simply got off the elevator on the wrong floor. In *F.M.*, which takes
place in a college writing class, a Faulkner-like novelist pours out his heart in
the classroom, incidentally reminding the teacher of her own sidetracked talent and writing career. The most ambitious collection of short plays, however, is *Pops*, a series of six short plays on the theme of love, designed to be
performed by the ideal company of actors: juvenile, ingenue, leading man,
leading lady, character man, and character woman. Sometimes working with
historical material (as in "Ave Maria") and sometimes with the present (as in
the delightful "Tonight We Love"), Linney finds the universal question in all
love stories: whether two people fall in love through fate or through their
own efforts.

Music, virtually always present in his work, is Linney's universal metaphor
for the harmonies and cadences of human interaction. *Childe Byron*, for
example, calls for some fourteen distinct musical pieces as accompaniment to

the action. Linney has stated that, because his plays are often episodic, they fall into a natural structural rhythm, like music. His words are musical as well; Linney's works reveal his fine ear for dialogue, especially for the regionalisms embedded in folktales, old saws and sayings, and figurative language born of the mountain life. An authenticity of expression, along with a sensitivity to linguistic rhythms, characterizes Linney's dialogue. From a position of healthy skepticism rather than cynicism, Linney sees a world of humor and warmth, in which the search for relationships based on mutual respect is never-ending.

Other major works
NOVELS: *Heathen Valley*, 1962; *Slowly, by Thy Hand Unfurled*, 1965; *Jesus Tales*, 1980.
TELEPLAY: *The Thirty-fourth Star*, 1976.

Bibliography
Spero, Bette. "Romulus Linney Looks at Love in Whole Theatre's Season Opener," in *The Newark Star Ledger*. October 3, 1986.
Williams, Christian. "Southern Discomfort," in *The Washington Post*. October 2, 1980.
Wynne, Peter. "An Evening of Variations on Love Themes," in *Morristown Record*. September 26, 1986.

Thomas J. Taylor

MARK MEDOFF

Born: Mount Carmel, Illinois; March 18, 1940

Principal drama
The Wager, pr. 1967, pb. 1975; *Doing a Good One for the Red Man*, pr. 1969, pb. 1974; *The Froegle Dictum*, pr. 1971, pb. 1974; *The War on Tatem*, pr. 1972, pb. 1974; *The Kramer*, pr. 1972, pb. 1976; *When You Comin' Back, Red Ryder?*, pr. 1973, pb. 1974; *The Odyssey of Jeremy Jack*, pr., pb. 1974 (with Carleene Johnson); *The Ultimate Grammar of Life*, pr., pb. 1974; *The Halloween Bandit*, pr. 1976; *The Disintegration of Aaron Weiss*, pr. 1977 (radio play); *Children of a Lesser God*, pr. 1979, pb. 1980; *The Hands of Its Enemy*, pr. 1984; *The Heart Outright*, pr. 1986.

Other literary forms
Mark Medoff is known only for his plays, but a story is anthologized in *Prize College Stories*, 1963.

Achievements
Although some of his early works found their way to the Off-Broadway circuit, Medoff's real achievement rests with his Tony Award–winning *Children of a Lesser God*, the first major play since *The Miracle Worker* to depict deafness onstage, but unique in that the play was written to be played by a deaf actress, Phyllis Frelich. Written in a stunning dramaturgical style, in which the speeches are signed in American Sign Language, Medoff explores not only the love story of the two protagonists but also the hidden assumptions about "being different" that result in prejudices in the "normal" person. The 1980 Tony Award was added to the Drama Desk Award and the Outer Critics Circle Award that same year; it was Medoff's second Outer Critics Circle Award, the first coming from *When You Comin' Back, Red Ryder?*, which also won an Obie Award and the Jefferson Award. A Guggenheim Fellowship in 1974-1975 allowed Medoff to pursue his writing while holding a faculty position at New Mexico State University. The film version of his play has also garnered many awards, including the Academy Award for Best Actress.

Biography
Mark Howard Medoff was born to educated parents (his father a physician and his mother a psychologist) and was educated at the University of Miami and at Stanford University. Intending to undertake a writing career, he gradually moved toward teaching, and found unexpected rewards. While pursuing his professional playwriting career, he advanced in academia,

chairing the Department of Drama at New Mexico State University, a position which would allow him to mount college productions of his work before attempting professional productions in the regional or New York market.

Medoff's relationship with Phyllis Frelich and her husband, Robert Steinberg, began in 1977, when Medoff promised Frelich, an accomplished deaf actress, to write a play for her. The resulting three-year collaboration moved to Broadway after Steinberg and Frelich helped Medoff refine the play's ideas into a finished script. John Rubenstein replaced Steinberg for the Broadway run, winning a Tony for his work, as did Frelich. After a long hiatus, during which Medoff wrote and rewrote his next two works, *Hands of Its Enemy* was performed Off-Broadway to mixed reviews, with Phyllis Frelich again cast as a deaf person and with Steinberg as her interpreter. *The Heart Outright* received a workshop production at the American Southwest Theatre Company, where Medoff serves as artistic director.

Analysis

Because of his practice of carefully rewriting every detail of his work and testing it in readings and workshops, and because his academic duties limit his writing time to the mornings, Medoff has only a modest number of plays to his credit. While some theatrical stylization is also present (as in his early *The War on Tatem*, in which a narrator helps the audience through several years of a young man's experiences, or in *Children of a Lesser God*, in which time is condensed by eliminating blackouts and other theatrical devices, allowing characters to move in and out of the stage frame at will), Medoff stays with realistic plots and psychologically believable characters. While on the surface Medoff deals with a variety of topics, placing his plays in quite different locales and social settings (a college dormitory room, a restaurant, a home for the deaf, a rehearsal stage, and the like), certain themes gradually emerge in Medoff's work as concerns which are central to the playwright's artistic vision and as recurring motifs important to understanding the larger ideas of his plays. Three major concerns can be discerned: the journey to self-realization; violence as an event which precipitates that journey; and the relation of language to meaning, in its ability to obfuscate as well as its limitations for full communication. Deafness is a built-in metaphor for all Medoff's themes, in that the deaf person must suffer not only the handicap but also the prejudices of the hearing public, who perceive deaf persons as somehow less than whole, as if the inability to speak the oral language somehow precludes their experiencing the same emotions and having the same thoughts as the hearing. This violence done to the deaf makes them highly sensitive to the limitations of all communication.

Thematically, there seems to be an underlying sense of incipient violence in many of Medoff's plays. The early one-act play titled *The War on Tatem*, far from a fully mature work, begins the exploration of a theme which seems to follow Medoff from play to play in steadily more sophisticated form. The "war" is a gang war in Miami Beach, between adolescents who do not even know the function of a gang, but know only that they must "fight it out" for some sort of vague control over an even vaguer territory. Here is the primeval impulse toward winning and keeping a territory; the young boys make a comedy of an inclination that becomes deadly serious a few years later in urban areas and that carries with it the seeds of nationalism and war. Tough-guy King Myron sends his challenge to Louis Dunbar via messenger. Louis, the leader of a sorry group of youngsters known as the Tatem Perch, knows that a showdown is inevitable, but he avoids it as long as he can, with glibness and clever talk. When, however, Myron picks on Louis's little brother, Louis sees that it is time for action. He gets a bloody nose for his trouble, but the lesson is learned and a reputation is saved. Most important, Louis comes to know things about himself that he carries with him into adult life and, as twenty-year-old narrator, explains in retrospect to the audience.

From this modest beginning, Medoff continued to explore the basic human trait of avoidance of violence. His notion is clearest in the two early full-length works that made their way to New York: *The Wager* and *When You Comin' Back, Red Ryder?* In *The Wager*, for example, two college men, Ward and Leeds, lounge in their dormitory room discussing the possibility of seducing Honor, the wife of a neighbor, Ron. Very early, and for no immediately explainable purpose, Leeds carries a revolver, an image which shadows the play as it moves toward its climax, exaggerated in a second-act scene in which Honor's husband brandishes a machine gun. The play moves within the possibilities of violence; Leeds is described in a stage direction: "A dangerous explosiveness rages beneath his very cool exterior." The sense is that underneath the complex patina of social conventions lies the ever-present possibility of physical violence, which exposes all the hypocrisy behind which normal personalities hide from raw forces. The "dance" of word games, double entendres, subtle reverse psychological ploys, and the like is interrupted by the unequivocal burst of energy implied in the violent act.

If the undercurrent of violence can be seen in *The Wager*, it bursts to the surface in *When You Comin' Back, Red Ryder?*, a play which explores more directly and visually the question of bravery and cowardice in the face of danger. Teddy, a dangerous man who is making his way across the country by his wits, confronts the self-protective and falsely safe inhabitants of a run-down wayside restaurant. At stake—besides the very expensive violin held "hostage" by Teddy throughout the play—is the presence or absence of bravery in the face of violence: Stephen, a frightened young man, is forced into humiliating acts before his girlfriend, Angel, and in the process discovers his own manliness. Teddy is not so much a real threat as he is the embodiment of all the threats to one's comfortable mental existence, a challenger not simply to the body but also to protective attitudes and self-deceit. Nor is Teddy a simpleminded brute; his cruelty is calculated and clever, and it stems from a rudimentary but accurate understanding of how humans act toward one another. He instinctively senses the affection of Angel for Stephen, and forces Stephen to "look bad" in front of her.

The violence he does to the married couple Richard and Clarisse, who have stopped for breakfast, is parallel to the Stephen-Angel plot: Richard is forced by Teddy to choose his wife's humiliation over the dollar value of the violin; when he turns his back on Clarisse, the false values of their marriage are exposed. It should be remembered, however, that Richard has been shot (a flesh wound) by this time and that Teddy still holds the gun, so the choice is not as simple as the wife chooses to interpret it. The dilemma, however, does seem to expose the duplicity and thinness of the marriage. Thus, Teddy, without destroying the violin, destroys the marriage. Ironically, after Teddy's departure, Richard himself destroys the violin in anger and as a gesture of what he has lost. Like Stephen, however, Clarisse is freed by the violence of the events to identify herself, finally, as a whole person no longer burdened with the falseness that the marriage forced on her. Thus, Medoff's plays explore how honest the characters are with themselves, given a situation which forces them to back away from all the façades and face who they really are behind the masks of social acceptability. While on the surface the plays are about violence, they are in fact about the realizations that come from the introduction of violence to an otherwise false and superficial life. Acting as a catalyst for the reaction that lies dormant within the human personality, violence, like agitation in a test tube, begins the chain reaction that results in a satisfaction, a neutralizing, of the disparate "chemicals" of the human personality.

Working alongside the themes of violence in Medoff's plays are his concerns with the manipulation of language to achieve the characters' ends. In every play, the dialogue hinges on wordplay: vague references, subtle and obscure distinctions in the language, a preciseness on the part of one character in order to intimidate another, less verbally accomplished person. Some of the battles are entirely verbal for a large part of the play. In *The War on Tatem*, for example, Louis does everything that he can, verbally, to avoid and then to ameliorate the actual fight, and he succeeds until his brother, less verbal and less cowardly, gets Louis to act on his principles with something besides words. The entire conflict of *The Wager* centers on Ward's ignorance of the subtleties of the (often unspoken) dialogue between Leeds and Honor. A typical line, showing how Leeds can manage the language to suit his ends, is: "You think I'm cleverer than you think I am, when in fact you think I'm cleverer than I am. And that's one of the reasons why I'm king and you clean the stables." Leeds, too, is possibly hiding something from himself. Hints of homosexuality or impotence are sprinkled through the play, and his ultimate discovery may be that his attraction to Honor may finally bring his sexual preferences to the surface. In *Children of a Lesser God*, the entire action revolves around the question of whether Sarah is somehow obligated to learn to read lips or whether she has a right to stay within her own range of expression and expect others to enter into it. The mode of communication becomes the arena of conflict not only for Sarah and James but for Sarah and the "real" world of the hearing as well.

Finally, the single most important aspect of Medoff's plays is the discovery by the protagonist of his or her own identity, a discovery often precipitated by the introduction of the possibility of violence. All of his plays are really moments when the search for self is intensified by circumstances. *Children of a Lesser God* is not merely James's play, in which he discovers that deaf people are whole people; it is, most important, a journey taken by Sarah into articulating a truth for herself, one which has lain embedded in her anger and defensive attitudes. When she tells James about the "joining" that they can never have, she is telling herself for the first time as well. The whole "speech" to the panel is in fact her manifesto for her future, and she comes to it only after her relationship with deafness is replaced by her relationship with James. It is no coincidence that James's last name is Leeds, the name of the character in *The Wager*, since in both cases a man hurries to assumptions about a woman, who must during the course of the action set him straight about those assumptions. Honor and Sarah are alike, too, in that they both are clearheaded about their defense systems against humanity but must discover who they are during the play itself. They both become more satisfied with themselves after the male (in both cases Leeds, a name which takes on significance in the abstract) helps them through the complexities of self-argument.

Continuing the themes of self-awareness and the difficulties of verbal communication, in Medoff's next play, *The Hands of Its Enemy*, it is a stage director who guides a woman on her journey to self-realization. The title refers to the existential saying "Life is in the hands of its enemies." Here, the play-within-a-play form is employed as a device for exploring the ways that a novice playwright (a deaf woman, played by Frelich in New York) hides the truth from herself about a violent incident in her past. As the rehearsals progress on her autobiographical play, the director admonishes her for writing a "little revenge play" instead of a "large play about domestic violence." The playwright has written a play about a wife's revenge on her husband, instead of about the pain and violence of her own experience. This self-disguise of one's real anguish is central to all Medoff's plays. He sees his characters as exposing themselves *to* themselves in the course of the play.

As Medoff's body of work grows and his dramaturgical skills become more refined, the recurring themes of self-realization, violence as catalyst, and the properties of language continue to identify his creative style. Given his habits of careful attention to detail and his obsession with drafts and workshops, the positive critical reception of his first plays in New York, and his opportunities for regional tryouts of all new work, Medoff is in a good position to continue a playwriting career offering high-quality drama to the American theatergoing public. This potential, if realized, along with his outstanding canon to date, puts him in the company of David Mamet, Sam Shepard, and Lanford Wilson, the best of contemporary American playwrights.

Bibliography

Barnes, Clive. *"Hands of Its Enemy* Has Firm Grip," in *New York Daily News.* November 19, 1986.

Beaufort, John. "Absorbing Mark Medoff Drama," in *Christian Science Monitor.* November 19, 1986.

Hall, S. Moore. "Ex-Faculty Bad Boy Mark Medoff Takes a Tony Home to New Mexico," in *People.* XV (January 12, 1981), p. 78.

"Locker Room Kid," in *Esquire.* LXXXIV (October, 1975), p. 190.

The New Yorker. Review of *Children of a Lesser God.* LVI (April 14, 1980), p. 101.

Rich, Frank. Review of *The Hands of Its Enemy* in *The New York Times.* CXXXVI (November 19, 1986), p. C29.

Simon, John. Review of *The Hands of Its Enemy* in *New York.* XIX (December 1, 1986), p. 150.

Thomas J. Taylor

PIETRO METASTASIO
Pietro Antonio Domenico Trapassi

Born: Rome, Italy; January 3, 1698
Died: Vienna, Austria; April 12, 1782

Principal drama

Gli orti esperidi, pr., pb. 1721; *Didone abbandonata*, pr. 1724, pb. 1733 (libretto; *Dido Forsaken*, 1952); *Siroe, re di Persia*, pr. 1726, pb. 1734 (libretto); *Catone in Utica*, pr. 1728, pb. 1734 (libretto); *Ezio*, pr. 1728, pb. 1733 (libretto); *Artaserse*, pr. 1730, pb. 1733 (libretto; *Artaxerxes*, 1761); *Adriano in Siria*, pr. 1731, pb. 1733 (libretto; *Adrian in Syria*, 1767); *Demetrio*, pr. 1731, pb. 1733 (libretto; *Demetrius*, pb. 1767); *Sant'Elena al Calvario*, pr. 1731; *Issipile*, pr. 1732, pb. 1733 (libretto; *Hypsipyle*, 1767); *La morte d'Abele*, pr. 1732, pb. 1734 (libretto; *The Death of Abel*, 1768); *L'Olimpiade*, pr., pb. 1733 (libretto; *The Olympiad*, 1767); *La clemenza di Tito*, pr. 1734, pb. 1737 (libretto; *The Mercy of Titus*, pb. 1767); *Temistocle*, pr. 1736, pb. 1737 (*Themistocles*, 1767); *Attilio Regolo*, wr. 1740, pr., pb. 1750 (libretto; *Atilius Regulus*, pb. 1767); *Zenobia*, pr. 1740 (libretto; English translation, 1767); *Isacco, figura del Redentore*, pr. 1740; *Il re pastore*, pr. 1751 (libretto); *L'eroe cinese*, pr. 1752; *The Works of Metastasio*, 1767 (two volumes).

Other literary forms

In addition to his plays, Pietro Metastasio wrote a number of oratorios, some stylized love songs of lyric charm called *canzonetta*, and several volumes of criticism and letters.

Achievements

Metastasio created the first great libretti in opera. Though they were written primarily as dramatic vehicles for music, his melodramas, as they were called, were so poetic and so dramatically effective that they were often performed as independent plays.

In the century or more before Metastasio, the libretto had sunk from its primacy in the works of the early operatic composers, such as Claudio Monteverdi, to mere episodic threads between scenes of spectacle and exaggerated action, even low comedy. The music, particularly as it allowed for feats of virtuosity and vocal fireworks, made the libretto an almost vestigial part of the performance; indeed, the poetry of most of the libretti during the hundred years before Metastasio was negligible.

Following the pioneering reform of his predecessor, Apostolo Zeno, Metastasio brought an impressive artistic integrity to the form. Subordinating the merely spectacular, he simplified plot structure, creating scenes which both enhanced the music and delineated character and idea. His melodramas were thematically controlled: logical, dignified, and poetic.

His lyric gift was the key to his art. The poetic language had a conciseness, a precision, a fluency that meshed the action perfectly with the music. In effect, he was not only the first great librettist but the first modern one as well. In his hands, the opera became genuinely dramatic as well as musical. His influence was such that almost all of his major works were set to music by every major composer of the age: Giovanni Battista Pergolesi, Antonio Vivaldi, Alessandro Scarlatti, Johann Sebastian Bach, George Frederick Handel, Wolfgang Amadeus Mozart, and Ludwig van Beethoven.

Biography

Pietro Metastasio was born Pietro Antonio Domenico Trapassi, the fourth child of a poor family living in Rome. Though little is known of his early years, he seems to have been a precocious child, gifted with the ability to create lyrics spontaneously. The first important event of his childhood years occurred in 1708, when, at the age of ten, he was reciting and singing extemporaneous verse to a group of playmates and he was noticed by the influential lawyer and literary man Gianvincenzo Gravina. So impressed was he with the boy's ability that Gravina secured permission from the parents to adopt him and carried the boy into a world of classical and legal studies.

Though the story sounds improbable, the practice of extemporary declamation was not an unusual one in Italy at that time. As a form of public entertainment, it often dazzled and frequently awed the audience, who watched as poets vied with one another to expatiate in eight-line rhyming stanzas on any subject offered. Metastasio himself relates in his letters how, one evening at Gravina's, he improvised eighty stanzas at a single sitting. Such a feat exhausted the youth, however, and Gravina, fearful for the boy's health, soon put a stop to such improvisations.

Gravina himself was a member of an important literary club. A coterie of artists and poets who had originally come together in a Roman garden in 1690, the group formalized its association, founding an academy called Arcadia. Its members were devoted to the writing of simple, classically inspired verse, poetry of pastoral clarity and elegance free from the artificial mannerism of the seventeenth century baroque poet Giambattista Marino and his followers.

Arcadia was an important early influence on the work of the young Pietro Trapassi. Indicative of his respect for the classics, Gravina had already changed the boy's family name to "Metastasio," a Greek translation of Trapassi, meaning "crossing" and symbolizing, appropriately, the crossing from a humble, untutored station to a position of cultivated study and discipline. Metastasio's admission to the Academy in 1718, at the age of twenty, provided him with examples of Italian neoclassical poetry which he was to bring to theatrical brilliance in his melodramas. The Academy taught him the importance of verse which was musical, precise, clear—verse in which importance was given to the sound of the word, the rhythm of the phrase.

Ironically, Gravina died shortly before Metastasio's formal admission to the Academy, but he left his protégé a large inheritance so that, for the first time in his life, Metastasio was independent. Both the law and literature now consumed his interest, and he continued to write lyric and conventional love poetry which began to attract notice. By 1719, he had moved to Naples, taking a position as law clerk in the office of one of that city's most respected jurists. Meanwhile, his fame as a poet was spreading.

Though he had produced only one minor dramatic work, *Justin* (1717), published in the same volume as his short poems, Metastasio received a commission from the viceroy in Naples to write a dramatic serenade in honor of the birthday of Elizabeth, the wife of Charles VI, Emperor of Austria and ruler of Italy. He responded with *Gli orti esperidi*, a short play which was to be a critical turning point in his life and career. The female lead of Venus was sung by Marianna Bulgarelli, one of the most famous actresses and singers of the era. Known as La Romanina, she was impressed by the lyric beauty of the piece and was further taken by the handsome young poet, whose courtliness and quiet elegance so naturally complemented his genius. She fell in love with Metastasio and took him as her protégé.

His relationship with La Romanina was the most significant in his career. Though married, she encouraged Metastasio to live in her household in Rome, where he would have more opportunity to pursue his art. That the two became lovers is probable but not certain. Metastasio's letters to her are complimentary, tactful, discreet; hers to him have not survived. What is certain is that Romanina convinced him to give up the law and to turn his attention full-time to poetry. She provided him with an intellectually stimulating environment, introduced him to theatrical friends, writers and artists, and, according to some biographers, served as a critical sounding board for the development of his craft. It was in her salon where he immersed himself in the study of music. Their relationship was to last until her death in 1734.

For her Metastasio wrote his first melodrama—a play meant to be performed with music. *Dido Forsaken* was a sensational success. Nothing like it had appeared in the Italian theater before. The melodrama was compact and logical and the poetry was of a high order, serving not as an excuse for the music but as an integral part of it. *Dido Forsaken* is one of the first truly modern operatic scripts.

Some half-dozen melodramas followed, and by 1730 Metastasio was one of the best-known dramatists in Italy. Upon the retirement of Apostolo Zeno as official poet to the Viennese court, Metastasio was offered the post. He arrived there in April, 1730, and from that date until his death more than half a century later, he wrote the works that were to establish him as the greatest of Italian librettists.

His life at court took on the regularity and the ease which made it possible for him to produce with great facility, though his life became, from a biographer's point of view, one of routine uneventfulness. The first decade of his stay in Vienna, the capital of the Holy Roman Empire, was the most productive of his career. From 1730 to 1740, he wrote the greatest melodramas—libretti—of the age. They appeared quickly, dazzlingly, in succession: *Demetrius*, *The Olympiad*, *The Mercy of Titus*, *Themistocles*, and *Attilius Regulus*.

The Countess D'Althan, who had first known Metastasio when he was in Naples, became his patron and his confidante during these Viennese years; it was she who filled the intellectual and emotional void left by Romanina's death at the height of his achievements. Refusing to learn German, he was even so, always courtly and diplomatic. Some contemporary accounts scorn his servility, his readiness to bow and to kiss the hand that fed him. He lived relatively isolated from the events at court, seemingly unconcerned with the momentous historical events of the era.

After 1740, Metastasio's powers began to wane. He had been engaged in almost ceaseless writing, often by command, always for an occasion; by 1750, his melodramas had become competent and crafty but little else.

His final years were not happy. Afflicted with a nervous disorder sometimes identified as hypochondria, Metastasio found writing increasingly difficult. He was aware, too, that the operatic world was beginning to turn away from his style of heroic tragedy—the *opera seria*—in preference for a more bourgeois, less aristocratic tradition which Christoph Willibald Gluck and Mozart were exemplifying. In addition, the lighter comic drama—the *opera buffa*—made the Metastasian conflicts of love and duty seem stodgy and old-fashioned, reliquaries of a pre-Enlightenment age.

By the time of his death in 1782, Metastasio's vogue had passed. Yet his influence was such that a medal was struck, bearing the phrase "The Italian Sophocles," in honor of Europe's most outstanding musical dramatist. His reputation is secure as a great librettist who was also a first-rate poet.

Analysis

The Metastasian themes which seemed so old-fashioned in the late eighteenth century were the very epitome of an artistic reflection of Order, of Monarchy, of a world controlled by reason and distrustful of the passions. The heroes and heroines of Pietro Metastasio's dramas are highborn princes, kings and queens who ultimately subdue their baser drives and who adhere to an ideal—patriotism, duty, honor. Conflicts in a Metastasian drama are thus not physical but psychological. Characters often philosophize and rarely bleed. The action of the drama—static by standards of a later theatrical tradition—revolves about the protagonist's resolution of the conflict, a resolution sometimes closed by death but more often also by happiness and salvation. In the end, dignity triumphs; order is restored.

Dido Forsaken, Metastasio's first melodrama and his earliest success, is an excellent introduction to his work, since it illustrates some of the major characteristics of his later Viennese period which produced his masterpieces. In his introduction to the drama, Metastasio notes that his source was Vergil's *Aeneid* (c. 29-19 B.C.), in deference to the classics, which typified the eighteenth century's idea of imitation and adaptation of Greek and Roman literary models. His plot is straightforward and uncomplicated. Dido, widowed queen of Carthage, has fallen in love with Aeneas, the Trojan warrior who has escaped from the fall of Troy and who has been shipwrecked on her North African shores. Aeneas loves Dido, as well, but his mission—he has been ordained by the gods to found Rome—must take precedence over his feelings. After declaring his love, he sets sail for Italy and his destiny. Angry, then forlorn, Dido hurls herself on her own funeral pyre, and in the concluding scene Neptune rises from the sea and quenches the flames.

To this basic plot, Metastasio fuses an element from Ovid, who, he declares in the same introduction, portrays Iarbas, King of the Moors, as one of Dido's suitors who destroys Carthage after Dido's death. In the interest of "good theater," however, Metastasio introduces Iarbas in disguise and pits him as a rival of Aeneas. Interestingly, the Elizabethan playwright Christopher Marlowe had earlier written with Thomas Nashe, *Dido, Queen of Carthage* (1586-1587), in which Iarbas is portrayed as Aeneas' chief rival. If Metastasio knew of Marlowe's play, however (which seemed unlikely), he took little from it.

Metastasio's piece on Dido, unlike that of Marlowe, is a tight, three-act tragedy which opens with Aeneas having already announced his intention of leaving Dido. Metastasio thus limited the action to the conflict of emotions and places dramatic emphasis on the psychological forces rather than on the physical. The epic sweep of Aeneas' story is distilled into a lyric cameo.

Moreover, Metastasio limited the number of characters. To the three major ones forming the basis of the action, he introduced only three others: Selene, Dido's sister ("Anna" in the *Aeneid*), who is secretly in love with Aeneas; Araspe, Iarbas' confidant, who is secretly in love with Selene; and Osmida, Dido's confidante, who is secretly plotting with Iarbas for the queen's overthrow. This use of confidants is a marked characteristic of Metastasian drama. The confidant is an effectively economical device for externalizing the conflict by providing alternative courses of action for the main character. The confidant is, in effect, a dramatization of the protagonist's inner voice, thus eliminating the need for the dramatic monologue or the soliloquy. This second group of characters also provides the grounds for a subplot of intrigue—as opposed to the honesty of Aeneas' and Dido's motives—and keeps the play from becoming static by maintaining a tension of opposing forces which alternates with each scene or clusters of scenes.

With almost mathematical precision, the scenes of swordplay between Aeneas and Iarbas—no one dies and there is no bloodshed or violence depicted—occur near the end of act 1 and again near the beginning of act 3, perfectly balancing the main, largely declamatory scenes portraying the emotions of love and hate and the sentiments of duty, honor, loyalty, and even repentance.

Declamation, in fact, is a strategic principle in the structure of *Dido Forsaken*. The characters declare their love, proclaim their intentions, and assert their feelings in neat, compact recitative—a middle way between speech and song, between spoken dialogue and sung verse. Significantly, major scene clusters conclude with a character's singing in arietta, or small aria, placed not only for virtuoso effect but also for dramatic emphasis and tension.

Despite the declamation, Dido herself is portrayed as a woman of genuine passion. Though she is willing to die for Aeneas, she is not an infatuated ingenue, but rather a queen who knows how to rule. Angry at Aeneas for denying her love, she reminds him shrewdly that she has presided over Carthage all these years without him, and without him has seen it prosper. She bitterly mocks him at his delay, sarcastically asking him why he was not already in Italy, subduing kings and winning other kingdoms. She is a woman of spirit; when she kills herself at the end, it is as much an act of strength as a gesture of despair.

Dido Forsaken is one of Metastasio's few melodramas in which the protagonist dies. Those representative of his best work end in reconciliation. These works of his Viennese period established the classic format and structure of the Metastasian drama. The first work of this period, one of his best, is *Demetrius*, a heroic melodrama suffused with idyllic sentiment. Its author claimed in his letters that the play brought tears to the eyes of even the most bearlike members of the audience when it was performed in 1731.

The plot, like that of *Dido Forsaken*, is clear and uncomplicated. There is the same limitation on the number of characters, the same logical distribution of arietta among the principals, and the same technique of using the confidant to externalize the conflict, which is resolved by the triumph of Reason and Order over emotional turmoil. Unlike *Dido Forsaken*, *Demetrius* ends happily; no one dies, no one is sacrificed.

Cleonice, Queen of Syria, is loved by Alcestes, a shepherd risen to the rank of soldier and reared by a nobleman, Phenicius, who is also the father of Olinthus. Alcestes is in reality Demetrius, son of King Demetrius, who died in exile and who gave his son to Phenicius to rear incognito until such time as he could assume his rightful throne.

Cleonice, meanwhile, must choose a husband to share her throne and is pressured by Olinthus to decide in his favor. The queen, however, loves Alcestes, though she is ignorant of his royal lineage. Urged by the people to choose a consort, she is torn between her love for Alcestes and her duty as queen to choose among the nobled blood and to respect "decorum." She is encouraged in her choice of a prince by her confidante, Barsene, who is secretly in love with Alcestes and wants him for herself.

The major scenes of the melodrama center on Cleonice's confrontations with Alcestes, during which she explains her dilemma and her reasons for choosing honor over love, loyalty to the idea of sovereignty over personal feelings. In the end, however, Phenicius arranges for Alcestes' true identity to be revealed, the lovers are united, and the play concludes with a grand chorus of reconciliation.

The theme of *Demetrius* is the triumph of harmony over the chaos consequent to the submission to personal desires. Writing for an absolute monarchy, Metastasio is stating in dramatic form the philosophical and political idea that reason, represented by the monarchy, brings order to a disordered world. Cleonice understands, as she tells Alcestes, that the crown is often a burdensome jewel, that the price of sovereignty is selflessness: "Tyrannical Honor! Because of you I must forever be deprived of what I hold dear."

That she is united with Alcestes in the finale is typical of the idyllic sentiment popular in the eighteenth century, and to later tastes, such an ending appears trite, even comic. In the world order that Metastasio was upholding, her union with the real Demetrius is the logical reward for her loyalty, the natural result of putting honor above personal happiness.

The plot of *Demetrius* is the reverse of that of *Dido Forsaken*. Where Aeneas spurned Dido's love in pursuit of a higher destiny, so Cleonice refuses Alcestes' love in deference to her high responsibility. Both Aeneas and Cleonice illustrate a glorious self-abnegation in the interest of what should be.

Demetrius is superior to *Dido Forsaken* in the greater depth of characterization. Olinthus, for example, who is reconciled at the end, is a Hotspur, a fiery, hot-tempered youth who has no false modesty about his preeminence as a match for Cleonice or his desire for the throne. He provides the main physical conflict in the melodrama, which succeeds in holding an audience's interest even though there are no spectacular effects. Only the verbal sparring keeps the play on the move.

The Olympiad is the most perfectly structured of Metastasio's melodramas and, like *Demetrius*, the product of his "golden age" of accomplishment. The play reveals both the strengths and the weaknesses of the poet's work. It illustrates Metastasio's mastery of the melodramatic formula already worked out in the previous plays, but it is a mastery that relies on repetition of and variation on established themes rather than on artistic experimentation, innovation, or growth. Metastasio simply reworked previous material and ideas, polishing, trimming, redressing.

The plot is drawn from classical sources, Herodotus and Pausanias, and the general story outline was probably already known to the courtly audience for whom the work—like all eleven of the melodramas of this period—was first performed. Such foreknowledge on the part of the audience allows the poet to begin, much in the manner of the classical Greek epics, late in the sequence of events. By means of this technique, called *in medias res*, the characters allude to previous actions, bringing the audience up to date naturally. Such a method provides for a remarkable compactness and for a direct, unflagging progress toward the denouement.

The source is a complicated, involved story which seems a cognate version of the Oedipus legend and which, curiously, anticipates the proxy idea contained in Edmond Rostand's late Romantic drama *Cyrano de Bergerac* (1897; English translation, 1898). Clistenes, king of Sicyon, is warned by an oracle that his infant son, twin to his sister Aristea, will one day kill his father. The king thus orders the boy to be thrown into the sea, but the baby is saved by Amyntus, who takes him to Crete, giving him to a childless royal couple to rear as their own. Years later, the young man, called Lycidas, falls in love with Argene, but the king forbids the relationship and Argene thus flees to Elis, where she lives as a shepherdess.

Meanwhile, Lycidas saves the life of Megacles, a young man famous for his athletic prowess. The two men become fast friends. When it comes to pass that the Olympic Games are to be held in Elis, Lycidas decides to participate, sees Aristea, and falls in love with her. She has arrived in Elis with her father, Clistenes, who was to preside over the Games. To win the love of Aristea—Lycidas is unaware that she is really his twin—he determines to win glory in the Games and sends for his friend, Megacles, persuading him to participate in the Games in his name. Disguised as Lucidas, Megacles wins the Games and gains the love of Aristea.

The major conflict is Megacles' loyalty to Lycidas, a loyalty which prevents him from returning Aristea's love. At the climax, Megacles is discovered as the false Lycidas, Lycidas almost strikes Clistenes in anger but relents, and by the final scene, all is made straight and reconciliation ensues. Happiness reigns for all. That Metastasio could create an effective vehicle from such a clumsy welter of detail is a tribute to his ability as a craftsman. He opens the play only a short time before the Games are to begin, and in the five short scenes of act 1, he has all the relationships drawn and the background clarified. Furthermore, *The Olympiad* relies less on the confidants and more on love scenes among the four principals. In addition, effective dramatic use is made of the chorus, especially in the climactic scenes in which the choral ariettas provide suspense and excitement. The action is thus condensed and the theme of loyalty is intensified.

The Olympiad remains one of Metastasio's finest achievements, not because of its subject matter but because of the way such potentially spectacular yet dangerously confusing material is handled. The play shows the reasons for Metastasio's reputation as one of the century's greatest musical dramatists—logical intensity, clarity of outline, quickness of movement, and, above all, structure remarkably adaptable to the musical score.

Other major works

POETRY: *Poesie*, 1717.

NONFICTION: *Estratto della Poetica d'Aristotele*, 1782.

Bibliography

De Sanctis, Francesco. *History of Italian Literature*, 1932. Translated by Joan Redfern.

Fucilla, Joseph. Introduction to *Three Melodramas by Pietro Metastasio*, 1981.

Grillo, Ernesto. "Metastasio and the Opera Musica," in *Studies in Modern Italian Literature*. 1930, pp. 51-90.

Kennard, Joseph Spencer. *The Italian Theatre*, 1932.

Lee, Vernon (Violet Paget). "Metastasio and the Opera," in *Studies of Eighteenth Century Italy*, 1907, 1978.

Edward Fiorelli

HEINER MÜLLER

Born: Eppendorf, East Germany; January 9, 1929

Principal drama

Das Laken: Oder, Die unbefleckte Empfängnis, wr. 1951, pb. 1966, pr. 1974; *Die Reise,* wr. 1951-1952, pb. 1977 (based on a Nō play by Motekiyo); *Die Schlact: Szenen aus Deutschland,* wr. 1951-1974, pr., pb. 1975 (*The Slaughter,* 1977); *Traktor,* wr. 1955-1961, pb. 1974, pr. 1975; *Germania Tod in Berlin,* wr. 1956-1971, pb. 1977, pr. 1978; *Der Lohndrücker,* pb. 1957, pr. 1958 (with Inge Müller); *Zehn Tage, die die Welt erschütterten,* pr., pb. 1957 (with Hagen Stahl; based on John Reed's *Ten Days That Shook the World*); *Die Korrektur: Ein Bericht vom Aufbau des Kombinats "Schwarze Pumpe,"* first version pb. 1958, second version pr. 1958, pb. 1959 (with Inge Müller; *The Correction,* 1958); *Klettwitzer Bericht,* pb. 1958; *Glücksgott,* wr. 1958, pb. 1975 (adaptation of Bertolt Brecht's fragment "Die Reisen des Glücksgotts"); *Die Bauern,* wr. 1964, pr., pb. 1975 (revision of the comedy *Die Umsiedlerin: Oder, Das Leben auf dem Lande,* 1961); *Philoktet,* pb. 1965, pr. 1968 (based on Sophocles' play; *Philoctetes,* 1981); *Der Bau,* pb. 1965, pr. 1980; *Herakles 5,* pb. 1966, pr. 1974; *Ödipus Tyrann,* pr., pb. 1967 (based on Friedrich Hölderlin's translation of Sophocles' play); *Prometheus,* pb. 1968, pr. 1969 (based on Aeschylus' play); *Drachenoper,* pr. 1969, pb. 1970 (libretto in collaboration with Ginka Tscholakowa for Paul Dessau's opera *Lanzelot*); *Horizonte,* pr. 1969, pb. 1975 (first scene of an adaptation of Gerhard Winterlich's play *Horizonte*); *Waldstück,* pr. 1969, pb. 1985 (compilation of different versions of Winterlich's *Horizonte*); *Weiberkomödie,* pr. 1970, pb. 1971 (based on Inge Müller's radio play *Die Weiberbrigade*); *Macbeth,* pr., pb. 1972 (based on William Shakespeare's play); *Der Horatier,* pr., pb. 1973 (based on Brecht's play; *The Horatian,* 1976); *Zement,* pr. 1973, pb. 1974 (based on a novel by Fyodor Vasilyevich Gladkov; *Cement,* 1979); *Mauser,* pr. 1975, pb. 1976 (based on Brecht's play *Die Massnahme*; English translation, 1975); *Medeaspiel,* pb. 1975 (scenario); *Leben Gundlings Friedrich von Pruessen Lessings Schlaf Traum Schrei: Ein Greuelmärchen,* pb. 1977, pr. 1979 (*Gundling's Life Frederick of Prussia Lessing's Sleep Dream Scream,* 1984); *Hamletmaschine,* pb. 1977, pr. 1978 (*Hamletmachine,* 1980); *Quadriga,* pb. 1978 (scenario); *Fatzer,* pr. 1978 (adaptation of Brecht's fragment "Fatzer"); *Der Auftrag: Erinnerung an eine Revolution,* pb. 1979, pr. 1980; *Philoktet 1979,* pb. 1979 (outline for a drama with ballet); *Quartett,* pb. 1981 (based on Pierre Choderlos de Laclos' novel *Les Liaisons dangereuses*; *Quartet,* 1984); *Herzstück,* pb. 1982; *Verkommenes Ufer Medeamaterial Landschaft mit Argonauten,* pb. 1983; *Wolokolamsker Chaussee I,* pr., pb. 1985; *Bildbeschreibung,* pr. 1985 (*Description of a Picture/Explosion of a Memory,* 1987).

Other literary forms

Since 1959, Heiner Müller, who began his career as a journalist and editor of a monthly journal on modern art, has devoted himself to the writing of plays, for which he is best known. He has, however, published lyric poetry, prose, and a great number of articles, interviews, and commentaries on the theory of drama.

Achievements

Although in 1970, in his critical introduction to postwar German literature, Peter Demetz named Peter Hacks as Bertolt Brecht's most sophisticated disciple, the American critic changed his mind when he assessed the problems of German theater in 1986, rating Heiner Müller's achievements as among the most important on the German stage. Müller is the only German playwright who has been able to combine his commitment to socialism with an avant-garde, if not postmodernist, consciousness. In the West German press of the early 1980's, he was named as the most famous East German dramatist since Brecht, who was, although successful abroad, most controversial at home. In terms of the theory and practice of drama, Arlene Akiko Teraoka, in her 1985 study of Heiner Müller's postmodernist poetics, regarded him as "the most significant playwright since Brecht to emerge out of East Germany, if not out of *any* of the German-speaking countries of postwar Europe."

By deconstructing both bourgeois and orthodox socialist models of drama, history, and revolution, Müller has gone beyond the conventions of dramatic action of individual characters in conflict with history or fate, and has created a new form of dramatic discourse which includes the anonymous voices of the oppressed, the nonrational, the nonmale, and the nonwhite of the Third World. In his ideology and dramatic idiom, Müller has traveled a long distance from Brecht, toward Jean Genet and Antonin Artaud, and has intersected with the postmodernist forms of Samuel Beckett, Edward Bond, Richard Foreman, and Robert Wilson. He has created a theater composed of the anarchic forms of montage, ritual, pantomime, comic-strip scenes, and street-theater demonstrations of terror, cruelty, and obscenity.

Biography

Born in Eppendorf, Saxony, in 1929, Heiner Müller was one of two sons of a working-class family. His father was a member of the Social Democratic Party and subject to the persecutions of the Nazi regime. Müller's childhood trauma began with the arrest of his father, who was put in a concentration camp in 1933, released, and reimprisoned when he refused to accommodate to the Nazi regime. After 1949, Müller's father was expelled from the Socialist Unity Party because of his "Titoism" (his opposition to the personality cult that had formed around Joseph Stalin) and left the German Democratic

Republic (GDR) for West Germany in the early 1950's in order to avoid the threat of government persecution.

During the last year of the war, Müller was drafted and experienced the total defeat of the German army in 1945. After the liberation of Germany, he was employed as an administrator for various cultural organizations in the GDR, and then worked as journalist and editor of the journal *Junge Kunst* (young art), until he was hired by the Maxim Gorky Theater in East Berlin (1958-1960), where he learned his stagecraft. In the late 1950's, Müller wrote a number of plays in collaboration with his wife, Inge Müller (1925-1966), for which they were awarded the Heinrich Mann Prize in 1959. After 1959, Müller continued to devote himself to the writing of plays. From 1970 to 1976 he served as dramaturge of the former Brecht company, the Berliner Ensemble, and later of the East Berlin Volksbühne. In 1979, Müller received the Drama Prize of the Mülheim Theater in West Germany, in 1985 the West German Büchner Prize.

Like many of his colleagues, Müller has had his share of conflicts with the Socialist Unity Party, the ruling party in the GDR, and with government officials responsible for the direction of cultural developments in the GDR. During the early 1960's, many of his plays were publicly criticized by party functionaries and were canceled after only a few performances or were never produced. At the same time, Müller was expelled from the East German Writers' Union. Therefore, from the mid-1960's to the early 1970's, Müller concentrated on adapting Greek, Shakespearean, and Brechtian plays. This was the period of a Socialist classicism, to which both Hacks and Müller contributed important plays.

Since 1971, when Erich Honecker came into office as first secretary of the Socialist Unity Party, a number of changes in official cultural politics have taken place which have allowed for a greater divergence of literary productions. The premiere of *Cement* by the Berliner Ensemble in 1973 was the first production of a major play by Müller since 1958. At the same time, many of his plays were made available in print in the GDR, while a West Berlin publishing house began with the publication of Müller's collected works. The production of *Mauser* by the Austin Theater Group at the University of Texas in 1975 brought international recognition to Müller.

In the mid-1970's, Müller had his breakthrough as a postmodernist playwright. While the East German theater reacted with some reservation to his development as a postmodernist, theaters in the West have welcomed the products of this phase. With the exception of *Der Auftrag* (the order), most of his postmodernist plays were premiered in West Germany or Belgium. *Hamletmachine* was premiered by the Théâtre Mobile in Brussels in 1978.

Müller resides in East Berlin and travels widely to participate in the production not only of his own plays but of other playwrights' works as well. For example, he collaborated with Robert Wilson on *the CIVIL warS* in 1984.

Analysis

Heiner Müller's development as a dramatist must be seen in the context of the international debate concerning a poetics for postmodernist drama. Since 1971, Müller has presented his work as a contemporary dramatist in terms of the poetic productions of a postmodernist artist in a postcapitalistic world system, as Teraoka has shown. In the works of this phase, beginning in 1971 with the completion of *Germania Tod in Berlin*, he has engaged in the deconstruction of certain models of Enlightenment or Socialist drama in favor of alternative models of Third World drama. Investigating the issues of cultural colonialism and the exportation of revolution, the role of the intellectual in the revolutionary process, and, especially, the role of the European Socialist intellectual in the conflicts of the Third World, Müller is current not only in terms of his topics but also in terms of his dramatic techniques. In his revolutionary postmodernist aesthetics, Müller has associated himself with the antiliterary traditions of contemporary literature, which work toward the elimination of the aesthetic autonomy of the work of art and the disappearance of the author behind the text as part of a universal discourse.

In an essay, "Der Schrecken, die erste Erscheinung des Neuen: Zu einer Diskussion über Postmodernismus in New York" (1979; "Reflections on Post-Modernism," 1979), Müller has defined his place and role within modernist and contemporary European literature. For Müller, quoting Franz Kafka, "literature is an affair of the people." The revolutionary artist must write from the standpoint of the oppressed people within the dominant structures of imperialism, capitalism, and colonialism. For Müller, the "oppressed people" are the masses of the Third World in Africa, Asia, and Latin America, living in a world that is divided between the two power blocs of capitalism and socialism. The author in the Socialist world, who is still privileged by virtue of his talent, has the goal of working toward his self-abolition. This goal is closely connected to the revolution of the Third World, which will establish, according to Müller, Marx's "realm of freedom," in which the author as privileged creator and art as private property no longer exist. In this situation, there are only two alternatives for the language of the contemporary author: either the self-abolition of the privileged voice or participation in a collective discourse—in Müller's words, "the silence of entropy, or the universal discourse which omits nothing and excludes no one."

Only gradually did Müller come to this perspective. His dramatic oeuvre can be divided into three major periods: from the early 1950's to the early 1960's, when Müller dealt with contemporary problems in industry and land reform in the GDR; from the mid-1960's to the early 1970's, when the playwright followed the trends of a Socialist classicism, employing mythology and the models of classical drama; and from the mid-1970's to the present, when Müller has explored the causes and consequences of failed revolutions in Germany and the demise of the German working-class movement. In this last period he has focused on the issues of cultural colonialism, the exportation of revolutions, and, especially, the struggles of the Third World.

In his first phase, Müller explored the contradictions, evolving from the collaboration of Communists and former Nazis, within the new collective work system under socialism. Plays such as *Der Lohndrücker* (the sweating man), *The Correction*, *Die Umsiedlerin* (the homeless one), which was to be revised as *Die Bauern* (the peasant), and *Der Bau* (the wall) belong to this period.

The play most typical for this period is *Der Lohndrücker*, dealing with the need for increased production under poor working and living conditions in the GDR in 1949. Following the Soviet model of rewarding exemplary workers, the GDR had singled out workers surpassing production norms for extra pay and special privileges. The protagonist of the play is such an "activist," hated and distrusted not only by his coworkers but also by management and the party. Their distrust is not without reason: The protagonist had denounced workers for sabotage during the Nazi regime in order to save his own life. The fulfillment of Socialist production plans, however, requires the collective labor of all workers. There is no room for private revenge. The protagonist, who is beaten by his coworkers after work, and his adversaries on different levels have to work together to complete an important project. The dialectics of the play show that collective labor under socialism is a matter not of individual choice but of historical necessity.

During the second phase of his work, in the late 1960's and early 1970's, Müller did adaptations of Greek, Shakespearean, and Brechtian plays: *Ödipus Tyrann* (based on Friedrich Hölderlin's translation of Sophocles' play), *Macbeth* (based on Shakespeare's play), *Philoctetes* (based on Sophocles' play), *Prometheus* (based on Aeschylus' play), *The Horatian* (based on Brecht's play), *Mauser* (based on Brecht's play *Die Massnahme*, and *Cement* (1972, based on Gladkov's novel) make up the corpus of his middle period.

The work most typical of this period is *Philoctetes*. The original play by Sophocles has a rare happy ending, returning the protagonist and his invincible bow from his isolation on the island of Lemnos to the Greek army before Troy, where his festering wounds are healed. In Müller's version, the return of Philoctetes is engineered by Ulysses for the sole purpose of rallying the troops for battle. Ulysses uses Achilles' son to carry out his plan, deceiving Philoctetes into believing that he is rescued to be taken home to Greece. When Achilles' son finally tells Philoctetes about the lie, a battle ensues, during which Philoctetes is killed. Now Ulysses exploits the death of Philoctetes, concocting a new lie in the service of the war against Troy. The Trojans are said to have invaded Lemnos and killed Philoctetes, because he refused to join their side. With this propaganda story, Ulysses hopes to inspire the Greek army to fight the Trojans with increased fury and desire for revenge. On its most obvious level of interpretation, the drama has been understood as an anti-imperialist play, showing the cynical exploitation of human values for the sake of aggressive wars, but the pervasive pessimism of the play that also informs the character of Achilles' young son has rendered the obvious interpretation questionable. The dialectics of Müller's *Philoctetes* are enigmatic, but not without direction.

That the dialectics of Müller's plays are not always in line with party-approved directions shows in *Mauser*, a "learning play," based on a theme from Mikhail Sholokhov's novel *Tikhii Don* (1928-1940; *And Quiet Flows the Don*, 1934). In this play, an old comrade who has administered revolutionary justice in the city of Vitebsk, to defend the Soviet system during the Civil War, is put to death by his own comrades because he continued killing people without party mandate. The revolution no longer needs him; it needs his death. As in Brecht's *Die Massnahme* of 1930, the death sentence is not executed, before the accused has confirmed his own sentence.

Although written in 1972 and instrumental in his rehabilitation in the GDR with its production by the Berliner Ensemble in 1973, Müller's *Cement*, based on Gladkov's novel of 1925, portraying the national effort of reconstruction in the Soviet Union after the October Revolution of 1917 and the subsequent Civil War, points in the same direction as *Mauser* and perhaps even Müller's earlier *Der Lohndrücker*. As during the Socialist reconstruction in the GDR, counterrevolutionaries were also needed for the reindustrialization in the Soviet Union after 1917. *Cement* is not, however, a historical drama, but rather a dramatic analysis of revolution in general and a thoroughgoing critique of the Soviet Revolution during the bureaucratic rationalization under the New Economic Policy after 1921. In this regard, *Cement* belongs to Müller's third phase. Of special interest is the concept of the role of women in the revolution, which is far more radical than the traditional Soviet interpretation. The female protagonist sacrifices her child for the revolution. Her daughter starves to death in a children's home. Her mother wants to construct a new world and is prepared to pay the price: her old love and her child. In reference to mythology, the true revolutionary woman is revealed as a second Medea.

During his third phase, Müller produced the most challenging and most avant-garde work of his career as a playwright. Plays such as *Germania Tod in Berlin*, *The Slaughter*, *Gundling's Life Frederick of Prussia Lessing's Sleep Dream Scream*, *Hamletmachine*, and *Der Auftrag* constitute Müller's breakthrough of the 1970's.

Germania Tod in Berlin (Germania dead in Berlin) is a dramatic collage of German history from the first century to 1953. According to Müller, Germany manifests itself through the fraternal strife of two brothers, from the Roman time of Arminius and Flavius to the divided Germany of the twentieth century. While one of the brothers loves freedom and fatherland and wants to liberate his people from servitude, the other brother is concerned only with his individual wealth, glory, and honor and thinks only about his personal freedom. This constellation repeats itself throughout German history, with the defeat and death of the altruistic brother at the hands of the egocentric brother. Still, the unselfish brother never gives up hope, in spite of defeat and death. In this play, Müller appears to be clinging to the last vestiges of hope in German history. In the play's final scene, the bricklayer Hilse, a counter-figure to Gerhart Hauptmann's quietist weaver Hilse in his drama, *Die Weber* (1892; *The Weavers*, 1899), is almost stoned to death by members of a juvenile gang who ridicule his Socialist work ethic. When he finally dies of cancer, Müller's Hilse sees in his hallucinations Rosa Luxemburg returning from her grave and red flags flying over a united Germany. In contrast to his namesake's meaningless death in Hauptmann's day—in which the old weaver is killed by a stray bullet after refusing to take part in the revolt against the ruling class—Müller's Hilse knows what he fought and died for, even though his final goal remains visionary.

Gundling's Life Frederick of Prussia Lessing's Sleep Dream Scream is a dramatized critique of the German Enlightenment in nine scenes. The synthetic title of the play lists the major figures of the comic-strip plot: Jacob Paul von Gundling (1673-1731), a professor of history and law and president of the Prussian Academy of Sciences; Frederick II, King of Prussia (1712-1786); and Gotthold Ephraim Lessing (1729-1781), the major dramatist of the German Enlightenment. The first scene portrays the degradation of Gundling as intellectual at the court of Frederick William I, King of Prussia. Scenes 2-7 present the transformation of Frederick II from poet-king and Enlightenment intellectual into a military tyrant, while scenes 8-9 show the resignation of Lessing and the self-destruction of the younger dramatist Heinrich von Kleist (1777-1811). In the concluding scene, Lessing meets with the last president of the United States in an American junkyard, while figures from his dramas embrace and kill one another. Enlightenment is exposed as treason of the intellectual, his adaptation to the authoritarian state and service to universal oppression. The reason of language is reduced to absurdity, resulting in the systematic deconstruction of the model of Enlightenment drama.

Hamletmachine, of 1977, is Müller's most enigmatic play, presenting the total deconstruction of European drama by means of a collage of fragments from that tradition. Consisting of five scenes, the play shows the Hamlet figure at the funeral of his father and raping his mother, while the Ophelia figure destroys the home, where she has been imprisoned, and takes to the street as a prostitute. While the Hamlet player represents the intellectual, betraying the revolution, the Ophelia player embodies the voice of the oppressed. In the end, Hamlet withdraws into a suit of armor, before murdering Marx, Lenin, and Mao, who appear totally defenseless as naked women. Ophelia is left behind on the stage in a wheelchair among the corpses. Her last words are a call to revolution in the Third World against European colonialism. Form and logic of classical bourgeois drama are abandoned in favor of an anarchic vision.

Der Auftrag, of 1979, is based on the model of the Brechtian learning play, specifically, Brecht's *Die Massnahme* (1930; *The Measures Taken*, 1960). While Brecht's play deals with the mission of four agitators, sent from Moscow, to export the revolution to China, Müller's play reconstructs the failure of three revolutionaries, sent from France, to accomplish a revolution in eighteenth century Jamaica. The three figures of Müller's play represent the various types of revolution in history: The bourgeois intellectual Debuisson stands for the French Revolution, the peasant Galloudec for the Communist revolution, and the former slave Sasportas for the revolution in the Third World. At the center of the play is a reenactment of Georg Büchner's drama *Danton's Tod* (wr. 1835, pb. 1850; *Danton's Death*, 1927) as "theater of the revolution," with Sasportas playing Robespierre and Galloudec playing Danton. Sasportas declares the "theater of the white revolution" historically finished.

As a black revolutionary, Sasportas adds a new voice to the revolutionary discourse, expressing its superiority over the dominant European models of the French Revolution as well as Marxist Communism. While Debuisson betrays the revolution by returning to his former life as a slave owner and Galloudec is not able to provide any leadership, Sasportas introduces an authentic alternative to the European models, continuing the revolutionary movement in Jamaica. As Antoine, the adjudicating voice in *Der Auftrag*, representing the "control chorus" of the Brechtian model, becomes directly involved in the betrayal of the revolution, Müller's play emerges as a deconstruction of the Brechtian learning play. By abandoning the indispensable control function of reason, *Der Auftrag* shows a shift from Brecht to the theater of Jean Genet and Antonin Artaud.

Bibliography
Demetz, Peter. *After the Fires: Recent Writing in the Germanies, Austria, and Switzerland*, 1986.
_____. *Postwar German Literature: A Critical Introduction*, 1970.
Girshausen, Theo. *Realismus und Utopie: Die frühen Stücke Heiner Müllers*, 1981.
_____, ed. *Die Hamletmaschine: Heiner Müllers Endspiel*, 1978.
Heuttich, H. G. *Theater in a Planned Society: Contemporary Drama in the German Democratic Republic in Its Historical, Political, and Cultural Context*, 1978.
Schulz, Genia. *Heiner Müller*, 1980.
Silberman, Marc. *Heiner Müller*, 1980.
Teraoka, Arlene Akiko. *The Silence of Entropy or Universal Discourse: The*

Postmodernist Poetics of Heiner Müller, 1985.
Wieghaus, Georg. *Heiner Müller*, 1981.

Ehrhard Bahr

NGUGI WA THIONG'O

Born: Kamiriithu village, near Limuru, Kenya; January 5, 1938

Principal drama
The Black Hermit, pr. 1962, pb. 1968; *This Time Tomorrow: Three Plays*, pb. 1970 (includes *The Rebels*, *The Wound in My Heart*, and *This Time Tomorrow*); *The Trial of Dedan Kimathi*, pr. 1974, pb. 1976 (with Micere Githae-Mugo); *Ngaahika Ndeenda*, pr. 1977, pb. 1980 (with Ngugi wa Mirii); *I Will Marry When I Want*, pb. 1982; "Mother, Cry for Me," wr. 1982 (with Ngugi wa Mirii).

Other literary forms
Ngugi wa Thiong'o is known primarily as a novelist, having published the first English-language novel by an East African, *Weep Not, Child* (1964). While that novel was the first one published, *The River Between* (1965) was written first. These two novels, together with *A Grain of Wheat* (1967) and *Petals of Blood* (1977), re-create the cultural history of the Gikuyu people and the emergence of modern Kenya. His fifth novel, *Caitaani Mutharaba-Ini* (1980; *Devil on the Cross*, 1982), combines elements of Gikuyu oral tradition with satire on neocolonial exploitation and realism portraying the victims of that exploitation. Writing fiction for the first time in his native Gikuyu, Ngugi completed his own translations into Kiswahili and English. In addition to his novels, Ngugi has also published a collection of early short stories, *Secret Lives and Other Stories* (1975), which gathers his work in this genre from the early 1960's to the mid-1970's.

Ngugi has also written extensively as a social and literary critic. His collection of literary criticism, *Homecoming: Essays on African and Caribbean Literature, Culture, and Politics* (1972), testifies to the maturation of his social vision, including speculations on Mau Mau, nationalism, socialism, and capitalism. A second collection of essays, *Writers in Politics* (1981), asserts that the function of the writer in society is essentially a political one, however explicitly mute or vocal the writer may choose to be on social issues. In *Detained: A Writer's Prison Diary* (1981), Ngugi records his experience during his politically motivated incarceration, openly indicting the corruption of neocolonial Kenya and offering insights into his development as a writer and an activist. In a subsequent collection of essays, *Barrel of a Pen: Resistance to Repression in Neo-Colonial Kenya* (1983), Ngugi employs the ideals of the Mau Mau movement to analyze the role of writing and education in contemporary Kenya. His fourth collection of essays, *Decolonising the Mind: The Politics of Language in African Literature* (1986), addresses the need for awareness of the dominating colonial legacies of British culture and the obligations of a neocolonial writer in Africa to address his countrymen, his cultural and historical milieu, and his global readership. Ngugi has also granted a number of interviews that have been published; in the 1960's, he contributed forty-four columns to the *Daily Nation*, a newspaper in Nairobi, useful for their witness to his humanistic and political growth as a writer and thinker. Because Ngugi's themes and concerns are often interwoven among his various modes of discourse, virtually all of his writings help provide an informative context for the reading of his drama.

Achievements

Ngugi is the foremost writer of modern East Africa. Through his novels, essays, and plays, he has garnered the respect of both Africans and others. His fiction offers the single most impressive record of an African country's precolonial history, its exploitation under colonial rule, its turmoil in gaining independence, and its subsequent struggles to maintain a democratic government in the midst of neocolonial corruption. His essays, often forthrightly polemical, have resulted in the emergence of East African literature as a serious topic of criticism among scholars of world literature; he has also made a significant contribution to curriculum reform in African universities, emphasizing the study of African literature.

Ngugi's plays, like his early fiction, reveal a well-schooled and well-read background in British and European literature, but they evolve, as do his novels, from a humanistic, ethical focus to one of a leftist, radical program for social reform. By adapting *The Trial of Dedan Kimathi* and *I Will Marry When I Want* to experimental forms that include aspects of the Gikuyu oral tradition, and by producing and writing the latter play in Gikuyu, Ngugi succeeded in reaching the masses with his drama and his concerns. His explicit commitment to democratic Socialist reform and the strong popular support of Ngugi's *I Will Marry When I Want* resulted in Ngugi's detention.

While Ngugi, as James Ngugi, was recognized early as a promising young writer, his later work—perhaps because of political circumstances and his refusal to desist from polemics and activism—has not been accorded the same official status. His first play, *The Black Hermit*, was selected for performance at the 1962 Ugandan independence celebration, and *Weep Not, Child*, his first published novel, received an award from the East African Literature Bureau in 1965 and first prize in the 1966 Dakar Festival of Negro Arts. In that same year, Ngugi traveled to the United States as an honored guest of the 1966 International PEN Conference. While formal recognition waned over the next two decades, Ngugi's reputation has continued to grow. Perhaps his greatest achievement has been his ability to appeal both to those who concern him most, the working classes of Kenya, and to a diverse international readership.

Biography

Ngugi wa Thiong'o was born James Ngugi in Kamiriithu village, twelve miles northeast of Nairobi, on January 5, 1938. His father, Thiong'o wa Nducu, was a farmer who had been dispossessed of his land in the White Highlands of the Kiambu District and forced to squat as a laborer on what had been his homeland. As a result of the British Imperial Land Act of 1915, many Gikuyu farmers—deprived of legal rights—had been reduced to farming the land of well-to-do British settlers or influential Africans who had been granted parcels in the confiscation of the fertile area by the British governor; Ngugi's father farmed for one of the few Africans who had retained property. His mother was one of four wives, and he was one of twenty-eight children in the extended family.

Until about the age of nine, Ngugi was reared according to a mixture of traditional Gikuyu customs and Christian principles. In 1947, he attended the mission school of Kamaandura in nearby Limuru for two years; subsequently, he completed his primary education in the village of Maanguu at a school established by the Karing'a, the Independence Schools Movement, a cooperative undertaking by Kenya's Africans who viewed education as a vital component in their struggle for freedom from British rule. From his earliest years in school, Ngugi experienced both the colonial and the nationalistic perspectives inherent in the respective curricula.

Ngugi's secondary education was at Alliance High School in Kikuyu. There Ngugi encountered Carey Francis, the principal, a man with rigid missionary views and a strict bias for the values of European civilization, who would become the prototype of the missionary headmaster in Ngugi's fiction. There, too, Ngugi acquired a complex religious sensibility, integrating biblical study and Christian mythology with his own Gikuyu background. His experiences at Alliance High School constitute one of the shaping influences of his adolescent life.

During this period, Ngugi's family was deeply involved in the Mau Mau resistance. His brother, Wallace Mwangi, fought with the clandestine Mau Mau forces in the forests from 1954 to 1956. His parents, as well as other relatives, were detained for the subversion of colonial rule. A stepbrother was killed by government troops, and his home village was relocated. Ngugi himself did not engage in combat, and although his youth provided him with a measure of justification, he suffered considerable guilt. Reflection on the Mau Mau as an ideal model for the fight against social injustices would be a central theme in his work.

After Ngugi's graduation from high school, he entered Makerere University College in Kampala, Uganda, the only school then conferring degrees in English literature in East Africa. An outstanding student, he completed work in the Honors English program in 1963. During this period, Ngugi began his creative writing, editing the student journal *Penpoint*, writing several short stories, drafting his first two novels, and writing his first play, *The Black Hermit*, as well as two one-act plays, *The Rebels* and *The Wound in My Heart*. He also began writing columns for the Nairobi newspaper *Daily Nation*, a task that was to lead to a stint as a junior reporter in Nairobi in the year following his graduation. Also during this period, Ngugi married Nyambura in 1961 and had the first two of his five children.

In 1964, Ngugi continued his education, pursuing a degree in English studies at Leeds University in England. Exposed to the radical views of fellow students and finding himself in a community which encouraged open inquiry into social and political issues, Ngugi began work on Caribbean literature as well as the extensive drafting of *A Grain of Wheat*, projects which helped him to delineate his views into the most systematic line of thought that he had yet achieved. He also traveled to literary conferences in Damascus, New York, and Moscow, meeting a number of writers and widening his access to diverse social and literary perspectives. Although his teachers at Leeds encouraged him to complete his M.A. thesis, Ngugi chose to pursue his writing and returned to Kenya in 1967.

At Nairobi University, Ngugi worked to reform the curriculum, encouraging an emphasis on African Studies, but he resigned in protest in March, 1969, siding with students who confronted the government for their lack of academic freedom. The next year found Ngugi in Makerere again, as a Fellow in creative writing, where he helped conclude curriculum revisions and organized a writers' workshop. In March, 1970, while addressing a church conference in Nairobi, at which he renounced Christianity, James Ngugi was challenged by an old man who pointed out that his name was contrary to his denial; thereafter, the writer used the traditional Gikuyu name. By then, however, he was well-known as simply Ngugi. Later that same year, he went to Northwestern University, where he taught African literature. While in Chicago, Ngugi witnessed the degraded conditions of Afro-American ghetto life, becoming convinced that American racism was the result of systematic economic and political exploitation. Returning to head, eventually, the Nairobi University English Department in August, 1971, Ngugi completed the curriculum changes which he had helped to initiate two years earlier. While his teaching was to continue until his detention, Ngugi had, by 1977, become the leading proponent of radical East African literature with the publication of *Petals of Blood*, his fourth novel.

After the successful and popular reception of *The Trial of Dedan Kimathi* and the release of *Petals of Blood*, Ngugi's activism provoked the anger of authorities during his staging of *I Will Marry When I Want* at the Kamiriithu Community Educational and Cultural Center in Limuru. While the play had been granted a license for production, a district official revoked permission after only a few performances, fearing that peasants would be moved to challenge the power of the upper class. The government, perhaps fearing Ngugi's outspoken convictions, arrested him on December 31, 1977. Despite international protests, appeals, and special delegations to Nairobi, Ngugi was detained without charges or trial in Kamiti Maximum Security Prison until December 12, 1978. Although the conciliatory climate in the early months of President Arap Moi's government probably facilitated Ngugi's release, he was not reinstated at Nairobi University, which terminated his appointment shortly after his detention, despite Ngugi's repeated attempts to regain his position. Ngugi continued to write, working on three collections of essays, his prison diary, his novel in Gikuyu and his own translation of it, *Devil on the Cross*, and a new play, a musical in Gikuyu written in collaboration with Ngugi wa Mirii. In March, 1982, the authorities dismantled the Kamiriithu center just when the new musical, "Mother, Cry for Me," was in its final rehearsal. Ngugi remains in Kenya, weathering the scrutiny of officials, as a powerful freelance voice, speaking and writing on behalf of the landless, ordinary people and social justice.

Analysis

Ngugi wa Thiong'o's drama explores the issues germane to the transition within Kenya from a colony to an independent nation. Often unabashedly didactic in his plays, Ngugi probes the challenges which young black intellectuals must overcome, if they are to alleviate conflicts of tribe, race, and religion that threaten the unity of nationalism. While his early plays of the 1960's usually revolve around the qualities of leadership, they also initiate themes concerning the tension between traditional, rural life and modern, urban life; the role of African women in developing a strong nationalism; and resistance to the continuation of colonial practices which perpetuate exploitation in the new country. As these themes evolve in the plays of the next decade, Ngugi's drama becomes even more decidedly didactic, using an idealized history of Mau Mau, straightforward calls to action, and realistic portrayals of the exploited that are interspersed with pageantry to evoke the grandeur of African culture and the tragedy of colonial history. From his earliest play *The Black Hermit* to his volatile *I Will Marry When I Want*, Ngugi gradually shifts his attention from the confusion of a central character beset by conflicts among his loyalties to the community's determination to achieve a democratic voice in the political and economic development of the nation.

In *The Black Hermit*, the protagonist, Remi, the only university-educated member of a small tribe, wavers between loyalty to his customs and desires for his own happiness. As the play opens, the villagers await Remi's return from the city. He is, however, returning to a bewildering array of anxious expectations in the village. Before he left for the city, Remi had fallen in love with Thoni, but, by the time he had mustered courage enough to propose, he learned of his brother's marriage to her. Six months later, his brother was killed in a car accident; custom required that Remi marry his dead brother's wife, which he did, hesitantly, believing that Thoni did not love him. Just after the ceremony, he fled to the city. Thoni, however, does love him, and, having remained faithful, she is hopeful of their reconciliation upon his return. His mother, Nyobi, expects him to comfort the abandoned Thoni and to start a family; the village priest wants Remi to reaffirm Christianity in the tribe; and the elders, having been convinced by Remi before his departure to support an African party in elections, hopes that his return signals his willingness to lead them to power in the government.

Act 2 finds Remi still in the city and entangled in an affair with a white woman, Jane. While he must end the affair before returning, Remi realizes that Jane does not have similar experiences under colonialism and cannot ever understand him, despite her sincere affection. Remi's belated admission that he has been married to Thoni while carrying on the affair provokes Jane's anger, and she leaves him, calling into question Remi's own sense of ethical standards. Meanwhile, Remi and his friend Omange debate the powers of the new black government. Both oppose tribalism and support the new nation, but Remi refuses to sanction the right of workers to strike, while Omange envisions a state based on black workers rather than foreign aid. Despite Remi's support for the government, he refuses to enter politics when the elders visit the city to plead for his return. When the priest visits him, he sends word of his return, but his motives are confused.

Upon his return to the anxious village, Remi rants against tribalism: Yet he reveals himself as an obsessed, arrogant intellectual whose egotism renders him incapable of recognizing the strengths and appreciating the values in his own people. He renounces Christianity, but he has sacrificed his own spiritual awareness and interpersonal sensitivity to his rigid, nearly desperate, adherence to unquestioned principles of nationalism. When Remi renounces his marriage to Thoni, she flees and kills herself. Having asserted his individuality as more important than the complexities of traditional, communal society, Remi realizes, too late, that he has not thwarted tribalism and custom but profaned the mutual love and respect upon which the traditions are founded. He recognizes, in short, that African traditions must inform the evolution of African nationalism. Although Omange, the priest, Jane, and Remi himself are type characters in *The Black Hermit*, the elders suggest a ceremonial dignity and ritual wisdom, represented by "Africa's anthem" and sung in Kiswahili. The women Nyobi and Thoni provide models of genuine sensitivity in their mutual support to overcome the literal and figurative departure of Remi: Leaders, they assert, cannot take leave of compassion.

The critique of leadership extends from *The Black Hermit* to the three one-act dramas in *This Time Tomorrow*. In *The Rebels*, a young man returns home with a Ugandan fiancée, Mary, only to find that his father has chosen a local girl to be his bride. When he hesitates to accept the arrangement dictated by custom, the humiliated prospective bride kills herself, and he loses

Mary as well. Implicitly, the play attacks the lack of black unity among the emerging nations of East Africa; by his use of a Ugandan for the character of Mary, Ngugi focuses on tribal prejudice rather than racial or colonial repression as the source of conflict. *The Wound in My Heart* portrays Ruhiu, a Mau Mau detainee, who eagerly returns to his village after his release only to find his wife with a child from an adulterous affair with a white man. Before she can hear Ruhiu's reaction, his wife kills herself. The fatalism inherent in *The Black Hermit* and these two one-acts, despite their sympathy with the role of African women in the emerging nation, yields to the undeveloped social protest of *This Time Tomorrow*, a later one-act, an attack on the affluent classes for their demolition of a slum in the interests of foreign investment and tourism. This play prefigures the social commitment of Ngugi's next two plays.

In *The Trial of Dedan Kimathi*, Ngugi shifts his concern from confused though well-intentioned leading characters to the strength of group commitment in reforming colonial practices which continue in independent Kenya. The play shapes the historical Dedan Kimathi into a heroic figure who embodies the idealistic principles of Mau Mau resistance. By idealizing a myth of Mau Mau, Ngugi and Micere Githae-Mugo, his collaborator, hoped to create a call to action, extolling Mau Mau glory and criticizing the neocolonial betrayal of the Mau Mau goals for social justice. An appeal to popular audiences, the play eulogizes Kimathi while celebrating his resistance to colonial enemies and staging re-creations of his tribulations, both in the courtroom and in private confrontations in his cell. Using an extremely loose structure—by Western standards—of three "Movements" rather than formally designed acts, each of which includes "Trials" and randomly juxtaposed rather than tightly meshed scenes, Ngugi creates an atmosphere of sad, undefined urgency in which characters, events, time, place, and conflict "flow into one another" until the play feels like and appears to be "a single movement."

As the play opens, the audience views a crowded courtroom and hears the charges against Kimathi for possessing a revolver. Although the date of this trial is 1956, Kimathi's refusal to plead guilty or not guilty gives way to a mimed pageant of "the Black Man's History," showing Kimathi's silence to be a gesture of disdain for repressive colonial law. As "phases" of the pageant progress, gunshots, voices, whiplashes, and drumbeats fade to a mime of mourning that evokes slavery, orphaned children, forced labor on Kenyan plantations, and black betrayals of the Mau Mau resistance, concluding with defiant shouts of "anti-imperialist slogans."

With the unfolding of the First Movement, the audience is witness to a number of rapidly shifting scenes; they see a village harassed and arrested for supporting Mau Mau fighters, and intimidating interrogation of peasants which is abetted by a black informer, and an important discussion between a

Woman and a Boy (a Girl later appears) who are symbolic of the birth of freedom and its hope for the future. Implicit in this First Movement is the African urban, colonial city as an archetype of corruption; the Boy is an orphan, who, with the Girl, hustles tourists in Nairobi and who himself eventually seeks to exploit the Girl for small sums of money. Confronting the Boy's sexist behavior toward the Girl, the Woman redefines manhood as possessing a Socialist, ethical awareness of the country's needs and conflicts. When the Boy agrees to deliver a loaf of bread, containing a gun, to the scene of Kimathi's trial, he does so out of a vivid clarity about his choice of political ideals. The threat to the Woman and the Boy in this Movement is not only from the colonial soldiers but also from the black soldiers, informers, and collaborators, the "black masters" who hope to profit by preserving colonial rule. While Ngugi keeps the play set safely in the 1950's, the premise is obvious to the audience: Present neocolonial corruption in land reform and court decisions began in the Mau Mau period and has continued to thrive in postcolonial Kenya. To attack that corruption will require the courage and dedication of the Mau Mau.

In the Second Movement, scenes move rapidly between the street outside the jail where Kimathi is imprisoned, the courtroom, and Kimathi's cell, in which his four Trials take place. (The cell becomes, in a sense the courtroom, and the courtroom, in turn becomes a cell.) Meanwhile, the historical pageant continues to be mimed in the dimly lit background onstage. In costuming, demeanor, and dialogue, the contrast between the peasants and the elite is pronounced. Kimathi, in his trial, repudiates the double standard of colonial law, favoring, in the Judge's words, "Civilization... Investment... Christianity... [and] Order," and condemns colonially inspired individual betrayals and tribalism. He rejects an offer to spare his life in return for naming fellow Mau Mau, and he refuses a banker's offer to make him wealthy. In rejecting colonial claims of progress and paternalistic benevolence, Kimathi, clearly a spokesman for Ngugi, espouses an anticapitalistic, classless society of laborers who draw upon their own customs for values rather than those of Christianity. In the Movement's closing, Kimathi, suffering from torture and beatings, refuses to surrender or to betray his compatriots.

The Third Movement begins with the Woman clarifying the plan to rescue Kimathi with the Boy and the Girl. She tells them stories that contribute to Kimathi's legendary status, honoring the qualities of his leadership. Thus, the Woman links respect for the oral tradition to qualities necessary for the people's support of a revolutionary leader. The major portion of the Movement consists of a flashback to Kimathi's command in a guerrilla camp in the Nyandarua forest. In long, didactic monologues, Kimathi, in the midst of directing the executions of British and African soldiers, justifies the Mau Mau war with minilectures on the pan-African arms supply to revolutionary movements, preaching self-sufficiency in weaponry, production, and education; the study of the lives of heroes as necessary training to comprehend history; and black pride as the basis for African self-determination. Calling for "unity and discipline in struggle," Kimathi touches on a number of issues, calling for the subordination of the individual's desires to the community's needs and calling explicitly for the implementation of an African Socialist philosophy. As the flashback closes, Kimathi, in a demonstrative act of compassion, spares the lives of several collaborators, among them his younger brother. They escape, however, and flee to the British, to betray the Mau Mau again with their testimony against Kimathi in the closing courtroom scene. When the Woman, having failed in the rescue attempt, is detained, Kimathi is sentenced to hang, and the Boy and the Girl fire their gun as darkness falls on the stage. A moment later, the stage erupts with the Boy and the Girl—the potential of the uneducated masses now having attained a vision of their own wisdom and power from the Woman—leading a crowd of workers and peasants in a freedom song in which the audience is encouraged to participate. The ambiguous end of Kimathi's life is thus downplayed, despite the construction of his legend throughout the play. Instead of merely celebrating a heroic revolutionary leader, the play's conclusion emphasizes a revolutionary spirit that remains potent long after Dedan Kimathi and the Mau Mau resistance have passed away.

Like *The Trial of Dedan Kimathi*, Ngugi's Gikuyu *I Will Marry When I Want* rejected the proscriptions for well-made drama in favor of an indigenous combination of mimed dance, historical realism, social vision, and heroic symbolism. While the former play is passionate in rhetoric and plain in diction, it was accessible only to those who comprehend English, and it was written by playwrights for an audience. *I Will Marry When I Want*, on the contrary, grew not only from Ngugi's collaboration with Ngugi wa Mirii but also from the collective contributions of the Kamiriithu community center. Changes by actors and crew were incorporated into the play both in its script and its performance, as there was much opportunity for improvisation. Consequently, the play includes a greater number of Mau Mau songs and Christian hymns, a much more extensive use of ritual and dance, and many more proverbs and striking images than the earlier play of the same period. Unlike *The Trial of Dedan Kimathi*, *I Will Marry When I Want* is set in contemporary neocolonial Kenya. Further, to a greater extent than does the earlier play, it embraces the entire history of the country—from before the coming of white settlers to a vision of a just, compassionate society of the future—centering on the village marriage ceremony as the symbol of a united, classless society. Ironically, Ngugi's dramas in the 1960's often presented marriage as an emblem of conflict and constraint; in *I Will Marry When I Want*, marriage is transformed from a deceptive scheme to swindle a poor family out of its land into an ideal that has the capacity to renew the strength of traditional family life in contemporary times.

The plot of *I Will Marry When I Want* pits the hypocritical piety of a Christian elite against the dignity and desperation of traditional Gikuyu, who are forced to work factory shifts or as farm laborers. The elite Ahab Kioi wa Kanoru and his wife Jezebel wa Kanoru conspire with foreign investors and Kenyan middlemen to swindle the poor Kiguunda and his wife, Wangeci, out of their last acre of land by coercing him to use his property as collateral for a loan to cover the costs of a Christian wedding between Kiguunda's daughter Gathoni and Kioi's son John Muhuuni. Kiguunda's land, on which stands his one-room house, has been selected for the site of an insecticide factory, thus keeping it at an agreeable distance from the homes of the wealthy and near the exploited laborers who will work there. Believing that Kioi plans a union of the two households, Wangeci condones the wedding, only to learn that John has abandoned the pregnant Gathoni. When Kiguunda insists on the marriage, Kioi dismisses them with contempt. When Kiguunda cannot meet the payments on the loan, he loses his furniture and, presumably, will eventually lose his house and his land as well. The play closes with Kiguunda drunk, Gathoni working as a prostitute in a local bar, and Wangeci crushed by hopelessness.

Both of Ngugi's plays of the 1970's call for adherence to traditional values in an egalitarian society. Those values, however anchored in the past, must be adaptable to changing conditions and responsive to the needs of the exploited, or they become only faint memories. Kiguunda's mimicry of Kioi's hollow Christian piety and his aspirations to the elite's ruthless materialism are as much responsible for his downfall as is Kioi's merciless conspiracy. Wangeci, for example, blinded by her own materialism, believes against all reason that Kioi actually wants to unite their two households. Kiguunda believes in neither a coherent social vision of freedom and justice nor a committed life-style of traditional values. Like the earlier betrayal of the Mau Mau, Kiguunda's betrayal of his own origins and values is a failure of leadership; Gicaamba, a factory worker and neighbor, provides the contrasting model. He opposes Kiguunda's flirtation with the elite Kioi and, throughout the play, portrays a leader who converts struggle and despair into pride in human dignity and protest against the elite. Echoed in the communal pageantry of song and dance, these attributes of leadership reverberate in speech rhythms of free verse, permitting easy identification and empathy by the audience. The audience, then, views a play wherein they themselves are the heroic force of social change, a dynamic relationship between stage and audience that evokes the drama of communal commitment overcoming the greedy whims of egocentric power brokers.

Entirely African in its design, *I Will Marry When I Want* represents the enactment of Dedan Kimathi's teaching: "unite, drive out the enemy and control your own riches, enjoy the fruit of your sweat." Ngugi's success as a dramatist is exemplified by the enthusiastic but violent reactions of audiences attending the first few performances before the government banned the play and detained Ngugi. Few playwrights in the history of drama have suffered so for their power to move an audience to action.

Other major works

NOVELS: *Weep Not, Child*, 1964; *The River Between*, 1965; *A Grain of Wheat*, 1967; *Petals of Blood*, 1977; *Caitaani Mutharaba-Ini*, 1980 (*Devil on the Cross*, 1982).

SHORT FICTION: *Secret Lives and Other Stories*, 1975.

NONFICTION: *Homecoming: Essays on African and Caribbean Literature, Culture, and Politics*, 1972; *Writers in Politics*, 1981; *Detained: A Writer's Prison Diary*, 1981; *Barrel of a Pen: Resistance to Repression in Neo-Colonial Kenya*, 1983; *Decolonising the Mind: The Politics of Language in African Literature*, 1986.

Bibliography

Chesaina, J. C. "Who Is on Trial in *The Trial of Dedan Kimathi?*" in *Busara*. XVIII, no. 2 (1976), pp. 21-37.

Cook, David, and Michael Okenimkpe. *Ngugi wa Thiong'o: An Exploration of His Writings*, 1983.

Killam, Gordon Douglas. *An Introduction to the Writings of Ngugi*, 1980.

_____, ed. *Critical Perspectives on Ngugi wa Thiong'o*, 1984.

Robson, Clifford B. *Ngugi wa Thiong'o*, 1979.

Michael Loudon

PETER NICHOLS

Born: Bristol, England; July 31, 1927

Principal drama

The Hooded Terror, televised 1963, pr. 1964; *A Day in the Death of Joe Egg*, pr., pb. 1967; *The National Health: Or, Nurse Norton's Affair*, pr. 1969, pb. 1970; *Forget-Me-Not Lane*, pr., pb. 1971; *Neither Up nor Down*, pr. 1972; *Chez Nous*, pr., pb. 1974; *The Freeway*, pr. 1974, pb. 1975; *Harding's Luck*, pr. 1974 (adaptation of E. Nesbitt's novel); *Privates on Parade*, pr., pb. 1977; *Born in the Gardens*, pr. 1979, pb. 1980; *Passion Play*, pr., pb. 1981; *Poppy*, pr., pb. 1982; *A Piece of My Mind*, pr. 1987.

Other literary forms

Peter Nichols is a prolific writer who is the author of dramatic works for motion pictures and television as well as for the stage. Among his many teleplays are *A Walk on the Grass* (1959), *The Continuity Man* (1963), and *Daddy Kiss It Better* (1969); he has adapted for the small screen works by F. Scott Fitzgerald and Evelyn Waugh. His film scripts include *Georgy Girl* (1966; with Margaret Foster; adaptation of her novel) and an adaptation of his stage play, *The National Health* (1972). In 1984, Nichols published his autobiography, *Feeling You're Behind*.

Achievements

Nichols has risen rather slowly through the ranks of his profession, with even *A Day in the Death of Joe Egg* undergoing limited runs in the initial London and New York productions. Nevertheless, he has become internationally recognized as one of Great Britain's leading playwrights, and his work has entered the standard repertory of professional, university, and community playhouses. His first official support came with an Arts Council Bursary, a small stipend, in 1961. With the first stage productions of his work, the awards began to accrue, including the John Whiting Award in 1969, four *Evening Standard* Best Plays awards, two Society of West End Theatres Best musical awards, the Ivor Novello Award for Best Musical Comedy, and the 1985 Tony Award for Best Revival. Though he has received limited critical attention, Nichols provides a rare blend of popular entertainment and intellectual challenge. Drawing on materials as diverse as English pantomime, military vaudeville, and intimate autobiography, Nichols has created plays with unique theatrical structures and intense, unusually extreme emotional effects. His work from the 1970's has been anthologized as representative of the best in contemporary British drama. Because he has so well captured the spirit of the times and done so in such wide-ranging topics and genres, his place in the history of dramatic literature has been secured.

Biography

Peter Richard Nichols was born and grew up in Bristol, in the generation that went through grammar school in the wake of local hero Cary Grant's rise to fame. Nichols has documented his early years in Bristol in two of his stage plays and, most extensively, in his autobiography, *Feeling You're Behind*. Nichols' family home, Palatine Lodge, was a rambling sort of unfashionable house located across the street from a large boys' orphanage that would serve during the war as an American military barracks. The presence of the orphanage, the example of Cary Grant, and the excitement of the American influx combined in Nichols' upbringing to create an environment that was alternatively either daunting or rife with the potential for upward mobility.

Both of Nichols' parents were performers of a sort. His mother, Violet Poole, had certificates in both piano and voice from the London Academy of Music and tutored students at home during the week. After the war broke out, she began to perform occasionally in service reviews but always when husband, Richard, a traveling salesman, was away. The interest her performances aroused in the audience almost led to a split in the family during the war, but Nichols' parents eventually reunited. Richard Nichols was a kind of self-styled musical-hall clown and classical music collector. The monologue passages in *Forget-Me-Not Lane* and the autobiography appear to have been lifted almost verbatim from the bitterly comic routines the elder Nichols rehearsed at home and then used in local club performances. The strong, eccentric style developed by his father later constituted an important obstacle for the younger Nichols, (who also had to overcome his father's admonition that motivation for success should come from making a habit of "feeling you're behind"), until he managed to master and use the style for his own effects. When Nichols first tried his hand at performance, as "the Miserable Mirth Maker" in wartime service reviews, his act owed something to his father's precedent.

While attending Bristol Grammar School, Nichols cultivated a comic self-image, and his exploits with his best friend, Cliff Browne, a gifted cartoonist, centered on the kind of irreverent ironic invention that would later pepper the sentiment of plays such as *A Day in the Death of Joe Egg*. When Nichols joined the military after the war, however, his attitude shifted; he became a dedicated diarist, trying hard to impress the other servicemen with his sophistication. Stationed in a dismal camp near Calcutta during the Indian independence movement, a melancholy Nichols observed with some detachment the effect of political conflict and maintained the discipline of keeping a journal, as he would for the rest of his life. Transferred to the Royal Air Force (RAF) entertainment unit in Singapore, he worked with mostly male performers, among whom were many homosexuals and transvestites, and he colorfully documented the experience in his musical comedy *Privates on Pa-*

rade. The flamboyance of the entertainment unit and its productions left an impression on Nichols that encouraged his bold choices in his use of theatrical technique.

Nichols was eventually "invalided out" of the service for repeated bouts with dysentery. On his return to Bristol, he enrolled in the Old Vic theater school and attempted a career in acting. Though he was able to gain occasional roles in local repertory companies, Nichols gradually became disillusioned with acting. First leaving on impulse to teach English for the Berlitz school in Florence, Nichols shortly returned to England and entered teacher training at the Trent Park Training College. Here, he met Bernie Cooper, the model for Ben Spray, and began the routine of classes and writing that would continue through his teaching years in the late 1950's and early 1960's. His academic years supplied Nichols with material for a number of television plays as well as parts of later stage works such as *Chez Nous.*

The first break came for Nichols through the British Broadcasting Corporation, and he began writing regularly for television until his *A Day in the Death of Joe Egg.* While his second teleplay was in production, Nichols suffered a collapsed lung and was hospitalized. Through his parents, he was reacquainted with Thelma Reed, a childhood friend of his brother whom he had used as a model for a television character. Her hospital visits led to their marriage in 1960. For the next few years, Nichols settled into a routine of television work and family life, though the latter was increasingly clouded by the realization of his eldest daughter's severe mental disability. When some screenplay work provided Nichols with the money to write daughter Abigail's story, she served as the model for Josephine—Joe Egg—in the play that would launch Nichols' career as a professional theater writer.

Since 1967, the year *A Day in the Death of Joe Egg* premiered in Glasgow, Nichols had worked steadily and produced a number of important plays, as well as some less successful thesis and autobiographical plays. The major plays have been regularly adapted by Nichols for the screen, and he has also continued to write occasional adaptations and scripts for television. His work for the stage has been generally acclaimed since 1967, when he began working with director Michael Blakemore. Later, Nichols would direct some of his own work, such as the Bristol Old Vic production of *Born in the Gardens* and the Guthrie production of *The National Health.* The intensity and theatrical inventiveness of *A Day in the Death of Joe Egg* continued through a series of plays on social issues and family life that peaked with his last straight drama, *Passion Play,* and his most accomplished musical play, *Poppy.*

Nichols announced his retirement from the stage in 1983, at a relatively early point in his career as a playwright. The decision was regrettable—and apparently not final. His plans to work on a trilogy of novels as of 1987 resulted in an adaptation for the stage titled *A Piece of My Mind,* which chronicles a writer's failure to write in narrative form.

Analysis

Critical analyses of Peter Nichols' major works have emphasized correspondences between events and characters in the plays and the playwright's personal experiences. For the most part, Nichols does not, in fact, write unadorned autobiography. When dealing with autobiographical material, Nichols has been able to bring much passion and insight to his work, but this material has been transformed in every instance by the bold use of theatrical devices. The difference in quality between Nichols' television work and his stage plays comes fundamentally from his skill in manipulating the communicative potential of the theatrical medium and not necessarily from his use of highly personal source material. His ability to sustain complex theatrical structures and to use them to exploit his subject matter makes Nichols unique in a generation of British playwrights that has typically written with great personal reflection and political commitment. Nichols might be considered somewhat conservative in comparison with his more radical peers, yet his use of theatrical resources allows the less controversial subject matter of his plays to have a strong emotional impact on his audiences.

The pattern of biographical reception for Nichols began with the international success of *A Day in the Death of Joe Egg*. Many details from the play were drawn from Nichols' personal experience as the father of a spastic child; his decision to represent such a character onstage had such a strong aesthetic impact at the time that biographical revelations only increased the play's potential for sensationalist responses. The central character within the play, however, is not Joe Egg but Bri, the father, a young schoolteacher, and it is the father's thoughts—in opposition to those of his wife—that direct the course of the play's events. The argument between the married couple over their responsibility to the daughter provides a classically simple dramatic plot that has no biographical parallel; other particular events, such as the attempt to kill the child through exposure, are also inventions.

The play's sense of intimacy in performance comes not so much from the audience's knowledge of the writer's biography as from the use of direct address. Nichols has acknowledged that the demands of expressing the couple's thoughts about their child seemed to defy the kinds of representational strategies he had employed as a writer of realistic television plays. The child herself could not realistically speak, and the characters were dealing with such a taboo subject in such a pressurized personal situation that it seemed implausible that they would express their thoughts openly to one another. Thus, Nichols chose to have the stage figures acknowledge the audience as listeners. This decision motivated a kind of ironic semantic split which has since proved to be the most enduring, characteristic aspect of Nichols' style.

A Day in the Death of Joe Egg begins with a "teacher skit" that Nichols wrote for an impromptu salon audience during his own teaching years. In the skit, the teacher speaks directly to the members of the audience, treating them as his class. This device served as a kind of bridge that allowed the audience gradually to be acknowledged at a time when modern realistic plays seldom did so. The teacher skit dissolves fairly quickly, but the apparent realism into which it dissolves remains pervaded with the trappings of theater: gag spiders, mad doctor bits, intentional comic misinterpretations. When Bri finally returns to soliloquy, the theatrical gesture seems more honest, more stable, than the troubled domestic scene.

The device of splitting the situations and characters into multiple semantic perspectives continues through both acts of the play and represents a kind of structural logic in the play's development. Soon after Bri's first monologue, describing the monotony of his daily life and the revulsion he feels, Sheila gets a chance to tell her side of the story in a pair of extended speeches. The final moment of the act is a *coup de théâtre* of the same order, in which the actress playing Joe Egg skips onstage jumping rope, apparently healthy and normal. The audience realizes that she is merely a projection of Sheila's maternal fantasy when the actress calmly undercuts the childish image with an announcement of the intermission. In the first act, Nichols progressively applies the semantic split between confessional monologue and dishonest realistic behavior, between the character's thoughts and actions, to both Bri and Sheila. Then, when the same device is applied to Joe Egg, there is no inner life to reveal, no consciousness, only an actress embodying a role. In act 2 the realistic action of the play gets split twice again. Because of the intimacy the audience acquired with the leading characters in the first act, it is able to see through the lies and delusions that occur in the parts that follow. The principal events in the second part are two visits, the first by married friends Freddy and Pam, the second by Bri's mother, Grace. These visits gradually intensify both the pressures on the couple to justify their decisions and the audience's sympathy for the couple, who must deal with the heartless, trivial behavior of the other adults. The ironic effect of the realistic dialogue continues through to the play's conclusion, when Sheila has returned with Joe Egg from the hospital after Bri's attempts to allow the child to die. Bri has finally abandoned his wife and child when Sheila has a last witless word with Joe about how devoted her Daddy is. The play ends enigmatically, with the handicapped child alone onstage. The multiple meanings encouraged by the other theatrical devices are finally distilled into the emblematic figure of Joe Egg, hopelessly alive.

The splitting of characters and situations in *A Day in the Death of Joe Egg* causes not only pathos but comedy as well. The same strategy of creating bitter comedy through ironic juxtapositon characterizes the form of Nichols' second major play, *The National Health*. The play draws on Nichols' repeated hospital stays during his military service and when suffering a collapsed lung. Nichols has removed this play more completely from autobiography, however, by adding an independent interior play, a send-up of hospital soap opera. This decision to split the play into two parts is again based on the need to manipulate audience response. The first version of *The National Health* was a realistic television play called *The End Beds*. This play, of which Nichols was particularly proud, was roundly rejected by television producers; they preferred conventional, romantic hospital drama to Nichols' grim, mordant chronicle play. Nichols responded by incorporating both attitudes toward hospital experience into the same play and changing to a theatrical venue where television norms could be viewed with more detachment. With the exception of the title character, the interior play has little contact with the unfolding of the more realistic hospital scenes, yet the principle of comparison deepens and informs the whole work.

A progressive principle applies again as well. When the play begins, there are six beds in the hospital ward; when it ends, there is only one. This image of gradual decay finds reinforcement in many other details, such as the gradual amputation of a cheerful, singing patient's limbs or the discharge of a vigorous young motorcyclist who returns from another accident brain-damaged and helpless. These patterns of progression replace what might ordinarily be considered a plot; each patient's background is sketched and his fate is sealed in the course of the action. The nearest approximation of a main character is Ash, a frustrated teacher with a stomach ulcer who worries himself helping the other patients while undergoing a more gradual decline of his own. His pathetic attempts to educate the helpless cyclist about his British heritage in a closing scene underline a second important irony in the play's title: the equation of the hospital with the failing welfare-state economy of contemporary England.

A third level of theatricality, providing the same kind of bridge between two dramatic levels as the teacher skit in *A Day in the Death of Joe Egg*, exists in the figure of Barnet, a hospital orderly. After his first entrance, in which the lowest man in the hospital, an orderly assigned not to attending the sick but to preparing the dead, has cajoled the ward's patients into good humor, Barnet begins to narrate the story of Staff Nurse Norton—not to the patients but to the theater audience. Barnet, beneath and beyond the hospital's concerns, also delivers a series of macabre monologues that serve to emphasize the difference between conventional representations of hospital life and its grim realities; for example, a comic rundown of his duties serves to mask the disappearance of Rees, one of the most endearing patients, so that his death seems like a successful magic trick. Barnet even provides a running commentary counterpointing the climax of the Nurse Norton melodrama, a spectacular kidney transplant, with the weary, unsuccessful attempts of the hospital staff to resuscitate Foster, another important sympathetic character. At the end of the play, Barnet appears surprisingly in blackface, a device that stresses his purely theatrical identity, and asserts that the audience members are themselves patients of a kind in the national health, not immune to the terrible suffering and humiliation that have befallen those in the hospital ward.

The National Health offers a broader scope on the problems of mercy killing and ethical responsibility explored by *A Day in the Death of Joe Egg*, pointing out that these are not mere personal problems but political issues. Biographical material has been reconstituted in both plays to achieve a layered, communicative structure that allows Nichols' characteristically ironic voice to emerge. The audience is encouraged to use one level of the play's action to see through others, and so the apparently simple situations and language of the plays take on a hidden depth, acquiring an unusual richness in their ability to encourage emotional response. Nichols' next few plays, though sometimes very successful, accomplish less, either because they address a limited range of concerns or because they employ less compelling theatrical techniques.

Forget-Me-Not Lane limits itself almost exclusively to Nichols' troubled memories of his family life. He uses a very flexible theatrical structure, with scenes shifting through three broad time periods, fluidly moving onstage and offstage through a series of hidden doors that constitute the only setting. In *Forget-Me-Not Lane*, this theatrical structure, with its Nichols-like author/narrator providing the usual direct address, serves also to facilitate a more important thesis about the structure of the family. Nichols views the family as a kind of trap, where heredity and the following of role models cause the mistakes of the parents to be repeated by their children, even when such patterns are acknowledged and challenged. The play juxtaposes scenes selected from Nichols' childhood to others from his early married years and his mature years as a parent—the time near his own father's death. Actors double roles, enacting similar events in each time frame to underline the patterns of familial repetition. Nichols deftly orchestrates the shifting scenes, incorporating material from five or more television plays while building slowly to the revelation of the father's death—the son's response to that death. Because the play is so scrupulously attentive to detail, the specific voices and cultural standing of the characters are difficult to translate beyond the time and place of the first British performance. Yet, for those same reasons, Nichols scored one of his largest popular successes in the play's original long-running London production. For critics such as John Russell Taylor, who can fund its themes with a wealth of similar experiences, the play seems to be Nichols' best, summarizing the feelings of an entire generation. From the distance of another culture, however, *Forget-Me-Not Lane* seems extremely eccentric, despite the attraction of its vaudeville elements and the cleverness of its theatrical structure.

Neither Up nor Down, like *The Hooded Terror*, made only a brief appearance onstage and has remained unpublished. The next popular success for Nichols came with *Chez Nous*, the least ambitious of his major works. The play's sensational subject involves an expert on child-rearing whose fourteen-year-old daughter has a child fathered by his closest friend. The two men and their wives undergo some doubts about the choices they have made in the past, but the play fails to arouse either the deep feelings or the theatrical excitement of Nichols' best work. Though his comic touch makes the play entertaining, particularly during a late visit to the expert by two American protégés, Nichols never introduces a specific political, moral, or personal problem with the scope of the earlier works. Unlike Joe Egg, the daughter never comes onstage, and the promising thematic potential of an itinerant French-speaking vagrant is never really exploited. Like Jean Anouilh, to whom he has been compared, Nichols appears to have employed his considerable theatrical talents in some plays written purely for diversion or profit.

The Freeway is Nichols' only attempt at a *pièce à thèse*. Once again, the amount of theatrical invention has been reduced, the only variety coming from the peculiar combination of comrades who are brought together by the national traffic jam serving as the play's premise. The work's most important aspect seems to be Nichols' new emphasis on narrative invention. Unfortunately, the world he imagines and the story he tells in *The Freeway* seem simplistic in comparison to the richness of plays drawn from biographical sources. The sort of futuristic society, based on the motor car, that Nichols uses to frame the action falls somewhere between fantasy and plausibility, satisfying neither sort of expectation. The various characters, intentionally chosen to represent different strata of British society, like their counterparts in *Forget-Me-Not Lane*, tend to lose their effectiveness when shown in another cultural context. The brief run of *The Freeway* in Jonathan Miller's National Theater production was followed shortly after by *Harding's Luck*, a children's story adaptation about the transformation of a crippled child, which must also be considered a minor work.

Privates on Parade, on the other hand, marks a new phase in Nichols' development. Here, the theatrical devices of the early plays combine with the techniques of musical comedy to produce one of the playwright's most dynamic works. The material for the play, a portrait of corruption in a Malaysian service entertainment company, comes from Nichols' postwar duty with a similar RAF troupe. As in the first two stage plays, he has transformed the material, breaking it up with a number of different performance techniques, tinkering with theatrical illusion and simultaneous action and manipulating his medium for the most intense emotional effects. Steve, a leading character loosely based on Nichols, provides a bridge into direct address for the other characters when he narrates his letters home. The military also provides a situation in which a wide variety of social classes can plausibly be put together in the same setting; at the same time, the experience of military service cuts across national boundaries, so that the play is readily accessible to non-British audiences. *Privates on Parade* was extremely successful in its London production, which was once again directed by Michael Blakemore, and will probably age well.

The technical advances which Nichols makes in *Privates on Parade* come in two areas. Most obviously, the switch to a musical comedy form allows another level of action to be introduced in the songs, much like the level provided by direct address in the early plays. Moreover, the freedom of writing lyrics rather than dialogue gives Nichols the chance to comment upon the action from an authorial perspective, whether these comments are directed toward characters and actions in the play or toward the broader political questions that Nichols asks about the nature of British colonialism. The use of music clearly marks this new level of writing for the audience, so Nichols is simply able to add it to the kind of complex theatrical structure he had already employed in his first three stage plays.

The second area of technical advance comes in Nichols' decision to use a theater as the location for much of the action. This choice allows Nichols to crosscut from song numbers directly into dramatic scenes that are frequently rehearsals, creating stinging ironic laughter and dazzling suspense by capitalizing on the audience's confusion between the immediate performance in their own theater and performances that may have some place in the dramatic structure of the play. Here, Nichols splits not only the actors but also the theater building and even the normal concept of the theater. As in his earlier extended pun on the hospital's "operating theater" in *The National Health*, in *Privates on Parade*, Nichols uses the conventional machinery of the English drag show to expose the brutality of the "theater of war." In this case, the hackneyed devices being exploited and ridiculed are not those of another form, television, but a juxtapositon of wartime bravado with the decadent cross-dress tradition that has been part and parcel of the popular English theater since before the time of William Shakespeare. The military comes off looking much like the kind of theater it sponsors: ridiculously outdated, empty, ineffectual, and above all, embarrassing.

Compared to *Privates on Parade*, Nichols' next play, *Born in the Gardens*, looks like a retreat. Here, the biographical materials are spread out into a larger, older family than the one so familiar from *Forget-Me-Not Lane* and the television plays. The central character, an elderly widow named Maud, resembles Nichols' mother, but there is no clear biographical parallel for the play's three children. The subject is really Bristol and how life there has changed. Consequently, Nichols chose to direct the first production himself at the Bristol Old Vic, where the slow-moving realistic play was warmly received for its local interest. *Born in the Gardens* reflects interestingly back upon the mother-child relationship in *A Day in the Death of Joe Egg* and complements the biographical plays centering on Nichols' father with an outstanding character study of the old woman. Unlike Nichols' major works, however, this play makes no attempt to explain or analyze the events as they are presented. *Born in the Gardens* shows the other side of the range Nichols has acquired, a naturalistic antithesis to the kind of flamboyant play he is most famous for writing.

Nichols followed this interesting but tangential play with one of his finest works. In *Passion Play*, Nichols took a very common, almost banal, topic, marital infidelity, and illuminated it through the clever use of a few theatrical devices. The most striking of these is his decision to introduce, at the point where each partner begins to lie to the other, a second stage figure for the character—one that the spouse cannot see or hear. Each character's double then serves as a kind of passionate alter ego: James spins off a Jim, while Eleanor acquires Nell. These new figures function like conventional whispering temptation figures, arguing in opposition to the consciences of the original characters. This device, quite old, has also been employed by modern writers such as Eugene O'Neill, Bertolt Brecht, and Brian Friel. Nichols uses the split masterfully, overlapping scenes and dialogue where the characters contradict one another's actions to create his usual blend of comedy, bitterness, and suspense. One might even suggest that Nichols wrote the play only for the sake of the trick's theatrical potential and not out of any interest in the subject or its resolution, for he notes that the play might well end with either Nell or Eleanor leaving the house. *Passion Play* seems to lack any specific biographical parallels; Nichols' lack of commitment to the resolution probably stems from a lack of personal commitment to the material itself.

The other devices that Nichols employs show the lessons he learned from *Privates on Parade*. Rather than writing musical numbers of his own, Nichols chooses to make Eleanor a singer of classical music. This characterization allows Nichols to quote liberally from music associated with Christ's Passion and (as the punning title suggests) to ask some important questions about the relation of Christian moral norms to the facts of human sexual desire. Similarly, Nichols makes James a restorer of modern paintings, allowing frequent allusions to art history that reinforce the same themes. For a playwright with Nichols' skill in the manipulation of audience response, such a topic provides ideal material: Temptation and passion are as universal as marriage, and when treated with the kind of riveting theatricality that Nichols can conjure, the aesthetic response called up becomes unusually intense and fulfilling. *Passion Play*, because of its universality and adept use of the medium, has become Nichols' most popular work.

Poppy, the last stage work before Nichols' announced retirement, may be the most accomplished of all of his plays. A musical comedy, *Poppy* draws on a unique set of theatrical resources to create a scathing seriocomic indictment of the imperial British opium wars. In a fairy tale gone wrong, Nichols presents the voyage of Dick Whittington, his merchant partner, his manservant, his mother, and his ward to Asia, where they propose to make their fortunes. A number of things go wrong with this ideal scenario: The fortunes will be made through a combination of evangelism and opium trading; Dick's ward, a schoolmistress who loves him, learns that she is his illegitimate half sister and becomes an opium addict; the efforts of the Chinese rulers to resist exploitation result in civil conflicts and eventually in their defeat by British gunboats. *Poppy* shows a strong commitment by Nichols to demonstrate the havoc wrought by the British empire overseas, inasmuch as the empire was built not on Christian values or on British forthrightness but on greed and deception.

The theatrical potpourri that Nichols uses to make his point is probably his most ambitious mixture ever. With a nod to W. S. Gilbert and Sir Arthur Sullivan's *The Mikado: Or, The Town of Titipu* (1885), Nichols utilizes conventional British images of the Orient in combination with the form and figures of the holiday pantomime. Unusual turns such as a 1950's-style newsreel report on nineteenth century India are deftly woven into the presentation, while the typical splitting of characters occurs in the cross-dressing of pantomime principals (Dick Whittington is a long-legged girl) and bits such as Queen Victoria's transformations into a statue of herself and a fortune figure. Story integrates with means of representation when Sally, the principal girl, is unable to marry her half brother, who is also played by a woman. The genius of the work comes in the way Nichols uses the traditional machinery of British imperial theater forms to expose the ideology of British imperialism. Tensions within the forms, such as cross-dressed stage figures and chauvinistic choruses, are exploited to reveal the decadence in the culture that created them. All this happens in a way that children might enjoy the colorful spectacle in the same way that they innocently enjoy a typical innuendo-ridden British pantomime. *Poppy* elevates the theme of innocence-gone-wrong to a national level and employs the materials of the nation's cherished "innocent" performances, holiday entertainments, to make its point.

Nichols' *A Piece of My Mind*, which marks Nichols' return to the stage after a five-year absence, moves his autobiographical method out of his obsessive memories of adolescence and into a concern with the struggle of a mature writer with his literary form, his personal limitations, and his rivals. Like *Forget-Me-Not Lane*, the play uses doubling of parts and shifts through time and place, movements in and out of character. The story, about a man who retires from playwriting to work on an autobiographical novel, closely parallels Nichols' life. Moreover, the rival writers bear resemblance to contemporary British playwrights Charles Wood and Tom Stoppard. The result is a Pirandellian collage of fact and fantasy, truth and fiction, that allows the technical virtuosity of Nichols to shine while underscoring it with a primary theme of failure. In *A Piece of My Mind*, Nichols continues to work with the tools and themes of his best plays, providing a balance between formalist effect and painful confession that confirms his status as a leading writer of ironic comedy.

The final impression of Nichols' work must include not only a high estimation of his technical abilities as a theatrical writer but also an appreciation of
his traditional humanism. Nichols consistently argues for mercy in a secular
world and does so in a way that typically avoids naïveté and maudlin sentiment. The laughter in his plays is not usually silly but based on a kind of
intellectual recognition that there is some overlooked truth behind the way
people ordinarily behave. In his domestic plays as well as his more political
musical comedies, Nichols appeals for understanding rather than violence,
for comprehension rather than conformity. He notes

> the danger of getting seduced by laughter for its own sake. But if understanding is the
> end of it all, or you manage to make the audience share your world view for a moment, or
> give them a glimpse of things they wouldn't have seen if they hadn't gone to the theater,
> then you've achieved something through laughter.

With such a point of view, Nichols cannot be dismissed as a merely "commercial" writer. He has created plays that entertain, but they often draw the
spectators in only to challenge them, to encourage them to face themselves
and their institutions from a new, more skeptically honest and intelligent van-
tage point.

Other major works
SCREENPLAYS: *Catch Us If You Can*, 1965 (U.S. edition, *Having a Wild
Weekend*, 1965); *Georgy Girl*, 1966 (with Margaret Foster; adaptation of her
novel); *Joe Egg*, 1971 (adaptation of his stage play *A Day in the Death of Joe
Egg*); *The National Health*, 1972; *Privates on Parade*, 1983 (adaptation of his
stage play); *Changing Places*, 1984 (adaptation of David Lodge's novel).
TELEPLAYS: *A Walk on the Grass*, 1959; *After All*, 1959 (with Bernie Coo-
per); *Promenade*, 1959; *Ben Spray*, 1961; *The Reception*, 1961; *The Big
Boys*, 1961; *The Heart of the County*, 1962; *The Continuity Man*, 1963; *Ben
Again*, 1963; *The Hooded Terror*, 1963; *The Brick Umbrella*, 1964; *When the
Wind Blows*, 1965; *The Gorge*, 1968; *Majesty*, 1968 (adaptation of F. Scott
Fitzgerald's short story); *Winner Takes All*, 1968 (adaptation of Evelyn
Waugh's short story); *Daddy Kiss It Better*, 1969; *Hearts and Flowers*, 1970;
The Common, 1973.
NONFICTION: *Feeling You're Behind: An Autobiography*, 1984.

Bibliography
Bryden, Ronald. "Playwright Peter Nichols: The Comic Laureate of Bad
    Taste?" in *The New York Times*. CXXIV (November 10, 1974), p. 5.
Canby, Vincent. "Peter Nichols, 'Joe Egg' Author, Found Humor in Des-
    peration," in *The New York Times*. CXVII (February 3, 1968), p. 22.
Davison, Peter. *Contemporary Drama and the Popular Dramatic Tradition in
    England*, 1982.

Foulkes, Richard. "The Cure Is Removal of Guilt: Faith, Fidelity, and Fertility in the Plays of Peter Nichols," in *Modern Drama.* XXIX, no. 2 (June, 1986), pp. 207-215.

Glendenning, Victoria. "Only Four Can Play," in *The Times Literary Supplement.* January 23, 1981, p. 83.

Jones, Mervyn. "Peter Nichols: The Playwright Who Has Had Enough," in *Drama: The Quarterly Theatre Review.* No. 148 (Summer, 1983), pp. 7-8.

Kerensky, Oleg. *The New British Drama,* 1977.

Miller, Brian. "Peter Nichols," in *British Television Drama*, 1981. Edited by George W. Brandt.

Schlueter, June. "Adultery Is Next to Godlessness: Dramatic Juxtaposition in Peter Nichols' *Passion Play*," in *Modern Drama.* XXIV, no. 4 (1981), pp. 540-545.

Taylor, John Russell. *The Second Wave: British Drama for the Seventies*, 1971.

Wertheim, Albert. "The Modern British Homecoming Play," in *Comparative Drama.* XIX (1985), pp. 151-65.

Michael Quinn

MARSHA NORMAN

Born: Louisville, Kentucky; September 21, 1947

Principal drama

Getting Out, pr. 1977, pb. 1978; *Third and Oak*, pr. 1978 (includes *The Laundromat* and *The Pool Hall*); *Circus Valentine*, pr. 1979; *The Hold-up*, pr. 1980; *'night, Mother*, pr. 1983; *Traveler in the Dark*, pr. 1984.

Other literary forms

Though known primarily as a playwright, Marsha Norman began her career as a journalist, writing a number of highly regarded feature articles and book, theater, and film reviews for the *Louisville Times* in the mid-1970's. During this same period, she created and edited that newspaper's celebrated children's weekend supplement, "The Jelly Bean Journal." She has continued to write reviews as well as articles on playwrights and on women's issues. Her first novel, *The Fortune Teller*, appeared in 1987.

Achievements

Norman's abilities as a playwright were first recognized in 1977 by Jon Jory, director of the Festival of New Plays, Actors Theatre of Louisville. Her first major play, *Getting Out*, was cowinner of the Actors Theatre's playwriting prize. Norman has subsequently garnered numerous other awards, among them the John Gassner New Playwright's Medallion, the Outer Critics Circle and George Oppenheimer *Newsday* Playwriting Award (1979), a playwright-in-residence grant from the National Endowment for the Arts (1978-1979), and a Rockefeller playwright-in-residence grant (1979-1980). Her masterwork, *'night, Mother*, won the Susan Smith Blackburn Prize, the Pulitzer Prize for Drama (1984), and several Tony Award nominations in 1983. The film version of the play appeared in 1986.

Norman's greatest strength is her ability to write compellingly about the psychic pain of ordinary, often inarticulate, and generally forgotten people. Inevitably, she seizes upon the single moment of greatest crisis in the lives of these people, that which allows them to rise to their greatest nobility. Though she is from the South, she makes every effort to create characterizations and settings that rise above regionalism to stand as contemporary and universal.

Biography

Marsha Williams Norman was born on September 21, 1947, in Louisville, Kentucky. She was a solitary child, and she inevitably cites childhood loneliness as having led to writing as a profession. Her mother, a Fundamentalist

Methodist, did not believe that the local children were "good enough," and so Norman spent her childhood reading, practicing piano, and playing with "Bettering," an imaginary friend, in her Audubon Park, Kentucky, home. A high school essay entitled "Why Do Good Men Suffer?" earned first prize in a local contest and was subsequently published in the *Kentucky English Bulletin*.

Norman's earliest works, whimsical reviews and essays published in the 1970's, appeared in local newspapers. Her most widely read pieces appeared in the *Louisville Times* starting in 1976 in "The Jelly Bean Journal," a weekend children's supplement which she created for that newspaper. It was only after Jory asked her to write a serious play that Norman recalled her counseling experiences with disturbed adolescents at Kentucky Central State Hospital (perhaps also the psychological imprisonment of her own childhood) and wrote *Getting Out*. This play was staged successfully by the Actors Theatre in 1977 and enjoyed Los Angeles and New York runs. Her most successful play is *'night, Mother*. *Third and Oak* achieved success in Louisville in its Actors Theatre production. *Traveler in the Dark* received mixed reviews when given by the American Repertory Theatre in Boston.

Norman's personal life changed greatly in the late 1970's, a period corresponding to her earliest theatrical success. Her first marriage, to Michael Norman, ended in divorce in 1974, and in November, 1978, she married Dann C. Buck, Jr., a Louisville businessman with an interest in the theater. After their marriage, Buck increasingly involved himself in theatrical production and support of Norman's work. The couple moved to New York despite Norman's apprehensions that Manhattan life would make her writing more difficult; in the event, Norman's most critically acclaimed works have all been written in New York.

Her work as a dramatist has led Norman to write for television, and two of her teleplays, *It's the Willingness* (1980), for the Public Broadcasting Service series *Visions*, and *In Trouble at Fifteen* (1980), for the National Broadcasting Company series *Skag*, have been popularly acclaimed. Indeed, it is probably true that Norman finds television such a congenial medium for her writing because of her gift in portraying the problems of ordinary and forgotten people. Though it is difficult to make definite judgments at this stage of Norman's career, it is clear that she is a playwright with an unusual gift for writing spare and taut dialogue and that her plays address the concerns of a very broad audience.

Analysis

Marsha Norman's plays have small casts and deal with a single moment of overwhelming importance for the protagonist. The dramatic conflict centers on the recognition of this problem and its resolution. Though this does not seem very different from the pattern of classical drama, Norman's plays focus on some difficulty which relates to the inner life of the protagonist. In consequence, her dramas depend greatly on dialogue rather than stage action, physical movement, or change of scene. They are often the cathartic conversations of ordinary people, given in simple language and without learned allusions but nevertheless profound, because they mirror the unexpressed thoughts of many individuals. Normally inarticulate, often nondescript protagonists find hidden strength and depth of feeling they had never before recognized in themselves, and they face their problems with determination. The solution is often a radical one, though it surprisingly affects directly only the protagonist rather than others in the play. Though the outcome may be tragic, the central character is usually personally triumphant.

Getting Out, for example, deals with the difficulties of Arlene Holsclaw, a newly released parolee who served an eight-year prison term for robbery, kidnaping, and manslaughter. Eight years have greatly changed her, but she must still come to terms with her past as well as face an uncertain future. Her past is first represented by Arlie, her younger and uncontrolled self, that part of her capable of the earlier crimes. Played by a second actress, Arlie literally invades Arlene's shabby apartment on the first day of Arlene's new freedom. Arlie is foulmouthed, crude, and cheap in contrast to Arlene's attempt to be quiet, reserved, and even refined. The alter ego declares that Arlene is not really free, that Arlene remains a prisoner to her younger self, and that this other part of her will surface again.

Though Arlene manages to expel Arlie, she is tormented by three other symbols of her past: a guard Arlene knew in prison who is concerned only with seducing her; her mother, who succeeds in revealing that she is domineering and selfish; and a former pimp who tries to enlist Arlene's help in supporting his addiction. The drama's tension mounts as Arlene, who could be destroyed at any moment, faces each of these temptations. She realizes that "getting out," winning personal freedom, must be accomplished by oneself and that psychological prisons are the most difficult to escape. Norman always mentions in interviews the feelings of isolation and terror she had while writing the play, that *Getting Out* represented her own emotional release. The play was much acclaimed in its 1977 Actors Theatre production in Louisville; it was voted best new play produced by a regional theater by the American Theatre Critics Association, and it was published in extract in *The Best Plays of 1977-78* (1980), the first non–New York production ever so honored. *Getting Out* was given an off-Broadway production at Marymount-Manhattan Theatre in the Phoenix Theatre's 1978-1979 season as well as a revival in May, 1979, at the Theatre De Lys, which ran eight months with highly favorable notices.

Third and Oak comprises a pair of one-act plays which explore psychological terrain similar to that of *Getting Out*. In *The Laundromat*, a widow and a woman trapped in a loveless marriage meet by chance in a local Laundromat and fall into a discussion of the ironic similarity of their lives. Both desperately need love, though neither can find it. As she would often do subsequently, Norman imposes a strict time limit on conversation and action, as long as it takes to finish a week's washing, and the commonplace setting further highlights the banality of her characters' lives. *The Pool Hall*, the second half of *Third and Oak*, takes the form of a parallel conversation between the owner of the hall and the son of a famous pool shark. It similarly deals with personal frustrations and unrealized hopes. *Third and Oak* was the major success of the Actors Theatre's 1978 season, but, more important, it marks a further development of the kinds of characterizations and situations typical in Norman's plays and anticipates the playwright's great achievement *'night, Mother*.

The simple language and ordinary women presented in *'night, Mother* contrast with the magnitude of the question with which it deals: whether a woman presumably in control of her life can rationally and with dignity end it if she chooses. Jessie Cates is, accordingly, typical of many suicide victims. She has no compelling or overwhelming crisis in her life at the time she chooses to end it. It is simply that she recognizes her life's mediocrity and tedium. Significantly, she blames neither herself nor anyone else for the failure of her marriage or the delinquency of her son. Indeed, she calmly tells her mother, Thelma Cates, what she plans to do, not to be dissuaded but to allow Thelma to understand better why she wants to die and to satisfy her mother's last wants.

Thelma has turned off her television set on the night of her daughter's suicide, no doubt the first time she has changed her usual routine in many evenings. The irony is that it has taken the crisis of Jessie's imminent suicide to force her into frank conversation with her daughter. Apparently, Thelma's life is as unfulfilling as her daughter's, but it is clear Thelma will never take her own life. She seems content with her small house, her sweets, her insipid friendships, and the superficial contacts she has with her son and daughter-in-law. Clearly, Norman has isolated a genuine paradox of the modern world: Crisis or impending catastrophe seems required for simple conversation; communication is otherwise limited to trivialities or sacrificed to television.

Her mother learns more about Jessie in her final ninety-minute conversation with her daughter than she has in a lifetime. The modern world ironically sets a premium on time; Norman emphasizes this with onstage clocks set at real time, 8:15 P.M. at the beginning of the performance, and running to the time of Jessie's suicide just before 10:00 P.M. Jessie makes repeated references to the time, particularly when her conversation with her mother falls into trivialities or becomes repetitive. Jessie's last act is to bequeath her wristwatch to her son. She is determined to kill herself on this evening, while she is in relative control of her own life. She is, therefore, certain that it is a rational decision, not influenced by her epilepsy or depression concerning her failed marriage or delinquent son.

The conversation between Thelma and Jessie which forms this play is a confrontation of life and death. While nearly all the audience obviously will choose life, it is ironic that Thelma clearly loses the argument with her daughter. She is never able to give Jessie a solid reason for continuing a life so obviously unsatisfactory. Indeed, Thelma appears completely reconciled, even childishly comforted, as she hears the gunshot which takes her daughter's life.

The play has only two characters: Jessie and Thelma. Their conversation takes place in the small living room of Thelma's house, a room filled with Thelma's possessions: magazines, candy dishes, afghans, quilts, and other examples of Thelma's needlework. The house is cluttered but comfortable, and it is clearly Thelma's: Nothing is clearly identifiable as Jessie's. She does not even own the gun with which she kills herself.

Jessie is in her late thirties or early forties and seems pale and physically unsteady. She has come through a difficult period following her illness and divorce but now seems in complete control. She is systematic and disciplined in her behavior, and the lists she writes, the pencil behind her ear, and the arrangements she makes throughout the play for Thelma's comfort serve to confirm that her decision to take her life, announced to her mother at the play's outset, is both rational and carefully considered.

Thelma is in her late fifties or early sixties and has begun to feel her age. She allows Jessie to do even the simplest tasks for her. Indeed, without realizing it, she has become inordinately dependent on her daughter. The audience, accordingly, comes to realize that the real objections Thelma has to Jessie's suicide involve her concern for herself, not her daughter. By the play's end, it is clear that Jessie, despite her younger age, shows far greater maturity than her mother.

It is a tribute to Norman's skill that she allows her audience to reach its own, albeit inevitable, conclusions about Jessie and Thelma. Aside from the plot's requirement that they live somewhere outside town, Thelma's house could be in any section of the country. Though nothing is said about their educational attainments, it is clear that neither woman is intellectually inclined. Jessie has the greater sensitivity and potential, but her inability to realize this potential is the very thing that causes her suicide.

Norman writes all of her plays about largely forgotten people, individuals whose lives seem small, perhaps even mean, but who, faced with some large and overwhelming problem, rise to their own variety of eloquence. It is for this reason that Norman keeps the dialogue simple in the extreme. There are few extended speeches and little that is philosophical. She does not intend her play as a polemic on the place of suicide in the modern world, and the audience correspondingly views Jessie and Thelma as individuals rather than as universals. Though this violates a norm of classical tragedy, it intensifies the drama, because the audience, while not admitting the inevitability or irreversibility of Jessie's decision, remains intent on discovering just what provoked it.

Norman has always maintained that it was precisely because she had no models that she came so late to drama. Nevertheless, it is clear from her studies at New York's Center for Understanding Media that she is a serious student of the theater in addition to being one of its most important developing playwrights. Her style is taut and spare, like that of Samuel Beckett, though her settings and characters are entirely realistic. She deals easily with psychological questions, as in *Getting Out*, in which a young woman moves easily between Arlene, her present self, and Arlie, the girl who committed the murder which sent her to prison. One recalls the spiritual and physical selves of Alma in Tennessee Williams' *Summer and Smoke* (1947). At the same time, Norman's characterizations are decidedly American, even though never regional. Her gift for portraying American life compares to that of Arthur Miller, though Norman has always avoided the political drama for which Miller is famous.

Other major works

NOVEL: *The Fortune Teller*, 1987.

TELEPLAYS: *It's the Willingness*, 1980; *In Trouble at Fifteen*, 1980.

Bibliography
Gill, Brendan. Review of *'night, Mother*, in *The New Yorker*. LXVI (April 11, 1983), p. 109.
Moritz, Charles, ed. *Current Biography*. XLV (1984), pp. 302-305.
The New York Times Magazine. Review of *'night Mother*. May 1, 1983, p. 22.
Tweeton, Leslie. "Art for Art's Sake: The American Repertory Theatre," in *Boston Magazine*. LXXVI (February, 1984), p. 23.

Robert J. Forman

ISTVÁN ÖRKÉNY

Born: Budapest, Hungary; April 5, 1912
Died: Budapest, Hungary; June 24, 1979

Principal drama

Voronyezs, pb. 1948, pr. 1969; *Sötét galamb*, pr., pb. 1957; *Tóték*, pr. 1966, pb. 1967 (*The Tóts*, 1982); *Macskajáték*, pr. 1969, pb. 1970 (*Catsplay*, 1976); *Pisti a vérzivatarban*, pb. 1970, pr. 1979; *Vérrokonok*, pr. 1974, pb. 1975 (*Blood Relations*, 1975); *Kulcskeresők*, pr. 1976, pb. 1977; *Forgatókönyv*, pr. 1979.

Other literary forms

As a writer, István Örkény is not easily categorized. In addition to dramatic works, he produced short stories, novels, and screenplays, several of which are adaptations of earlier works. Örkény's *Sötét galamb* (dark pigeon) is a stage adaptation of his novel *Glória* (1957). *Macskajáték* (1966; catsplay) and *Tóték* (1964; the Tóts), two of Örkény's most celebrated novels, were first conceived as film scenarios but were left unfinished when the original film projects were abandoned. The unused material was salvaged in the form of novels, which were subsequently adapted for the stage and finally recast as two critically acclaimed films: *Macskajáték* (1974) and *Isten hozta, őrnagy úr!* (1969; welcome, dear major). The difficulty of categorizing Örkény is further demonstrated by his *Egyperces novellák* (1968; one-minute short stories). These writings are sketches imbued with wit and concentrated meaning. As the title of the collection suggests, these stories are highly condensed, bearing a relationship to the conventional-length short story analogous to that of the terse haiku to lyrical poetry.

Achievements

Örkény is, more often than not, labeled a writer of the absurd and grotesque. The sardonic and often understated wit that he brings to his writing makes his work unique and readily identifiable. He has been a favorite with many critics and, as far as Hungarian writers go, has enjoyed some commercial success as well. He is practiced and accomplished in several genres: drama, the novel, the short story, and the screenplay. His mature works are historical probes which reach back to retrieve and record the collective psychological plight of a nation—his native Hungary—in its difficult transition from a backward and semifeudal order to a Socialist state characterized by lofty ideals and Stalinist abuses of power alike. The distinctive ambience of Örkény's plays and other writings is in no small part achieved by his terse, pared-down style, in which rhetoric and decorativeness give way to plain diction and simple syntax.

Örkény was twice the winner of the Attila József Prize (in 1953 and 1967), and in 1970, his *Tóték* won the Grand Prize for Black Humor in France. In 1973, he was at long last the recipient of the most coveted award in Hungary, the Kossuth Prize.

Biography

István Örkény was born in Budapest, Hungary, on April 5, 1912. His father, a well-to-do pharmacist, was by Örkény's account a generous man with his money, and through sheer improvidence he eventually lost all four of his Budapest pharmacies. A man of a dying age, he participated in no fewer than twelve duels. Örkény was, on his father's side, of Jewish descent, but was reared a Catholic, if not a particularly devout one. He attended the Piarist *gymnasium* in Budapest, where he studied Latin and Greek. By the time Örkény was graduated in 1930, he was conversant in German, French, and English as well. After an inauspicious two years at the Polytechnic University at Budapest, where he studied chemical engineering, in 1932 Örkény enrolled at the University of Arts and Sciences.

In 1934 he received his diploma, and in the same year he cofounded the short-lived periodical *Keresztmetszet*, of which he would also be main financier. It was in this periodical that Örkény's first writings were to appear, but they did not yet bespeak any great talent. In 1937, he became involved with the liberal-radical periodical *Szép Szó*, where the first version of his short story "Tengertánc" (sea dance) was published. Also in 1937, Örkény married Flóra Gönczi. He spent 1938 in London and much of 1939 in Paris, eking out a living. In 1939, upon Hungary's declaration of war, Örkény returned home. That year he reenrolled at the Polytechnic University, earning his degree in 1941.

In 1942, Örkény was recruited into forced labor, was later transported (together with the second Hungarian army) to the Soviet front, and had to march on foot all the way from Gomel to the Don. Winter set in, and Örkény and his companions endured the cold in summer clothes. Örkény was eventually wounded and taken prisoner by the Soviets. During his long tenure as a prisoner of war, Örkény wrote three pieces: *Voronyezs*, *Lágerek népe* (1947; people of the camps), and *Emlékezők* (1945; those who remember), a drama and two reportages respectively.

Several years and three prison camps later, Örkény was set free in 1946. One of the first things he would do upon his return to Hungary was join the Communist Party. At first Örkény shared the general enthusiasm for the future exhibited by the utopianists and party ideologues, and in the late 1940's and early 1950's he himself contributed to the building of that future with politically unassailable writings. With the publication in 1952 of the short story "Lila tinta" (purple ink), however, dogmatists and ideologues strongly censured Örkény, accusing him, among other things, of immorality.

In 1948, Örkény married Angéla Nagy, with whom he would have two children. From 1951 to 1953, he worked periodically as a dramaturge. In 1956, Örkény's volume of short stories *Ezüstpisztráng* (silver trout) was published, signaling a new period for the writer. In the same year, the Hungarian revolt was suppressed, and Örkény, along with several other writers, would be practically unpublishable until the early 1960's. He was divorced from Angéla Nagy in 1958, but in the same year became acquainted with Zsuzsa Radnóti, a dramaturge, whom he married in 1965. In that decade, Örkény slowly rejoined Hungarian literary life, creating in succession works both profound and humorous. He died in Budapest on June 24, 1979.

Analysis

The oeuvre of István Örkény is characteristically described as absurd and grotesque. The description is accurate, yet the world he depicts is also quite familiar, rendered with realistic details which readers or theatergoers— particularly if they are Hungarian—immediately recognizes. At his best, Örkény presents the absurd as he finds it in real life and does not go out of his way to manufacture the strange and bizarre. His *ars poetica* argues for clarity and brevity in the service of the truth as he sees it. Rhetorical devices have little or no place in the works of his mature years. His characters are on the whole likable and sympathetic. Yet though they breathe with life, they straddle the border between the realm of flesh-and-blood characters, on the one hand, and that of the stereotype and archetype, on the other. The figures that inhabit the world of Örkény are happy to the extent that they are in communication with one another, but as a rule they seem barely to elude one another's reach. Nevertheless, the possibility of establishing and securing bonds between people is affirmed and reaffirmed by Örkény. By the same token, historical forces seem to act as determinants, making the balance that he postulates between man and the controlling environment very delicate and tenuous indeed.

Örkény's earliest writings, which at most document the writer's search for a voice of his own, do not offer interesting reading for anyone today but the specialist. In 1941, his first complete volume of short stories was published. *Tengertánc* (1941), named after the 1937 short story, signaled the arrival of a bona fide writer. The combination of realist and surrealist elements so characteristic of his mature years is already in evidence here. The collection is not without distinct left-wing political overtones, another recurring feature in Örkény.

Örkény's next few works were written in prisoner-of-war camps in the Soviet Union. *Voronyezs*, *Lágerek népe*, and *Emlékezők* are clearly the works of a much maturer man than the Örkény who wrote "Tengertánc," one who had since seen and himself suffered the hardships of war and prison. In the late 1940's and early 1950's, Örkény, who had in the meantime joined the

Communist Party, produced writings heavily influenced by Socialist Realism. They were overly schematic and heavy-handed treatments of social and political issues which were, however, worthy of being addressed. The most glaring example of this—mercifully brief—period is the novel *Házastársak* (1951; married couple). Set in Hungary in the spring and autumn of 1949, it depicts the life of fairly idealized workers, among whose proudest moments will be their observances of May Day and "Uncle Joe" Stalin's seventieth birthday. The novel strikes one today as a biting satire of the conventions of the time, though in fact the absurd situations and characters are not treated with irony but earnestness.

By 1956, Örkény had been writing seriously for two decades, yet he still found himself experimenting with subjects, themes, and forms alike. He had not yet found his own voice. In 1956—the year which saw a series of dramatic events in Hungary culminate in the earthshaking anti-Soviet revolt—important changes came for Örkény, too. *Ezüstpisztráng*, which appeared in that year, marked the beginning of Örkény's truly mature period. This volume of short stories struck just the right balance between realism, on the one hand, and the grotesque, on the other. It also signaled, according to Örkény, the end of a brief flirtation with colorful and rhetorical language and a return to the laconic and economical style of "Tengertánc."

Örkény's works of this period are all, in one way or another, reflections and commentaries on the peculiar conditions of post–World War II Hungary—indeed of all Eastern Europe—owing in part to, and characterized by, the peculiar "chemical reaction" of a fledgling socialism and a millennium of feudalism. This basically absurd world, fraught with terrible and seemingly irreconcilable contradictions, is starkly rendered by Örkény with language plain and direct. It is not merely the common rhetorical devices such as metaphor that Örkény shuns, it is essentially anything that might call attention to itself and distract the reader from the heart of the matter.

Obviously this is no "art for art's sake" writer here, nor one who would argue that the medium is the message. Still, how did Örkény, after some two decades of trial and error, finally decide on the simple, uncluttered prose of *Ezüstpisztráng*? The writer himself attributed it to his scientific-technical (as opposed to liberal arts) education. To express thoughts and ideas like a scientist putting together the building blocks of a theory, this was the ideal for which Örkény aimed. The condensibility of language is submitted to the acid test with the writer's *Egyperces novellák*, containing as it does writing as compact and concentrated as prose can get. The syntax is characterized by the simple sentence (this term is to be understood in both the general and the grammatical senses), yet is still richly textured and capable of resonance.

The world of Örkény seems at a glance too infected with humor to be taken seriously. Beneath the armor of wry wit, however, lurks a much darker dimension. Yet even this is a place less sad than it appears. Overcast though it may be, it is penetrated by a ray of hope. Örkény might well be called a realistic optimist. This basic orientation was, Örkény says, formed during his long tenure in the Soviet prison camps. It was there that he experienced how an apparently heterogeneous collection of people, comprising several different nationalities and social classes, can transcend the plane of mere coexistence to cohere into a genuine community. Örkény's conviction that solidarity is the most that one can give to another derives from those years. Even in the contemporary world, where many writers seriously doubt whether real communication is possible, Örkény affirms that true and lasting bonds can be formed.

As noted above, Örkény's oeuvre is extremely varied; he wrote novels, plays, reportages, and novellas without seeming to show preference for one over another. Nevertheless, the last two decades of his career were particularly rich in dramatic works, ones that won critical acclaim abroad no less than at home.

Catsplay was adapted by Örkény for the stage in 1969. Its epigraph reads:

> We all want something from each other.
> It is only old people whom no one wants anything from.
> But when old people want something from each other, we laugh.

Catsplay is the story of two elderly sisters—the uncouth Mrs. Orbán and the distinguished Giza—and their relationship. It is set around the late 1950's and early 1960's, when the Iron Curtain, understood in a broad sense, still represented a serious barrier of communication between East and West. The déclassé Mrs. Orban is living in her native country, while Giza has for several years been living in the West, where she occupies an even higher position on the social scale than that which she enjoyed during her childhood years in Hungary.

The differences between them are substantial. Giza is an invalid confined to her wheelchair and is perhaps for that reason more willing than her able-bodied but unshapely sister to see that the sweet flower of youth is gone. It is perhaps their attitude toward aging and death that most distinguishes them from each other. Giza, by all appearances, accepts death as the inevitable and final stage of life; her sister jousts with it like Don Quixote with his windmill. The epigraph, like a musical theme which is varied and developed, appears in many guises and forms. Giza's thoughts on old age recall, and at the same time amend, its message. The only way, she says, that young people can forgive the elderly their old age is if old people themselves show that they accept and are reconciled to their old age.

Though the sisters keep in touch by telephone and by letter, these imperfect means of communication prove insufficient to bridge the cavernous gap between them, caused by two diverse ways of life and thinking. Yet the fact that the sisters persevere, against great odds, to reestablish the bond that has been lost between them is courageous and portends some faint hope.

The Tóts, set during World War II, is the story of a certain visit paid one day by a certain major to a certain family. The family is temporarily without their son, who is away at war. The major who has come as their guest is the boy's commander. Apparently there for only a short visit, the major's stay begins to look like one of indefinite duration. The family waits in vain to hear from their boy, while in the meantime the major takes over the house, issuing gratuitous and nonsensical commands. His favorite command, repeated with the frequency and force of a recurring nightmare, is that the family assist him in making paper boxes. This they do, with the assistance of a paper cutter that calls to mind the guillotine.

The village in which the story is set serves as a microcosm of the country as a whole, and the major's dictatorial reign over the Tóts suggests the unequal relationship of the Fascists and the common people over whom they rule. As the country in the end deposes the Fascists, so the Tóts, upon learning that their son is dead and has been for some time, oust from power the maniacal major, turning the force of the paper cutter against him. The overall effect of *The Tóts* is in no small part achieved by the balance Örkény strikes between absurdism and realism. Indeed, the very distinction between the realistic and the absurd becomes blurred. Örkény, here as elsewhere, does not so much invent the absurd as he discovers it in real life.

Pisti a vérzivatarban (Pisti in the bloodbath) was finished by Örkény in 1969 but was not actually performed until a decade later, in 1979. Whereas *The Tóts* and *Catsplay* are small chamber works, set in a well-defined space and time, *Pisti a vérzivatarban* is a grand production which encompasses all of Central-Eastern Europe and the second third of the twentieth century. It is, particularly in comparison to other Örkény plays, highly experimental theater. It is characterized by lengthy discussions, thought fragments, and flights of the imagination. It is an epic of the absurd, the twentieth century counterpart of Imre Madách's *Az ember tragédiája* (1862; *The Tragedy of Man*, 1933). Örkény, not wont in general to instruct or preach, does not assume an omniscient view of history but rather confides in his audience, as a patient might confide in his psychoanalyst, with self-revelatory statements connected only by the thread of free association.

Who or what is the Pisti of the title? It is not a single character as such but, in Örkény's language, the collective noun for the people or masses. "Pisti" in Hungarian is the diminutive form of the name István (Stephen). Its use therefore might suggest some condescension on the part of the playwright toward his subject, particularly when he uses the emphatic "pistipisti." Yet such is not the case. Örkény, no doubt aware of the tendency in Socialist Realism and even Brechtian drama to idealize the "people," bestowed upon the subject of his sympathy a name of endearment rather than risk evoking the familiar image of the people as a race of native geniuses.

Pisti is no less the hero of Örkény's play for his colloquial nickname. Like Christ, he tries to die, for a good cause, a martyr's death. In the twentieth century, however, when the relativity of good and bad has overturned absolute morality, his well-meaning gesture looks absurd. Besides, Pisti can be different things at different times. Now he is a murderer, now a man at the gallows, now a tyrant, now Moses before the burning bush. It is not, however, the interchangeability of slayer and victim that interests Örkény. He merely demonstrates that even the people are only as good or bad, virtuous or wicked, as their historical circumstances will permit.

Blood Relations had its debut on March 28, 1974, and a year later appeared in book form. The characters are all railway employees and their wives, all going by the name of Bokor. They have a single passion in common: the railroad. If another subject by chance enters their conversations, it soon becomes apparent that this topic too has, in the minds of the Bokors, some association with the railroad. It would seem, therefore, that the railroad provides for its devotees a very strong bond, and so it does: It is the bonding force of the family, in whose embrace all is one and one is all. The members of the family seem, however, somewhat out of touch with one another, as though they occupied noncontingent planes. Their apparently common obsession is in fact experienced by each person differently and separately. It is as if, when any two of them stand on either side of the tracks or semaphore, they are cut off from each other no less certainly than if they were separated by *Catsplay*'s Iron Curtain.

Örkény would not be Örkény if behind the absurd and bizarre situations of the story there did not lurk a historical examination. One of the Bokors, the most likable of them all, is one day arrested for a crime he never committed, coerced into a phony confession, and eventually "rehabilitated." The reference is to the Stalinist years of Hungary, the late 1940's and early 1950's, during which time such practices were all too common.

In *Kulcskeresők* (the key hunters), Örkény probes into the Hungarian collective psyche, doing so examining an ordinary character with few distinguishing features. At most, the psychoanalysis turns up these facts: Hungarians are a dreaming people whose best successes may well come from their worst failures.

The play is a return to the small-studio format, focusing as it does upon a single character. It forms an integral part of Örkény's oeuvre, sketching in details omitted from other works. Just as *Pisti a vérzivatarban* studied the relationship between historical forces and the collective consciousness of a people, so *Kulcskeresők* examines the way a national character can shape the individual.

Örkény was active until his death in 1979. He left behind him a body of published work neither very big nor very small. The manuscripts of his unfinished and discarded writings could fill several volumes. In reviewing his entire oeuvre from beginning to end, particularly the works of his mature years, it is impossible not to notice the common themes, recurring motifs, and characteristic style which forge them into a grand unity.

Other major works

NOVELS: *Házastársak*, 1951; *Babik*, 1953; *Glória*, 1957; *Macskajáték*, 1966; *Tóték*, 1964; *Rózsakiállítás*, 1977 (*The Flower Show*, 1982).

SHORT FICTION: *Tengertánc*, 1941; *Budai böjt*, 1948; *Hóviharban*, 1954; *Ezüstpisztráng*, 1956; *Jeruzsálem hercegnője*, 1966; *Egyperces novellák*, 1968.

SCREENPLAYS: *Becsület és dicsőség*, 1951; *Babik*, 1953; *Isten hozta, őrnagy úr!*, 1969; *Macskajáték*, 1974.

NONFICTION: *Emlékezők*, 1945; *Amíg idejutottunk*, 1946; *Lágerek népe*, 1947.

Bibliography

Bales, Ken. "An American Catsplay," in *The New Hungarian Quarterly*. XIX (Spring, 1978), pp. 198-202.

Földes, Anna. "Three Short Story Collections," in *The New Hungarian Quarterly*. VIII (Summer, 1967), pp. 201-210.

Szántó, Judit. "Three Kinds of Theatre," in *The New Hungarian Quarterly*. XII (Autumn, 1971), pp. 207-209.

Tomai, József. "The Subject and the Style," in *The New Hungarian Quarterly*. XV (Winter, 1974), pp. 212-213.

Varga, László. "The Metamorphosis of a Writer," in *The New Hungarian Quarterly*. XV (Summer, 1974), pp. 141-146.

Gregory Nehler

ROBERT PINGET

Born: Geneva, Switzerland; July 19, 1919

Principal drama

Lettre morte, pb. 1959, pr. 1960 (*Dead Letter*, 1963); *La Manivelle*, pr., pb. 1960 (*The Old Tune*, 1960); *Ici ou ailleurs*, pr., pb. 1961 (*Clope*, 1963); *L'Hypothèse*, pr., pb. 1961 (*The Hypothesis*, 1967); *Architruc*, pr., pb. 1961 (English translation, 1967); *Plays*, pb. 1963, revised 1967; *Identité*, pr., pb. 1971; *Abel et Bela*, pr., pb. 1971; *Paralchimie*, pr., pb. 1973.

Other literary forms

Robert Pinget began his literary career with the 1951 publication of *Entre Fantoine et Agapa* (1951; *Between Fantoine and Agapa*, 1982), a collection of short stories. Since then he has written more than a dozen experimental, highly innovative novels. Among these are *Mahu: Ou, Le Matériau* (1952; *Mahu: Or, The Material*, 1966), *Baga* (1958; English translation, 1967), *Le Fiston* (1959; *No Answer*, 1961; also as *Mr. Levert*), *Clope au dossier* (1961), *L'Inquisitoire* (1962; *The Inquisitory*, 1966), *Quelqu'un* (1965; *Someone*, 1984), *Le Libéra* (1968; *The Libera Me Domine*, 1972), *Passacaille* (1969; *Recurrent Melody*, 1975), *Cette Voix* (1975; *That Voice*, 1982); *Monsieur Songe* (1982), and *Le Harnais* (1984).

Achievements

In his fiction, and in the plays that derive from it, Pinget has created and peopled the mapless region of Fantoine and Agapa. This is a world not of being but of becoming, constantly changing from work to work and even within particular books. As Pinget described his fictional universe in a lecture at Williams College on April 21, 1970, his characters and setting "exist not as defined but as in the process of definition." This "continual metamorphosis"—Pinget's term—mirrors the uncertainty and instability of the late twentieth century.

For many readers and viewers, Pinget's techniques render his works inaccessible. Although his works have been translated into eleven languages, he has enjoyed less recognition than such fellow experimenters as Samuel Beckett and Eugène Ionesco. Still, critical response has been warm. *The Inquisitory* won the Prix des Critiques (1963), and two years later, *Someone* received the Prix Femina. The Ford Foundation awarded him a grant in 1960, and more recently the French government recognized his achievements with a subsidized sabbatical (1975-1976).

Biography

Robert Pinget was born in Geneva, Switzerland, on July 19, 1919. After receiving a law degree from the University of Geneva and practicing briefly (1944-1946), he turned to painting. A one-man showing of his works was fairly successful, but he grew dissatisfied with this career as well. He taught design and French in England; then, in 1951, after settling in Paris, he completed a manuscript collection of stories, *Between Fantoine and Agapa*, which was published by a provincial press at the author's expense.

Having at last found his vocation, he began to write extensively, publishing his first novel, *Mahu*, in 1952. This book won for him the admiration of another avant-garde writer, Alain Robbe-Grillet, who reviewed the work favorably. Pinget's second novel gained for him another significant admirer; he submitted the manuscript to the prestigious publishing house Gallimard, whose reader, Albert Camus, was much impressed. Subsequently, Pinget has continued producing a series of novels that have received critical acclaim.

Pinget's dramatic career began in 1959 when he translated Beckett's *All That Fall* (1957) as *Tout ceux qui tombent*; Beckett soon reciprocated by translating *La Manivelle* into *The Old Tune*, broadcast by the British Broadcasting Corporation (BBC) on August 23, 1960. Pinget's first original play, *Dead Letter*, followed shortly afterward, and in the spring of 1960 it shared the stage with Beckett's *Krapp's Last Tape* (1958). Although Pinget claims to prefer the novel, he has used his plays to explore more fully the themes, characters, and situations that he presents in his fiction.

Analysis

Although Martin Esslin includes Robert Pinget among the playwrights examined in *The Theatre of the Absurd* (1961), Pinget himself claims that he more accurately belongs to the "theater of the ear." In a 1962 interview he replied to the question "What am I trying to do?" by stating that he sought "to translate into the language of today the problems of today." Elsewhere, he has talked of his efforts to capture the proper tone that will reify his characters. "Only the manner of speaking interests me," he observed in a lecture in Philadelphia (May 7, 1964).

Consequently, there is little action on the stage. Instead, all the emotion and energy are concentrated into highly evocative, often poetic language, which is itself one of the chief concerns of these works. How can people communicate? Can people communicate? While rejecting the antiliterary bias of many contemporary playwrights, Pinget shares their interest in the pitfalls that seem hidden within words.

For Pinget, language is the only means to recapture the past, know the present, establish a personality, and bond with others. Yet because this language is so elusive, characters often are isolated from their own history and identity, divided from relatives and associates. An existential anxiety pervades Pinget's writing, as each person fails to understand himself or make himself understood to others. Clope's groping for his past in the darkness at the beginning of the second act of *Clope* represents the universal plight of mankind. At the same time, Pinget finds much humor and even occasional glimmers of hope in this struggle for sense in what may be a meaningless world.

Like the dramas to follow, Pinget's first play, *Dead Letter*, derived from a novel, in this case *No Answer*. In the first act, set in a bar, Edward Levert talks about his son, who has left him, as a waiter listens to this story that he has heard many times before. The second act resembles the first, except that the setting is a post office. Levert again speaks of his son, while a clerk, who is the bartender in another guise, half-heartedly listens. This repetition highlights the futility of Levert's quest, indicating that it will be repeated in various settings but never achieve a successful resolution.

Pinget further emphasizes the hopelessness of the situation by introducing a play-within-a-play. Toward the end of the first act, Fred and Lili enter the bar and perform part of a piece they have just finished, *The Prodigal Son*. In this conventional play, the father's letters succeed in winning back his son, but Pinget implies that such happy endings occur only in artificially contrived dramas. In the real world that his work represents, such happy resolutions are unlikely if not impossible.

The father's failure to reach his son with his letters represents language's inability to connect people, for the son never responds. The bartender/clerk, despite his irritation with Levert and his oft-told tale, tries to be comforting, but his words, too, become in effect dead letters. At the end of the first act he can offer only the cliché, "Oh, you know how it is." The second act concludes even less satisfactorily, as he tells Levert, "Letters don't matter. What matters is . . . What matters is . . . What matters. . . ."

The play raises questions about identity as well as about language. The bartender metamorphoses into a postal clerk, and he may be Levert's missing son, too. In the first act his title is *garçon*, meaning either waiter or boy. The bartender's father, like Levert, owns a villa on the Mediterranean, and the bartender, like Levert's son, never writes letters to is father. Physically, too, there seems to be some similarity; at least Levert tells the man, "You're like my son."

Other incidents raise further questions about who is who. Fred and Lili's fellow actors have names like theirs—Bed and Quiqui—and in the bar, Fred and Lili assume their colleagues' roles. In the second act, the clerk and Levert watch the funeral of a girl whose history mirrors that of the clerk's sister. The clerk tells Levert of a man who used to come in looking for a letter from Heaven; that man may have been Levert.

As Levert observes, "We never know anyone." He does not know the history of the bartender; he cannot even be sure who the bartender is. In an attempt to learn more about him, he asks the man to strip himself, and he offers to undress also, but the bartender tells him that the mystery of existence lies deeper than the skin. The quest for truth must therefore proceed in a bewildering universe that holds out little hope for success.

The Old Tune raises a number of the same issues as *Dead Letter*, letting the audience eavesdrop on Pommard and Toupin, two old men trying to review their youth. Since this is a piece for radio, the audience would rely on the voices to distinguish the characters, but the two sound alike. Both have cracked voices; both stop for breath even in the middle of a word or sentence; both whistle their sibilants. Moreover, Pommard seems to know Toupin's past better than Toupin, and the reverse is also true. Hence, their attempt to reestablish a friendship through their conversation leads instead to quarrels. Also, at times they seem not to be paying attention or are unable to hear each other because of the roar of the traffic. The resulting confusion is both humorous and sad. One cannot help laughing as the "happy memories" repeatedly prove false, yet one also realizes that these characters are doomed to fail in their effort to rekindle a former alliance. Symbolic of this failure is their attempt to smoke a cigarette. Neither has a match, nor will any passerby provide one. The cigarettes thus remain unlit, unsmoked, just as their old friendship remains unrevived and cold.

Clope once more traces this search for union. Clope and Madame Flan live in a railway station kiosk, where she sells newspapers and he tells fortunes with a Tarot deck. While their trades are therefore similar—telling others what is happening in their world—their personalities differ. Madame Flan is the idealist, dreaming of an escape to China or Clysterea. Clope, on the other hand, is the cynic. He tells Madame Flan that a trip to China—or anywhere—would be pointless; he does not believe that life will change for her or anyone else. Hence, he gives everyone the same reading of the cards, and when they return the next week, he repeats that reading yet again.

Devoid of illusions and hope, Clope persuades a would-be traveler, Pierrot, to abandon his intention of seeking a better life elsewhere. Instead, Pierrot builds a second kiosk at the train station and becomes a surrogate son to Clope. As in *Dead Letter*, though, this son finally goes away, but he does leave hope behind. Clope resolves to pursue him and so embarks on another of Pinget's quests. As the play ends, each character clings to an expectation: Pierrot thinks that he will find a better life somewhere else, Clope wants to find Pierrot to reestablish their former relationship, and Madame Flan, clutching Clope's old grammar book, longs for her colleague to return.

In a poetic sequence opening the second act of *Clope*, Clope searches for something in his past that will allow him to make sense of his life. This search for self-understanding, already evident in *Dead Letter*, serves as the central issue of the aptly named *Identité*. The protagonist, Mortin, had already appeared in *The Hypothesis* and the radio drama based on it, *Autour de Mortin* (1965; *About Mortin*, 1967), in which he vainly attempted to determine why a manuscript, perhaps his own, had been tossed into a well. As

Identité opens, Mortin, apparently a writer, sits before a stack of papers and urges his physician to leave so that he, Mortin, can get on with his work.

Quickly, however, confusion sets in, for the doctor is not onstage as Mortin makes his request; two scenes later, at the urging of the maid, Naomi, Mortin reverses his position, but again the doctor does not hear a word of what is being said to him. To add to the confusion, Naomi afterward tells Mortin to send the doctor away, and the doctor threatens to leave the other characters. Just as one is uncertain as to who wants whom to do what, so one cannot tell who is interfering with whose work—assuming that anyone has work to do. Naomi claims that Mortin prevents her from doing her job, Mortin blames the doctor, and the doctor blames Mortin. As Naomi and the doctor say, "One is never sure of anything."

This lack of certainty results from and is reflected in the slippage of language. When, for example, Mortin speaks of *l'analyse* (analysis), Naomi hears Anne-Lise and begins a conversation about that woman, sidetracking their discussion about the doctor. Also indicative of the treachery of words is the frequent discussion of an anticipated duck dinner, but in the end Naomi produces only an empty plate. Words have lost their significance; they do not represent real objects, and at times they lose all coherence, as when the doctor and Naomi speak at once, telling two stories by uttering selected phrases from each. The result is gibberish. In the final scene, the audience remains with noise followed by silence, both of which are as meaningful—or meaningless—as the dialogue that has filled the preceding two acts.

As an artist, Pinget frequently explores the creative process. *The Inquisitory* is on one level an examination of how to write a novel, and Mortin in both *The Hypothesis* and *Identité* attempts to produce a coherent manuscript. *Abel et Bela* translates this problem to the stage, as the two title characters discuss a projected play. Initially, they consider a traditional, elegant piece set before World War II and filled with upper-class characters circulating in opulent settings. The first act soon degenerates into an orgy, though, and the projected second and third acts merely repeat the first, indicating that in the contemporary world, one no longer can compose a conventional or traditional work for the theater because life has become too chaotic. *Dead Letter*, rather than *The Prodigal Son*, should serve as the playwright's model.

Abel and Bela therefore propose a psychological examination of their own lives, but they fail again because they realize how dull their existence has been. Since reality lacks the stuff of drama, and since the old forms no longer serve, they next turn to surrealism, imagining a play about the lives they have not led. Even this idea does not work, though, for their plot becomes too bizarre. Bela imagines himself a nun, Abel a swan. As with *Clope*, the ending does leave room for hope nevertheless, for as Pinget's piece ends, the audience sees the beginning of Abel and Bela's first suggested play.

Like all of Pinget's other works for the stage, *Abel et Bela* explores questions of identity and language. The very names of the two characters are virtually identical, as are their accounts of their past. Moreover, Pinget acted in this piece, so he is both writer and a character trying to write. Since the similarities between Abel and Bela are linguistic, however, they can create new lives by saying other words. "Everything is a question of vocabulary," Abel insists; if they tell other stories about themselves, they can give themselves different, fantastic histories.

In fact, language may change itself and its users. "One word changes and all the rest follow," Abel insists. When Abel begins to speak of the playwright's freedom and uses the word "liberty," Bela immediately adds "fraternity," one word drawing forth the other. Like Lewis Carroll, Pinget here poses the question every communicator, certainly every writer, must face: Do people control words or do words control people? *Abel et Bela* implies that the latter is closer to the truth.

This transforming quality of language provides the title for *Paralchimie*, a word itself exhibiting linguistic shifts. It can mean "by alchemy" (*par alchimie*), "word chemistry" (*parole chimie*), or, by extension, "word alchemy." For Mortin, who appears yet again, words are the philosopher's stone that can transform the dross of his life into gold. Despite the abundance of words, though, all the efforts of the first act produce only sleep and silence.

In the second act, Naomi and the doctor return from *Identité* to continue their shaggy dog stories. Mortin joins them in constructing a fable about a shepherd, but its meaning never becomes clear, nor can they complete their tale. The play concludes with a thunderstorm that leaves Mortin blind and speechless; the quest for the magical "two or three key words" has ended in sound and fury that signify nothing.

In 1968, frustrated by the inability of language to retain or convey meaning, Pinget vowed to stop writing. The fascination with the quest for those key words has, however, driven him back to his desk to explore the central dilemma of the age. In *Le Mythe de Sisyphe* (1942; *The Myth of Sisyphus*, 1955), Albert Camus observed that in the modern world man has become "an exile because he is deprived of memories of a lost homeland as much as he lacks the hope of a promised land to come." At the end of *Clope*, Pierrot and Clope embark on an actual quest for that land, in which Madame Flan also believes. More often in Pinget's works, the search is verbal. Always, though, the conclusion, whether more or less promising, remains open-ended, the answer still unfound, and Pinget's characters seem condemned, like Sisyphus, to continue the never-ending search for meaning and fulfillment in a world that may not contain either.

Other major works

NOVELS: *Mahu: Ou, Le Matériau*, 1952 (*Mahu: Or, The Material*, 1966);

Baga, 1958 (English translation, 1967); *Le Fiston*, 1959 (*No Answer*, 1961; also as *Mr. Levert*); *Clope au dossier*, 1961; *L'Inquisitoire*, 1962 (*The Inquisitory*, 1966); *Quelqu'un*, 1965 (*Someone*, 1984); *Le Libéra*, 1968 (*The Libera Me Domine*, 1972); *Passacaille*, 1969 (*Recurrent Melody*, 1975); *Cette Voix*, 1975 (*That Voice*, 1982); *Monsieur Songe*, 1982; *Le Harnais*, 1984.

SHORT FICTION: *Entre Fantoine et Agapa*, 1951 (*Between Fantoine and Agapa*, 1982).

Bibliography

Bann, Stephen. "Robert Pinget," in *The London Magazine*. IV (October 7, 1964), pp. 22-35.

Cismaru, Alfred."Robert Pinget: An Introduction," in *American Benedictine Review*. XIX (June, 1968), pp. 203-210.

Esslin, Martin. *The Theatre of the Absurd*, 1961.

Henkels, Robert M., Jr. *Robert Pinget: The Novel as Quest*, 1979.

The Review of Contemporary Fiction. III (Summer, 1983). Special Kerouac and Pinget issue.

Joseph Rosenblum

RONALD RIBMAN

Born: New York, New York; May 28, 1932

Principal drama

Harry, Noon and Night, pr. 1965, pb. 1967; *The Journey of the Fifth Horse*, pr. 1966, pb. 1967 (based in part on Ivan Turgenev's short story "The Diary of a Superfluous Man"); *The Ceremony of Innocence*, pr. 1967, pb. 1968; *Passing Through from Exotic Places*, pr. 1969, pb. 1970 (includes three one-acts, *The Son Who Hunted Tigers in Jakarta*, *Sunstroke*, and *The Burial of Esposito*); *Fingernails Blue as Flowers*, pr. 1971, pb. 1973; *A Break in the Skin*, pr. 1972; *The Poison Tree*, pr. 1973, pb. 1978; *Cold Storage*, pr. 1977, pb. 1978; *Buck*, pr., pb. 1983; *Sweet Table at the Richelieu*, pr. 1987; *The Cannibal Masque*, pr. 1987; *A Serpent's Egg*, pr. 1987.

Other literary forms

Ronald Ribman has worked extensively as a screenwriter, both for film and for television. Among those scripts that have been produced are *The Final War of Olly Winter*, an original television play produced by CBS in 1967; *The Angel Levine*, a screenplay written with William Gunn and based on a story by Bernard Malamud, produced by United Artists in 1969; and *Seize the Day*, a teleplay based on the novel by Saul Bellow, produced by PBS in 1987. Three of Ribman's stage plays have also been adapted for television: *The Journey of the Fifth Horse* for NET in 1966 and for the Canadian Broadcasting Company in 1969. *The Ceremony of Innocence* for NET in 1972 and for Granada Television in London in 1974, and *Cold Storage* for the Entertainment Channel in 1983.

Achievements

Since the beginning of his career in the late 1960's, Ribman has been recognized by a relatively small number of discriminating critics, and by foundations dedicated to improving the literary merit of the American theater, as one of the most significant and promising voices of the stage, one that rings out with poetry in the face of the prosaic norm, that values language itself: a language that emphasizes the beauty and fluidity of words. Though *The Journey of the Fifth Horse* was savaged by the mainstream critics, it received the Obie Award for the best Off-Broadway play of the 1965-1966 season. *The Final War of Olly Winter* was nominated for five Emmy Awards; *The Poison Tree* won the Straw Hat Award for Best New Play in 1973, and *Cold Storage* won the Hull-Warriner Award of the Dramatists Guild in 1977. Ribman received Rockefeller grants in 1966 and 1968, and in 1975 the Rockefeller Foundation awarded him a fellowship "in recognition of his sustained contribution to American theatre." He has also been awarded a Guggenheim Foundation grant in 1970, and National Endowment for the Arts fellowships in 1973 and 1986-1987.

Biography

Ronald Burt Ribman was born in New York City on May 28, 1932, the son of Samuel M. Ribman, a lawyer, and Rosa Lerner Ribman. As a teenager he took an aptitude test that indicated that he should be a writer, but it made no sense to him; at that time he despised all forms of literature. His earliest career choice was science. "I was the worst chemistry major in the history of Brooklyn College," he has said. "Things bubbled strangely and blew up in my retorts." He abandoned science, and for his sophomore year he transferred to the University of Pittsburgh, where in 1954 he received his bachelor's degree in business administration.

Soon after graduation he was drafted. To while away the long hours off duty while he was stationed in Germany, he began to write: long letters at first, and then poetry. "I wrote a lot of terrible poems which they broadcast over the Armed Forces Network, which led to all kinds of suspicions about me—whether I was the right kind of gung-ho military material the Army was looking for."

Upon his discharge, he started working at one of his father's business concerns, a coal brokerage in Pennsylvania. He continued to write—short stories as well as poetry—and decided to apply to the graduate school at the University of Pittsburgh to study the very subject he had once despised above all others, English literature. He supported his application with copies of his recent writing and was accepted. (His writing was returned with a critical comment: "Mr. Ribman has a penchant for the bizarre, which a few writing courses that stress concrete imagery will take out of him"). After earning his M.Litt. in 1958, he was accepted for doctoral work at the Universities of Edinburgh and Minnesota. "Faced with a choice, I of course picked the wrong one." After "one freezing quarter" in Minnesota, he returned to "Pitt," where he earned his Ph.D., with a dissertation on John Keats, in 1962. He then entered the academic world as an assistant professor of English at Otterbein College in Westerville, Ohio. This career lasted only one year. He resigned to devote himself full-time to writing, which he has done ever since.

In New York, Ribman collaborated with his father on an article about the poor treatment indigent defendants were getting in the federal court system; the piece appeared in *Harper's*. He was thus a published writer, but he had not yet discovered his form. That discovery came while he was watching an amateur production of Edward Albee's *The Sandbox* (1960) in Johnstown, Pennsylvania. It hit him rather suddenly: "I'm a playwright. That's what I am. I recognize myself now."

Ribman wrote a one-act play called "Day of the Games," and sent it to the American Place Theatre in New York. The artistic director, Wynn Handman, came across it while slogging through a stack of manuscripts one Saturday morning in 1963, and it leaped out at him. "It was the language: fantastic, actable language, rich, evocative, poetic." He immediately telephoned Ribman and asked him to write a companion piece that would fill up an evening of theater.

The "companion piece" turned out to be a full-length play, *Harry, Noon and Night*, which was staged as the second major production in the American Place Theatre's first season, with two then-unknown actors in the leads, Joel Grey and Dustin Hoffman. Another Off-Broadway production followed immediately, with Robert Blake in the cast. In 1966, the American Place Theatre produced Ribman's second full-length play, *The Journey of the Fifth Horse*, with Hoffman as Zoditch and Michael Tolan as Chulkaturin.

A number of critics—among them Robert Brustein, Martin Gottfried, and Gerald Weales—immediately identified Ribman as one of the few playwrights who represented the future of American playwriting and a rejection of the relatively mindless fare that was becoming the staple of Broadway. Mainstream critics have never embraced him, though, and only two of his plays have been produced on Broadway: *The Poison Tree* in 1976 and *Cold Storage* in 1977. Most of his subsequent plays have been produced by Handman at the American Place Theatre and by Brustein at the Yale Repertory Theatre in New Haven, Connecticut, and the American Repertory Theatre in Cambridge, Massachusetts.

Ribman has refused to create his plays according to any notion of what an audience might want to see. "The thing for me that has always been the most difficult," he has said,

> is to be faithful to my own creative instincts, to what I want to do. There are powerful market forces out there that push you into more conservative directions because more conservative directions are what pay. To be true to yourself means that if you are going to find your authentic, individual voice you may at first be pushed aside because it doesn't sound like anyone else, and if it doesn't sound like anyone else they don't know what to do with it. It's been said that we are all born originals, but most of us die as copies. That's what an artist must avoid.

Ronald Ribman lives and writes in South Salem, New York, with his wife, Alice Rosen, a nurse, whom he married on August 27, 1967. They have two children, James and Elana.

Analysis

Ronald Ribman is a virtuoso of style. The shape of his imagination is protean, its colors those of a chameleon. He has the ability to project himself, from play to play, into different locales, times, levels of reality and fantasy, and to sound, against all odds, persuasive, consistent, compelling.

Each of his plays adopts a different approach to the question of how reality is to be refracted through the playwright's prism before being presented to the audience. He can write snappy, amusing dialogue, and he can adopt the tone of a parable: simple, lapidary, but suggestive. He can hew very close to realism, but at other times he approaches surrealism, jumping back and forth in time, presenting different levels of fantasy and reality simultaneously, with a poet's eye and ear journeying deep into the thickets of the imaginary to create new worlds—worlds that resemble our own but differ in time, locale, and in their idiosyncratic approaches to reality.

As a result of this virtuosity, it is difficult to identify Ribman with any one particular style. "Some writers," he has said,

> are very fortunate in that they find the vein, the seam in their mind that they can mine right at the beginning and they just keep hacking away at it. I keep finding it and I keep losing it and keep picking it up somewhere else. People have told me, "None of your plays looks like the one that went before. They all look very different from each other." That's because I'm mining different areas.

Nevertheless, there are certain themes and patterns that have recurred from play to play throughout his career, preoccupations and threads of consistency that tie together all the disparate forms of his protean shape. One of these is an interest in the process of victimization, in which, frequently, the victim and the victimizer reverse roles; both are revealed as no more than clowns, and the conflict itself as nothing more than an absurd game. Often the characters and the plots are created with a bizarre, dreamlike logic, a grotesque, nightmarish quality. Sometimes the fevered imagination of one character seems to create the rest of the cast, as distorted reflections of his fears or preoccupations; they speak and act as if they had never felt the inhibitions of civilization, as if they were capable of keeping nothing inside, as if every unspeakable thought had to emerge immediately—as if, in fact, they had no insides, as if their insides were all on the surface. Grotesque images and incidents appear, too, that are distorted images of what is disturbing the protagonist.

Characters often speak past one another, rather than to one another. They misunderstand one another, and so make it easy for the audience to misunderstand them. In fact, as Ribman himself has often insisted, the plays are ambiguous; there are no single meanings, and each will and should be understood in a number of different ways. Their exact natures are as difficult to seize as Proteus. Ribman's poetry, then, is not simply a matter of rich, supple language; it is also a matter of poetic ambiguity, of ineffability.

One other recurring concern of Ribman is his preoccupation with the persistence of the past in the present—a recognition that all people carry a heavy baggage of seeds, each of which began sprouting at a different time in the past, and never stopped shooting out tendrils: a bag of memories which can never simply be dumped. The figure that embodies this preoccupation, in play after play, is a character who seldom appears onstage: the lost one, the dear one who has disappeared, never to be recovered. He has often been swept away in a horrifying instant, a moment that can never be forgotten, that will always live in the present but can never be reversed.

Harry, Noon and Night, the first of Ribman's plays to be produced, is set in Munich in 1955, during the American occupation. Each of the three scenes of this black comedy is essentially a confrontation between two people. In the first, Harry, posing as an impossibly inept journalist, is interviewing a thick-witted soldier in a bar while both of them fondle a local prostitute. The interview is a wild, improvisatory put-on; the soldier submits to all of Harry's addled questions because Harry promises to give him money for the girl when it is over, but the audience never learns Harry's reason for going through this charade. In the second scene, the audience meets Immanuel, Harry's insectlike roommate (and bedmate), in their chaotic, filthy apartment; he is conducting a similar put-on of Harry's brother Archer, a gung-ho Air Force gunner during the war, now a can-do Ohio businessman. Harry is an artist who has abandoned the sugary, commercial pictorial realism he learned at home in favor of an ugly, inchoate expressionism that he has never succeeded in selling; Archer has come to fetch him home. Immanuel conducts a masterful put-on of Archer, posing alternately, and successfully, as a student of philosophy, a raging queen, and a vendor of religious relics, and befuddling him with fish scales, dry-cleaning fluid, talcum powder, and an overflowing toilet. In the last scene, Harry returns to the apartment to pack his bags to meet Archer at the train station, but causes such an uproar—he ties Immanuel up in the bedding and assaults the neighbors—that he is arrested and misses the train.

The plot is as chaotic as Harry's life and art, but through it, by indirection, the audience begins to see relationships and histories; it is never made clear exactly what Harry's problem is, or what his youth with Archer was like, but, subtly, a picture emerges. The one image that emerges most clearly is that of Moko the failure clown, whom Archer had brought Harry to see at the circus; Archer had found him hilarious, but Harry had seen only his pain.

One of the clowns in *The Journey of the Fifth Horse* is Chulkaturin, an impoverished landowner in czarist Russia, whose story is adapted from Ivan Turgenev's short story "Dnevnik lishnyago cheloveka" ("The Diary of a Superfluous Man"). Dying at the age of twenty-eight, Chulkaturin confides to his diary that he has never really lived, never succeeded in love, or indeed in making any impression at all on his fellowman. Ribman creates another clown as counterpoint to Chulkaturin: Zoditch, the lowly first reader in a publishing house, whose task it is to evaluate the manuscript of Chulkaturin's diary. As he reads the diary in his miserable rooming house, Chulkaturin's story comes to life, and Zoditch peoples it with analogous characters from his own loveless, pointless existence. In the end, Zoditch, dripping with scorn for Chulkaturin—especially for those qualities that resemble his own—rejects the manuscript and consigns him to oblivion.

Throughout the play, scenes from Chulkaturin's diary alternate with scenes from Zoditch's life and fantasies. This interweaving of plots and levels of reality is quite ingenious, but the technical ingenuity only enhances the pain and ludicrousness of the two protagonists. It is a bittersweet play, its laughter tinged with death. One of its most remarkable aspects is the way Ribman, through his mastery of language, convincingly creates two separate levels of nineteenth century Russian society.

His leap of imagination is even greater in *The Ceremony of Innocence.* This play was written, in a sense, as a response to the war in Vietnam, but the story that Ribman tells is a fanciful revision of the history of Ethelred the Unready, King of England in the eleventh century. Ribman creates a sense of war as an entity unto itself, with its own momentum and a tenacious hold upon the minds and spirits of the people. Ethelred (who is generally seen by historians in a harsher light) is depicted as standing alone for peace, for common prosperity and the spread of literacy, and for justice; appalled at the prejudice and treachery of his court—even his son and his mother—toward the Danes, he simply refuses, as a matter of principle, to take the field at the head of his troops in defense of England.

Ribman begins his play with Ethelred's refusal to meet with the Earls of Sussex and Kent and the Bishop of London, who have come to his retreat on the Isle of Wight to importune him to do battle. His refusal seems bullheaded, a bit deranged, and positively untenable—especially in that the subject matter inevitably calls to mind William Shakespeare's histories, in which the welfare of the English throne is assumed to be the greatest good. The playwright then leaps backward a full year to reveal the underpinnings of Ethelred's convictions; then he works forward to the last scene, which is set a few hours after the first; and by the end of the play Ribman has managed to justify, both ethically and emotionally, the king's refusal to lead his country into war even in defense of its borders. Ribman's achievement is all the more remarkable in that he creates a persuasive language for his characters, a diction that mixes some of the direct, prosaic idiom of modern American speech with Elizabethan locutions—a factitious language that, in less skillful hands, might have come across as clumsy or downright silly, but which Ribman wields into an eloquent sort of poetry.

The linguistic audacity of *The Poison Tree* is very different, but no less perilous, and no less successful; Ribman sets the play in a prison, for the most part among black prisoners, and writes for them a number of varieties of black dialect. (A few years earlier, in 1967, another white writer, William Styron, had been excoriated for using black dialect—and, indeed, for daring to imagine the workings of a black man's mind—in *The Confessions of Nat Turner*, 1967.) The racism of the white prisoners and guards is a palpable, oppressive force throughout the play, but it is only one of a number of oppressions wearing away at the souls of prisoners and guards alike.

The play begins with the murder of a white guard by a black prisoner. The victim, his neck snapped, falls into the arms of another guard, Di Santis. He becomes obsessed with the senseless loss of his comrade, and, through direct violence and covert manipulation, he wreaks a terrible vengeance on the innocent as well as on the guilty. In the end, though, the tables are turned again, and the victimizer becomes the victim.

In *Cold Storage*, Ribman's most successful play commercially, the language is very close to his own natural speech: modern New York. In technique, it is his most realistic, straightforward play. It dares, though, to forge snappy comedy from a situation of inevitable catastrophe; set on the roof garden of a hospital, it presents the relationship between two patients: an old man who is dying and a prosperous middle-aged designer who may have cancer.

Buck, also set in modern New York, is somewhat more complex stylistically. It concerns a television director who is hired to make sleazy exploitation tapes for a cable channel but gets so involved in trying to create a true picture of the realities he is restaging that the scenes he films take on a life of their own.

Sweet Table at the Richelieu is set in a mysterious, elegant spa in an unspecified (though probably Germanic) corner of Europe. It consists of nothing but an after-dinner conversation among the guests; the guests, however, are a most curious, nightmarish assemblage of Eurotrash, and the discussion is brutal, feral, flaying—more direct, probing, and yet poetical than any real-life chitchat could ever be. Among the guests are a widowed baroness avid to enforce the prerogatives of her rank despite the humiliations of a more democratic age; a half-man, half-beast clairvoyant; a best-selling American author of pulp novels and her lover, a Moroccan given to violent fantasies; and a French Lothario who constantly humiliates his wife, who is always hanging on his neck. The presiding figure is Dr. Atmos, a cheerful but treacherous unlicensed physician who attracts guests to the Richelieu with promises of eternal youth.

The central character, Jeanine Cendrars, is a Pennsylvania woman who speaks very little. Early in the play, the audience learns that her marriage is in trouble, and toward the end Dr. Atmos, who dabbles in psychology as well as in rejuvenation, reveals to all that she is haunted by the loss of a child who was swept from her side on a boat by a wave during a moment of inattention. While the other characters are intent on obliterating their pasts, Jeanine clings tenaciously to the image of her lost child, keeping him alive in her mind. In fact, the entire play can be seen as an emanation of her mind, and all the other characters as dream-figures brought to palpable form as combatants in her struggle with a tragic past that remains ever present.

The Cannibal Masque and A Serpent's Egg are one-act plays that were conceived to form a trilogy with Sweet Table at the Richelieu. Each of the three plays has for its central image people eating: in Sweet Table at the Richelieu, a cornucopia of sweets from a groaning board; in The Cannibal Masque, a fat pork dinner in the midst of a famine in Bavaria in 1923; and in A Serpent's Egg (set some thirty years later), a skimpy picnic on a German mountainside under the greedy eye of a rapacious landowner. While the longer play deals with excess through luxuriant verbiage, the one-acts are spare and parabolic, like little allegories of inhuman victimization, but each with a sudden shift of fortunes.

Though there are similarities with Sweet Table at the Richelieu, the other plays in the trilogy are very different in form and feel. Indeed, one of the most curious aspects of Ribman's playwriting career is its diversity, the breadth of imagination that puts him into so many different times, places, idioms, and styles. "I think of Keats," he has said, "who likened a career to the sun which gradually rises, reaches its zenith, and gradually sets. A playwright produces a body of work—he doesn't just produce one or two plays—because what he's doing is mining his life, and a life encompasses more than one or two plays." Ronald Ribman has mined many different veins of his life—a life of imagination as well as experience, rich in words, emotions, and fantasies—and has produced a body of work that reveals the absurd and often grotesque mixture of comedy and tragedy, reality and dream, that constitutes human existence.

Other major works

SCREENPLAY: *The Angel Levine*, 1969 (with William Gunn; based on a story by Bernard Malamud).

TELEPLAYS: *The Final War of Olly Winter*, 1967; *The Most Beautiful Fish*, 1969; *Seize the Day*, 1987 (based on Saul Bellow's novel).

Bibliography

Brustein, Robert. "Journey and Arrival of a Playwright," in *The Third Theatre*, 1969.

DiNovelli, Donna. "Ronald Ribman's Journey to the Sweet Table," in *A.R.T. News*. VII, no. 2 (February, 1987).

Gottfried, Martin. *Opening Nights: Theater Criticism of the Sixties*, 1969.

_____. *A Theater Divided: The Postwar American Stage*, 1967.

Weales, Gerald. "Drama," in *Harvard Guide to Contemporary American Writing*, 1979. Edited by Daniel Hoffman.

_____. *The Jumping-Off Place: American Drama in the 1960's*, 1969.

Jonathan Marks

ALFONSO SASTRE

Born: Madrid, Spain; February 20, 1926

Principal drama

Ha sonado la muerte, pr. 1946, pb. 1949 (with Medardo Fraile); *Uranio 235*, pr. 1946, pb. 1949; *Cargamento de sueños*, pr. 1948, pb. 1949; *Comedia sonámbula*, pb. 1949 (with Fraile); *Teatro de vanguardia*, pb. 1949; *Prólogo patético*, wr. 1950, pb. 1964 (*Pathetic Prologue*, 1968); *El cubo de la basura*, wr. 1951, pb. 1965; *Escuadra hacia la muerte*, pr. 1953, pb. 1960 (*The Condemned Squad*, 1961; also as *Death Squad*, 1964); *La mordaza*, pr. 1954, pb. 1956; *La sangre de Dios*, pr. 1955; *El cuervo*, pr. 1957, pb. 1960; *El pan de todos*, pr. 1957, pb. 1963; *Medea*, pr. 1958, pb. 1967 (adaptation of Euripides' play); *Asalto nocturno*, wr. 1959; *Ana Kleiber*, pr., pb. 1960 (*Anna Kleiber*, 1962); *La cornada*, pr., pb. 1960 (*Death Thrust*, 1964); *Guillermo Tell tiene los ojos tristes*, pb. 1960 (*Sad Are the Eyes of William Tell*, 1970); *Muerte en el barrio*, pb. 1960; *Teatro*, pb. 1960; *Tierra roja*, pb. 1960 (*Red Earth*, 1962); *En la red*, pr. 1961, pb. 1966 (*In the Web*, 1964); *Oficio de tinieblas*, wr. 1962, pr. 1967; *Los acreedores*, pr. 1962, pb. 1967 (adaptation of August Strindberg's *Fordringsägare*); *Mulato*, pr. 1963 (adaptation of Langston Hughes's play); *Teatro*, pb. 1964; *MSV: O, La sangre y la ceniza; Flores rojas para Miguel Servet*, wr. 1965, pb. 1977; *Marat-Sade*, pb. 1966, pr. 1968 (adaptation of Peter Weiss's play); *Teatro selecto*, pb. 1966; *Obras completas*, pb. 1967; *Crónicas romanas*, wr. 1968, pb. 1979; *Rosas rojas para mí*, pr., pb. 1969 (adaptation of Sean O'Casey's *Red Roses for Me*); *Los secuestrados de Altona*, pr. 1972 (adaptation of Jean-Paul Sartre's *Les Séquestrés d'Altona*); *Las cintas magnéticas*, pb. 1973 (radio play; *The Magnetic Tapes*, 1971); *Ejercicios de terror*, pb. 1973.

Other literary forms

Alfonso Sastre has written hundreds of articles and essays. He has also published several collections of poetry, a volume of short stories, and books on dramatic theory, as well as a novel entitled *El paralelo 38*, written in 1958 but not published until 1965.

Achievements

Sastre is credited with attempting to revive the national theater during the years following the Spanish Civil War (1936-1939). After the war, economic hardship and strict censorship caused many Spanish intellectuals either to quit writing or to emigrate. Sastre was one of the few playwrights who opted to stay in Spain and to continue the effort to create meaningful, politically involved drama. Sastre's entire life has been a struggle to reform Spain's political and theatrical institutions. In 1945, before completing his university studies, he helped to found the Arte Nuevo (New Art), an experimental theater group that sought to offer an alternative to the shallow, conventional plays that dominated the stage during post–Civil War Spain. It also attempted to incorporate new methods of staging and acting. Although the group lasted only two years and had no immediate impact, it provided valuable training to several young men who would later be instrumental in the revitalization of Spanish theater.

In 1948, Sastre became the first theater editor of a student magazine called *La hora* (the hour), thereby initiating his career as an essayist. His essays usually addressed political questions—in particular, the relationship between art and politics.

In 1950, Sastre and José María de Quinto, who had also been involved in New Art, founded Teatro de Agitación Social (Theater of Social Agitation, known as T.A.S.), another new theater group. T.A.S. attempted to introduce major foreign playwrights such as Arthur Miller, Bertolt Brecht, Jean-Paul Sartre, and Eugene O'Neill to the Spanish public. In their manifesto, Sastre and Quinto explained that their purpose was to make the spectator think about major political and social issues. The group was censured immediately by the authorities. Yet Sastre was building a reputation and, in 1956, he received a grant from UNESCO.

In 1960, Sastre and Quinto again combined forces to form the Grupo de Teatro Realista (Realist Theater Group), another dissident troupe. The formation of the G.T.R. reflected Sastre's interest in realism in the arts. Its purpose was to bring serious, politically provocative plays to the Spanish stage, as well as to explore realism in drama. Although the G.T.R., like its predecessors, fell victim to censorship, it met with some success. In 1961, it presented three major plays: *Vestire gli ignudi* (1922; *Naked*, 1924), by Luigi Pirandello; *El tintero* (1961; the inkwell), by Carlos Muñiz; and *In the Web*, by Sastre. A relationship was established between G.T.R. and UNESCO's International Institute of the Theatre. One of the greatest contributions that Sastre has made to theater in Spain is the introduction of European and American playwrights to Spanish audiences through the T.A.S. and G.T.R., as well as through his numerous essays.

In 1964, Sastre participated in a Festival of Latin American Theater, held in Cuba. He returned to Havana in 1968 to attend the Cultural Congress. Although Sastre's production has dwindled since the early 1970's, his plays continue to be popular among Spanish youth and in parts of Europe and Latin America. *The Condemned Squad, Death Thrust, La mordaza* (the gag), and *Muerte en el barrio* (death in the neighborhood) have appeared in student editions in the United States. With the political liberalization of Spain following the death of General Francisco Franco, Sastre's radical stance has diminished in significance.

Biography

Alfonso Sastre was a child of ten when the Spanish Civil War erupted and an adolescent during the harsh years following the conflict. He developed professionally during the dictatorship of Franco, when severe censorship was in effect. Like that of many other Spanish artists of his generation, his work has been a response to the political absolutism that prevailed until late 1975, when Franco died.

Sastre is from an artistic family, several of whose members he characterizes as "Bohemian." His father did some acting and then gave it up for economic reasons. Sastre began his theater career in 1945, when he participated in the founding of the New Art theater group. New Art performed Sastre's first plays, *Uranio 235* (uranium 235) and *Ha sonado la muerte* (death has sounded), the latter written in collaboration with Medardo Fraile. In 1947, Sastre and Fraile wrote another play, *Comedia sonámbula* (sleepwalker's comedy), which was not performed. New Art presented one more drama by Sastre, *Cargamento de sueños* (cargo of dreams), before it collapsed in 1948. That same year, Sastre became theater editor of a new student magazine, *La hora*. During his student years and beyond, Sastre acted in several plays.

In the late 1940's, a theater of social concern was beginning to develop in Spain. Antonio Buero Vallejo's *Historia de una escalera* (1949; *Story of a Staircase*, 1955) was staged to critical acclaim. While Buero Vallejo's works were not adamantly countercultural, Sastre's were, and they therefore provoked the animosity of the theater establishment. In 1950, when Sastre and José María de Quinto issued their manifesto for the T.A.S., the effort was largely futile. In 1951, when Sastre submitted his *Pathetic Prologue* to the María Guerrero National Theater, it was rejected. The next year, it was rejected a second time. Finally, in 1953, a university theater group presented *The Condemned Squad* at the María Guerrero. Audiences responded enthusiastically, and, although authorities closed the play after three performances, Sastre became known as a promising young playwright. That same year, Sastre completed his university studies. He also finished writing *El pan de todos* (community bread), begun the year before.

During this period (from 1949 until 1953), Sastre wrote prolifically. His output included essays as well as plays. His articles appeared in several periodicals and consisted of commentaries on the nature of drama, criticism of Spanish theater, and reviews of books and films.

During the years prior to 1953, Sastre underwent a religious crisis resulting from his struggle with the absolute values of Catholicism. On the one hand, he advocated a relativistic approach to life, arguing that any doctrine must be constantly questioned and reevaluated. On the other, he sought some sort of creed to replace the vacuum left by the disintegration of the faith of his childhood. Politically, Sastre was becoming more and more radical. Marxism, with its emphasis on change and, at the same time, its insistence on moral purism,

was increasingly attractive to him. In addition to suggesting a means to reconcile the opposing extremes that dominated Sastre's thought, Marxism provided a basis for the theater of agitation.

In the early 1950's, Sastre was influenced by Jean-Paul Sartre's doctrine of
artistic *engagement*, which claimed that the artist must put his work at the
service of an ideology. In 1951, however, he opposed a proposed festival of
Catholic theater on the basis that it would be nothing more than an instrument of Catholic propaganda and agitation. That is, he was drawn to the
concept of an ideological theater when it promoted the goals of political reform but opposed such a theater when it promoted the ideals of Catholicism.
Sastre's essays of this period reveal much vacillation. Although he adhered to
the principles of *engagement*, Sastre was aware of the doctrine's weakness: If
an artist seeks to advance one particular ideology exclusively, he must necessarily close his eyes to the advantages of other ideologies. The need to
remain open-minded while at the same time advocating a new political system created a major dilemma for the young playwright.

During this period, Sastre continued to identify himself as a Christian, although not as a Catholic. For him, Christianity signified a truth and purity
that contrasted radically with the hypocrisy and corruption of society. After
1953, Christianity ceased to be a major theme in Sastre's work; later in his
life, he became an atheist. Still, the conflicts that emerged during his early
years continued to appear in his mature writing. Instead of attempting to
provide solutions, however, he strove to make his audiences confront the contradictions that they might face in their own lives. His mature plays do not
advance a rigid ideology, but, rather, pose questions.

The early and mid-1950's were an active time for Sastre. In 1954, the government prohibited the staging of *Pathetic Prologue* and *El pan de todos* although Sastre's new play, *La mordaza*, was performed in Madrid under the
direction of José María de Quinto. The author's first professional production, the play had a successful run. He wrote one more work that year and
four the next. One of them, *La sangre de Dios* (the blood of God), was performed in Valencia, but two others, *Muerte en el barrio* and *Sad Are the Eyes
of William Tell*, were banned.

In 1955, Sastre married Genoveva Forest, a psychologist and social activist.
In 1956, the year of the birth of their first son, Juan, Sastre collaborated with
José María Forqué on a film entitled *Amanecer en Puerta Oscura* (dawn in
Puerta Oscura). That year, he was imprisoned for his political activities. At
about the same time, *Drama y sociedad* (1956; *Drama and Society*, 1962) was
published. A collection of essays on the nature of theater, the book contained the most important of the essays that had appeared previously in
periodicals. In the years following *Drama and Society*, Sastre continued to
write essays and, although he did not depart radically from the positions he
adopted early in his career, he continued to grow intellectually. Many critics

consider his 1957 analysis of Samuel Beckett's *En attendant Godot* (1952; *Waiting for Godot*, 1954) which appeared in *Primer acto*, one of his most perceptive pieces.

In 1957, an edited version of *El pan de todos* was performed in Barcelona. Many critics interpreted the play as an antirevolutionary statement. In response, Sastre ordered the play closed. That year and the following, Sastre wrote several film scripts. One of them, *Carmen*, was banned twice before it met with official approval. In 1958, Sastre wrote his first and only novel, *El paralelo 38* (the thirty-eighth parallel); the same year, his son Pablo was born.

In the late 1950's, Sastre developed an intense interest in the theories of Bertolt Brecht, and in 1960 he published the first of several essays in which he analyzed Brecht's epic theater. Brecht wished to engage the audience intellectually, but not emotionally, and at first Sastre objected to the distance the German playwright strove to create between spectator and spectacle. Later, he modified his views. During the 1960's, Sastre cultivated the epic drama himself, although with modifications. Sastre shared with Brecht the concept of theater as an instrument for societal transformation. The Spanish dramatist attempted to expose the spectator to experiences of change, however, rather than to convince him rationally. His techniques included shock treatment in sound, light, and scenic effects. *Asalto nocturno* (nocturnal assault), written in 1959, is Sastre's earliest epic play.

In 1960, *Death Thrust* premiered in Madrid and *Anna Kleiber* in Athens. That same year, Sastre and Quinto founded the G.T.R., and Sastre, along with 227 other intellectuals, signed a statement condemning censorship in Spain. In the next year, G.T.R. performed *In the Web*, which was subsequently banned in the provinces. Sastre was once again imprisoned for his political participation, although only briefly.

In 1962, the year of the birth of his daughter Eva, Sastre wrote *Oficio de tinieblas* (office of darkness), which was prohibited by the authorities. In 1963, he joined other playwrights in protesting alleged atrocities against miners who were striking in Asturias, in the northern part of the country. As a result, Sastre's works were banned from national theaters throughout Spain.

Following his trip to Cuba in 1964, Sastre attempted to visit the United States, where he had received invitations to lecture at universities, but was unable to obtain a visa. He did travel to Portugal, however, where there was considerable interest in his theater. Several of his plays have been translated into Portuguese. In 1968, Sastre, an avid supporter of Fidel Castro, made a second trip to Cuba.

In the fall of 1974, Sastre and his wife were imprisoned for crimes against the state. Genoveva was implicated in bomb explosions that took place in Madrid. She was also accused of involvement with Basque terrorists and charged with murder in the assassination of Premier Admiral Luis Carrero

Blanco in 1973. Sastre was incarcerated with Genoveva because, under Spanish law, a husband was legally responsible for crimes committed by his wife. Many of Sastre's plays written after 1963 have not been published. In 1967, *Oficio de tinieblas* premiered in Madrid but was received unenthusiastically. The increasing popularity of motion pictures, spectator sports, and television, as well the democratization of Spain after Franco's death, have contributed to the dwindling interest in Sastre's theater. Nevertheless, Sastre the man continues to be an important figure in international theater circles.

Analysis

Alfonso Sastre sees drama as an instrument of social reform. For him, a successful play is one that works on the spectator's conscience and produces a reaction. Through his works, Sastre seeks to investigate the causes of social injustice and of individual unhappiness. He asks himself, "Why does man suffer and who is the guilty party?" In his article "El teatro de Alfonso Sastre visto por Alfonso Sastre" (Alfonso Sastre's theater seen by Alfonso Sastre), he states that he approaches theater as a form of criminal investigation. It is not surprising that some of his works, such as *Muerte en el barrio*, revolve around the investigation of a crime.

Sastre's purpose is not to provoke anarchy but to create an atmosphere of inquiry and analysis that will lead to the establishment of a new order. His plays often present no clearly defined answers, but, rather, raise questions that produce a catharsis by leading the spectator to agonize over possible solutions. This is what Sastre calls "theater of anguish." Thus, although Sastre reflects Sartre's influence in that his plays convey existential pain and the need for reform, the Spanish playwright does believe that theater must promote a definite political ideology.

The vehicle that Sastre prefers is tragedy. According to ideas set forth in *Drama and Society*, tragedy awakens in the spectator a profound sense of guilt. This experience purifies him and makes him susceptible to change. The result may be a social revolution or, at least, a new willingness to address social problems.

Sastre's works deal with a variety of subjects, although nearly all have reformist or existential overtones. Political revolution is the theme of *Pathetic Prologue*, *El pan de todos*, *Red Earth*, *Sad Are the Eyes of William Tell*, *In the Web*, and *Crónicas romanas* (Roman chronicles). *Uranio 235* and *Asalto nocturno* deal with atomic terror. *El cuervo* (the raven) and *Cargamento de sueños* deal with existential anguish. *Anna Kleiber* is a love story.

Structurally, Sastre's plays range from the classically Aristotelian to the highly experimental. As a rule, his plots are functional and unadorned. His language is concise, conversational, and nonrhetorical. His characters are real people with real problems, victims of an unjust society or of their own weaknesses.

Like that of Sartre, Sastre's theater is largely situational. Characters find themselves in predicaments in which they are forced to act or be overcome by circumstances. In several plays, especially among the earlier ones, characters are alienated from society and from one another. They are swept up by history; they are not makers of history. They do not act, but are acted upon. These plays convey a sense of anguish and frustration.

Anna Kleiber is an example of this type of drama. The play begins at a hotel in Barcelona, where The Writer, identified as Sastre, is being interviewed by two reporters who systematically misinterpret his responses. In a separate conversation, a man urges his distraught mistress to have an abortion, while she complains of feeling emotionally abandoned. This preliminary dialogue introduces the major themes of the work: lack of communication, isolation, and the individual's inability to find happiness in love. The Writer's involvement suggests a secondary theme: the creative process by which a dramatist writes a play.

Anna Kleiber, nervous and upset, asks for a room and requests that she be awakened early the next morning because she has an appointment so important that it will determine her future. During the night, she dies of a heart attack. At her funeral, The Writer encounters Anna's former lover, Alfredo Merton, who, through a series of flashbacks, tells Anna's story.

Anna and Alfredo met in Paris, when Anna was on the verge of suicide. After spending eight wonderful days with Alfredo, Anna abandons him, unable to bear the happiness and fearful of bringing him misfortune. Alfredo follows her to Germany, where she is acting in a small theater company. Cohen, Anna's former impressario, torments Alfredo with allusions to his previous relationship with her. In a rage, Alfredo kills him. Then, overcome with terror at the act he has committed, he yields to the entreaties of a young Nazi fanatic who praises him for killing the Jew and offers to recommend him to the Nazi authorities. Anna is disgusted by Alfredo's cowardliness, and once more the lovers separate. Anna, a libertine ever in search of new experiences, seeks thrills through sex and alcohol. When she once again joins Alfredo, however, they set up a household and she becomes a "model housewife."

When the war breaks out, Alfredo obeys the call to duty unquestioningly. In the meantime, Anna amuses herself with a series of lovers. Wounded in battle, Alfredo returns and hurls insults at Anna, who responds that his abuse "purifies" her. Alfredo, now bored with Anna's complexities and angry at her infidelities, attacks and almost kills her. Then he returns to the front. After the war, they write to each other and fix a date to meet at the hotel in Barcelona, where Anna dies.

Anna Kleiber explores the dark, self-destructive aspect of man. Throughout the play, Anna's sadomasochistic tendencies prevent her from attaining happiness. She refers to herself repeatedly as "diabolical," and, indeed, she

has a diabolical need to destroy what is dearest to her. She resists content-
ment because she fears routine and stagnation. She insists that she wants to
live "intensely" and therefore rejects bourgeois domesticity in favor of a life
of passion and freedom. Yet Anna is not free. She is a pawn of her persona—that of the depressive, nonconformist actress. Alfredo's disdain for
her shallowness is evident in his ironic comment: "You retain a crumb of
bourgeois dignity. . . which doesn't become an enigmatic, open woman like
you."

Alfredo, however, is no more authentic than Anna. He runs to her when
she flees him but flees from her when he senses that she really needs him. He
kills a man, then fails to accept responsibility for his act, preferring, rather,
to disappear into the ranks of Nazism, a cause in which he does not believe.
When the war starts, Alfredo goes willingly. "It's not something you think
about . . . you just hand yourself over to it. . . . Maybe I'll get to be a hero."
He is a man without convictions who allows himself to be swept by circumstances. Perhaps Anna and Alfredo are unable to be true to each other because they are not true to themselves.

Each sees in the other something pure. After Anna's death, Alfredo remarks that, in spite of everything, Anna is "clean"—although during her lifetime she repeatedly describes herself as "dirty." Who is Anna, really? Would
she and Alfredo have found happiness had she lived? Sastre does not answer
these questions. Rather, he shows that it is impossible for one human being
ever really to know another. "Everyone must bear his own pain," The Writer
tells Alfredo. "In that respect, we can help each other very little." All The
Writer can do is observe and record. It is after he has heard Alfredo's story
that he sits down to write _Anna Kleiber_, reproducing what he has seen and
heard.

While _Anna Kleiber_ focuses on alienation, _Muerte en el barrio_ focuses on
solidarity and political action. In the prologue, a police inspector interrogates
Pedro the bartender about the murder of Dr. Sanjo, and the story emerges.
In a working-class neighborhood, a child is struck by a car and rushed to a
clinic. Dr. Sanjo, who is supposed to be on duty, is absent, and the child dies.
Anger mounts in the neighborhood, and violence erupts in the bar on the following Sunday, when a crowd attacks and kills Dr. Sanjo.

The events leading up to the outburst are depicted in flashbacks. It becomes clear that Dr. Sanjo represents a cold, impersonal system that dehu-
manizes the poor. He holds both his patients and his nurses in contempt. Yet
he does not bear the sole responsibility for the child's death. While he is
guilty of abandoning his post, he is a cog in the wheel of social inequality and
injustice.

The death of the child unifies the community and prompts people to act.
Dr. Sanjo's murder constitutes a rebellion against the system. "Justice
depends on us," not on the authorities, maintains the child's father. The po-

lice inspector finds it consoling that people "can kill attaching importance to what they're doing. That they can kill united by rage, dirtying their clothes with blood . . . suffering in order to kill." The experience purifies the collective psyche of the community. Yet will eliminating one element in an oppressive system really prove constructive?

Throughout their dialogue, the police inspector and the bartender complain of the asphyxiating heat. The constant mention of the weather serves to raise another question. To what extent were the neighbors impelled to act by the sheer discomfort of their physical situation? Was the doctor's murder a conscious, deliberate act or was it the result of several factors, some unrelated to Sanjo's irresponsibility? In *Muerte en el barrio*, as in other plays, Sastre raises important issues about the nature of political violence.

Other major works

NOVEL: *El paralelo 38*, 1965.

SHORT FICTION: *Las noches lúgubres*, 1964.

POETRY: *Te veo, Viet Nam*, 1973; *Balada de Carabanchel*, 1976; *El espanol al alcance de todos*, 1978; *T.B.O.*, 1978.

NONFICTION: *Drama y sociedad*, 1956 (*Drama and Society*, 1962); *Anatomía del realismo*, 1965; *La revolucíon y la critica de la cultura*, 1970; *Critica de la imaginación*, 1978; *Lumpen, margenación, y jerigonça*, 1980; *Escrito en Euskadi*, 1982.

Bibliography

Anderson, Farris. *Alfonso Sastre*, 1971.

_____. "The New Theater of Alfonso Sastre," in *Hispania*. LV (December, 1972), pp. 840-847.

Bryan, T. Avril. *Censorship and Social Conflict in the Spanish Theater: The Case of Alfonso Sastre*, 1982.

Pasquariello, Anthony. "Alfonso Sastre, Dramatist in Search of a Stage," in *Theater Annual*. XXII (1965-1966), pp. 16-23.

Pronko, Leonard C. "The 'Revolutionary Theater' of Alfonso Sastre," in *Tulane Drama Review*. V (December, 1960), pp. 111-132.

Schwartz, Kessel. *The Meaning of Existence in Contemporary Hispanic Theater*, 1969.

_____. "Tragedy and the Criticism of Alfonso Sastre," in *Symposium*. XXI (Winter, 1967), pp. 338-346.

Wellwarth, George. *Spanish Underground Theater*, 1972.

_____. *The Theatre of Protest and Paradox*, 1971.

Barbara Mujica

NTOZAKE SHANGE
Paulette Williams

Born: Trenton, New Jersey; October 18, 1948

Principal drama

For Colored Girls Who Have Considered Suicide When the Rainbow Is Enuf, pr., pb. 1976; *A Photograph: Still Life with Shadows; A Photograph: A Study in Cruelty*, pr. 1977 (revised as *A Photograph: Lovers in Motion*, pr. 1979, pb. 1981); *Where the Mississippi Meets the Amazon*, pr. 1977; *From Okra to Greens: A Different Kinda Love Story*, pr. 1978, pb. 1985; *Spell No. 7*, pr. 1979, pb. 1981; *Boogie Woogie Landscapes*, pr. 1979, pb. 1981; *Mother Courage and Her Children*, pr. 1980 (adaptation of Bertolt Brecht's play); *Three Pieces*, 1981.

Other literary forms

Ntozake Shange's three genres—plays, poems, and novels—so overlap that one might say she has invented a new genre, the "choreopoem." She has published four volumes of poetry: *Nappy Edges* (1978), parts of which were included in her 1976 play *For Colored Girls Who Have Considered Suicide When the Rainbow Is Enuf*; *Natural Disasters and Other Festive Occasions* (1979); *A Daughter's Geography* (1983); and *Ridin' the Moon in Texas: Word Paintings* (1987). Her novels are *Sassafrass, Cypress and Indigo* (1982) and *Betsey Brown* (1985). She has gathered writings about her work from 1976 to 1984 into *See No Evil: Prefaces, Essays, and Accounts, 1976-1983* (1984), essential for study of her art.

Achievements

Shange's work embodies a rich confusion of genres and all the contradictions inherent in a world where violence and oppression polarize life and art. These polarizations in Shange's work both contribute to her artistry and complicate it. She has been criticized and praised for her unconventional language and structure, for her almost religious feminism, and for her stand on black/white and male/female issues. Her first play, *For Colored Girls Who Have Considered Suicide When the Rainbow Is Enuf*, produced in 1976 by Joseph Papp's New York Shakespeare Festival, was honored in that year by the Outer Critics Circle, comprising those who write about the New York theater for out-of-town newspapers. Shange's 1980 adaptation of Bertolt Brecht's *Mother Courage and Her Children* won one of the *Village Voice's* Obie awards.

Biography

Ntozake Shange (pronounced "En-to-zaki Shong-gay") was born Paulette

Williams in Trenton, New Jersey, on October 18, 1948, daughter of a surgeon and a psychiatric social worker. She grew up surrounded by music, literature, art, and her parents' prominent friends, among them Dizzy Gillespie, Chuck Berry, and W.E.B. Du Bois, as well as Third World writers and musicians. Her ties with her family were strong; she also was close to her family's live-in black maids. She was graduated from Barnard College with honors in 1970, then received a graduate degree at the University of Southern California in Los Angeles. While in California, she began studying dance, writing poetry, and participating in improvisational works (composed of poems, music, dance, and mime) at bars, cabarets, and schools. These gradually grew into *For Colored Girls Who Have Considered Suicide When the Rainbow Is Enuf*, which she carried across the country to perform in workshops in New York, then at the Public Theatre, and eventually on Broadway. The contrasts between her privileged home and education and the realities of the lives of black women led her, in 1971, to change her name legally from what she called the "slave name" of Paulette Williams to Ntozake Shange, meaning "she who comes with her own things" and "she who walks like a lion" in Xhosa (Zulu). Her two failed marriages, her suicide attempts, and her contact with city violence resulted in an anger which found its outlet in her poems. During the late 1970's, she lived in New York City, but she later moved to Houston, Texas, with her daughter, Savannah. She has taught and lectured at many colleges and universities, including Mills College in Oakland, California, The State University in Rutgers, New Jersey, the University of California, Berkeley, and the University of Houston.

Analysis

Ntozake Shange's plays have evoked a range of critical responses commensurate with their unconventional nature. Should her work be characterized as poetry or drama, prose or poetry, essay or autobiography? All these forms can be found in her plays, which are unified by a militant feminism in which some critics have seen a one-sided attack on black men. Others, however, point out the youthful spirit, flair with language, and lyricism that carry her plays to startling and radical conclusions. Her style and its contradictions (embracing black English and the erudite vocabulary of the educated) are at the heart of her drama. Influenced by their method of development—public poetry reading in bars, cafés, schools, Off-Off-Broadway theaters—the plays are generally somewhere between a poetry reading and a staged play.

First among the contrasts is her blending of genres: Her poems shade into drama, her dramas are essentially verse monologues, her novels incorporate poetic passages. Second, her language varies radically—on a single page and even in a single phrase—from black dialect ("cuz," "wanna," "awready," "chirren") to the language of her middle-class upbringing and education ("i cant count the number of times i have viscerally wanted to attack deform n maim the language that i waz taught to hate myself in/"). In the published texts of her poetry, plays, and essays, in addition to simplified phonetic spellings, she employs the slash instead of the period and omits capitalization. Many recordings of her work are available, and these will provide the reader with a much fuller sense of the dynamic quality of her language in performance.

Shange's first dramatic success, *For Colored Girls Who Have Considered Suicide When the Rainbow Is Enuf,* she called a "choreopoem"—the recital, individually and in chorus, of the lives and growth of seven different black women, named according to their dress colors: "lady in red," "lady in blue," "lady in orange," "lady in brown," "lady in yellow," "lady in purple," and "lady in green." The term "colored girls" in the title evokes a stereotype of black women yet also contains a germ of hope for the future (the "rainbow," both of color and of eventual salvation).

These seven stylized figures are representative voices of black women, and they express their fury at their oppression both as women and as blacks. The first segment shows high school graduation and the social and sexual rite of passage for "colored girls" in the working-class suburbs. Some of the women who have been cruelly disappointed in relationships with men discuss their spiritual quest. A black woman pretends to be Puerto Rican so that she can dance the merengue in Spanish Harlem. A woman breaks up with her lover by returning to him his plant to water. The scenes become more somber, portraying rape, abuse, city dangers, and abortion. Ties with a more heroic black past appear in "Toussaint," while the glamorized prostitute evicts her lover from her bed. The women begin to analyze their predicament and to assert their independence in segments entitled "somebody almost walked off wid alla my stuff" and "pyramid," in which three women console one another for the actions of the faithless lover whom they share. In the brutal culminating scene, a crazed Vietnam veteran, Beau Willie Brown, abuses his woman Crystal and kills their infant children, dropping them from a window.

Ultimately, the theme of the play is the thwarting of dreams and aspirations for a decent life by forces beyond one's control: war, poverty, and ignorance. There is, however, a saving grace. Toward the end of the play, the seven women fall into a tighter circle of mutual support, much like a religious "laying on of hands" ceremony, in which say,

> i found god in myself
> & i loved her/ i loved her fiercely

Their bitter pain, shown throughout the dramatic episodes, turns into a possibility of regeneration. Thus, the play is a drama of salvation for women who do not receive their full value in society.

Though it was a landmark in the emergence of new black women playwrights, *For Colored Girls Who Have Considered Suicide When the Rainbow*

Is Enuf has been criticized for its lack of discussion of black traditions in religion, family, and ordinary work, and for its omissions of both black literary and political history and the influence of whites. Its style, considered as an attack on language, part of blacks' "enslavement," has also been criticized. Later plays, however, include these elements in a constantly enriching network of allusions.

Shange's second major work, *A Photograph: A Still Life with Shadows; A Photograph: A Study in Cruelty*, was produced in 1977; its title was changed in a later version to *A Photograph: Lovers in Motion* (which is the source of the text analyzed here). *A Photograph* is a set of meditations and sketches involving an ideal black woman named Michael and her lover Sean, a failed photographer. Sean, trying to objectify the world about him in his photographs, provides both the play's title and the technological representation of the play as a picture or mirror of the world. Rich allusions such as these, as in most of Shange's plays, are thickly sown throughout the characters' speeches and typically not explained. Sean and Michael's world is not that of *For Colored Girls Who Have Considered Suicide When the Rainbow Is Enuf* (New York slums, ridden with violence) but that of San Francisco's arty world, peopled with dancers, lawyers, and intellectuals. The problems addressed are not those of Shange's previous play but those of middle-class, professional, and artistic blacks in a complicated urban society. In this play, Shange expands her black world's boundaries.

Sean tells Michael that she must share him, just as all sorts of women shared Alexandre Dumas in nineteenth century France. Michael dreams of an idealized lover who is not "all-American," while Sean boasts that "lil sean david who never got over on nothing but bitches/ is building a world in his image/" when one of his women, Nevada, an attorney, tears up his photographs. Michael expresses the world of her grandmother as "alla the blood & the fields & the satchels dragging in the dust. all the boogies & stairways late at night oozing the scent of love & cornbread/ the woods smelling of burnt flesh & hunger."

In addition, the idea of art as either survival (Sean's view) or love (Michael's) emerges. All the characters show insecurity and find no solution for their dilemmas, sexual or political. In manipulating one another, they realize how much they have been manipulated in the way they were reared and by the environment in which they live. They cannot love one another enough.

After examining the identity of isolated young black women in *For Colored Girls Who Have Considered Suicide When the Rainbow Is Enuf* and of couples in *A Photograph*, Shange concentrates in her next play on one woman's visions, dreams, and memories. *Boogie Woogie Landscapes* was first produced as a one-woman poetry piece in 1978 and then cast as a play in 1979, with music and dance. Layla, a young black woman, entertains in her dreams a series of nightlife companions who exemplify her perceptions of herself and her memories. "Layla" means "born at night" in Arabic, and the whole play exists in Layla's subconscious, in her dreams. Layla's memories of Fidel Castro's Cuba, of primitive cruelties to African women, and of rock-and-roll and blues, interweave with her feelings about growing up, family, brothers and sisters, parents, maids (some of which appear later in Shange's semiautobiographical novel *Betsey Brown*).

Shange's 1979 play *Spell No. 7*, like her first play, is structured like a highly electric poetry reading, but this time the cast is mixed male and female. A huge blackface mask forms the backdrop for actors and actresses of an imitation old-time minstrel show, where actors did skits, recited, and joked, all under the direction of a Mr. Interlocutor. The actors come offstage, relax at an actors' bar, and gradually remove their masks, revealing their true selves. One magician says that he gave up the trade when a colored child asked for a spell to make her white. The new spell the actors discover is a pride in their blackness. They arrive at this through telling classic "tall stories"; one of these concerns a child who thought blacks were immune to dread diseases such as polio since television pictures show polio victims as all white. She is disillusioned when she finds that blacks can hurt one another, so she buys South African gold to remind her of that pain. Another woman loves her baby while it is in the womb but kills it after it is born. Still another girl vows to brush her "nappy" hair constantly so that she can toss it like white girls. By these contrasts and by wry lists and surprising parallels, Shange shows the pain and difficulty, as well as the hopefulness, of being black. She concludes, "we gonna be colored & love it." As in her play *For Colored Girls Who Have Considered Suicide When the Rainbow Is Enuf*, the power of love and self-realization becomes their salvation.

Shange has also done distinguished work as a director, of both her own work and that of others, notably Richard Wesley's *The Mighty Gents* in 1979. In 1980, Shange adapted Bertolt Brecht's *Mutter Courage und ihre Kinder* (1940; *Mother Courage and Her Children*, 1941), changing the scene from mid-seventeenth century Europe to post–Civil War America, making the protagonist an emancipated slave doing business with the army oppressing the Western Indians, and changing the language to black English.

Though she has not always succeeded, Shange's bold and daring use of language, her respect for people formerly given little value, and her exploration of the roles of black men and women have opened a new dimension in theater. Her blendings of poetry, music, and dance bring theater back to its origins and simultaneously blaze a trail toward the drama of the future.

Other major works

NOVELS: *Sassafras: A Novella*, 1976; *Sassafras, Cypress, and Indigo*, 1982; *Betsey Brown*, 1985.

POETRY: *Nappy Edges*, 1978; *Natural Disasters and Other Festive Occa-*

sions, 1979; *A Daughter's Geography*, 1983; *Ridin' the Moon in Texas: Word Paintings*, 1987.

NONFICTION: *See No Evil: Prefaces, Essays, and Accounts, 1976-1983*, 1984.

Bibliography

Blackwell, Henry. "An Interview with Ntozake Shange," in *Black American Literature Forum*. XIII (Fall, 1979), pp. 134-138.

Buckley, Tom. "The Three Stages of Ntozake Shange," in *The New York Times*. CXXVII (December 16, 1977), sec. C, p. 6.

Christ, Carol P. *Diving Deep and Surfacing: Women Writers on Spiritual Quest*, 1980.

Dong, Stella. "Ntozake Shange," in *Publishers Weekly*. CCXXVII (May 3, 1985), pp. 74-75.

Flowers, Sandra Hollin. "*Colored Girls*: Textbook for the Eighties," in *Black American Literature Forum*. XV (Summer, 1981), pp. 51-54.

Mitchell, Carolyn. "'A Laying on of Hands': Transcending the City in Ntozake Shange's *For Colored Girls Who Have Considered Suicide When the Rainbow Is Enuf*," in *Women Writers and the City: Essays in Feminist Literary Criticism*, 1984. Edited by Susan Merrill Squier.

Murray, Timothy. "Screening the Camera's Eye: Black and White Confrontations of Technological Representation," in *Modern Drama*. XXVIII (March, 1985), pp. 110-124.

Peters, Erskine. "Some Tragic Propensities of Ourselves: The Occasion of Ntozake Shange's *For Colored Girls Who Have Considered Suicide When the Rainbow Is Enuf*," in *Journal of Ethnic Studies*. VI (Spring, 1978), pp. 79-85.

Rich, Frank. "*Mother Courage* Transplanted," in *The New York Times*. CXXIX (June 15, 1980), sec. D, p. 5.

Richards, Sandra L. "Conflicting Impulses in the Plays of Ntozake Shange," in *Black American Literature Forum*. XVII (Summer, 1983), pp. 73-78.

Rushing, Andrea Benton. "*For Colored Girls*: Suicide or Struggle," in *Massachusetts Review*. XXII (Autumn, 1981), pp. 539-550.

Tate, Claudia, ed. *Black Women Writers at Work*, 1983.

Anne Mills King

WALLACE SHAWN

Born: New York, New York; November 12, 1943

Principal drama

The Hotel Play, wr. 1970, pr. 1981; *Play in Seven Scenes*, pr. 1974; *Our Late Night*, pr. 1974; *In the Dark*, pr. 1976 (libretto); *Three Short Plays: Summer Evening, The Youth Hostel, Mr. Frivolous*, pr. 1976; *The Mandrake*, pr. 1977 (adaptation of Niccolò Machiavelli's play *La mandragola*; *Marie and Bruce*, pr. 1979, pb. 1980; *My Dinner with André*, pr. 1980, pb. 1981 (with André Gregory); *The Music Teacher*, pr. 1982 (libretto); *Aunt Dan and Lemon*, pr., pb. 1985.

Other literary forms

In addition to his stage plays, Wallace Shawn has also written two opera librettos (*In the Dark* and *The Music Teacher*) and a screenplay (*My Dinner with André*, 1981, adapted from his stage play).

Achievements

After a slow start, Shawn has established himself as a leading writer in the Off-Broadway theater. His first play to receive a major production, *Our Late Night*, as staged by André Gregory's Manhattan Project at the Public Theatre, received an Obie Award in 1975. His play *Aunt Dan and Lemon* shared that same award with several other plays in 1985. Shawn's work, though often taking as its subject extremely violent thoughts or antisocial behavior, has been praised for its accuracy in representing the emotional qualities of contemporary American life. His plays make unusual demands upon audiences, who must respond to his characters with comic insight and intellectual energy. Shawn's distinctive voice is one of insidiously timid argumentation, an impression that is reinforced by his frequent appearances as a humorously innocuous character in contemporary films, yet he is also capable of writing shrill, viscerally affecting drama. Shawn's major works are distinctively provocative and unconventional, and he is among the most promising writers in the American theater today.

Biography

Wallace Shawn's upbringing was without question a privileged one. His father, William Shawn, was the editor of *The New Yorker* for several decades, and so Shawn grew up in the atmosphere of Manhattan literary society. His education has been extensive, including the best schools in the English-speaking world. From the Dalton School (1948-1957) and Putney School (1958-1961), Shawn went on to take a B.A. in history from Harvard (1965).

He then took additional degrees at Magdalen College, Oxford: a B.A. in philosophy, politics, and economics (1968) and an M.A. in Latin under G.J. Warnock (1968). The time between universities was spent teaching English on a Fulbright Scholarship at Indore Christian College, India.

Shawn's dramatic talents were encouraged by his parents, who provided him with creative tools such as a toy theater and a motion-picture camera. His childhood theatrics included the composition and performance of lurid murder mysteries with his younger brother Allen. Shawn recalls that an important turning point in his perception of drama came when his father took part in a different kind of play, about a botanist in Japan. From this point, Shawn developed the conviction that a play could be almost anything, and other performances included a four-hour version of John Milton's *Paradise Lost* (1667), a play featuring Ludwig Wittgenstein, and a Chinese dynastic drama. Many of these performances featured music by Allen Shawn, with whom Wallace still collaborates.

The young Shawn attended frequent professional productions in New York, including acclaimed productions of work as varied as Eugene O'Neill's *The Iceman Cometh* (1946) and the early classics of the absurdist drama. This exposure reinforced Shawn's conviction that the potential topics for dramatization are infinite.

Shawn's career after Oxford started with two years of teaching Latin at the Church of the Heavenly Rest Day School in Manhattan. During that time, Shawn began to write regularly, drafting plays such as *Four Meals in May* and *The Old Man*. Shawn then took a succession of odd jobs, including work as a shipping clerk in the garment district and as a copy-machine operator, while drafting a number of short plays and one full-length script, *The Hotel Play*. During this time, Shawn also studied acting with Katherine Sergava at the H.B. studio.

Shawn has maintained a long-term relationship with writer Deborah Eisenberg. His play *Marie and Bruce* is dedicated to her, and she is mentioned several times in *My Dinner with André*. Her book of short stories, *Transactions in a Foreign Currency* (1986), carries a dedication to Shawn, and her long story "A Cautionary Tale" (published in *The New Yorker*) features characters resembling them both. Eisenberg has also authored one play, *Pastorale* (1982), which features the same sort of casually cryptic dialogue and frustrated young characters that characterize much of Shawn's dramatic output.

Shawn's first break came through André Gregory's Manhattan Project. The hour-long production of *Our Late Night*, Shawn's first professional production, was awarded an Obie for Best Play Off-Broadway. Shawn was then engaged by the Public Theater to prepare the adaptation of Niccolò Machiavelli's *La mandragola*. The production was staged by Wilford Leach, and Shawn was featured as an actor in the prologue. Leach later directed *Marie and Bruce*, with Louise Lasser and Bob Balaban, in a widely reviewed Public Theater production in 1980 that led to Shawn's publishing contract with Grove Press.

Shawn's plays have also received several productions in London, including an early stage version of *My Dinner with André* in 1980. The first British production of his work was a *succès de scandale*, a staging of the trilogy *Three Short Plays* by Max Stafford-Clark for the Joint Stock Company in 1977. One part of the trilogy, an orgiastically sexual play called *The Youth Hostel*, aroused a public outcry over alleged obscenity. The author fortunately escaped prosecution, but concern over the representation of sex precluded any impression that might have been created by the play's artistic qualities. Later productions of *Marie and Bruce* and *Aunt Dan and Lemon* were received more responsibly.

The development of Shawn's acting career since 1977 has allowed him the comfort of a regular income and the time to pursue his writing projects. Shawn has had large character roles in a number of films, such as an obsessed psychiatrist in Marshall Brickman's *Lovesick* (1983), a depraved priest in the schoolboy drama *Heaven Help Us* (1985), and the diminutive innkeeper Freud in *The Hotel New Hampshire* (1984), but he is still perhaps best known for a brief appearance as Diane Keaton's former lover in Woody Allen's *Manhattan* (1979), as well as his role as himself in the film version of *My Dinner with André*. Shawn has also appeared frequently in his own plays, including the 1981 La Mama E.T.C. production of *The Hotel Play*, the stage and screen versions of *My Dinner with André*, and the London and New York productions of *Aunt Dan and Lemon*.

By his own admission, writing does not come particularly easily to Shawn. Nevertheless, he has consistently pursued the images and themes that capture his imagination, always with the assumption that a personal concern with the material will arouse some similar response in the audience. Shawn has not developed any formulaic approach, though his work has distinctive stylistic traits and persistent themes. His plays have shown a steady improvement, and his following has continued to grow as his works enter the repertoire of major regional playhouses such as the Magic Theater and the Mark Taper Forum.

Analysis

Wallace Shawn's major plays exhibit a concern with vivid images of violence, whether political or sexual, as they are manifested in the imaginations and behavior of his contemporary characters. These images connect Shawn's work with the traditional themes of surrealism, yet the apparently harmless characters and situations in the plays' narrative structures cause a kind of contradictory tension between the force of obsessive imagination and the ordinary experience of daily life. Shawn has consistently improved his ability to express this juxtaposition of qualities, while emphasizing the immediate importance of his major themes. No detailed line of development can be established in Shawn's career because so much of his work has not yet been published or professionally produced, but the recent major plays show a definite connection to the material of his early writings.

Shawn's first play to receive a major production, *Our Late Night*, raised the eyebrows of critics with its simultaneously scatological and intelligent style. The situation involves a young couple and their party guests and proceeds anecdotally from the final preparations of the couple, through the recitations of their guests' unusual feelings and experiences, to the empty moments after the party ends. The play's action—or what there is of action in the play—concerns the lusts of the partygoers for one another in combination with their visceral reactions to what gets said (and eaten). The longest, most memorable monologue is an impassioned shaggy-dog story about one single-minded male guest's sexual exploits in the tropics.

The language of the play reveals one of Shawn's characteristic devices: the polite utterance of unconscionably rude sentiments. Obscenity begins to flow so freely that it becomes the normal discourse of the play, along with the frequent use of proper names, salutations, and other conventionally respectful phrases. The language becomes the stylistic equivalent of the characters themselves: well-dressed and pleasant-seeming, but sexually obsessed at the core. The final effect of the play, in the right sort of sophisticated performance situation, is not obscene but satirical, exposing the thin veneer of manners that strains to hold back the force of human desire.

Shawn's second professional production raised more than eyebrows. The London production of *Three Short Plays* provoked antiobscenity complaints that resulted in a government investigation of the theater and an initiative to rewrite British obscenity laws. Of the three plays which constituted the production, the objectionable material was contained in *The Youth Hostel*. The play is unique for Shawn because the actors do not merely talk about their fantasies, they enact the fulfillment of their sexual desires onstage. Yet stylistically, the play has passages very similar to the successful satire of *Our Late Night*. Characters copulate, masturbate, and have violent fistfights, but they continue to express themselves in the polite, matter-of-fact idiom of contemporary young Americans.

The other two plays in the trilogy are less likely to offend audiences than *The Youth Hostel*, but they address the same themes. In *Summer Evening*, a young couple in a foreign hotel pass the time between meals by trying on clothes, discussing the mundane details of their vacation, and snacking. Yet lurking under the surface of the action, which Shawn suggests should have an extremely quick, unrealistic pace, are the desires of the man to possess the woman to the point of death, and the woman's fears of the injury that could come with her submission. The language, dotted with interruptions to encourage the tempo, remains oddly formal and polite, even while the intimacy of the characters' revelations gradually leads them to make love at the play's end. The last play of the set, a monologue titled *Mr. Frivolous*, features the eponymous character at breakfast, fantasizing about companionship and sexual pleasure. The title suggests the principal theme: Despite the intimacy and even the quaintness of his recitation, the young man is vacuous to the point of complete superfluity.

In *Marie and Bruce*, Shawn combines his stylistic habits with his psychological thematic concerns to create an elegantly crafted, if sometimes painful, portrait of a woman's life. Marie narrates the action, a typical day that includes abusing her husband at breakfast, going about her housework, taking a walk, going to a party with her husband, and then abusing him again over dinner. The shrillness of Marie's scatological vilifications of Bruce are countered by a patient, quizzical humility on his part, which carries the relationship through a final, horrible denunciation by Marie and back into a pattern of everyday life. The language of the play contains descriptive passages of unusual beauty that are deeply felt by the characters and are strangely moving. Both of the main characters also have an extended narrative solo, in which they describe their adventures when they leave the familiar surroundings of home and office. The images in these monologues are almost lush— erotically charged with the power of each character's frustrated sexuality.

As in *Our Late Night*, Shawn uses the device of a party scene. The supporting characters' scenes are short, with quick crosscutting between snatches of dialogue and actors doubling the many characters in such a way that the overall impression is like an overheard pastiche of party conversation. Some of the scenes, as they are juxtaposed to Marie's narration and short scenes with Bruce, are very funny. Later, at a restaurant, the couple is forced to overhear another conversation, this time a disgusting description of an intestinal ailment. This encounter triggers a blast from Marie that causes the amusing frustration and sexual flirtation of the earlier scenes to be seen from the tragic perspective of human mortality. Her enormous anger and disappointment expressed, Marie settles down at home with Bruce for the quiet end of her Sisyphean day. The dehumanizing experiences of the party scene, of urban confinement, and of powerlessness are reinforced in even the smallest details of the play, such as Bruce's search for the typewriter that Marie has destroyed, a machine made to express human feelings.

The Hotel Play is much less accomplished than *Marie and Bruce* and much more diffuse and vague. Its tropical setting suggests that the play has some connection to the sexual narration of the guest in *Our Late Night*. In fact, the central character of this episodic nightmare play is a diminutive but mysterious hotel clerk. The action shifts between various settings in the hotel, with a human menagerie passing through the more public scenes, while sex and gunfire punctuate the play's more private encounters. Shawn notes in a foreword that the play's atmosphere is intentionally dreamlike, and the most prominent themes are, like those of dreams, full of sexual fascination, eating, laughter, and the fear of death. The random ordering of the work creates the impression of a dream logic as well, which finally culminates in the death of one of the clerk's several paramours. Like the young people in *The Youth Hostel*, the impulsive characters of *The Hotel Play* have a detached, casually polite attitude toward the extreme situations that confront them.

My Dinner with André shows a considerable shift away from this relaxed attitude, mostly because André Gregory's part of the extended conversation that constitutes the play is so fraught with concern over the state of humanity and the nature and potential of the human condition. The play's tight form, even as it pretends to be a rambling dialogue in a restaurant, has an important antecedent in the balance and meticulousness of composition in *Marie and Bruce*. Shawn provides a narrative frame for the action, which consists almost entirely of Gregory's extended description of his search for an absolute human meaning in places such as Jerzy Grotowski's retreat in the Polish forest, in Findhorn, in Tibet, and in the Sahara. Once Gregory has almost concluded his fascinating litany of hope and despair, Shawn begins to answer from his domestic perspective, which he views as potentially infinite in its extension. *My Dinner with André*, while not a play in the conventional sense, is a carefully edited, scripted, and objectified conversation with a range of dynamic effects and a wealth of themes that recapitulate those of Shawn's other work: the emptiness of sex, the automatizing influence of routine, the frustrations of desire, and even the horror of the Nazi cruelties. This last point is much more clearly amplified, however, in Shawn's most ambitious play, *Aunt Dan and Lemon*.

The narrative frame for *Aunt Dan and Lemon* is provided by Leonora, nicknamed Lemon, as she shares her thoughts and memories with an audience that she welcomes into the theater. The play's progress begins along autobiographical lines, as the audience becomes familiar with Lemon's parents and their friends. Then the action begins to focus on one of the friends, an articulate and conservative Oxford intellectual called Aunt Dan, who forms a peculiar, destructive attachment to Lemon. Once Aunt Dan is introduced, much of the play consists of her storytelling, as she describes sordid acquaintances and political situations to Lemon from her confused, eccentric perspective. The squalid events from Aunt Dan's stories, her conservative background and political instruction, and the impression made on Lemon by her friend's eventual illness and death are gradually coalesced into a fascination on the girl's part for the Nazi war crimes. The primary theme of the play, then, seems to be Shawn's demonstration of how an intelligent, sensitive, privileged individual can be persuaded, through the influence of a few frustrated teachers and poor examples, to take a political position sympathetic to radical Fascism.

Interestingly, Shawn includes very little material in the play's dialogue that confronts or questions the despicable beliefs of the main characters. Their voices and attitudes, through conventional habits of expression such as those used in the earlier plays, disarm the audience, leading spectators to suppose that the characters are normal, pleasant people. Yet once the stage material begins to include political content, Shawn depends upon the audience to carry on a perceptive dialogue of its own, a kind of internal running commentary in the mind of each viewer that confronts and ridicules the beliefs of the characters. Shawn's only manipulation of the audience comes in his choices for the humorous juxtaposition of images and the improbable choice of characters: Aunt Dan's explanation of the Vietnam bombing uses stuffed animals to demonstrate her points, and her story about a seedy group of London friends involves the seduction and murder of an exaggerated Latin Lothario. In the right kind of performance situation, where an educated audience is likely to have strong views that they can oppose to those of the characters, the play is instructive, terrifying, and often quite amusing. Yet the ideological aspect of this play is much like its affective side, almost completely dependent upon the competence and the insight of the audience response. For this reason, Shawn was accused of irresponsible playwriting in some of the New York reviews, an accusation that prompted him to write a special afterword on the context of the play.

Despite problems with its critical reception and its potential for misunderstanding, *Aunt Dan and Lemon* is probably Shawn's most challenging and absorbing play. Shawn's most important works, such as *My Dinner with André* and *Marie and Bruce*, tend to proceed from a narrative framework into a carefully constructed series of dialogues and monologues, arriving finally at a kind of stillness in resolution. Shawn's strengths as a playwright include an unusual flair for formal innovation, in plays as different as *The Hotel Play*, with its innumerable sets and characters, and *My Dinner with André*, almost minimalist in its simple structure and tight focus. He also writes dialogue of enormous sophistication, allowing him to represent the language of intellectuals by credibly imitating rather than satirizing their discourse. Yet his most remarkable quality as a writer comes in his persistent posing of difficult, even painful, questions about contemporary life. Given the temptations of the commercial marketplace, Shawn could easily use his comic skills to write successful teleplays or screenplays. Yet he has sustained his commitment to the exploration of obsessive, subconscious desire and the way it shapes human experience, not only in daily life but also in the broader perspective of one's appreciation of the history and value of human culture.

Other major work
SCREENPLAY: *My Dinner with André*, 1981.

Bibliography

Bennets, Leslie. "Hunt and Pogson on Dan and Lemon," in *The New York Times*. CXXXV (November 14, 1985), sec. 2, p. 17.

Billington, Michael. "A Play of Ideas Stirs Political Passions," in *The New York Times*. CXXXV (October 27, 1985), sec. 2, p. 1.

Franks, Lucinda. "Interview with William and Wally Shawn," in *The New York Times*. CXXIX (August 3, 1980), sec. 2, p. 1.

"Wally and André Dissect the Theater," in *The New York Times*. CXXXI (January 17, 1982), sec. 2, p. 1.

"Why Write for the Theater? A Roundtable Report," in *The New York Times*. CXXXV (February 9, 1986), sec. 2, p. 1.

Michael Quinn

MEGAN TERRY

Born: Seattle, Washington; July 22, 1932

Principal drama

Ex-Miss Copper Queen on a Set of Pills, pr. 1963, pb. 1966; *Calm Down Mother*, pr. 1965, pb. 1966; *Keep Tightly Closed in a Cool Dry Place*, pr. 1965, pb. 1966; *Comings and Goings*, pr. 1966, pb. 1967; *The Gloaming, Oh My Darling*, pr. 1966, pb. 1967; *Viet Rock: A Folk War Movie*, pr., pb. 1966 (music by Marianne de Pury); *The Magic Realists*, pr. 1966, pb. 1968; *The People vs. Ranchman*, pr. 1967, pb. 1968; *Megan Terry's Home: Or, Future Soap*, televised 1968, staged 1974, pb. 1972; *Massachusetts Trust*, pr. 1968, pb. 1972; *The Tommy Allen Show*, pr. 1969, pb. 1971; *Approaching Simone*, pr. 1970, pb. 1973; *Couplings and Groupings*, pb. 1973; *Nightwalk*, pr. 1973, pb. 1975 (with Sam Shepard and Jean-Claude van Itallie); *Hothouse*, pr., pb. 1974; *The Pioneer, and Pro-Game*, pr. 1974, pb. 1975; *100,001 Horror Stories of the Plains*, pr. 1976, pb. 1978 (with Judith Katz, James Larson, and others); *Willa-Willa-Bill's Dope Garden*, pb. 1977; *Attempted Rescue on Avenue B: A Beat Fifties Comic Opera*, pr., pb. 1979; *Goona Goona*, pr. 1979, pb. 1981; *Advances*, pb. 1980; *Mollie Bailey's Traveling Family Circus: Featuring Scenes from the Life of Mother Jones*, pr. 1981, pb. 1983.

Other literary forms

Megan Terry authored lyrics for *Thoughts* (1973), a musical by Lamar Alford, and she has contributed prose pieces to *The New York Times* and *Valhalla: A Modern Drama Issue.* She has also written teleplays and radio plays.

Achievements

One of the most prolific playwrights of the "New Theater" in the United States, Terry is linked with the Open Theatre, which she helped form with Joseph Chaikin and Michael Smith in 1963. The work which brought international attention to Terry is *Viet Rock*, the first well-publicized play about Vietnam to be produced in the United States. Terry and the Open Theatre created an improvisational workshop atmosphere, in which actors, directors, and playwrights could form a living theater experience, disorienting audience expectations through "transformations" in which actors, settings, times, or moods may alter without transition or apparent logic. While some critics find this experience alienating or confusing, others hail the technique as a significant contribution to the development of a truly living theater experience. Terry's earthy language, sexual and political content, musical segments, humor, and vaudeville touches all blend to create lively, dynamic experiences for audiences. Her innovative work has received numerous awards, including the Stanley Drama Award (1965), WGBH Award (1968), Latin American Festival Award (1969), Obie Award (1970), Earplay Award (1972), and grants from the National Endowment for the Arts, Creative Artists Public Service Grant, and the Guggenheim Foundation.

Biography

Megan Terry was born in Seattle, Washington, on July 22, 1932, and was named Marguerite Duffy. Throughout grade school, Terry was fascinated with the theater, and she was exposed at an early age to the influence of the Seattle Repertory Playhouse. In 1951, the theater closed under pressure from a state committee investigating so-called un-American activities, an event which both radicalized the young Terry and confirmed her in her view of the theater as a powerful political tool. Terry received a B.Ed. from the University of Washington, and she taught at the Cornish School of Allied Arts. She traveled to New York, where she became involved with the Playwrights' Unit Workshop, which included Edward Albee, Richard Barr, and Clinton Wilder, in the 1963 production of *Ex-Miss Copper Queen on a Set of Pills*, a work based on her fascination with a pill-popping prostitute who had once been a beauty queen. Terry's career includes several attempts at realistic drama, including *Hothouse* and an early version of *Attempted Rescue on Avenue B*, but she found that she wanted to create new techniques for conveying her messages about the destructiveness of the United States' economic and political power structures. In working with the Open Theatre on *Calm Down Mother* and *Keep Tightly Closed in a Cool Dry Place*, Terry created two of her most successful one-act transformation plays. Using three female actors, *Calm Down Mother* explored what is possible for women and what role limitations women encounter in society. In a similar fashion, *Keep Tightly Closed in a Cool Dry Place* used three male actors, whose characters begin in a prison setting and transform from gangsters to drag queens to soldiers, testing various kinds of enclosures, both imagined and real. Her fascination with sexuality appeared in another transformation play entitled *Comings and Goings*, which stretched actors' technique and delighted its original audiences, many of whom were actors themselves. The first collaboration play to be created in a workshop situation was also Terry's most renowned, *Viet Rock*. Gerome Ragni was among the actors in the workshop, and he later collaborated with James Rado to produce *Hair* in 1967. *Viet Rock* created a number of firsts, including the combination of rock music with the traditional musical-theater genre, treatment of the controversial Vietnam war theme, and the intrusion of actors touching and interacting with audience members.

After receiving an American Broadcasting Company "Writing for the Camera" Fellowship from Yale, Terry wrote *The People vs. Ranchman*, a work dealing with the creation of stars out of people such as Charles Manson and Angela Davis. After receiving negative reviews for this work, Terry went on to produce *Megan Terry's Home*, a futuristic play commissioned by Channel Thirteen's "New York Television Theater," the first commissioned play ever presented on National Educational Television (NET) Playhouse. With an increasing interest in feminist issues, Terry wrote *Approaching Simone* (winner of the Obie Award for Best New Play of 1969-1970) in 1970, studying the life of Simone Weil, a Jewish-French philosopher who starved herself to death in protest over the World War II soldiers who were starving at the front. Turning again to historical sources, Terry created *100,001 Horror Stories of the Plains* in 1976 from the accounts of family stories, poems, and songs collected while Terry was playwright-in-residence for the Magic Theater in Omaha, Nebraska. Another controversial work combining her concern over violence and women's rights was *Goona Goona*, a burlesque treatment of child abuse and wife abuse in the imaginary Goon family. Terry further explores feminist themes in *Mollie Bailey's Traveling Family Circus*, first produced in 1981 at the Mark Taper Laboratory Theater of Los Angeles, a play dealing with real and imagined events in the lives of Mollie Bailey and Mother Jones.

Analysis

Megan Terry's works, although varied in structure, length, technique, and subject matter, are linked by a dynamic emphasis on emotion over reason; a lively use of earthy language, humor, music, metaphors, and symbols; a fearless treatment of timely controversial subjects; and a dedication to collaboration and spontaneity in acting and production. Because of her quickness to address controversial issues, some of her most noted works may not be her best plays, but rather those works which elicited the strongest public reaction at the time of first production. *The Magic Realists* drew sharp criticism and publicity for its failure to touch ground with some realistic setting or situation, but it merits analysis in that it marks the beginning of Terry's shift to her own distinctive theatrical style, rooted in the traditions of vaudeville and early film comedy. *Viet Rock*, while characterized by some critics as naïve and simplistic, clearly captures the spirit of early protest reactions to the war in Vietnam, and as such it is Terry's best-known play. Two of her most representative works, *Keep Tightly Closed in a Cool Dry Place* and *Megan Terry's Home*, explore the theme of enclosure and entrapment, at both personal and cultural levels. *Mollie Bailey's Traveling Family Circus* represents yet another phase in the development of Terry's playwriting, combining her love of music and strong female characters with a deep commitment to exploring ethical and political issues.

The Magic Realists premiered in 1966 at La Mama Experimental Theatre Club in New York, and drew sharp criticism from *Village Voice* reviewer

Michael Smith for its lack of connection to any outside reality. Terry's first break from realistic theater styles, *The Magic Realists* presents a combination of obscure dialogue and stereotyped characterizations. The action of the play centers on T. P. Chester's attempts to find a clone of himself who can carry on his nonstop wheelings and dealings. He chooses Don, a teenage escaped convict, in whom he recognizes the same total lack of scruples and the same "hunger" that have brought him to his esteemed position in the world of high finance. Occasionally, a "person" enters the stage, representing one of his numerous children, whom Chester views solely as tax exemptions. When a beautiful black woman named Dana arrives on the scene, she manages to seduce Don from Chester's influence. Dana, a Japanese American, and an American Indian, who all turn out to be secret agents, attempt to arrest Chester, but one of Chester's offspring persons appears to rescue him with a submachine gun. At last united, the father and child inadvertently gun down the secret agents as the weapon is held between them in a wild, whirling embrace.

The action demonstrates in vaudeville style how the capitalist economic power structure creates machinelike human beings whose sense of family, justice, and human emotion are entirely subordinated to the drive for money. While the plot and characterizations are admittedly thin, this early work reveals several of Terry's strong points. She captures natural speech rhythms and the comedy inherent in juxtaposition of radically differing character types. The combined elements of violence and sexuality create lively slapstick comedy and a few thought-provoking insults to the status quo.

In a similar vein, *Viet Rock* garnered much attention but little praise for its earnest, naïve attack on the brutality and absurdity of the Vietnam War. The play uses all the familiar clichés about honor, duty, and love of country to demonstrate that the soldiers who deliver these lines are basically automatons. Women in the play share responsibility for creating males who are infantile, obedient, and easily manipulated by brainless sentimentality. *Viet Rock* depicts events as varied as senate hearings and soldiers writing home to mothers and sweethearts in a collection of vignettes linked by few or no transitions. Although the music and satire received negative reviews for failure to achieve depth or complexity, Terry also drew admiration for her canny sense of theater and her ability to create a "happening" that captured the current mood of public outrage. Critics argued, however, that the play did very little to deepen anyone's understanding of issues or to undermine self-satisfaction, two principal aims of satire. The play may not be notable for its depth, but its innovative use of rock lyrics and interaction between actors and audience broke ground for the creation of *Hair*, one of the best-known rock musicals to come out of the Vietnam War era.

Receiving much more critical acclaim but less publicity, *Keep Tightly Closed in a Cool Dry Place* premiered at the Sheridan Square Playhouse in

1965 under the aegis of the Open Theatre. Dedicated to Joseph Chaikin, one of the founders of the group, the play typifies the concept of "transformation," a theater style in which actors, setting, and mood metamorphose, often without transition. The play has only three characters: Jaspers, an intellectual lawyer; Michaels, a burly type; and Gregory, a bewildered, handsome young man destined to become victim of the other two characters. In jail, Jaspers and Michaels consider how to undermine Gregory's confession, which has revealed that Jaspers hired Michaels to get Gregory to kill Jaspers' wife. The first transformation turns Jaspers into General George Armstrong Custer, with Michaels as one of his soldiers, whom he instructs to kill Gregory, now a "redskin." Just as abruptly, the characters become themselves again, and Gregory dreams of rape, achieving orgasm as Jaspers and Michaels berate him for his lack of control, his ineptitude, and his unprofessionalism.

If the audience members believe that they understand the character types established in the opening, the remainder of the play shatters these assumptions. The three men join to become a machine, apparently a gun, and each actor describes a part of the machine's features. In the next transformation, Jaspers becomes a dying English soldier under Captain John Smith, alias Gregory. Later, Jaspers becomes mother to Michaels, then victim of a murderer, then an evangelist, and finally father to Michaels and Gregory. The play closes with a dancing chant in which the three form a human wheel, with Jaspers offering the closing line, "This side should face you!" Although the unexpected transformations are jarring and disorienting, the play offers the unifying notion that all human beings go through a series of roles, presenting different facets of human behavior, as dictated by society and circumstance. The prison setting suggests that people are locked into these roles, just as unwillingly and randomly as prisoners are incarcerated.

Another play examining confinement, this time in a futuristic setting, is *Megan Terry's Home*, originally created for Channel Thirteen in New York and later commissioned for NET and nationally broadcast in January of 1968. The principal characters, Mother Ruth, Cynthia, and Roy, constitute part of a unit of nine people, forced by overpopulation to live and die together in a room smaller than a jail cell. Central Control, the governing body, ministers to their physical, spiritual, and psychological needs, through the total organization of their sleeping and waking time. They pop pills for nourishment and psychological well-being, watch multiple television screens for news of past and present, and dream, chant, and perform isometrics for social and physical interaction.

The central conflict of the play rests in Cynthia and Roy's desire to marry and have their own real baby for the group, a privilege rarely granted to units, regardless of how obedient, efficient, or patient they are. When the air-venting system temporarily breaks down, allowing another human to enter their cell, Ruth panics, overrides her socialization, and kills the intruder. The group of nine quickly disposes of the body and the marriage ceremony of Roy and Cynthia continues, with all nine hoping that they may one day be allowed by the state to have a baby of their own.

Terry's play cleverly creates an alternative world, complete with values, customs, and mannerisms convincingly appropriate to a highly technological civilization coping with overpopulation and limited resources. It confronts the idea that human instincts for survival may be exactly the impulses that will lead to self-destruction. The overcrowded society places a premium on cooperation, self-sacrifice, obedience, and nonviolence, but it is unable to overcome the women's urges to become mothers to their own children. One of her most sophisticated and intellectually complex works, *Megan Terry's Home* calls on audiences to question human nature, media culture, religious values, and Western notions of progress. The action of the play suggests the possibility that brutality in the name of survival may be unavoidable, and it does so in a way that creates dramatic suspense and empathy for believable characters. Terry effectively exploits the medium of television, but stage directions make the work easily adaptable for live presentation as well.

Terry's dedication to feminism appears in numerous plays, nowhere more openly than in *Mollie Bailey's Traveling Family Circus*. This piece, dedicated to Mollie Bailey and Mother Jones, alternates between scenes of Mollie and Gus Bailey and children and the life of Mother Jones. As with some of her earlier work, this play is at times heavy-handed in its delineation of good and evil, with heartless capitalists and their flunkies as adversaries to Mother Jones, who bravely seeks justice and protection for victimized children. Women are portrayed as the preservers of civilization, of all that is good and brave and true, and males appear in the play as little more than sperm banks. For all its didacticism, however, music and humor carry the play, creating an entertaining spectacle with the timely obsessions of contemporaneous culture at its heart.

Megan Terry's work demonstrates adaptability, variety, and a consistent dedication to political and ethical ideals, qualities that provoke criticism as well as praise. Analysis of the body of her work reveals a prolific and imaginative mind at work, constantly striving and reworking themes as old as drama: family and gender roles, violence and pacifism, individual and social welfare, subordination and freedom. Her plays, numbering more than fifty, represent a substantial contribution to American drama, both in their innovative forms and in their political and philosophical substance.

Other major works

TELEPLAYS: *The Dirt Boat*, 1955; *One More Little Drinkie*, 1969.

RADIO PLAYS: *Sanibel and Captiva*, 1968; *American Wedding Ritual Monitored / Transmitted by the Planet Jupiter*, 1972.

Bibliography
Clurman, Harold. "Theater," in *The Nation*. CCIII (November 28, 1966), p. 587.
Feldman, Peter. "Notes for the Open Theatre Production of *Keep Tightly Closed*," in *The Tulane Drama Review*. X, no. 4 (1966), pp. 200-208.
Gent, George. "TV: The Sterilized Nightmare of Megan Terry," in *The New York Times*. January 20, 1968, p. 59.
Kerr, Walter. "The Theater: *Viet Rock*," in *The New York Times*. November 10, 1966, p. 38.
Pasolli, Robert. *A Book on the Open Theatre*, 1970.

Rebecca Bell-Metereau

MICHEL TREMBLAY

Born: Montreal, Canada; June 25, 1942

Principal drama

Le Train, wr. 1959, televised 1964; *Cinq*, pr. 1966, pb. 1971 (English translation, 1976; includes *Berthe, Johnny Mangano and His Astonishing Dogs*, and *Gloria Star*); *Les Belles-sœurs*, pr., pb. 1968 (English translation, 1973); *En pièces détachées*, pr. 1969, pb. 1970 (revision of *Cinq*; *Like Death Warmed Over*, 1973, also as *Broken Pieces* and *Montreal Smoked Meat*); *La Duchesse de Langeais*, pr. 1969, pb. 1970 (English translation, 1976); *Demain matin, Montréal m'attend*, pr. 1970, pb. 1972 (musical); *À toi, pour toujours, ta Marie-Lòu*, pr., pb. 1971 (*Forever Yours, Marie-Lou*, 1972); *Les Paons*, pr. 1971; *Hosanna*, pr., pb. 1973 (English translation, 1974); *Bonjour, là, bonjour*, pr., pb. 1974 (English translation, 1975); *Surprise! Surprise!*, pr. 1975, pb. 1977 (English translation, 1976); *Les Héros de mon enfance*, pr., pb. 1976 (musical; music by Sylvain Lelièvre); *Sainte-Carmen de la Main*, pr., pb. 1976 (*Saint Carmen of the Main*, 1978); *Damnée Manon, Sacrée Sandra*, pr., pb. 1977 (English translation, 1979); *Les Socles*, pb. 1979 (*The Pedestals*, 1979); *L'Impromptu d'Outrement*, pr., pb. 1980 (*The Impromptu of Outrement*, 1981); *Les Anciennes Odeurs*, pr., pb. 1981 (*Remember Me*, 1984); *Albertine en cinq temps*, pr. 1985, pb. 1986 (*Albertine in Five Times*, 1986).

Other literary forms

Although Michel Tremblay is best known for his drama, he is also the author of a number of short stories, film scripts, and television plays; in addition, he translated into French Aristophanes' *Lysistrata* (411 B.C.), Paul Zindel's *And Miss Reardon Drinks a Little* (1967) and *The Effect of Gamma Rays on Man-in-the-Moon Marigolds* (1965), four short plays by Tennessee Williams, and Dario Fo's *Mistero buffo* (1969). He has also published two well-received novels, *La Grosse Femme d'à côté est enceinte* (1978; *The Fat Woman Next Door Is Pregnant*, 1981) and *Thérèse et Pierrette à l'École des saintes-anges* (1980; *Thérèse and Pierrette and the Little Hanging Angel*, 1984).

Achievements

Tremblay is part of a new generation of playwrights that emerged in Quebec during the 1960's and 1970's, a time of profound political and cultural change for this province. Led by Tremblay, these writers saw as their primary task the liberation of Quebec culture from the shackles of foreign domination. With very few exceptions, the theater of Quebec to the mid-twentieth century had never treated issues genuinely French-Canadian; it was a theater enslaved to the thematic, stylistic, and linguistic control of "mother" France. With the opening of Tremblay's *Les Belles-sœurs*, at the Théâtre du Rideau Vert in Montreal on August 28, 1968, a new and autonomous Quebecois theater was born. Significant partly for its thematic focus on the realities of the working class of Quebec, *Les Belles-sœurs* is the first play to be written in the distinctive French of Tremblay's people—*joual*. A peculiar mixture of Anglicanisms, Old French, neologisms, and standard French, *joual* (from the Quebecois pronunciation of the French word *cheval*) is the popular idiom of Quebec and especially of Montreal's working class. To the French and to Quebec's cultural elite, *joual* was a bastard tongue, emphasizing the pitiful nature of Quebec culture. To Tremblay, however, *joual* was a symbol of identity, a language not to be silenced but to be celebrated for its richness and for its distinctive flavor. To discuss Tremblay's greatest achievements is thus not simply to focus on the fact that he has become Canada's leading playwright, that his enormous creative output in the areas of theater, literature, film, and television has won for him international fame, that he has influenced the development of Canadian drama, that he has won countless awards for his work; though all of this is true, it is also important to recognize him as a cultural leader with a commitment to articulate and grapple with the problems of an oppressed community.

Biography

Michel Tremblay was born in east-end Montreal on June 25, 1942, the youngest child of a working-class family. His family lived in a small seven-room house with two other families, and Tremblay remembers distinctly the first voices of his life: women who would speak candidly to one another about their lives and who would censor nothing in front of the young child. Indeed, these are the voices sounded in many of his plays, especially *Les Belles-sœurs*. In 1955, he won a scholarship to a school for gifted children; his innate distaste for the cultural elite soon caused him to return to the public schools.

Tremblay speaks of his adolescence as a time of personal anguish, a time when writing became his primary channel of expression. Moreover, as a young man he became obsessed with television: "It was the only theatre I knew." In 1959, he took a job as a linotype operator and during this period wrote his first television play, *Le Train*, for which he eventually won first prize in the 1964 Radio-Canada Contest for Young Authors. It is also in 1964 that he met André Brassard, who became one of his closest friends, his principal collaborator, and the director of many of the premier performances of his plays. His publishing career began in 1966 with a book of short stories, *Contes pour buveurs attardés* (*Stories for Late Night Drinkers*, 1978). In the same year, he submitted his first full-length play, *Les Belles-sœurs* (written in

1965), to the Dominion Drama Festival, but the revolutionary piece was rejected. Two years later, however, it was produced, with great success, at the Théâtre du Rideau Vert in Montreal, and later in Paris.

The years following 1968 marked a creative and prolific period for Tremblay. For English-speaking Canadians, however, Tremblay was not so widely publicized, partly because of the playwright's desire to restrict his work to his French compatriots. It was only after 1976, the year the Separatists' Parti Québécois under René Lévesque took power in the provincial House, that Tremblay opened his work to the English-speaking world. After 1976, translations of his plays appeared, productions abounded, and Tremblay emerged as Canada's leading playwright, recognized as such in both North America and Europe. That he has achieved international acclaim testifies to the fact that his work is as universal in meaning as it is specific to contemporary Quebec life.

Analysis

Antecedents in the history of dramatic literature help to characterize the plays of Michel Tremblay. The playwright himself cites as most influential the ancient Greek tragedians, on the one hand, and Samuel Beckett, on the other. The influence of the ancient playwrights shows itself most notably in Tremblay's repeated use of choruses and in the rhythmic precision of his work. Indeed, much of his theatrical power stems from a native musical sensibility that informs the structure of his plays. Like the Greeks, Tremblay writes dramatic pieces that operate, at least in part, as rhythmic scores for performance; his plays abound with overlapping voices and interwoven monologues, and possess a rhythm so peculiar to the language and intonations of the Quebecois that there is often as much power in how his characters speak as there is in what they say.

Beckett's influence on Tremblay manifests itself in the specific context in which Tremblay places his characters and in the way those characters grapple with the struggles of life. Tremblay celebrates the notion that, despite the seeming despair of Beckett's figures, there is a beauty in their struggle to face and accept their lives. "I never read or see a Beckett play without experiencing a lift." His appreciation of Beckett is significant; although Tremblay's characters seem trapped in the underbelly of culture, in seedy nightclubs, confined apartments, in a world of whores, pimps, and transvestites, or trapped even in their own social roles and family relationships, still there is a sense of uplift in their struggles and in the courage they find in themselves.

Stylistically, Tremblay's dramas are eclectic, not only when looked at as a body of work, but also within single plays. In *Les Belles-sœurs*, for example, he creates a realistic setting, utilizes realistic dialogue, and then counters that realism with stylized elements reminiscent of the Theater of the Absurd. The premise of the play is simple: Fifteen women of the neighborhood gather to help Germaine Lauzon paste a million Blue Chip stamps in booklets for a contest she has won. The women of the title ("the sisters-in-law" or "the beautiful sisters," an ambiguity in French that accounts for the original title maintained in translation) gossip as they paste. When Germaine is not looking, however, the women secretly steal the stamps. This ostensible, realistic line of the story unfolds in a dynamic relationship with stylized, isolated monologues spoken by the women to express the more honest, individual problems of their miserable, trapped lives: Marriage, family, and sex—the basis of their worlds—have achieved a level of banality that seems to reduce all of life to sheer endurance.

Perhaps the clearest example of the juxtaposition of styles comes at the end of the play. Germaine discovers the thieves, throws them out of her home, and feels profoundly a sense of loneliness and isolation. She falls to her knees to pick up the stamps that scattered on the floor during the chaos of discovering the theft. At that moment, Tremblay breaks out of the realistic structure once again. From offstage the women begin to sing a chorus of "O Canada" while simultaneously a rain of stamps falls from the ceiling. The stylized "shower" of prosperity is parallel to Germaine's windfall of stamps at the beginning of the play. Yet the playwright creates his final image as a self-consciously artificial construct, an image that contrasts with the conventionally realistic form used at the outset. Like a Euripidean *deus ex machina*, Tremblay's rain of stamps is a theatrical joke; humanity is in turmoil and has reached an impasse within the realistic conventions of the play. The playwright's ending undercuts that impasse, however, and, with a broad satirical gesture, he clarifies the source of the problem itself; the values of the Canadian middle class have their price.

The body of Tremblay's dramatic work possesses a remarkable consistency both in theme and in focus. His *dramatis personae* are the underprivileged, the people on the fringe of society, people who live in disguise. His plays also have a striking similarity of context; indeed, in the bulk of his work, he examines two specific worlds. On the one hand, he looks at the family, at the home, and at the nature of the individual within the family construct. On the other hand, he looks to a horrifying world external to the family: the world of the Main in Montreal, with its host of transvestites, whores, and pimps, all set against a backdrop of "gambling joints, cabarets, lights and noise." In the words of André Brassard, "The Main is the Kingdom of the marginals . . . the underprivileged and forgotten part of the proletariat . . . the underlayer of society." The Tremblay opus can thus be examined to a large degree in two major cycles: the family cycle and the Main cycle. The two worlds do intersect at points, creating a potent juxtaposition; indeed, when considered as a whole, Tremblay's work is interesting not only because of his investigation into these two separate worlds but also because of his ability to show how those worlds mirror each other. In effect, the two cycles intersect to illuminate the "family" of the Main and the "underbelly" of the home.

Like Death Warmed Over, the first play of the family cycle, was actually written, in its original version, before *Les Belles-sœurs* but published and performed at a later date. It unfolds in four loosely connected episodes. The play begins in the inner courtyard of an east-end Montreal tenement on a sweltering summer afternoon. For the chorus of neighbors, the single point of interest is the window across the way—the home of Robertine, her daughter Hélène, Hélène's husband, Henri, and their daughter Francine. The neighbors are fascinated with the peculiar and unsavory domestic battles in Robertine's home. They offer a detailed description of the troubled family and its history as they wait for Hélène to come home, for the "show" of the evening to begin.

The middle two episodes tell the story of Hélène, how she spends her time slinging smoked meat in a cheap restaurant on Papineau Street after having lost her job in a bar on the Main. She gets drunk, returns to the bar, only to have the frustrations of her life become that much more glaring as she confronts the figures of her past. The final episode takes place back in Robertine's living room. Hélène comes home, verbally abuses Henri (who spends all of his time watching cartoons on television) and Robertine, and gives the neighbors the "show" for which they have waited. Toward the end, Claude, the retarded brother, returns home for a visit after escaping from his sanatorium. He wears "sunglasses and speaks English" and believes that doing so gives him ultimate power: It makes him invisible. In Tremblay's world, the madman overturns his alienation to make it an illusory source of strength. Claude's presence thus provides a sharp contrast to the feeling of humiliation and powerlessness among the other members of the family. Typically, the play ends in a series of stylized monologues in which the family members express their despair. They repeat a refrain in unison during this final section, a refrain that sums up their despondency and languor: "There's not a goddamn thing I can do."

While *Like Death Warmed Over* is a play about failure and ultimate despair in family relationships, Tremblay's next play in the family cycle, *Forever Yours, Marie-Lou*, presents the attempt of two sisters, Carmen and Manon, to find refuge from the traumas of family life. In this play, two conversations transpire simultaneously, one between Marie-Louise and her husband, Leopold, and the other between their daughters Carmen and Manon. The two conversations take place in the family home, but ten years apart. Carmen and Manon (in the 1970's) recall the past, ten years earlier, when their parents and younger brother Roger died in a car accident. For Manon, a religious zealot, her father Leopold was responsible for the accident, an act of suicide and filial murder. Carmen denies this account, although her rejection is undermined when Leopold (in the action of the 1960's) threatens

Marie-Louise with that very scenario.

Structurally, the play is a quartet of interweaving voices as each level of action comments on the other through a powerful theatrical juxtaposition. Each character has complaints about the others, each feels abused, each feels as if life has dealt him or her an unfair blow. In the turbulence of the marriage, Marie-Louise turns to religion and Leopold to his drinking and television. The daughters, too, have their share of trouble, not only as products of their repressive and abusive home but also as individuals who must cope with the tragic past. Carmen has turned to the Main and to singing in cabarets. Manon has, on the other hand, withdrawn entirely into a lonely life of religious fanaticism. The two women have clearly gone in opposite directions, but it is evident that they are both striving to find shelter from the traumas of the family.

While Marie-Louise and Manon hide in an existence of religious repression, and Leopold in an escape into alcohol and boredom that finally erupts in the violence of murder and suicide, Carmen achieves a degree of liberation from her repressive past. This is evident only when one realizes that the core of Tremblay's play is the collision of real human needs with the religious and social constructs that make the fulfillment of those needs impossible. That Carmen turns to the Main is perhaps only a limited alternative, another subculture with its own restrictions. Yet, within the context of the play, Carmen's choice is the most fruitful; she has at least discovered a part of herself that opens the way toward personal creativity. This notion is the center of the play in which she next appears: *Sainte Carmen of the Main*, a play in which issues of the family and the Main intersect in a subtle but provocative way.

In this later play, Carmen is returning from a stay in Nashville, where she has been sent to improve her yodeling technique; the play opens with the chorus (the people of the Main) celebrating her return. Indeed, her education away from the Main was more than simply a time to improve technique: Carmen comes back as a leader of the people, as their voice; it is a voice expressed through her new lyrics and songs that relate directly to the concerns of the community. Carmen's journey from repression to release is a model of realized human potential and gives her strength to speak for others. Despite the ecstasy of the people over their newfound leader, however, Carmen must face her antagonists: the cabaret owner Maurice, who wants her to sing the "old songs," and Carmen's rival, Gloria, who fights for her "rightful place." When he challenges Carmen, Maurice articulates the political question of the play, a question that perhaps haunts the playwright himself: "All right. Let's say they take our advice. Let's say they smarten up, they wake up and they get mad. Then what? It's fine to wake people up, but once they're awake, what do you do with them?"

Shortly after her performance at the cabaret, Carmen is brutally murdered; she is denounced as a lesbian so that the crime may be pinned on her innocent dresser, Harelip. "The lights go out completely on the Choruses"; the sun is down, the fire of awakening quelled. This is a play about the possibility of awakening, of fighting repression, of the change that can come about when human beings are acknowledged for their strengths. Carmen has found that strength within herself and is a beacon for the people. Yet the figures of the status quo—threatened for reasons both political and financial—end the triumph of humanity that lit the world for an instant.

If in the story of Carmen, Tremblay suggests that personal strength can come only from a freedom discovered outside the repressive home, then in *Bonjour, là, bonjour* he explores the act of personal acceptance within the family itself. Again, this play is inspired by musical principles; there are thirty-one sections entitled "solo," "duo," "trio," and so forth, up to "octuor," depending on the number of voices involved in a given episode. The central figure in *Bonjour, là, bonjour*, Serge, is a young man who has just returned from a three-month stay in Paris, where he has tried to deal with his love for his sister Nicole. Though the odds are against him, Serge breaks through the oppressive structures of his family life to assert his integrity and express his love both to Nicole and to his aging and deaf father, Gabriel. Serge must defend himself against the invasion of his relatives (two spinster aunts and three sisters other than Nicole), who try to use his vitality to serve their needs. Once he sees past moral taboo to admit fully his incestuous love, he is able to triumph and communicate with his father. Like Carmen, in her relationship to the people of the Main, Serge becomes a figure who releases his father from a suffocating life. He invites his father to live with him and Nicole and, in the end, finds the strength to shout the words "I love you" into Gabriel's deaf ears.

The plays of the family cycle are clearly parables of the political and cultural repression Tremblay sees within Quebec culture. Like Tremblay's characters, the Quebecois must begin a long journey to self-acceptance. Still, there is another "family" Tremblay explores: the family of the Main. In the Main cycle, he focuses on the individual desperately trying to find himself in a chaotic and frightening world, a world in which the search for identity is no less difficult, nor alienation less painful, than it is within the home. Perhaps most indicative of his concern is the recurring transvestite figure, whose multiple personas epitomize the alienation of the individual in the Main.

Tremblay began his investigation of the Main in three short plays written early in his career: *Berthe, Johnny Mangano and His Astonishing Dogs*, and *Gloria Star*. The three plays function as a trilogy and were originally part of the collection entitled *Cinq*, written in 1966. The trilogy examines the individual's alienation from the self by focusing on the collision of one's dreams and fantasies for fame and glory with the stark realities of a boring and desperate life. Tremblay once again works toward a stylized ending to the trilogy in which he communicates how dreams of success and perfection are the offspring of artifice; the playwright makes this abundantly clear in a surrealistic conclusion of theatrical make-believe.

La Duchesse de Langeais, a piece in which the past of an aging transvestite unravels in monologue, is the next play of the Main cycle and represents Tremblay's first treatment of this sexually complex figure. The Duchesse is a human being who is desperately alone. She speaks of how she became the Duchesse, "the biggest faggot ever," how she envisions herself as a "woman of the world," how she spent her life whoring for hundreds of men, how she was sexually abused as a child by her cousin Leopold (later to appear in *Forever Yours, Marie-Lou*), and how she entered a life of obsessive sexual activity from the age of six.

The theme of alienation operates on many levels in *La Duchesse de Langeais*. She is a transvestite locked in a sexually ambiguous role. She is aware of her age and feels a frightening sense of attenuation in her life. She has a history of being a female impersonator, trapped in a Pirandellian disparity between the roles performed and the actress/actor underneath. Yet the monologue itself attests her alienation in a more immediate way. Is there any possibility of verifying the past she describes? Is she merely creating a fiction for the audience? Is she creating the fiction for herself? Indeed, reality and illusion are so disconnected in this play that it is impossible to verify much. Tremblay (the primary illusion-maker) communicates through this onslaught of unverifiable information the pain and suffering that accompanies the life of one lost in a labyrinth of insubstantiality and artifice.

Hosanna, on the other hand, probes deeper into the tensions of the multiple roles of the transvestite and female impersonator. The play takes place in the early hours of the morning in the confined and oppressive apartment of Hosanna, a transvestite whose original name is Claude, and "her" lover Cuirette ("Leatherette" in French, but also suggesting the English "Queerette"), whose original name is Raymond. Hosanna has returned from a night of humiliation and ridicule, a night that will ultimately lead her to a painful acceptance of self.

Hosanna and Cuirette represent two extremes. The former is a highly effeminate drag queen whose excessive perfume, makeup, jewels, and clothing constitute her mask. The latter is a "leather-man," who has grown too fat for the clothes that once expressed his exaggerated machismo image; nevertheless, his leather jacket, motorcycle, and tough persona are all the accoutrements through which he defines himself. The first act deals with the tensions and collisions of the relationship, the inability of the two individuals to recognize the needs of the other and, more important, to recognize and accept themselves for who they are. When the second act begins, Hosanna is alone; she tells the story of how the people of the cabaret (including the Duchesse) played a practical joke on her, how they faked plans for a costume party for which they were all to dress as famous women in history. Hosanna prepares for weeks her role as Elizabeth Taylor playing Cleopatra; when she arrives, however, everyone at the club is dressed in a Cleopatra costume— "Everyone made up better than me!" She tries to keep her composure, even through the taunting repetition of the chant that haunts the audience as much as Hosanna herself: "Hosanna, Hosanna, Hosanna, Ho!"

The event is enough to shock Hosanna into a state of self-reflection and to force her to confront the mask she wears. Cuirette, who is absent for most of the second act in a frustrated sexual escapade, and who had been privy to the joke played on Hosanna, returns home to shed his own mask and to be with the one he loves. It is, thus, Raymond and Claude present at the last moment of the play, not Cuirette and Hosanna. In the end, Tremblay shows two human beings who have begun the difficult journey involved with the abandonment of self-hatred. Raymond and Claude must accept who they are, together and as individuals.

The theme of reconciliation with the self dominant in the Main cycle is also at the core of *Damnée Manon, Sacrée Sandra*. (The literal English translation would be "doomed Manon, holy Sandra," but is finally inadequate because of the ambiguous implication of *sacrée* in French, a word with meanings both sacred and profane. Indeed, this ambiguity is precisely what this conceptually complex piece is about.) Manon, the religious sister from *Forever Yours, Marie-Lou*, and Sandra, the transvestite cabaret owner from *Hosanna*, are the characters of the drama. Tremblay again creates a double action by juxtaposing two monologues. The double action eventually moves to a single point that articulates the place where the sacred and profane meet. Moreover, the play ends with the kind of theatrical self-consciousness that informs much of the playwright's work: Both characters realize that they are the invention of the same author. As Manon comes to recognize the erotic nature of her religious devotion and Sandra the obsessive religiosity of her sexual escapades, the playwright himself seems to imply a reconciliation of seeming opposites within himself. He is the creator of both characters; indeed, as an individual, he, too, embodies both the sacred and profane.

Tremblay wrote three major plays after 1979: *The Impromptu of Outrement, Remember Me*, and *Albertine in Five Times*. In these plays, he plucks his characters out of the Main and places them back in a domestic context. In *The Impromptu of Outrement*, Tremblay presents four sisters who were brought up in a middle-class Montreal suburb, Outrement, and who are meeting for the occasion of Yvette's birthday; the party has become an annual custom, a time for a little "impromptu." The real purpose of their meeting, however, is to have a chance to lash out against one another, to complain about one another's lives, to scream about one another's failures and life choices. Ultimately, however, it is an occasion when they feel disgust with who they are; the sisters mirror to one another what they deem ugliest in themselves. The play is Tremblay's version of Anton Chekhov's *Tri sestry* (1901; *Three Sisters*, 1940), a work that explores the torture of languishing potentiality, of the trap of the middle class, of unrealized dreams and bourgeois isolation.

Remember Me examines two men who are meeting long after the end of their relationship of seven years. Each man has continued with his career and with other relationships; each, however, feels the burden of his own mediocrity and a profound discontent with life. Like *The Impromptu of Outrement*, therefore, *Remember Me* centers on the individual who feels disenfranchised from his own potential; both plays demonstrate how middle-class promise quickly turns to mundane routine. In addition, by focusing on four women in the one play, and two homosexual men in the other, Tremblay makes a clear statement about the frustrations minorities feel with the false promises of acceptance in bourgeois society.

Albertine in Five Times is a play about the life of one woman at five different points in her life. Tremblay presents the fragmented individual in many of his dramas, but this time he exploits his art to realize all pieces simultaneously. In this play, Tremblay pursues his preoccupation with self-alienation by grappling with the problem of the ever-changing self in time; as in Beckett's *Krapp's Last Tape* (1958), *Albertine in Five Times* creates a picture of the individual estranged from the past and from the self that has emerged over time. Nevertheless, the play provides a moving portrait of the stages of one woman's struggle. Like so many of Tremblay's characters, Albertine, though desperate, does struggle; the search for identity is the most challenging task for any individual. Tremblay celebrates the courage of his characters, and of the Quebecois themselves; he celebrates their strength to look at themselves and begin the long journey to freedom.

Other major works

LONG FICTION: *La Cité dans l'œuf*, 1969; *C't'à ton tour, Laura Cadieux*, 1973; *La Grosse Femme d'à côté est enceinte*, 1978 (*The Fat Woman Next Door Is Pregnant*, 1981); *Thérèse et Pierrette à l'École des saintes-anges*, 1980 (*Thérèse and Pierrette and the Little Hanging Angel*, 1984).

SHORT FICTION: *Contes pour buveurs attardés*, 1966 (*Stories for Late Night Drinkers*, 1978); *Manoua*, 1966.

SCREENPLAYS: *Françoise Durocher, Waitress*, 1971; *Backyard Theatre*, 1972; *Il était une fois dans l'est*, 1974; *Parlex-nous d'amour*, 1974.

TELEVISION PLAYS: *Trois Petits Tours*, 1969; *En pièces détachées*, 1971; *Le Soleil se lèvue en retard*, 1975; *Bonheur d'occasion*, 1977; *Les Belles-sœurs*, 1978.

TRANSLATIONS: *Lysistrata*, 1964 (of Aristophanes' play); *L'Effet des rayons gamma sur les vieux garçons*, 1970 (of Paul Zindel's play *The Effect of Gamma Rays on Man-in-the-Moon Marigolds*); *Et Madame Roberge boit un peu*, 1971 (of Zindel's play *And Miss Reardon Drinks a Little*); *Mistero buffo*, 1973 (of Dario Fo's play).

Bibliography

Anthony, G., ed. *Stage Voices: Twelve Canadian Playwrights Talk About Their Lives and Work*, 1978.
McQuaid, Catherine. "Michel Tremblay's Seduction of the Other Solitude," in *Canadian Drama*. II, no. 2 (1976), pp. 217-221.
"Michel Tremblay Casebook," in *Canadian Theatre Review*. Fall, 1979.
Nardocchio, Elaine F. *Theatre and Politics in Quebec*, 1986.
Usmiani, Renate. *Michel Tremblay*, 1982.
_____ . "Michel Tremblay's *Sainte Carmen*: Synthesis and Orchestration," in *Canadian Drama*. II, no. 2 (1976), pp. 206-218.

Lorne M. Buchman

RODOLFO USIGLI

Born: Mexico City, Mexico; November 17, 1905

Principal drama

El niño y la niebla, wr. 1936, pr., pb. 1951; *Medio tono*, pr. 1937, pb. 1938; *Estado de secreto*, pr. 1938, pb. 1963; *La mujer no hace milagros*, pr. 1939, pb. 1949; *La familia cena en casa*, pr., pb. 1942; *El gesticulador*, pb. 1944, pr. 1947; *Otra prima vera*, pr. 1945, pb. 1947 (*Another Springtime*, 1961); *Corona de sombra*, pr., pb. 1947 (*Crown of Shadows*, 1946); *Jano es una muchacha*, pr., pb. 1952; *Corona de fuego*, pr., pb. 1960; *Corona de luz: La virgen*, pr. 1963, pb. 1965.

Other literary forms

Although Rodolfo Usigli is recognized principally as a playwright, he has worked in other genres as well. His theoretical works on the theater, in general, and the Mexican theater, in particular, include: *México en el teatro* (1932; *Mexico in the Theater*, 1976), *Caminos del teatro en México* (1933; paths of the theater in Mexico), *Itinerario del autor dramático* (1940; itinerary of a dramatist), and *Anatomía del teatro* (1966; anatomy of the theater). He has also produced two theoretical essays on the theater titled "Ensayo sobre la actualidad de la poesía dramática" (essay on the actuality of dramatic poetry) and "Epílogo sobre la hipocresía del Mexicano" (epilogue on the hypocrisy of the Mexican). Usigli's poetry is collected in a volume entitled *Conversación desesperada* (1938; desperate conversation). He has also produced a novel, *Ensayo de un crimen* (trial of a crime), which was published in 1944.

Achievements

Usigli has been hailed as the father of the Mexican theater. He introduced authentic dramatic representations of Mexico through works that addressed its history, its politics, and the psychological makeup of its people. The psychological factor is the core of his theater.

Usigli does not merely criticize the Mexican people and their society: Rather, he seeks to ennoble them by offering them models of their own potential greatness. Usigli accomplishes this by introducing the concept of myth formation. The concept of myth formation has its roots in Georg Wilhelm Friedrich Hegel's conception of the historical process as a series of syntheses that revolve around transcendental historical figures such as Maximilian and Montezuma, who represent superior cultural symbols. From a cultural and theatrical perspective, a myth is a transcendental synthesis embodied in one of these figures which offers a new perspective, a positive direction for the country's future growth. Its direct appeal to the faith of the Mexican audience causes them to reevaluate their mythical past and to experience a catharsis of nationality with those national sentiments and values that most ennoble it. In recognition of his efforts to create a Mexican national theater, Usigli was awarded the Premio Nacional de Letras in 1972.

Usigli's determination to forge a sense of national identity for Mexico, his sense of the Mexican spirit and the originality with which he expresses it in his plays, and the increased awareness he offers Mexican audiences of their national identity, culture, history, and values constitute his most important achievements.

Biography

Rodolfo Usigli was born in Mexico City, Mexico, on November 17, 1905, the product of Italian, Austrian, and Polish ancestry. Usigli demonstrated his interest in the theater at an early age. When he was eleven years old, he worked as an extra in the Castillo-Taboada troupe at Mexico's Teatro Colón. He wished to study drama, but there were no established schools of drama in Mexico at that time. Therefore, he designed his own curriculum whereby he read and analyzed on a daily basis six plays by well-known dramatists. He then attended local performances, at which he compared the dramas he studied with the actual stage productions. His commentaries were published in Mexican newspapers. By the time he reached the age of twenty, he had become a respected theater critic.

Usigli met with little success in finding producers for his first dramatic attempts. His difficulties with managers, producers, and critics may perhaps be traced to unhappy childhood experiences. Usigli was born with slightly crossed eyes, a person the Spaniards call *bizco*. His classmates punned on the word and nicknamed him *Visconde* (Viscount), which also alluded to his conviction of being superior to them. He later underwent corrective surgery for his eyes but never lost his conviction about his superiority, which often expressed itself in an arrogance and defensiveness that theater authorities found unappealing.

From 1932 to 1934, Usigli offered courses in the history of the Mexican theater at the University of Mexico and served as director of the Teatro Radiofónico, which broadcast plays in conjunction with the Ministry of Education. During this period, he was also associated with the Teatro Orientación, which was created to introduce Mexico to the masterpieces of world theater, performing plays translated from French, Italian, English, German, and Russian. Usigli prepared the Spanish versions for the stage. In 1935, Usigli was awarded a scholarship to study dramatic composition at Yale University. During this period, he wrote *El gesticulador* (the pretender), one of his greatest works. Upon his return to Mexico, he was appointed director of the school of drama and theater and director of the department of fine arts at the University of Mexico. In 1940, he founded his own theater, the Teatro Media Noche, in order to produce his Mexican plays, but ongoing problems with producers soon ended this venture.

During the period from 1943 to 1946, Usigli served Mexico in a diplomatic capacity, becoming the cultural attaché at the Mexican embassy in Paris. During his tenure in Europe, he had the opportunity to meet his idol, playwright George Bernard Shaw. Also during this period, he completed another of his great works, *Crown of Shadows*, part of a trilogy about the three Mexican myths of sovereignty. (The other works comprising the trilogy are *Corona de fuego*—crown of fire—and *Corona de luz*—crown of light.) After completing his tour of duty, Usigli returned to Mexico and offered courses at the University of Mexico in the history of the theater and playwriting. He completed The Corona Trilogy and several other plays.

Usigli resumed his diplomatic career from 1956 until 1962, serving as Mexico's ambassador to Lebanon and Norway. During this period and after his return to Mexico, he continued to produce dramatic works.

Analysis

Mexico and its people have furnished the material for almost all of Rodolfo Usigli's dramatic works. Psychology is the essential component of his writing and the soul of his interpretations.

Usigli's dramatic works can be classified into two major categories: the social satire of contemporary Mexico, and the treatment of certain historically significant figures or periods in the development of Mexico. The themes most frequently treated are insanity, hate, love, hereditary illness, stagnant lifestyle, cruelty, sex from a Mexican perspective, and culminating moments in Mexican history.

There are four elements which constantly recur in Usigli's plays: fantasy, myth, family types, and humor. Fantasy is present in all of his works. Through examples which illustrate his philosophy, he sets the course which propels the action and motivates the characters: madness, absurdity, dreams, superstition, double identity, and illusions. The element of the fantastic is reinforced by dramatic techniques such as the play of lights, visions, flashbacks, and anonymous voices. Myth is of utmost importance in Usigli's works. He sees Mexico as an outstanding example of a fusion of two cultures, the indigenous and the Hispanic, both of which are myth-oriented. Within the framework of Usigli's Hegelian view of history, the central characters become transcendental myth figures. He uses myth to reinterpret historical events, clarifying their significance and offering a new and positive direction for Mexico's future. Another recurring element found in Usigli's dramatic productions is the character types based on members of the family. He treats all social levels—lower, middle, upper, and aristocratic—to portray segments of Mexican society. Usigli's acute awareness of the inconsistencies in

Mexican life and culture are often expressed in witty dialogue and amusing episodes.

Medio tono (middle class), *El gesticulador*, and *Crown of Shadows* are considered to be Usigli's finest works. Each portrays a conflict that tests the spirit. Human emotions are presented so as to diminish the distance between the public and the stage. Ridicule is not provoked from pathetic situations; rather, the audience feels a sense of spiritual elevation at the conclusion of each of these dramas.

In the sociological drama *Medio tono*, the mundane Sierra family is transformed by Usigli into a universal symbol of middle-class family life. This play depicts the problems which beset a typical middle-class family, not only in Mexico but anywhere in the world as well. Each family member has his own particular problem. The father has lost his job with the government because of his political affiliation and has taken refuge in pursuing other women. The mother's overwhelming religious character prevents her from seeing that anything is wrong. Their sons have problems. David, the eldest son and moderator of the family, suffers from tuberculosis. Victor is unhappy because he has no money with which to court a girl whom he has just met. Julio finds that everyone is hostile to him because of his Communist sympathies. Martin, the youngest son, is interested only in animals and is unhappy because animals are not allowed in their apartment. The daughters are also unhappy with their situations. Gabriela is frustrated because she cannot find a political party compatible with her beliefs; Enriqueta is suffering from the banalities of married life and from grave financial problems after the bankruptcy of her husband's store; Sarah is in love with someone of whom the family does not approve. David alone realizes that the only form of salvation is unity. Still, it seems that each one must find his way by himself because each finds the others to be incapable of understanding and compassion. An atmosphere of dissension, pessimism, confusion, and egotism prevails. Unknowingly, however, the family members share a sense of unity which will surface during a grave crisis.

At the end of the drama, the circumstances are much more serious than at the beginning. The father moves the family to another province, which is very poor, and he must sell much of the family furniture in order to pay the rent. The mother is able to recognize and acknowledge her family's difficulties and suffers much, knowing that Gabriela spent the night in jail for attending a Communist rally. David enters the hospital to seek help for his illness; Julio leaves for Spain to fight against the forces of Francisco Franco and the Fascists; Sarah is pregnant. The difference, however, lies in the sense of consolidation and unity among the members of the family and their attempts to rescue one another. They feel a new freedom in thought and action, born of the now-prevailing atmosphere of mutual love and respect.

The Sierra family is a typical example of the trials and tribulations of any middle-class family anywhere in the world. The value of this drama lies in the fact that Usigli, by presenting the life of the Sierra family in a universal light, successfully transcended national boundaries and won the empathy of other frontiers. Psychologically, Usigli appealed to a fundamental element of Mexican society: the clan instinct, the overpowering desire of family members to overcome their personal differences, no matter what the sacrifice or price, in order to ensure the continuation of their line.

El gesticulador, like *Medio tono*, deals with conflict and the psychology of human emotions. They are presented from a political perspective, however, and involve the concept of myth formation. *El gesticulador* is the story of a professor of revolutionary history, César Rubio, who loses his job for political reasons and returns with his family to his native province. He realizes that his life has been a failure and is afraid that he has been a sorry example to his children. During a chance meeting with a historian from the United States, César, on a promise of secrecy, assumes the identity of a glorified revolutionary general of the same name whose fate had been a mystery. César then uses his acquired identity to run for provincial governor. He is assassinated and dies a famous man. César's son finally learns the truth but is powerless to proclaim it. If he exposes his father as an impostor and is believed, it would arouse little indignation; if he is not believed, he would be incarcerated as an insane political agitator.

In the structure of *El gesticulador*, there is a clear progression toward the formation and propagation of a myth. The work is divided into three acts. Act 1 introduces César and the character he assumes, General César Rubio. The arrival of Bolton, the historian from the United States, looking for information about the general, causes a psychological change in the personality of César, who almost instantly believes himself to be the general. This enables Usigli to introduce the element of predestination, which is made manifest in three ways: by the arrival of the failed professor and his family to his native town, where, coincidentally, two men share the same name and one is a hero; by the attitude of the other family members toward César; and by the arrival of the American historian Bolton. César, desperate because of his family's rejection of him, acts solely on his instincts in an effort to save himself.

Act 2 traces the development of the myth, César's assumption of the false identity which permits him to overcome his sense of inadequacy. His family plays a large part in this. The family functions as a chorus—they are César's conscience and externalize his inner conflict. His wife represents the part of his conscience which wants to liberate itself from the lie. His precocious son suspects that something is amiss and becomes very disgusted. His daughter, however, represents the other side of his conscience. She shares her father's sense of failure because she believes that she is ugly and socially unacceptable. Because she aspires to be loved and to live well, she sees something positive in her father's new life-style and encourages him. Finally, César accepts the lie, the past becomes the present, the myth begins to take root, and optimism becomes the prevailing mood of the play.

Act 3 presents the propagation of the myth. At the beginning of the act, César is converted into the universal candidate who has reached the peak of glory. He is respected and loved by his people. Yet the confrontation between César and his colleague Navarro interrupts the euphoria. The meeting between the two rivals illustrates the theme of truth against illusion. Navarro wants to denounce him as a fraud to all the people. The most important event of act 3 is César's assassination. With his death, the myth will never be separated from the man. Navarro immediately changes his attitude toward César and proclaims him a true hero. The myth is engraved in the public mind; it is stronger than reality.

In this work, Usigli uses the Revolution to focus on Mexico and its people. The false César Rubio is not regarded in a negative light. Rather, he is revered as a hero for assuming a new identity to affirm his faith in the Revolution and ultimately to die for it. Psychologically, the Mexican concept of heroism is infantile. A hero is not expected to perform only one great deed but rather constantly to provide examples of heroism during his lifetime. Mexico had no such heroes. The hero César Rubio evolved because a conflict arose which created a need for one of these heroes in a historical event that was purely Mexican. Thus, Usigli was able to save the intention of the Revolution, metamorphose it, and convert it into a positive growth symbol for Mexico. It is interesting to note that Usigli dedicated *El gesticulador* to his hypocritical countrymen because of their tendency to hide from reality and avoid the truth by putting on other faces. By exposing this character flaw, Usigli hoped to chide his countrymen out of this weakness.

Crown of Shadows shares with *Medio tono* and *El gesticulador* the theme of conflict and an acute psychological analysis of the Mexican people and their ideologies. Like *El gesticulador*, it deals with myth. It is part of a trilogy devoted to three fundamental Mexican myths: political sovereignty (*Crown of Shadows*: Benito Juárez versus Maximilian), territorial or national sovereignty (*Corona de fuego*: Cuauhtémoc versus Hernán Cortés), and spiritual sovereignty (*Corona de luz*: the synthesis of paganism and Catholicism).

Crown of Shadows is a reinterpretation of the history of Maximilian and Carlota presented as a modernized version of an Aristotelian tragedy. In this setting, the psychological projection of his characters, rather than the action, is emphasized.

This drama involves the conflict between fate and justice. Maximilian and Carlota abide by completely opposite moral codes yet share an adverse fate. Maximilian is a novice in the political world and dies, without ever having committed any wrongdoing, for a country that never accepted him. He is sacrificed for the deeds of other politicians, namely Napoleon Bonaparte.

Carlota, on the other hand, is driven by a strong sense of ambition for which she is punished by the death of her husband and seventy years of madness. This play has been widely lauded for its innovative theatrical techniques. The stage is divided, which helps to evoke and reconstruct the past and allows for rapid shifts of space, simultaneous action, and the juxtaposition of time using flashbacks. Some psychological symbols are presented by crossing planes of reality. For example, in the first scene, when the doorman is guiding Erasmo Ramírez, the Mexican historian, through Carlota's home, visible reality, such as the terrace and the garden, is described using the verb "to seem." An unreal environment as well as a sense of atemporality is constructed. Another example occurs when Carlota becomes confused and believes that she is speaking to Juárez, her husband's rival. The error establishes the symbolism present in the title: It alludes to her insanity and her illusion of power. Her constant demands for more light symbolize a brief recovery of her reason, during which time she clarifies historical reality to her listener.

Usigli's purpose in writing *Crown of Shadows* was to justify the misfortune suffered by Maximilian and Carlota by suggesting its ultimate positive significance. He classifies the play as antihistorical, treating his characters as human beings rather than historical figures. Thus, he was able to present them at various levels: husband and wife, rulers, foreigners. He succeeded in ennobling this period of Mexican history through Erasmo Ramírez, the Mexican historian: His name recalls the Dutch scholar who sought reforms from within. The audience, and the historian, are able to review and reconcile themselves to the past. They are able to see that Maximilian loved Mexico and sensed the essence of the nation—its ancient symbols and bloody upheavals—and that his death was in fact a catalyst for the birth of Mexican nationalism.

Usigli dedicated his life to the creation of a Mexican national theater. He combined practical experience, a keen sense of the Mexican spirit, a thorough knowledge of the theater, stylistic creativity, and a new ideology to establish the basis for a new Mexican theater. His dramas are neither didactic nor doctrinal, but objective in their thematic treatment. Usigli's desire was to bring the past and the present into harmony, to see them in a positive light, and to appeal to the faith of the Mexican people to overcome their weaknesses and gain a new and optimistic perspective on their country's future. Through his acting, translating, teaching, and writing, he played a decisive part in the creation of a Mexican national theater.

Other major works

NOVEL: *Ensayo de un crimen*, 1944.
POETRY: *Conversación desesperada*, 1938.
NONFICTION: *México en el teatro*, 1932 (*Mexico in the Theater*, 1976);

Rodolfo Usigli 365

Caminos del teatro en México, 1933; *Itinerario del autor dramático*, 1940; *Anatomía del teatro*, 1966.

Bibliography

Clark, Barrett H., and George Freedley. *A History of Modern Drama*, 1947.
Drew, Elizabeth A. *Discovering Drama*, 1937.
Ragle, Gordon. "Rodolfo Usigli and His Mexican Scene," in *Hispania*. XLVI (1963), pp. 307-311.
Savage, Ronald Vance. "Rodolfo Usigli's Idea of Mexican Theatre," in *Latin American Theatre Review*. IV, no. 2 (1971), pp. 13-20.
Tilles, Solomon H. "Rodolfo Usigli's Concept of Dramatic Art," in *Latin American Theatre Review*. III, no. 2 (1970), pp. 31-38.

Anne Laura Mattrella

LUIS MIGUEL VALDEZ

Born: Delano, California; June 26, 1940

Principal drama

The Theft, pr. 1961; *The Shrunken Head of Pancho Villa*, pr. 1965, pb. 1967; *Las dos caras del patroncito*, pr. 1965, pb. 1971; *La quinta temporada*, pr. 1966, pb. 1971; *Los vendidos*, pr. 1967, pb. 1971; *Dark Root of a Scream*, pr. 1967, pb. 1973; *La conquista de Mexico*, pr. 1968, pb. 1971 (puppet play); *No saco nada de la escuela*, pr. 1969, pb. 1971; *The Militants*, pr. 1969, pb. 1971; *Vietnam campesino*, pr. 1970, pb. 1971; *Huelguistas*, pr. 1970, pb. 1971; *Bernabé*, pr. 1970, pb. 1976; *Soldado razo*, pr., pb. 1971; *Actos*, pb. 1971 (includes *Las dos caras del patroncito*, *La quinta temporada*, *Los vendidos*, *La conquista de Mexico*, *No saco nada de la escuela*, *The Militants*, *Vietnam campesino*, *Huelguistas*, and *Soldado razo*); *Las pastorelas*, pr. 1971 (adaptation of a sixteenth century Mexican shepherd's play); *La Virgen del Tepeyac*, pr. 1971 (adaptation of *Las cuatro apariciones de la Virgen de Guadalupe*); *Los endrogados*, pr. 1972; *Los olivos pits*, pr. 1972; *La gran carpa de los rasquachis*, pr. 1973; *Mundo*, pr. 1973; *El baille de los gigantes*, pr. 1973; *El fin del mundo*, pr. 1975; *Zoot Suit*, pr. 1978; *Bandido!*, pr. 1981; *I Don't Have to Show You No Stinking Badges*, pb. 1986.

Other literary forms

Although Luis Miguel Valdez is known primarily for his plays, his writing on Chicano culture has had a significant impact. In a number of essays in the 1960's and 1970's ("Theatre: El Teatro Campesino," "Notes on Chicano Theatre," and several others), he elaborated an aesthetic based on what he believed to be the special features of Chicano reality: bilingualism, *mestizaje* (mixed race), and cultural disinheritance. Valdez's commitment to Chicano nationalism is reflected in two important works of nontheatrical writing— *Aztlan: An Anthology of Mexican American Literature* (1972; coedited with Stan Steiner), whose lengthy introduction recounts the history of the Chicano people as the original inhabitants of "Aztlan" (the contemporary American Southwest), and *Pensamiento Serpentino: A Chicano Approach to the Theatre of Reality* (1973), which explores the influence of Aztec and Mayan spirituality on Chicano art and thought. It is in this latter book that all of Valdez's published poetry can be found.

Achievements

Without Valdez, the Chicano theater would not exist in its present vibrant form. At the age of twenty-five, in the fields of rural California, without financial backing and using farm laborers as actors, Valdez single-handedly created a movement that has since become international in scope, leading to the founding of Chicano theater troupes from Los Angeles, California, to Gary, Indiana. Although not usually mentioned in the company of revered American playwrights of his generation, such as Sam Shepard, David Mamet, and Richard Foreman, he is in many ways as distinguished and as well-known internationally, both in Europe and in Latin America.

In one respect especially, Valdez has accomplished what no other American playwright has: the creation of a genuine worker's theater, completely indigenous and the work of neither university intellectuals nor producers of a commercialized "mass culture." He has made "serious" drama popular, political drama entertaining, and ethnic drama universal.

Valdez has won acclaim in two parallel but distinct artistic communities. If his early career fits neatly within the contours of the cultural nationalism of the Civil Rights movement (whose Chicano forms in the American Southwest are perhaps less well-known than the Afro-American forms of the South), he found a hearing also in more established circles. One of the original organizers for the United Farm Workers Union, a tireless propagandist for Chicano identity, and a founder of a still-fourishing annual cultural festival in Fresno, California, he has also been a founding member of the California Arts Council, a congressional subcommittee of the National Endowment for the Arts, the board of directors of the Theatre Communications Group, and an actor in teleplays and films based on his own work. Winning an honorary Obie Award in 1968 for his work on the West Coast, he, appropriately, was the first, ten years later, to produce a Chicano play on Broadway, the highly acclaimed *Zoot Suit.*

He cannot, however, be seen simply as a major playwright. His fortunate position as a public figure at the first serious outbreak of Chicano nationalism in the mid-1960's—which he helped articulate, and which helped articulate him—makes him also an emblematic representative of American cultural politics, especially as it regards the important (and often forgotten) Latino community.

Crucial in this respect is his groundbreaking book, *Aztlan*, which brings together documents from the pre-Columbian period to the present, sketching a picture of Chicanos as a distinct people with a long tradition and an active history. Valdez's passionate commitment to Chicano nationalism must be seen as a driving force of his art. If *Aztlan* defiantly underlined the uniqueness of the Chicano in an alienating landscape of oppressive "Anglo" institutions, his next book, *Pensamiento Serpentino*, emphasized the evils of artificially separating peoples on the basis of race and culture; it argued for a common North American experience in a spirit of forgiveness and mutual cooperation and derived its moral approach to contemporary social problems from Aztec and Mayan teachings.

The rarity of someone from Valdez's background and interests finding so distinctive a public voice cannot be underestimated. Nevertheless, his greatest work is probably the legacy he leaves to Chicano culture itself. The Centro Campesino Cultural, a nonprofit corporation which he founded in Del Rey, California, in 1967, became a clearinghouse for Chicano artists around the country and operated film, publishing, and musical recording facilities for their use. Inspired by the success of Teatro Campesino, many other groups have come into being. Some of the most important are Teatro Urbano, El Teatro de la Esperanza, El Teatro de la Gente, and El Teatro Desengañó del Pueblo. It is the pioneering work of Valdez that has allowed these vital regional theaters to operate in a coordinated and organized fashion under a national network known as TENAZ (El Teatro Nacional de Aztlan), a direct offshoot of the Centro Campesino Cultural.

Biography

Luis Miguel Valdez was born on June 26, 1940, in Delano, California, the second of ten brothers and sisters. His father and mother were migrant farmworkers. Already working in the fields by the age of six, Valdez spent his childhood traveling to the harvests in the agricultural centers of the San Joaquin Valley. Despite having little uninterrupted early schooling, he managed to win a scholarship to San Jose State College in 1960.

Soon after his arrival at college, he won a regional playwriting contest for his first one-act play, *The Theft*. Encouraged by his teachers to write a full-length work, Valdez complied with *The Shrunken Head of Pancho Villa*, which was promptly produced by the San Jose State Drama Department. Graduating with a bachelor's degree in English in 1964, Valdez spent the next several months traveling in Cuba; upon his return, he joined the San Francisco Mime Troupe under Ron Davis, where he worked for one year, learning from the troupe's *commedia dell'arte* techniques, which he was later to adapt in new ways.

Partly as a result of the sense of solidarity which he gained from his experiences while in Cuba, Valdez returned home to Delano, where the United Farm Workers Union was then being formed under the leadership of César Chávez. Amid a strike for union recognition, the union officials responded enthusiastically to Valdez's offer to create an educational theater group. Using volunteer actors from among the strikers, he formed the Teatro Campesino in 1965. Traveling on a flatbed truck from field to field, the troupe produced a series of one-act political skits dubbed *actos* (actions, or gestures), performing them in churches, storefronts, and on the edges of the fields themselves.

Enormously successful, the plays soon won outside attention, and led to a United States tour in the summer of 1967. Later that year, Valdez left the fields to found the Centro Campesino Cultural in Del Rey, California. Similar recognition followed, with an Obie Award in New York in 1969 for "creating a workers' theater to demonstrate the politics of survival" and an invitation to perform at the Theatre des Nations festival in Nancy, France—one of four tours to Europe between 1969 and 1980. Later in 1969, Valdez and the troupe moved to Fresno, California, where they founded an annual Chicano theater festival, and Valdez began teaching drama at Fresno State College.

The Centro Campesino Cultural relocated once again in 1971 to San Juan Bautista, a small rural California town, where it would stay for the next several years, rooting itself in the community and transforming its dramaturgy to reflect local concerns—particularly through its adaptations of earlier devotional drama dating from the Spanish occupation. Teatro Campesino there underwent a fundamental transformation. Living more or less in a commune, the group began increasingly to emphasize the spiritual side of their work, as derived not only from the prevalent Christianity of the typical Chicano community but also from their own newfound Aztec and Mayan roots. This shift from the agitational *actos* to a search for spiritual solutions was met with anger by formerly admiring audiences at the Quinto Festival de los Teatros Chicanos in Mexico City in 1974.

From its base in San Juan Bautista, the Centro Campesino Cultural continued to flourish, touring campuses and communities on a yearly basis; giving financial support, training, and advice to other theater troupes; and hosting visitors such as English director Peter Brook, who brought his actors from the International Centre of Theatre Research in 1973. After a career of refusing to participate in the commercial theater, Valdez determined finally, in 1978, to try reaching a middle-class audience. The result was *Zoot Suit*, a polished, full-length dance-musical based on the "Sleepy Lagoon" murder trial of 1943. It premiered at the Mark Taper Forum in Los Angeles in 1978 and ran for eleven months. The play opened at the Wintergarden Theatre on Broadway in 1979 but was forced to close after a month because of bad reviews. A film version of the play was made in 1981. In 1985, *Soldado razo* and *Dark Root of a Scream* were performed for the first time in New York at the Public Theater as part of a Latino theater festival.

Analysis

Luis Miguel Valdez's genius was to reach an audience both Chicano and working-class, not only with political farces about strikers, "scabs," and bosses in a familiar street-theater concept but also by incorporating the popular theatrical forms of Spanish America itself—the *carpas* (traveling theater shows), *variedades* (Mexican vaudeville), *corridos* (traditional Mexican folk ballads), and others. It is a unique combination to which Valdez added his own distinctive forms. Appraising Valdez's work is, however, different from appraising that of most other playwrights of his stature. By political conviction and by necessity, much of his oeuvre is a collective product. While he has always been Teatro Campesino's major creative inspiration, and although entire passages from the collective plays were written by him alone, Valdez's drama is largely a joint project under his guidance—a collective political and religious celebration.

The starting point for all of Valdez's work is his evocation of what he calls *la plebe, el vulgo*, or simply *La Raza*, that is, the Chicano people. It is from this outlook that the first *actos* were created—a genre very close to the Brechtian *Lehrstück* (teaching piece), with its episodic structure, its use of broad social types, its indifference to all but the most minimal of props and scenery, and its direct involvement of the audience in the solving of its dramatized social problems. In Valdez's words, the *actos* "must be popular, subject to no other critics except the pueblo itself, but it must also educate the pueblo toward an appreciation of *social change*, on and off the stage."

According to various accounts, the form was first developed in a Delano storefront, where Valdez had assembled his would-be performers from among the strikers. He hung signs around their necks which read: *huelguista* (striker), *esquirol* (scab), and *patroncito* (little boss) and then simply asked them to show what had happened that day on the picket line. After some hesitation, the actors performed an impromptu political play, alive with their own jargon and bawdy jokes and inspired by the passions of the labor dispute within which they found themselves.

One exemplary early *acto* is *Las dos caras del patroncito* (the two faces of the boss), in which a typical undocumented worker, recruited fresh from Mexico by a California landowner in order to scab on the strike, exchanges roles with his *patroncito*. Dressed in a pig mask and speaking in an absurd Texas drawl, the *patroncito* playfully suggests that he temporarily trade his own whip for the *esquirol*'s pruning sheers. The two quickly assume the inner reality of these symbolic outward forms. The climactic moment occurs when the owner removes his mask, at which point the *esquirol* has the revelation that worker and boss look (and therefore are) the same. Calling now for help, the boss is mistaken by the police for a troublemaker and is hauled off-stage, shouting for César Chávez and declaring his support for *La huelga* (the strike). The social tensions and contradictions of this role-reversal are central to all the *actos*. If the boss is brought down to a vulnerable stature and the worker is shown to be capable of leadership, there is no simplistic identification of one or the other as totally good or evil.

In the next stage of his career, Valdez explored the legends and myths of the Chicano's *indio* past. *Bernabé* is perhaps Valdez's most fully realized *mito* (myth-play). The hero is a thirty-one-year-old village idiot who has never had sexual relations with a woman. At the same time, he is a symbolic embodiment of the Chicano who possesses what Valdez calls "divinity in madness." After a series of taunts by the village toughs and an embarrassing encounter with Consuela, the local prostitute, Bernabé flees to a favorite hiding place in the countryside, where he has dug a gravelike hole in which he frequently masturbates in a kind of ritual copulation with *La Tierra* (the earth). The climactic scene occurs when the elemental surroundings take on the forms of an Aztec allegory. *La Luna* (the moon) appears dressed as a *pachuco* (an urban Chicano zoot-suiter), smoking marijuana and acting as a go-between for his sister *La Tierra*, who then enters in the costume of a Mexican revolutionary camp follower (the proverbial "Adelita"). In the interchange, *La Tierra* questions the extent of Bernabé's love for her—whether he is "Chicano" enough to kill and to die for her. It is precisely his status as *loco* (crazy) that gives him the courage finally to say yes, and *El Sol* (the sun), as father, is pleased. As if mimicking the sacrifices to the Aztec sun god, Huitzilopochtli, Bernabé offers his physical heart to *La Tierra* and immediately ceases being the village idiot he was before, buried now within the earth but living on as a lesson to his people.

Valdez was to refine further this allegorical (and less immediately political) approach to Chicano identity in his plays throughout the 1970's, particularly in *La gran carpa de los rasquachis* (the great tent of the underdogs) and *El fin del mundo* (the end of the world), which further developed the use of the Mexican *corrido* (musical ballad), the split-level staging designed to evoke a mythical and suprahistorical realm of action, and the traditional images from Spanish American religious drama—particularly the *calavera* (skeleton) costume. In *El fin del mundo*, his play had become a full-scale allegorical ballet—a great dance of death.

With his first deliberate turn to the commercial theater in 1978, Valdez incorporated the *mito*, *acto*, and *corrido* in the unlikely framework of a play about the urban Chicano of the 1940's. *Zoot Suit*—filled with stylized scenes from the Los Angeles barrio—was a drama about a celebrated murder trial and the racist hysteria surrounding it. A panorama of American life of the time, the play deliberately adopted many of the outward features of the "professional" theater, while transforming them for its purposes. It displayed immense photographic projections of newspaper headlines, slickly choreographed dances and songs, and the overpowering central image of the narrator himself, dressed in a zoot suit—the mythical *pachuco*. To an extent greater than in any other of his plays, the work addressed Americans as a whole, reviving for them a historical moment of which they had never been aware and bringing them face-to-face with their latent prejudices.

Valdez's theatrical vision is inseparable from the conditions under which he founded the Teatro Campesino in the farmworkers' strike of 1965. Born in struggle, his early plays all have a vitality, directness, and urgency that cannot be divorced from their lasting appeal. His achievement blossoms finally with his successful incorporation of the deep cultural roots of the Chicano nation, which are found in the religious imagery of the *indio* past. Both facets of his career have been widely copied by other Chicano directors and playwrights and admired widely outside the Chicano community as well.

Other major works

ANTHOLOGY: *Aztlan: An Anthology of Mexican American Literature*, 1972 (with Stan Steiner).

MISCELLANEOUS: *Pensamiento Serpentino: A Chicano Approach to the Theatre of Reality*, 1973.

Bibliography

Bagby, Beth. "El Teatro Campesino: Interviews with Luis Valdez," in *Tulane Drama Review*. XI (Summer, 1967), pp. 71-80.

Cárdenas de Dwyer, Carlota. "The Development of Chicano Drama and Luis Valdez's 'actos,'" in *Modern Chicano Writers*, 1979. Edited by Joseph Sommers and Tomás Ybarra-Frausto.

Cizmar, Paula. "Luis Valdez," in *Mother Jones*. June, 1979, pp. 47-64.

Harrop, John, and Jorge A. Huerta. "The Agitprop Pilgrimage of Luis Valdez and El Teatro Campesino," in *Theatre Quarterly*. V (March/May, 1975), pp. 30-39.

Huerta, Jorge A. *Chicano Theatre: Themes and Forms*, 1982.

Kanellos, Nicolás. "Chicano Theatre in the Seventies," in *Theatre*. XII (Fall/Winter, 1980), pp. 33-37.

Morton, Carlos. "The Teatro Campesino," in *The Drama Review*. XVIII (December, 1974), pp. 71-76.

Shank, Theodore. "A Return to Aztec and Maya Roots," in *The Drama Review*. XVIII (December, 1974), pp. 56-70.

Timothy Brennan

MARUXA VILALTA

Born: Barcelona, Spain; September 23, 1932

Principal drama

Los desorientados, pr. 1960 (adaptation of her novel); *Trio*, pr. 1964, pb. 1965 (includes *Un país feliz, Soliloquio del tiempo*, and *La última letra*); *El 9*, pr. 1965, pb. 1966 (*Number 9*, 1973); *Cuestión de narices*, pr. 1966, pb. 1967; *Esta noche juntos, amándonos tanto*, pr., pb. 1970 (*Together Tonight, Loving Each Other So Much*, 1973); *Nada como el piso 16*, pr. 1975, pb. 1977 (*Nothing Like the Sixteenth Floor*, 1978); *Historia de El*, pr. 1978, pb. 1979 (*The Story of Him*, 1980); *Una mujer, dos hombres, y un balazo*, pr. 1981, pb. 1984 (*A Woman, Two Men, and a Gunshot*, 1984); *Pequeña historia de horror (y de amor desenfrenado)*, pb. 1984, pr. 1985 (*A Little Tale of Horror (and Unbridled Love)*, 1986).

Other literary forms

Although Maruxa Vilalta is known primarily as a playwright, she also is the author of three novels and one collection of short stories.

Achievements

Vilalta is known at home and abroad as an experimentalist, a playwright who with every new work further explores the possibilities of the theatrical medium. Her plays are showcases for significant theatrical innovations since the mid-twentieth century, and they have been associated with names such as Eugène Ionesco, Samuel Beckett, Harold Pinter, and Bertolt Brecht. Vilalta has been concerned with the most pressing issues of the twentieth century, such as the loss of direction in a seemingly absurd world, humankind's horrifying capacity for cruelty, the corrupting allure of power. Given these concerns, it is not surprising that Vilalta's plays are themselves often violent and shocking and that her characters are dehumanized grotesques.

Vilalta's work, like much experimental theater since the 1960's, means to assault rather than comfort audiences, and has a definite political intent while not being allied with any specific ideology. Instead, it makes a statement with a broad application, regardless of geography or culture. As a result, Vilalta has won audiences throughout Latin America, in the United States, Canada, and numerous European countries. In Mexico itself, Vilalta has three times received that country's most prestigious drama award, the Alarcon Prize of the Mexican Critics Association—for *Together Tonight, Loving Each Other So Much, Nothing Like the Sixteenth Floor*, and *The Story of Him. Number 9* was selected for publication in the United States as one of the best short plays of 1973. Vilalta's major plays have been published in English as well as in French, Italian, Catalan, and Czech.

Biography

Maruxa Vilalta was born in Barcelona, Spain, on September 23, 1932. Exiles of the Spanish Civil War, her family emigrated in 1939 to Mexico, where Vilalta has continued to reside. After completing her primary and secondary education at the Liceo Franco Mexicano in Mexico City, Vilalta studied Spanish literature at the College of Philosophy and Letters of the Autonomous National University of Mexico. She was married in 1951 and has two children.

Vilalta began her writing career as a novelist in 1957, with *El castigo* (the punishment). When, in 1960, she adapted her second published novel, *Los desorientados* (the disoriented ones), for the stage, Vilalta was so impressed by the immediacy of the theatrical medium and the concrete life it gave to her characters that she has since dedicated herself almost exclusively to playwriting. While her early plays, especially *Number 9*, won for her considerable critical attention, it was in 1970, with *Together Tonight, Loving Each Other So Much*, that she really established herself as one of Mexico's leading experimental dramatists. This was the first of three plays that would win for her the coveted Alarcon Prize for the best play of the year; in 1978, *The Story of Him* won that prize on a unanimous vote, something rather rare in the award's history.

In 1975, with the prizewinning *Nothing Like the Sixteenth Floor*, Vilalta began directing her own plays, and as a director, she has been closely associated with the National Autonomous University of Mexico, which is considered the major locus for experimental play production in Mexico. Vilalta is also a noted essayist and theater critic for Mexico's leading daily newspaper, *Excelsior*.

Analysis

Maruxa Vilalta's playwriting fits within a universalist trend in Latin American theater, and for this reason, her plays are not peculiarly Mexican, either in their language, their characters, or their setting. This goes hand in hand with Vilalta's rejection of more realistic stage conventions, which she considers too much associated with a local theater of customs or manners, what in Spanish is called *costumbrismo*. Instead, Vilalta usually prefers a nonrepresentational theater, whose characters belong to no specific country. When she does place them geographically, as in *Nothing Like the Sixteenth Floor*, it is in Manhattan, New York, and not in Mexico City.

Vilalta's conscious effort to avoid things typically Mexican clearly places her on one side of a long-standing debate among fellow playwrights about how indigenous their art should be and the degree to which it should be valued based on international appeal. A similar debate has been waged by artists in most Latin American countries, who recognize the necessity to deal with their own reality but also do not want to be potentially isolated from world audiences. Many have chosen the same solution as Vilalta, which is to write plays that can be read as allegories. Thus, while on one level they may not have anything overtly Mexican about them, the issues with which they deal—the dehumanization of the labor force, the cruelty individuals inflict on one another, the institutionalization of violence—most certainly do. It is by indirection, then, that Vilalta makes a powerful commentary on the specific world in which she lives, while not actually having to place her characters there.

Vilalta often expresses her thematic concerns through the theatrical metaphor of game playing. Usually she keeps the number of players at two or three, and the intensity of the games may well explain her preference for one-act plays. The rules for the games her characters play are not always easy to follow, because they do not necessarily adhere to everyday logic. Their logic resides in the games themselves, which should be interpreted as metaphors and not concrete depictions of reality offstage.

Vilalta's first important play, *Number 9*, takes place in a small yard, behind a large factory. Everything there, which is not much—a wall, a bench, a trash can, some barbed wire—is a depressing, prisonlike gray color; the workers, themselves dressed in dull gray overalls, are the inmates of this dehumanized workplace. The game here is an unevenly matched one—the powerful forces of capitalism against the ordinary men and women who keep its machinery running. The violence done to them is camouflaged behind a smokescreen of cleanliness, order, and paternalism. The workers for Sunshine of Your Life, Ltd., labor with the most modern conveniences and under employers who care about their well-being, or so they are constantly told by a throaty female voice blaring at them over the loudspeaker in the yard. They supposedly have a spotless cafeteria, immaculate working areas, a complaints bureau—everything the labor force could ask for.

What this disembodied voice fails to mention, however, is that the workers to whom and of whom she speaks have no names, only numbers; they have become automatons, indistinguishable from the machines they operate, and their lives are as anesthetized as the colorless surroundings at the factory. The workers are cogs in a superefficient system which does not even stop to mourn the death of Number 9, who, in desperation to assert his individuality, has allowed himself to be mangled to death by the very machine that made his life intolerable. Only then does Number 9 regain an identity and his name—José.

In writing this play, Vilalta certainly felt the influence of the Theater of the Absurd, which gained popularity in the early 1960's. The dominant mood of *Number 9*, with its often disjointed dialogue, sense of a repetitive action leading nowhere, schematic characters, and the gloomy picture painted of a pointless existence, is that of absurdism, but with one fundamental difference. Unlike the European variety, absurdism here is not an ontological or existential dilemma but a specifically socioeconomic one instead. Number 9 and his fellow workers are the playthings not of a disinterested or irrational god but rather of the cruel demigods of exploitative capitalism. Vilalta's adaptation of the Theater of the Absurd was not an unusual one among Latin American playwrights of the period, many of whom emulated the movement's theatrical innovations while not necessarily embracing its philosophical premises.

This same kind of adaptation takes place in Vilalta's next important play, *Together Tonight, Loving Each Other So Much*, except that in this case the game playing is a much more salient motif, and her mastery of the stage is more evident. Whereas *Number 9* sometimes seems safe and unimaginative, with its obvious, if not clichéd, symbolism (the gray walls, the characters' mechanical movements and speech patterns, Number 9's suicide), here Vilalta is far bolder and innovative. The principal characters in this play, Rosalía and Casimiro (also referred to as Her and Him), are a vicious old couple who have barricaded themselves behind the walls of their filthy apartment, where they delight in playing a humiliating game of one-upmanship. They cackle with glee as they debase each other, all the while congratulating themselves on the love they share and on their generous hearts, an ironic self-appraisal that explains the play's title and that is reinforced by the way Rosalía and Casimiro refuse to aid a dying neighbor and by the nearly erotic pleasure they take in reading all the bad news about what is going on in the real world outside of their wretched little apartment.

In *Together Tonight, Loving Each Other So Much*, Vilalta once again writes the kind of illogical, sometimes quirky dialogue that is associated with the Theater of the Absurd. In many ways, Rosalía and Casimiro are rather nastier versions of the old couple in Eugène Ionesco's *Les Chaises* (1952; *The Chairs*, 1957), but they are also reminiscent of two other famous absurdist couples. Like Didi and Gogo in Samuel Beckett's *En attendant Godot* (1952; *Waiting for Godot*, 1954), Rosalía and Casimiro live a routinized life of waiting. She spends her days knitting and he smoking his pipe, always in anticipation of a dinner hour that never comes. Like George and Martha in Edward Albee's *Who's Afraid of Virginia Woolf?* (1962), Vilalta's husband and wife fill their time with cruel and maiming verbal games.

As in *Number 9*, however, Vilalta molds aspects of the Theater of the Absurd to her own purposes. In this instance, she combines them with multimedia techniques and methods that were popularized by the German playwright Bertolt Brecht in the creation of his so-called epic theater. A notable example of this is when Vilalta has Rosalía and Casimiro read the newspaper, while other characters appear onstage—a General, a Dictator, a Hangman—at the same time that slides depicting real events having to do with war, famine, torture, and repression are projected onto a screen. In this way, Vilalta is able to connect her characters' private, domestic horror with the public horrors of twentieth century life, without ever having to verbalize it. In *Nothing Like the Sixteenth Floor*, the theatrical kinship is closer to the English dramatist Harold Pinter, who writes seemingly realistic plays which are in fact quite strange and offbeat. The stage set in this Vilalta play is meant to be a realistic depiction of an elegant apartment in Manhattan. The three characters—Max, Stella, and Jerome—are not such obvious abstractions as Number 9 or Him and Her. Jerome, a young electrician, is called to the apartment by Max, who has actually tampered with the electrical systems in order to lure him there. Max insults Jerome because of his working-class background and then bullies him into having sex with his live-in prostitute, Stella. During the following months, Stella shares her favors with both men and their *ménage à trois* becomes a power struggle with shifting roles of dominance. At first, Jerome is repulsed by the game, but he finds that he cannot resist the allure of sex, power, and material goods with which Max and Stella entice him. By the end of the play, he is no different from his tormentors, and it is only then, with the three characters equally matched, that they can play their games for even higher stakes.

While there is nothing obviously unrealistic about this play, the subtle undercurrents in its mood signal that these characters are not quite what they appear to be. Vilalta manages to create this mood mostly through the dialogue, which sounds very ordinary but which, on closer inspection, proves to be too loaded with double meanings, sinister innuendos, ambiguities, and symbolism to be simple, everyday talk. Characterization is also deceptive, for although the characters at first seem the sort to be readily defined by their surface, there is something not quite concrete about them. This is especially true of the woman, who changes her name from Jane to Stella to Samantha, depending on her male partner, and is actually more a product of masculine wishful thinking than a real person, rather like Ruth in Pinter's *The Homecoming* (1965). Similarly, the characters in *Nothing Like the Sixteenth Floor*, despite superficial touches of realism, are more (and less) than they appear to be. The play is not a psychological exploration of the sexual games that a few people play; the characters represent what could become of all human society. As one of them says, "Three on the sixteenth floor, or a million all over the world."

The Story of Him marks a notable change in both the form and content of Vilalta's plays. The story it tells is of a lowly bank clerk named simply El (Him) and his rise through the world of finance into the political arena and, ultimately, the highest office of an unspecified country. In the process, he leaves behind a trail of broken hearts and bodies, only to end up a hollow shell of a man, a twisted tyrant who blabbers about revolution while tyrannizing his people.

Because this is such a familiar tale in Latin American history, *The Story of Him* is easily Vilalta's most overtly political play and marks the first time that she makes repeated reference or allusion to Mexico. Whereas before she relied on a single setting and casts of two or three, here there are eighty-seven characters and at least thirteen different settings in seventeen different scenes that are given continuity by one character—The Reader—who functions as a narrator and commentator. The rapid set changes and broadly sketched characters give the play a cartoonlike quality that is very effective in ridiculing the madness of power politics without ever trivializing it. In fact, even though he is a caricature, the central character has an emotional depth that makes him the most human and pathetic of Vilalta's creations and *The Story of Him* the most satisfying of her plays.

The broad brushstrokes used to render the cast of characters in *The Story of Him* become even broader in *A Woman, Two Men, and a Gunshot* and *A Little Tale of Horror (and Unbridled Love)*, where Vilalta tries her hand at humor. *A Woman, Two Men, and a Gunshot* comprises four brief one-acts which parody certain theatrical styles: melodrama, Theater of the Absurd, surrealism, and Broadway musicals. Since Vilalta herself has used some of these styles, she is also poking fun at herself; one of these playlets, "In Manhattan That Night," is in many ways a humorous rendition of *Nothing Like the Sixteenth Floor*. *A Little Tale of Horror (and Unbridled Love)* is more farce than parody and revolves around mistaken identities, gender confusions, a murder, and the inevitable sinister butler. With these plays, Vilalta explores new territory without leaving behind her usual thematic concerns, although these do seem secondary to her preoccupation with humorous effect—a shift in emphasis which might explain why these plays have not received the degree of critical success that her others have enjoyed.

Maruxa Vilalta represents a considerable presence in Mexican experimental drama, and her plays show the clear influence of many major theater innovators of the twentieth century. Vilalta is not merely derivative, however, for she adapts these influences to her own ends. The result is a very personal theater, one that is not particularly Mexican in any obvious way but that still manages to make an indirect commentary on the social and political realities of Mexican culture. Moreover, although the vision of humankind that Vilalta paints is bleak in the extreme, critical and audience enthusiasm for her plays, both in Mexico and abroad, would seem to indicate playgoers' recognition that, by emphasizing the negative, Vilalta ultimately hopes to provoke change for the better.

Other major works

NOVELS: *El castigo*, 1957; *Los desorientados*, 1958; *Dos colores para el paisaje*, 1961.

SHORT FICTION: *El otro día, la muerte*, 1974.

Bibliography
Bearse, Grace, and Lorraine E. Roses. "Maruxa Vilalta: Social Dramatist," in *Revista de estudios hispánicos*. XVIII (October, 1984), pp. 399-406.
Holzapfel, Tamara. "The Theatre of Maruxa Vilalta: A Triumph of Versatility," in *Latin American Theatre Review*. XIV (Spring, 1981), pp. 11-18.

Kirsten F. Nigro

MARTIN WALSER

Born: Wasserburg, Germany; March 24, 1927

Principal drama

Überlebensgross Herr Krott: Requiem für einen Unsterblichen, pr. 1913, pb. 1964; *Der Abstecher*, pr., pb. 1961 (*The Detour*, 1963); *Eiche und Angora*, pr., pb. 1962 (*The Rabbit Race*, 1963); *Der schwarze Schwan*, pr., pb. 1964; *Die Zimmerschlacht*, pr., pb. 1967; *Wir werden schon noch handeln*, pr. 1968 as *Der schwarze Flügel*, pb. 1968; *Ein Kinderspiel*, pb. 1970, pr. 1972; *Das Sauspiel: Szenen aus dem 16. Jahrhundert*, pr., pb. 1975; *In Goethes Hand: Szenen aus dem 19. Jahrhundert*, pr., pb. 1982; *Ein fliehendes Pferd*, pr. 1985 (dramatization of his novella).

Other literary forms

Martin Walser's earliest literary efforts resulted in several radio plays, written while he was employed by the South German Radio Network. These contained the seeds, both in terms of form and content, for his earliest plays. His real breakthrough as a writer of serious fiction came with the publication of his first book of short stories, *Ein Flugzeug über dem Haus und andere Geshichten* (1955; an airplane over the house and other stories), and his first novel, *Ehen in Philippsburg* (1957; *The Gadarene Club*, 1960; U.S. edition, *Marriage in Philippsburg*, 1961). Walser's place as one of the most important, most controversial, and most talented West German prose writers was clearly established through his trilogy of novels, *Halbzeit* (1960; half-time), *Das Einhorn* (1966; *The Unicorn*, 1971), and *Der Sturz* (1973; the crash). The protagonist of all three works, Anselm Kristlein, is the prototypical main character for virtually all of Walser's writing (the major characteristics of which are delineated in the Analysis section of this essay).

Among Walser's other notable fiction works are *Die Gallistl'sche Krankheit* (1972), *Jenseits der Liebe* (1976; *Beyond All Love*, 1982), *Ein fliehendes Pferd* (1978; *Runaway Horse*, 1980), *Seelenarbeit* (1979; *The Inner Man*, 1984), *Das Schwanenhaus* (1980; *The Swan Villa*, 1982), and *Brandung* (1985). The reception of Walser's prose works in general, by critics and the public alike, has been more favorable than that of his plays. The critical acclaim, for example, of such a work as *Runaway Horse* has been as positive as that accorded virtually any other single literary work in West Germany in the postwar period. Even among those critics who have been quite negative about Walser's plays, there are several who have praised his prose works both for their content and for their form. It appears that the nontraditional qualities of Walser's writing in general find greater acceptance as prose fiction than they do as drama, but that says more about the inclinations of several German theater critics, perhaps, than it does about Walser's talent as a dramatist.

The last area of Walser's writing worth noting here is that of the essay, a form in which Walser has established himself as a leading figure in West Germany. His essay topics range from literary criticism to cultural, political, and social criticism in general. Among his numerous publications one can find several volumes of essays in which his attitudes about and analyses of matters cultural, social, and political are powerfully and effectively expressed. The most important of these volumes are *Erfahrungen und Leseerfahrungen* (1965; experiences and reader-experiences), *Heimatkunde* (1968; home-arts), *Wie und wovon handelt Literatur* (1973; how and what literature concerns) and *Wer ist ein Schriftsteller?* (1978; who is an author?).

Achievements

One of the most important authors of post–World War II German literature, Martin Walser has distinguished himself with an extensive and impressive output of plays, novels, short stories, and essays. Like others in his generation of (West) German authors, such as Günter Grass and Siegfried Lenz, Walser was born at the end of the 1920's, grew up in Germany during the Third Reich, and then, once he began writing in the 1950's, directed his literary efforts at forcing his fellow Germans to confront rather than suppress their history and to recognize that their recent, terrible past is a part of their present, whether they are willing to admit it or not, and it cannot and must not be conveniently, uncritically, and irresponsibly swept under the rug. In all Walser's diverse works, he has retained that critical sensibility toward his society, analyzing in particular the power structures in both private and public, historical and contemporary realms, and exposing how those structures oppress individuals as well as keep genuine social progress from occurring. He grants a certain amount of sympathy and understanding to his protagonists, virtually all of whom come from the middle and lower-middle classes, yet they are anything but heroic and, in fact, usually end up as failures—in their occupations, in their private and political lives, and in their attempts to find lasting meaning or realize their aspirations. Walser's dramas and prose works alike, despite all of their variety, display these basic thrusts consistently.

Although the critical and popular acclaim for Walser's literary and dramatic creations has not been unanimous, nor the reception of the individual works even, he is undoubtedly one of the most important writers in German in the postwar period. He has attracted considerable scholarly attention and has been awarded numerous prestigious literary prizes, including the Prize of the Gruppe 47 (1955), the Hermann Hesse Prize (1962), the Gerhart Hauptmann Prize (1962), and the Georg Büchner Prize (1982).

Biography

Martin Walser was born the son of relatively poor innkeepers in the small but picturesque south German town of Wasserburg on Lake Constance, on March 24, 1927. He claims that he was shielded from the most blatant Nazism by his very Catholic family, but even if that was true, there were other kinds of hardship in his youth, especially after the death of his father in 1938. His schooling was often interrupted, particularly toward the end of the war when he was forced into civilian and then military service. He was captured by allied troops but was released at war's end. He then resumed his schooling, receiving his diploma (*Abitur*) in 1946. Walser studied initially at the Theological-Philosophical College in Regensburg; in 1948, he transferred to the University in Tübingen. He completed his studies in literature, history, and philosophy with an important Ph.D. dissertation on Franz Kafka in 1951. Both as a student and afterward, between 1949 and 1957, Walser worked for the South German Radio Network, and it was during that time that he began his career as an author, writing numerous radio plays.

After the critical success in 1957 of his first novel, *Marriage in Philippsburg*, Walser and his wife moved to Lake Constance, where they took up permanent residence, rearing four artistically talented daughters. Walser's literary productivity has been prolific and steady, as has his production of significant work in the areas of literary and social criticism. Even though Walser "withdrew" to the idyllic shores of Lake Constance, he has remained a committed public figure since the days of his radio work. During the 1960's, he spoke out frequently and consistently for social and political progress, moved steadily toward the political Left, and championed many of the causes associated with the student movement of those turbulent years. Walser's political engagement, evident in his literary works only indirectly and never dogmatically, has never been undertaken for a specific political party, such as was the case with Günter Grass's well-publicized engagement for the Social Democrats. For a time, some observers placed Walser close to the Communists; yet, even though his social and economic analyses are definitely informed by certain Marxist principles, Walser did not join, nor would he have been at home in, the small and rather dogmatic West German Communist Party. The "revolutionary" momentum of the late 1960's and early 1970's slowed and then halted, in West Germany as well as in the United States, and Walser's direct engagement decreased in a corresponding fashion; although it is never altogether absent, his works and public statements in the later 1970's indicated an increased pessimism with regard to hopes for lasting social and political change.

Walser's reputation as a writer was solidified by the success of novels and dramas alike, particularly that of the novel trilogy (which had begun with *Halbzeit* in 1960, continued with *The Unicorn* in 1966, and culminated in *Der Sturz* in 1973), as well as the plays *The Detour* in 1961, *The Rabbit Race* in

1962, and *Die Zimmerschlacht* (the indoor battle) in 1967. The reception of Walser's works in general has been marked by vocal disagreements, contradiction, and controversy. In certain of Walser's works, most directly in the play *Wir werden schon noch handeln* (we're going to get to the plot soon), he turns the reception of his works into a literary theme. Although the balance between the positive and negative reactions to Walser's works has varied with the individual works, it can be asserted that politically and aesthetically conservative critics have tended to be more negative in their assessment than have those whose politics are more liberal and whose artistic expectations are less traditional. In any case, Walser and his works continue to inspire lively commentary from scholars, critics, and reviewers across the political-cultural spectrum. The one work which has elicited virtually universal praise from critics and readers is the novella *Runaway Horse*, which Walser later adapted into a stage version that was first performed in 1985.

The main protagonist of that novella appears later as the central figure in the novel *Brandung*. This novel is an anomaly among Walser's works in that it is not set primarily in Germany, but in California. This is a reflection of the fact that Walser has spent considerable time, particularly during stints as a visiting professor (at universities in West Virginia, Texas, and California) in the United States. The novel is based largely on those experiences. Walser continues to live in Nussdorf on Lake Constance, but makes frequent trips to teach and lecture, both in Europe and abroad.

Analysis

Critics have frequently, and correctly, claimed that Walser writes the story of the everyday. The characters that populate his plays are not the movers and shakers of history, but rather singularly unexceptional individuals. These antiheroes are generally struggling, somewhat neurotic types who display middle-class, even lower-middle-class, sensibilities and behavior. Often the larger moments of history are evident in the background, but the protagonists are usually far too passive and acquiescent to be major actors on that level. Walser's perspective on history as well as on contemporary society is thus from below rather than from above, and, although it is obvious that he is highly critical of his unheroic figures, it is also obvious that he identifies with them.

Several main topics run throughout Walser's dramatic works, whether these focus specifically on dealing with Germany's immediate past (*The Rabbit Race, Der schwarze Schwan*), on its more distant past (*Das Sauspiel, In Goethes Hand*), or on contemporary domestic (*The Detour, Die Zimmerschlacht, Ein Kinderspiel*) or artistic situations (*Wir werden schon noch handeln, In Goethes Hand*). In all of his plays, Walser is concerned with power structures, master-servant relationships, and the tensions which are inherent in such structures and relationships. The tensions usually have a deleterious,

even crippling effect on the protagonists who struggle but never quite succeed in getting out of the dependent positions in which they find themselves.
Exploitation, opportunism, and subservience are all important catchwords.
Walser is consistently critical of those who abuse their power as well as of
those who acquiesce and allow such abuse to occur. He is concerned as well
with the German past, not for its own sake, even in his history plays, but because of the shadows it casts on the German present. Whether it is the Germany of the sixteenth century (*Das Sauspiel*, "the pig-play"), the nineteenth
century (*In Goethes Hand*, "in Goethe's hand"), or Nazi Germany (*The Rabbit Race, Der schwarze Schwan*) that is in question, it is the patterns of behavior, the attitudes, the traditions developed in those eras yet still present in
Walser's Germany, usually in infelicitous ways as far as he is concerned, that
command his attention. The third major topical category found in Walser's
plays is that of the artist and intellectual—his (they are all men) status in
society, responsibility (and irresponsibility) to society, as well as the use of his
position and talent either to legitimize or to challenge and criticize the reactionary and oppressive structures and characteristics of their society.

The major literary influences on Walser, especially early in his career, were
Franz Kafka, Samuel Beckett, and Bertolt Brecht. Although these writers
may seem to make rather strange bedfellows, one thing they have in common
is their break with traditional literary forms. Walser has followed their lead
and, with few exceptions, has rejected traditional dramatic form, choosing
instead a loosely connected, open, or epic (in the Brechtian sense) structure
instead. As the individual scenes or sections of the play have gained in
importance, the significance of overall plot or character development has
decreased, at times becoming even minimal, as is the case, for example, in
Wir werden schon noch handeln. The subtitle to *Das Sauspiel*, which means
"scenes from the sixteenth century," and the subtitle to *In Goethes Hand*,
meaning "scenes from the nineteenth century," also point up the relative
autonomy of the individual scenes over the general, chronological plot. Furthermore, where any substantial changes occur in the protagonists, it is
clearly as disintegration or diminution rather than any positive growth.

Some of Walser's earliest plays, particularly *The Detour* and *Überlebensgross Herr Krott*, display some elements of the Theater of the Absurd and,
hence, the influence of Beckett and Existentialism. Most of Walser's plays,
however—even though they can be read on one level as parables or allegories, and even though symbols play a very significant role—are far more
grounded in clearly recognizable reality. Other significant features of Walser's style are his strong sense of irony, a satirical bent, wit and witticisms,
love of wordplay, and an inclination toward lightly grotesque situations and
figures.

The Detour, Walser's first play, enjoyed an enthusiastic response from
West German theatergoers following its premiere in 1961, and it was staged

in numerous theaters in the following few years. The play is divided into three parts: a prologue, the main section, and an epilogue. The prologue and epilogue consist of conversations between the now-successful West German businessman Hubert Meckel and his subservient chauffeur Berthold. More or less on a whim, Hubert has decided to take a short detour from the freeway and visit his former lover, now married, in Ulm. At the beginning of the main section, he has found her at home, but as Frieda responds to his lighthearted flirtation with accusations of shabby treatment earlier, the mood of the play gradually becomes tense, frightening, and even rather grotesquely absurd. When Frieda's husband arrives home, the two of them decide to put Hubert "on trial" for the way he had treated Frieda several years before. A sense of terror arises when they bind Hubert and conclude that he should be put to death. Ultimately, however, this terror subsides, as Frieda's husband shifts positions and aligns himself instead with Hubert against Frieda, in a show of a kind of "good old boys" solidarity.

The surrealistic, absurd atmosphere of the "trial" is thus abandoned, only to be replaced, however, by the rather grotesque and cruel irony of the men (in this case, the oppressors) joining forces against the woman (the victim). "Everyday reality" returns, Hubert bids adieu, rejoins his chauffeur, and they drive off. During the ensuing conversation between them, as well as in parts of their discussion in the prologue, the same kind of master-servant, oppressor-oppressed, exploiter-victim structures, attitudes, and behavior patterns become evident in the relationship between boss and chauffeur. Walser's intent is to analyze various kinds of power structures and the negative tensions which are inherent in them, both in the more private realm of male-female relationships and in the more public, capitalistic business world.

The didactic thrust of the play is illuminated during the "trial" when Hubert, scared out of his wits, is forced to recognize the corruption of his behavior and the abuse of power which he exerted and exerts through his position and attitudes. For the reader or viewer, he clearly becomes a symbol of the system he represents. The fact that he is to remain a "negative hero," however, whose cathartic moment of insight is only fleeting, is evident when he dismisses the whole episode as a "joke" as he and Berthold drive off, back into their everyday routines. Walser thus poses the challenge to repressive structures, but the reality of his society will not allow him to portray, optimistically, any real changes in that society, its structures, and attitudes. It is not possible to overlook the fact that Walser's play can be read, on one level, as a kind of parable of how West German society, seduced into amnesia and a false sense of righteous security by its overwhelming "economic miracle" of the 1950's, refused to deal honestly, openly, and self-critically with its own shabby past, even though the attitudes which prevailed in that past remain visible in the present for those who dare to look.

In Walser's next play, *The Rabbit Race*, he attacked this topic more directly. Divided into three main parts set in 1945, 1950, and 1960, respectively, the play follows Alois Grubel through his ill-timed political transformations. The audience learns that, during the Nazi period, Alois was a Communist and was sent to a concentration camp for his views. While in the camp, he was castrated and, in a rather grotesque twist, became converted to Nazism and was released. At the war's end, where the play begins, Grubel and his acquaintances in the small southern German town where they live attempt to shed the signs of their Nazism as the Allies approach. The others do so successfully, even though only the signs and rhetoric change, certainly not the attitudes. These are not shown to be mean people; they are not real Nazi criminals, but they embody the banality of evil in their subservience, their gullibility, and their petty opportunism. Grubel, though, does not make the transformation from one ideological setting to another, and in 1950 he is still making statements that reveal Nazi sentiments. He is sent to an asylum, betrayed by those who had shared his sentiments earlier. Grubel is a pathetic figure, powerless and easily manipulated, both by ideologies and by other people. The fact, however, that his ultimate failure to survive in his society derives not from his views but his timing is a clear indictment of a German society which has survived by its timing and opportunism, rather than by any real changes in attitudes and behavior. Walser's criticism of his fellow West Germans for their smug righteousness while steadfastly refusing to look hard and deep at the relationship between their past and present is perhaps nowhere expressed as strongly as in this play.

Walser's next play, *Überlebensgross Herr Krott*, whose subtitle translates into English as "requiem for an immortal," is one of his most allegorical. Set in a rather surrealistic Alpine hotel, the play abounds in deaths, but Mr. Krott, the immensely wealthy industrialist, who actually wants to die, cannot. Krott is an insatiable power broker who uses everything and everyone around him for his own gain, convenience, and enjoyment. It is hinted that Krott's alienation from all others and even from any human decency has its roots in the Nazi years, including war experiences, but that is not offered as an excuse. Krott is far more representative than a flesh-and-blood character, standing for an aggressive and brutal capitalistic system which, even though corrupt and inhumane, remains "alive" while causing the death, literal and metaphorical, of countless others.

Walser's other play from 1964, *Der schwarze Schwan* (the black swan), marks an intensification of his attempt to confront German society with its terrible, recent past and its efforts to suppress or deny its responsibility, even guilt, for that past. The timing of the play coincided with the Frankfurt trials of Nazi criminals, trials which pointed up very clearly the need for Germans to deal with the unfinished business of their Nazi past. This was also the time when serious generational conflicts in Germany began to show themselves, not least of all because teenagers and young adults began to ask their parents about their roles, activities, and attitudes during the Third Reich. Forthright answers to such questions were infrequent, and youth began to criticize and rebel against the older generation. That, in fact, becomes the main focus of Walser's *Der schwarze Schwan.*

Walser sets the play in a postwar insane asylum, which is directed by a former Nazi doctor. This doctor, Professor Libere, has withdrawn to the asylum for two seemingly contradictory reasons: to atone for his role in the medical atrocities which occurred, but also to invent an imaginary past, for himself and his family, in which he had no part in the Third Reich. Libere's rather schizophrenic manner of dealing with guilt appears to be representative, for Walser, of the way his society has dealt with it. There is more of a plot in this play than in most other Walser plays, and it starts with the arrival of Rudi Goothein, a young man about twenty years old, who claims that he is a former SS man. His father, also a former Nazi doctor, brings him to the asylum, thinking his son has had a nervous breakdown. Rudi demands a "trial" for his own "imagined" crimes, during which he wants to confront his father with the latter's unacknowledged crimes. Rudi has discovered a letter in which his father's responsibility for atrocities is evident. The "trial," which takes place in the asylum as a kind of play-within-a-play, suggests comparison with *Hamlet*. It leads to outrage on the part of Libere and Rudi's father when they are forced to recognize themselves, their guilt, and their elaborate attempts to deny and suppress their true pasts, but they refuse, nevertheless, to abandon their false masks and claims of innocence. Realizing that he has failed to force his father to confess and recognizing that the foundation for his own life and future is therefore corrupt, Rudi commits suicide rather than live with this lie. He views his death as a protest and symbolic statement about the futility and impossibility of building a sound future on a mendacious past. Rudi's situation, then, is clearly meant to be allegorical for that of postwar German youth in general. It is also a bitter admonition to the older members of German society to come clean and face their past honestly, if not for their own sake, then at least for that of their children.

Walser's fifth play, *Die Zimmerschlacht*, was written about the same time as *Der schwarze Schwan*, but was not performed or published until 1967. A pattern for Walser's dramatic works begins to show itself clearly by this time, and that is his movement back and forth from more public questions and situations to those of a more private nature. The themes tend to be similar, but are emphasized differently in each kind of play. *Die Zimmerschlacht* presents a kind of domestic nightmare, somewhat in the mode of August Strindberg's marriage plays or Edward Albee's *Who's Afraid of Virginia Woolf?* (1962). The only two characters, Felix and Trude, have been married for many years and, by suppressing feelings and expectations, have managed to coexist with a certain degree of innocuous harmony. On the evening that is the focus of the play, however, aided by too much alcohol, they both let down their guard and begin to speak honestly with each other. The result is disastrous, for their pseudoharmony is unmasked as a lie, as a kind of ritual to cover the genuine sadomasochistic nature of their relationship. Walser is not asserting that glossing over the truth is better, however, for it is obvious that they could not have lived this lie much longer, with or without alcohol. Once again, then—although in a much different situation from those he posited before—Walser focused on the theme of truth, the difficulty of confronting it openly, but the necessity, regardless of the consequences, of doing so.

In Walser's next play, *Wir werden schon noch handeln*, he very cleverly and ironically presents a self-conscious analysis of the contemporary German world of theater, performances, and reviewers. It is a play which attacks and satirizes those critics who expect and demand traditional form even for radically nontraditional, contemporary topics. It is also, therefore, a defense, though not without self-irony, of Walser's own theatrical style and attitudes about contemporary drama.

The last play which Walser wrote before taking a significant break of five years' duration was *Ein Kinderspiel*, written and performed in 1970. The title is bitterly ironic, for this play is anything but a "children's game." The topic is once again the conflict between the generations, a conflict which was virtually everywhere in evidence in Germany, as in many other places, during the late 1960's. What the play actually portrays as black, psychological comedy is an almost absurdly dysfunctional family. The mother in the family has recently died, and Asti, the twenty-year-old son, his twenty-three-year-old sister Bille, their estranged father, and his new, young wife, come to the family cottage for a kind of reunion. There are hints of incest between mother and son, as well as between brother and sister, and the plot thickens as Asti tries to enlist his sister's help in killing their father upon his arrival. Asti plans patricide not only because he believes that his father is responsible for his mother's death but also because he holds him "responsible" for his own *birth* and his sister's. The murder never occurs, as the father unwittingly calls Asti's bluff, but the rest of the play teems with intensely bizarre and cruel provocations. This is private drama, psychological drama of consciousness, and Walser seems to be highly critical of everyone. One can sense not only Walser's criticism of the older generation but his growing disenchantment as well with the younger one that appears, at least in Asti, to engage in infantile and destructive self-indulgence. The question presents itself whether Walser sees before him, reflected in such dysfunctional domestic situations, the end of bourgeois, capitalistic society.

After *Ein Kinderspiel*, five years passed before Walser presented his next play, his first genuine history play, *Das Sauspiel*. In a series of loosely connected scenes, Walser concentrates on the post-Reformation, postrevolutionary situation in Nuremberg in the years 1525 to 1527. The city is now Lutheran, free of the oppressive control of the Catholic Church and the Bishop of

Bamberg. It is governed by those who had revolted, an illustrious group of artisans, merchants, teachers. Many of their names are famous, either from Albrecht Dürer's paintings or from historical and fictional sources, including Hans Sachs and Dürer himself. Walser does not place them in the key roles, however, and the protagonist is a poor street-singer who feigns blindness in order to increase donations, Jörg Graf. This device allows Walser to portray the events, characters, and historical dilemmas from the perspective of those who are less the shapers of history than its victims. Walser uses much documentary material in the play, but it is not a documentary drama in the well-known style of Rolf Hochhuth, Peter Weiss, or Heinar Kipphardt.

Walser is interested in what happens *after* a revolution has apparently succeeded, and he concludes that, if not inevitably, then certainly often, a reaction sets in whereby the revolutionaries of old, now in power, become reactionary and distance themselves from their old ideals in order to establish their power and position. In this play, Walser shows how these former revolutionaries begin to persecute those former allies who are not yet satisfied with what has happened and who want to extend the benefits of the successful revolution to others. Representative of these former allies are the Anabaptists, the so-called radical reformers, who were not only persecuted but also, according to Walser and numerous progressive historians, have been unjustly maligned by historical, fictional, and theological accounts up to the present day.

Walser is thus keen on challenging traditional interpretations of these historical events and characters, but he is equally intent on exploring post-revolutionary patterns in general. The disappointment that Walser felt over the return of what he viewed as reactionary patterns in West German society after the "revolutionary" changes in the progressive 1960's is certainly in evidence here, as well as his attempts to find explanations for that reaction. In *Das Sauspiel*, he is critical not only of idealists-turned-establishment-politicians but also of opportunistic artists and intellectuals who abandon their "ideals" when the wind changes directions, as does Jörg Graf.

Das Sauspiel, which was performed in numerous German theaters, both West and East, elicited a genuine controversy among reviewers and critics, in part because Walser had challenged both the legitimacy of Nuremberg's legendary humanistic tradition and the traditional ways of interpreting the events, characters, and results of the Reformation. During the next seven years until 1982, Walser focused most of his literary energy on novels and other prose forms, and this was a period in which he firmly established himself, even in the eyes of critics who had been former detractors, as a novelist of international significance. In 1982, however, his ninth play appeared, and it, too, caused much controversy.

The play, *In Goethes Hand*, like *Das Sauspiel*, is a history play, which, despite its title, concentrates not directly on the famous title character but on his rather subservient assistant, Eckermann, and on what Walser views as the negative, inhibitory, and even reactionary legacy of the "Goethe legend" for the subsequent development of German culture.

Once again, Walser's interest in history is not merely for its own sake but for the ways in which it still informs and affects the present. Walser does not criticize Goethe's literary works but rather his ego, monumental posing, and later conservative views toward politics and art. Eckermann, with whom Walser's sympathies partially reside, also is subject to criticism for his subservience and his part in perpetuating a bigger-than-life image of Goethe. There is no doubt that Goethe is the central figure in modern German literature, and Walser would not dispute that, but he does want to view the man and his legacy critically. *In Goethes Hand* is a play about the tensions between traditional and modernist art, about the reception of culture, about history and its, sometimes burdensome, relationship to the present. It is also, however, a play about the venerable German problem of subservience, about dependence and exploitation.

In his uncompromising attempts to confront his fellow Germans with critical portrayals of the past they consistently try to suppress, of the relationship of that past to the present, of traits and developments in private and public behavior which inhibit progress toward liberation of all kinds, Walser is one of the most vociferous spokesmen in contemporary German letters for honesty, openness, and critical thinking. And even though some of his plays do show weaknesses in structure and consistently convincing style, others are masterpieces of postwar German drama. Walser's refusal to follow trends in modern drama, to cave in to criticism of his unconventional dramatic forms, is one of his greatest strengths, even though it sometimes means that his plays, because of their experimental nature, fall short of "masterpiece" status. It is to be hoped, though, that he will continue to experiment with and seek new forms that are appropriate both for contemporary theater and for the crucial contemporary topics with which Walser is concerned. It is also to be hoped that American audiences will soon gain the opportunity to see some of Walser's plays performed and thereby become acquainted with one of West Germany's most important and controversial playwrights.

Other major works

NOVELS: *Ehen in Philippsburg*, 1957 (*The Gadarene Club*, 1960; U.S. edition, *Marriage in Philippsburg*, 1961); *Halbzeit*, 1960; *Das Einhorn*, 1966 (*The Unicorn*, 1971); *Die Gallistl'sche Krankheit*, 1972; *Der Sturz*, 1973; *Jenseits der Liebe*, 1976 (*Beyond All Love*, 1982); *Ein fliehendes Pferd*, 1978 (novella; *Runaway Horse*, 1980); *Seelenarbeit*, 1979 (*The Inner Man*, 1984); *Das Schwanenhaus*, 1980 (*The Swan Villa*, 1982); *Brief an Lord Liszt*, 1982 (*Letter to Lord Liszt*, 1985); *Brandung*, 1985.

SHORT FICTION: *Ein Flugzeug über dem Haus und andere Geschichten*, 1955;

Lügebgeschichten, 1964; *Selected Stories*, 1982; *Gesammelte Geschichten*, 1983; *Messmers Gedanken*, 1985 (anecdotes).

NONFICTION: *Beschreibung einer Form*, *Franz Kafka*, 1961; *Erfahrungen und Leseerfahrungen*, 1965; *Heimatkunde*, 1968; *Wie und wovon handelt Literatur*, 1973; *Wer ist ein Schriftseller?*, 1978; *Liebeserklärungen*, 1983.

Bibliography

Fetz, Gerald A. "Martin Walser's *Sauspiel* and the Contemporary German History Play," in *Comparative Drama*. XII, no. 3 (1978), pp. 249-265.

Nelson, Donald F. "The Depersonalized World of Martin Walser," in *German Quarterly*. XLII (1969), pp. 204-216.

Thomas, R. Hinton. "Martin Walser: The Nietzsche Connection," in *German Life and Letters*. XXXV, no. 4 (1982), pp. 319-328.

Waine, Anthony Edward. *Martin Walser: The Development as Dramatist, 1950-1970*, 1978.

Gerald A. Fetz

PATRICK WHITE

Born: London, England; May 28, 1912

Principal drama

Return to Abyssinia, pr. 1947; *The Ham Funeral*, wr. 1947, pr. 1961, pb. 1965; *The Season at Sarsaparilla*, pr. 1962, pb. 1965; *A Cheery Soul*, pr. 1963, pb. 1965; *Night on Bald Mountain*, pr. 1963, pb. 1965; *Four Plays*, pb. 1965 (includes the preceding four plays); *Big Toys*, pr. 1977, pb. 1978; *Signal Driver*, pr. 1982, pb. 1983; *Netherwood*, pr., pb. 1983.

Other literary forms

Patrick White is best known for his novels. In addition, he has published numerous short stories and an autobiographical volume that he called a "self-portrait." He has also written a screenplay based on one of his short stories, "The Night the Prowler."

Achievements

In 1973, White received the Nobel Prize for Literature for his fiction. Thereafter he wrote several more novels and several plays, which have been staged along with revivals of his earlier plays. Because his dramatic works are not widely known outside Australia, White's international reputation rests on his novels, which constitute an astounding achievement. In their grandeur and metaphysical use of the Australian landscape and character, they altered the course of that country's fiction, previously marked, for the most part, by self-conscious realism and nationalism. Although many critics in Australia scoffed at his complex philosophical work before he received the Nobel Prize, White had steadily built a following abroad, beginning with the publication of *The Aunt's Story* in 1948. He has often been credited with putting Australian literature into the mainstream, as well as setting free and influencing an entire generation of fiction writers in Australia whose work is now highly esteemed among those bodies of literature written in English. Whether White is a major dramatist may be open to argument; he does, however, deserve attention for a limited but solid achievement in plays characterized by originality in structure, powerful language, and expression of universal concerns. Although a number of Australian dramatists have achieved widespread recognition, White remains one of the first to experiment on the stage. His example posed a challenge in the 1960's, when realistic and provincial plays constituted the few native works that appeared in a country where theatergoers most often looked to Great Britain and the United States for "real plays."

Biography

Although born in London, Patrick Victor Martindale White was the son of wealthy, third-generation Australian landowners, who were visiting England in 1912 but sailed for home six months after their son's birth. He spent his first thirteen years in and around Sydney, then left for Great Britain to attend school in Cheltenham. Returning to Australia in 1929, he worked for three years at a sheep station in the New England area northwest of Sydney before entering King's College, Cambridge. After he took his degree in modern languages, he remained in London to pursue his theatrical and writing ambitions. Travel through Europe and the United States followed, and in 1939 his first novel, *Happy Valley*, appeared. With the outbreak of World War II, he joined the Royal Air Force, serving in North Africa, Alexandria, the Middle East, and Greece. He returned to London after the war and there saw his first play, *Return to Abyssinia*, produced; the manuscript, lost (or destroyed), was never published. At this time, he wrote another play, *The Ham Funeral*, which did not receive a production until 1961. He returned to Australia during 1947 and except for brief trips abroad has remained there. For the next twenty-five years, he wrote novel after novel, all of which gained for him more recognition in Great Britain and the United States than in Australia. Following the award of the Nobel Prize for Literature in 1973 for his impressive achievement as a novelist, he emerged as something of a public figure in Australia, often criticizing his countrymen, voicing his opinion—at one time or another—on politics and politicians, literary criticism and its practitioners, the Australian involvement in the Vietnam War, preservation of natural resources, nuclear disarmament, and the treatment of aborigines. He invested his Nobel Prize money in a fund to assist other Australian writers, has established scholarships for aboriginal students, and has donated paintings from his extensive private collection to the New South Wales Art Gallery in Sydney. He continues to write both fiction and drama, although he once vowed never to write for the stage again. His plays, now seen throughout Australia, have yet to be produced elsewhere even though they have appeared abroad in published form. In 1986, one of his most famous novels, *Voss* (1957), was turned into an opera; another Australian novelist, David Malouf, wrote the libretto for the production, which enjoyed tremendous success in Australia.

Analysis

Patrick White's plays address the same thematic concerns as the novels: the role of the artist, the conflict between the visionary and the materialist, the moral desolation and decay prevailing in modern life. Their language and structure intensify and heighten experience by combining the poetic with the mundane, the experimental with the traditional, the events of ordinary life with the metaphysical quest for truth. In general, the plays owe much to the

European tradition of expressionism, which depends on the use of anti-naturalistic stage devices; compression of language; symbolic picture sequences achieved through short, unrealized scenes; lofty themes of spiritual regeneration or renewal; and a declamatory tone.

The best known of the plays, *The Ham Funeral*, illustrates these points. The Young Man, the only name given to its major character, reveals in the prologue that he is a poet and, like all poets, knows too much, then adds: "That is the poet's tragedy. To know too much and never enough." He proceeds to explain that the audience must enter with him into the house before which he stands and there learn what it means to be a poet. The scenes that follow bring together the disparate parts of The Young Man's psyche and give him direction as an artist. In the first scene, he lies on his bed in silence, considering the "great poem," when the Landlady interrupts to tell him that her husband has died. He assists in preparation for the funeral, at which the relatives eat the ham the widow has provided to give the funeral class. Later, the Landlady attempts, unsuccessfully, to seduce The Young Man, who returns to his room and carries on a long conversation with The Girl, actually his anima. At the end of the play, The Young Man leaves the house—its back wall dissolving, the stage directions say—and walks into the "luminous night."

Through this fluid series of fragmented scenes, the self-absorbed artist has learned to identify himself with the raw stuff of life: love and lust, hate and compassion, the beautiful and the ugly. Henceforth his poetry will no longer resemble "self-abuse in an empty room," as he describes it, but a discovery of the human condition in all of its forms.

If *The Ham Funeral* may be taken as an autobiographical statement—and there exist substantial grounds for such an interpretation—then The Young Man (White) set his hand to the novel, forsaking poetry altogether and not returning to the drama for almost fifteen years. When he did, he took up in *The Season at Sarsaparilla* the plight of the visionary thrust into a world that is mundane, respectable, conventional, materialistic—but altogether lacking in awareness. The name given to an imaginary Sydney suburb, Sarsaparilla, comes to life on the stage through a setting that represents the kitchens and backyards of three adjoining houses. As the action moves from house to house, the families' lives intertwine in the most ordinary of ways, thus giving the outward texture of the play a deceptive air of naturalism. A dog in heat, or in season, interrupts the quiet lives of the three families when she goes under one of the houses, pursued by a pack of excited dogs. This ironic use of "season" in the title extends to the growing awareness of the central character, Pippy, a young girl on the verge of womanhood, who learns through the dogs' natural actions that life embraces passion, violence, birth, death, that it goes through its seasons, as she will hers.

A Cheery Soul takes for its setting the Sundown Home for Old People and centers its action on Miss Docker. This at once comic and bitter portrayal of a cheery soul, the very soul of suburban respectability and morality, offers a superbly drawn character in Miss Docker, who destroys herself and others as she goes about doing good and remaining cheerful in the face of every disaster. The destructive force, which she manifests unknowingly, stems from an absolute belief in the rightness of her actions, an attitude so pervasive that it leaves no room for sensitivity toward other people.

Probably the least successful of all the plays, *Night on Bald Mountain* sets out to portray the disintegration of Western civilization. The means it uses fail to rise to the loftiness of the theme: A woman more devoted to a herd of goats than to humankind, an embittered professor, his alcoholic wife, and a young woman with incestuous longings lack the universal appeal to make convincing so significant a message. Still, the play's artistry in language and structure and its striking use of setting lend to it a pure theatrical excitement in spite of its defects.

Disheartened by the reception of his plays, White left the drama for the novel and shunned playwriting for fourteen years. Some critics believe, though, that his early plays, so different from anything native ever produced on the Australian stage, sowed the seeds for the new theater movement that got under way there in 1967, when several young writers demanded that Australian theater make room for the country's linguistic vigor, concern itself with matters contemporarily Australian, and liberate the imagination to experiment with new forms. Whereas these playwrights moved in directions different from White, they surely benefited from his earlier attempts to establish a distinctly Australian drama.

In 1977, *Big Toys* opened in Australia to a new breed of theatergoers, ones who not only took Australian drama seriously but also accepted work that ignored the conventions of theatrical realism. Set in a fashionable Sydney suburb, *Big Toys* depicts the empty lives of Mag and Ritchie Bosanquet, who have what should make life full—wealth, beauty, social position, every imaginable material possession, indeed all the "big toys." As they rise in the material realm, however, in reality they are rushing to their downfall: In White's world, outward success leads to inward failure. *Big Toys* employs the elegant form of comedy of manners and relies on a conflict created by industrial exploitation to draw this bleak picture. Yet the realistic conflict and the stylized form that frames it expand in such a way that they merge into White's earlier devotion to the expressionistic mode. The three characters—as real as those who appear in the daily newspaper, and their personal, social, and business connivances—move into abstract and symbolic dimensions to declaim, albeit subtly, the moral bankruptcy that dominates the lives of those who control the course of the late twentieth century.

Signal Driver is White's purest dramatic venture into expressionism and one of his most impressive plays. Taking its title from Sydney bus signs that

instruct potential riders to "signal driver," the play follows Theo and Ivy
Volkes from youth to old age, the telling of their stories amplified by two
music-hall characters who serve as the Volkeses' alter egos. The entire action
takes place at a bus stop, its environs and conditions changing to show the
passage of time. Buses go by, but the Volkeses never board; when old age
levels them, they realize that they have metaphorically missed the bus of life.
Simplistic though the concept might sound, the talented application of the
expressionistic techniques governing language, character development, staging, and handling of theme turns the play into a powerful and memorable
statement on the desolate human condition.

Netherwood follows theatrical conventions more closely than *Signal Driver*,
at least on the surface. The action takes place in a once-grand Australian
country house, called Netherwood, where a group of half-comic, half-mad
characters live together on parole from the local mental institution, Bonkers
Hall, under the supervision of a couple who are determined to do good. During act 1, the events unfold on a believable level and suggest that this play
might be an Australian version of the English manor-house comedy. In the
second act, however, all pretense toward representation of reality vanishes.
Characters take on multiple identities and serve as one another's alter egos,
thereby revealing to the audience their sexual repressions and perversions,
their hidden failures, suppressed fears, and inability to grasp meaning. With
the personal struggles of the characters unable to be solved by a tidy plot, the
play ends on an apocalyptic note. Amid gratuitous gunfire, one of the characters says: "Comical bastards, us humans. Seems like we sorter *choose* ter
shoot it out . . . to find out who's the bigger dill." At the end, White appears
to voice his rising concern with nuclear armament through this statement, so
very Australian in its syntax and diction. In Australia, a "dill" is a fool—a
description that seems to express White's view of mankind.

Although White's plays will not gain the kind of recognition his fiction has
achieved for him, they should not be discounted or ignored. They stand as
accomplished works in their own right, especially in their author's original
handling of techniques that made expressionism so vital a force in twentieth
century theater. Finally, an understanding of the dramas will lead to a richer
appreciation of the novels, for both literary forms show how the artist can
meld opposites: symbolism which employs the trivial to clarify the universal;
characters who emerge as both real human beings and metaphysical abstractions; settings which rely on the tangible, which are microcosmic, but suggest
the elusive, the universal.

Other major works

NOVELS: *Happy Valley*, 1939; *The Living and the Dead*, 1941; *The Aunt's
Story*, 1948; *The Tree of Man*, 1955; *Voss*, 1957; *Riders in the Chariot*, 1961;
The Solid Mandala, 1966; *The Vivisector*, 1970; *The Eye of the Storm*, 1973;

A Fringe of Leaves, 1976; *The Twyborn Affair*, 1979; *Memoirs of Many in One*, 1986.

SHORTH FICTION: *The Burnt Ones*, 1964; *The Cockatoos: Shorter Novels and Stories*, 1974.

SCREENPLAY: *The Night the Prowler*, 1976.

POETRY: *The Ploughman and Other Poems*, 1935.

NONFICTION: *Flaws in the Glass: A Self-Portrait*, 1981.

Bibliography

Bray, J. J. Review of *The Ham Funeral*, in *Meanjin Quarterly*. XXI (March, 1962), pp. 32-34.

Brisbane, Katharine. Preface to *Big Toys*, 1978.

Brissenden, R. F. "The Plays of Patrick White," in *Meanjin Quarterly*. XXIII (September, 1964), pp. 243-256.

Burrows, J. F. "Patrick White's Four Plays," in *Australian Literary Studies*. II (June, 1966), pp. 155-170.

Robert Ross

ROBERT WILSON

Born: Waco, Texas; October 4, 1941

Principal drama

Dance Event, pr. 1965; *Solo Performance*, pr. 1966; *Theater Activity*, pr. 1967; *Spaceman*, pr. 1967 (with Ralph Hilton); *ByrdwoMAN*, pr. 1968; *The King of Spain*, pr. 1969, pb. 1970; *The Life and Times of Sigmund Freud*, pr. 1969; *Deafman Glance*, pr. 1970; *Program Prologue Now, Overture for a Deafman*, pr. 1971; *Overture*, pr. 1972; *KA MOUNTAIN, GUARDenia TERRACE: a story about a family and some people changing*, pr. 1972; *king lyre and the lady in the wasteland*, pr. 1973; *The Life and Times of Joseph Stalin*, pr. 1973; *DIA LOG/A MAD MAN A MAD GIANT A MAD DOG A MAD URGE A MAD FACE*, pr. 1974; *The Life and Times of Dave Clark*, pr. 1974; *Prologue to a Letter for Queen Victoria*, pr. 1974; *A Letter for Queen Victoria*, pr. 1974, pb. 1977 (with Christopher Knowles); *To Street*, pr. 1975; *$ Value of Man*, pr. 1975; *DIA LOG*, pr. 1975 (with Knowles); *Einstein on the Beach*, pr., pb. 1976 (music by Philip Glass); *I Was Sitting On My Patio This Guy Appeared I Thought I Was Hallucinating*, pr. 1977, pb. 1978; *Prologue to the 4th Act of Deafman Glance*, pr. 1978; *DIALOG/ NETWORK*, pr. 1978; *Death Destruction and Detroit*, pr. 1979; *DIALOG/ Curious George*, pr. 1979; *Edison*, pr. 1979; *Medea*, pr. 1981; *The Golden Windows*, pr. 1982; *the CIVIL warS*, partial pr. 1983 and 1984 (includes *Knee Plays*); *Alcestis*, pr. 1985 (based on Euripides' play); *Knee Plays*, pr. 1986.

Other literary forms

Although Robert Wilson has produced some artwork exhibited in various galleries, no other substantial literary works are attributed to him.

Achievements

An experimental performing artist whose major work has been compared to Pablo Picasso's painting *Guernica* and Igor Stravinsky's ballet, *The Rite of Spring* (1913), and who has been characterized by Surrealist Louis Aragon as "a miracle," Wilson is considered by many to be the single most gifted and creative theater artist of the twentieth century. In scope, vision, imagination, and sheer size, Wilson's marathon "operas" (as he insists on calling them) are giant panoramas of all the possibilities of the stage, physical and temporal (one environmental event in Iran lasted a whole week). His reputation in Europe as the modern theater's most significant avant-garde director/ playwright is not so universally acknowledged in his native country, the United States, but, with the performance of major works on Broadway and at the Metropolitan Opera House, as well as the Brooklyn Academy of Music and the studios of Wilson's theater group, the Byrd Hoffman School of Byrds, his place in the history of American contemporary theater, especially the strong and widespread experimental movement of the 1960's and 1970's, is assured.

Wilson has won several distinguished European awards for his work, including the Grand Prize for *Einstein on the Beach* at the International Festival of Nations in Belgrade in 1977. In the United States, an Obie Special Award Citation for Direction was presented to Wilson in 1974; he has held numerous Guggenheim and Rockefeller Foundation fellowships.

Biography

Born in Waco, Texas, to white, middle-class, Protestant and Southern parents, Robert Wilson attended high school in his hometown. A gangly, shy, but likable young man he had a speech impediment that was "cured" by a dance teacher, Mrs. Byrd Hoffman, who simply made Wilson realize that he could "take his time" to express himself. Following his early impulse to be a visual artist, Wilson studied at the University of Texas and privately in Paris, graduating from Pratt Institute in Brooklyn in 1965. During these years his patience with and sympathy for learning disabilities led him to work with autistic and disturbed children in Texas, where he discovered not only a unique talent for helping them but also a personal metaphor for his own anguish at the virtually universal inability to communicate that is part of the existential condition.

After several striking visual projects such as "Poles" (an "installation" of more than six hundred telephone poles in rural Ohio) and the creation of giant puppets for Jean-Claude van Itallie's experimental play *America Hurrah* (1966), Wilson found that performance art offered the best medium for self-expression. Several small works in which Wilson was the primary performer were followed by increasingly ambitious projects, incorporating more and more "actors" (many of whom were untrained laypersons drawn to Wilson's charismatic personality) and more and more special effects, stage props, and scenery. By 1967, he had gathered a group of friends and theater experimenters into the Byrd Hoffman School of Byrds (named in honor of the woman who helped Wilson in high school) and began an impressive series of long performance works, first in the modest studios of downtown New York, then at the Brooklyn Academy of Music (BAM), and finally throughout Europe, where the combination of his genius and the more benign attitude of political and cultural institutions toward the support of experimental art allowed Wilson to create his best work. The return of his work to America met with both unreserved acclaim and scathing criticism, culminating in the financial failure of the monumental multinational project *the CIVIL warS*, rehearsed and also performed, in part, in six separate countries and scheduled to be performed during the Olympics in Los Angeles in 1984. The only surviving portion of that work, the American connective sections known as *Knee Plays*, has toured the country in truncated form.

Analysis

Robert Wilson's "Theatre of Visions" can best be described as a series of stage tableaux and slowly moving, apparently nondramatic activities which, in the individual minds of the witnesses, connect to form a nonreductive, nonrhetorical, nonnarrative but subjectively unified theatrical experience. This experience may or may not bear a relationship to the piece's title, often referring to a famous person, as in *The King of Spain*, *The Life and Times of Sigmund Freud*, *A Letter for Queen Victoria*, and *Edison*. In the course of the performance (always extremely long by traditional standards), the witness is presented with an opportunity to form whatever subjective connections the images suggest, either intellectually or subconsciously, during which process new "bisociations" are created. Although appearing arbitrary and unrehearsed, the activities are carefully arranged for maximum visual effect. Wilson, however, does not prescribe that effect; it remains for the witness to make what he or she will of the series of "visions," adding to the mix the private experiences and perceptions each one brings to the theatrical event.

The Life and Times of Joseph Stalin, performed first in Denmark, then at BAM, provides access to Wilson's prevailing imagery, because it is in large part a retrospective of all of his work up to that time. In seven acts, each with its own prologue, the piece lasted twelve hours (7:00 P.M. to 7:00 A.M.) and survived four performances in December of 1973. The actors cross and move in seven planes parallel to the proscenium arch; objects hang from the flies against a sky backdrop; silent, immobile figures fill the stage (act 2 alone, originally part of *The King of Spain*, contains "a boy who stands on a stool for the entire act, a blind man and two other men who play chess, Freud, Anna, Stalin, a photographer who takes their picture, a piano player, and a walrus," as well as the King of Spain himself). Processions, choruses, minstrel-show performers, historically costumed, nude, and white-draped figures troop on and off; a cave, a pyramid, "two-dimensional trees and a three-dimensional house" are among the stage scenery; the menagerie includes four turtles with a pool on their backs, wooden fish that swim in it, a bull (beheaded during act 4), nine apes, and twenty dancing ostriches. Yet the huge size of the stage and the unimaginably long duration of the performance dwarf the props, performers, and action, and virtually every activity seems to take place in slow motion. The witness, partly lulled by the slow pace and absence of dramatic intensification, and partly prompted by its uniqueness to perceive everything with a new "vision," eventually succumbs to the rhythms of the performance, coming away from the experience freed from stale habits of passive receptivity and re-energized by the aesthetic euphoria of visual stimulation.

The dialogue passages in this monumental retrospective point to a transition in Wilson's work about this time. Earlier pieces (such as *Deafman Glance*) were essentially silent, with occasional songs, incomprehensible utterances, or sounds, but after the ambitious outdoor piece entitled *KA MOUNTAIN, GUARDenia TERRACE*, Wilson turned in another direction, marked by an increasingly concentrated examination of language as partial, failed, or desensitized communication. The spoken word, often in the form of seemingly meaningless phrases repeated and repeated, begins to draw the focus of the work. In stark contrast to the virtual silence of his early work, Wilson now exhaustively examined the nature of the word onstage.

A Letter for Queen Victoria is the best illustration of this new concern. The "text," edited by Bonnie Marranca with her introductory essay and a preface by Wilson, immediately identifies the nonnormative nature of Wilson's language experiments during this period. While the spoken word transliterates theoretically into the written word, no simple recitation of the "text" could reproduce the immediacy of the spoken performance, especially taking into account the participation of Christopher Knowles, a young man who shares authorship in the piece, clinically "autistic" but, according to Wilson, possessing perceptual powers different from but not inferior to normal perceptions. Knowles's and Wilson's "performance" of the phrases, neither concatenative nor "meaningful," reduces the text to "architectonic" sounds that express the actors' personal relationship in untranslatable ways.

From the backdrops of projected sound-words to the concrete layout of the poetry of the script page, Wilson's main arena of theatrical inquiry during this period becomes the word, the script, and its tenuous relationship to the spoken aspect of theatrical experience. For example, a "press conference" in Yugoslavia consisted of Wilson's repeating the word "dinosaur" for twelve hours while cutting an onion. A thwarted radio project called for actors to say "Hmm," "O.K.," and "There" for five hours. When a word is repeatedly uttered in this fashion, it loses its denotative meaning, resurfacing in the consciousness as pure sound, and, according to Wilson, helping to reestablish emotional responses which have been dulled by the everyday use of language. Wilson's close association with Knowles, Raymond Andrews, and other children with limited hearing and speech has inspired him to experiment with language as "weather," that is, as atmospheric pressures that alter accompanying movements and gestures, transforming them into highly subjective but effective personal communications.

The difficulties of "reading" a Wilson text should serve as a reminder: It is important to understand Robert Wilson's work as performance art rather than primarily as literary expression. While the "scripts" of Wilson's works are theoretically available, often in obscure and out-of-print formats, the complexity and visuality of the experiences are best captured in the form of "performance documentation." This genre, originating in such journals of experimental theater as *The Drama Review* and *Performing Arts Journal*, seeks to record nonscripted or partially scripted theatrical events by means of carefully detailed description of the nature, sequence, and duration of those events, told from the standpoint of a neutral, informed witness who avoids as much as is humanly possible any evaluative or subjective interpretations of those events. Necessarily, some interpretation is inevitable, but the reader can re-create, however imperfectly, some of the visual "semiotics" of the original performance. In Wilson's case, the German critic Stefan Brecht has reported all the significant performance pieces of the Byrd Hoffman Studio up to 1978 in his exhaustively comprehensive study, *The Theatre of Visions: Robert Wilson* (1978), a title which is descriptive of Wilson's whole aesthetic approach.

After a very successful European tour of *Einstein on the Beach* (a collaboration with experimental music composer Philip Glass) in 1976, culminating in sold-out performances at the Metropolitan Opera House in New York City, Wilson found himself with increasingly complex production difficulties, brought on by his limitless vision and his refusal to compromise it with the petty realities of financial exigency. Forced to try smaller works such as *I Was Sitting On My Patio This Guy Appeared I Thought I Was Hallucinating*, Wilson seemed to be gathering his energy for his masterpiece, *the CIVIL warS*, a work that was to combine the most striking scenes and activities from earlier work with new visions on a grand scale. Yet after years of preparation in six countries and countless fund-raising trips and meetings, Wilson was forced to abandon his epic cycle, expressly designed in scope and theme for the Olympic Arts Festival in 1984. Efforts to mount it in Austin, Texas, in 1986 fell to financial realities as well; American audiences could only glimpse the tattered fragments of the Wagnerian vision in a tour of the diminutive *Knee Plays*, whose original purpose was to link the larger segments together.

An unusual gallery tour in 1980 of the artifacts from Wilson's plays brought some money to the Byrd Hoffman Foundation, but brought little relief. It may be that Wilson's theatrical genius is too large for the American stage. It would seem that an institutional or corporate vision of the size and vigor of Wilson's own commitment to his art will be needed if his greatest work is to come to fruition. Perhaps for Wilson the theatrical vision has no limitations of size or duration, and he will be satisfied only when the world stages itself.

Bibliography

Belloli, Andrea, ed. *Robert Wilson's "CIVIL warS": Drawings, Models, and Documentation*, 1984.

Brecht, Stefan. *The Theatre of Visions: Robert Wilson*, 1978.

Coe, Robert. "The Extravagant Mysteries of Robert Wilson," In *American*

Theatre. II, no. 7 (October, 1985), pp. 4-11, 46-47.
Croyden, Margaret. *Lunatics, Lovers, and Poets: The Contemporary Experimental Theatre*, 1974.
Deák, František. "Robert Wilson," in *The Drama Review*. XVIII, no. 2 (June, 1974), pp. 67-80.
Hoffman, William, ed. *New American Plays*. Vol. 3, 1970.
Stearns, Robert. *Robert Wilson: The Theater of Images*, 1980.
Wilson, Robert. ". . . I thought I was hallucinating," in *The Drama Review*. XXI, no. 4 (December, 1977), pp. 75-78.
_____. "A Letter for Queen Victoria," in *The Theatre of Images*, 1977. Edited by Bonnie Marranca.

Thomas J. Taylor

UPDATES

UPDATES

Albee, Edward
BORN: Washington, D.C.; March 12, 1928
DRAMA
Marriage Play, pr. 1987

Ayckbourn, Alan
BORN: Hampstead, England; April 12, 1939
DRAMA
Joking Apart and Other Plays, pb. 1979
A Chorus of Disapproval, pr. 1985, pb. 1986

Beckett, Samuel
BORN: Foxrock, near Dublin, Ireland; April 13, 1906
DRAMA
Three Occasional Pieces, pb. 1982 (includes *A Piece of Monologue*, *Rockaby*, and *Ohio Impromptu*)
The Collected Shorter Plays of Samuel Beckett, pb. 1984
Enough, pb. 1984
Imagination, Dead Imagine, pr. 1984

Gibson, William
BORN: New York, New York; November 13, 1914
DRAMA
Raggedy Ann and Andy, pr. 1984 (libretto, music and lyrics by Joe Raposo)
Handy Dandy, pr. 1984

Gray, Simon
BORN: Hayling Island, England; October 21, 1936
DRAMA
The Common Pursuit, pr., pb. 1984
Otherwise Engaged and Other Plays, pb. 1984
The Rear Column and Other Plays, 1985

Hochwälder, Fritz
BORN: Vienna, Austria; May 28, 1911
DIED: Zurich, Switzerland; October 20, 1986

Kopit, Arthur
BORN: New York, New York; May 10, 1937
DRAMA
End of the World, pr., pb. 1984

Kroetz, Franz Xaver
BORN: Munich, West Germany; February 25, 1946
DRAMA
Reise ins Glück, pr. as radio play 1975, staged 1976, pb. 1976 (*Journey into Happiness*, 1983)
Mensch Meier, pr., pb. 1978, televised 1982 (English translation, 1984)
Wer durchs Laub geht . . ., pb. 1979, pr. 1981 (*Through the Leaves*, 1984)
Furcht und Hoffnung der BRD, pr., pb. 1984 (*Help Wanted*, 1986)

McNally, Terrence
BORN: Saint Petersburg, Florida; November 3, 1939
DRAMA
The Rink, pr. 1984 (libretto, music by John Kander, lyrics by Fred Ebb)
The Lisbon Traviata, pr. 1985
It's Only a Play, pr. 1986

Mamet, David
BORN: Chicago, Illinois; November 30, 1947
DRAMA
The Spanish Prisoner, pr. 1985
The Shawl, pr. 1985
The Frog Prince, pr. 1985
ACHIEVEMENTS
Pulitzer Prize in Letters, 1984, for *Glengarry Glen Ross*

New York Drama Critics' Circle Award, 1983-1984, for *Glengarry Glen Ross*

Miller, Arthur
BORN: New York, New York; October 17, 1915
DRAMA
The American Clock, pb. 1982
The Archbishop's Ceiling, pr., pb. 1984

Pinter, Harold
BORN: London, England; October 10, 1930
ACHIEVEMENTS
New York Drama Critic's Circle Award, 1979-1980, for *Betrayal*

Rabe, David
BORN: Dubuque, Iowa; March 10, 1940
DRAMA
The Rabbit and the Toyota Dealer, pr. 1985

Schisgal, Murray
BORN: Brooklyn, New York; November 25, 1926
DRAMA
The New Yorkers, pr. 1984 (with Adolph Green and Phyllis Newman)

Shepard, Sam
BORN: Fort Sheridan, Illinois; November 5, 1943

DRAMA
Cowboys #2, pr. 1984
The Sad Lament of Pecos Bill on the Eve of Killing His Wife, pr., pb. 1984
Lie of the Mind, pr. 1986
The Unseen Hand and Other Plays, pb. 1986

Simon, Neil
BORN: New York, New York; July 4, 1927
DRAMA
Broadway Bound, pr. 1986
ACHIEVEMENTS
Tony Award, 1985, for *Biloxi Blues*

Soyinka, Wole
BORN: Abeokuta, Nigeria; July 13, 1934
DRAMA
A Play of Giants, pr. 1984
Six Plays, pb. 1984
ACHIEVEMENTS
Nobel Prize for Literature, 1986

Stoppard, Tom
BORN: Zlin, Czechoslovakia; July 13, 1937
DRAMA
Squaring the Circle, televised 1984, pb. 1984
Four Plays for Radio, pb. 1985
Rough Crossing, pb. 1985 (music by André Previn; adaptation of Ferenc Molnár's play *Játék a kastélyban*)

CRITICAL SURVEY
OF
DRAMA

INDEX

À toi, pour toujours, ta Marie-Lòu. See *Forever Yours, Marie-Lou.*
Abel et Bela (Pinget), 306-307.
About Face (Fo), 114.
Abstecher, Der. See *Detour, The.*
Accidental Death of an Anarchist (Fo), 112-113.
Actos, 368, 370-371.
Agitprop theater, 110.
Ahl al-kahf (Hakim), 174.
Ahl al-qamar. See *Poet on the Moon.*
Akalaitis, JoAnne, 1-7; *Dead End Kids*, 4-5; *Dressed Like an Egg*, 2-3; *Green Card*, 5; *Southern Exposure*, 3-4.
al-Hakim, Tawfiq. See **Hakim, Tawfiq al-.**
Albee, Edward, 407.
Albertine in Five Times (Tremblay), 356.
Alphabetical Order (Frayn), 127-128.
Anciennes Odeurs, Les. See *Remember Me.*
Angels' Prayer (Hakim), 178.
Anna Kleiber (Sastre), 323-324.
Arcangeli non giocano a flipper, Gli (Fo), 110.
Armer Mörder. See *Poor Murderer.*
Auf dem Chimborazo (Dorst), 96.
Auftrag, Der (Müller), 262.
August, August, august (Kohout), 223.
Aunt Dan and Lemon (Shawn), 337-338.
Avant-garde, 2.
Aveva due pistole con gli occhi bianchi è neri (Fo), 110-111.
Ayckbourn, Alan, 407.
Aydi al-na'imah, al-. See *Tender Hands.*

Barnes, Peter, 8-15; *The Bewitched*, 12-13; *Laughter!*, 13-14; *Leonardo's Last Supper*, 12; *Noonday Demons*, 12; *Red Noses*, 14; *The Ruling Class*, 11-12.
Beast's Story, A (Kennedy), 216.
Beckett, Samuel, 407.
Belles-sœurs, Les (Tremblay), 349-350.
Benefactors (Frayn), 130-131.
Bernabé (Valdez), 370-371.
Berthe. See *Cinq.*
Bewitched, The (Barnes), 12-13.
Beyond Therapy (Durang), 104.

Big Toys (White), 395-396.
Birth of the Poet (Foreman), 123.
Black Hermit, The (Ngugi), 268-269.
Blood Relations (Örkény), 300.
Bloody Poetry (Brenton), 35.
Bonjour, là, bonjour (Tremblay), 353.
Boogie Woogie Landscapes (Shange), 329-330.
Born in the Gardens (Nichols), 283-284.
Bösen Köche, Die. See *Wicked Cooks, The.*
Boys in the Band, The (Crowley), 71-72.
Braun, Volker, 16-27; *The Great Peace*, 25-26; *Guevara*, 25; *Hinze und Kunze*, 22-23; *Die Kipper*, 20-22; *Schmitten*, 23-24; *Simplex Deutsch*, 26; *Tinka*, 23-24.
Brecht, Bertolt, 17, 25, 116, 118-119, 321.
Breeze from the Gulf, A (Crowley), 71-72.
Brenton, Howard, 28-37; *Bloody Poetry*, 35; *Christie in Love*, 32-33; *The Churchill Play*, 36; *The Genius*, 34-35; *Magnificence*, 33-34; *Pravda* (with Hare), 187-190; *Weapons of Happiness*, 34.
Bridal Dinner, The (Gurney), 164-165.
Broken Pieces. See *Cinq* and *Like Death Warmed Over.*
Buck (Ribman), 315.
Byrne, John Keyes. See **Leonard, Hugh.**

Camp, The (Gambaro), 147-148.
Campo, El. See *Camp, The.*
Cannibal Masque, The (Ribman), 316.
Carpas, 369.
Catsplay (Örkény), 298-299.
Cement (Müller), 260.
Centro Campesino Cultural, 368-369.
Ceremony of Innocence, The (Ribman), 314.
Césaire, Aimé, 38-44; *Et les chiens se taisaient*, 41-42; *A Season in the Congo*, 42-43; *The Tempest*, 43; *The Tragedy of King Christophe*, 42.
Cesta kolem světa za 80 dni (Kohout), 223.
Cheery Soul, A (White), 394-395.

I

II